Roman Roads

Roman Roads

New Evidence – New Perspectives

Edited by Anne Kolb

DE GRUYTER

ISBN: 978-3-11-076334-8
e-ISBN (PDF): 978-3-11-063833-2
e-ISBN (EPUB): 978-3-11-063631-4

Library of Congress Control Number: 2018967637

Bibliografische Information der Deutschen Nationalbibliothek
Die Deutsche Nationalbibliothek verzeichnet diese Publikation in der Deutschen National-
bibliografie; detaillierte bibliografische Daten sind im Internet über http://dnb.dnb.de abrufbar.

© 2021 Walter de Gruyter GmbH, Berlin/Boston
This volume is text- and page-identical with the hardback published in 2019.
Einbandabbildung: Ruines romaines de Timgad (Wilaya de Batna, Algérie). Rue menant à l'Arc de Trajan. © Photograph by PhR61 on Wikimedia Commons, https://commons.wikimedia.org/wiki/File:Timgad_rue.jpg
Satz: Dörlemann Satz, Lemförde
Druck: CPI books GmbH, Leck
Printed in Germany

www.degruyter.com

Contents

Preface —— VII

I A Broader View

Anne Kolb
Via ducta – Roman Road Building: An Introduction to Its Significance, the Sources and the State of Research —— 3

Richard Talbert
Roads in the Roman World: Strategy for the Way Forward —— 22

Grant Parker
Roots to Routes: Gandhara's Landscapes of Mobility —— 35

Michael A. Speidel
Rom und die Fernhandelswege durch Arabien —— 53

Hélène Cuvigny
Le livre de poste de Turbo, curateur du *praesidium* de Xèron Pelagos (*Aegyptus*) —— 67

II The Roads of the Empire

Anthony Comfort
Travelling between the *Euphrates* and the *Tigris* in Late Antiquity —— 109

Chaim Ben David
Milestones near Roman Army Installations in Desert Areas of the Provinces of Palaestina and Arabia —— 132

Mustafa H. Sayar
Römische Straßen und Meilensteine im Ebenen Kilikien —— 147

Hamdi Şahin
CIL XVII, 5, 3: Neue Meilensteine und Straßen aus der *Cilicia Aspera* —— 166

Stefan Groh – Helga Sedlmayer
Via publica vel militaris: Die Bernsteinstraße in spätantoninischer und severischer Zeit —— 191

Florin-Gheorghe Fodorean
The Peutinger Map, the Roman Army and the First Military Roads in Dacia —— 215

Miroslava Mirković
Roman Roads in *Moesia Superior* at Six Points —— 236

Vladimir P. Petrović
Some Considerations about the Roman Road Network in Central Balkan Provinces —— 252

François Mottas
Du premier milliaire au dernier palimpseste: cinq siècles et demi de présence romaine en Grèce —— 272

Michael Rathmann
Miliaria in der Provinz *Lusitiania* —— 303

Stéphanie Guédon
Road Network and Roman Frontier in Numidia: the Region of Tobna —— 323

Mariette de Vos Raaijmakers
Twin Roads: the Road Carthage-Theveste and the *via nova Rusicadensis*; some Observations and Questions —— 338

Alfredo Buonopane – Chantal Gabrielli
Miliari e viabilità dell'Etruria romana: un aggiornamento e alcune considerazioni —— 375

Patrizia Basso
Excavations in the North of Italy along the *via Claudia Augusta* —— 404

Autorenliste —— 423
Index —— 425

Preface

Studying the roads of the Roman Empire has always raised larger questions of Roman history, politics and culture. These routes form the basis of all processes of communication and exchange that allow not only for military conquest and security but also for the organisation of the state and for trade, food supply and cultural transfer. In doing so, the study of roads, in particular the so-called imperial roads (*viae publicae*), must always be based on a combination of written and archaeological sources in order to adequately take into account both the geographical location of the road and the spatial conditions of this location.

Due to various new editions of source material, as well as new archaeological and historical studies, many new insights into the installation and use of the main roads have been gained recently, especially in the last 10 years. Bringing these new developments together was the aim of the international conference "*Viae Romanae –* Roman Roads: New evidence – new perspectives" held at the Historical Seminar of the University of Zurich on the 1st and 2nd of June 2017. The conference examined the current state of research in both its historical and archaeological dimensions and synoptically established the complexity of the imperial Roman road network in recently studied regions of the empire and partly even beyond its borders.

This volume presents the papers delivered at this international conference. For its generous funding I am very grateful to various institutions: the Swiss National Fund, the Swiss Academy of Humanities and Social Sciences, the Higher Education Fund of Zurich University, the Zurich University Society, as well as the University of Zurich itself.

My colleagues at Zurich provided invaluable support both in organising the conference and in editing the volume. My profound gratitude is due above all to Monika Pfau and Miriam Bastian, further to Dr. Jens Bartels, Yannick Baldassarre, Dr. Ursula Kunnert as well as to the staff at De Gruyter (Berlin) for the productive collaboration.

Anne Kolb
Zurich, July 2018

I A Broader View

Anne Kolb
Via ducta – Roman Road Building: An Introduction to Its Significance, the Sources and the State of Research

Zusammenfassung: Der Fall des Marcus Dunius Paternus, eines Angehörigen der städtischen Elite in der römischen Kolonie *Aventicum* (Provinz *Germania superior*), beleuchtet exemplarisch Quellen und Forschungsstand zum römischen Straßenbau im etablierten *Imperium Romanum* der Kaiserzeit. Der vermögende Unternehmer bekleidete das lokale Oberamt in der nach römischem Recht verfassten Stadt und scheint nicht zuletzt aufgrund seiner eigenen ökonomischen Interessen mit privaten Mitteln den Ausbau einer *via publica* finanziert zu haben. Der Nutzen von Straßen auch für die Wirtschaft des Imperium Romanum wird einmal mehr demonstriert. Die Bedeutung des römischen Straßennetzes als Grundlage, Instrument und Symbol der römischen Herrschaft ist durch die Jahrhunderte der staatlichen Entwicklung zu verfolgen. Ein Überblick über die Quellenlage und den Stand der Forschung, insbesondere zu den heute bekannten über 8000 römischen Meilensteinen, ergänzen das Bild.

Abstract: The case of Marcus Dunius Paternus, a member of the urban elite in the Roman colony of *Aventicum* (in the province of *Germania superior*), serves to exemplify the sources and state of research on Roman road construction in the High Roman Empire. The wealthy entrepreneur held the highest local magistracies available in his city, and seems to have used his private means to finance the construction of a *via publica*, not least due to his own economic interests. The beneficial effects roads had upon the Roman Empire and its economy are thus demonstrated once again. The importance of the Roman road network as a foundation, instrument and symbol of Roman rule can be traced through the centuries of the state's development. An overview of the sources and the state of research, especially on the more than 8,000 Roman milestones known today, complete the picture.

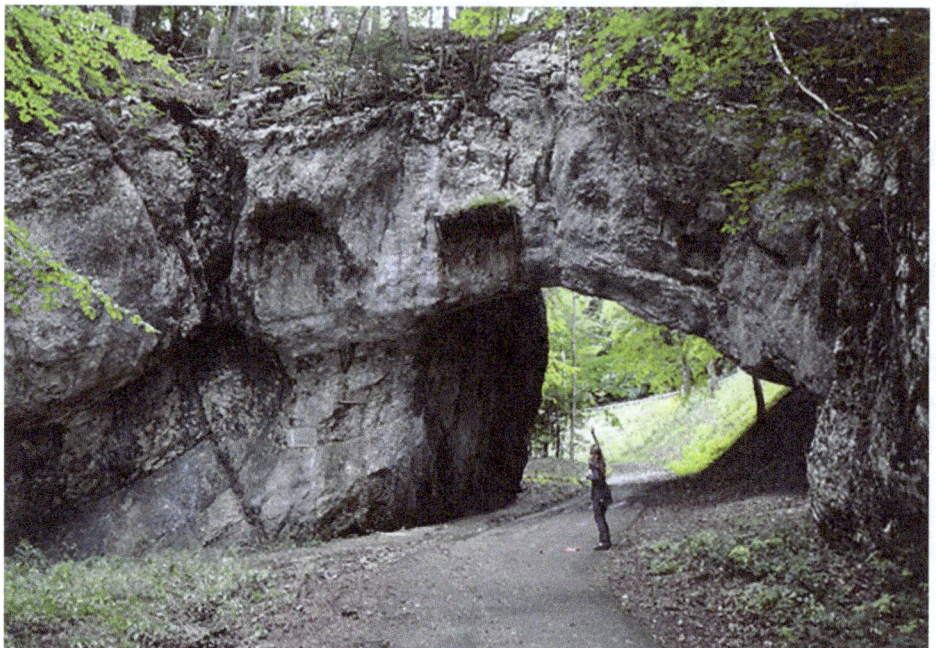

Fig. 1: Pierre Pertuis, Foto J. Bartels

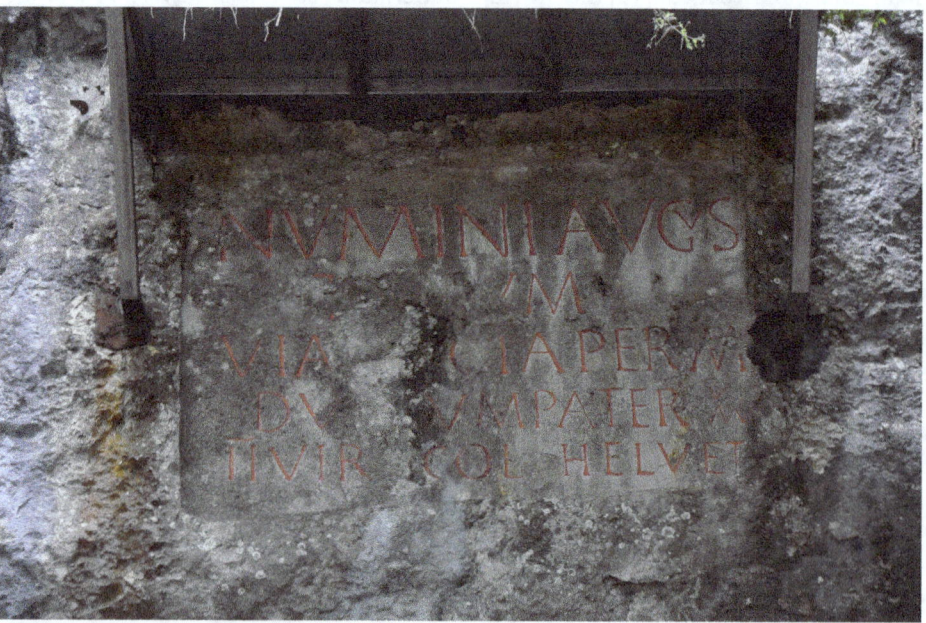

Fig. 2: Pierre Pertuis Inschrift, Foto J. Bartels

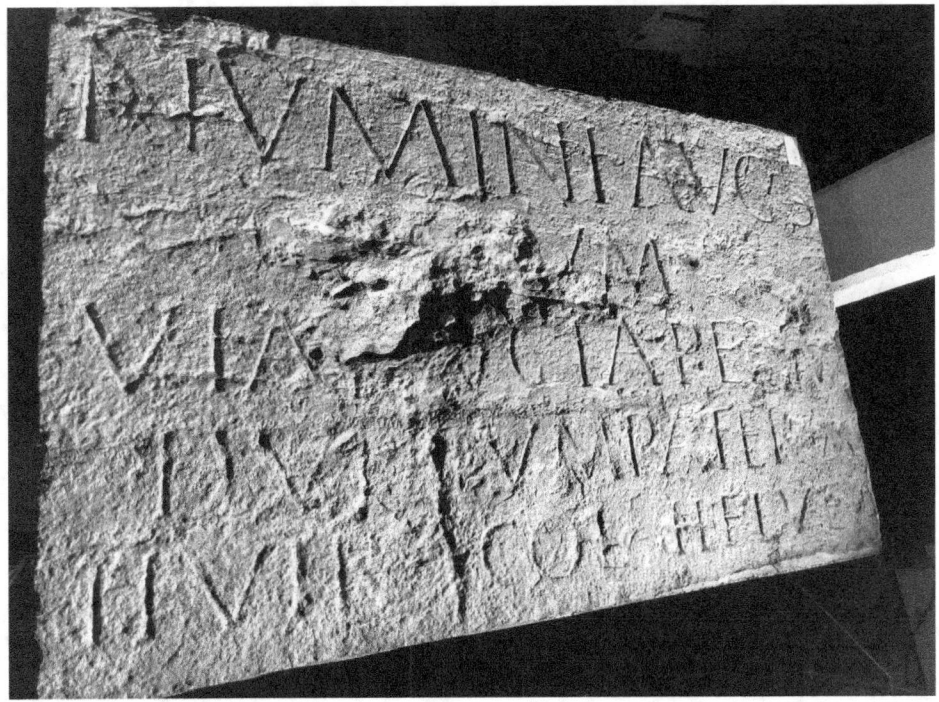

Fig. 3: CIL XIII 5166 cast in the Nationalmuseum Zürich (Nr. A-85164 Depot Affoltern am Albis), Foto A. Kolb

1 The Case of Marcus Dunius Paternus

Numini Augus/t[or]um / via [d]ucta per M(arcum) / Dunium Paternum / IIvir(um) col(oniae) Helvet(iorum).[1]

In the Swiss Jura mountains, above the rock gateway of Pierre Pertuis south of Tavannes, a Latin inscription documents construction work on the road that traversed the Jura from the area around Lake Biel to the Birs Valley. This monumental arch and the inscription it bears can here serve to exemplify the significance of the Roman road system, the sources used in its historical reconstruction and, last but not least, the recent developments in research.

The inscription above the rock arch refers to a route that may have followed a Celtic path, which the Romans expanded up to the mid first century in order to connect

---

1 CIL XIII 5166, HOWALD/MEYER 1940, 271 no. 244; WALSER 1980, 34–35 no. 125. The inscription is carved into the rock above the north exit of the gate (815 mamsl), which probably marked the border between the areas of the *Raurici* and the *Helvetii*.

the two main routes of the region.² The inscription further attests to local construction work being done on this route, causing one to wonder who paid for it and why. Given the lack of the usual formulae, such as *sua pecunia*, the inscription does not offer any overt answers to these questions; but it might be assumed that M. Dunius Paternus, *IIvir coloniae Helvetiorum*, financed the work on his own.³ That said, the fact that neither the second duumvir nor the community are mentioned as builders seems to substantiate that conclusion.

His motives were hardly simply altruistic or even solely prestige-oriented. In fact, it seems more likely that his decision was informed by concrete economic interests. As other sources attest, M. Dunius Paternus was probably an active entrepreneur who dealt in lumber and architectural ceramics.⁴ These resources were the source of his wealth, which was usually the prerequisite for a leading role in local politics.⁵ It is even possible that the road ran along his private holdings.⁶ While cases in which private economic interests and public interest coincided are rarely attested due to our patchy source record, this dynamic should thus not be underestimated as a driving force behind ancient road building.⁷

The inscription and the rock gate further stand for two key genres of source material used in studying ancient Roman roads: the rock gate is an important archaeological marker for the route the Jura road followed through the terrain, but also for the labour involved in road construction; both these aspects are now being studied in a more comprehensive perspective.⁸ The route connecting the Lake Biel area and the

---

2 These led from Avenches via Solothurn to Augst and from Besancon via Mandeure to Kembs. The Roman Jura road that split off at Petinesca (and led to Porrentruy and Delle) is dated based on archaeological finds; see the overview in HERZIG 2006, 96–99, who assumes that there was an older Celtic structure due to the numerous ore deposits in the Jura.
3 Similarly FREI-STOLBA 2017, 164, though she thinks of money contributed by the colonia and external subsidies.
4 Most recently FREI-STOLBA 2017, 162–167.
5 His prominent role in the *colonia* seems to be documented by the fragments of an honorary inscription that may refer to his construction of a *schola*: AE 2009, 940 (= CIL XIII 5101. 5114. 5144).
6 This might make sense in the mountain region, especially for a lumber producer. A parallel case could possibly be seen in the Arco di Barà in Hispania Tarraconensis. This arch, built by the senator L. Licinius Sura, may have bridged the Via Augusta where this road reached his family's land, as was suggested by G. ALFÖLDY in CIL II²/14, 2332; RATHMANN 2003, 141, likewise argues that this large landowner financed the section of the Via Augusta that passed through his holdings; he further proposes the arch of Berà as another parallel case.
7 A likely parallel is a rock inscription near Soria (Spain) naming only one duumvir as well: CIL II 2886: *Hanc viam / Aug(ustam?) possibly better: usto/ustis) / L(ucius) Lucret(ius) Densus / IIvir{um} / fecit*. A few other inscriptions attest extra urban road building by private donors: CIL II 3167. 3221. 3271; CIL III 600; CIL V 1863. 1864; CIL XIII 4549; SEG 17, 315; IK 59, 152; cf. RATHMANN 2003, 141 Anm. 807, who has doubts about the status of "Reichsstraße"; HAENSCH/WEISS 2012, 451; for the low rate of utilitarian gifts such as roads ZUIDERHOEK 2009, 77.
8 Scholars generally agree that the gate is a natural formation (see already CIL XIII 5166) that was widened in Roman times to 10,5 m; see for instance DRACK/FELLMANN 1998, 524. By contrast, GREWE 2004,

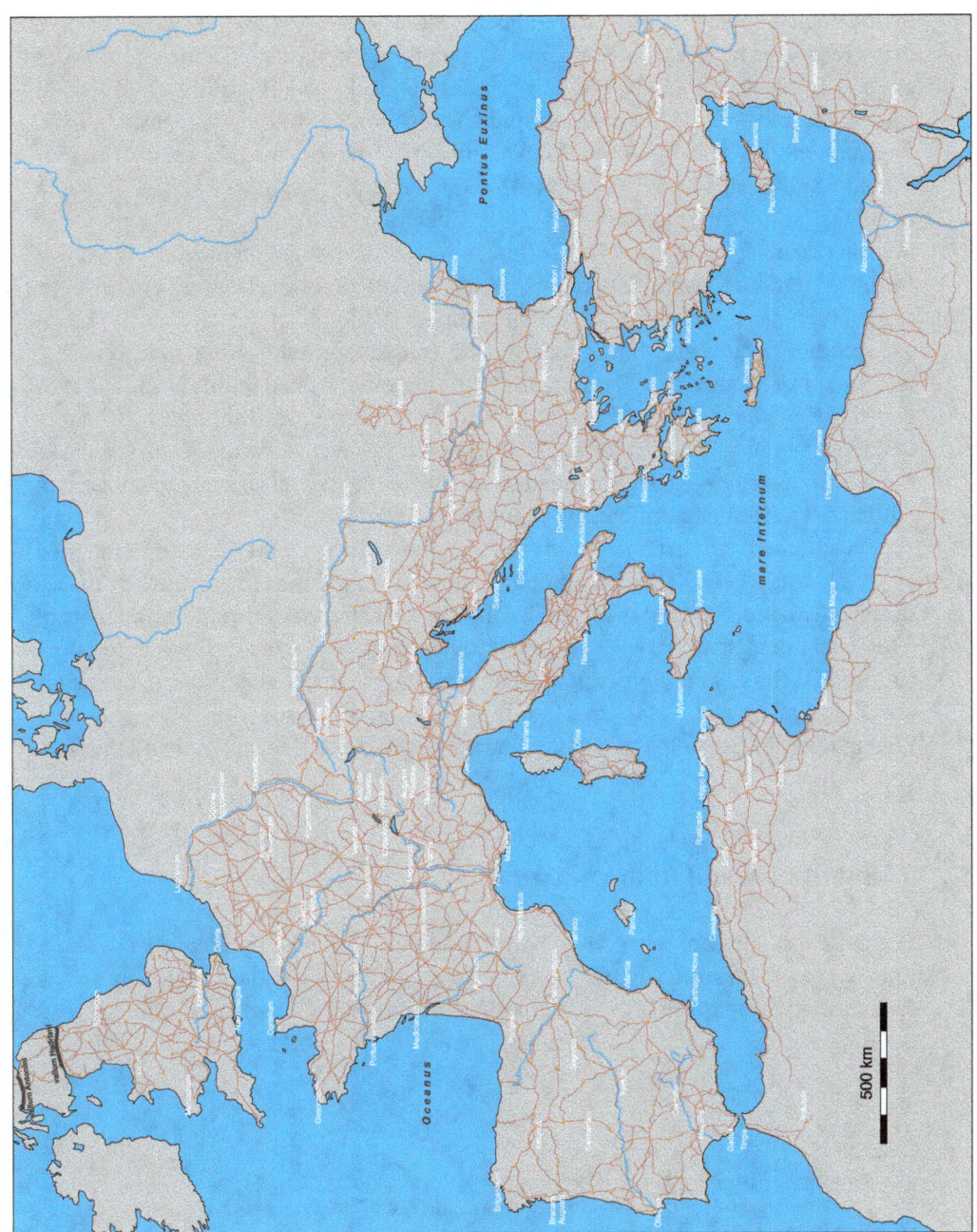

Fig. 4: M. Herchenbach/A. Kolb

13–14 argued that the rock was artificially cut (6m deep and 9m wide). Since the workers followed the natural slant of the limestone layers, the cut's ceiling slopes from 7 m down to 5 m; the argument is repeated in GREWE 2016, 773.

Birs Valley via the Swiss Jura Mountains is otherwise attested only by various traces of the roadway and the scanty remains of a potential waystation.⁹ Though it had been previously thought unlikely, the first century date suggested by this archaeological evidence could well fit the inscription. Its invocation of multiple emperors (*numini Augustorum*) had been interpreted as a *terminus post quem* of the joint reign of Marcus Aurelius and Lucius Verus (161–169). Already ERNST MEYER, however, had uttered a well-founded warning against dating inscriptions so late solely on the grounds of *Augusti* occurring in the plural.¹⁰ If this indicator for dating is removed, M. Dunius Paternus' building inscription can be placed earlier, after the elevation of the *gentis caput Aventicum* as *colonia Helevtiorum* in the year 71.

Another peculiarity that stands out by comparison with other road building inscriptions is the *via ducta* formula that is hitherto unattested in this form. The verb *ducere* (or *perducere*) most frequently occurs on inscriptions that deal with aqueducts (*aquae*) and trenches (*fossae*), which often involved excavation work.¹¹ While the phrasing may have been intended to emphasize the technical accomplishment of cutting the rock, that point must remain speculative.

The duumvir's inscription further allows one to deduce that the road functioned and ranked as a *via publica*, i.e. a public main road maintained by the public purse.¹² In sum, therefore, the combined study of inscription and rock gateway as an element of a regional interdisciplinary research perspective exemplifies the changes in research culture that the field of Roman roads has seen in recent years. In order to introduce these changes in a summary fashion, the following will discuss the significance of Roman roads in general, as well as review the available source material and the state of research.

2 Significance of Roman Roads

In the Roman Empire, roads were both foundation and means of power – a claim that can easily be substantiated by pointing to the history and development of the Roman road system. Already in Antiquity, the particular intensity of Roman road building was considered a characteristic feature of this world empire, since already

---

9 Summarised by HERZIG 2006, 96–99.
10 The sources use this phrase also for successive rulers and the ruling family; see most recently MEYER 1970. This formula first occurs in inscriptions securely dated to the year 139 (RIB I 707).
11 See for instance CIL XIV 85: ...*fossis ductis*; CIL VIII 4204: ...*aqua vic[o] / Augustor[um] / Verecundens(ium) / perducta*; RIB I 1463: ... *aqua adducta*; a number of milestones from Sardinia (and only there) have the phrase *via qui ducit a Nora* ... CIL X 7996–8001 etc.
12 HERZIG 2006, 99 points out that the itineraries do not list the road, which seems to indicate that its importance declined over time.

Greek and Roman authors listed the roads among Rome's greatest achievements.[13] A good example is Aelius Aristides, whose famous speech on Rome, delivered before Emperor Antoninus Pius, praises the Romans for opening up the entire world with their roads: *"You have surveyed the entire globe, spanned rivers with bridges of all kinds, pierced mountains to create roadways, established waystations in uninhabited areas and introduced a cultured and orderly way of living everywhere"*.[14] The author's obeisance to the Empire concentrates on the civilising impact it has on other peoples by virtue of its technical and political-administrative superiority, which finds its material expression in road building. The Romans' ability to rule, which Aristides highlights elsewhere, thus finds its concrete expression in their road system.[15] His praise further implies that the Empire's inhabitants are the main beneficiaries of these roads, since they provide infrastructural access to their places of residence, while also bringing order and culture. It is not difficult to imagine that the general principles of Roman rule in practice that Aristides praises here will have met with the approval of the Emperor and the imperial elite. That the Romans saw themselves as the bringers of salvation and civilising order is a familiar theme, beautifully expressed for instance in the memorable phrase Vergil formulated under the impression of the *pax Augusta* and the new monarchy: *tu regere imperio populos Romane, memento – haec tibi erunt artes – pacique inponere morem, parcere subiectis et debellare superbos*.[16] The Roman road system remained a quintessential symbol of Roman power even in the 6th century when Procopius used a project of road repair undertaken by the Emperor Justinian to illustrate the excellence of Roman rule.[17]

For Rome, the roads were not merely a symbol of power, but also served as a concrete instrument of rule. The Empire was pervaded by an extensive network of main roads (*viae publicae*), built or expanded under imperial direction, with a total length of around 100.000 km, as well as around 200.000 km of regional and local roads of lower standard.[18] The Roman road system did not reach this density, level of quality, and structure before the mid-2nd century CE. Before that, it had grown gradually in the wake of Rome's military expansion, driven by the needs of the army and the developing territorial state. These were served by making existing or new paths passable and reinforcing them, or even by turning them into *viae publicae* of the highest level of quality, which allowed even waggons to pass without being hindered by either terrain

---

13 Dion. Hal. ant. 3,67,5; Strab. 5,3,8; Plin. nat. 36,125.
14 Aristeid. 26, 101.
15 Aristeid. 26, 51. 58.
16 Verg. Aen. 6,847–853.
17 Prokop, De aedificiis 4,8.
18 On the Roman road system of the provinces see fundamentally Pekáry 1968; Rathmann 2003; situation of Italy see Eck 1979; on the technology Quilici 2008; Grewe 2013, 128–135; Raepsaet 2016; significance and development Rathmann 2007; Kolb 2012; Rathmann 2014; Kolb 2015; Kolb 2016b.

or weather. This gradual growth began already in the 4th century BCE on the Italian peninsula and served to secure the newly acquired territory by connecting newly founded cities to Rome. From the 3rd century BCE onwards, Rome extended its interests beyond Italy into the Mediterranean world, gradually conquering and provincializing first the Western and then the Eastern half of it. This expansion of Roman rule is clearly visible in the roads built.[19] In doing so, Rome made use of and expanded upon the existing structures, while also systematically adding new connections. This not only improved the ability of people to move over land, for instance for the purposes of travel or troop deployment, but also affected the movement of resources, especially of goods extracted from subjects or those required to supply Rome and its armies, while also benefiting communication.

After the growth it saw under Augustus, Roman road building was at its most intense during the imperial period. The need to consolidate the empire caused Roman administration to be intensified and its infrastructural basis needed to grow accordingly, giving rise to a wide-reaching and high-quality network of roads that connected even the most peripheral parts of the empire. According to Aristides, the emperor could then, as we know for Antoninus Pius, keep in close and uninterrupted contact with all his legates and emissaries. Like a conductor, he directed their moves using written instructions: "Hardly written, they already arrive, as if borne on wings."[20]

This network of roads was particularly beneficial to the economy,[21] which is well known to have flourished in the 2nd century, at least in most provinces. Later, maintenance work and repairs predominate, as is documented primarily by the many milestones that have survived even from the 4th century. In the West, these sources seem to disappear in the 5th century.[22] In the East, by contrast, concern and care for the road system remains significant in the 6th century and continues under the Byzantine Empire.[23]

---

19 The oldest known provincial milestone stems from Sicily. It was evidently set up by the consul L. Aurelius Cotta (cos. 254 and 248 BCE) after the Roman victories over the Carthaginians (262 BCE Agrigentum, 254 BCE Palermo) according to AE 1957, 172; for this stone see most recently DIAZ ARINIO 2015, 104–105 no. 24, who gives the older research but offers no new insights. In Narbonensis a milestone of the consul Domitius Ahenobarbus (CIL XVII/2, 294) attests to the extension of the route from Italy to Spain in 118 BCE. In Asia the first milestones are likewise set up when the province was established and bear the name of Manlius Aquilius (e.g. IK 17/2, 3602), consul in 129 BCE.
20 Aristeid. 26, 33.
21 Most recently ADAMS 2012, 229–230; ROTHENHÖFER 2013; by employing network applications DE SOTO/CARRERAS 2009 and CARRERAS/DE SOTO 2013 discuss mobility, transportation costs and motives of Roman road building.
22 The last known milestone dates to the reign of Theodosius II and Valentinian III (435 CE) and was found at Arles: CIL XVII/2, 53.
23 As we saw, Procopius mentions Justinian's concern with road building, but milestones seem to vanish, see DESTEPHEN 2018. The youngest known milestone dates to the reign of Justin (518–527 CE)

3 Sources

Research on the so-called imperial or public roads (*viae publicae*) has always been based on a variety of sources. The starting point is provided by ancient itineraries, practical aids used by travellers that consisted of written lists of routes that corresponded to actual roads through the terrain. One of the most extensive lists of this kind, which exist not only in literary, but also in epigraphic form, is the 3rd century *Itinerarium Antonini*.[24] Comprising 225 routes, more than 2000 places names, and just as many distance figures, this imperial Roman travel handbook offers an excellent overview of the main routes one could take to navigate the Empire. The famous *Tabula Peutingeriana* (created around 1200), named after the second and most famous owner of this manuscript, the humanist KONRAD PEUTINGER (1465–1547), has usually been interpreted as an illustrated version of such an itinerary (of early 5th century date). While the *Tabula* maintains the systematic arrangement of a linear list, it expresses it visually on a more than 6m long scroll that shows a compressed and distorted landscape view of the greater Mediterranean area, with the routes being marked out by largely parallel lines. Using this format, the scroll gives 2700 settlements and the corresponding distance measurements between them, presenting not only the Roman world but also a few areas far beyond the Empire's borders, such as Sri Lanka and China. In addition, this ancient world map also shows stylised topographical features, characterises the settlements with 555 little iconic vignettes, and also gives miscellaneous further information. As RATHMANN has recently demonstrated, the *Tabula Peutingeriana* derives from the Greek chorographic tradition and thus probably had a Hellenistic archetype that was created around 200 BCE. As such, it seems appropriate today to categorise it as a chorographic map.[25]

In order to verify the exact course taken by a road referenced by a route listed in the itineraries, it is necessary to consult archaeological finds. While these are not preserved everywhere, they are relatively common for the Empire overall, which allows for a good understanding of construction techniques and the relative dates of roads. What is preserved below the surface reveals that not only the foundation and structure of the road itself vary depending on the road's location, the topography, and the condition of the terrain, but that these factors also affected the use of built structures to overcome obstacles or difficult stretches, such as bridges, tunnels, steps or stone furrows. The famous and much-lauded paved surface[26] of Roman roads is common in

---

RRMAM III 5, 119, as does the youngest road-building inscription MACKAY/MACKAY 1969, 139–140. In the 7th/early 8th century, the Umayyads continued the tradition in Palestine by setting up milestones in Arabic; see VAN BERCHEM 1922, 17–29.
24 See the overview of itineraries in KOLB 2016b, 235–237.
25 RATHMANN 2018, 14–31.
26 Strab. 5,3,8.

the environs of towns, but was not a general standard for overland roads, which were frequently gravelled earth roadways.

Besides the rather sporadic mentions of roads in the corpus of ancient literature – ranging from poetry to technical and legal literature – inscriptions provide the most informative testimony. This documentary material reveals not only the course of a road, but also its function and use, and thus sheds light on the significance of a given road as well as on that of road building more generally. Besides votive offerings – for instance those dedicated at crossroads – and city laws that provide information on road administration, the most important types of inscription are building inscriptions and milestones. At the same time, these are also the most common and conspicuous epigraphic monuments.

Milestones, a characteristic feature of the *viae publicae*, marked the distance, mile for mile, a road had progressed and further communicated that it had been built on the initiative of or funded by Roman magistrates, emperors or communities. Their purpose was thus not purely practical, but also to immortalise Roman rule on stone columns along the Empire's main lines of communication. Ancient travellers were thus constantly confronted with Roman power, as well as the Empire's capacity for organisation and public welfare. Despite the over 8,000 *miliaria* that have survived from all over the Roman Empire, we possess only a tiny fraction of the original number.[27] That notwithstanding, these largely monotonous texts are extremely important sources for political history, the spatial and administrative organisation of the Empire, and for imperial ideology. Besides the hard data they provide in the form of titulatures, place names and distance figures, their find spots and the regularities and irregularities of their formulae can also allow for significant insights. Up to the 4th century CE, their inscriptions often document construction work – either *ex novo*, repairs or improvements, or even the act of setting up new miliaria – on the *viae publicae*, which explains why milestone-inscriptions are often considered a special type of building inscription. At the same time, they increasingly take on features of dedications, as they come to be phrased in the Dative and references to road building become increasingly rare, especially from the 4th century onwards; finally they seem to loose any practical function.[28]

Building inscriptions are particularly conspicuous if they are preserved on monumental structures, such as archways or honorary columns and bases.[29] They supplement our understanding of road construction and in some cases even reveal how the

---

27 This includes inscribed and uninscribed stones. See below the figures given as review of the state of research. In general see Hirschfeld 1907; Kolb 2001; Kolb 2004.
28 The dative is first attested for Caligula (CIL II 4640), but becomes more common in the 2nd/3rd century; accoding to Sidon. carm. 24,5 a traveller saw old columns with imperial names *(satis vetustis nomen Caesareum viret columnis)*; Destephen 2018 on the development of late Roman milestones.
29 On monumental archways that spanned roads see Eck 2004, 23–39.

Romans planned the networks, which took place after new areas were added to the Empire and provincialized.[30] This can be seen on representative monuments, such as the so-called "Stadiasmus Patarensis / Stadiasmus provinciae Lyciae". It is a huge pillar or statue base (6,72 m high, dating to the year 45/46), which not only records 65 routes in the province of Lycia as being built by the emperor Claudius, but also preserves the honorific dedication of the provincials to Claudius.[31] As two years (after the Roman annexation of Lycia in 43) seem too short a time span to build such a road network, the previous existing and already measured ways seem to have been included into the Roman road network. Another example is the great building inscription of the Illyrian governor P. Cornelius Dolabella from the time of Tiberius.[32] The preserved stone panels could come from a monument comparable to the Stadiasmus, though an arch is also possible. Although both inscriptions list overland routes and give distances, they are not to be understood as road directories for use by travellers. Rather, in praising road building, they propagate the efforts and accomplishments of Rome in integrating new territories and their inhabitants into the Empire. Inscriptions of this kind should thus be considered emphatic expressions of the structures and practices of Roman imperial organisation.

4 The State of Research

The Roman *viae publicae* have long been the subject of historical and archaeological research. As such, the history of this research cannot be exhaustively presented here. Instead, a few important contributions shall be singled out. The fundamental historical studies are still those of PEKÁRY 1968 and RATHMANN 2003.[33] They deal with the organization and administration of the main road network inside the Empire. In research, the *viae publicae* are often called imperial roads, which differ from private and regional roads on various counts, as set forth by the jurist Ulpian (Dig. 43,8,2,20–24). Closely related and occasionally overlapping fields of historical study are those of

---

[30] KOLB 2013, 206–221; KOLB 2016b, 229–230; see further on this process for the example of the province of Thracia (e.g. CIL III 6123) KOLB 2018.
[31] SEG 51, 1832; cf. ŞAHIN/ADAK 2007, esp. 6 for the measures (6,72 x 2,38 x 1,62 m) which might refer to a base of an equestrian statue of the emperor; ONUR 2016a; ONUR 2016b.
[32] CIL XVII/4 (fasc. 2) p. 129–132.
[33] In addition for the Republic WISEMAN 1970; for the organisation of the system in Italy ECK 1979; well-illustrated but popular summaries are provided by HEINZ 2003, STACCIOLI 2003 and KLEE 2010; on civic road administration KAISER 2011 and CAMPEDELLI 2014 (in Italy); more recent work on the building of *viae publicae* in RATHMANN 2004 (*capita viarum*); RATHMANN 2006a; RATHMANN 2014; BARTELS 2014.

'travel', 'transportation' and 'the state infrastructure of the *cursus publicus*', research into which has increased during recent years.[34]

Recent conferences have already helped to collect the new results being achieved in current historical and archaeological research on Roman roads. So far, however, the regional diversity of the Empire has not been represented. Furthermore, the focus was on other questions, such as on the significance of *viae publicae* for settlements[35] or the relevance of road systems in the pre-modern world more generally.[36] Finally, these edited volumes applied very broad conceptions of roads and often had diachronic interests.[37] The small number of recent contributions to roads in the ancient world thematise the fundamental economic role of roads in the northern Roman Empire (ROTHENHÖFER, POLLAK) and the Celtic *leuga* as a unit of measure, which is being empirically reassessed once more (GREWE).[38]

The numerous available archaeological detail studies and excavation reports predominantly document individual finds relating to roads, their facilities and their course. More recently, scholars have begun to treat larger regions with an eye to more interdisciplinary road research.[39] Of particular interest are those regions that have so far been neglected, such as the Roman-Persian border region recently considered by COMFORT 2009 and COMFORT/MARCIAK 2018. In recent years, archaeological research has further expanded our knowledge of the infrastructure travellers used along the roads, such as waystations and overnight quarters, as well as of military posts. This data also serves to improve our understanding of the relevance and usage of the road network; a recent example is the re-evaluation of the amber road through Pannonia and of its waystations.[40] Another related development is that the *stationes* are now thematised more explicitly.[41]

The study of Roman milestones is primarily carried out in a wealth of detail studies that engage with individual stones, individual roads, or with certain regions or time periods.[42] An example of the latter approach is the new monograph by DIAZ ARINIO 2015 stands out, who assembled all milestones known from the Republican

---

[34] Important monographs to the named topics deliver CASSON 1994; LAURENCE 1999; KOLB 2000; ADAMS/LAURENCE 2001; ADAMS 2007; VAN TILBURG 2007; GUÉDON 2010; ZWINGMANN 2012; LEMCKE 2016; RAEPSAET 2016.
[35] FREI-STOLBA 2004.
[36] ALCOCK/BODEL/TALBERT 2012.
[37] KOSCHIK 2004; KUNOW 2007; SCHWINGES 2007; FISCHER/HORN 2013.
[38] ROTHENHÖFER 2013; POLLAK 2013; GREWE 2013.
[39] E.g. BEKKER-NIELSEN 2004; GRABHERR/WALDE 2006; HERZIG 2006; HERZIG 2007; BISHOP 2014; CUVIGNY 2014.
[40] GROH/SEDLMAYER/ZALKA 2013.
[41] Useful collected volumes on the topic are those of FRANCE/NELLIS-CLÉMENT 2014 and BASSO/ZANINI 2016; for a recent brief account of the *mansiones* of the *cursus publicus* KOLB 2016a.
[42] The state of research is reviewed in KOLB 2004. The following listed publications refer to the most recent or important works.

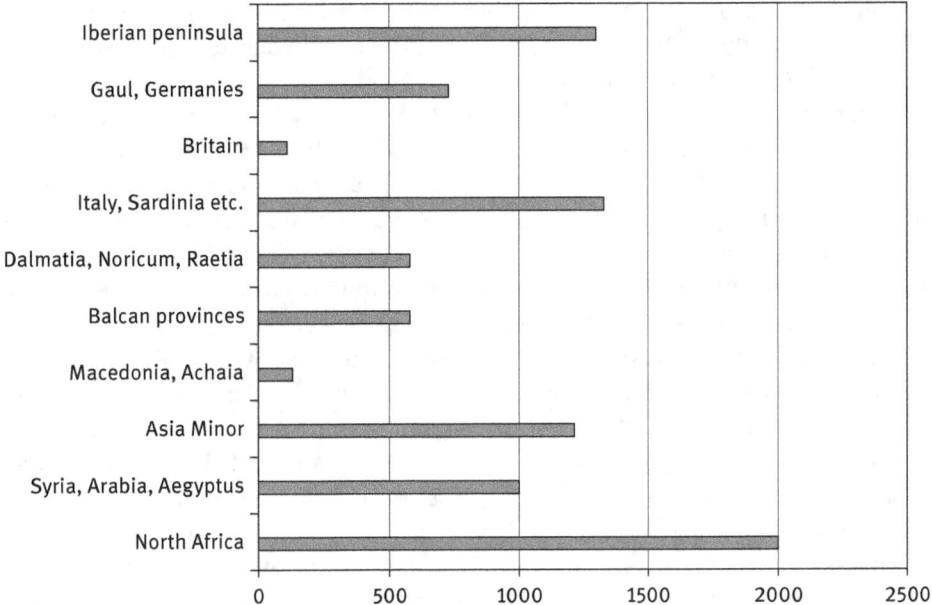

Fig. 5: Roman milestones: occurrence in the Empire (A. Kolb)

period (a little under 50 in number) in a catalogue with commentary and historical analysis.

Today the number of known milestones (both inscribed and as well anepigraphical stones) must nowadays be roughly assembled from the various regions of the empire (most figures are approximations): We know about 1300 from the provinces of the Iberian peninsula (*Hispania citerior, Baetica, Lusitania*),[43] the Gallic and Germanic provinces have rendered around 730,[44] 110 have been found in Britain,[45] in Italy (including the islands of Sardinia, Corsica and Sicily) around 1300,[46] in western Illyricum (*Dalmatia, Noricum, Raetia*) 580,[47] in the Balkan provinces (*Pannoniae, Dacia,*

---

43 SILLIÈRES 1990 (for *Baetica:* ca. 100); RODRIGUEZ COLMENERO et al. 2004 (*Asturia* and *Gallaecia:* 674, but not deducting 41 dedications); CIL XVII/1, fasc. 1 (*Hisp. citerior:* 307); ESPAÑA-CHAMORRO 2017, 619–653 who counts 708 milestones for all Iberian provinces (519 alone for *Hisp. citerior* without *Gallaecia*) excepting the number given by RODRIGUEZ COLMENERO et al. 2004; RATHMANN (in this volume) counts 266 for the *Lusitania*.
44 CIL XVII/2; HERZIG 2006; RATHMANN 2006b.
45 SEDGLEY 1975; RIB I 98. 598. 2219–2314; RIB III 3516–3527.
46 HERZIG 1970; DONATI 1974; BASSO 1987; OGGIANU 1991; BANZI 1999; GROSSI/ZANCO 2003; GROSSI 2019; further information about numbers by P. BASSO, A. BUONOPANE, P. GROSSI who are preparing the manuscipt for CIL XVII 3,1 (Northern Italy).
47 CIL XVII/4, fasc. 1–2.

Moesiae, Thracia) 570,[48] in the Greek provinces of *Macedonia* and *Achaia* 130,[49] in Asia Minor 1274,[50] in the eastern provinces of *Syria, Arabia* and *Aegyptus* perhaps around 1000,[51] in North Africa around 2000.[52]

All these publications provide important preparatory work for the forthcoming edition of the known milestones in the volume XVII of the *Corpus Inscriptionum Latinarum* (CIL XVII), which aims at collecting and making available only this category of source material province by province. Therefore it will offer a systematic and consistent presentation of the *miliaria* as part of the *Corpus Inscriptionum Latinarum*. The project "Roman milestones", which was originally founded by GEROLD WALSER in the 1960ties, creates the basis for such research in aiming at the complete edition by the Berlin-Brandenburgische Akademie der Wissenschaften as "CIL XVII Miliaria Imperii Romani". The edition is being prepared as a joint-venture of an international group of scholars around the mediterranean collaborating with the University of Zürich and the Berlin-Brandenburgische Akademie der Wissenschaften.[53] Following the criteria of the CIL the edition will cover all the milestone material from Roman Italy and the provinces; it is presented in a standardized form with text, commentary, drawing and photographs. Besides the already published volumes on Gaul and *Germania superior et inferior* (CIL XVII/2), as well as the provinces of the western Illyricum (*Raetia, Noricum, Dalmatia)*, the latest published volume to date now covers *Hispania Tarraconensis* (2015).[54] Other volumes are currently in preparation for the regions of: *Britannia* (XVII/1), Italy (CIL XVII/3), *Pannonia* (XVII/4), the eastern Balkan and Greek provinces (XVII/4,3: *Moesia superior, Moesia inferior, Thracia, Macedonia and Achaia*) and the provinces of Asia minor.[55]

---

48 HOLLENSTEIN 1975; HOLLENSTEIN 1995; PANAITE 2015; MIRKOVIC (in this volume); PETROVIC (in this volume); SOPRONI/LÖRINCZ/KOVACS et al. manuscript in preparation for CIL XVII; HOLLENSTEIN/KOLB manuscript in preparation for CIL XVII.
49 MOTTAS 1989; MOTTAS/DECOURT 1997; MOTTAS (in this volume).
50 FRENCH 1981–1988; FRENCH 2012–2015 who notes that 576 of the 1214 milestones are anepigraphic.
51 THOMSEN 1917; ISAAC/ROLL 1982; BAUZOU 1989; FISCHER/ISAAC/ROLL 1995; BAUZOU 1998; GRAF 2004; ROLL/AVNER 2008; BALTY 2008; ISAAC 2015; see now the full bibliography for *Judaea*: http://milestones.kinneret.ac.il/en/bibliography/. For the region as a whole THOMSEN 1917 counted 706 milestones; but now BEN DAVID (paper below in this volume) records already almost 700 milestones for the province of *Judaea* alone.
52 According to SALAMA 2001, 26; SALAMA 1987. In his unpublished MA thesis HUGENBERG 2004 counted 1926 milestones which were published up to the year 2001.
53 Financial aid was graciously provided by the aid of the Deutsche Forschungsgemeinschaft.
54 CIL XVII/2 (*Galliae, Germaniae*) ed. G. WALSER; CIL XVII/4, fasc. 1 (Raetia, Noricum) ed. A. KOLB/G. WALSER/G. WINKLER and CIL XVII/4, fasc. 2 (*Dalmatia*) ed. A. KOLB/G.WALSER as well as CIL XVII/1, fasc.1 (*Tarraconensis*) ed. M.G. SCHMDIT/C. CAMPEDELLI.
55 The overall publication plan forsees the following volumes:
CIL XVII/1 *miliaria provinciarum Hispaniae, Britanniae*: fasc. 1,1 *miliaria Hispaniae citerioris*, Berlin 2015.
CIL XVII/2 *miliaria provinciarum Galliarum et Germaniarum*, Berlin 1986.

Due to this state of the project the established regions are mostly omitted in the papers of this conference volume which aims at reassessing current research on the construction and use of the Roman *viae publicae* in a combined historical and archaeological perspective. This reassessment tries to take into account recently studied regions of the Empire and some territories beyond, as well as to consider new sources and approaches to deliver new results.

Bibliography

ADAMS 2007 = C. ADAMS, Land Transport in Roman Egypt, Oxford, 2007.
ADAMS 2012 = C. ADAMS, Transport, in: W. SCHEIDEL (ed.), The Cambridge Companion to the Roman Economy, Cambridge 2012, 218–240.
ADAMS/LAURENCE 2001 = C. ADAMS/R. LAURENCE (ed.), Travel and Geography in the Roman Empire, London/New York 2001.
ALCOCK/BODEL/TALBERT 2012 = S. ALCOCK/J. BODEL/R. TALBERT (ed.), Highways, Byways, and Road Systems in the Pre-modern World, Malden, MA/Oxford 2012.
BALTY 2008 = J.-C. BALTY, Un nouveau milliaire de Domitien et le gouvernement syrien d'A. Lappius Maximus (note d'information), *CRAI* 152, 2008, 835–846.
BANZI 1992 = E. BANZI, I miliari come fonte topographica e storica. L'esempio della XI regio (Transapadana) e delle Alpes Cottiae, Roma 1999.
BARTELS 2014 = J. BARTELS, Meilensteine und Barbaren. Die Straßenbaupolitik auf dem Balkan unter Maximinus Thrax und Gordian III., in: A. KOLB (ed.), Infrastruktur und Herrschaftsorganisation im Imperium Romanum, Berlin 2014, 222–245.
BASSO 1987 = P. BASSO, I miliari della Venetia Romana, Padova 1987.
BASSO/ZANINI 2016 = P. BASSO/E. ZANINI (ed.), Statio Amoena. Sostare e vivere lungo le strade romane, Oxford 2016.
BAUZOU 1989 = T. BAUZOU, A finibus Syria. Recherches sur les routes des frontières orientales de l' Empire romain, PhD Université Paris I, Paris 1989 unpublished.
BAUZOU 1998 = T. BAUZOU, Le secteur nord de la *via nova* en Arabie de Bostra à Philadelphia, in: J.-B. HUMBERT/A. DESREUMAUX (ed.), Fouilles de Khirbet Es-Samra en Jordanie I, Turnhout 1998, 101–255.
BEKKER-NIELSEN 2004 = T. BEKKER-NIELSEN, The Roads of Ancient Cyprus, Copenhagen 2004.
BISHOP 2014 = M.C. BISHOP, The Secret History of the Roman Roads of Britain, Barnsley 2014.
CAMPEDELLI 2014 = C. CAMPEDELLI, L' amministrazione municipale delle strade Romane in Italia, Bonn 2014.
CARRERAS/DE SOTO 2013 = C. CARRERAS/P. DE SOTO, The Roman Transport Network: A Precedent for the Integration of the European Mobility, *Historical Methods: A Journal of Quantitative and Interdisciplinary History* 46, 117–133.

CIL XVII/3 *miliaria Italiae* (in 4 parts)
CIL XVII/4 *miliaria provinciarum Illyrici et Europae Graecarum*: fasc. 4/1*miliaria provinciarum Raetiae et Norici*, Berlin 2005; fasc. 4/2 *miliaria provinciae Dalmatiae*, Berlin 2012.
CIL XVII/5 *miliaria provinciarum Asiae*
CIL XVII/6 *miliaria provinciarum Syriae, Arabiae, Aegypti*
CIL XVII/7 *miliaria provinciarum Africae*

Casson 1994 = L. Casson, Travel in the Ancient World, Baltimore/London 1994².
Chevallier 1976 = R. Chevallier, Roman Roads, London 1976 (transl. from French orig. 1972).
Comfort 2009 = A. Comfort, Roads on the Frontier between Rome and Persia, PhD Univ. Exeter 2009.
Comfort/Marciak 2018 = A. Comfort/M. Marciak, How did the Persian King of Kings Get His Wine?: The upper Tigris in antiquity (c.700 BCE to 636 CE), Oxford 2018.
Cuvigny 2014 = H. Cuvigny, Le système routier du désert Oriental égyptien sous le Haut-Empire à la lumière des ostraca trouvés en fouille, in: France/Nellis-Clément 2014, 247–278.
De Soto/Carreras 2009 = P. De Soto/C. Carreras, La movilidad en época romana en Hispania: aplicaciones de análisis de redes (SIG) para el estudio diacrónico de las infraestructuras de transporte, *Habis* 40, 2009, 303–324.
Destephen 2018 = S. Destephen, The Late Milestones of Asia Minor, *Gephyra* 16, 2018, 173–184.
Diaz Arinio 2015 = B. Diaz Arinio, Miliarios romanos de época republicana, Roma 2015.
Donati 1974 = A. Donati, I miliari delle regioni IV e V dell'Italia, *Epigraphica*, 36, 1974, 155–222.
Drack/Fellmann 1998 = W. Drack/R. Fellmann, Die Römer in der Schweiz, Stuttgart 1988.
Eck 1979 = W. Eck, Die staatliche Organisation Italiens in der hohen Kaiserzeit, München 1979.
Eck 2004 = W. Eck, Straßen und ihre Denkmäler, in: Frei-Stolba 2004, 17–39.
España-Chamorro 2017 = S. España-Chamorro, Límites y territorios de la Bética romana, PhD Madrid 2017.
Fischer/Horn 2013 = T. Fischer/H.G. Horn (ed.), Straßen von der Frühgeschichte bis in die Moderne. Verkehrswege – Kulturträger – Lebensraum. Akten des Interdisziplinären Kolloquiums Köln, Februar 2011, Wiesbaden 2013.
Fischer/Isaac/Roll 1995 = M. Fischer/B. Isaac/I. Roll, Roman Roads in Judaea II: The Jaffa-Jerusalem Roads, Oxford 1996, 289–293.
France/Nellis-Clément 2014 = J. France/J. Nellis-Clément (ed.), La statio. Archéologie d'un lieu de pouvoir dans l'empire romain, Bordeaux 2014.
Frei-Stolba 2004 = R. Frei-Stolba (ed.), Siedlung und Verkehr im Römischen Reich: Römerstrassen zwischen Herrschaftssicherung und Landschaftsprägung: Akten des Kolloquiums zu Ehren von Prof. H. E. Herzig, Bern/New York 2004.
Frei-Stolba 2017 = R. Frei-Stolba, Holzfässer. Studien zu den Holzfässern und ihren Inschriften im römischen Reich mit Neufunden und Neulesungen der Fassinschriften aus Oberwinterthur/Vitudurum. Zürcher Archäologie Heft 34, Zürich/Egg 2017.
French 1981–1988 = D. French, Roman Roads and Milestones of Asia Minor, Vol. 1–2, Oxford 1981–1988.
French 2012–2015 = D.H. French, Roman Roads and Milestones of Asia Minor Vol. 3: Milestones, Fasc. 3.1–8: Galatia (BIAA Electronic Monograph 2), London 2012–2015.
Grabherr/Walde = G. Grabherr/E. Walde (ed.), Via Claudia Augusta und die Römerstraßenforschung im östlichen Alpenraum, Innsbruck 2006.
Grewe 2004 = K. Grewe, Alle Wege führen nach Rom – Römerstraßen im Rheinland und anderswo, in: Koschik 2004, 9–42.
Grewe 2013 = K. Grewe, Streckenmessung im antiken Aquädukt- und Straßenbau, in: Fischer/Horn 2013, 123–146.
Grewe 2016 = K. Grewe, Urban Infrastructure in the Roman World, in: G.L. Irby (ed.), A Companion to Science, Technology, and Medicine in Ancient Greece and Rome, Volume II, Chichester 2016, 768–83.
Groh/Sedlmayer/Zalka 2013 = S. Groh/H. Sedlmayer/C. V. Zalka, Die Straßenstationen von Nemesco und Sorokpolany an der Bernsteinstraße (Panonien, Ungarn), Wien 2013.
Grossi 2019 = P. Grossi, Politics, Administration and Propaganda along Ancient Roman Roads in the Center and North Italy, Oxford 2019 in print.

GROSSI/ZANCO 2003 = P. GROSSI/A. ZANCO, Miliari romani nel Nord Italia: materiali, provenienza, lavorazione. L'esempio dell'area veneta e friulana, *Quaderni di Archeologia del Veneto* 19, 2003, 192–202.
GUÉDON 2010 = S. GUÉDON, Le voyage dans l'Afrique romaine, Bordeaux 2010.
HAENSCH/WEISS 2012 = R. HAENSCH/P. WEISS, Ein schwieriger Weg. Die Straßenbauinschrift des M. Valerius Lollianus aus Byllis, *Römische Mitteilungen* 118, 2012, 435–454.
HEINZ 2003 = W. HEINZ, Reisewege der Antike. Unterwegs im römischen Reich, Stuttgart 2003.
HERZIG 1970 = H.E. HERZIG, Le réseau routier des régions VI et VIII d'Italie, Bologna 1970.
HERZIG 2006 = H.E. HERZIG, Römerstrassen in der Schweiz, *Helvetica Archeologica* 146/147, 2006, 42–112.
HERZIG 2007 = H.E. HERZIG, Historische Strassen- und Wegforschung in der Schweiz, in: SCHWINGES 2007, 119–159.
HIRSCHFELD 1907 = O. HIRSCHFELD, Die römischen Meilensteine, *Sitzungsberichte der Königlich Preussischen Akademie der Wissenschaften* 9, 1907, 165–201 (= Kleine Schriften, Berlin 1913, 703–743).
HOLLENSTEIN 1975 = L. HOLLENSTEIN, Zu den Meilensteinen der römischen Provinzen Thracia und Moesia Inferior, *Stud. Balc.* 10, 1975, 23–44.
HOLLENSTEIN 1995 = L. HOLLENSTEIN, Neue Meilensteininschriften aus Bulgarien, in: R. FREI-STOLBA/M.A. SPEIDEL (ed.), Römische Inschriften – Neufunde, Neulesungen und Neuinterpretationen. Festschrift für Hans Lieb, Basel 1995, 179–189.
HOWALD/MEYER 1940 = E. HOWALD/E. MEYER, Die römische Schweiz, Zürich 1940.
HUGENBERG 2004 = R. HUGENBERG, Strassen und Meilensteine in den römischen Provinzen Africa proconsularis, Numidia und Mauretania, Zürich 2004 unpublished MA thesis.
ISAAC 2015 = B. ISAAC, The Roman Road System in Judeaea, *Scripta Classica Israelica* 34, 2015, 41–48.
ISAAC/ROLL 1982 = B. ISAAC/I. ROLL, Roman Roads in Judaea I: The Legio-Scythopolis Road, Oxford 1982.
KAISER 2011 = A. KAISER, Roman Urban Street Networks, New York 2011.
KENNEDY 2004 = D.L. KENNEDY, The Roman Army in Jordan, London 2004[2].
KLEE 2010 = M. KLEE, Lebensadern des Imperiums. Straßen im römischen Weltreich, Stuttgart 2010.
KOLB 2000 = A. KOLB, Transport und Nachrichtentransfer im Römischen Reich, Berlin 2000.
KOLB 2001 = A. KOLB, Meile und Meilenstein, in: Reallexikon der Germanischen Altertumskunde 19, 2001, 505–507.
KOLB 2004 = A. KOLB, Römische Meilensteine: Stand der Forschung und Probleme, in: FREI-STOLBA 2004, 135–155.
KOLB 2011 = A. KOLB, Miliaria: ricerca e metodi. L'identificazione delle pietre miliari, in: F. PAVAN (ed.), I miliari lungo le strade dell'Impero. Atti del convegno. Isola della Scala 28 novembre 2009, Verona 2011, 9–18.
KOLB 2012 = A. KOLB, The Conception and Practice of Roman Rule: the Example of Transport Infrastructure, *Geographia Antiqua* 20–21, 2011/2012, 53–69.
KOLB 2013 = A. KOLB, Antike Strassenverzeichnisse – Wissensspeicher und Medien geographischer Raumerschließung, in: D. BOSCHUNG/TH. GREUB/J. HAMMERSTAEDT (ed.), Morphome des Wissens: Geographische Kenntnisse und ihre konkreten Ausformungen. Beiträge der Tagung vom 15.-17. Juli am Internationalen Kolleg Morphomata, München 2013, 192–221.
KOLB 2015 = A. KOLB, Communications and Mobility in the Roman Empire, in: C. BRUUN/J. EDMONDSON (ed.), Oxford Handbook of Roman Epigraphy, Oxford 2015, 649–670.
KOLB 2016a = A. KOLB, Mansiones and *cursus publicus* in the Roman Empire, in: BASSO/ZANINI 2016, 3–8.

Kolb 2016b = A. Kolb, The Romans and the World's Measure, in: S. Bianchetti/M.R. Cataudella/ H.-J. Gehrke (ed.), Brill's Companion to Ancient Geography, Leiden/Boston 2016, 223–238.

Kolb 2018 = A. Kolb, Transport in Thracia, in: Cities, Territories and Identities. 1st International Roman and Late Antique Thrace Conference. Plovdiv, 7–10 October 2016, *Bulletin of the National Archaeological Institute of the Bulgarian Academy of Science* 44, 2017 (2018), 1–9.

Koschik 2004 = H. Koschik (ed.), „Alle Wege führen nach Rom ..." Internationales Römerstrassenkolloquium Bonn, Pulheim 2004.

Kunow 2007 = J. Kunow (ed.), Erlebnisraum Römerstraße Köln-Trier. Erftstadt-Kolloquium 2007, Treis-Karden 2007.

Laurence 1999 = R. Laurence, The Roads of Roman Italy: Mobility and Cultural Change, London 1999.

Lemcke 2016 = L. Lemcke, Imperial Transportation and Communication from the Third to the Late Forth Century: The Golden Age of the *cursus publicus*, Bruxelles 2016.

Mackay/Mackay 1969 = T.S. Mackay/P. A. Mackay, Inscriptions from Rough Cilicia East of the Calycadnus, *Anatolian Studies* 19, 1969, 139–142.

Meyer 1970 = E. Meyer, Nochmals Augusti, *Klio* 52, 1970, 283–285.

Mottas 1989 = F. Mottas, Les voies de communication antiques dans la Thrace égéenne, in: H.E. Herzig/R. Frei-Stolba (ed.), Labor omnibus unus. Gerold Walser zum 70. Geburtstag dargebracht von Freunden, Kollegen und Schülern, Stuttgart 1989, 82–104.

Mottas/Decourt 1997 = F. Mottas/J.-C. Decourt, Voies et milliaires romains de Thessalie, *BCH* 121, 1997, 311–354.

Oggianu 1991 = M.G. Oggianu, Contributo per una riedizione dei miliari sardi, in: L'Africa Romana. Atti dell'VIII convegno di studio, Cagliari, 14–18 dicembre 1990, Sassari 1991, 863–897.

Onur 2016a = F. Onur, Parerga to the Stadiasmus Patarensis 16, The roads, settlements and territories, *Gephyra* 13, 2016, 89–118.

Onur 2016b = F. Onur, Patara Yol Anıtı / «The Monument of Roads» at Patara, in: H. Işık/ E. Dündar (ed.), Lukka'dan Likya'ya: Sarpedon ve Aziz Nikolaos'un Ülkesi/From Lukka to Lycia: The Country of Sarpedon and St. Nicholas, Yapı Kredi Yayınları Anadolu Uygarlıkları Serisi 5, İstanbul 2016, 570–577 (online: http://adkam.akdeniz.edu.tr/sp-en-text).

Panaite 2015 = A. Panaite, Roman Roads in *Moesia inferior*. Archaeological and Epigraphic Evidence, in: L. Vagalinski/N. Sharankov (ed.), Limes XII. Proceedings or the 22nd International Congress of Roman Frontier Studies. Ruse, Bulgaria Spetember 2012, Sofia 2015, 593–600.

Pekáry 1968 = T. Pekáry, Untersuchungen zu den römischen Reichsstrassen, Bonn 1968.

Pollak 2013 = M. Pollak, Wege zum Wohlstand. Technologie und Infrastruktur in den Zentralalpen, in: Fischer/Horn 2013, 11–42.

Quilici 2008 = L. Quilici, Land Transport Part 1: Roads and Bridges, in: J. P. Oleson (ed.), The Oxford Handbook of Engineering and Technology in the Classical World, Oxford 2008, 571–579

Raepsaet 2016 = G. Raepsaet, Land Transport and Vehicles, in: G.L. Irby (ed.), A Companion to Science, Technology, and Medicine in Ancient Greece and Rome, Volume II, Chichester 2016, 768–83.

Rathmann 2003 = M. Rathmann, Untersuchungen zu den Reichsstraßen in den westlichen Provinzen des Imperium Romanum, Bonn 2003.

Rathmann 2004 = M. Rathmann, Die Städte und die Verwaltung der Reichsstraßen, in: Frei-Stolba 2004, 163–226.

Rathmann 2006a = M. Rathmann, Statthalter und die Verwaltung der Reichsstraßen in der Kaiserzeit, in: A. Kolb (ed.), Herrschaftsstrukturen und Herrschaftspraxis. Konzepte, Prinzipien und Strategien der Administration im römischen Kaiserreich, Berlin 2006, 201–259.

Rathmann 2006b = M. Rathmann, Die Reichsstraßen der *Germania Inferior*, *Bonner Jahrbücher* 204, 2004 [2006], 1–45.

RATHMANN 2007 = M. RATHMANN, Die Bedeutung der Straßen im Römischen Reich, in: KUNOW 2007, 17–30.
RATHMANN 2014 = M. RATHMANN, Der Princeps und die *viae publicae* in den Provinzen. Konstruktion und Fakten eines planmäßigen Infrastrukturausbaus durch die Reichszentrale, in: A. KOLB (ed.), Infrastruktur und Herrschaftsorganisation im Imperium Romanum. Herrschaftsstrukturen und Herrschaftspraxis III. Akten der Tagung in Zürich 19.-20. 10. 2012, Berlin 2014, 197–221.
RATHMANN 2018 = M. RATHMANN, Tabula Peutingeriana. Die einzige Weltkarte aus der Antike, Darmstadt 2018³.
RODRIGUEZ COLMENERO et al. 2004 = A. RODRÍGUEZ COLMENERO/S. FERRER SIERRA/R.D. ALVAREZ ASOREY, Miliarios e outras inscricións viarias romanas do noroeste hispánico (conventos bracarense, lucense e asturicense), Santiago de Compostela 2004.
ROLL/AVNER 2008 = I. ROLL/U. AVNER, Tetrarchic Milestones found near Yahel in the Southern Aravah, *ZPE* 165, 267–286.
ROTHENHÖFER 2013 = P. ROTHENHÖFER, Die Wirtschaft der Römer: Produktionszentren und Handelswege in römischer Zeit, in: FISCHER/HORN 2013, 109–121.
ŞAHIN/ADAK 2007 = S. ŞAHIN/M. ADAK, Stadiasmus Patarensis. Itinera Romana Provinciae Lyciae, Istanbul 2007.
SALAMA 1987 = P. SALAMA, Bornes milliaires d'Afrique provonsulaire. Un panorama historique du Bas Empire Romain, Rome 1987.
SALAMA 2001 = P. SALAMA, Les bornes milliaires du territoire de Tipasa (Maurétanie Césarienne), Roma 2001.
SCHWINGES 2007 = R.C. SCHWINGES (ed.), Strassen- und Verkehrswesen im Hohen und Späten Mittelalter, Ostfildern 2007.
SEDGLEY 1975 = J. P. SEDGLEY, The Roman Milestones of Britain: their Petrography and probable Origin, Oxford 1975.
SILLIÈRES 1990 = P. SILLIÈRES, Les voies de communication de l'Hispanie méridionale, Paris 1990.
STACCIOLI 2003 = R.A. STACCIOLI, The Roads of the Romans, Rome 2003.
THOMSEN 1917 = P. THOMSEN, Die römischen Meilensteine der Provinzen Syria, Arabia und Palästina, *ZDPV* 40, 1917, 1–103.
VAN BERCHEM 1922 = M. VAN BERCHEM, Matériaux pour un Corpus Inscriptionum Arabicarum II,1, Le Caire 1922.
VAN TILBURG 2007 = C.R. VAN TILBURG, Traffic and Congestion in the Roman Empire, London/New York 2007.
WALSER 1980 = G. WALSER, Römische Inschriften in der Schweiz. II. Teil: Nordwest- und Nordschweiz, Bern 1980.
WISEMAN 1970 = T.P. WISEMAN, Roman Republican Road Building, *PBSR* 38, 1970, 122–152 (= Roman Studies, Liverpool 1987, 126–156).
ZUIDERHOEK 2009 = A. ZUIDERHOEK, The Politics of Munificence in the Roman Empire. Citizens, Elites and. Benefactors in Asia Minor, Cambridge 2009.
ZWINGMANN 2012 = N. ZWINGMANN, Antiker Tourismus in Kleinasien und auf den vorgelagerten Inseln, Bonn 2012.

Richard Talbert
Roads in the Roman World: Strategy for the Way Forward

Abstract: TALBERT urges that wide-ranging investigation of the roles of Roman roads in the cultures and mindsets of the Empire's peoples has untapped potential; in the same vein so, too, does comparison of Rome's roads with those of other pre-modern states worldwide noted for their highways. Also recommended and outlined is an initiative to create a digital, Empire-wide collection of Roman milestones; this would be first-rate scholarship, but designed to be accessible to non-specialists.

Zusammenfassung: TALBERT fordert eine umfassende Untersuchung der Rolle römischer Straßen in den Kulturen und Mentalitäten der Reichsbevölkerung, da eine solche ungenutztes Potential berge. In gleicher Weise gelte dies auch für den Vergleich der Straßen Roms mit denen anderer vormoderner Staaten weltweit, die bekannt sind für ihre Fernstrassen. Ebenso empfohlen und skizziert wird eine Initiative, um eine digitale, reichsweite Sammlung römischer Meilensteine zu schaffen. Dabei sollte es sich um exzellente Forschung handeln, die jedoch so konzipiert wäre, dass sie auch Fachfremden zugänglich wäre.

The kind invitation to give the keynote lecture on this occasion is both an honor and a daunting challenge. A breadth of perspective is called for, as well as more general reflection than might prove practical or appropriate within the scope of a single paper. Permit me to use this opportunity, therefore, to draw attention tactfully to two concerns, and to present some recommendations about them. My aim is no more than to stimulate productive discussion among us all. There is no intent here to expose faults, or to win arguments, or to press for radical changes to current approaches.

The first concern relates to my reactions when I seek to gain (so far as is possible) an informed overview of the work at present being pursued on Roman roads, milestones and associated matters – as demonstrated not least, for instance, by the papers at this conference. There is every reason to find current work sound and useful, not to say vital. Our understanding of the courses of many roads certainly needs improvement, for example. Undiscovered milestones, documents and archaeological finds are always emerging; naturally, the entire scholarly community benefits from their methodical study and publication. However, just because there continues to be so much to preoccupy us in these typically very focused basic respects, other approaches are liable to remain relatively neglected by contrast and so still await realization of their latent potential. This observation applies in particular, I suspect, to the wider roles of Roman roads in the cultures and mindsets of the Empire's peoples. To be sure, far be it from me to overlook or to devalue the explorations that have been made

https://doi.org/10.1515/9783110638332-003

of such roles, and that continue to be made – for example, in the entire substantial volume 24 (2016) of *Antiquité Tardive*, just published, devoted to *Le voyage dans l'Antiquité tardive: réalités et images*. I merely urge the cultivation of such broader approaches as an aspect of our own work if it is not already present there. We should also welcome interest in this level of approach on the part of colleagues who make no claim to be experts on roads, but who recognize that their place in the Roman physical, cultural and mental landscape repays attention.

As in the study of antiquity from any perspective, it is essential to keep in mind the fundamental point that Romans' vision of their roads did not necessarily match our vision of them today. In Chapter 12 of a *Highways* volume (the outcome of a conference at Brown University in 2008), I dared to question provocatively "how far even [Roman] emperors or their better-educated subjects were in the habit of conceptualizing the empire's highways as a 'network'."[1] This is a perspective which comes so naturally to us today – with our scientific and cartographic grasp, and our planned national highway systems – that we may too readily project it back into antiquity (as other contributors to the same volume did). I concluded with reference to Rome:

> "Even at the highest level, it seems, the mindset, motivation, reference tools, and administrative resources to recognize the empire's highways as an interconnected network and to exploit their potential as such were all absent."[2]

Clearly, there is ample scope for discussion here. Major issues arising include, for instance, the degree to which the Roman authorities sought to control and exploit their subjects, as well as the authorities' ability to produce maps at a reasonable scale that marked the course of roads, and then their inclination to use such maps. Specifically, how typical is the featuring of roads on the Peutinger Map?[3] Was it intended to have some practical use? Would it have prompted viewers to think of the roads as a network? My altogether skeptical conclusions failed to convince at least one reviewer, RAY LAURENCE, whose discussion of the entire book, and of its Chapter 12 in particular, was notably generous and thoughtful.[4] However, as so often in scholarship, the new questions opened up by a book or a chapter may prove more influential in the long term than the conclusions advanced in the first instance.

One approach that the *Highways* volume aimed to encourage specifically was comparison of the experiences of pre-modern states worldwide noted for their highways. The initial impetus came one morning during an earlier conference that KURT RAAFLAUB and I organized at Brown University in 2006 on ideas about geography and

---

1 TALBERT 2012, 247.
2 TALBERT 2012, 250.
3 See TALBERT 2010.
4 LAURENCE 2016.

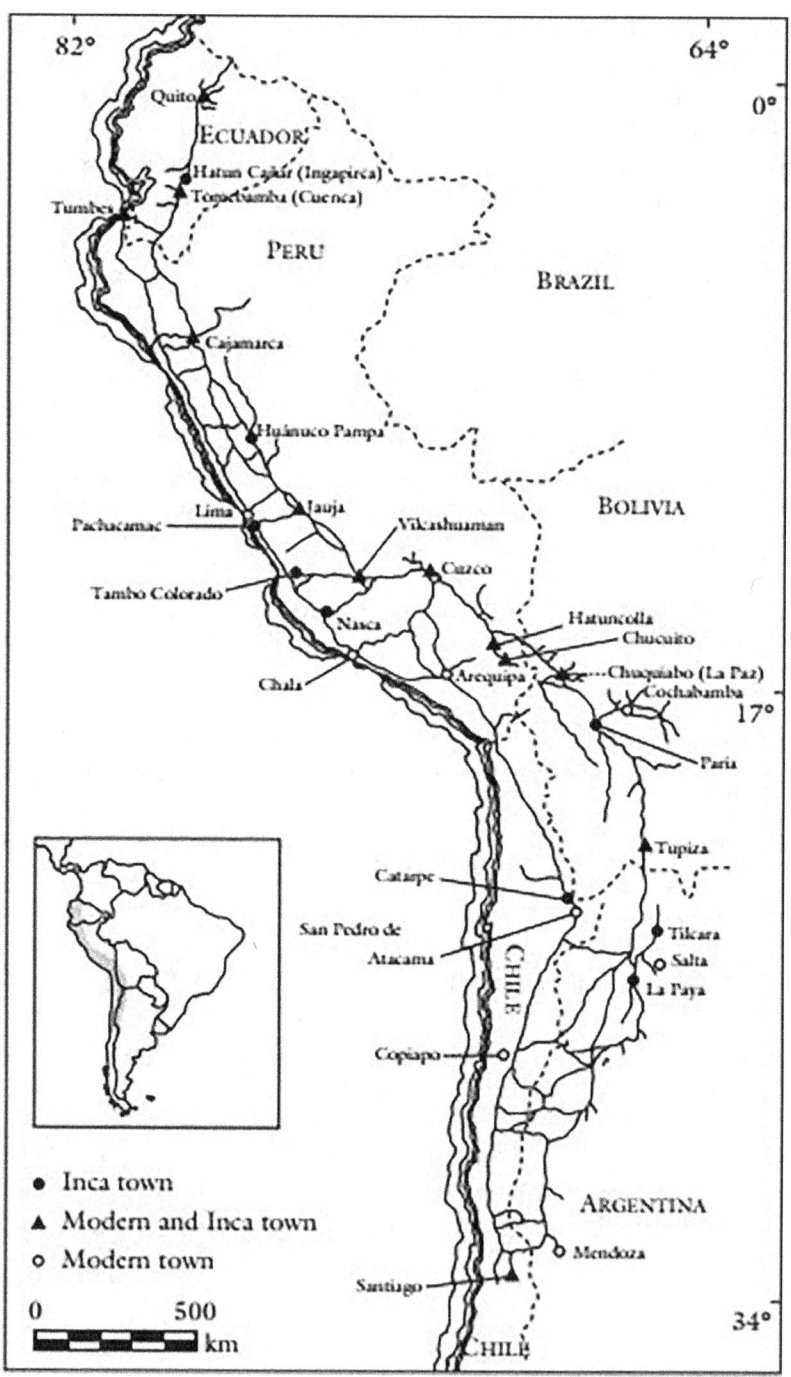

Fig. 1: The Inca Empire (Tawantinsuyu) in the early 1500s, featuring its highways.
[RAAFLAUB/TALBERT 2010, fig. 9.1 (Catherine Julien), courtesy of John Wiley and Sons]

ethnography in pre-modern societies.⁵ In the course of our breakfast Catherine Julien, an Inca expert, referred in passing to how the sixteenth-century Spanish conquerors of Peru often made comparisons between Roman and Inca roads. [FIG. 1] It struck me that such comparisons could usefully be extended and deepened worldwide. When I proposed this topic, Kurt agreed without hesitation that we should organize a second conference for the purpose, although subsequently pressure of multiple commitments forced him to ask other colleagues at Brown to take his place in realizing the prospect.

During the planning stage, two memorable surprises emerged. The first was that an effort to make such comparisons on the global scale seemed almost unprecedented. We could find no published record of an earlier such initiative, although we were delighted to discover that one of our contributors, James Snead, was co-editing a volume (the outcome of a conference like ours) *Landscapes of Movement: Trails, Paths, and Roads in Anthropological Perspective* that was to be published in 2009. In fact almost all its twelve chapters relate to the American continent only, but the broad premise on which they are based clearly invites application elsewhere. The co-editors state in their Preface:

"Our discussion began from the shared premise that trails, paths, and roads are the manifestation of human movement through the landscape and are central to an understanding of that movement at multiple scales. The study of these features connects with many intellectual domains, engaging history, geography, environmental studies, and, in particular, anthropology and its subfields. In the process we are developing a better understanding of infrastructure, social, political, and economic organization, cultural expressions of patterned movement, and the ways that trails, paths, and roads materialize traditional knowledge and engineering, world view, memory, and identity."⁶

The second surprise was that in several instances colleagues with the relevant expertise were very hard to find; and of those that we did find eventually, none (we learned) had ever been involved in a comparative initiative. Securing an expert for the Classical Era (late fourth century BCE to early fourth century CE) in China of all states was an exceptional challenge. Prof. Michael Nylan at Berkeley was highly recommended to us, but her initial response when approached was discouraging. She was unable to help, she replied, and in any case (she assured us) there was next-to-nothing to say about highways in pre-modern China. In desperation we begged her to contribute whatever she could all the same. She kindly agreed, and then three months later reported in a very different mood that she had found plenty to say in fact. For this reason, we accepted from her a chapter double the length of any other in view of the importance and range of her findings. These extended to the road as metaphor, as well as to road deities, cults and rituals.⁷

---

5 Raaflaub/Talbert 2010 was the outcome.
6 Snead/Erickson/Darling 2009, xv.
7 Nylan 2012.

To be sure, the Roman case is different insofar as specialist interest in Rome's roads is long established. Even so, to compare Rome's roads with those of other pre-modern states still remains a novel perspective where there is surely unrealized potential to be tapped. My own initial efforts have at least acted to highlight formative characteristics that I suspect go unappreciated, or at best underappreciated, by those of us in today's first-world Western societies who limit our attention to Roman roads. Let me identify, and briefly comment upon, three such characteristics.

The first characteristic is the quality and empire-wide range of Rome's highways or 'public' roads. The level of organization, along with the deployment of immense manpower and material resources, that were required to construct and maintain these roads for centuries merit recognition as an astonishing achievement and investment for any state worldwide at any period, especially in a pre-modern era. Specialists on Roman roads are well aware of the achievement, naturally; but they have hardly been concerned to set it in the global context of time and space. It may have slipped their notice, too, that the 'pre-modern' era can extend to less than a century ago. In a major geographic overview of China, GEORGE CRESSEY (who had traveled very widely there during the 1920s) could state:

> "Inaccessibility and poor communications have handicapped China for centuries. Except where railroads or modern automobile service is available, travel is on foot, by sedan chair, on muleback, in two-wheeled carts, or by boat. Twenty miles a day is a good average, and in place of a journey of a few hours as by rail one spends days jolting along in a two-wheeled cart."[8]

Within former Roman territory, conditions in Asia Minor towards the end of Ottoman rule a century ago were similar to those in China. The *Handbook of Asia Minor* issued by the British Naval Staff Intelligence Department around the end of World War I gives a vivid sense of them, and of the sketchiness of available data. The header to the itinerary from Adalia (Antalya) to Selefke (Silifke), for example, draws attention to the kinds of difficulties routinely encountered, as well as warning users that distance-figures are liable to be estimates derived from the time spent on the journey in the absence of accurate measurement on the ground:

> "The greater part of this route is merely a track. It does not appear to be passable for wheels, except possibly over short stages, and is not in regular use. The main authorities used for the itinerary are archaeological reports, and the route described may in places not be the track most commonly followed. The distances are calculated from the times noted by the various travellers whose reports have been consulted, and can only be regarded as approximate."[9]

---

8 CRESSEY 1934, 24–25.
9 Naval Staff Intelligence III.3 1919, 92. The Handbook was planned to appear in four volumes, with vol. III in three parts, and vol. IV in two. In the event, vol. III part 1 (to cover north of the Bosphorus to the Halys) and vol. IV part 2 (to cover the area between the Black Sea and Kayseri) never appeared.

The itineraries in the *Handbook* can also serve as a reminder that, in focusing on well-engineered Roman roads or highways, we may be unduly neglecting secondary roads, tracks and even paths that were also much used in antiquity, especially in areas of rugged landscape. An effort to redress such imbalance would no doubt prove rewarding.

The second formative characteristic to mention is that Roman highways are designed and built with gradients and a width that can accommodate wheeled traffic. We are prone to take these design features for granted, but again in a global context they need to be recognized as conscious choices which bring both costs and benefits. With good reason, the toll which the emperor Hadrian allowed Milevis in Africa to levy in order to recoup the costs of road construction was termed on the local milestones a *vectigal rotare*, "wheel-toll".[10] Inca roads present an extreme contrast: they were envisaged as a network for certain, but still for individuals on foot only, together with no more than pack-animals.[11] Hence they could be graded far more steeply than Roman roads. The Andean environment, needless to add, presents far more extreme elevations than any in the Roman empire. In New Granada (today Colombia) during the early 1850s, at a time when the cost of constructing new roads for wheeled traffic would severely deplete the state's limited means, the compromise recommended by the head of its Chorographic Commission, Agustín Codazzi, is instructive: paths just wide enough for mules and horses should be built at once, he urged, but in such a way that subsequently they could be widened to accommodate wagons.[12]

The third formative characteristic is the openness of Roman roads to all comers and to vehicles of all kinds. Slaves needed their owners' permission for any movement, of course; exiles were restricted; and Roman senators' private travel beyond Italy, Sicily or Narbonese Gaul was subject to the emperor's approval. But otherwise, generally speaking, anyone could use these roads without requiring prior authorization or the equivalent of a modern passport.[13] While freedom of movement was indeed a prized feature of the Roman citizen's *libertas*, throughout the Empire this freedom was by no means limited to citizens. Moreover, tolls were the exception, not the rule; individuals and their vehicles could usually travel along a road without charge. All this is very different from the arrangements in both Japan and China, for instance. Here the authorities exercised tight control on who could take which roads, for what fee, with what documentation, and even at what date during the year. In early modern Japan there was added discrimination by gender on the highways of the 'Gokaidô'

---

10 CIL VIII 10327–10328.
11 Julien 2012.
12 Appelbaum 2016, 112. Notoriously, in some regions of New Granada the trails were so steep and eroded that it was safest for a traveler to submit to being carried in a chair on the back of a local porter (Appelbaum 2016, 81–83).
13 Talbert 2012, 244–245.

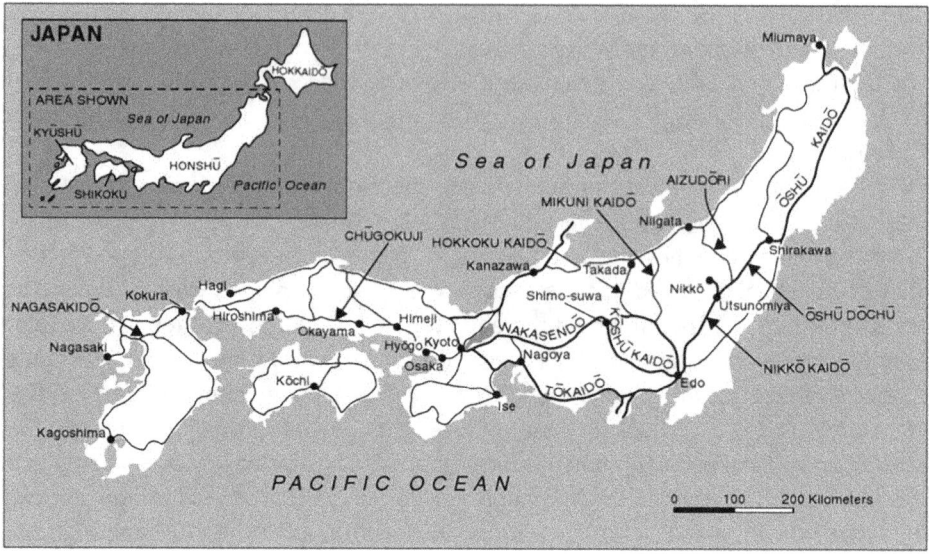

Fig. 2: The Gokaidô highway network in Early Modern Japan (1603–1868). [VAPORIS 2012, fig. 4.1., courtesy of Harvard University Asia Center]

network; not only the authorities (until 1867 !), but also family pressure, especially discouraged travel by females.[14] **[Fig. 2]** NYLAN says of China in its Classical Era:

> "Obviously, the dynasty hoped to control the flow of people, things, and ideas as much as possible, lest too much commerce and too much movement disrupt subject populations engaged in sedentary agriculture, the basis of stable rule within civil society."[15]

If our focus remains confined to Rome's world, there is the risk that we shall take almost for granted the empire's "connectivity" (as we like to call it), without maybe acknowledging quite how remarkable a phenomenon this was. Connectivity overland, after all, is a product not just of the construction and maintenance of so many roads. As noted with reference to Japan and China, a state where the authorities place severe limits on who can travel creates a connectivity inferior in quality to Rome's. A further contributing factor easily overlooked is Rome's lack of restrictions on vehicles. In China, by contrast, who could use what vehicles was closely regulated; in Japan the public road network could accommodate wheeled vehicles, but their use on it was banned.[16]

---

14 VAPORIS 2012, 93, 95–98.
15 NYLAN 2012, 42.
16 NYLAN 2012, 39–40; VAPORIS 2012, 101.

By the same token, there may be marked variation in the components of a state's highways and its investment in them, with serious consequences for travelers and their rate of progress. In particular, the provision of bridges built in stone – perhaps the most challenging, expensive, and impressive single component of a Roman highway – is not to be taken for granted. Inca suspension bridges, by contrast, were made of straw and other plant materials.[17] In Japan, for a variety of reasons (rather than merely cost), the Tokugawa authorities mostly opted not to build bridges. So even on Japan's most developed highway – the 'Tokaido', running for 500 km between Kyoto and Edo (modern Tokyo) – travelers were compelled to cross eight major rivers by ferry and to ford four others; only over two further rivers were bridges built. Considered in this light, the smoothness of Roman connectivity overland for travelers and their vehicles is all the more striking. Thus to place this Roman achievement within a global context seems a perspective ripe for further exploitation.

****

The second of my two concerns is different and more delicate: the publication of Roman milestones. As everyone here knows, the inscriptions on them have long been treated by scholars as a distinct type of document, most notably in the *Corpus Inscriptionum Latinarum*, where volume XVII gathers this material. Undeniably, the quality of the presentation in this volume's fascicles remains very high. My concern, rather, is that the pace of publication is too slow (a problem that may indeed lie more with the publisher than the contributors), and that the format is no longer satisfactory in today's academic environment. This is not to advocate the abandonment of the volume, or radical change to its format (which has been modestly updated, and is not determined by the contributors). However, I do see sound reason to launch an associated, secondary initiative: it would be able to achieve empire-wide coverage much sooner than CIL XVII can be expected to, and would be designed to benefit extensively from up-to-date digital technology.

The current situation could be regarded as comparable to that in a related area during the late 1980s, when I was commissioned by the American Philological Association (APA) to plan and produce a major, comprehensive atlas of the classical world. This feat had only been achieved successfully once before, in wholly different circumstances, during the 1850s to 1870s. Some colleagues objected that APA had no cause to take such an initiative, because the *Tabula Imperii Romani* project (TIR) was fulfilling the need. To be sure, this project (begun around 1930) was still proceeding, but at a painfully slow pace. According to the rule set by the sponsor, the Union Académique Internationale (UAI), each modern nation's territory had to be mapped by it and not by any other. However, some nations whose territory was vital to the

---

17 JULIEN 2012, 151.

project, like Turkey, were unconcerned to contribute to it (and were not necessarily even members of UAI). Several other nations would not co-operate on sheets which spanned the territory of one or more adjacent nations as well as their own. An agreed set of conventions for the presentation of the maps remained lacking, and adherence to a uniform scale was being abandoned. Typically, moreover, the maps were expensive items by no means easy to obtain, and the original vision that they should fit together had been lost. Above all, by the late 1980s the likelihood of TIR actually being completed in the foreseeable future was remote. And even were the full quota of its sheets ever to be completed, they would not provide a set of maps of the Roman Empire uniform in scale and presentation. It was in these circumstances that the project to produce what became the *Barrington Atlas of the Greek and Roman World* was designed and pursued as a secondary initiative.[18] The goal was to finish – within about ten years – a classical atlas that would be both complete in its coverage and as uniform as possible. This project was separate from TIR, which continued as before and is still ongoing.

Today, the publication of Roman milestones may reflect certain limitations comparable to those of TIR during the late 1980s, but these can be addressed more effectively than was conceivable then, thanks to the development of robust and versatile digital technology (the *Barrington Atlas*, by contrast, was planned in a pre-digital era). One marked difference from the state of mapping during the late 1980s that must be taken into account is the continued publication of collections of Roman milestones in addition to, and independent of, CIL XVII fascicles. Aside from the rich array of publications with more localized scope, most notable are the volume for Galicia published by ANTONIO RODRÍGUEZ COLMENERO and colleagues in 2004,[19] and the fascicles for Asia Minor published by DAVID FRENCH between 1981 and 2016.[20] To their credit, both RODRÍGUEZ COLMENERO and FRENCH, as well as the CIL XVII fascicles, all include maps, but their presentation is far from uniform.

In these circumstances what could have immense lasting value is an initiative to develop a digital, Empire-wide collection of Roman milestones, with a single seamless map, as well as photographs and drawings, all accessible without charge. The initiative should be organized so as not to impede working across national boundaries. The record of each milestone's inscription should conform to a standard format, a concise one, limited to presenting and translating its text and explaining the important features, with a minimum of bibliography. Normally, therefore, there would be no account of an inscription's publication history such as CIL XVII offers, often at length. Even though scholarly in character, the record would be written to render it accessible

---

18 For this background, and the planning of the *Barrington Atlas*, see briefly TALBERT 2000, xix–xxii.
19 RODRIGUEZ COLMENERO 2004.
20 FRENCH 1981–2016.

to non-specialists. Consequently, it would not be written in Latin (like CIL), but rather in a widely understood modern language.[21]

Looking to the future, the standard format developed for each milestone's record might also serve as a useful guide to the compilers of further collections to be published. When I was asked recently to comment on a proposal for publishing a nation's Roman milestones after several decades of preparation, the absence of a sample of the presentation format seemed an unjustified omission; there was no sample map provided either, even though the publication was to include maps. What the proposal did carefully explain, however, was that prior to completion of the collection, a little further archaeological work would be undertaken to investigate two further possible milestones. To me, this is a far from sound work-plan (one which might point to why the collection had been so puzzlingly long in preparation). Without doubt, the zeal to identify and study new finds, and to make a collection as complete as possible, is admirable. But a stage must be reached when these efforts – for all their importance – are separated from the assembly and publication of a substantial collection. There will always be the prospect of new finds, and no collection can ever expect to be the last word.

However, in today's digital era, if a digital format is adopted for the publication of a collection rather than a print one, it is a matter of no great difficulty to introduce corrections, modifications and additions. CIL XVII suffers in this important respect because it appears only in a print format. Inevitably, this has also become a more and more expensive format. As a result, access to CIL XVII is reduced, since fewer libraries can afford its fascicles (let alone individual purchasers). That is an unwelcome development at a time when, in my view, we should be striving to broaden the audience for our work, to engage non-specialists, and to facilitate a global perspective.

An attempt to engage a broader audience does not require lowering the standards of our scholarship. However, it will be essential to abandon any lingering traces of the exclusivity that I encountered at a Colloquio in Rome hosted by the Accademia dei Lincei twenty-five years ago. This was a meeting of a UAI group, at which I had been offered the opportunity to broach inclusion of APA's Classical Atlas Project among the *projets* of UAI. That application was the last item on the agenda. After I had spoken, there was no comment from any member. Faced with such baffling silence, I dared to ask the president very humbly whether the group could make a positive recommendation to UAI's *assemblée générale*. His response was a single word: "no." Once it was evident that he did not intend to elaborate, I further dared to request some explanation. This temerity unleashed a crescendo of expostulations, as the president proceeded to explain what to him (and presumably his fellow-members) was obvious. Three objections to APA's atlas stood out: first, that it was "not scholarly" [by compar-

---

21 The choice of Galician for RODRIGUEZ COLMENERO et al. 2004 did not meet with the approval of KOLB 2006, 582.

ison with TIR], a dubious allegation indeed; second, that the goal was to finish it so quickly [within a decade, by contrast with TIR which was nowhere near completion after six decades]; and third, that once published the APA atlas was sure to be *used*! [whereas, ideally, true scholarship should remain accessible only to specialists][22]

I need no reminder that both the preparation and the long-term maintenance of a digital resource which is accessible free of charge will still incur substantial costs. But an initiative to present Roman milestones empire-wide, including a seamless map and photographs, is surely the type of international project that would be competitive for funding. One potentially suitable geo-referenced map base (available free) is the *Antiquity-A-La-Carte* tool created at Chapel Hill's Ancient World Mapping Center.[23] It returns the modern landscape, so far as possible, to its ancient aspect. The scale at which the landscape may be displayed is of course variable, up to no more than around 1:50,000. This zoom limit may suffice, however, given the fact that the findspots of most milestones were never recorded with the precision accuracy now attainable with Global Positioning Systems data. In *A-La-Carte*, landscape can be edited both by removing features and adding them as well as altering them; lines and polygons can be drawn, colors chosen and changed, distances on the map calculated. The ancient landscape can be removed altogether, and today's substituted, in either Open Street Map or satellite rendering. When a placename is selected from the accompanying database, it will automatically be sited correctly on the map (or, if need be, it can be shifted). New names and sites can be introduced; name-formats, type-styles (including Greek and other alphabets), font-sizes, symbols can all be chosen. Differentiation by time-period can be achieved by use of separate layers, thus offering a valuable option for distinguishing milestones by period or emperor's reign.

A digital format can accommodate many more photographs – such as the large quantity taken by DAVID FRENCH – than any print product can reasonably be expected to include. Also feasible is the provision of images where the object in effect rotates, allowing a view of entire inscriptions which cannot be encompassed by a regular still image. Equally, in the case of milestones with text that is more or less illegible to the naked eye, photographs taken using Reflectance Transformation Imaging can be included. The project's record of a milestone, the photographs of it, and its location on the map can, and should, all be linked; further links to reference works such as Pleiades, Pelagios and epigraphic databases can also be incorporated.

None of this is to suggest that a project as just outlined would prove wholly straightforward to design and implement. However, at least some potential obstacles could be avoided by ensuring from the start that an international group of acknowledged milestone experts and epigraphers steers the project; it should not be undertaken

---

[22] Even so, in due course UAI did adopt the APA Project as its projet XLVIII.
[23] URL: awmc.unc.edu/wordpress/alacarte.

merely by an individual or two, who may have only limited contacts. To design the framework with care, and then to implement a pilot phase for inspection, comment and adjustment, should be the first steps. At the same time, to engage an institution willing to shoulder the onerous responsibility of hosting the project's site long-term is vital. Consideration should be given to the matter of accessibility for users who do not enjoy the highest-speed internet connections. And a title should be formulated for the project that is meaningful as well as appealing to non-specialists (not, therefore, a Latin one!). Only once all these preparations are securely achieved would it be prudent to proceed further.

This said, while not belittling the difficulties to be expected, I do believe that such a project could be accomplished successfully within a few years. Moreover, as a digital product it can be released in stages. It does not have to incur the risk that persistently haunted the *Barrington Atlas* project, namely that a print product designed to cover the classical world in 100 maps cannot be completed (with gazetteer, etc) and submitted for publication until all 100 have been prepared satisfactorily; delays involving even a handful of them could be crippling. By contrast, to correct slips in a well-designed digital product, and to add supplementary material (new discoveries especially), should be routine tasks.

In short, all this is far from an easy undertaking, but it is feasible nonetheless, and sure to be invaluable for the long term, not least as a means of broadening interest worldwide. Such a digital product would definitely be *used* too! Altogether, then, here is a sound strategy for enhancing and linking all the valuable work currently being done on Roman roads and milestones.

Bibliography

APPELBAUM 2016 = N.P. APPELBAUM, Mapping the Country of Regions: The Chorographic Commission of Nineteenth-Century Colombia, Chapel Hill NC 2016.
CRESSEY 1934 = G.B. CRESSEY, China's Geographic Foundations: A Survey of the Land and its People, New York 1934.
FRENCH 1981–2016 = D.H. FRENCH, Roman Roads and Milestones of Asia Minor, Ankara 1981–2016.
JULIEN 2012 = C. JULIEN, The Chinchaysuyu Road and the Definition of an Inca Imperial Landscape, in: S.E. ALCOCK/J. BODEL/R.J.A. TALBERT (ed.), Highways, Byways, and Road Systems in the Pre-Modern World, Malden MA 2012, 147–167.
KOLB 2006 = A. KOLB, Die Meilensteine von Galicien und Asturien, *JRA* 19, 2006, 577–582.
LAURENCE 2016 = R. LAURENCE, Connectivity, Roads and Transport: Essays on Roman Roads to Speak to Other Disciplines?, *JRA* 29, 2016, 692–695.
NAVAL STAFF INTELLIGENCE III.3 1919 = NAVAL STAFF INTELLIGENCE DEPARTMENT, A Handbook of Asia Minor, vol. III part 3, 1919.
NYLAN 2012 = M. NYLAN, The Power of Highway Networks during China's Classical Era (323 BCE–316 CE): Regulations, Metaphors, Rituals, and Deities, in: S.E. ALCOCK/J. BODEL/R.J.A. TALBERT (ed.), Highways, Byways, and Road Systems in the Pre-Modern World, Malden MA 2012, 33–65.
RAAFLAUB/TALBERT 2010 = K.A. RAAFLAUB/R.J.A. TALBERT (ed.), Geography and Ethnography: Perceptions of the World in Pre-Modern Societies, Malden MA 2010.

Rodriguez Colmenero 2004 = A. Rodriguez Colmenero et al., Miliarios e outras inscricións Viarias Romanas do Noroeste Hispánico (Conventos Bracarense, Lucense e Asturicense), Santiago de Compostela 2004.

Snead/Erickson/Darling 2009 = J.E. Snead/C.L. Erickson/J.A. Darling (ed.), Landscapes of Movement: Trails, Paths, and Roads in Anthropological Perspective, Philadelphia PA 2009.

Talbert 2000 = R.J.A. Talbert (ed.), Barrington Atlas of the Greek and Roman World, with Map-by-Map Directory, Princeton NJ 2000.

Talbert 2010 = R.J.A. Talbert, Rome's World: The Peutinger Map Reconsidered, Cambridge 2010, with www.cambridge.org/9780521764803.

Talbert 2012 = R.J.A. Talbert, Roads Not Featured: A Roman Failure to Communicate?, in: S. E. Alcock/J. Bodel/R.J.A. Talbert (ed.), Highways, Byways, and Road Systems in the Pre-Modern World, Malden MA 2012, 235–254.

Vaporis 2012 = C.N. Vaporis, Linking the Realm: The Gokaidô Highway Network in Early Modern Japan (1603–1868), in: S.E. Alcock/J. Bodel/R.J.A. Talbert (ed.), Highways, Byways, and Road Systems in the Pre-Modern World, Malden MA 2012, 90–105.

Grant Parker
Roots to Routes: Gandhara's Landscapes of Mobility

Abstract: Gandhara's place in world history seems beyond dispute: enriched by its connection with the so-called Silk Road, it became a decisive area for the history of Buddhism, both in terms of its art and architecture and as an area from which Buddhism spread eastwards. Located on the southern areas of the Hindu Kush, far from the historical Buddha's journeys, Gandhara became integrated into Buddhist tradition via the cult of relics. On its western side, however, how exactly Gandhara was linked with the Mediterranean world and with Arsacid Iran is little known. For this reason it is all the more important to comb through the little evidence that exists. The main texts in question (all from the first and second centuries AD) are the *Parthian Stations* by Isidore of Charax; the *Periplus of the Erythraean Sea*; and Ptolemy's *Geographical Description*. From these we seek to make sense of Gandhara and its land-routes in relation to the Roman empire. These atomistic but tantalizing clues offer not just historical data but also an opportunity for methodological reflection. How does the Roman Mediterranean connect with the vast Eurasian world? What evidence is there for overlap between the seaborne and land networks? The specific case of Gandhara requires us to negotiate between its originary status in Buddhism (thus 'roots') on the one hand and the land-routes linking Mediterranean and east Asia on the other.

Zusammenfassung: Gandharas Rolle in der Weltgeschichte scheint unbestritten: Bereichert durch seine Anbindung an die sogenannte Seidenstraße wurde es zu einer entscheidenden Region für die Geschichte des Buddhismus, sowohl im Hinblick auf die dort entwickelte Kunst und Architektur als auch als Ausgangspunkt, von dem aus der Buddhismus sich in Richtung Osten verbreitete. Da Gandhara in den südlichen Gebieten des Hindu Kush weit von der Reiseroute des historischen Buddha entfernt lag, wurde es über den Reliquienkult in die buddhistische Tradition integriert. Wie Gandhara auf seiner Westseite mit dem Mittelmeerraum und dem von den Arsakiden beherrschten Iran verbunden war, ist allerdings kaum bekannt. Umso wichtiger ist es, die wenigen Belege, die es dafür gibt, zu analysieren. Als Quellen kommen in erster Linie die *Mansiones Parthicae* des Isidoros von Charax, der *Periplus Maris Erythraei* und die *Geographia* des Ptolemaios in Frage (alle aus dem ersten und zweiten Jahrhundert n. Chr.). Von diesen versuchen wir Anhaltspunkte für die Landwege zwischen Gandhara und dem römischen Reich zu erhalten. Die geringen, aber interessanten Hinweise bieten nicht nur historische Daten, sondern auch eine Gelegenheit für methodische Reflektionen. Wie war der römisch beherrschte Mittelmeerraum mit dem riesigen Gebiet der eurasischen Welt verbunden? Welche Belege gibt es für die Überschneidung der Wegenetze zu Wasser und zu Land? Der besondere Fall von Gandhara erfordert es, zum einen seinen einzigartigen Status im Buddhismus (daher

„die Wurzeln") und zum anderen die Landwege, die den Mittelmeerraum und Ostasien miteinander verbinden, zu berücksichtigen.

The name Gandhara has adhered, in the first instance, to a small valley around Peshawar, in what is now Pakistan. Beyond that, it has signified a substantial area nestled on the south side of the Hindu Kush, principally via particular art-historical and religious contexts.[1] Its world-historical significance comes most obviously from its role in Buddhism, both the development of figurative art and the diffusion of the religion. The enabling circumstance was Gandhara's relative proximity to the transasiatic land routes, commonly but misleadingly known as the Silk Road. The connection of this so-called Silk Road with Greco-Roman history is problematic, to say the least. Yet it has clear relevance to the overall project of understanding roads in the ancient Roman world, broadly conceived. The aim of the present essay is to take up the challenge of making sense of Gandhara and its land-routes in relation to key Greek and Latin texts which seem to offer direct and indirect evidence: these vague but tantalizing clues offer not just historical data but also an opportunity for methodological reflection. In the context of the current volume we ask what such clues can tell us, whether suggestively or in detail, about roads and mobility in the vast Eurasian world stretching eastward from – and overlapping with – the Roman Mediterranean. The specific case of Gandhara requires us to negotiate between its originary status in Buddhism (thus 'roots') on the one hand and the land-routes it occupied between Mediterranean and east Asian states on the other hand.

I Locating Gandhara

The question of where to place Gandhara on a map is more complicated than it might initially appear. Here the earliest evidence is from the Sanskrit tradition. In the *Rig Veda*, the Gandhari are named as one of the groups inhabiting the northwest of India (1,126,7). The high quality of the wool from their sheep is their distinctive feature. This is the earliest reference in a literary source, less to Gandhara per se than its inhabitants. Likewise, the *Atharvaveda* refers not exactly to Gandhara per se but to Gandharis.[2] A vague, distant people in *Atharvavedas*, they are more positively represented in later Vedic texts as pure and orthodox.[3] While the historical-topographical evidence emerging from the Sanskrit sources is somewhat impressionistic, we are on

---

1 Among the vast and disparate literature, three edited volumes seem especially worth mentioning: BEHRENDT/BRANCACCIO 2007; LUCZANITS 2008; and now RAY 2018.
2 MACDONELL/KEITH 1912, 219.
3 ZWALF 1996, 15; cf. now MOITRA 2018.

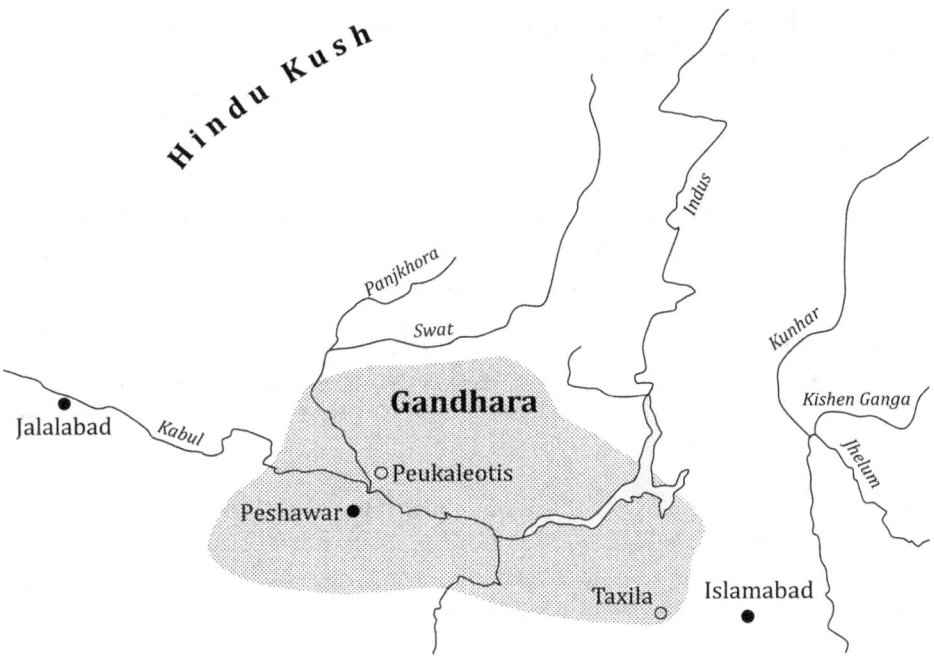

Fig. 1: Maps by Nicholas Hächler (Zürich).

firmer footing with documents from the Achaemenid empire, the first of several states to conquer the valley – one might say the first of a series stretching to the British annexation of the valley into the Raj in 1849. We also know that the Achaemenids used a road network to consolidate their power within Iran and beyond.[4] About the Persian conquest we hear from both Herodotus (Hdt. 3,91,4) and Darius I's Behistun inscriptions, in a list of 'countries which fell to [his] lot'.[5] Here Gandhara is part of the seventh satrapy. The area succumbed to Alexander in 330 BCE. Following a period of instability, it came under the sway of Chandragupta Maurya. In the second and first centuries BCE Gandhara was variously under Greek, Scythian (Shakas) and Parthian rule, until the Kushanas entered the scene. It was under the Kushanas that Gandharan art reached its apogee. After the Hephthalites arrived in the early fifth century CE Gandhara continued to flourish, its decline apparently coinciding with the end of the Hephthalite empire in the early sixth century. By the time the monk Xuanzang visited Gandhara in 640 CE he could reflect on the decline the area had undergone by that

---

[4] GRAF 1995; and BRIANT 2012, emphasizing long-term continuities with previous states. BRIANT'S approach here seems to substantiate Earle's thesis that road-building was a means of consolidating power (EARLE 2009), see section V below.
[5] E.g. DB I 12–17 = section 6. See SCHMITT 1991, 49. KHATCHADOURIAN 2016 has recently reframed the Achaemenid empire.

time. Indeed, decline is a major theme in the Buddhist accounts, with religious sites in particular having suffered ruin:

> There are about 1000 *sangharamas*, which are deserted and in ruins. They are filled with wild shrubs and solitary to the last degree. The stupas are mostly decayed.[6]

This note of decline in Buddhist observance marks Xuanzang's account of the broader region, and Gandhara is no exception. Nonetheless, Gandhara remained agriculturally productive even in this supposedly lean period.

> [t]he country is rich in cereals, and produces a variety of flowers and fruits; it abounds also in sugar-cane ... The climate is warm and moist, and in general without ice or snow. The disposition of the people is timid and soft: they love literature; most of them belong to heretical schools; a few believe in the true law.[7]

Early accounts of this kind have been triangulated to create a generalized account of Gandhara. To take a well-known example, SIR ALEXANDER CUNNINGHAM describes the location by drawing on both Xuanzang and to a lesser extent on Alexander histories, though these are divided by a millennium:

> The boundaries of Gandhara ... may be described as Lamghan and Jalalabad on the west, the hills of Swat and Bunir on the north, the Indus on the east, and the hills of Kalabagh on the south. Within these limits stood several of the most renowned places of ancient India; some celebrated in the stirring history of Alexander's exploits, and others famous in the miraculous legends of Buddha, and in the subsequent history of Buddhism under the Indo-Scythian prince Kanishka.[8]

Indeed, CUNNINGHAM quotes the elder Pliny's *Natural History* (6,61) as an epigraph on the title page of his *Ancient Geography of India*, to the effect that the optimal way to make sense of India is 'in the footsteps of Alexander' – a classicising detail that ill fits the designation of the Buddhist period in his subtitle. So great is the significance of Alexander as a landmark in historical consciousness.[9]

The key fact in a religious context, overlooked by scholars with surprising ease, is that Gandhara lies several hundred kilometres from the original seat of Buddhism. The Buddha's life has only very limited direct association with Gandhara. Despite this disjunct, Gandhara played a major role in the diffusion of Buddhism particularly in the Kushan era. The need of Buddhists to come to terms with this fact may be considered formative in the development of Buddhism in the Kushan age: relics played

---

[6] BEAL 1884, 98.
[7] BEAL 1884, 98.
[8] Thus CUNNINGHAM 1871, 41, cf. SINGH 2004, ch. 2. On CUNNINGHAM's relation to Buddhist pasts see RAY 2014, 66–67.
[9] VASUNIA 2013, chs. 1–2.

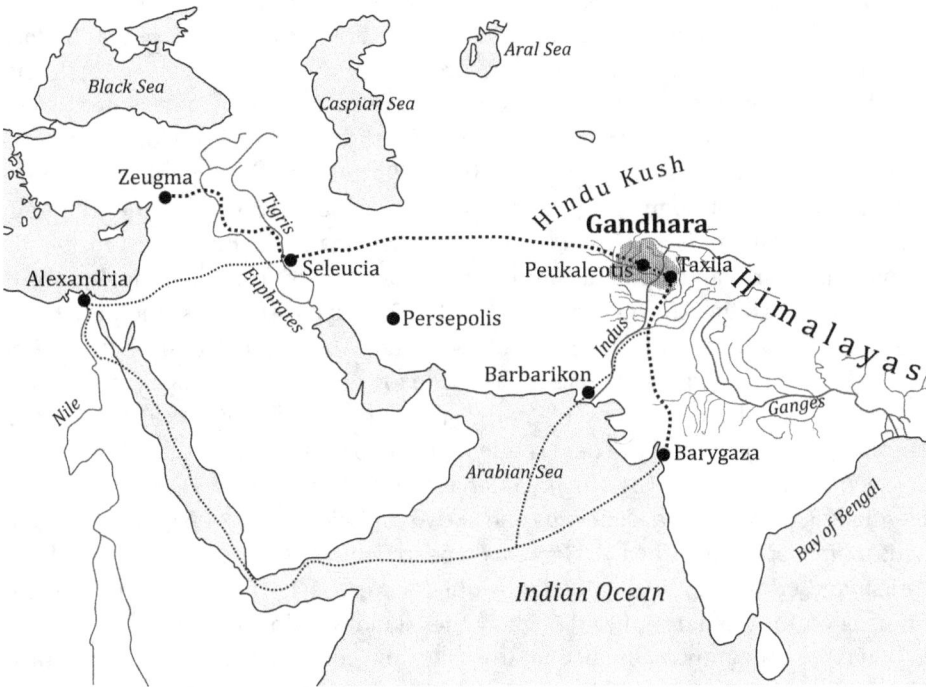

Fig. 2: Maps by Nicholas Hächler (Zürich).

a major role in the diffusion of Buddhism by allowing a wider geographical area to be included.[10] Such broader considerations necessarily complicate any mappings of Gandhara, and need to be borne in mind alongside seemingly uncomplicated descriptions such as that of Cunningham.

II Isidore of Charax, *Parthian Stations*

The first text to consider is the *Parthian Stations* of Isidore of Charax: some two dozen texts of diverse character are linked to his name, most of them purporting to trace a route from Zeugma on the Euphrates as far as Alexandria in Arachosia. The relevance of this text to Gandhara and its routes is indirect, it must be emphasized, but nonetheless they provide potentially valuable clues to the land network system connecting the Mediterranean with continental Asia.[11]

---

10 Neelis 2014a; Neelis 2014b.
11 By way of editions of this fragmentary text, Roller 2016 in *Brill's New Jacoby* (*BNJ*) no. 781 provides the new gold standard.

Isidore himself we may date to the Augustan age, around 2 BC to AD 4.[12] The texts may be summed up as follows: (a) Several references in Pliny's *Natural History* suggest a primary concern with the measurement of the earth (e.g. 2,242. 245), and here he is often paired with Artemidorus of Ephesus (fl. ca. 100 BC) as a source. These references constitute the *terminus ante quem* for the shadowy figure of Isidore: the text must have predated Pliny, who died in AD 79, and it has been plausibly connected with the time of Augustus. (b) A mysterious text survives via a medieval manuscript, Codex Parisinus 443, listing a route from Zeugma on the Euphrates, eastwards through the Parthian empire, as far as Arachosia, here ending emphatically: 'Thus far this place is under the rule (*enkrateia*) of the Parthians.' (*BNJ* F2 section 19). Nineteen regions are listed with distances between them. An unusual feature in itineraries of this kind is the naming of regions alongside towns. This text is highly schematic, and is so generalized as to provide no reason to imagine that its author undertook any such a journey himself. There is much greater detail given for the initial stretch of Zeugma to Seleukia, whereas the later sections are mostly very jejune, typically mentioning only the area name plus one or two capital cities. (c) A passage in Athenaeus' *Deipnosophists* (Athen. 3,93e-94b) on pearl fishing (*BNJ* F1), rich in natural historical and ethnographic detail, stands out from the rest. The location to which it refers is on the Persian Gulf, most likely the island of Tylos, modern Bahrain, and is otherwise topographically distinct from the land-route described in the itinerary. (d) Finally, a brief text by Lucian or Pseudo-Lucian refers to long-lived kings in the Persian-Arabian world.[13] It is immediately obvious that the coherence of these passages is open to question, particularly the relation of (c) to the rest. Nonetheless their confluence around the name of Isidore suggests some Ur-text involving a land route across Arsacid Iran.

The western part of this territory is better known from Achaemenid-era sources, particularly the substantial number of 'travel ration texts' in the Persepolis Fortification Texts and the stations (*stathmoi*) listed by Herodotus (Hdt. 5,52–53).[14] In such texts we hear about guard stations, inns and caravanserais en route. A journey of some 2,400km from the Aegean to the Persian capital would have required 90 days. Such evidence suggests a communications system centred on a mounted courier service. Whereas we gain some knowledge here about a road network for official travellers, we have much less information about commercial travel.

A specific question that arises from itinerary conveyed in (b) has to do with the fact that it charts the western end of a terrestrial route between the Mediterranean and Central Asia. The text in itself suggests trade relations between the Parthian empire

---

12 Plin. Nat. 6,141 (*BNJ* T1) links him to Gaius' Armenian expedition in that time-frame. There is a textual problem in that 'Dionysius' is transmitted, but comparison with Pliny's corresponding list of sources securely corrects that problem. See ROLLER commentary on T1.
13 Lucian or Pseudo-Lucian, *Macrobioi* 15 and 18 = *BNJ* 781 F3–4 (ROLLER).
14 From Jewish tradition compare Est 3,13 and 8,9–14.

and Rome, and strikingly takes the eastern extent of the Parthian state as its textual limit. As such the text constitutes an invaluable clue about the Iranian world. It is significant that the initial route, certainly from Zeugma to Seleucia on the Tigris, coincides to a considerable degree with the course of the Euphrates and Tigris; it is even possible that some of the travel implied by the text is by river rather than by land. Possibly, the use of the river for travel might account for the jarringly unusual detail about king Phraates IV cutting the throats of his concubines at the time of invasion by Tiridates (section 1): the story focuses on the island Belesi Biblada. Another unresolved point is that geographically the route mapped by the *Parthian Stations* is considerably south of what is usually conceived as the Silk Road.[15] Though many of the settlements mentioned seem to have been founded by Alexander, this is mentioned only once, in the case of Nikophorion on Euphrates (also section 1).

In sum, the *Parthian Stations* gives us an itinerary-style lead through the Arsacid empire, apparently at a time of military hostility between the Roman and Parthian worlds. Though the precise geography does not fit well with the usual tracings of long-distance trade, this does seem to make best sense when linked to long-distance commercial travel in the direction of Gandhara. Its existence is intriguing in that no commodities are mentioned; yet the key point is that it does give a sense of the Persian world as integrated within commercial networks stretching beyond. It is thus all the more valuable given that evidence of this kind is strangely lacking for Iran, whereas there is a fair amount of evidence for the Indus Valley and subcontinent.[16]

III *Periplus of the Erythraean Sea*

The anonymous *Periplus of the Erythraean Sea*, dated to the mid-first century (AD 40–60) provides a uniquely valuable account of commercial sea-travel from the Red Sea via two routes: south of the Horn of Africa to roughly the region of Zanzibar; and eastwards to the western coast of peninsular India.[17] Its relevance here is unexpected, given its seaborne focus, but it is all the more valuable for that element, for it does touch on Gandhara in the broader context of its sea-routes.

As Millar aptly comments, the *Periplus* 'provides just what we do not know, or hardly know, of land-trade with Asia: the various different routes of exchange, the political relations involved, and above all detailed accounts of the objects of trade'.[18]

---

15 MILLAR 1998, 135.
16 MILLAR 1998.
17 CASSON 1989 remains the point of departure.
18 MILLAR 1998, 120; RAY 2018, 9.

> Inland behind Barygaza there are numerous peoples: the Aratrioi, Arachusioi, Gandarioi, and the peoples of Proklais, in whose area Bukephalos Alexandreia is located. And beyond these there is a very warlike people, the Bactrians [Kushans] under a king ...

Given that the *Periplus* includes very little information that is not immediately relevant to commercial travel, it is striking that the text continues by directly mentioning Alexander's expedition, the memory of which survives in coins honouring leaders that claimed linear descent from Alexander:

> Alexander, setting out from these parts, penetrated as far as the Ganges but did not get to Limyrike and the south of India. Because of this, there are to be found on the market in Barygaza even today old drachmas engraved with the inscriptions, in Greek letters, of Apollodotus and Menander, rulers who came after Alexander. (peripl. m. r. 47)

To be sure, it is a geographical anomaly to put any part of Alexander's expedition beyond the Ganges.[19] On the other hand, the *Alexander Romance* tradition makes a reality out of Alexander's dream.[20] What matters for present purposes is the extent to which the river valleys are connected with the seaborne *Periplus* route. It is evident that when the *Periplus* sea-route moves south to Barygaza, its author makes a detour inland up the Indus – far enough north to get caught up in apparent confusion between the Indus and Ganges river valleys. Though the reference to Gandhara here is brief and only in passing, it is telling that the river valley is connected with the sea-route, via commercial networks that interest the *Periplus* author.

IV Claudius Ptolemy, *Geographical Description*

Our third case study provides a different perspective on several counts. Claudius Ptolemy's *Geographical Description*, composed around 150 CE at Alexandria, has been seen as the culmination of ancient geographical thought and also the point of departure for modern cartography.[21] While little is known about Ptolemy's life, he is thought to have lived approximately AD 90–168. The maps associated with Ptolemy stem from his *Geographical Description (Geographike Hyphegesis)*, or to be precise his 'Guide to drawing a world map'.[22] The Greek text is known today on the basis of manuscripts the 12th century onward, in other words a good millennium after the fact; there is no clarity as to whether the original text contained maps or whether these were added

---

19 TARN 1923, esp. 96: at issue is the location of the Prasii.
20 For references see PARKER 2008, 38.
21 STÜCKELBERGER/GRASSHOFF/MITTENHUBER 2006.
22 BERGGREN/JONES 2000, 4.

later.²³ In a way that foreshadows modern geographers, Ptolemy is at least as much concerned with the methodology of mapping as he is with the results. Despite the early modern importance of the *Geographical Description*, Ptolemy was in the first instance an astronomer: his *Almagest* far exceeded his *Geographical Description* in being read and copied in the Byzantine world.

The *Geographical Description* caps several centuries of Greco-Roman scientific tradition. Its early chapters (Ptol. 1,1–21) are a detailed critique of one Marinos of Tyre, an even more obscure figure.²⁴ To judge from Ptolemy, a hostile but solitary historical source, Marinos addressed the very same questions that occupy Ptolemy in his own theoretical chapters. Map projections are one example. It is clear from the *Geographical Description* that Ptolemy draws on Marinos even as he differs from him. Foremost among the criticisms of Marinos is that he overestimates both the latitude and the longitude of the known world; Ptolemy systematically proposes reductions in both of these.

Ptolemy's pointedly broad span should be seen in its geopolitical context. The Roman state, which fully encompassed the Mediterranean by 30 BC under Octavian (later called Augustus), would reach its maximal territorial extent under the emperors Trajan (AD 98–117) and Hadrian (117–38). It is of this period that EDWARD GIBBON famously claimed that 'the condition of the human race was most happy and prosperous' of all world history.²⁵ It is true that the systematic detail of the work is unthinkable without Rome's huge military and imperial infrastructure, just as the Roman state had supported two earlier imperial-age geographers, Strabo of Amaseia and Pliny the Elder. Roman power enabled commercial activity, even though the imperial-age geographers ostensibly placed less value on commercially generated information.²⁶ The downplaying of traders' information is undoubtedly exaggerated, as we shall discuss below, reflecting social prejudice against the traders.

As it is, the surviving text of the *Geographical Description* consists of three parts: first a theoretical section (Ptol. book 1) that discusses methodological matters, especially instructions for cartographic projections (Ptol. 1,22–24); the bulk of the work, constituting a gazetteer of locations in the 'known world' (*oikoumene*), grouped by regions and listed by latitude and longitude (Ptol. 2,1–7.4), followed by further instructions (Ptol. 7,5–7); and, third, a description of how to divide the known world into 26 regional maps (Ptol. book 8). The work may thus be considered a practical guide for mapmakers – regardless of whether Ptolemy himself created maps – just as the *Almagest* (esp. Ptol. 7,4) provides practical instructions for the makers of celestial globes.

---

23 BERGGREN/JONES 2000, 45–50.
24 His dates are usually given as 'fl. AD 100', but this must be considered broad inference.
25 GIBBON 2009, 53, strictly referring to the period AD 96–180, marked by the death of Domitian and the accession of Commodus.
26 Strabo (from Augustus' time) and Ptolemy.

It should by now be clear that Ptolemy's project in the *Geographical Description* is an ambitious one of enormous scale, systematically integrating a mass of topographical information within a lengthy tradition of mathematical theory. Indeed the concept of tradition is important in making sense of Ptolemy, in that he is explicit about balancing specific empirical data with theoretical considerations of a more *a priori* nature. It is not surprising, then, that Ptolemy is aware of the contingent nature of his own conclusions, going so far as to warn mapmakers. He argues for relative certainty, in which less sure inferences are explicitly made on the basis of more secure knowledge (Ptol. 2,1,2).

In relation to Gandhara, Claudius Ptolemy' coverage is disappointingly sparing (Ptol. 7,1,44). The relevant passages are quoted below, complete with geographical coordinates:

Between the Suastos[27] and the Indus live the Gandharai with the following cities:

Poklais: 123 [degrees longitude], 33 [degrees latitude]
Naulibis: 124° 20' [longitude], 33° 20' [latitude]

Thereafter come Ithaguros[28] and Taxila, located between the Indus and the Bidaspes[29] rivers in the land of Varsa[30] (Ptol. 7,1,45). The relevant section heading (Ptol. 7,1,42) that precedes these locations provides a framework of orientation, in particular the relative position of rivers, their sources, and mountains. In this instance Ptolemy refers to 'Gandharai', that is, via an ethnonym rather than a toponym. Further, of his two 'Gandharan' locations, Poklais is especially important. Also known as Peukaleotis in Greek, or Pukkhalavati in Middle Indian, it lies some 25 km north of Peshawar.

It is Peukaleotis that is also named in the *Periplus of the Erythraean Sea* (peripl. m. r. 47). Since that text describes seaborne trade routes between Egypt's Eastern Desert and the Indian subcontinent (along with a southerly route from the Red Sea to the region of Zanzibar), we may infer that Gandhara was known to travellers on this 'monsoon' route.

If Ptolemy's references to Gandhara itself are disappointing, his references to transasiatic land routes are intriguing, particularly since they are part of his project to frame the known world as a whole. Whereas Marinos was apparently the first Greek geographer to extend the known world to eastern Asia, Ptolemy subjects Marinos calculations to close scrutiny (Ptol. 1,11–12). For Ptolemy, the ends of the known world are marked by the Makaros ('Blessed') Islands in the west and Sera, capital of the Seres ('Silk people') in the east. In calculating the intervening distance as systematically

---

27 Modern Swat River.
28 Modern Isaguros.
29 Modern Jhelum River.
30 Known in modern times as Byarsa or Hazara.

as possible, Ptolemy mentions a certain 'Stone Tower' in Central Asia.³¹ Though its location is unknown, it emerges from the context as a trading station. Typical of Ptolemy's detailed argumentation on geographical accuracy, he accepts as a given that a journey from the Stone Tower to Sera lasts seven months, which equates to 36,200 stadia. These two locations are on the same parallel, but allowance must be made for deviation therefrom; in other words, land journeys on the route connecting them are not as the crow flies (Ptol. 1,11,4).³² As Ptolemy repeats in the following section (Ptol. 1,12), it is reasonable to imagine that there were pauses in the journey caused by weather and other factors, so that the correlation of time and distance travelled is an imperfect one. On these grounds Ptolemy faults Marinos' calculations, and reduces the distance supposedly covered in seven months. He adds:

> Moreover, it was because of the opportunity for commerce that [the route] came to be known. Marinos says that one Maes, also known as Titianos, a Macedonian and a merchant by family profession, recorded the distance measurements, though he did not traverse it himself but sent certain [others] to the Seres. (Ptol. 1,11,7)

This comment is made en passant, but it is telling for several reasons. Such a passage points – with surprising singularity – to a long-distance land route across Central and East Asia, indeed the Silk Road itself.³³ This would seem to be the route, or more correctly network, bordering Isidore's route to the far west, and the *Periplus* route to the south. Furthermore, the Ptolemaic passages quoted also allude to commercial sources of topographical knowledge, even as it give that lower status, as Strabo also commented in relation to seaborne commerce with India.³⁴ A passage such as this shows Ptolemy to be aware of the deficiencies of his sources, so much so that he warns mapmakers (Ptol. 2,1,2). Arguing for relative certainty, he encourages his readers to make educated guesses, inferring less certain locations on the basis of more certain ones.

The striking aspect of Claudius Ptolemy is that he integrates individual journeys – in some ways not unlike those implied by the *Parthian Stations* or even the *Perip-*

---

31 The exact identity and location of this 'Stone Tower' is today a matter of speculation (THOMSON 1948, 307–9; BERGGREN/JONES 200, 72 n. 44). The name equates to Tash Kurgan in Turkic languages, which is used of several locations in Central and East Asia, but it cannot be assumed that Ptolemy's 'Stone Tower' coincides with any of these.

32 SIR AUREL STEIN tried to identify Ptolemy's route and in part to trace it (STEIN 1928, 848–50, 893–894). For a modern account, see RIENJANG 2012.

33 Thus BERGGREN/JONES 2000, 150–56. Caution is in order in so far as it would be incorrect to conclude, on the basis of such texts, that this 'Silk Road' was a single path as opposed to an extended, overlapping network: see HANSEN 2012 and FRANCOPAN 2016 for recent overviews.

34 'As for the merchants who nowadays sail from Egypt via the Nile and Arabian Gulf as far as India, few have sailed as far as the Ganges, and even these are merely private individuals (*idiotai*) and are useless with regard to accounts of the places they have seen.' (Strab. 15,1,4 C686) This passage is further contextualized by PARKER 2008,190–91.

lus – into an overall geographical scheme. This is a massive universalizing project that self-evidently rests on the judicious evaluation and incorporation of a mass of empirical data.

V Some Problems of Context

From the main texts under discussion, four general problems may be identified, all of which involve contextualization in different ways. First and most obviously, historians face a problem of how to connect disparate sources, different languages and different media, material and textual. In some cases there is overlap of sources but in other cases overlap is eminently lacking. From a Mediterranean point of view, the most striking absence involves the Kushans, who ruled Gandhara at its apogee and controlled the trade to its north, yet do not appear in Greco-Roman sources barring one textual conjecture. In this regard, the single reference in the *Periplus* is especially important here in connecting sea and land networks of exchange in the mid-first century AD. In the process they steer us away from an overly linear notion of space and instead encourage us to think of the complexities involved in a far-flung networks.

Generally speaking, the challenge of integrating sources is one that pervades different fields of ancient history, especially as compared with modern. In the case of Gandhara, groups of sources are placed into linguistic piles: here the collections of HILL 2015 and COEDÈS 2010 are good examples, focused on Chinese-language and Greco-Latin sources respectively. While several scholars have done groundbreaking work in combining different kinds of text, in different languages, there remains much room. This is precisely where *Großforschung*, the meat and drink of western Europe's learned academies in the 19th century but today more typical of the sciences than the humanities, may bring benefits. The ancient languages involved are an obstacle in their own right. In our own age, a starting point might involve mapping known data, yet – and this is important but hard and too often overlooked – indicating a considerable degree of uncertainty in the process of cartographic location. How does one map uncertainty?

Second, it is apparent that different sources are variously interested in either topographical particulars or larger systems, seldom both. Here TALBERT's research on the Peutinger Map holds valuable lessons of potentially broader relevance. Clearly, at some level, the routes marked in red represent roads, but as TALBERT points out they are not necessarily the most direct routes: rather its maker aimed rather at the 'cumulative effect of the detail' rather than any topographic specifics, in the interests of ideological value – maximized if it were physically displayed in an apse, in front of which an emperor might receive visitors. TALBERT concludes that the map was 'not seriously concerned to make the route network a practical guide for travellers'.[35] It

---

[35] TALBERT 2012, 18.

does not even use one uniform scale but several different ones, in keeping with the considerable distortion involved in its peculiarly flattened shape.³⁶ The point here is that, though the Peutinger Map contains a vast amount of data, its maker's – if TALBERT is correct – was emphasis on an impressive whole, an aggregate. Comparable arguments have been made for Trajan's Column: given its height, a viewer would not be able to see more than a small percentage of the intricate detail carved into the relief. The same phenomenon has been identified in the donative inscriptions on Buddhist monuments, some of which were placed on portions of monuments that would never have been seen.³⁷ On this analogy we may be able to see Gandhara as part of a broader network, spanning as far west as the Parthian territory of Isidore of Charax. In the setting of such a network, seemingly isolated bits of knowledge make a different kind of sense as systems instead.

This is one of several problems of generality and specificity that come to the fore. We have discussed at the start the difference between Gandhara proper and 'Greater Gandhara'.³⁸ As we have seen, whereas Gandhara proper is a small area in the vicinity of Swat, its impact has caused the term to be used much further, particularly in art historical and philological contexts. This is a distinction between the topographic specifics of place and the larger impact of space. It can be owed to some extent to the diffusion of objects, especially of the Kushan period, that began in earnest with CHARLES MASSON in the Northwest Frontier Province (NWFP), removing all the sculptures they could find, so that today Gandharan statues are mostly to be found in a small number of museums the British Museum, Indian Museum in Calcutta, the Metropolitan Museum of Art and – worst of all from both scholarly and heritage points of view – private homes. This dislocation means that sculptures have no provenance, and this has contributed to the confusingly wide use of 'Gandharan' as a term in Buddhist contexts.

There are other kinds of generalizing too, that we face, such as that between individual travelers such as Ptolemy's Maes and the abstract scientific knowledge that could be gleaned from it. Certainly ancient science, with its emphasis on *ktisteis* or first inventors, readily extrapolates from such personalized information, and in this respect ancient geographic discourse is not so far from modern. Syntheses such as that of McLAUGHLIN 2016 typically make this move.³⁹ It is not necessarily incorrect, but at the very least scholars should show awareness of the move they are making.

Third, we have seen within a Roman frame hierarchies of geographical knowledge. Ptolemy is dismissive of mercantile information, as Strabo had been before him: yet the vast topographical compendia of both are unimaginable without it. Tellingly, both raise this point in dealing with some of the most remote locations, from their Mediter-

---

36 TALBERT 2012, 179.
37 SCHOPEN 2002, 66.
38 On the pointed uses of the latter term, see for example BEHRENDT 2004, 12–38.
39 More cautious and self-aware is EVERS 2016.

ranean perspectives – the Seres and peninsular India. Such prejudices are reminders of the constraints surrounding what little information we do have. In all, Gandhara comes through both in a topographic or chorographic sense of place, with implications of specificity, as geography defined by particular human experiences; but at the same time also as space, the potentiality of movement, connected to various kinds of power. In early Buddhism its status is mystified by the presence of the Buddha's relics. On the one hand the physical reality of Gandhara has everything to do with the harshness of its mountainous conditions that adjoin it; on the other hand, imaginations are fuelled by the piety of Buddhist pilgrims such as Xuanzang, and the lure of commodities in the world of Pliny the elder. In this context it is not surprising that geographical information can serve many different purposes, whether practical or ideological, sometimes both at the same time: the Peutinger map makes that clear by way of a comparandum. In this case we are dealing with distance and scale, in that Ptolemy, like Xuanzang later and from the east, is making sense of Gandhara and its routes from a far distant perspective, but nonetheless a perspective that requires this area to be integrated into its system, whether scientific (Ptolemy) or religious (Xuanzang).

Fourth and finally, we are faced with the paradox that Gandhara is indeed a territory in its own right, yet our Roman sources (not unlike the Chinese of Xuanzang and others) would present it as a landscape of movement. To follow the lead of EARLE, SNEAD and other others,[40] it is as well to be reminded that human geography is the study of the ways in which humans interact with the natural landscape. Imagination itself is one kind of interaction, as is abundantly clear in the case of Ptolemy. Ptolemy's Gandhara is by implication a place of movement, for what we might see as commercial enterprises. In this remote part of the Eurasian continent, Ptolemy gives us a sense of through-movement, a sense of space contingent on routes: contrast the Buddhist narratives mentioned, where Gandhara gained significance via the Buddha's relics and received pilgrimage accordingly. A sense of movement – to the degree we can reconstruct it from historical accounts – is the way to relate the specificities of place with the dynamics and potentialities of space.[41]

VI Gandharan mobility today

But objects travel too, not merely persons. By way of a coda, let us ask what would eventuate if we brought this historical topic into the present time. For any critical approach to this topic today, the elephant in the room is the endangered status of anti-

---

[40] EARLE 2009; SNEAD/ERICKSON/DARLING 2009a; BEAUDRY/PARNO 2013. EARLE articulates a useful set of variables to promote comparative study, including frequency of use; the level of labour investment; use (ceremonial, military, economic, etc.). A key criterion for us might be the degree of state involvement, which seems low.
[41] The foundational text in human geography is still that of TUAN 1977.

quities in the region. The Taliban's destruction of the Buddha colossi at Bamiyan in March 2001 received a great deal of international attention.[42] As huge as these statues themselves were, they represent only the tip of the iceberg in relation to the wartime destruction of the cultural heritage of Afghanistan and Pakistan over several decades and most extensively since the War in Afghanistan (2001–14). Extreme poverty in the region is another, related factor in the compromising of heritage sites. The larger backdrop is the illicit trade in antiquities: even as UNESCO and other bodies have sought international agreements by which to curb the traffic in heritage objects, the illegal market has reached new levels in a context of long-term regional instability and failed statehood.[43] Against this background, it comes as no surprise that archaeological activity has been severely limited: in fact the Italian team in the Swat valley has been unique its perseverance amidst the most trying circumstances.[44]

New initiatives such as CyArk, which digitizes large-scale archaeological sites and connects them to state-of-the-art virtual reality software, are a contemporary response to urgent challenges of preservation.[45] It is all the more to be regretted that there are no apparent plans to extend CyArk to Afghanistan's sites, in view of that country's precarious situation. On the other hand, ancient Merv in Turkmenistan is already part of the CyArk site, currently the sole Silk Route site. This relative absence surely reflects safety concerns rather than any lack of interest in the Silk Road per se.

While such projects bring about new possibilities of digital preservation and public outreach, archaeological sites themselves remain in danger and artifacts have long been detached from their find contexts. The prime offender in this respect is soldier-turned-excavator, CHARLES MASSON (1800–1853), who visited and despoiled Eastern Afghanistan sites in the 1830s. On the one hand, MASSON appropriated Afghan cultural property on a scale that has not been seen since, removing items from their original sites; on the other hand these very acts of appropriation have in effect saved artefacts from destruction and looting and made them available to researchers. What does it mean to save an object? By a bitter paradox, one person is both a destroyer of archaeological context and at the same time preserver of fundamental archaeological records of as well as a prime donor of the British Museum's early Buddhist collec-

---

42 MORGAN 2012 provides one account, among many, of the Bamiyan Buddhas, whereas STEIN 2015 is an overview of Afghanistan's heritage situation. Updated information is available at the UNESCO website, https://en.unesco.org/countries/afghanistan. At the time of writing (June 2018), several of the recent posts concerned the murder of journalists and infrastructure rebuilding, in other words heritage in an archaeological sense is merely one part of UNESCO's remit.
43 To take a prominent instance from southwest of Gandhara proper, the Buddhist site of Mes Aynak has until very recently (June 2018) been subject to Chinese mining interests: https://www.npr.org/sections/goatsandsoda/2015/08/30/435570591/whats-better-for-afghanistans-future-buddha-tours-or-a-copper-mine.
44 OLIVIERI 2018.
45 http://www.cyark.org/projects/

tion.⁴⁶ By the same token, the Musée Guimet in Paris owes its extraordinary quality to excavations of the Délégation archéologique française en Afghanistan (DAFA), begun in 1922 under the leadership of ALFRED FOUCHER (1865–1952) and later interrupted by war.⁴⁷ While transnational collections such as those at the British Museum and the Musée Guimet could not have been made after the UNESCO Convention of 1970, those very collections served a visible role of cultural preservation amid the violent conflicts in the late 20th and early 21st centuries – even though in many cases (and especially for Masson's collection) the find contexts and thus archaeological value were lost in the process. The success of highly visible traveling exhibits such as *Gandhara, das Buddhistische Erbe Pakistans*⁴⁸ and *Afghanistan: hidden treasures from the National Museum, Kabul.*⁴⁹ According to the website of the Afghan Ministry of Information and Culture, the exhibit has functioned as a kind of cultural ambassador for Afghanistan, and precipitated the return of several Afghan-origin artifacts to the country and spurred the building of capacity within Afghanistan's heritage sector.⁵⁰ Gandhara in this sense involves post-antique routes, determined no longer by the so-called Silk Road on land but by two international juggernauts: the illegal market in antiquities and the museum-exhibit industry.⁵¹

Bibliography

ALCOCK/BODEL/TALBERT 2007 = S.E. ALCOCK/J. BODEL/R.J.A. TALBERT (ed.), Highways, Byways and Road Systems in the Pre-Modern World, Chichester 2007.
BEAL 1884 = S. BEAL, *Su-yi-ki:* Buddhist records of the western world, London 1884.
BEAUDRY/PARNO 2013 = M.C. BEAUDRY/T.G. PARNO (ed.), Archaeologies of Mobility and Movement, New York 2013.
BEHRENDT 2004 = K.A. BEHRENDT, The Buddhist Architecture of Gandhara, Leiden 2004.
BEHRENDT/BRANCACCIO 2007 = K. BEHRENDT/P. BRANCACCIO (ed.), Gandharan Buddhism, Vancouver 2007.
BERGGREN/JONES 2000 = J.L. BERGGREN/A. JONES, Ptolemy's Geography: an annotated translation of the theoretical chapters, Princeton 2000.
BRIANT 2012 = P. BRIANT, From the Indus to the Mediterranean: the administrative organization and logistics of the Great Road of the Achaemenid Empire, in: ALCOCK/BODEL/TALBERT 2007, 185–201.

---

46 ERRINGTON 2014; GARG 2018.
47 RAY 2018, 3.
48 Bonn-Berlin-Zurich, 2008–9; New York, 2011.
49 Inter alia Washington, 2008; New York, 2009; Sydney, 2014; Tokyo, 2016; China, 2018.
50 http://moic.gov.af/en/page/1291/2122
51 Warm thanks to Professor Anne Kolb for the invitation and fellow conferees for engaging discussion; beyond that to Professor Himanshu Prabha Ray, whose own project on Gandhara initially brought me to the topic. Dan Tuzzeo (Stanford) has provided valuable input over several years. The usual disclaimer applies.

Casson 1989 = L. Casson, The Periplus Maris Erythraei: text with introduction, translation and commentary, Princeton 1989.

Coedès 2010 = G. Coedès, Texts of Greek and Latin Authors on the Far East, from the 4th century BCE to the 14th century CE. Tr. John Sheldon, Turnhout 2010.

Cunningham 1871 = A. Cunningham, The Ancient Geography of India, vol. 1: the Buddhist period, including the campaigns of Alexander and the travels of Hwen-Thsang, London 1871.

Earle 2009 = T. Earle, Routes the landscape: a comparative approach, in: Snead/Erickson/Darling 2009, 253–269.

Errington 2004 = E. Errington, 'Charles Masson', *Encyclopedia Online*, online edition http://www.iranicaonline.org/articles/masson-charles (accessed 29th June, 2018).

Evers 2016 = K.G. Evers, Worlds Apart Trading Together: the organisation of long-distance trade between the Mediterranean and the Indian Ocean, 1st-6th centuries CE, Copenhagen 2016.

Frankopan 2016 = P. Frankopan, The Silk Roads: a new history of the world, New York 2016. Digital edition.

Garg 2018 = S. Garg, Charles Masson: a footloose antiquarian in Afghanistan and the building up of numismatic collections in the museums of India and England, in: Ray 2018, 130–153.

Gerini 1909 = G.E. Gerini, Researches on Ptolemy's Geography of Eastern Asia (Further India and Indo-Malay Archipelago), London 1909.

Gibbon 2009 = E. Gibbon, The Decline and Fall of the Roman Empire, abridged by Hans-Friedrich Müller, New York 2009.

Graf 1995 = D. Graf, The Persian Royal Road system, in: A. Kuhrt/M. Cool Root/H. Sancisi-Weerdenburg (ed.), Achaemenid History VIII: continuity and change, Leiden 1995, 167–189.

Gurukkal 2016 = R. Gurukkal, Rethinking Classical Indo-Roman Trade: political economy of eastern Mediterranean exchange relations, Oxford 2016.

Hansen 2012 = V. Hansen, The Silk Road: a new history, Oxford 2012.

Hill 2015 = J.E. Hill, Through the Jade Gate, China to Rome: a study of the Silk Routes through the later Han Dynasty, 1st to 2nd centuries CE. An annotated translation from the Hou Hanshu 'The Chronicle of the Western Regions', 2 vol., Marston Gate 2015.

Khatchadourian 2016 = L. Khatchadourian, Imperial Matter: Ancient Persia and the Archaeology of Empires, Oakland 2016.

Luczanits 2008 = C. Luczanits (ed.), Gandhara, the Buddhist Heritage of Pakistan: legends, monasteries and paradise, Mainz 2008.

Macdonell/Keith 1912 = A.A. Macdonnel/A.B. Keith, Vedic Index of Names and Subjects, 2 vol., London 1912.

McLaughlin 2016 = R. McLaughlin, The Roman Empire and the Silk Routes: the ancient world economy and the empires of Parthia, Central Asia and Han China, Barnsley 2016.

Millar 1998 = F. Millar, Caravan Cities: The Roman Near East and long-distance trade by land, in: M. Austin/J. Harrie/C. Smith (ed.), Modus Operandi: essays in honour of Geoffrey Rickman, London 1998, 119–137.

Moitra 2018 = T. Moitra, Region through text: representation of Gandhara in the *Mahabharata*, in: Ray 2018, 104–128.

Neelis 2002 = J. Neelis, La vieille Route Reconsidered: Alternative Paths for Early Transmission of Buddhism beyond the Borderlands of South Asia, *Bulletin of the Asia Institute* 16, 2002, 143–164.

Neelis 2007 = J. Neelis, Overland shortcuts for the transmission of Buddhism, in: Alcock/Bodel/Talbert 2007, 12–32.

Neelis 2014a = J. Neelis, Literary and Visual Narratives in Gandhāran Buddhist Manuscripts and Material Cultures: Localization of Jātakas, Avadānas, and Previous-Birth Stories, in:

B. Fleming/R. Mann (ed.), Material Culture and Asian Religions: Text, Image, Object. Routledge Research in Religion, Media and Culture, New York 2014, 252–264.

Neelis 2014b = J. Neelis, Localizing the Buddha's Presence at Wayside Shrines in Northern Pakistan, in: V. Rabens/P. Wick (ed.), Religions and Trade: Religious Formation, Transformation and Cross-Cultural Exchange between East and West. Dynamics in the History of Religion, vol. 5, Leiden 2014, 45–64.

Olivieri 2018 = L.M. Olivieri, Vajirasthana/Bazira and beyond: foundation and current status of the archaeological work in Swat, in: Ray 2018, 173–212.

Parker 2008 = G. Parker, The Making of Roman India, Cambridge 2008.

Ray 2014 = H.P. Ray, The Return of the Buddha: ancient symbols for a new nation, London 2014.

Ray 2018 = H.P. Ray (ed.), Buddhism and Gandhara: an archaeology of museum collections. Archaeology and Religion in South Asia, London 2018.

Rienjang 2012 = W. Rienjang, Aurel Stein's work in the Northwest Frontier Province, in: H. Wang (ed.), Sir Aurel Stein: colleagues and collections, London 2012, British Museum, online edition.

Robson 2009 = J. Robson, Buddhist sacred geography, in: J. Lagerway/M. Kalinowski/P. Lü (ed.), Early Chinese Religion, Leiden 2009.

Robson 2012 = J. Robson, Changing places: the conversion of religious sites in China, in: J. Benn/ J. Chen/J. Robson (ed.), Images, Relics and Legends: the formation and transformation of Buddhist sacred sites, Oakville 2012, 90–111.

Roller 2008 = D.W. Roller, Isidoros of Charax (781), *Brill's New Jacoby*. Online edition.

Ruffing 2014 = K. Ruffing, Cultural encounters between Rome and the east, in: I. Lindstedt et al. (ed.), Case Studies in Transmission, The Intellectual Heritage of the Ancient and Mediaeval Near East, vol. I, Münster 2014, 143–157.

Schmitt 1991 = R. Schmitt, The Bisitun Inscriptions of Darius the Great, London 1991.

Schopen 1997 = G. Schopen, Filial Piety and Monk in the Practice of Indian Buddhism: A Question 'Sinicization' Viewed from the Other Side in: G. Schopen, Bones, Stones and Buddhist Monks: Collected Papers on the Archaeology, Epigraphy, and Texts of Monastic Buddhism in India, Honolulu 2002, 56–71.

Singh 2004 = U. Singh, The Discovery of Ancient India: early archaeologists and the beginnings of archaeology, Delhi 2004.

Snead/Erickson/Darling 2009 = J.E. Snead/C.L. Erickson/J.A. Darling (ed.), Landscapes of Movement: trails, paths and roads in anthropological perspective, Philadelphia 2009.

Snead/Erickson/Darling 2009a = J.E. Snead/C.L. Erickson/J.A. Darling (ed.), Making human space: the archaeology of trails, paths and roads, in: Snead/Erickson/Darling 2009, 1–19.

Stein 1905 = Sir A. Stein, Report of the Archaeological Survey World in the North-West Frontier Province and Baluchistan, Peshawar 1905.

Stein 1928 = Sir A. Stein, Innermost Asia: detailed report of explorations in Central Asia, Kan-su and Eastern Iran, 4 vol., Oxford 1928.

Stein 2015 = G.J. Stein, The war-ravaged cultural heritage of Afghanistan: an overview of projects of assessment, mitigation and preservation, *Near Eastern Archaeology* 78.3, 2015, 187–195.

Stückelberger/Grasshoff/Mittenhuber 2006 = A. Stückelberger/G. Grasshoff,/F. Mittenhuber (ed.), Klaudios Ptolemaios, Handbuch der Geographie, Basel 2006.

Talbert 2012 = R.J.A. Talbert, Urbs Roma to Orbis Romanus: Roman mapping on the grand scale, in: R.J.A. Talbert (ed.), Ancient Perspectives: maps and their place in Mesopotamia, Egypt, Greece and Rome, Chicago 2012, 162–191.

Tarn 1923 = W.W. Tarn, Alexander and the Ganges, *Journal of Hellenic Studies* 43.2, 1923, 93–101.

Tuan 1977 = Y.F Tuan, Space and Place: the perspective of experience, Minneapolis 1977.

Vasunia 2013 = P. Vasunia, The Classics and Colonial India, Oxford, Oxford 2013.

Zwalf 1996 = W. Zwalf, Catalogue of the Gandhara Sculpture in the British Museum, London 1996.

Michael A. Speidel
Rom und die Fernhandelswege durch Arabien

Abstract: Road maps of the Roman Empire usually show a reticulate network of local and long distance routes stretching to the very limits of the *Imperium Romanum*, where all roads suddenly appear to end. Although the physical remains of Roman roads clearly show that Rome constructed its road system only within the empire's boundaries, they also reveal that this was not done to a single empire-wide standard. Nor did Rome's interest in road connections end where provincial territory did. This contribution discusses new epigraphic and archaeological evidence from the territory of the former Nabataean kingdom that illustrates how, in the early decades of the new province of Arabia, the purpose a certain road was expected to serve determined the standards to which it was constructed. Purpose and construction standards, in turn, therefore shed light on various aspects of Roman imperial interests in the wider region.

Zusammenfassung: Straßenkarten des Römischen Reiches zeigen ein zumeist verästeltes Netzwerk von Fern- und Lokalstraßen, das sich bis an die äußersten Grenzen des *Imperium Romanum* erstreckt, wo die Verbindungen dann abrupt enden. Zwar zeigen die physischen Reste römischer Verkehrsinfrastruktur, dass der römische Ausbau des Straßennetzes sich nicht über das Provinzgebiet hinaus erstreckte, doch bekanntlich geschah der Ausbau innerhalb des Reiches keineswegs gleichförmig oder nach einem einheitlichen Standard. Auch endete das römische Interesse an Verbindungsrouten nicht an den Reichsgrenzen. Die in diesem Beitrag besprochenen neuen archäologischen und epigraphischen Funde vom Gebiet des ehemaligen Nabataeerreiches zeigen, wie der vorgesehene Zweck, dem bestimmte Straßen in der frühen Phase der Erschließung der neuen Provinz dienen sollten, die Art des römischen Ausbaus der vorgefundenen nabatäischen Routen bestimmte. Zweck und Ausbau werfen somit auch neues Licht auf verschiedene Aspekte römischer Interessen in der weiteren Region.

Das Netz von Fernstraßen, das sich bis in die Peripherie des Römischen Reiches erstreckte, gehörte zu den kennzeichnenden Merkmalen des *Imperium Romanum*. Das ist bekanntlich keine neuzeitliche Einschätzung moderner Historiker und Archäologen, sondern das hat bereits Dionysios von Halikarnassos gegen Ende des 1. Jahrhunderts v. Chr. in seinem Werk zur römischen Frühgeschichte so geäußert. Für diesen augusteischen Historiker aus Kleinasien gehörten die Straßen (zusammen mit den Aquaedukten und den Kloaken) zu den drei größten Errungenschaften der Römer.[1]

---

[1] Dion.Hal.ant. 3,67,5. Research for this contibution was carried out in the context of the author's fellowship no. UMO-2016/23/P/HS3/04141 of the National Science Centre, Poland. This project has received funding from the European Union's Horizon 2020 research and innovation programme under the Marie Skłodowska-Curie grant agreement No 665778 [EU-Logo].

https://doi.org/10.1515/9783110638332-005

Nur wenige Zeilen vor dieser Aussage beschrieb Dionysios wie die Römer im Kampf gegen die Sabiner Straßen mit militärischen Festungen versahen und dadurch einen wichtigen Sieg errangen.² Auch an zahlreichen anderen Stellen seines Geschichtswerks beschreibt Dionysios wie die Römer seit ihrer frühesten Geschichte, Straßen in ihre militärischen Pläne einbezogen, oft auch befestigten und damit nahezu immer Erfolge im Kampf erzielten.³ Dionysios' Aussagen sind trotz oft zweifelhaftem Wahrheitsgehalt im Einzelnen vor allem deshalb von Bedeutung, weil sie zeigen, wie ein Historiker aus Kleinasien zu Beginn der Kaiserzeit ganz selbstverständlich die römischen Kriegserfolge schon seit der Frühzeit mit dem Ausbau und der militärischen Nutzung von Straßen und ihrer Befestigung mit Kastellen verband.

Ein weit verbreitetes Verständnis vom Verhältnis zwischen römischen Straßen und römischer Herrschaft gründet noch heute auf solchen Vorstellungen und lässt dabei Bilder und Karten entstehen, die das *Imperium Romanum* als verästeltes Netzwerk von Fern- und Lokalstraßen bis an seine äußersten Grenzen darstellen, wo diese dann aufhören. Roms Herrschaftsgebiet wird somit durch das römische Straßennetz geradezu definiert. Diese Sichtweise hat in der Verbreitung der physischen Reste römischer Verkehrsinfrastruktur tatsächlich eine gewisse Stütze. Denn sie lässt einen römischen Ausbau des Straßennetzes nur in Italien und innerhalb des eigenen Provinzgebiets erkennen. Allerdings findet sich in den schriftlichen Quellen der Kaiserzeit durchaus auch der Ausdruck römischen Interesses an Straßen außerhalb des eigenen Herrschaftsgebiets. Besonders deutlich wird dies etwa in der Darstellung eines weltumspannenden Straßennetzes auf der *Tabula Peutingeriana*. Aber auch in den Texten von Isidor von Charax, Claudius Ptolemaeus, oder im *Periplus Maris Erythraei* (und andernorts) wird weder der Eindruck vermittelt, dass die Verkehrswege noch das römische Interesse an ihnen an den Reichsgrenzen endeten. Nach diesen Quellen führen Fernverbindungen aus dem Römischen Reich heraus oder in das Reich hinein und werden stets so beschrieben, als seien sie mit den römischen Straßen nahtlos verbunden gewesen. Die einheitliche Darstellung der Verkehrswege auf der gesamten *Tabula Peutingeriana* ist dabei aber kaum als Ausdruck einer römischen Weltherrschaftsphantasie zu verstehen, wie dies vor kurzem vorgeschlagen wurde.⁴ Vielmehr sollte wohl eine zentrale Aussage dieser bemerkenswerten Darstellung in der Verbundenheit der römischen mit der übrigen Alten Welt liegen, die durch ein umfassendes Verkehrsnetz ermöglicht wurde, das vom Atlantik bis an den östlichsten Rand Asiens reichte.⁵

Der Bau der *via nova Traiana* unmittelbar im Zusammenhang mit der Einrichtung der *provincia Arabia* ist zweifellos zu Recht als ein Musterbeispiel für das kaiserzeitliche römische Verhältnis von Straßenbau und der Schaffung einer neuen Provinz

---

2 Dion.Hal.ant. 3,65,2.
3 Dion.Hal.ant. 5,60,1. 6,4,3. 6,5,3. 6,47,1. 8,21,2. 8,36,3. 9,19,1. 9,26,5. 9,26,8. 9,70,2. 10,16,4. 10,44,2–4; 10,46,1. 11,33,4–5. 15,3,14–15.
4 PARKER 2008, 246; TALBERT 2010, bes. 149; ARNAUD 2014, 48; dazu etwa SPEIDEL 2016a, 107.
5 Zur Darstellung verschiedener „Welten" auf der Tabula Peutingeriana siehe SPEIDEL 2016a, 108.

bezeichnet worden.[6] Neue Inschriften und archäologische Befunde aus dem Gebiet der römischen *provincia Arabia* werfen indes neues Licht nicht nur auf außerordentliche *via nova Traiana* sondern auch auf die Bedeutung, die Rom dem Netz von Fernverkehrswegen in der neuen Provinz insgesamt beimaß. Denn mit dem Herrschaftsgebiet des ehemaligen nabatäischen Königreichs übernahm Rom von den Nabatäern bekanntlich auch ein weit gespanntes Netz von Fernverkehrsrouten. So war die königliche Residenzstadt Petra, die zugleich politisches, ökonomisches, kulturelles und religiöses Zentrum der Nabatäer war, durch zahlreiche Verkehrswege mit Südarabien, Syrien, Nordmesopotamien und dem Persischen Golf, mit Rhinocolura und Gaza am Mittelmeer, sowie mit Ägypten und dem Roten Meer verbunden.

Die Existenz von Fernverbindungsrouten allein führte freilich noch nicht zum Wohlstand der Nabatäer. Entscheidend war vielmehr der Fluss und das Volumen der Handelsgüter auf diesen Routen. Daraus erst ergab sich die Höhe des Einkommens aus Wegzöllen und der Erfolg als Zwischenhändler von Weihrauch, Myrrhe und weiteren Gütern.[7] Der Fluss und das Volumen des Handels wurde aber nicht nur von der Nachfrage nach den gehandelten Gütern bestimmt, sondern ebenso von der Sicherheit der Handelsrouten, von der Zusammenarbeit mit weiteren Zwischenhändlern auf diesen Strecken, sowie von der Zahl und der Höhe der Abgaben, die den verschiedenen lokalen Herrschern unterwegs zu entrichten waren.[8] Wollte eine Karawane, wie jene unter der Führung des Hadramiten Hārith^{um} im 1. Jahrhundert n. Chr. mit einer Eskorte von bewaffneten Männern aus dem Hadramaut mehrere Herrschaftsgebiete auf dem Weg von Süden nach Norden durchqueren, wie eine altsüdarabische Inschrift berichtet,[9] so war dies kaum möglich, ohne Vereinbarungen oder Bündnisse entlang der Reiseroute. Dennoch blieb die Begleitung durch bewaffnete Mannschaften wegen des außerordentlichen Werts der transportierten Güter und der Gefahr von Überfällen zu Land und zu Wasser oft notwendig.[10] Ihren Wohlstand verdankten die Nabatäer deshalb auch den wichtigen Bündnissen und ihrem Einfluss, über den sie auf weiten Teilen der arabischen Halbinsel verfügten.[11] Zudem unterhielten sie, wie archäologische und epigraphische Zeugnisse zeigen, in ihrem Herrschaftsgebiet militärische Einrichtungen und Garnisonen an mehreren wichtigen Knotenpunkten der Fernhandelsrouten und trugen damit zweifellos ebenfalls zur Sicherheit der Handelsrouten bei.[12]

---

6 So etwa RATHMANN 2006, 209.
7 Diod. 19,94,4–5; Strab. 16,4,19 (siehe auch 4,18–25); Plin. nat. 12,32,63–65; vgl. dazu etwa YOUNG 1997.
8 Strab. 16,4,19 und 22. Plin. nat. 12,32,63–65. Zur politischen und ökonomischen Geschichte Südarabiens in dieser Zeit siehe etwa ROBIN 2012, 247–254; ROBIN 2015, 94–98.
9 ROBIN 2013.
10 Peripl. m. r. 20; Plin. nat. 6,26,101; Philostr. Ap. 3,35; ROBIN 2013 (zu R 1850).
11 Strabo 16,4,24; SPEIDEL 2015, 247–249 zu weiteren Zeugnissen.
12 SAVIGNAC/STARCKY 1957; GRAF 1979, 123–126; BOWERSOCK 1983, 94, 104; EADIE 1986, 247; GRAF 1997; vgl. SPEIDEL 2009, 647–48; SPEIDEL 2015, 247–48.

Nach der Durchquerung der Arabischen Halbinsel gelangten die für Italien und die römischen Provinzen bestimmten Güter schließlich ans Mittelmeer oder an die Provinzgrenzen, wo nun auch Rom Zölle auf die Importgüter einforderte, die hier bekanntlich 25% des Warenwertes (τετάρτη) betrugen.[13] Die wenigen überlieferten Zahlen zum Einkommen der römischen Staatskassen aus diesen Importzöllen auf Waren östlicher Herkunft legen dabei nahe, dass diese Einnahmen zu den bedeutendsten der römischen Staatskasse insgesamt gehörten und sogar ausgereicht hätten, den größten Teil der laufenden Ausgaben für das römische Heer zu decken.[14] Die Nabatäer erzielten somit als Zwischenhändler und als Zollerheber an den Routen durch ihr Herrschaftsgebiet nicht nur bedeutende Einnahmen für die eigenen Kassen, sondern sie trugen durch ihre militärischen und diplomatischen Aktivitäten zu einem steten und bedeutenden Fluss und Volumen des Fernhandels bei und verhalfen damit auch der Staatskasse Roms zu erheblichen Einnahmen. Auch das nabatäische Rechtswesen scheint die Erwartungen römischer und anderer ausländischer Händler erfüllt zu haben und trug damit ebenfalls zur Stabilität der Herrschaft und des Reiches mit bei.[15]

Natürlich wusste man auch in Rom um den Wert der Routen und des Handels durch Arabien und das Rote Meer und begann deshalb schon früh, Maßnahmen zu treffen, die den Fernhandel zum Vorteil Roms beeinflussen sollten. So sollte kurz nach der Eroberung Ägyptens ein römischer Feldzug nach Südarabien unter der Beteiligung jüdischer und nabatäischer Truppen die Sabäer im Süden der Halbinsel zu „Freunden" machen oder sie unterwerfen und jedenfalls für Rom großen Gewinn einbringen.[16] Die Lage des Königreichs der Sabäer verlieh diesen einen bedeutenden Einfluss auf den Karawanenhandel. Durch die Expansion ihres Herrschaftsgebietes an die Küsten Südarabiens dehnten sie im Laufe des ersten Jahrhunderts v. Chr. zudem ihren Einfluss auf den Fernhandel zur See aus.[17] Der Feldzug der Jahre 26 / 25 v. Chr. scheint schliesslich trotz großer römischer Verluste zu einer Veränderung der politischen Lage in Südarabien geführt zu haben, die römischen Vorstellungen entsprach und zudem offenbar nabatäische Positionen im Süden der Arabischen Halbinsel stärkte. Auch scheint Rom schon im ersten Jahrhundert n. Chr. eine militärische Flotte im Roten Meer unterhalten zu haben.[18] Die militärischen Operationen der „Statthalter und Könige Arabiens" gegen die Stützpunkte und Siedlungen von Piraten an der Ostküste

---

[13] Siehe etwa YOUNG 1997; JÖRDENS 2009, 355–370; AST/BAGNALL 2015.
[14] Vgl. Cic. Manil. 7,17: *vectigalia nervos esse rei publicae semper duximus*. Zu den konkreten Zahlen siehe MCLAUGHLIN 2014, 94; WILSON 2015, 23; SPEIDEL 2016b, 165–167 mit weiterer Literatur.
[15] Strab. 16,4,21.
[16] Strab. 16,4,22–24; Plin. nat. 6,32,160; Cass. Dio 53,29,8. Dazu ausführlich MAREK 1993; DEBIDOUR 2012; SPEIDEL 2015. Römische Kenntnisse der Handelsrouten: Strab. 16,4,21.
[17] AVANZINI 2016, 188–190.
[18] Dazu SPEIDEL 2015, 249–250; NAPPO 2015, 57–62; SADDINGTON 2016.

des Roten Meeres geschahen ebenfalls wenigstens zum Teil zweifellos in Erfüllung römischer Erwartungen an seine Verbündeten.[19]

Aber Rom stärkte seine Positionen auf der Arabischen Halbinsel schon im ersten Jahrhundert auch mit Blick auf die Routen durch das Nabatäerreich. So wurde in Leuke Kome, dem südlichsten Hafen der Nabatäer am Roten Meer, den eine Karawanenroute über Hegra mit Petra verband und den Aelius Gallus als Ausgangspunkt seiner Expedition im Jahre 26 v. Chr. nach Südarabien benutzt hatte, eine römische Zollstation eingerichtet und durch einige Soldaten unter einem Zenturionen bewacht.[20] Vermutlich wurde hier, ähnlich wie an den ägyptischen Häfen am Roten Meer, zunächst nur der genaue Umfang und Wert jener Güter festgestellt, die ins Römische Reich importiert werden sollten. Von Leuke Kome führte eine wichtige Route über Hegra nach Petra.[21] An den Mittelmeerhäfen war dann beim Import der Waren ins Provinzgebiet des *Imperium Romanum* der Zoll zu entrichten.

So lag Petra als politisches, gesellschaftliches, juristisches und militärisches Zentrum im Mittelpunkt eines Netzes von außerordentlich gewinnbringenden Fernhandelsbeziehungen. Bemerkenswert ist dabei, dass eine Rekonstruktion der nabatäischen Handelsverbindungen in einer jüngeren Studie von Karen Borsted keine Karawanenroute verzeichnet, die Petra direkt mit Bostra auf der Linie der späteren *via nova Traiana* verband. Unter den wichtigsten Gründen dafür nennt die Autorin zum Einen das vollständige Fehlen positiver Nachweise für eine solche Streckenführung in nabatäischer Zeit und zum Anderen den steilen Auf- und Abstieg, der eine Durchquerung der tiefen Wadis (vor allem des großen Wadi Mujib) auf der späteren römischen Strecke für beladene Kamele unmöglich gemacht hätte.[22] Die nabatäischen Karawanenrouten hätten deshalb die großen Wadis umgangen. Ist es tatsächlich kein Zufall, dass bisher auf diesem Abschnitt der späteren *via nova Traiana* keine archäologischen Überreste einer vorrömischen Karawanenroute entdeckt wurden, so muss man in Traians neuer Straße mehr als nur den Ausbau einer bereits vorhandenen, nabatäischen Handelsverbindung erkennen, wie dies zumeist getan wird.[23] Vielmehr gewinnt Traians Behauptung an Glaubwürdigkeit, er habe *redacta in formam provinciae Arabia viam novam a finibus Syriae usque ad mare rubrum aperuit et stravit*.[24]

---

19 Peripl. m. r. 20; SPEIDEL 2016b, 167–169.
20 Peripl. m. r. 19; Strab. 16,4,23–24. Hierzu und zum folgenden bes. YOUNG 1997; JÖRDENS 2009, 364–365; AST/BAGNALL 2015; NAPPO 2015; SPEIDEL 2016b, 159. Gegen die These, es handle sich um Funktionsträger und Militärs in nabatäischen Diensten (so etwa BOWERSOCK 1983, 71) demnächst SPEIDEL, im Druck. Zur Lokalisierung von Leuke Kome bei El Wajh an der Saudi Arabischen Rotmeerküste siehe NAPPO 2010.
21 Strab. 16,4,24; peripl. m. r. 19.
22 BORSTAD 2008.
23 So etwa BOWERSOCK 1983, 83; ISAAC 1992, 120; GRAF 1995, 264; YOUNG 2001, 108; RATHMANN 2006, 209 n. 36.
24 Z.B. ILS 5834, Kera. Anders etwa noch etwa ISAAC 1992, 120: "not necessarily true". FREEMAN 1996, 109: "commemorative".

Jedenfalls kann kein Zweifel bestehen, dass die römische Übernahme des nabatäischen Königreichs und seine Umwandlung in eine Provinz tiefgreifende Veränderungen mit sich brachten, zu denen vor allem auch der Bau der *via nova Traiana* zu zählen ist. Denn wie kein anderes römisches Bauwerk prägte diese gepflasterte Straße mit ihren zahlreichen beschriebenen Meilensteinen das Gesicht der neuen Provinz, zumal Straßenpflaster und Meilensteine nicht zum Erscheinungsbild nabatäischer Straßen gehört hatten.[25] Gerade die Meilensteininschriften betonen den Zusammenhang der Provinzgründung und des Straßenbaus sehr deutlich. Der eigentliche Grund jedoch, weshalb der Kaiser dieses außerordentlich aufwändige und kostspielige Denkmal seiner Umwandlung des nordarabischen Königreichs in eine römische Provinz befahl, ist in keiner Quelle überliefert. In der Forschung hat man vor allem ökonomische, militärische oder administrative Gründe angenommen.[26] Für die Beurteilung der Bedeutung von Traians neuer Straße ist neben dem technisch aufwändigen und teuren Ausbau des Bauwerks sicherlich von besonderem Gewicht, dass die Straße durch das urbane Siedlungsgebiet der neuen Provinz verlief, dass sich die zahlreichen frühen Meilensteine im Umfeld der Siedlungszentren häuften, dass deren Texte alle in lateinischer Sprache abgefasst waren, und schließlich dass diese die Ausweitung des römischen Provinzgebietes bis ans Rote Meer verkündeten. Damit war Traians neue Straße für die überwiegende Mehrheit der Bewohner der Provinz vor allem ein gegenwärtiges Zeichen ihrer Zugehörigkeit zur Welt der römischen Provinzen und diente ganz wesentlich der Integration der neuen *provincia Arabia* in das von Rom direkt beherrschte Reich.

Zwar sollten wohl weder einzelne mögliche Beweggründe für die Errichtung dieses außerordentliche Bauwerks ausgeschlossen noch als allein zutreffend angesehen werden, doch vornehmlich als große Handelsstraße dürfte die *via nova Traiana* zunächst kaum konzipiert gewesen sein. Denn weder lässt die archäologische Hinterlassenschaft den Schluss zu, Aila am Roten Meer sei schon während der ersten beiden Jahrhunderte n. Chr. ein bedeutender Handelshafen gewesen, noch verband in nabatäischer Zeit anscheinende eine bedeutende Karawanenroute den Küstenort mit der Residenzstadt Petra.[27] Dennoch spielten auch die Fernhandelsrouten des ehemaligen Nabatäerreiches bei der Einrichtung der Provinz Arabia unter Traian eine weit bedeutendere Rolle als das bisher zu erkennen gewesen war. Darauf lassen jedenfalls vor allem neuere archäologische und epigraphische Funde schließen. Denn ein jüngst in der Stadt Hegra entdecktes römisches Militärlager sowie mehrere lateinische, griechische und nabatäische Inschriften legen nahe, dass die Stadt wohl unmittelbar bei der Übernahme des nabatäischen Königreichs von römischen Soldaten besetzt und – wie zweifellos alle Regionen des ehemali-

---

25 Straßenpflaster und Meilensteine in der Wüste Negev sind nach BEN DAVID 2012 allesamt römisch (3. Jh. n. Chr.?) und im Rahmen militärischer Neustrukturierungen entstanden.
26 Siehe etwa ISAAC 1992, 131–132; FREEMAN 1996, 108; YOUNG 2001, 108; BORSTAD 2008, 68.
27 Aila: PARKER 1996; SIDEBOTHAM 2017, 129–132. Karawanenroute: BORSTAD 2008, 62 fig. 4.

gen Königreiches – der neuen Provinz zugeschlagen wurde.[28] Letzteres legen auch drei nabatäische Graffiti aus Hegra nahe, die das Jahr nach der neuen Provinzära zählen.[29] Mehrere lateinische, griechische und nabatäische Inschriften und Graffiti des zweiten (und dritten?) Jahrhunderts nennen zudem die regelmässige (oder zumindest wiederholte) Anwesenheit von römischen Soldaten und Offizieren, darunter auch von solchen der *legio III Cyrenaica*.[30] Eine der in Medâ'in Sâlih kürzlich entdeckten und bekannt gemachten Inschrift nennt *stationarii*, wie sie auch aus der ägyptischen Ostwüste bekannt sind, und die in Hegra offenbar unter dem Befehl zweier Zenturionen der *legio III Cyrenaica* standen.[31] Bemerkenswerterweise gehört das in Hegra entdeckte römische Militärlager nach Auffassung der Ausgräber zu den frühesten bisher auf dem Gebiet der neuen *provincia Arabia* bekannt gewordenen militärischen Strukturen insgesamt.[32]

Nur wenige Kilometer entfernt, auf der Route nach der Oase Al-'Ulâ sind zudem seit langem an zwei verschiedenen Orten Graffiti aus dem zweiten Jahrhundert von Reitersoldaten erhalten, die sich seit der jüngst erfolgten Veröffentlichung dreier Militärdiplome der Jahre 126, 142 und 145 für *auxiliarii* des *exercitus Arabicus* den beiden Einheiten der *ala I Ulpia dromadariorum Palmyrenorum milliaria* (Graffiti bei Qubūr al-Jundī) und der *ala veterana Gaetulorum* (Graffiti bei Jabal Ithlib) zuordnen lassen.[33] Beide Einheiten gehörten offenbar zur frühesten Besatzung der neuen Provinz.[34] Vor allem die Stationierung von Soldaten der *ala I Ulpia dromadariorum Palmyrenorum milliaria* bei Hegra hilft, Roms Vorgehen bei der Einrichtung der neuen

---

28 Provinz: vgl. dazu YOUNG 2001, 109 und 242 Anm. 178; SPEIDEL 2009, 634 mit weiterer Literatur. Zum römischen Militärlager von Hegra jetzt FIEMA 2016a, FIEMA 2018 und VILLENEUVE/FIEMA, im Druck.
29 NEHMÉ 2009, 44.
30 AE 1974, 662 = SEG 40, 1523; AE 2007, 1639; VILLENEUVE 2015, 37–40; VILLENEUVE 2016, 20–23.
31 VILLENEUVE 2015, 37–38; VILLENEUVE 2016, 20–21 (mit „verbesserter" Lesung). Ägyptische Ostwüste: SIDEBOTHAM 2011, 166. Zu *stationarii* siehe jetzt auch FUHRMANN 2012, 207–220.
32 FIEMA 2016b, 44: „The fort in Area 34 should be dated to the early/mid-2nd century and thus it is probably, after Humayma, the second earliest Roman military structure in Arabia."
33 Militärdiplome: AE 2004, 1925; ECK/PANGERL 2016. Graffiti: JAUSSEN/SAVIGNAC 1914, 644–649; SEYRIG 1940, 163; SPEIDEL 1984, 245–248; SARTRE 1982, 30–33; GRAF 1988, 192–196; YOUNG 2001, 109f.; jetzt bes. GATIER 2017. Zur Datierung siehe den Namen Ulpius Magnus eines der in den Graffiti an der Route nach Al-'Ulâ genannten Reiter der *ala dromadariorum*.
34 *Ala I Ulpia dromadariorum*: siehe unten. *Ala veterana Gaetulorum*: Auf dem Diplom des Jahres 126 ist ihr Name vermutlich zu ergänzen: ECK/PANGERL 2016, 230. Ein Altar aus Tomis bezeugt in der zweiten Hälfte des zweiten oder zu Beginn des dritten Jahrhunderts die Stationierung der Einheit in Arabia: AE 1974, 579 = SEG 24, 1064 = ISM II 127 = SEG 27, 401: Σηδάτιος [Ἀ]πολλώνιος ἔπαρχος ἱππέων εἴλης Γαιτούλων τῶν ἐν Ἀραβίᾳ. Der Stifter stammte zweifellos aus Tomis oder der näheren Umgebung (A. CHANIOTIS in SEG 61, 588), da er in Tomis für einem einheimischen Heros (Manibazos) und den Göttern seiner heimatlichen Vorfahren (*theoi patrioi*: SEG 61, 588 = AE 2011, 1146 vom selben Stifter) Altäre stiftete. Eine Herkunft aus einer östlichen Provinz vermutet hingegen MATEI-POPESCU 2011, 308. Spätere Zeugnisse für das Reiterregiment sind bisher nicht bekannt.

Provinz besser zu verstehen. Denn diese Einheit dürfte wohl sogar eigens für die neue Besatzung der Provinz aufgestellt worden sein.³⁵ In den Jahren 153 und 157 lag die *ala* dann in *Syria*.³⁶ Dennoch sind auch am Ende des zweiten Jahrhunderts *dromedarii* als Elitereiter im *exercitus Arabicus* bezeugt, es ist aber keineswegs sicher, dass es sich dabei um Reiter der *ala I Ulpia dromadariorum Palmyrenorum milliaria* handelte.³⁷ Auf jeden Fall ist aber die Aufstellung einer eintausend Mann starken Einheit von palmyrenischen Dromedarreitern ein deutlicher Hinweis auf Traians Absicht, die neu erworbenen Karawanenrouten durch die Steppen und Wüstengebiete zu sichern.³⁸ Denn darauf deutet einerseits der Begriff *dromadarius,* der vom griechischen δρομάς (κάμηλος) abgeleitet den Reiter eines schnellen Reitkamels bezeichnet (und nicht etwa den Führer eines Lasttiers),³⁹ sowie andererseits die Herkunft der überwiegenden Mehrheit dieser Reiter aus einer Region, in der sowohl vergleichbare topographische und klimatische Verhältnisse als auch ein großes Maß an Erfahrung im Karawanenschutz zu finden war.⁴⁰ Aber auch die Stationierung römischer Soldaten mitten in der Wüste des Hedschas rund 900 km südlich der Provinzhauptstadt Bostra und an der alten Weihrauchstraße in dieser Grenzregion im Süden der *provincia Arabia* ist kaum anders als mit dem Auftrag zu erklären, der Kontrolle und dem Schutz des Karawanenhandels zwischen dem Mittelmeer und Südarabien zu dienen, zumal die (meist palmyrenischen) *dromadarii* in *Syria* und *Aegyptus* offenbar ähnliche Aufträge hatten.⁴¹ Eine Statue, die zu Ehren eines aus Palmyra stammenden ritterlichen Befehlshabers der *ala I Ulpia dromadariorum Palmyrenorum milliaria* in den 150er Jahren in seiner Heimatstadt errichtet wurde, und deren beschrifteter Sockel in Palmyra teilweise erhalten geblieben ist, war möglicherweise Ausdruck der

---

35 So auch GATIER 2017, 284. Weniger wahrscheinlich, wenn auch nicht ganz auszuschliessen, ist dass die Einheit erst während der Vorbereitung für Traians Partherkrieg ausgehoben wurde (so erwogen von SPEIDEL/WEISS 2004, 253).
36 WEISS 2006, 283; vgl. CIL III 123 = CIL III 14160,1 = ILS 2541 = IGLS 15,2,392 (Rimet al-Lohf / Rimea, Syria).
37 CIL III 93 (p. 969) = IGLS 13,1, 9071 (Bosra/Bostra): *eq(uites) sing(ulares) exerc(itus) Arab(ici) item drom(adarii)*.
38 Ob die Einheit auch Kavalleristen enthielt, die als *equites* von den eigentlichen *dromadarii* zu unterscheiden waren, wie dies GATIER 2017, 282 annimmt, muss offen bleiben. Seine Identifizierung eines Flavius Beryllios, *dromedarius* auf einer griechischen Inschrift aus Qasr al-Abyad im Süden Jordaniens (IGLS 21, 94) mit einem gleichnamigen, jedoch als *eques* bezeichneten Soldaten der *ala dromadariorum Ant(oniniana)* auf einem von ihm neu veröffentlichten griechischen Graffito aus Bayīr spricht eher dagegen.
39 LSJ 450 s.v. δρομάς. Darauf weist auch GATIER 2017, 284 zurecht hin. Kamele dienten im Osten freilich durchaus auch als Lasttiere im römischen Heer: Tac. ann. 15,12: *vis camelorum*.
40 YOUNG 2001, 147–148.
41 So zu Recht schon YOUNG 2001, 109–110. Den selben Auftrag hatten zweifellos auch für die bei Hegra bezeugten Reiter der *ala veterana Gaetulorum*. Zu den *dromedarii* im römischen Heer allgemein siehe DĄBROWA 1991; YOUNG 2001, 146–148 und 155–156; RANCE 2015.

Dankbarkeit eines Karawanenführers für den Schutz der Dromedarreiter, wie dies bei ähnlichen Denkmälern in Palmyra gut bekannt ist.[42]

Traian hat aber nicht nur die Verbindungsrouten der „Weihrauchstraße" in den Süden der Arabischen Halbinsel von den Nabatäern übernommen und mit Soldaten des römischen Heeres neu besetzt. Auch die Befestigung und Besetzung der Hauptinsel des Farasanarchipels im Roten Meer mit Soldaten der damals in *Arabia* stationierten *legio VI Ferrata* geht mit größter Wahrscheinlichkeit auf seinen Befehl zurück.[43] Zudem berichten spätrömische Quellen, Traian habe im Roten Meer eine römische Flotte eingerichtet.[44] Aber auch den ehemals von Nabatäern bewachten Handelskorridor an den Persischen Golf durch das Wadi Sirhan in der arabischen Wüste hat bereits Traian im Zuge der Provinzialisierung des Nabatäischen Königreichs in römischen Besitz übernommen. Die Oasenstadt Dumata (Dûmat al Jandal, Saudi Arabien) am östlichen Ausgang des Wadi Sirhan war zumindest im Jahre 44 n. Chr. von nabatäischen Soldaten bewacht gewesen, dennoch wird meist angenommen, der Platz sei erst in severischer Zeit von römischen Soldaten (darunter mindestens ein Zenturio der *legio III Cyrenaica*) besetzt worden.[45] Die jüngsten archäologischen und epigraphischen Funde in dieser Region (al-Jawf und Sakākā) legen jedoch einen ganz anderen Schluss nahe. Denn in Dumata wurden nicht nur Überreste eines während des ersten bis ins vierte Jahrhundert n. Chr. durchgehend genutzten Wachtturms entdeckt, sondern unweit von Dumata fanden sich auch nabatäische Graffiti römischer Soldaten des zweiten Jahrhunderts. Auch hier legen die Quellen nahe, dass Traian im Jahre 106 (oder unmittelbar danach) sogleich die wichtigen militärischen Kontrollpunkte an dieser Karawanenstraße besetzen ließ.[46] Denn eine der nabatäischen Ritzinschriften, in der ein einheimischer Offizier *centurio* genannt wird, konnte von der Herausgeberin (wenn auch mit der gebotenen Vorsicht) ins Jahr

---

42 AE 1947, 171 = STARCKY 1949, 128 = HILLERS/CUSSINI 1996, 1422; siehe dazu HARTMANN 2001, 56. Ähnliche Denkmäler: z.B. SEG 15, 849 = HILLERS/CUSSINI 1996, 197 (132 n. Chr.); SEG 46, 1797 (144 n. Chr.); AE 1931, 54 = SEG 7, 135 = HILLERS/CUSSINI 1996, 1062 (145/6 n. Chr.); STARCKY 1949, 96 = HILLERS/CUSSINI 1996, 1403 (157 n. Chr.); STARCKY 1949, 91+95 = HILLERS/CUSSINI 1996, 2763 (157 n. Chr.).
43 AE 2005, 1640 = AE 2007, 1659; dazu ausführlich SPEIDEL 2009, 639–640; SPEIDEL 2016b, 161–163; vgl. auch NAPPO 2015.
44 Eutr. 8,3,2 (vgl. auch Hieron. Chron. 7,1 ed. R. Helm p. 194): *in mari Rubro classem instituit, ut per eam fines Indiae vastaret*. Jord., *Rom*. 268: *in mari Rubro classem, unde Indiae fines vastaret, instituit, ibique suam statuam dedicavit*. Ohne Verweis auf *India* und eine Statue berichtet auch Fest. 14f.: *in mari Rubro classem instituit*. Dazu zuletzt SPEIDEL 2016, 161–162.
45 Handelskorridor: Plin. nat. 6,32,146; Ptol. 5,19,7. Nabatäische Soldaten: SAVIGNAC/STARCKY 1957; BOWERSOCK 1983, 154–159. Zenturio: AE 2001, 1979. Ältere Literatur zum Wadi Sirhan in römischer Zeit (und bes. zu AE 1987, 964 = AE 1996, 1623, Azraq): SPEIDEL 1992, 369–370; ISAAC 1992, 126; CHRISTOL/LENOIR 2001, 164–165; YOUNG 2001, 83, 85, 99–100, 104. Siehe jetzt vor allem NEHMÉ 2017, 148–150.
46 Wachtturm (L2018): CHARLOUX 2016, 206–228. Weitere römische Funde aus Dumata: CHARLOUX/COTTI/THOMAS 2014, 200; Graffiti: NEHMÉ 2017.

114 / 115 n. Chr. datiert werden.[47] Die Einheit dieses Offiziers ist zwar nicht genannt, doch wenn die Datierung zutrifft, so handelt es sich offensichtlich um eine römische Hilfstruppe. Eine zweite der insgesamt 17 neu entdeckten nabatäischen Ritzinschriften nennt einen nabatäischen Reitersoldaten und ist ins Jahr 135/136 n. Chr. datiert.[48] Auch in zwei weiteren, allerdings undatierten Texten erscheinen Reiter. Der verwendete nabatäische Begriff *prš'* legt dabei nahe, dass es sich bei um Kavalleristen und nicht um Dromedarreiter handelte.[49]

Zusammen zeigen die neuen und schon bekannten epigraphischen und archäologischen Zeugnisse, dass die neue römische Provinzherrschaft in *Arabia*, zweifellos unmittelbar nach der Übernahme des ehemaligen Königreichs, ihre Aufmerksamkeit u.a. auch allen bedeutenden Fernverbindungsrouten auf dem gesamten Territorium des vormaligen Nabatäerreiches zuwandte. Zwar stand hinter diesen Bemühungen in allen Fällen wohl gleichermaßen die Absicht, die Bewohner und die als nützlich eingeschätzten Strukturen und Institutionen der Nabatäer (natürlich mit Ausnahme des Königs und seiner Berater) in die Welt der römischen Provinzen einzugliedern. Das römische Vorgehen war dabei allerdings keineswegs einheitlich. Wenn aber die *via nova Traiana* mit Steinen gepflastert, mit Meilensteinen ausgestattet und durch eine beeindruckende, teils wohl auch ganz neue Streckenführung gekennzeichnet war, so muss man fragen, weshalb andere Fernrouten weder im Zuge der Eingliederung des Nabatäerreiches noch später in vergleichbarer Art ausgebaut wurden. Denn die Verbindung von Leuke Kome, dem damals wohl wichtigsten nabatäischen Hafen am Roten Meer, zur bedeutenden nabatäische Oasenstadt Hegra, wo sie auf die Karawanenrouten der Weihrauchstraße aus dem Süden der Arabischen Halbinsel traf, sowie ihre Fortsetzung nach Petra, dienten während der ersten drei Jahrhunderte als zentrale Handelsverbindungen in diesem Raum.[50] Auch die Fernhandelsroute durch das Wadi Sirhan wird zweifellos während dieses gesamten Zeitraums dem gewinnbringenden Fernhandel mit dem Osten gedient haben. Die Bedeutung Arabiens (und natürlich auch Ägyptens) für den Import östlicher Waren wird etwa auch in Cassius Dios griechischer Bezeichnung der dafür bestimmten Lagerhäuser im Zentrum Roms deutlich, denn er nennt die *horrea piperataria* nicht wie im Lateinischen nach der bedeutendsten dort gelagerten Ware und auch nicht nach deren Herkunft, sondern er bezeichnet sie als „Lagerhäuser ägypti-

---

47 DaJ144Nab10; Nehmé 2017, 136–137 und 142. Die Datierung beruht auf der unmittelbaren Nachbarschaft einer weiteren Inschrift auf demselben Stein, die sicher ins Jahr 114/115 datiert. Der ins Nabatäische transkribierte Titel *centurio* hilft vermutlich für die Datierung wenig, denn er erscheint in einem bekannten Fall bereits in einer nabatäischen Inschriften des 1. Jh. n. Chr.: Nehmé 2017, 142.
48 DaJ144Nab8; Nehmé 2017, 135–136.
49 Nehmé 2017, 148.
50 Zum fortgesetzten Fernhandel auf der Weihrauchstraße bis ans Mittelmeer auch nach der römischen Provinzialisierung des Nabatäerreiches siehe etwa Erickson-Gini 2010, 50, 58, 191; Erickson-Gini 2014, 102.

scher und arabischer Waren", offenbar nach den Ländern, über welche diese Güter importiert wurden.[51]

Allein ökonomische Gründe können somit kaum helfen, den unterschiedlichen Ausbau der großen Fernverkehrsrouten in der neuen Provinz zu erklären. Aber auch militärische Überlegungen, die die Verteidigung der Provinz gegen äußere Feinde im Jahre 106 n. Chr. in den Vordergrund stellen, können nicht überzeugen. Die erhaltenen Zeugnisse legen vielmehr den Schluss nahe, dass diese Routen gemäß ihren unterschiedlichen Zwecken ausgebaut wurden. Denn während die *via nova Traiana* den am stärksten urbanisierten Bereich der *provincia Arabia* erschloss und dem überwiegenden Teil der Bevölkerung (sowie natürlich auch allen Fremden) deutlich vor Augen führte, dass dieser Teil der Welt nun von Rom direkt beherrscht wurde, so stand hier der lukrative Import östlicher und südarabischer Güter wohl kaum im Zentrum der römischen Planungen. In der *provincia Arabia* scheint die für die römischen Staatskassen so bedeutende Einfuhr dieser Waren vielmehr im Wesentlichen nach den traditionellen und bewährten Vorgehensweisen weitergeführt worden zu sein. Die sichtbarste Änderung betraf dabei wohl die Übernahme der Sicherheitsdienste entlang der Fernhandelsrouten, die zuvor nabatäische Soldaten erbracht hatten, durch Hilfstruppen- und Legionssoldaten des römischen Heeres. Diese scheinen ihre bewaffnete Präsenz zwar oft an denselben Stellen eingerichtet zu haben, an denen bereits die Nabatäer eigene Anlagen unterhalten hatten, passten aber die baulichen Strukturen ihren eigenen Vorstellungen und Bedürfnissen an. Ein Ausbau der für Rom wirtschaftlich zweifellos sehr bedeutenden Fernhandelsrouten im Hedschas und im Wadi Sirhan nach dem Vorbild der *via nova Traiana* wäre im Hinblick auf den ganz anderen Zweck dieser Routen somit kaum sinnvoll gewesen. Der Ausbau selbst der für Rom wichtigsten Verkehrswege in der neuen *provincia Arabia* geschah somit nicht nach einheitlichen Vorgaben sondern war von Beginn an unterschiedlich und stark zweckgebunden.[52]

Literatur

ARNAUD 2014 = P. ARNAUD, Mapping the Edges of the Earth: Approaches and Cartographical Problems, in: A.V. PODOSSINOV (Hg.), The Periphery of the Classical World in Ancient Geography and Cartography, Leuven 2014, 31–57.

AST/BAGNALL 2015 = R. AST/R.S. BAGNALL, The Receivers of Berenike. New Inscriptions from the 2015 Season, *Chiron* 45, 2015, 171–185.

AVANZINI 2016 = A. AVANZINI, By Land and By Sea. A History of South Arabia before Islam Recounted from Inscriptions, Rome 2016.

---

51 *Horrea piperataria*: Chron. a. 354, p. 16 f. 64 (Chron min. I 146); AE 1994, 297; Cass. Dio 73,24,1: τὰς ἀποθήκας τῶν τε Αἰγυπτίων καὶ τῶν Ἀραβίων φορτίων. Zum Wert dieser Importe für die römische Staatskasse siehe oben zu Anm. 14.

52 Ganz ähnlich zum römischen Strassenbau in der nördlichen Negev PAŽOUT 2018.

Ben David 2012 = C. Ben David, Nabataean or Late Roman? Reconsidering the Date of the Built Sections and Milestones along the Petra–Gaza Road. in: L. Nehmé/L. Wadeson (Hg.), The Nabataeans in Focus: Current Archaeological Research at Petra, Oxford 2012, 17–26.

Borstad 2008 = K. Borstad, History from Geography: The Initial Route of the Via Nova Traiana in Jordan, *Levant* 40, 2008, 55–70.

Bowersock 1983 = G. Bowersock, Roman Arabia, Cambridge MA 1983.

Charloux/Cotty/Thomas 2014 = G. Charloux/M. Cotty/A. Thomas, Nabataean or Not? The Ancient Necropolis of Dumat. First stage: a Reassessment of al-Dayel's excavations, *Arabian Archaeology and Epigraphy* 25, 2014, 186–213.

Charloux 2016 = G. Charloux, The Western Settlement Sector C, in: G. Charloux/R. Loreto (Hg.), Dûma 2. The 2011 Report of the Saudi–Italian–French Archaeological Project at Dûmat al-Jandal, Saudi Arabia, Riyadh 2016, 183–225. https://hal.archives-ouvertes.fr/hal-01509443/file/Duma%202%202011%2016092014.pdf (7. 3. 2018).

Christol/Lenoir 2001 = M. Christol/M. Lenoir, Qasr el-Azraq et la reconquête de l'Orient par Aurélien, *Syria* 78, 2001, 163–178.

Dąbrowa 1991 = E. Dąbrowa, Dromedarii in the Roman Army: A Note, in: V.A. Maxfield/B. Dobson (Hg.), Roman Frontier Studies 1989, Exeter 1991, 364–366.

Debidour 2012 = M. Debidour, Un général romain au-delà des frontières: l'expédition d'Aelius Gallus en Arabie (26/25 av. J.-C.), in: B. Cabouret/A. Groslambert/C. Wolff (Hg.), Visions de l'occident. Mélanges Y. Le Bohec, Paris 2012, 766–786.

Eadie 1986 = J.W. Eadie, The Evolution of the Roman Frontier in Arabia, in: Ph. Freeman/D. L. Kennedy (Hg.), The Defence of the Roman and Byzantine East, Oxford 1986, 243–252.

Eck/Pangerl 2016 = W. Eck/A. Pangerl, Ein Diplom für die Hilfstruppen der Provinz Arabia, ausgestellt unter Hadrian wohl im Jahr 126, *ZPE* 197, 2016, 227–231.

Erickson-Gini 2010 = T. Erickson-Gini, Negev Settlement and Self Organized Economy in the Central Negev: Crisis and Renewal, Oxford 2010.

Erickson-Gini 2014 = T. Erickson-Gini, Oboda and the Nabataeans, *Strata* 32, 2014, 81–108.

Fiema 2016a = Z.T. Fiema, The Military Camp, Area 34. Preliminary Report on the 2015 Season, in: L. Nehmé (Hg.), Madâ'in Sâlih Archaeological Project. Report on the 2016 Season, May 2016, o.O. 2016, 24–33. https://halshs.archives-ouvertes.fr/halshs-01311865/document (7. 5. 2018).

Fiema 2016b = Z.T. Fiema, Area 34. Preliminary Report on the 2016 Season, in: L. Nehmé (Hg.), Madâ'in Sâlih Archaeological Project. Report on the 2016 Season, December 2016, o.O. 2016, 19–46. https://hal.archives-ouvertes.fr/hal-01518460 (7. 5. 2018).

Fiema 2018 = Z.T. Fiema, Area 34: the Roman Fort. Preliminary Report on the 2017 Season. In: L. Nehmé (Hg.), Report on the 2017 Season of the Madâ'in Sâlih Archaeological Project. o.O. 2018, 17–36. https://hal.archives-ouvertes.fr/hal-01804965 (3. 7. 2018).

Freemann 1996 = P. Freeman, The Annexation of Arabia and Imperial Grand Strategy, in: D. Kennedy (Hg.), The Roman Army in the East. Ann Arbor, MI, 1996, 91–118.

Fuhrmann 2012 = C. Fuhrmann, Policing the Roman Empire. Soldiers, Administration, and Public Order, Oxford 2012.

Gatier 2017 = P.-L. Gatier, Méharistes et cavaliers romains dans le désert jordanien, in: L. Néhmé/A. Al-Jallad (Hg.), To the Madbar and Back Again. Studies in the Languages, Archaeology and Cultures of Arabia, dedicated to Michael C. A. Macdonald, Leiden 2017, 270–297.

Graf 1979 = D.F. Graf, A Preliminary Report on a Survey of Nabataean-Roman Military Sites in Southern Jordan, *ADAJ* 23, 1979, 121–127.

Graf 1988 = D.F. Graf, Qura Arabiyya and Provincia Arabia, in: P.-L. Gatier/B. Helly/J.-P. Rey-Coquais (Hg.), Géographie historique du Proche-Orient (Syrie, Phénicie, Arabie, grecques, romaines, byzantines), Actes de la Table Ronde de Valbonne, 16–18 septembre 1985, Paris 1988, 171–211.

GRAF 1995 = D.F. GRAF, The Via Nova Traiana in Arabia Petraeam, in: J.H. HUMPHREY (Hg.), The Roman and Byzantine Near East: Some Recent Archaeological Research, Ann Arbor 1995, 241–68.
GRAF 1997 = D.F. GRAF, Rome and the Arabian Frontier: From the Nabataeans to the Saracens, Aldershot 1997.
HARTMANN 2001 = U. HARTMANN, Das palmyrenische Teilreich, Stuttgart 2001.
HILLERS/CUSSINI 1996 = D.R. HILLERS/E. CUSSINI, Palmyrene Aramaic Texts, Baltimore 1996.
ISAAC 1992 = B. ISAAC, The Limits of Empire, Oxford 1992².
JAUSSEN/SAVIGNAC 1914 = A. JAUSSEN/R. SAVIGNAC, Mission archéologique en Arabie, vol. II, Paris 1914.
JÖRDENS 2009 = A. JÖRDENS, Statthalterliche Verwaltung in der römischen Kaiserzeit. Studien zum praefectus Aegypti, Stuttgart 2009.
MAREK 1993 = C. MAREK, Die Expedition des Aelius Gallus nach Arabien im Jahre 25 v. Chr., *Chiron* 23, 1993, 121–156.
MATEI-POPESCU 2011 = F. MATEI-POPESCU, A Greek Inscription from Tomis, in: Scripta Classica. Radu Ardevan sexagenario dedicata, Cluj Napoca 2011, 307–310.
MCLAUGHLIN 2014 = R. MCLAUGHLIN, The Roman Empire and the Indian Ocean. The Ancient World Economy & the Kingdoms of Africa, Arabia & India, London 2014.
NAPPO 2010 = D. NAPPO, On the Location of Leuke Kome, *JRA* 23, 2010, 334–348.
NAPPO 2015 = D. NAPPO, Roman Policy on the Red Sea in the Second Century CE, in: F. DEROMANIS/M. MAIURO (Hg.), Across the Ocean: Nine Essays on Indo-Mediterranean Trade, Leiden 2015, 55–72.
NEHMÉ 2009 = L. NEHMÉ, Quelques éléments de réflexion sur Hégra et sa région à partir du IIe siècle après J.-C., in: C. ROBIN/J. SCHIETTECATTE (Hg.), L'Arabie à la veille de l'Islam, Paris 2009, 37–58.
NEHMÉ 2017 = L. NEHMÉ, New Dated Inscriptions (Nabataean and pre-Islamic Arabic) from a Site near al-Jawf, Ancient Dūmah, Saudi Arabia, *Arabian Epigraphic Notes* 3, 2017, 121–164.
PARKER 2008 = G. PARKER, The Making of Roman India. Greek Culture in the Roman World, Cambridge 2008.
PARKER 1996 = S.T. PARKER, The Roman Aqaba Project: The Economy of Aila on the Red Sea, *The Biblical Archaeologist* 59.3, 1996, 189.
PAŽOUT = A. PAŽOUT, Early Roman Fortifications in the Northern Negev – A Spatial Analysis, in: C.S. SOMMER/MATEŠIĆ (Hg.), Limes XXIII, Mainz 2018, 174–180.
RANCE 2015 = P. RANCE, Camels: Late Empire, in: Y. LEBOHEC et al. (Hg.), The Encyclopedia of the Roman Army, vol. 1, Cichester 2015, 125–126.
RATHMANN 2006 = M. RATHMANN, Der Statthalter und die Verwaltung der Reichsstraßen, in: A. KOLB (Hg.), Herrschaftsstrukturen und Herrschaftspraxis. Konzepte, Prinzipien und Strategien der Administration im römischen Kaiserreich, Berlin 2006, 201–259.
ROBIN 2012 = C.J. ROBIN, Arabia and Ethiopia, in: S.F. JOHNSON (Hg.), The Oxford Handbook of Late Antiquity, Oxford 2012, 247–332.
ROBIN 2013 = C.J. ROBIN, À propos de Ymnt et Ymn: « nord » et « sud », « droite » et « gauche », dans les inscriptions de l'Arabie antique, in: F. BRIQUEL-CHATONNET/C. FAUVEAUD/I. GAJDA (Hg.), Entre Carthage et l'Arabie heureuse. Mélanges offerts à François Bron, Paris 2013, 119–140.
ROBIN 2015 = C.J. ROBIN, Before Himyar: Epigraphic Evidence for the Kingdoms of Saudi Arabia, in: G. FISHER (Hg.), Arabs and Empires Before Islam, Oxford 2015, 90–126.
SADDINGTON 2016 = D.B. SADDINGTON, Did the Romans have a Fleet on the Red Sea?, in: N. HODGSON/P. BIDWELL/J. SCHACHTMANN (Hg.), Roman Frontier Studies 2009, Oxford 2016, 696–698.
SARTRE 1982 = M. SARTRE, Trois études sur l'Arabie romaine et byzantine, Brüssel 1982.

SAVIGNAC/STARCKY 1957 = R. SAVIGNAC/J. STARCKY, Une inscription nabatéenne provenant du Djôf, *RBibl* 64, 1957, 196–217.

SEYRIG 1940 = H. SEYRIG, Postes romains sur la route de Médine, *Syria* 21, 1940, 218–223 (= id., *Antiquités Syriennes* 3, Paris 1946, 162–167).

SIDEBOTHAM 2011 = S.E. SIDEBOTHAM, Berenike and the Ancient Maritime Spice Route, Berkeley 2011.

SIDEBOTHAM 2017 = S.E. SIDEBOTHAM, Roman Ports on the Red Sea and their Contacts with Africa, Arabia and South Asia: Ancient Literary, and Recent Archaeological Evidence, in: K.S. MATHEW (Hg.), Imperial Rome, Indian Ocean Regions, and Muziris. New Perspectives on Maritime Trade, London 2017, 129–178.

SPEIDEL 2009 = M.A. SPEIDEL, Heer und Herrschaft im Römischen Reich der Hohen Kaiserzeit, Stuttgart 2009.

SPEIDEL 2015 = M.A. SPEIDEL, 'Almaqah in Rom? Zu den Beziehungen zwischen dem kaiserzeitlichen Imperium Romanum und Südarabien im Spiegel der dokumentarischen Überlieferung, *ZPE* 194, 2015, 241–258.

SPEIDEL 2016a = M.A. SPEIDEL, Augustus-Tempel in Indien und im Partherreich? Zur Tabula Peutingeriana und zum römischen Herrscherkult ausserhalb des Reiches, in: A. KOLB/M. VITALE (Hg.), Kaiserkult in den Provinzen des Römischen Reiches – Organisation, Kommunikation und Repräsentation, Berlin 2016, 101–121.

SPEIDEL 2016b = M.A. SPEIDEL, Fernhandel und Freundschaft. Zu Roms a*mici* an den Handelsrouten nach Südarabien und Indien, *Orbis Terrarum* 14, 2016, 155–193.

SPEIDEL IM DRUCK = M.A. SPEIDEL, Roman Red Sea Politics, in: C.J. ROBIN/M. WISSA (Hg.), Aksum, Himyar and Egypt.

SPEIDEL 1984 = M.P. SPEIDEL, Roman Army Studies I, Amsterdam 1984.

SPEIDEL 1992 = M.P. SPEIDEL, Roman Army Studies II, Stuttgart 1992.

SPEIDEL/WEISS 2004 = M.P. SPEIDEL/P. WEISS, Das erste Militärdiplom für Arabia, *ZPE* 150, 2004, 253–264.

STARCKY 1949 = J. STARCKY, Inventaire des inscriptions de Palmyre X, Damascus 1949.

TALBERT 2010 = R.J.A. TALBERT, Rome's World. The Peutinger Map Reconsidered, Cambridge 2010.

VILLENEUVE 2015 = F. VILLENEUVE, The Rampart and the South-Eastern Gate (Area 35). Survey and Excavation Seasons 2011 and 2014, in: L. NEHMÉ (Hg.). Report on the Fifth Season (2014) of the Madâ'in Sâlih Archaeological Project, March 2015, o.O. 2015, 17–45. https://halshs.archives-ouvertes.fr/halshs-01122002/document

VILLENEUVE 2016 = F. VILLENEUVE, La porte Sud-Est, Zone 35, in: L. NEHMÉ (Hg.), Madâ'in Sâlih Archaeological Project. Report on the 2015 Season, April 2016, o.O. 2016, 8–23. https://halshs.archives-ouvertes.fr/halshs-01311865/document

VILLENEUVE/FIEMA IM DRUCK = F. VILLENEUVE/Z.T. FIEMA, The Roman Military Camp in Ancient Hegra, Akten des 2015 Limeskongresses, Ingolstadt im Druck.

WEISS 2006 = P. WEISS, Die Auxilien des syrischen Heeres von Domitian bis Antoninus Pius. Eine Zwischenbilanz nach den neuen Militärdiplomen, *Chiron* 36, 2006, 249–298.

WILSON 2015 = A. WILSON, Red Sea Trade and the State, in: F. DE ROMANIS/M. MAIURO (Hg.), Across the Ocean: Nine Essays on Indo-Mediterranean Trade, Leiden 2015, 13–32.

YOUNG 1997 = G. K. YOUNG, The Customs-Officer at the Nabataean Port of Leuke Kome (Periplus Maris Erythraei 19), *ZPE* 119, 1997, 266–268.

YOUNG 2001 = G. K. YOUNG, Rome's Eastern Trade: International Commerce and Imperial Policy, 31 BC – AD 305, London 2001.

Hélène Cuvigny
Le livre de poste de Turbo, curateur du *praesidium* de Xèron Pelagos (*Aegyptus*)

Abstract: Edition of amphora fragments, which served as a base from which to copy out the postal register of Turbo. The mention of a prefect of Egypt, L. Volus(s)ius Maecianus, suggests a date in February of 161 CE. Two other individuals who were previously known – from an inscription (OGIS 707) and a papyrus – are also mentioned: the *tabularii* Fortunatus and Narcissianus. Turbo's register belongs to one of the three types of postal registers known for the *praesidia* of the Eastern Egyptian desert: the mail-sack delivery register. It includes a copy of the packing slip, followed by a note from the curator certifying proper receipt of the items listed in the slip and indicating the identity of the messengers involved, as well as the date and hour the package arrived at. Turbo distinguishes the objects that passed through his hands into categories, mentioning "sealed letters", "opened letters" and ἀπόδεσμοι (letter bundles?), which I understand as documents (probably mostly letters) that were tied together. In one of the fragments the ἀπόδεσμοι are described as σεσαβανωμένος and δεδερματωμένος, which means "in an envelope of linen or leather", respectively.

Zusammenfassung: Edition von Amphora-Fragmenten, die dazu gedient haben, das Postverzeichnis Turbos zu kopieren. Aus der Erwähnung des Präfekten von Ägypten, L. Volus(s)ius Maecianus wird eine Datierung auf den Februar 161 abgeleitet. Zwei weitere Personen, die bereits bekannt sind – aus einer Inschrift (*OGIS* 707) und einem Papyrus – werden erwähnt: die *tabularii* Fortunatus und Narcissianus. Das Verzeichnis Turbos gehört zu einem der drei bekannten Typen von Postverzeichnissen auf dem Posten der orientalisch-ägyptischen Wüste: das Register der Übermittlung von Postsäcken. Es beinhaltet die Kopie des Begleitbriefes, gefolgt von einer Notiz des *curator*, mit der er den Empfang der im Begleitschreiben aufgelisteten Gegenstände bescheinigt und die Identität der Boten nennt sowie das Datum und die Stunde, in der die Briefsendung eingetroffen ist. Unter den Gegenständen, die durch seine Hände gingen, unterscheidet Turbo die „versiegelten Briefe", die „geöffneten Briefe" und die ἀπόδεσμοι (Briefbündel?), worunter ich Dokumente (wahrscheinlich vor allem Briefe) verstehe, die zusammengebunden sind. In einem der Fragmente, werden die ἀπόδεσμοι σεσαβανωμένος und δεδερματωμένος genannt, d.h. in einem Umschlag aus Leinen beziehungsweise Leder.

Résumé: Édition de fragments d'amphore ayant servi à copier le journal de poste de Turbo. La date, février 161, est déduite de la mention du préfet d'Égypte L. Volus(s)ius Maecianus. Deux autres personnages déjà connus – par une inscription (*OGIS* 707) et un papyrus – sont également mentionnés : les *tabularii* Fortunatus et Narcissianus. Le journal de Turbo appartient à un des trois types de journaux de poste attestés dans les *praesidia* du désert Oriental égyptien : le registre de transmission des sacs postaux ; il comporte la copie du bordereau d'envoi, suivie d'une note du curateur certifiant la bonne réception des items énumérés dans le bordereau et indiquant l'identité des messagers impliqués ainsi que la date et l'heure d'arrivée du courrier. Parmi les items qui passent entre ses mains, Turbo distingue les « lettres scellées », les « lettres déliées » et les ἀπόδεσμοι (liasses ?), ce que je comprends comme des documents (sans doute surtout des lettres), liés ensemble. Dans un des fragments, les ἀπόδεσμοι sont dits σεσαβανωμένος et δεδερματωμένος, c'est-à-dire dans une enveloppe de lin et de cuir respectivement.

I Les *praesidia*, relais de la poste publique

Les ostraca publiés ci-après ont été trouvés dans le dépotoir du *praesidium* de Xèron Pelagos dont j'ai dirigé la fouille entre 2010 et 2013.[1] Ce fortin est situé entre Dios et Phalakron sur la route de Bérénice, dans une vaste plaine sablonneuse d'où il tire son nom de « Sèche Mer » **(fig. 1)**. Le toponyme figure sous la forme abrégée Xèron, également bien attestée par les ostraca, dans la Table de Peutinger et dans la Cosmographie de Ravenne. La route de Bérénice (ὁδὸς Βερενίκης) était, avec la route de Myos Hormos, l'une des deux grandes transversales structurant cette partie du désert Oriental essentiellement vouée au commerce érythréen que les Romains avaient appelée *Mons Berenicidis* (var. *Berenices*). Ce territoire, dont les frontières nord et sud étaient un peu floues (du moins pour nous), correspondait plus ou moins au *ḏw Gbtyw* (« désert de Koptos ») de l'époque pharaonique et à l'« isthme » si maladroitement conceptualisé par Strabon.[2] L'*hodos Berenikès* n'était matérialisée que par les fortins qui la jalonnaient tous les trente kilomètres en moyenne : pas de chaussée empierrée, pavée ou même simplement épierrée comme la *via Hadriana*. Le sable meuble des oueds était ce qui convenait le mieux au principal moyen de transport empruntant cette route : le chameau. Y circulaient également des ânes, mais pas de chars (alors qu'il y en avait sur la route de Myos Hormos, qui traversait des terrains plus fermes).[3] Et bien sûr aussi des hommes – et des femmes. Dans une lettre trouvée à Didymoi, Nemesous, une maquerelle qui emmenait une prostituée sur son lieu de travail, décrit ses démêlés avec les âniers : on avait chichement loué un seul âne qu'elles monteraient à tour de rôle et les âniers profitèrent de la faiblesse de ces deux femmes isolées.[4]

---

[1] Cette fouille a été la dernière du programme « *Praesidia* du désert Oriental » financé par le Ministère des affaires étrangères et l'IFAO. La fouille du dépotoir était conduite par Jean-Pierre Brun, épaulé par Emmanuel Botte et le raïs Baghdadi Mohammed. Je remercie Rudolf Haensch et Naïm Vanthieghem pour leur relecture critique et attentive du manuscrit de cet article.
[2] Cuvigny 2003a, 3–10.
[3] Bülow-Jacobsen 2013, 567.
[4] O.Did. 400.

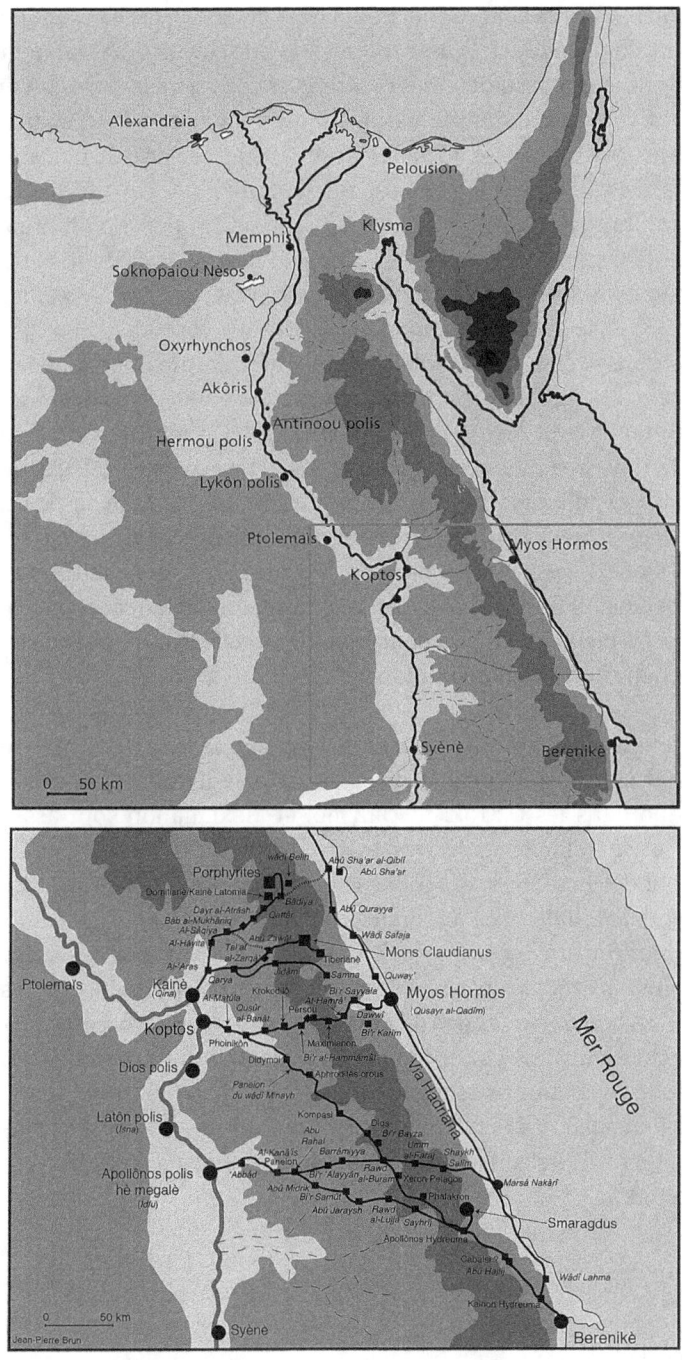

Fig. 1: Carte du désert Oriental ©J.-P. Brun

Entre autres fonctions, les *praesidia* routiers du désert de Bérénice servaient de relais pour le transport du courrier officiel : un nombre réduit de cavaliers s'y tenaient prêts, de jour et de nuit, à emporter dans l'heure lettres et colis vers le *praesidium* suivant. Le *curator praesidii* commandant la garnison, qui remplissait le rôle attribué dans les armées françaises modernes au vaguemestre, tenait registre du courrier passant entre ses mains. Dans mon édition des ostraca de Krokodilô, j'ai attribué ce dispositif à la « poste militaire ». C'était, je pense, une erreur :[5] « poste militaire » signifierait une organisation propre à l'armée et à son seul usage. Or des lettres du préfet d'Égypte et de l'administration centrale alexandrine étaient transportées par les cavaliers des *praesidia*. Je pense donc à présent que les ostraca « postaux » du désert de Bérénice témoignent du système de la poste publique dans la province romaine d'Égypte, même si cette poste publique est fortement marquée par la particularité régionale : pour communiquer avec les ports de la mer Rouge, l'administration centrale s'appuyait, dans la traversée du désert, non pas sur le réseau des stratèges de nomes,[6] mais sur le maillage militaire. Par la force des choses, une grande partie du courrier officiel, en particulier les circulaires adressées aux curateurs, était aussi d'intérêt local, mais l'importance de ce courrier « militaire » se laisse aisément surestimer parce qu'il s'agit essentiellement de circulaires dont les curateurs prenaient copie. Le courrier de l'administration civile, qui ne les concernait pas, était clos, et par conséquent moins « visible » dans notre documentation.

La plupart des fortins fouillés sous ma direction dans le désert de Bérénice ont livré des fragments de tessons inscrits témoignant de l'existence de livres de poste. J'ai publié ceux de Krokodilô dans les O.Krok. I.[7] Didymoi et Maximianon sont assez pauvres en matériel de ce genre. En revanche Dios et Xèron ont livré chacun les débris du livre de poste tenu par des curateurs dont nous connaissons les noms : Dinnis[8] à Dios, Turbo à Xèron. Leurs habitudes diplomatiques sont différentes

Reconnaissables à leur écriture, la plupart des fragments de livres postaux issus des poubelles de Xèron ont été rédigés par ce Turbo (ou sous sa responsabilité). Les tessons sont disséminés dans plusieurs carrés du dépotoir. Des raccords ont permis de reconstituer notre n° **1**, qui donne une bonne idée de la présentation en colonnes des livres de Turbo. Plus modeste, **2** donne des informations inédites sur le conditionnement du courrier officiel. Beaucoup d'éclats n'ont cependant pu être raccordés, mais presque tous valaient la peine d'être édités, parce qu'ils apportaient une date, un nom ou confirmaient une lecture.

---

5 Déjà corrigée in Cuvigny 2013, 421.
6 Cf. P.Ryl. II 78.
7 Cuvigny 2005.
8 Voir Cuvigny 2013, 426.

Liste complète des fragments du livre de poste de Turbo

1	inv. 618 + inv. 1015	US 50904, 60514	Mecheir, 14, 20, 22
2	inv. 257	US 80803	?
3	inv. 279	US 80807	Phamenôth
4	inv. 1030	US 60509	Phamenôth
5	inv. 1241	US 50507, 50510	Pharmouthi
6	inv. 46	US 50618	Pharmouthi
7	inv. 106	US 50618	?
8	inv. 58	US 40844	?
	inv. 1013	US 60506	?
	purgatoire	US 50619	?

II Date

Aucun quantième d'année régnale ne figure dans les documents, mais la date est assurée par la mention, aux lignes 29–30 de **1**, du préfet d'Égypte L. Volusius Maecianus (13 février–15 novembre 161) ; si son nom est non seulement mutilé, mais aussi estropié, la lecture en est confirmée par la mention des *tabularii* Narcissianus et Fortunatus (**1**, III, 35–36). Cette paire est attestée l'année suivante en SB XIV 11612, copie d'une lettre du préfet d'Égypte qui a succédé à Volusius Maecianus, Annius Syriacus (fin 161 ou début 162–2 mars 164) : dans cette circulaire adressée à des stratèges de nomes, Syriacus évoque un rapport financier qui lui a été remis par les ταβλάριοι Narcissianus et Fortunatus ; la circulaire, dont la date est perdue, est copiée dans un registre de correspondance officielle à la suite d'une lettre en date du 23 novembre 162. Le *diplôma* reproduit dans la col. III de notre **1** est daté du 20 Mecheir, qui ne peut être que le 14 février (jul.) de l'an 24 d'Antonin (le *dies imperii* de Marc Aurèle est le 7 mars 161).[9]

Il se trouve qu'un Fortunatus est également connu, cette fois-ci l'année précédente, dans les hautes sphères de l'administration alexandrine : c'est le dédicant d'OGIS 707,[10] qui honore T. Furius Victorinus, lequel, après avoir été préfet d'Égypte (10 juillet 159–28 septembre 160), vient d'être nommé préfet du prétoire ; cette promotion se place donc entre octobre 160 et janvier 161. Dans l'inscription, Fortunatus se décrit comme Σεβαστοῦ ἀπελεύθερος, ἀρχιταβλάριος Αἰγύπτου καὶ ἐπίτροπος προσόδων Ἀλεξανδρείας. S. DARIS, le premier éditeur de SB XIV 11612, l'identifie au Fortunatus collègue de Narcissianus. Cela supposerait qu'il ait été rétrogradé sous

---

9 Éminent juriste, conseiller apprécié d'Antonin et de ses successeurs, Maecianus a fait toute sa carrière à Rome (PFLAUM 1960, n° 141). Pour R. HAENSCH, la parenthèse que représente sa courte préfecture d'Égypte a eu pour objet d'assurer la loyauté de la province au moment où arriverait la nouvelle de la mort d'Antonin (courriel du 14/4/2017).
10 = I.Alex.imp. 21.

Maecianus de chef des *tabularii* à simple *tabularius*, ou bien qu'il ait embelli ses titres dans sa dédicace ; cette dernière explication, formulée par S. Daris,[11] est accueillie avec scepticisme par F. Kayser[12] et par R. Haensch, qui remarque que Fortunatus est un nom répandu.[13] Ce n'est certes pas le cas dans le corpus papyrologique et épigraphique de l'Égypte, mais ce corpus rend sans doute mal compte de l'anthroponymie dans l'administration centrale de la province, remplie de bureaucrates appartenant à la *familia Caesaris*.

III De quel type de livre de poste s'agit-il ?

L'activité d'un *curator praesidii* en tant que vaguemestre générait divers types de documents apparentés mais distincts. Les informations susceptibles d'y figurer sont les suivantes :
- descriptif du courrier : nature, nombre, expéditeurs, destinataires, caractéristiques matérielles ;
- teneur des lettres : simple mention de l'objet de la missive[14] aussi bien que copie plus ou moins intégrale ;
- identité des messagers apportant ou emportant le courrier ;
- date et heure d'arrivée, éventuellement de départ, du courrier.

Avant de classifier les livres de poste du désert de Bérénice, il est utile de distinguer les types de missives qui passaient entre les mains d'un curateur :
- les circulaires adressées à des officiers et sous-officiers, dont les curateurs (et souvent seulement ces derniers).[15] On en connaît des copies indépendantes (O.Krok. I 13) ou intégrées dans des livres de correspondance reçue (*infra*). Elles circulent ouvertes et les curateurs en prennent connaissance et les copient avant de les remettre en circulation. Elles sont souvent appelées δίπλωμα (au lieu de ἐπιστολή) ;
- les lettres adressées à des fonctionnaires individuels. Elles ne sont pas nécessairement closes (autrement dit scellées), mais les curateurs se contentent de les transmettre sans les recopier ;[16]

---

11 *Studia Papyrologica* 11, 1972, 27 sq.
12 I.Alex.imp., p. 83, n. 1.
13 4102 occurrences dans la base EDCS (courriel du 2/4/2018).
14 E.g. O.Krok. I 30, 44 : μετὰ διπλώματο(ς) Ἀρτωρίου Πρισκ(ίλλου) ἐπάρχου περὶ ξύλων.
15 E.g. O.Krok. I 13.
16 La face convexe d'O.Krok. I 10 fait exception : c'est la copie d'une lettre adressée au préfet de Bérénice par un curateur qui ne semble pas être celui de Krokodilô. Pourtant, Capito, le curateur de Krokodilô, l'a copiée dans son livre de poste.

– les bordereaux d'envoi accompagnant un sac postal. Leur nom technique est δίπλωμα τῆς ἐπιθέσεως.[17] Ils ont en fait la forme de circulaires adressées aux responsables des relais postaux, qui sont essentiellement les *curatores praesidiorum*.

Nous venons de voir que les circulaires, qu'il s'agisse de bordereaux d'envoi ou de lettres contenant des ordres ou des informations adressés à plusieurs destinataires, tendent à s'appeler δίπλωμα. Cet appellatif a-t-il un sens affaibli, dénotant simplement la pluralité des destinataires, ou signifie-t-il que ces circulaires étaient des documents doubles avec *scriptura interior* protégée par des sceaux, puisque tel est le sens traditionnel de δίπλωμα, qu'il s'agisse de tablettes ou d'un document sur papyrus ?[18] J'ai longtemps considéré qu'il était peu probable que les διπλώματα mentionnés dans les ostraca du désert fussent des documents doubles, mais le cas des bordereaux postaux m'incite à revoir ma position : il n'est pas inconcevable qu'ils aient présenté une copie scellée de façon à prévenir toute tentative de supprimer la mention d'une missive égarée en cours de route, ou de modifier une indication horaire pour dissimuler un retard.

Les livres de poste des curateurs du désert de Bérénice appartiennent à trois types :[19]
1) Procès-verbaux des mouvements journaliers, indiquant l'identité des cavaliers arrivant et sortant, avec l'horaire.[20] La transmission du courrier officiel n'est pas l'unique raison de ces mouvements : il y a aussi les escortes (O.Krok. I 4 semble enregistrer des arrivées et des départs sans rapport avec le service postal). Les items transportés sont identifiés par le nom de l'expéditeur quand il s'agit d'une personne importante et éventuellement, s'il s'agit d'une circulaire, par le contenu; le tout-venant des lettres, simplement désigné comme ἐπιστολαί, n'est pas dénombré.

Ces procès-verbaux pourraient résulter de la compilation de fiches journalières établies à chaque arrivée ou départ, telles que O.Krok. I 120 (Trajan/Hadrien), SB XXIV 16187 (Maximianon, *c.* 150^p), O.Did. 52 (III^p). Mais il est curieux, dans cette hypothèse, qu'on ait retrouvé si peu de ces fiches.

2) *Libri litterarum allatarum* (registres de copies de circulaires reçues) :
Deux exemples significatifs sont fournis par O.Krok. I 41 et 44 où seul le jour de la réception est indiqué en tête de certaines des copies ; en O.Krok. 47, 36, seule l'heure de réception est notée avant une copie. En O.Krok. 50, la présentation est variable : aucune note de réception avant la première copie ; date et heure (l. 14) ; seulement la date (l. 24) ; seulement? le nom du messager (l. 30).

---

[17] P.Worp 51.
[18] P.Oxy. LI 3642, 17–21n.
[19] Cuvigny 2013, 425.
[20] O.Krok. I 1 (exemple le plus complet); 24–40; 89; 90.

3) Registres de transmission des sacs postaux. Ils comportent la copie du bordereau d'envoi, suivie d'une note du curateur dans laquelle il certifie la bonne réception et la réexpédition immédiate des items énumérés dans le bordereau, en indiquant l'identité des messagers impliqués ainsi que la date et l'heure d'arrivée du courrier.

4) Mentionnons enfin la possibilité que le curateur ait tenu un registre de ses propres lettres envoyées à sa hiérarchie. O.Krok. I 91, très délabré, pourrait être un *liber litterarum missarum*, contenant la copie de lettres envoyées par le curateur lui-même, suivies du nom du messager ayant emporté le pli (date et heure du départ, en lacune, étaient sans doute indiquées). Il est significatif que le courrier, même à caractère « professionnel », échangé entre curateurs, n'ait pas été enregistré dans les livres postaux, ce qui n'empêchait pas qu'il fût transporté par les mêmes cavaliers, avec le reste des envois privés que ces derniers voulaient bien prendre en charge. Cette correspondance non enregistrée entre curateurs était d'ailleurs écrite, au moins en partie, sur des ostraca.

Les registres de Turbo relèvent de notre type 3. Mis à part **2**, 17–26, tous les tessons sont de la même main que je lui attribuerai par commodité, même si l'intervention d'un secrétaire n'est pas à exclure. L'écriture est expérimentée, mais peu soignée et sans la moindre prétention à l'élégance, ce qui s'explique en partie par le caractère de ces documents, qui étaient des copies officieuses : le « vrai » livre de poste de Turbo était vraisemblablement couché sur papyrus. Question aussi de personnalité : à Dios, le curateur Dinnis (ou son secrétaire) a de toute évidence la passion de la calligraphie.[21]

IV Diplomatique

Les livres de poste de Turbo étaient rédigés en plusieurs colonnes sur des panses d'amphores AE3 bitronconiques. Ces amphores représentaient-elles le livre de poste lui-même ?[22] J'ai peine à le croire. Sans pouvoir le démontrer, il me semble plus probable que les curateurs rédigeaient une belle copie sur papyrus de leur livre de poste, qu'ils envoyaient à intervalle régulier à la préfecture de Bérénice pour contrôle. J'imagine qu'on comparait les dates et heures de départ et d'arrivée à chaque extrémité des deux routes et que, si le transport d'une sacoche postale se révélait avoir pris trop de temps, on épluchait les registres des *praesidia* intermédiaires pour localiser l'origine du retard. Les registres sur amphores ou ostraca ne sont à mon avis que des brouillons ou des copies personnelles, inscrits sur ce support afin d'économiser le papyrus, dont il pouvait y avoir pénurie dans les *praesidia*, même pour les curateurs.[23]

---

[21] Cuvigny 2013, 427 : photo d'un ostracon du livre de poste de Dinnis, rédigé en grec, mais en caractères latins et dans une belle *scriptura actuaria*.
[22] Ainsi Remijsen 2007, 139.
[23] Cuvigny 2003b, 266.

1 Le bordereau d'envoi

A Le prescrit
Seuls trois auteurs de ces bordereaux sont identifiés :
- Volussius Vindicianus (**1**, col. I et col. III), plusieurs fois appelé ὁ κράτιστος ἔπαρχος. Son courrier part de Koptos : il a donc toute chance d'être préfet du désert et/ou préfet de l'aile de cavalerie stationnée à Koptos, qui est alors l'*ala Vocontiorum* ;
- Lucianus, seulement connu par son cognomen (**2**, 17). Il faut sans doute l'identifier avec le décurion Lucianus mentionné comme destinataire de courrier dans le bordereau **1**, III, 29. Il était peut-être stationné à Apollônos Hydreuma, grande station au sud de Phalakron ; situé sur la route de Bérénice, Apollônos Hydreuma commandait aussi un diverticule vers les mines d'émeraude ;
- Didymianus, seulement connu par son cognomen (**6**, 6), qui était peut-être aussi un décurion.

D'autres bordereaux indiquent que le courrier est parti de Bérénice (**2**, 10 ; **5**, 4), mais l'identité de leur auteur est perdue.

Ces bordereaux sont nécessairement des circulaires. Ils s'adressent collectivement non seulement aux curateurs de la route de Bérénice mais aussi à des centurions et des décurions, simplement désignés par les symboles ρ̄ (**1**, I, 2) et ῑ (**5**, 9).[24] Les grades de centurion et de décurion sont également abrégés (contrairement à ἐπάρχοις, δουπλικαρίοις, κουράτορσι) dans un prescrit de circulaire bien conservé en O.Krok. 87, 15. En **2** et **5**, les décurions (ῑ) sont les premiers destinataires nommés, ce qui exclut, puisque ces prescrits observent l'ordre hiérarchique, que le borderau ait été adressé aussi à des centurions ; c'est d'autant plus curieux que les occurrences **1**, I, 2 et **5**, 9 se trouvent dans des bordereaux émanant du préfet du Désert. Je me demande s'il n'y a pas erreur de copie dans un ou plusieurs cas.

B La liste des items
Cette partie du bordereau est assez bien conservée en **1** et **2**. Elle permettait de vérifier à chaque étape la présence de tous les items de l'envoi. Ces items sont identifiés par un descriptif ou par la mention de l'expéditeur et/ou du destinataire, mais seulement s'il s'agit de personnages d'une certaine importance, ce que j'avais déjà observé dans mon introduction à l'édition du journal de poste trajanien O.Krok. I 1.

Les items énumérés sont presque systématiquement à l'accusatif dans les deux bordereaux du préfet Vindicianus (**1**) ; ces accusatifs dépendent du verbe introduisant les circonstances de l'envoi.[25] Ils sont au nominatif dans deux bordereaux de courrier

---
24 Je ne tiens pas compte de **2**, 17, qui est un cas ambigu.
25 Cf. infra C.

parti de Bérénice (**2** et **5**). Cette différence reflète-t-elle la rédaction des originaux ou a-t-elle été introduite par Turbo ? La question pose aussi, de manière plus intéressante, pour la présentation du nom du préfet Volussius Vindicianus en **1**, III, 32–33.

1, III, 23–50 est un bordereau dont l'auteur est Vindicianus lui-même, et pourtant une des lettres énumérées dont il est l'expéditeur est décrite comme émanant de « son Excellence notre préfet Vindicianus ». Cette marque de respect figurait-elle dans le bordereau original ? J'imagine mal une telle maladresse d'énonciation de la part d'un secrétaire appartenant à l'*officium* d'un *praefectus*. Cet ajout reflète à mon avis une initiative du curateur qui, en recopiant le bordereau, a trouvé bon de marquer son respect envers son supérieur (il peut s'agir aussi d'un simple automatisme). Le fait que les livres de poste étaient destinés à être contrôlés pour détecter les retards et les manquements[26] n'est peut-être pas pour rien dans cette petite infidélité à l'original. L'adaptation circonstancielle des copies de documents officiels était une pratique normale : cf. l'adjonction de γενόμενος devant le titre d'un fonctionnaire sorti de charge au moment de la copie, ou celle de θεός devant le nom d'un empereur désormais défunt.

C Circonstances de l'envoi du paquet postal et de son bordereau

Elles sont introduites par le verbe ἔπεμψα ou plus souvent ἀπέλυσα, suivis chaque fois du lieu d'expédition (ἀπὸ Κόπτου, ἀπὸ Βερνείκης).[27] La question de la fidélité à l'original se pose aussi à propos de la suite : dans les deux bordereaux du préfet Vindicianus, la date et l'heure de l'envoi, ainsi que l'identité du ou des messagers qui ont emporté le courrier vers la première étape sont indiqués (**1**, I, 9–11 et III, 46–50) ; dans le bordereau écrit à Bérénice, ces informations sont omises. Est-ce parce qu'elles n'étaient pas sur l'original, ou parce que Turbo modulait la fidélité de sa copie selon l'importance de l'auteur de l'original ?

Enfin, on se serait attendu à ce que les bordereaux, lettres circulaires, se terminent sur une *formula valedicendi* qui, écrite sur l'original de la main même de l'auteur, avait une indispensable valeur d'authentification. Les ostraca du désert de Bérénice en livrent quelques exemples. Deux se trouvent dans le livre de poste O.Krok. I 51 (109ᵖ), lignes 19 (en latin) et 29 ; O.Did. 28 (176 ou 208ᵖ), fragment d'un document analogue à ceux du dossier de Turbo, conserve le bas d'un bordereau d'envoi dont subsistent la recommandation faite aux curateurs de réexpédier le courrier sans retard, l'identité du *monomachès* qui l'a emporté de Koptos[28] et la *formula valedicendi*, sous laquelle le curateur de Didymoi a ajouté sa note de réexpédition. Or aucun des bordereaux d'envoi copiés par Turbo ne présente de salutation finale ; si Turbo a ajouté, outre ses

---

26 Cf. P.Worp 51.
27 ἔπεμψα : **1**, 45 ; ἀπέλυσα : **1**, 8 ; **2**, 10 ; **5**, 4 ; **6**, 5. En O.Krok. I 51, 18, le verbe est ἐδόθη, calqué sur le *datum* ou *data* de la correspondance officielle en latin.
28 Malheureusement sans date ni heure.

fautes d'orthographe, des marques de respect autour du nom du préfet, il a retranché la fin des bordereaux : non seulement la *formula valedicendi*, mais sans doute aussi les recommandations de routine sur la nécessité de remettre le courrier en circulation le plus rapidement possible.[29] De fait, il semble s'être ravisé en **1**, ɪ, 8 où il a rajouté, dans l'interligne, les deux ou trois premiers mots de cette recommandation.

La copie des bordereaux n'est donc pas un reflet parfaitement fidèle des originaux. D'abord à cause du phénomène de l'adaptation ; ensuite parce qu'il s'agit de copies hâtives et abrégées.

2 La note du vaguemestre

À la fois accusé de réception et déclaration d'envoi, elle commence par le sujet des deux verbes qui la structurent, « Turbo, curateur du *praesidium* de Xèron ». Le premier verbe, παρέλαβον/-βα, ἔλαβα « j'ai reçu », est immédiatement suivi de la formule καθὼς πρόκειται, qu'on trouve habituellement dans la souscription d'un déclarant au pied d'un contrat ou d'une déclaration et qui sert à authentifier, en les confirmant, les données contenues dans le texte qui précède. Dans le cas présent, καθὼς πρόκειται exprime la conformité entre la liste des items énumérés dans le bordereau et ceux que Turbo a effectivement réceptionnés et réexpédiés : autrement dit, Turbo certifie qu'aucun item ne s'était égaré quand le sac postal est passé entre ses mains. Ensuite, l'ordre d'énonciation étant indifférent, viennent la date et l'heure de la réception ainsi que l'identité du/des messagers ayant apporté le courrier des deux fortins voisins (Dios et Phalakron), introduite par παρά ou ἀπό. Seul **1** a conservé les données permettant de calculer la vitesse de transmission du courrier : parti de Koptos le 20 à la 9e heure du jour, il arrive le 22 à la 5e heure du jour, soient 44 heures pour couvrir 192 km, ce qui fait une moyenne étonnamment basse de 4,3 km/h. Il faut évidemment compter avec le temps nécessaire au curateur de chacune des cinq étapes entre Koptos et Xèron pour vérifier le courrier et pour copier les bordereaux et d'éventuelles circulaires, mais cette opération n'était pas très longue : d'après O.Krok. I 83, il suffisait d'une demi-heure, si bien que les curateurs pouvaient écrire, comme le fait aussi Turbo, qu'ils réexpédiaient le courrier dans l'heure : καὶ εὐθέως ἀπέλυσα τῇ αὐτῇ ὥρᾳ. L'identité du/des messagers qui partent de Xèron est introduite par διά.

Les instructions énoncées cinquante ans plus tôt dans la circulaire O.Krok. I 47, 52–58 (109[p]) sont donc toujours en vigueur : « ces lettres pour son Excellence le préfet (d'Égypte) et pour Artorius Priscillus, ayant noté à quelles heures et de qui vous les recevez, et à qui vous les remettez, faites-les suivre en vitesse à son Excellence le préfet Artorius Priscillus ».

---

29 On trouve ces recommandations aussi bien dans des circulaires que dans des bordereaux d'envoi. Pour ces derniers : O.Krok. I 51, 17–18, 26–27 ; O.Did. 28, 3–6.

V L'identité des messagers et les heures de circulation

En P.Ryl. II 78, les messagers de la poste officielle dans la *chôra* égyptienne, qui sont au service des stratèges de nomes, sont appelés ἐπιστολαφόροι. Dans le désert de Bérénice, territoire contrôlé par l'armée, les estafettes mises à la disposition des curateurs pour la transmission du courrier par relais sont, d'une part, des cavaliers auxiliaires, d'autre part des μονομάχαι (ou μονομάχοι) à l'anthroponymie souvent pittoresque. Ce technonyme, qui à cette époque se réfère habituellement aux gladiateurs, est, dans cet emploi, propre au désert Oriental, Mons Claudianus inclus. Le recours aux μονομάχαι pour le service la poste officielle semble être un phénomène postérieur à Trajan : le mot n'apparaît pas dans les ostraca trajaniens du Claudianus[30] non plus qu'au *metallon* d'Umm Balad, où le corpus ostracologique date majoritairement de Domitien et de Trajan, nonobstant une occurrence dans une *entolè* ouvrière, genre apparu à la fin du règne d'Hadrien dans les carrières du désert Oriental.[31] Les ostraca de Krokodilô, qui datent de Trajan et du début du règne d'Hadrien, comportent des mentions de μονομάχαι, mais ceux-ci n'apparaissent jamais alors comme messagers de la poste officielle. Il semble que leur emploi dans ce service soit intervenu plus tardivement.

Le journal de Turbo pourrait donner l'impression que les *monomachai* étaient stationnés dans les *praesidia* du désert et non au camp de Koptos : tous les messagers partis de Koptos sont en effet des *equites*. Mais O.Did. 28 (176 ou 208ᵖ) signale que la liaison postale Koptos-Phoinikôn a été assurée par le *monomachès* Chrysoplokamos.[32]

On ignore si les *monomachai* étaient des courriers à pied ou montés : aucun ostracon du désert Oriental ne les associe à des montures. Il me paraît néanmoins improbable qu'on ait laissé partir des piétons, comme les ἡμεροδρόμοι des cités grecques, dans le désert avec le courrier officiel (ou alors avec des ânes, se serait-ce que pour porter les fardeaux et une nécessaire ration d'eau ?).

Le tableau suivant donne la liste complète des messagers mentionnés dans les bordereaux et dans les notes de réception-réexpédition de Turbo. Comme le sac postal est remis aussitôt en circulation, l'heure d'arrivée à Xèron depuis Dios ou Phalakron est la même que l'heure de départ. Les équivalences en heure moderne locale sont données d'après les heures de lever et de coucher du soleil le 1ᵉʳ mars 161 à mi-chemin entre Koptos et Xèron, en ajoutant deux heures aux données en temps universel.[33] J'avais cru déceler dans les journaux de poste trajaniens de Krokodilô une répugnance

---

[30] À l'exception possible d'O.Claud. inv. 312, issu d'une couche peut-être antoninienne du South Sebakh, dépôt essentiellement trajanien.
[31] O.KaLa. inv. 574.
[32] Chrysoplokamos peut évidemment avoir été attaché au *praesidium* de Phoinikôn, d'où il aura été envoyé à Koptos avec du courrier venu du sud, et où il sera rentré avec du courrier qu'on lui aura confié à Koptos.
[33] Lever du soleil : 4 h 10 TU, coucher : 15 h 45 TU.

à laisser les cavaliers voyager de nuit (sauf lorsqu'ils transportaient du poisson).³⁴ Ce n'est pas le cas dans notre dossier : à trois reprises, le courrier arrive à Xèron à la 9ᵉ heure de la nuit (vers 2 heures du matin) pour être aussitôt réexpédié par Turbo. Lorsqu'il arrive à la 11ᵉ heure du jour et que Krènitès l'emporte aussitôt, c'est une heure avant le coucher du soleil.

n°	lieu de départ	messager	date	heure de départ	heure d'arrivée à Xèron
1, I	Koptos	Isidôros f. Ammônianos (turme de Salvianus [*sic*])	14 Mecheir	8ᵉ h	
	Dios	Gigas et [...], *monomachai*	[...]		9ᵉ h de la nuit = *c.* 2 h du matin
	Xèron	Narkissos et [...], *monomachai*	[...]	9ᵉ h de la nuit	
1, III	Koptos	Posidônios (turme d'Apollinaris) et Isidôros f. Ammônianos (turme de Sabinus)	20 Mecheir	9ᵉ h du jour = *c.* 12 h 30	
	Dios	[...] (turme de [*gentilice*?] Alexandros)	22 Mecheir		5ᵉ? h du jour = *c.* 10 h 15
	Xèron	Marôn (turme de Salvianus)	22 Mecheir	5ᵉ? h du jour	
3	Dios ou Phalakron	[...] (turme de [*gentilice*?] Alexandros) et Serenus (turme de S...)	[...]		9ᵉ h de la nuit
	Xèron	[...] (turme de Salvianus)	[...]	9ᵉ h de la nuit	
4	Dios ou Phalakron	[...] *monomachès*	Phamenôth		
5	Xèron	Glaphyrinos, *monomachès*	Pharmouthi	9ᵉ h de la nuit	
6	Dios ou Phalakron	...ax et Chenos, *monomachai*	Pharmouthi		11ᵉ h du jour = *c.* 16 h 45
	Xèron	Krènitès, *monomachès*?	Pharmouthi	11ᵉ h du jour	

---

34 O.Krok. I, p. 17; REMIJSEN 2007, 137.

En **1**, Le cavalier Isidôros fils d'Ammônianos, probablement stationné à Koptos, est rattaché d'abord à la turme de Salvianus, puis à celle de Sabinus. Il y a nécessairement lapsus dans un des deux cas, ce qui peut s'expliquer du fait qu'au moins un cavalier stationné localement, donc familier à Turbo, Marôn, appartient à la turme de Salvianus. Le plus probable est par conséquent que la turme dont relève Isidôros est celle de Sabinus.

VI L'aspect matériel du courrier

Mis à part trois pots contenant des roses envoyés à Bérénice pour des fêtes d'Isis, les objets transportés sont des lettres (ἐπιστολαί), des circulaires (διπλώματα) et des liasses (ἀπόδεσμοι).

Certaines lettres sont signalées comme étant ἀναγκαῖαι, « importantes, urgentes, prioritaires » (**1**, III, 25–26 et comm., **5**, 10). Dans le désert Oriental, cette épithète est propre au journal de Turbo. Les unes sont ἐσφραγισμέναι, « scellées », les autres λελυμέναι, « déliées », donc « ouvertes ». Je pense que λελυμέναι fonctionne simplement comme antonyme de ἐσφραγισμέναι et n'implique pas que ces lettres ouvertes aient été scellées à l'origine.[35]

Il serait naturel de supposer que ces dernières sont des circulaires destinées à être lues par tous les curateurs entre les mains desquels elles passaient. Pourtant, l'une de ces lettres « déliées » est adressée à un centurion par un autre (**1**, III, 41–43). Avait-elle un intérêt général, si bien que l'expéditeur avait jugé opportun que les curateurs puissent en prendre connaissance ? Mais un tel raccourci n'est pas dans les habitudes de la communication officielle : on s'attend à ce que la lettre figure sous forme de copie introduite par quelques mot dans une circulaire adressée aux centurions, décurions et curateurs.[36] Antérieur de quelques années seulement à notre dossier, P.Ryl. II 78 (157ᵖ) nous met peut-être sur la voie d'une solution : cette lettre adressée par un personnage dont l'identité est en lacune[37] à Hèrakleidès, stratège du Busirite, est principalement un bordereau d'envoi, nonobstant un passage concernant du courrier égaré et le rappel d'un envoi précédent. Il n'y est pas question d'ἐπιστολαὶ λελυμέναι, mais les trois listes de courrier[38] identifient chaque lettre par un court résumé et par leur destinataire (généralement un stratège). Quoique brefs, les résumés sont trop détaillés pour avoir été composés à partir d'une éventuelle mention dorsale indiquant l'objet du pli. Il faut donc en déduire que ces lettres n'étaient pas scellées. Pour les

---

35 Dans le cas contraire se poserait la question de savoir par quelle autorité et à quel moment du processus ces lettres, confiées scellées à la poste publique, auraient été ouvertes.
36 Voir par exemple O.Krok. 87, 14–50 ou P.Oxy. III 474 (post 184 ou 216).
37 KRUSE 2002, 817 et THOMAS 1999, 189 estiment que c'est le stratège d'un nome voisin.
38 Lignes 2–17 et 27–36 : lettres arrivées avec le bordereau ; lignes 36–38 : rappel des lettres d'un précédent envoi.

éditeurs du P.Ryl. II 78, l'intérêt de faire circuler ainsi ouvert le courrier officiel était d'étendre l'information à ceux qui n'en étaient pas destinataires.³⁹ Je ne le pense pas : ces lettres, d'après les résumés, concernent des affaires aussi diverses que spécifiques et cela aurait demandé un effort intellectuel soutenu d'identifier des cas locaux analogues pour lesquels elles étaient pertinentes. Et quel fonctionnaire, déjà accablé de paperasse, se sentirait concerné par celle de ses collègues ? Lorsque l'administration jugeait utile de porter à la connaissance d'autres destinataires une lettre adressée à un fonctionnaire, elle avait soin de la personnaliser en la faisant précéder d'une lettre d'envoi dont le prescrit mentionnait les nouveaux destinataires. La non-clôture des lettres avait peut-être comme objet d'en permettre l'identification et le suivi pour le cas où elles se perdraient, accident qui ne devait pas être exceptionnel : cf. P.Oxy. LX 4060, 57–58, ἐπεὶ δὲ συμβ[α]ίνει παρ' αἰτίαν τῶν διακομιζόντων παραπείπτειν τ[ι]νάς, « comme il se trouve que certaines (lettres) se sont perdues par la faute des messagers ». Aucune des lettres énumérées en P.Ryl. II 78 ne semble donc avoir été scellée et l'impression se dégage qu'il n'était pas dans les habitudes de sceller la correspondance confiée à la poste publique. R. HAENSCH était déjà parvenu, par d'autres cheminements, à cette conclusion : si les lettres privées, qui n'étaient pas prises en charge par la poste officielle, semblent avoir habituellement été scellées, la correspondance administrative ne l'est que lorsque l'auteur tient à la confidentialité ou lorsque, dans des circonstances exceptionnelles, le sceau est nécessaire pour authentifier l'origine de la lettre.⁴⁰

À côté des lettres scellées et des lettres « déliées », les documents **1** et **2** mentionnent des ἀπόδεσμοι. L'emploi de ce terme pour désigner des lettres empaquetées ensemble est, dans le désert Oriental, propre au journal de Turbo. Dans les papyrus, on ne le relève qu'en P.Oxy. VII 1070, 39, lettre privée du IIIᵉ s. p.C.,⁴¹ et en P.Ryl. II 78, 18 et 36, antérieur de quatre ans seulement à notre dossier. Le contenu de telles liasses n'est pas détaillé, parce qu'elles n'étaient pas censées être défaites au cours du transport. Par conséquent, elles sont seulement identifiées par leurs caractéristiques matérielles extérieures. En **1**, III, 38–39, l'*apodesmos* est scellé avec un sceau de plomb ; les deux *apodesmoi* mentionnés en **2**, 3–4 et 8–9 sont enveloppés l'un de cuir, l'autre de lin. KATELIJN VANDORPE fournit une liste de six sceaux en plomb datant du Haut-Empire et d'origine égyptienne⁴² dont les éditeurs considèrent qu'ils servaient à sceller des conteneurs de la poste officielle, sacs ou caisses en bois. Quatre ont été

---

39 Interprétation acceptée par KRUSE 2002, 817.
40 HAENSCH 1996, 451–454, 474.
41 L'épistolier de P.Oxy. VII 1070, qui est à Alexandrie, a dû envoyer sa lettre, adressée à sa femme, dans l'ἀπόδεσμος τῶν ἐπιστολῶν qui contenait sans doute des lettres pour les autres membres de la famille, ainsi que, dit-il, les copies de deux pétitions dirigées contre ses beaux-parents.
42 VANDORPE, 1996, p. 285 (n° 302–307). Sauf pour le sceau FRŒHNER, elle s'appuie sur le catalogue de TURCAN 1987, 17–19 et pl. I. Pour l'iconographie, voir aussi le dessin du sceau CIL XV 7974a in FRŒHNER 1890, 236 sq. ; sur cet objet, cf. ALPERS 1995, 283 et n. 978.

trouvés à Rome et un à Lyon. Le revers de certains de ces sceaux a conservé l'empreinte de la surface de l'objet sur lequel ils étaient apposés : bois, mais aussi toile, ce qui fait penser à notre ἀπόδεσμος σεσαβανωμένος. On trouve sur ces sceaux en plomb diverses indications écrites, en sus des portraits impériaux : année régnale alexandrine, mention *fisc(us) alex(andrinus)*,[43] ou numéral que ROBERT TURCAN interprète comme un numéro d'envoi. Notre ostracon **1** montre que le courrier officiel interne à la province d'Égypte pouvait aussi être scellé au plomb.

On sait que la liasse scellée au plomb contenait une lettre du préfet d'Égypte, grâce à une information orale du porteur (spécial ?) qui l'a remise à la préfecture de Bérénice : cette information (de même que le nom de son auteur) était jugée assez importante pour être consignée dans le bordereau d'envoi. En P.Ryl. II 78, 18–19, un *apodesmos* contient aussi une lettre du *praefectus Aegypti*. Ces précisions ne pouvaient pas servir à identifier visuellement l'*apodesmos*, mais à faire savoir aux responsables du transport postal que c'était un objet à traiter avec une attention spéciale. Lorsque, en P.Worp 51, on signale que le cavalier Hèrakleidès a retardé de plusieurs heures la transmission du courrier parce qu'il était au lit avec une femme, le scripteur qui signale l'infraction ne manque pas de préciser qu'il s'agissait de lettres du préfet d'Égypte : c'était une circonstance aggravante. Certains envois étaient donc « recommandés » de diverses manières, qu'ils soient qualifiés de « prioritaires » dans les bordereaux, ou que la présence de lettres du préfet d'Égypte soit signalée, oralement si nécessaire. Ces envois importants ne faisaient cependant pas l'objet d'un acheminement spécial et accéléré : à quoi bon dès lors les recommander ? Simple manière de stimuler le zèle des curateurs ? Il n'est pas exclu qu'un sac postal ne contenant pas d'envois recommandés circulât moins vite. On pourrait imaginer, par exemple, que le cavalier de service n'était pas tenu d'effectuer sa mission de nuit si la sacoche ne contenait que du tout-venant.

VII Expéditeurs et destinataires. Un nouveau préfet de Bérénice et un procurateur de Bérénice

Les auteurs de bordereaux sont le *praefectus Montis* Volussius Vindicianus et deux décurions, Lucianus et [Did]ymianus.

Volussius Vindicianus n'est pas autrement connu. En Égypte, le gentilice Volus(s)ius est plutôt rare : mis à part le préfet d'Égypte alors en fonction L. Volusius Maecianus, on ne connaît que Volussius Sabinianus fils d'un G. Volussius [...] en BGU III 709, 4 (138–161ᵖ) et M. Volusius Rufus associé à T. Volusius [...] en P.Marmar. rº VIII, 37–38 (191ᵖ). Volussius Sabinianus est un vétéran qui acquiert au Fayoum, au mois de Phaophi d'une année régnale inconnue d'Antonin le Pieux, plusieurs par-

---

[43] CIL XV 7974a.

celles de terre catécique en se faisant représenter par un autre vétéran, Marcus Antistius Capitolinus,[44] connu dans trois autres documents du règne de Marc-Aurèle. Le préfet du Désert Vindicianus serait-il alors un parent du préfet d'Égypte Maecianus ? RUDOLF HAENSCH m'incite à la prudence et à ne pas prendre à la légère, en dépit de l'orthographe défaillante de Turbo, la question de la graphie du gentilice avec ou sans géminée. Il observe que le gentilice du préfet Maecianus est toujours écrit, dans les papyrus et les inscriptions, Volusius, l'emploi de la géminée étant caractéristique de l'Afrique du nord.[45]

Egnatuleius Gallus, centurion de la *legio II Traiana Fortis*, figure dans trois bordereaux, chaque fois comme destinataire : d'une lettre scellée partie de Koptos (**1** I 7–8), d'une lettre déliée que lui envoie un collègue (**1**, III, 41–42), et enfin en **5**, 12 où le contexte est lacuneux. Les centurions légionnaires sont rares dans les ostraca du désert de Bérénice : celui-ci est le troisième attesté, les deux autres apparaissant en O.Did. 49 (88–96ᵖ) et en O.Krok. I 41, 7 (109ᵖ). O.Did. 49 étant un laissez-passer délivré par le centurion (de la XXIIᵉ légion) à des âniers pour un voyage vers Koptos, il est vraisemblable que ce centurion était stationné à Bérénice, comme c'est sans doute aussi le cas d'Egnatuleius Gallus. Le centurion d'O.Krok. I 41, qui semble être l'auteur d'une circulaire adressée aux curateurs de la route de Myos Hormos, pourrait être, lui, posté dans ce dernier port. Egnatuleius n'est autrement attesté en Égypte que comme gentilice de l'épistratège de Thébaïde L. Egnatuleius Sabinus, connu par le cursus ILS 1409 trouvé à Thysdrus.[46] JÉRÔME FRANCE préfère fixer comme *terminus post quem* à ce cursus le règne d'Hadrien et non, comme PFLAUM, celui de Commode.[47] Il y a donc peut-être un lien entre le nom du procurateur et celui du centurion.

Autre destinataire : Aelius Gemellus (**1**, I, 6 et III, 33–34). Le 14 Mecheir, une lettre à lui destinée part de Koptos. Mais le 20 Mecheir, une lettre adressée au décurion Lucianus et qui, si je comprends correctement le texte, est un écrit conjoint du préfet Vindicianus et d'Aelius Gemellus, quitte Koptos (où Gemellus serait donc retourné entre temps). Gemellus est « procurateur de Bérénice » (ἐπίτροπος Βερενίκης, *procurator Berenices*). Ce titre est nouveau. Il figure dans un autre ostracon de Xèron, inédit, mais plus tardif, puisqu'il appartient à une série de comptes trouvés dans un contexte archéologique du IIIᵉ siècle.[48] Il arrive que le préfet de Bérénice, dont le poste était procuratorien, soit appelé non pas ἔπαρχος, mais ἐπίτροπος. En ce cas, ἐπίτροπος est spécifié par Σεβαστοῦ ou par Ὄρους (*procurator Augusti, procurator Montis*), jamais par Βερενίκης seul. Ce personnage a parfois le titre de *praefectus Berenicidis*/ἔπαρχος Βερενίκης, mais jamais après 72ᵖ. Dans deux cas seulement, la titulature d'un préfet de

---

44 NACHTERGAEL 2002, 252–254. Il est plus difficile d'imaginer un scénario qui lierait ce Volussius Sabinianus au préfet Maecianus.
45 Courriel du 2/4/2018.
46 PFLAUM 1960, n° 217 ; THOMAS 1982, 186.
47 FRANCE 2001, 162–165.
48 O.Xer. inv. 727.

Bérénice cumule les termes de *praefectus* et de *procurator* : Licinius Licinianus, destinataire d'une pétition, est appelé ἐπίτροπος Σεβαστοῦ καὶ ἔπαρχος ἴλης Βουκουντίων (encore ἔπαρχος se réfère-t-il alors à son commandement militaire et non à sa préfecture territoriale, les préfets du désert de Bérénice étant souvent en même temps préfets de l'aile de cavalerie stationnée à Koptos) ;[49] l'autre exemple concerne Artorius Priscillus qui, lui, n'avait pas de commandement militaire et qui semble être désigné une fois comme ἔπαρχος ὄρους καὶ ἐπ[ίτ]ροπος ὄρους Βερενίκης.[50] Mais, dans le cas présent, le préfet Volussius Vindicianus est flanqué d'un *procurator Berenices*. Dépourvu de prédicat honorifique, contrairement à Vindicianus, Aelius Gemellus a des chances d'être un procurateur affranchi, ce que son gentilice impérial tendrait à confirmer.[51] Le lieu où se trouve le décurion Lucianus destinataire de la lettre apporte peut-être un indice : il pourrait s'agir du *praesidium* d'Apollônos Hydreuma. Situé sur la route de Bérénice, ce fortin (dont il ne reste aujourd'hui qu'une aile), était plus grand que les autres *praesidia*, ce qui expliquerait la présence à sa tête d'un décurion et non d'un simple *curator praesidii*. Son importance pourrait venir de sa situation à l'entrée de la route conduisant aux carrières d'émeraudes de Sikayt et de Nugrus.[52] Le *procurator Berenices* était peut-être responsable des *metalla* du désert de Bérénice.

VIII Les documents

1	inv. 618 + 1015	février 161
US 50904, 60514	14 x 15,5 cm	pâte alluviale

Le texte était inscrit en trois colonnes sur la panse d'une amphore AE3. Deux de ces colonnes (I et III) sont relativement bien conservées et contiennent chacune la copie d'un *diplôma* accompagnant un envoi de courrier officiel parti de Koptos, suivi de la note dans laquelle le curateur Turbo en accuse réception et déclare l'avoir réexpédié. De la colonne II ne subsistent que des débuts de lignes au niveau des l. 6–9 de la col. I, et des fins de lignes au niveau des lignes 55–63 de la col. III. Je n'ai pas jugé utile de reproduire ces lettres isolées. Les deux bordereaux d'envoi sont émis par le préfet du Désert Volussius Vindicianus. Celui de la col. I date du 14 Mecheir, celui de col. III du 20 Mecheir (février). Nous sommes dans la 24ᵉ année régnale d'Antonin le Pieux, qui mourra le 7 mars.

---

[49] O.Dios inv. 1460 (inédit).
[50] O.Krok. 41, 47n.
[51] À cette époque, ce peut être un affranchi d'Hadrien ou d'Antonin.
[52] Supposition faite par SIDEBOTHAM/HENSE/NOUWENS 2008, 299–301.

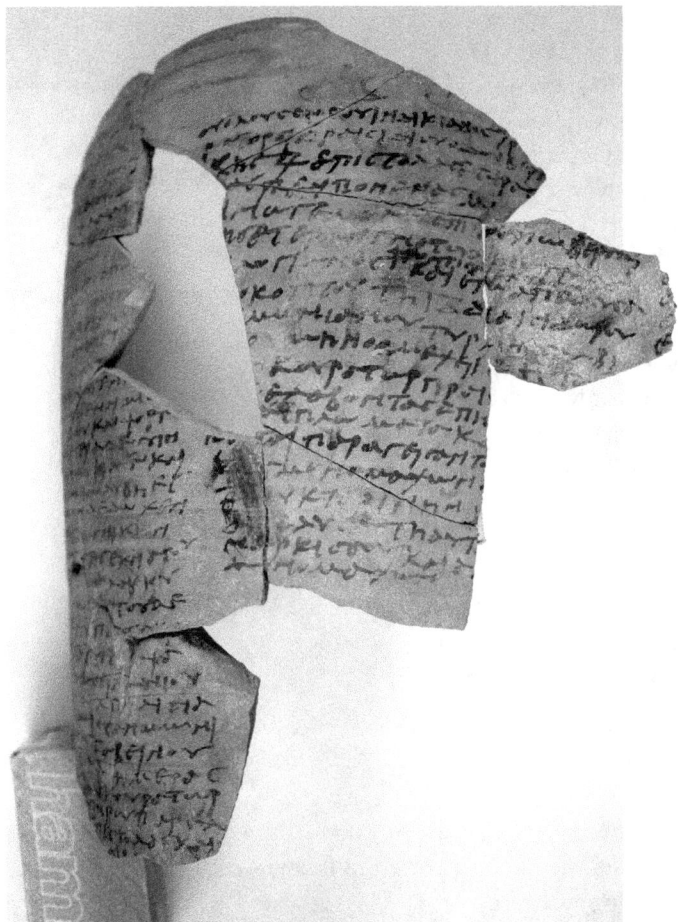

Fig. 2: 1 col. I ©A. Bülow-Jacobsen

Colonne I **(fig. 2)**

Le bordereau d'envoi notifie l'expédition d'un nombre inconnu de lettres scellées, dont deux sont identifiées par leur destinataire : le procurateur de Bérénice Aelius Gemellus et le centurion Egnatuleius Gallus. La date à laquelle ce courrier a atteint Xèron est en lacune. La fin des lignes 6–11 se trouve sur le tesson inv. 1015 ; ce raccord crucial, qui m'avait échappé sur le terrain, ne m'est apparu qu'au moment de la publication.[53]

---

[53] Je remercie FLORENT JACQUES pour le montage photographique du raccord.

marge
〚. . . .〛 .[
Οὐολούσσιος Οὐινδικιανὸς (ἑκατοντάρχαις) [(δεκαδάρχαις)]? κου-]
ράτορσι πραισιδίου ὁδοῦ Βερν[εί-]
4   κης χα(ίρειν). ἐπιστολὰς ἐσφραγ[ισμέ-]
[ν]ας πενπονένας μί[αν . .]δ̣[. . .].
[Α]ἰλίῳ Γεμέλῳ ἐπιτρόπῳ Βερνεί-
[κ]ης, ἑτέραν Γνατουληίῳ Γάλλῳ
8   (ἑκατοντάρχῃ) λογιῶνος `φροντίσατε κταχ . . ϛ´ καὶ ἐγὼ ἀπέλυσα
[ἀπ]ὸ Κόπτου τῇ ιδ̄ διὰ Ἰσιδώρου
[Ἀ]μωνιανοῦ τύρμης Σαλβι-
[αν]οῦ μηνὸς Μεχειρ ὥρ(αν) η̄. Τού[ρ-]
12 [βω]ν κουράτωρ πραισ[ιδίου Ξηροῦ]
[πα]ρέλαβον τὰς ἐπισ[τολὰς καὶ]
[τὰ] διπλώματα κα[θὼς πρό-]
κ̣ε̣ιται παρὰ Γείγαντο̣[ς καὶ c. 3]
16 δ̣ο̣ς μονομαχῶν Μ̣[εχειρ . . ὥρ(αν)]
θ̄ νυκτερινὴν κ̣[αὶ εὐθέως]
ἀπέλυσα τῇ αὐτῇ [ὥρᾳ διὰ]
Ναρκίσσου καὶ Α .[c. 8]
20 μονομαχῶν.
vacat

2, 8 ρ̃   3 *l.* πραισιδίων   3, 4 *l.* Βερενίκ-   4 χ̊   5 *l.* πεμπομ-
6 *l.* Γεμέλλῳ   7 *l.* Ἐγνατουληίῳ, ω *post corr.*   8 *l.* λεγιῶνος   10 *l.* [Ἀ]μμων-
11 ϕ   15 *l.* Γίγ-   16 -δος *post corr.*

« Volussius Vindicianus aux centurions, [aux décurions]?, aux curateurs des fortins de la route de Bérénice, salut. Lettres scellées : une pour Aelius Gemellus, procurateur de Bérénice, une autre pour Egnatuleius Gallus, centurion légionnaire. Veillez à rapidement? <les transmettre>. Pour ma part, je les ai envoyées de Koptos par les soins d'Isidôros fils d'Ammônianos, de la turme de Salvianus, le 14 du mois de Mecheir (8 février [jul.]) à la 8e heure.

« Turbo, curateur du fortin de [Xèron], j'ai réceptionné les lettres et les bordereaux comme spécifié des mains de Gigas et de [...], *monomachai*, le [n] Mecheir à la 9e [heure] de la nuit et je les ai aussitôt réexpédiées à la même [heure par les soins] de Narkissos et de [...], *monomachai*. »

2.   (δεκαδάρχαις)?. La présence du symbole ῑ dans la lacune n'est pas certaine.
4.   ἐ̣πιστολάς. Le *epsilon* est corrigé de *alpha* : le scribe avait peut-être commencé à écrire ἀπόδεσμον.

5. μί[αν μέν] (cf. l. 34–35) ne suffit pas à remplir cette fin de ligne dont les traces, le long du bord supérieur du fragment raccordé, montrent qu'elle était plus longue.

8. λογιῶνος. Autres attestations papyrologiques de la graphie λογ- : P.Oslo II 33 v° 7 (29ᵖ), λογιῶνος ; P.Mich. IX 551, 30 (103ᵖ), λογηῶνος (et non pas λογεῶνος : le *èta* est assez effacé, mais ses deux jambages sont bien perceptibles sur la photo en ligne).

φροντίσατε κταχ . .ς. On lit spontanément φροντίσαι, qui serait difficile à intégrer dans la syntaxe. Le *tau* a l'avantage de rendre compte du trait horizontal qui barre le *èta* de -ληίῳ à la ligne précédente. De plus, l'impératif φροντίσατε est courant dans les circulaires où il introduit normalement un infinitif (« veillez à... ») ; dans le désert Oriental, on ne le trouve cependant qu'en O.Did. 29, 9. La suite est incertaine. On lit assez bien ταχ, et spontanément ταχέως (ou τάχους, proposé par N. VANTHIEGHEM), mais que faire du *kappa* ? φροντίσατε <ἐ>κ ταχέως ? Mais l'expression ἐκ ταχέως est sans parallèle (et ἐκ τάχους a un autre sens que « rapidement ») ; ou, en admettant la présence d'un *alpha* effacé entre *kappa* et *tau*, φροντίσατε κατὰ <τά>χους / (l. κατὰ τάχος). L'idée générale est vraisemblablement : « veillez à transmettre rapidement (les deux lettres précédemment mentionnées) » (cf. O.Krok. I 47, 56 : ἐν τάχ<ε>ι διαπέμψεσθε). Ces lectures supposent l'omission d'un infinitif (que Turbo a peut-être jugé n'avoir pas la place d'écrire, le prolongement du *sigma* final indiquant alors qu'il faut restituer implicitement la suite). Imaginer un substantif au génitif complément de φροντίσατε serait une autre possibilité, mais je ne vois pas lequel on pourrait lire.

καὶ ἐγώ, assez inattendu, s'oppose à mon avis au sujet de φροντίσατε. Turbo, qui avait décidé d'omettre, pour abréger, la recommandation de routine, s'est peut-être ravisé afin de donner sens à καὶ ἐγώ.

9–11. L'auteur du bordereau (ou Turbo en recopiant) a écrit par erreur le quantième du mois avant le nom du messager, disloquant ainsi l'expression de la date.

10. [Ἀ]γμωνιανοῦ. Ce qui reste du *nu* ne saurait appartenir à un *mu*. Même faute sur ce patronyme à la ligne 48.

10–11. Σαλβι|[αν]οῦ. Il est plus probable qu'Isidôros appartient à l'escadron de Sabinus (*supra* pag. 80).

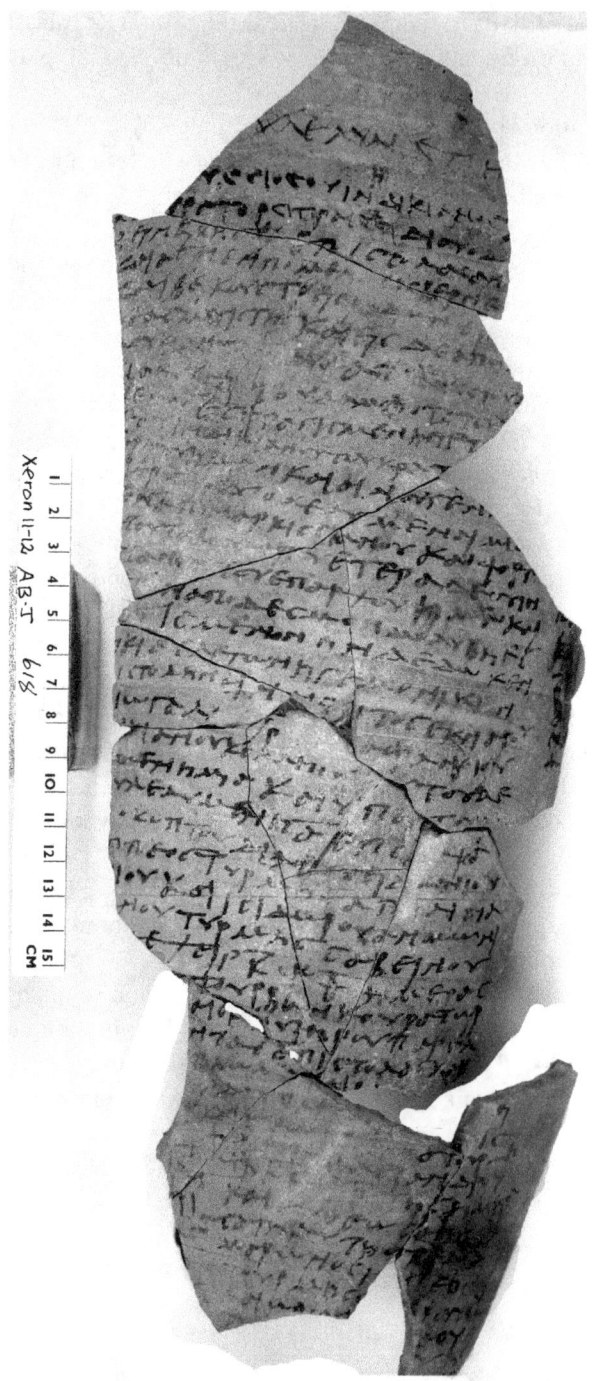

Fig. 3: 1 col. III ©A. Bülow-Jacobsen

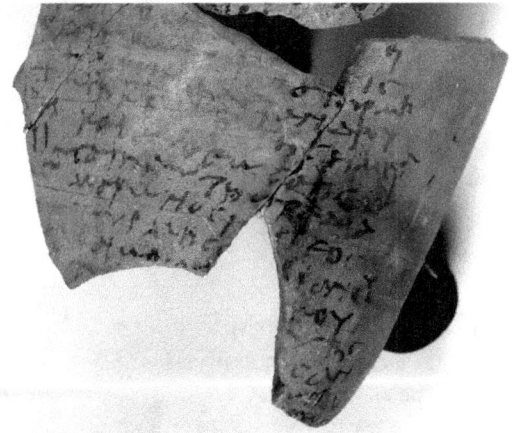

Fig. 4: 1 col. III (détail du bas) ©A. Bülow-Jacobsen

Colonne III **(fig. 3 et 4)**

À partir de la ligne 55, l'emprise de la col. II oblige le scribe à décaler vers la droite le bord gauche de la colonne. La détérioration du texte empêche d'établir avec une parfaite certitude la liste des objets énumérés dans le bordereau d'envoi de Volussius Vindicianus ; voici comment je la comprends :

– des lettres urgentes à destination de Bérénice (sont-ce des lettres non identifiées, ou est-ce un chapeau annonçant des items mentionnés plus loin ?) ;
– trois pots contenant des roses pour la déesse Isis ;
– deux lettres adressées au décurion Lucianus : une, scellée, du préfet d'Égypte Volusius Maecianus, une autre du préfet Vindicianus et du procurateur Aelius Gemellus.
– deux lettres ouvertes dont le destinataire n'est pas mentionné : une envoyée par les directeurs d'un bureau des comptes alexandrin, les *tabularii* Narcissianus et Fortunatus ; l'autre envoyée par Vindicianus ;
– une liasse scellée au plomb contenant, aux dires du messager qui l'a remise à la préfecture du Désert, une lettre du préfet d'Égypte (il n'est pas clair si le destinataire de la lettre préfectorale est anonyme ou s'il s'agit du centurion Egnatuleius Gallus) ;
– une lettre ouverte du centurion Flavius Flavianus adressée au centurion Egnatuleius Gallus ;
– une lettre ouverte (expéditeur et destinataire anonyme, à moins que ce dernier ne soit aussi Egnatuleius Gallus).

marge
21   ]υ λελυμένη[
            1–2
      [Οὐολο]ύσσιος Οὐινδικιανὸς (ἑκατοντάρχαις?) [(δεκαδάρχαις)?]
24   κ[ο]υράτορσι πραισειδίου ὁδοῦ
      Βερνείκης χα(ίρειν). ἐπιστολὰς ἀνα[γ-]
      καίας πενπομένας ἰς Βερνεί[κην]
      καὶ βείκους τρεῖς ῥόδων Εἴσ[ιδος]
28   θεᾶς μεγίστης καὶ εἰς δὲ Ἀπο . . [
      Λουκιανῷ (δεκαδάρχῃ) δύο ἀπ . λ . . . σίου Μ[αι-]
      κιανοῦ {(ἑκατοντάρχου)} τοῦ λαμπροτάτου ἡ[γε-]
      μένος ἐσφραγισμένην, ἑτέ[ραν]
32   [δ]ὲ Οὐινδικιανοῦ τοῦ κρατί[στου]
      [ἐπ]άρχου ἡμῶν καὶ Αἰλίου Γεν . [
      [ἐπ]ιτρόπου · δύο λελυμέναι, μία
      [μ]ὲν ἀπὸ Ναρκισσιανοῦ καὶ Φορτο[υ-]
36   [ν]άτου ταβουλαρίου, ἑτέρα δὲ Οὐιν-
      [δι]κιανοῦ τοῦ ἐπάρχου ἡμῶν · καὶ
      [ἕτ]ερον ἀπόδεσμον μολυβῇ ἐσ-
      [φρ]αγισμένον ἦν δέδωκεν
40   [.] . ικίας λέγων ἡγεμονικὴν
      [ἐπ]ιστολὴν εἶναι ἐντός · Ἐκνατου-
      [λη]ίῳ Γάλλ[ῳ] (ἑκατοντάρχῃ) [παρ]ὰ Φλαυίου
      [Φλ]αυιανοῦ κολλήγας [α]ὐτοῦ λε-
44   [λυ]μένη μία καὶ ὑπὲρ του . . -
      [. ο]υ λελυμένη ā ἔπε[μ]ψα
      [ἀ]πὸ Κόπτου διὰ Ποσειδωνίου
      [ἱ]ππέος τύρμης Ἀπολινα-
48   ρίου καὶ Ἰσιδώρου Ἀνμωνι-
      ανοῦ τύρμης Σαβείνου
      Μεχειρ κ̄ ὥρ(αν) θ̄ ἡμέρας.
      [2–4] . Τούρβων κουράτωρ
52   [πρ]αισιδίου Ξηροῦ παρέλα-
      [βο]ν τὰς ἐπιστολὰς καὶ τ[ὸ]
      [δ]ίπλωμα καὶ βε[ί]κ[ους Εἴσ]ει-
      δι ὑπάρχον[τας τρε]ῖς
56   και . ρω . . . . . ος τούρμη(ς)
      φ . . . . Ἀλεξάνδρου
      τῇ κ̄β̄ ὥρ(αν) ε̄ τῆς ἡμέρα(ς)
      καὶ εὐθέως ἀπέλυ-
60   σα τῇ αὐτῇ ὥρᾳ διὰ
      Μάρωνος ἱππέος

```
                τούρμης Σ[αλ]βιανοῦ
                [κ]αὶ ὥρᾳ .[. . . .]κου
        64      ..[           ]υης
                              ]cαν
                              ]ων.
                              ]. . . .
        – – – – – – –
```

24 *l.* πραισιδίων   25, 26 *l.* Βερενίκ-   25 χ̅   26 *l.* πεμπ-, εἰς   27 *l.* βίκ-, Ἴσιδος   29 ῑ   30 ρ̅   30–31 *l.* ἡγεμόνος   31 ἐσφραγισμένην : ην *ex* ας *corr.*   33 *l.* Γεμ-   36 *l.* ταβουλαρίων   37 ημν̅   39 *l.* ὃν   41 εκνατο^υ *l.* Ἐγν-   42 ρ̅   Φλαυίου : υ *post corr.*   47 *l.* ἱππέως   48 *l.* Ἀμμωνι-   56 τουρμ^η   58 ημερ^α   61 *l.* ἱππέως   62 -βιανο^υ   64]υη^c

« Volussius Vindicianus aux centurions?, [aux décurions?] (et) aux curateurs des fortins de la route de Bérénice. Envoyé à Bérénice : lettres urgentes et trois pots de roses pour Isis, très grande déesse ; à destination d'Apollônos?, pour Lucianus, décurion, deux lettres : une scellée, de Volusius Maecianus, le clarissime gouverneur, l'autre de son Excellence notre préfet Vindicianus et du procurateur Aelius Gemellus. Deux (lettres) ouvertes : une de Narcissianus et de Fortunatus, agents comptables, l'autre de Vindicianus, notre préfet. Une autre liasse, scellée au plomb, remise par Nikias?, qui a indiqué qu'elle contenait une lettre gouvernorale. Une lettre ouverte pour Egnatuleius, centurion, de la part de Flavius Flavianus, son collègue, et une lettre ouverte ... J'ai envoyé (les items énumérés) de Koptos, par les soins de Poseidônios, cavalier de la turme d'Apollinaris, et d'Isidôros fils d'Ammônios, de la turme de Sabinus, le 20 Mecheir (14 février [jul.]) à la 9ᵉ heure du jour.

« Turbo, curateur du fortin de Xèron, j'ai réceptionné les lettres, le bordereau et les pots pour Isis qui sont au nombre de trois, des mains de ..., de la turme de ... Alexandros le 22 à la 5ᵉ heure du jour et je les ai réexpédiés aussitôt dans l'heure par les soins de Marôn, cavalier de la turme de Salvianus et de... »

21. Cette ligne, écrite en surcharge, est de la même main que ce qui suit, mais d'un module supérieur ; le calame est plus fin. Est-ce un titre, λελυμένη étant la lettre ouverte (le δίπλωμα τῆς ἐπιθέσεως) qui suit ? Ou est-ce un début de texte abandonné ?

23. (ἑκατοντάρχαις?) [(δεκαδάρχαις)?]. Du premier symbole ne subsiste qu'une partie du *chi*. L'autre lettre, disparue, était-elle un *rho* comme à la ligne 2 de la colonne I, ou un *iota* comme en **5, 9** ? Et si les premiers nommés sont des centurions, le symbole pour décurions figurait-il dans la lacune ?

24. κ[ο]υράτορσι. Le deuxième point d'encre en début de ligne n'appartient probablement pas à l'*omicron* ; c'est plutôt l'extrémité de la branche inférieure du *kappa*.

25–26. ἀνα[γ]|καίας. Je n'ai pas trouvé d'autre exemple d'ἀναγκαῖος qualifiant ἐπιστολή, sinon chez Philostrate, Ap. 4, 46 : τὰς δὲ οὐχ ὑπὲρ μεγάλων ἐπιστολὰς ἐάσαντες τὰς ἀναγκαίας παραθησόμεθα κἀξ ὧν ὑπάρχει κατιδεῖν τι μέγα, « laissant de côté les lettres insignifiantes, nous citerons celles qui sont importantes et qui donnent à voir quelque chose de grand » (à propos d'une correspondance philosophique). Mais, dans nos bordereaux, le sens est technique : il s'agit de lettres prioritaires (voir *supra* pag. 80). Cette qualification permettait peut-être de marquer comme urgentes des lettres dont les auteurs ou les destinataires n'étaient pas des personnages suffisamment importants pour que leur nom figure dans le bordereau et que leur courrier soit automatiquement considéré comme prioritaire.

27. βείκους. Le terme βῖκος est susceptible de désigner des récipients de formes et de tailles très variées.[54] Il devait s'agir de conteneurs à large embouchure où les fleurs coupées encore en bouton étaient maintenues au frais (sans doute les mouillait-on à chaque étape).

27–28. ῥόδων Εἴσ[ιδος]|θεᾶς μεγίστης. Ces « roses d'Isis » (si le génitif n'est pas une faute pour le datif, employé par Turbo aux lignes 54–55) sont peut-être destinées à des fêtes saluant le retour du printemps, connues pour être célébrées en Mecheir. À Soknopaiou Nèsos, les *rhodophoria* s'étendent du 12 au 24 Mecheir (SPP XXII 183, 76 [(*post*) 138ᵖ], P.Louvre 4, 56n.).[55]

29. ἀπ.λ...σίου. Le scripteur a cafouillé et les traces, dont certaines semblent suspendues, ne se laissent pas interpréter avec certitude ; c'est curieux, puisque le même gentilice (nonobstant la question de la géminée évoquée pag. 83) est écrit sans peine dans le cas du préfet du Désert. Quoi qu'il en soit, l'intention était ἀπὸ Οὐολουσίου.

30. λαμπροτάτου. *Rho* écrit en surcharge sur *pi*, formant un monogramme qu'on retrouve dans πρόκειται en **3**, 7. Ce prédicat (*vir clarissimus*) est en vigueur pour le préfet d'Égypte entre 145 et 267.[56]

33 Γεν.[. Il serait très improbable qu'il s'agisse d'un autre *procurator* qu'Aelius Gemellus, même si le peu qui reste de la lettre qui suit le *nu* ne fait pas penser spontanément à *epsilon*.

38. [ἕτ]ερον suppose en principe qu'un autre ἀπόδεσμον a déjà été mentionné, ce qui n'est pas le cas.

---

54 BONATI 2016, 27–31.
55 Cf. YOUTIE 1951, 193. YOUTIE identifie tacitement cette fête à celle de la « germination des plantes divines », célébrée à Edfou entre le 22 et le 30 Mecheir. Une lettre trouvée à Bérénice, O.Berenike II 195 (50–75ᵖ), commentée in O.Berenike III, p. 14, évoque un achat en gros de roses pour un montant de 100 drachmes, sans le prix du transport.
56 ARJAVA 1991, 19 sq., n. 11 et 13.

μολυβῆ. σφραγῖδι est sous-entendu ou oublié : cf. O.Krok. I 17 (σφρ[αγ]εῖδι βολυμ[ῆ). La fiche éphéméride O.Did. 23 mentionne aussi un item postal indéterminé scellé au plomb.

40. [Ν]ε̣ικίας ?

44-45. ὑπὲρ το̣υ̣ ̣ ̣|[̣ο]υ. ὑπὲρ τοῦ ̣ ̣|[̣ο]υ est tentant, mais que faire de la haste descendante qui suit ? Penser à ὑπὲρ Ταυρί̣|[νο]υ ? τοῦ φί̣|[λο]υ ?

48-49. Ἀνμωνιανοῦ. Cf. Ἀνμωγ[ίου en P.Hamb. IV 270, 3 et le nom de la carrière Νειλάνμων en O.Claud. IV 734-738.

51. [2-4] ̣ Τούρβων. On ne sait s'il faut évaluer l'étendue de la lacune d'après la ligne précédente ou la suivante. Il y a visiblement quelque chose avant Τούρβων. Un gentilice ?

54-56. Je ne suis pas entièrement certaine de la correspondance entre le début et la fin de ces trois lignes.

55. Les deux lettres qu'on aperçoit devant δι appartiennent à la colonne II.

56. ἱππέος est le mot attendu devant τούρμης et n'est pas une lecture impossible. Mais il reste alors peu de place pour le nom du cavalier.

57. Φλαουίου sous toute réserve.

2	inv. 257	161
US 80803, 80804	14 x 15,5 cm	pâte alluviale

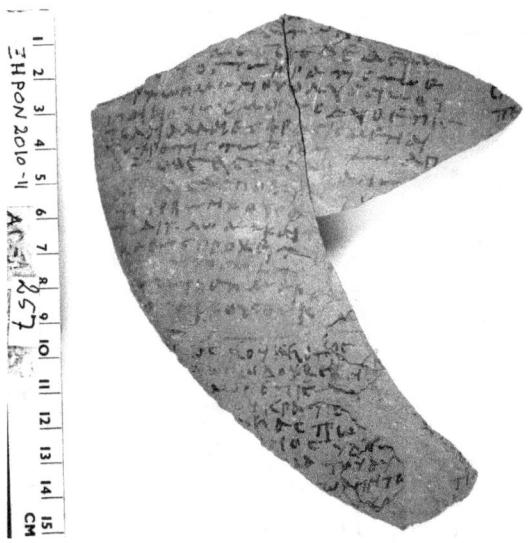

Fig. 5: 2 ©A. Bülow-Jacobsen

Contrairement à la présentation de **1**, il y a deux *diplomata*, séparés par une ligne, dans la même colonne. De plus, ils pourraient avoir été copiés par des scribes différents : si la première main est bien celle du reste du dossier, la seconde, pour autant que ce mince échantillon permette d'en juger, me semble présenter des tracés significativement différents pour certaines lettres (ω, β) et surtout pour υ, systématiquement en y.

```
                    _ _ _ _ _ _ _ _
                              ].[
            [τῷ λαμπ]ρ[ο]τάτῳ ἡγε[μόνι·]
            [ἀπόδε]σμος εἷς δεδερμα-
   4        [τωμ]ένος τῷ κρατίστῳ ἐ-
            [π]άρχῳ ἡμῶν Οὐολυσσίῳ Οὐ-
            ινδικιανῷ · ὁμοίως δύο ἐπισ-
            τολαὶ ἄλλαι ἐσφραγισμέναι
   8        τῷ κρατίστῳ ἐπάρχῳ, ἀπό-
            δεσμος εἷς σεσαβανωμ[ένος·]
            ἀπ[έ]λυσα ἀπὸ Βερνείκ[ης.]
            Τούρβων κουράτ[ωρ 5–6 ]
  12        τὸ δίπλωμα καὶ τ[7–8 ]
            καθὼς πρόκειται  [c. 8  ]
            [ἐ]νεστῶτος μηνὸς Φ[
            [?] ω   τῆς ἡμέρα[ς
  16        [.]  [.]εικουσουκ[.].[
            _____[
  m.2       [2–3]2–3 ος  Λουκειανὸς (δεκαδάρχ-) [
            [πραισι]δίων ὡδοῦ Βε[ρε]νε[ίκης
            [ἀπόδεσ]μον ἐπιστ[ο]λῶ[ν
  20             ] τοῦ κρατίσ[του
                ] ειαστρω [
            -- Ἀπόλλ]ωνος ὑδρευ[μα--
            -- δίπλω]μα τοῦ αὐ[τοῦ
  24        -- ἐπισ]τωλὴν το[ῦ
            ].κ.[.....]τι.[
                       ].[
                    _ _ _ _ _ _
```

10 *l.* Βερενίκ[ης   17 *l.* Λουκιανός, ϊ   18 *l.* ὁδοῦ Βε[ρε]ν[ίκης   24 *l.* ἐπισ]τολὴν

« ... pour le clarissime gouverneur ; une liasse enveloppée de cuir pour son Excellence notre préfet Volussius Vindicianus. De même, deux autres lettres scellées pour son

Excellence le préfet ; une liasse enveloppée de lin. J'ai expédié (les items énumérés) de Bérénice. Turbo, curateur, [j'ai réceptionné] le bordereau et [...] comme indiqué ci-dessus, le [jour] du mois courant de Ph[amenôth (heure) et les ai réexpédiés?] le même jour [heure, identité des messagers].

[Gentilice] Lucianus, décurion (ou aux décurions), [aux curateurs] des *praesidia* de la route de Bérénice [salut.] Une liasse de lettres... »

3-4. δεδερμα[τωμ]ένος. *S.v.* δερματόω, LSJ indique, pour le passif, le sens « be turned into a hide ». Mieux inspirés, le *Th.Gr.L.* traduit *pelliculo*, et le *DGE* s.v. δερματόομαι, *formar piel*, traduction appropriée pour le passage de Galien référencé où le sujet est σάρξ. Ce verbe n'est pas attesté à la voix active, où il aurait le sens général de « couvrir de peau ou de cuir ».

4. κράτιστος (*vir egregius*) devient épithète de rang des procurateurs équestres sous Marc Aurèle, mais on le trouve avant, dans un emploi non protocolaire, pour le préfet d'Égypte et les procurateurs équestres et affranchis.

9. σεσαβανωμ[ένος. Le verbe σαβανόω est dérivé de τὸ σάβανον, emprunt à l'égyptien *sbn* (bandelettes de momie en lin). Τὸ σάβανον désigne dans les papyrus une pièce de lin aux usages divers (serviette, écharpe...). En P.Kellis I 72, 34, le diminutif σαβανίον se réfère à une étoffe de lin servant à protéger des fils ou des flocons de laine teints en pourpre lors d'un transport. Certains des manuscrits de Qumrân étaient enveloppés dans des rectangles de lin pourvus de liens en cuir.[57] Quant au verbe, on ne le connaissait jusque-là que dans des textes très tardifs : dans le Digenis Akritas, poème épique du XIIe s. en langue démotique, et dans la traduction en grec, faite au XIVe s. dans le Péloponnèse, du Roman de Troie, poème en langue romane de Benoît de Sainte Maure (poète normand ou tourangeau du XIIe s.). Il signifie chaque fois « mettre (un cadavre) dans un linceul ».

Il n'est pas certain que la liasse enveloppée de lin soit destinée à Volussius Vindicianus. Il se peut que, comme dans le journal de poste O.Krok. I 1 (*c.* 107[p]), on ne prenne pas la peine de spécifier les destinataires de moindre importance. Dès lors, il n'est pas exclu que le choix du cuir ou du lin pour envelopper le courrier soit un indicateur de la qualité des destinataires.

10. C'est la fin du bordereau d'envoi. Cette version de journal de poste est visiblement abrégée, car ἀπέλυσα (var. ἔπεμψα, cf. **1**, II, 45) introduit alors normalement le jour et l'heure du départ ainsi que l'identité du ou des messagers.

11. C'est le seul endroit où placer ἔλαβον, employé en O.Xer. inv. 574 (plutôt que παρέλαβον qu'on trouve aussi à Xèron dans ce contexte, mais qui serait trop long). Le nom du *praesidium* n'est donc pas indiqué comme c'est le cas ailleurs.

---

57 Bélis 2003.

13. τ[ῇ 1–2 τοῦ] ?
15. On attend ici la fin du verbe ἀπέλυσα, lecture qui ne s'accorde pas aux traces.
16. Identification du messager attendue ici.
17. (δεκαδάρχης) ou (δεκαδάρχαις). Cf. **6**, 6.
19. ἀπόδεσμος ἐπιστολῶν : P.Ryl. II 78, 18 et 36 (157p).
21. χ]ρείας τρωχ[, l. τροχ[οῦ ? Les mentions de τροχοί, roues à eau, sont rares et toujours douteuses dans les ostraca du désert (O.Did. 61, 4 ; O.KaLa. inv. 619).

3	inv. 279	25 février-26 mars 161
US 80807	14 x 14 cm	paroi Dressel 2/4

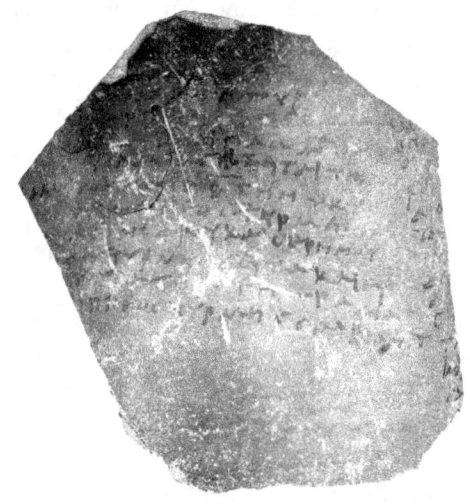

Fig. 6: 3 ©A. Bülow-Jacobsen

L'ostracon est tellement effacé que les traces d'encre sont à peine perceptibles à l'œil nu. Il contient les restes de deux colonnes. De celle de droite ne restent que les débuts de treize lignes, à raison de deux à quatre lettres, de lecture souvent incertaine. De la colonne de gauche, éditée ci-dessous, subsiste le coin inférieur droit, qui correspond à l'accusé de réception de Turbo.

```
          – – – – – – – – – – –
               traces de 3 lignes
   4                ] . . . . . . . .  Τούρ-
          [βων κουράτ]ωρ πραισειδίου
          [Ξηροῦ] παρέλαβα τὸ δίπλωμα
          [καὶ τὰς ἐπισ]τολὰς ὡς πρ(ό)κειται τῇ [1–2]
   8      [τοῦ μηνὸς] Φαμενωθ ὥρᾳ θ τῆς νυκτὸς
          [ἀπὸ --] . . . . . . . ἱππέος τύρμης
                 ] . . Ἀλεξάνδρου καὶ Σερήνου
          ἱππ]έος τύρμης Σειτα καὶ εὐ-
  12      [θέως ἀπέ]λυσα τ[ῇ αὐ]τῇ ὥρᾳ διὰ
          [Μάρωνος?] ἱππέος τύρμης Σαλβιανοῦ.
                 vacat
```

5 *l.* πραισιδίου   6 διπλωμ^a 8 τη^ς 9, 11, 13 *l.* ἱππέως

6. τὰ διπλώμα(τα) n'est pas à exclure.
7. πρ(ό)κειται. Même monogramme *pi-rho* dans λαμπροτάτου en **1**, 30, mais ici le monogramme représente toute la syllabe προ. En P.Oxy. XL 2915n., JOHN REA relève des exemples de ce monogramme représentant le préverbe προσ-.
11. Σειτα. On peut envisager ρ ou υ au lieu de ι et υ au lieu de τ.
13. Restitution Μάρωνος d'après **1**, II, 61.

| **4** | inv. 1030 | 25 février-26 mars 161 |
| US 60509 | 5,6 x 6,8 cm | pâte alluviale |

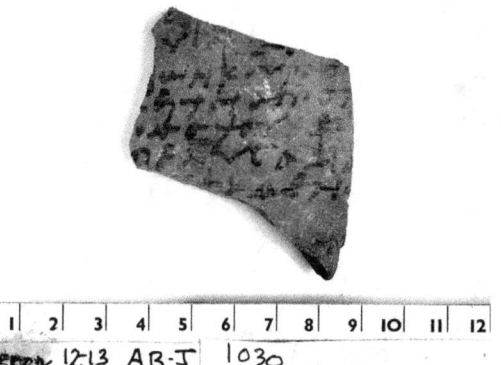

Fig. 7: 4 ©A. Bülow-Jacobsen

Note de réexpédition du curateur.

```
           ] . . . . [
           ] . υ . . . . [
        Τούρ]βων κουράτω[ρ
4       πρό]κειται ἀπὸ Στρ[
        μον]ομάχου ὥρ(αν) [
        ἀ]πέλυσα διὰ [
        ] .  Φαμενω[θ
        ] vacat [
8       ] . . . . [
```

5 ϕ

| 5 | inv. 1241 | 27 mars-25 avril 161 |
| US 50507, 50510 | 9 x 11 cm | pâte alluviale |

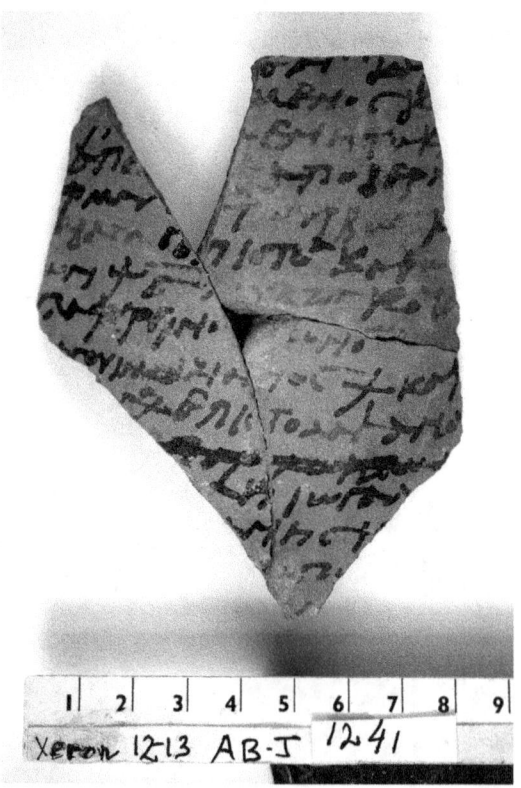

Fig. 8: 5 ©A. Bülow-Jacobsen

Le livre de poste de Turbo, curateur du *praesidium* de Xèron Pelagos (*Aegyptus*) — **99**

Le fragment conserve la fin d'un bordereau de courrier parti de Bérénice (lignes 1–5), la note du curateur (lignes 5–8) et le début d'un second bordereau émanant du préfet du Désert (lignes 9–15).

```
                    ]σαι` ΄και[
                    ]μενος κ[
           ἐσ]φρ[αγισ]μένη τῷ κρ[ατίστῳ
  4        ] ἀπέλ[υσ]α ἀπὸ Βερν[είκης
           Φ]αρμουθ[ι.] Τούρβων κ[ουράτωρ
           παρέλ]αβα τὰς ἐπιστολ(ὰς) καθὼ[ς
           ]ων ὥρ(αν) ϛ̅ νυκτὸς καὶ ε[ὐθέως
  8        ] Γλαφυρείνου μονομ(άχ-)  vac. [
           [Οὐολούσσι]ος Οὐινδικιανὸς (δεκαδάρχαις) καὶ [
           ] . χα(ίρειν). ἐπιστολὰς ἀνα[γκαίας
                    ἐ]⟦πάρχῳ ἡμῶν⟧[
  12                Ἐγνατου]ληίῳ Γάλ[λῳ
                    Τραι]ανῆς Ἰσ[χυρᾶς
                    ]απο[
                    ] . . [
```

4 *l.* Βερεν- 6 επιστο^λ 7 ϕ 8 μονο^μ

7.]ων. Peut-être παρά τινος καί τινος μονομαχ]ῶν. En ce cas, le quantième du jour devrait être directement après καθὼ[ς πρόκειται.

6	inv. 46	3 avril 161
US 50618	14,5 x 7,5 cm	pâte alluviale

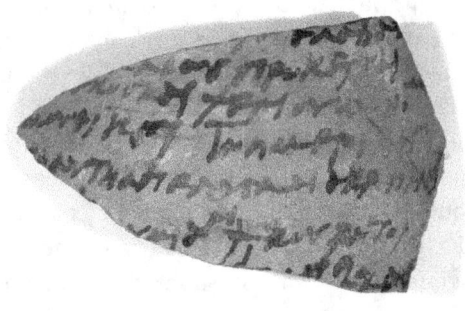

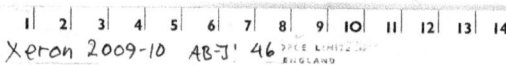

Fig. 9: 6 ©A. Bülow-Jacobsen

Les lignes 1–5 appartiennent à la notice de réception de Turbo, les lignes 6–7 sont le début d'un nouveau *diplôma*.

```
               ] ̣ ̣ ἔλαβα τ[
           ] καθὼς πρόκειται vac. ([)
        ] ̣ ακος καὶ Χένου μονομ(αχῶν) ([)
4       Φαρ]μουθι η̄ ὥρ(αν) ιᾱ ἡμερινήν vac. ([)
        ὥρᾳ] τῇ αὐτῇ ἀπέλυσα διὰ Κρηνείτ(ου) ([)
           ] ̣ [ ̣ ̣ ̣ ]υμιαν(ὸς) (δεκαδάρχ-) κουράτορ(σι?) ([)
               ] Βερνεί(κης) χα(ίρειν). α ̣ ([)
```

3 μονο^μ   4 ημερινη^ν   5 κρηνει^τ   6]υμια^ν ϊ   7 l. Βερενί-^α χ

1. ἔλαβα. Les traces n'autorisent pas παρέλαβα.
3.] ̣ ακος καὶ Χένου. Ces noms sont nouveaux dans la prosopographie des *monomachai* du désert. Χένος n'existe ni comme anthroponyme, ni comme terme lexical (sinon chez les lexicographes et les grammairiens qui le présentent comme un dérivé de χέω et une variante orthographique de κενός (παρὰ τὸ χέω χενὸς καὶ κενός). Serait-ce alors une graphie de Χέννος, surnom du grammairien alexandrin Ptolemaios Chennos, qui vivait au temps de Trajan et d'Hadrien ?[58] Ce surnom pourrait être tiré d'un appellatif *χέννος, dont τὸ χέννιον, bien attesté en revanche, serait la forme diminutive. De *χέννος sont peut-être également tirés les anthroponymes Χεννᾶς (O.Berenike I 75, cf. O.Berenike I, p. 27) et le féminin Χενοῦς (SB XX 14116, 3). D'après LSJ, χέννιον serait un emprunt à l'égyptien *chennu* (précisément ḫnn.t, graphié aussi ḫnnw, tiré de ḫn, « se poser ») et signifierait « caille ». Cette identification vient d'Athénée, en particulier 9,48,40 Kaibel = 9,393c Casaubon : τῶν δὲ καλουμένων ΧΕΝΝΙΩΝ (μικρὸν δ' ἐστὶν ὀρτύγιον) μνημονεύει Κλεομένης ἐν τῇ πρὸς Ἀλέξανδρον ἐπιστολῇ γράφων οὕτως· « φαληρίδας ταριχηρὰς μυρίας, τυλάδας πεντακισχιλίας, χέννια ταριχηρὰ μύρια », « Cléomène mentionne les "chennia" – il s'agit d'une petite caille – dans sa lettre à Alexandre : "dix mille foulques salées, cinq mille grives, dix mille cailles salées" ». Au témoignage d'Athénée et des lexicographes, mais aussi d'Hérodote (2, 72, cité *infra*), les Égyptiens consommaient la caille en salaison. Athénée cite au même endroit des vers d'Hipparque, représentant de la nouvelle comédie, dans lesquels le poète se moque des Égyptiens qui passent leur vie à plumer des χέννια. L'origine égyptienne du mot semble donc s'imposer, non sans rencontrer deux problèmes : en premier lieu, ḫnn.t est rare après le Nouvel Empire et n'est

---
58 Suda, π 3037.

pas du tout attesté en démotique ;⁵⁹ ensuite, ḫnn.t, ḫnnw est un terme générique pour « oiseau » ;⁶⁰ en égyptien, caille se dit pʿrt, pʿr en démotique. Plus précisément, les ḫnn.t sont les oiseaux qu'on chasse et qu'on mange par opposition aux oiseaux de proie, comme l'a bien expliqué MAURICE ALLIOT : « Les Égyptiens divisaient les oiseaux en deux catégories : p3yt nbt ḫnnt nbt voulait dire : "tous les oiseaux". Ceux de la première catégorie sont non seulement ceux qui s'envolent, mais ceux qui *volent haut*, et qui passent la majeure partie de leur existence en vol (les rapaces, par exemple) ; ceux de la deuxième sont non seulement ceux qui "se posent", mais ceux qui *volent bas*, marchent ou nagent (les oiseaux d'eau ou de basse-cour, par exemple, la "volaille", sauvage ou domestique) ».⁶¹ Comment le générique ḫnn.t en serait-il venu, une fois emprunté par le grec, à signifier « caille » ? La réponse est peut-être chez Hérodote (2, 72) : ὀρνίθων δὲ τούς τε ὄρτυγας καὶ τὰς νήσσας καὶ τὰ σμικρὰ τῶν ὀρνιθίων ὠμὰ σιτέονται προταριχεύσαντες, « quant aux oiseaux, (les Égyptiens) mangent crus et préalablement salés les cailles, les canards et les petits oiseaux ». *χέννος pourrait se référer à tout petit oiseau entrant dans la confection de ce type de salaison (ḫnn.t se serait spécialisé dans ce sens à basse époque ?), la caille étant le plus emblématique, d'où le glissement vers le sens de « caille » dont témoignent les sources littéraires. Mais qu'en est-il des papyrus ? Les attestations de χέννια sont peu nombreuses, mais s'étirent du IIIᵉ s. a.C. jusqu'à l'époque byzantine. Deux papyrus des archives de Zénon montrent qu'on faisait la différence entre un pot de *chennia* et un pot de cailles.⁶² Si, dans les papyrus, les ὄρτυγες (cailles) sont parfois décomptés à l'unité ou même mentionnés comme des animaux vivants qu'on nourrit, les *chennia* forment une masse indistincte, conditionnée, presque toujours expressément, en pot. La forme diminutive constante χέννιον pourrait s'expliquer par le fait que ces oiseaux sont évoqués moins comme volatiles que comme produit alimentaire.⁶³ Si le lien entre l'anthroponyme Χένος et l'égyptien χέννιον est correct, notre *monomachès* « Pitoiseau » serait particulièrement malingre, à moins que ce ne soit, par antiphrase, un malabar.

5. Κρηνείτ(ου). Le nom de ce *monomachès* est également attesté en O.Xer. inv. 847, 1144 et 1199, étrangers au dossier de Turbo. Il est homonyme de deux gentilés : d'après Artémidore chez Hérodien, De prosod. 3.1 (ed. A. Lentz 1867, p. 188, l.19), les Κρηνῖται sont les habitants de la ville de Κρηνίδες en Macédoine, rebaptisée Φίλιπποι par Philippe après qu'il l'eut secourue contre les Thraces. Il peut aussi s'agir de la forme grécisée d'un ethnique arménien devenu nom de famille

---

59 MARIE-PIERRE CHAUFRAY et FRANÇOIS HERBIN, *per litt*.
60 FOURNET 1989, 74.
61 ALLIOT 1946, 72, n. 3. Je remercie FR. HERBIN pour cette référence.
62 P.Iand. Zen. 53, 12; 55; 81 et PSI VII 862, 10–11 : ὀρτύγων βανωτὸν α, χεννίων βανωτὸν α.
63 Cf. S. AMIGUES, comm. ad Theophr. h.plant. 7,1, CUF, 79, citant notamment l'opposition entre ἧπαρ qui appartient au lexique de l'anatomie et ἡπάτιον, terme culinaire.

à l'époque byzantine ; on trouve alors aussi la forme Κρινίτης, d'ailleurs présente en O.Xer. inv. 1199.[64]

6.] . [. . .]υμιαν(ός). Le seul anthroponyme qu'on trouve en Égypte à cette époque correspondant à cette finale est Διδυμιανός, porté aussi par des militaires, par exemple le décurion Aponius Didymianus, qui adresse le court message O.Florida 5 (II^p) au curateur Iulianus. À Xèron même, on a retrouvé une capsule d'amphore avec un dipinto au nom du décurion Ulpius Didymianus (inv. 1212). La première trace de la ligne est trop haute pour appartenir à ce nom et doit correspondre à une lettre suspendue du mot précédent.

(δεκαδαρχ-). S'agit-il du grade de Didymianus ou de destinataires de cette circulaire ? Même incertitude en **2**, 17.

7. α . ([). Peut-être le début d'ἀπόδεσμον (suggestion de N. Vanthieghem).

7	inv. 106	161
US 50618	10,5 × 7,5 cm	pâte alluviale

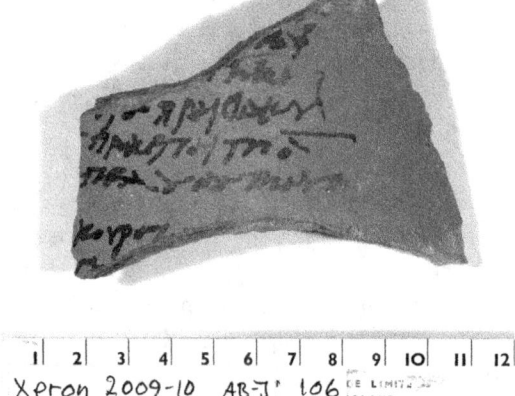

Fig. 10: 7 ©A. Bülow-Jacobsen

Les lignes 4–6 appartiennent à la note de réception de Turbo, la ligne 7 est le début d'un nouveau *diplôma*. La main de Turbo se fait erratique, ce qui complique la lecture.

```
           – – – – – –
                    ] .
                  ] . α .
              ] τῆ κθ
```

---

64 Porph. Const., de administrando imperio, 165, comm. ad 43/137.

```
4                  ] . . α πραισιδίου .
             καθὼ]ς πρόκειται τῇ ᾱ
                   ] ἀπέλυσα τῇ αὐτῇ
                   ] vacat
                   ] κουράτορσι [
8                  ] . . [
                   — — — —
```

2. En fin de ligne, on dirait un monogramme (φρ ?), à moins qu'il n'y ait une rature.
4. Je ne sais comment expliquer la sinusoïde après πραισιδίου. Elle monte trop pour représenter Ξ(ηροῦ).

8	inv. 58	161
US 40844	6,6 x 8 cm	pâte alluviale

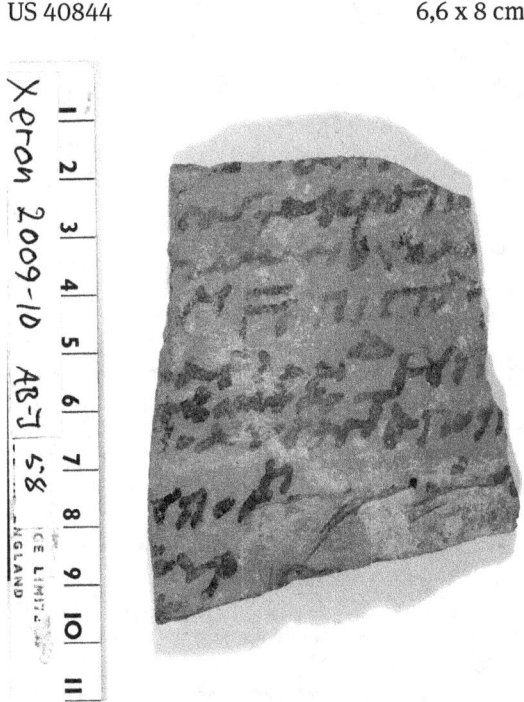

Fig. 11: 8 ©A. Bülow-Jacobsen

Fragment de bordereau. Plusieurs termes y figurent qu'on ne trouve pas dans les autres fragments.

```
          — — — — — — — —
              ] . . . α . . [
            ]σαγ( ) τῷ κρατίσ[τῳ
```

```
            ] ἡμῶν Οὐολο[υσσίῳ
    4      ]`γ´ γ̄ ἐπιστολ(αὶ) τ[
            ] Ἀλεξανδ( ) Εὐπ[
            ] . . β . ντες
            ἀ]πολύσαντ( ) ἀπὸ π . [
    8      ] ὑποση( ) . . . . . . . [
            ] τουρ[
            ]κ . [
            _ _ _ _ _
```

2 σα^χ   4 επιστο^λ   5 αλεξαν^δ   7]πολυσαν^τ   8 υποσ^η

2.]σαγ( ). La lettre suspendue qui ressemble à un *gamma* pourrait être un *sigma* (cf. les *sigma* de -καίας en **1**, III, 26 et de -μενος **1**, III, 31). Chez ce scribe, la suspension n'implique pas toujours l'abréviation, cf. τῆς en **3**, 8.
6.] . . β . ντες. Interligne.]λαβόντες, à quoi on pense spontanément, ne s'accorde pas très bien aux traces.
7. πρ[αισιδίου ?
8. Mention d'une souscription (ὑποσημείωσις) ?
9. Τούρ[βων ou τούρ[μης.

Bibliographie

ALLIOT 1946 = M. ALLIOT, Les rites de la chasse au filet, aux temples de Karnak, d'Edfou et d'Esneh, *RdE* 5, 1946, 57–118.

ALPERS 1995 = M. ALPERS, Das nachrepublikanische Finanzsystem: Fiscus und Fisci in der frühen Kaiserzeit, Berlin 1995.

ARJAVA 1991 = A. ARJAVA, Zum Gebrauch der griechischen Rangprädikate des Senatorenstandes in den Papyri und Inschriften, *Tyche* 6, 1991, 17–35.

BÉLIS 2003 = M. BÉLIS, Les textiles de Qumrân: catalogue et commentaires, in: J.-B. HUMBERT/J. GUNNEBERG (ed.), Fouilles de Khirbet Qumrân et de Aïn Feshka, vol. 2, Fribourg–Göttingen 2003, 207–276.

BONATI 2016 = I. BONATI, Il lessico dei vasi e dei contenitori greci nei papiri. Specimina per un repertorio lessicale degli angionimi greci, Berlin 2016.

BÜLOW-JACOBSEN 2013 = A. BÜLOW-JACOBSEN, Communication, Travel, and Transportation in Egypt's Eastern Desert during Roman Ttimes (1st to 3rd Century AD), in: F. FÖRSTER/H. RIEMER (ed.), Desert Road Archaeology in Ancient Egypt and Beyond, Köln 2013, 557–574.

CUVIGNY 2003a = H. CUVIGNY, Introduction, in: H. CUVIGNY (éd.), La route de Myos Hormos. L'armée romaine dans le désert Oriental d'Égypte, I, Le Caire 2003, 1–35.

CUVIGNY 2003b = H. CUVIGNY, Les documents écrits de la route de Myos Hormos à l'époque gréco-romaine (inscriptions, graffiti, papyrus, ostraca), in: H. CUVIGNY (éd.), La route de Myos Hormos. L'armée romaine dans le désert Oriental d'Égypte, II, Le Caire 2003, 265–294.

CUVIGNY 2005 = H. CUVIGNY, Ostraca de Krokodilô. La correspondance militaire et sa circulation, Le Caire 2005.

Cuvigny 2013 = H. Cuvigny, Hommes et dieux en réseau: bilan papyrologique du programme « désert Oriental », *CRAI* 2013, 2013, 405–442.
Fournet 1989 = J.-L. Fournet, Les emprunts du grec à l'égyptien, *BSL* 84, 1989, 55–80.
France 2001 = J. France, Quadragesima Galliarum. L'organisation douanière des provinces alpestres, gauloises et germaniques de l'empire romain (Ier siècle avant J.-C. – IIIe siècle après J.-C.), Rome 2001.
Frœhner 1890 = W. Frœhner, Variétés numismatiques, *Annuaire de la Société française de numismatique* 14, 1890, 469–478.
Haensch 1996 = R. Haensch, Die Verwendung von Siegeln bei Dokumenten der kaiserzeitlichen Reichsadministration, in: M.-F. Boussac/A. Invernizzi (éd.), Archives et sceaux du monde hellénistique, *BCH* Supplément 29, Athènes 1996, 449–496.
Kruse 2002 = T. Kruse, Der Königliche Schreiber, II, Leipzig 2002.
Nachtergael 2002 = G. Nachtergael, Papyrologica I, *CdE* 77, 2002, 249–258.
Pflaum 1960 = H.-G. Pflaum, Les carrières procuratoriennes équestres sous le Haut-Empire romain, vol. 1, Paris 1960.
Remijsen 2007 = S. Remijsen, The Postal Service and the Hour as a Unit of Time in Antiquity, *Historia* 56, 2007, 127–140.
Sidebotham/Hense/Nouwens 2008 = S.E. Sidebotham/M. Hense/H.M. Nouwens, The Red Land, Cairo/New York 2008.
Thomas 1982 = J.D. Thomas, The Epistrategos in Ptolemaic and Roman Egypt. Part 2. The Roman Epistrategos, Opladen 1982.
Thomas 1999 = J.D. Thomas, Communication Between the Prefect of Egypt, the Procurators and the Nome Officials, in: W. Eck/E. Müller-Luckner (ed.), Lokale Autonomie und römische Ordnungsmacht in den kaiserzeitlichen Provinzen vom 1. bis 3. Jahrhundert, München 1999, 181–195.
Turcan 1987 = R. Turcan, Nigra Moneta, Lyon 1987.
Vandorpe 1996 = K. Vandorpe, Seals in and on Papyri of Greco-Roman and Byzantine Egypt, in: M.-F. Boussac/A. Invernizzi (éd.), Archives et sceaux du monde hellénistique, *BCH* Supplément 29, Athènes 1996, 231–291.
Youtie 1951 = H.C. Youtie, The Heidelberg Festival Papyrus: A Reinterpretation, in: P.R. Coleman-Norton/A.C. Johnson/F.C. Bourne (ed.), Studies in Honor of Allan Chester Johnson, Princeton 1951.

II The Roads of the Empire

Anthony Comfort
Travelling between the *Euphrates* and the *Tigris* in Late Antiquity

Abstract: The paper discusses roads in the eastern Roman provinces, especially in south-eastern Anatolia, with material obtained by the author during visits between 1996 and 2008. It examines the presence of milestones, paving, forts and cisterns using specific examples, which are illustrated also with satellite images.

Zusammenfassung: Der Beitrag behandelt Straßen in den römischen Ostprovinzen, besonders im südöstlichen Anatolien. Dafür legt der Autor Material vor, das er während Besuchen zwischen 1996 und 2008 selbst erhoben hat. Anhand mehrerer Beispiele wird geprüft, ob Meilensteine, Pflasterung, Kastelle und Zisternen vorhanden sind. Alle Beispiele werden durch Satellitenbilder illustriert.

Introduction

There is not much new evidence in regard to this part of the Roman world for reasons connected principally with the security situation. In 1966 FREYA STARK published a book intended for a popular audience on this area ('Rome on the Euphrates').[1] It would be wrong to say that there has been no public interest at all since then concerning the Roman presence in Northern Mesopotamia, but the conditions for working in that area have always been difficult and are now almost impossible. Those difficulties have not prevented a few scholarly books from being written on this subject while some excavations and surveys have taken place before the present crisis, for example in the northern Jazira. But for 60 years little research that is new has emerged in northern Mesopotamia which is of relevance to roads during the period from the birth of Christ to the Arab invasions – apart from the work of JÖRG WAGNER[2] and DAVID and JOAN OATES.[3] There have been studies of the churches and monasteries of the Tur Abdin[4], reports of rescue excavations at Zeugma[5] and further to the south sites of great importance have been excavated at Dura Europos (*Euphrates*) and Se Qubba (*Tigris*),[6] but little has emerged concerning roads since LOUIS DILLEMANN's 'Haute Mésopotamie orientale et pays adjacents' of 1962. However, TONY WILKIN-

---
1 STARK 1966.
2 WAGNER 1983, 1985.
3 OATES 1956, OATES 1968, OATES/OATES 1990.
4 See especially WIESSNER 1981–1993.
5 See the various publications of the Institut français d'Etudes anatoliennes.
6 The most recent excavations at Dura were published in 'Syria' (LERICHE 1986–1992); those at Se Qubba (possibly 'Castra Maurorum') in BALL 2003.

son's work on landscapes in the Near East, especially on the 'hollow ways', has helped to inspire further research, including studies of that part of northern Mesopotamia south of the Tur Abdin.[7] He conducted surveys in the northern Jazira and many other areas of the Near East; although his work concerns landscape studies in the first instance, it is of great importance for the history of the region and of its roads.

Although in recent decades study of the Roman road network has rarely been possible, in the 1930s investigations were carried out by the Reverend POIDEBARD in what is currently north-eastern Syria and by SIR AUREL STEIN in northern Mesopotamia, both using aerial photography, then in its infancy as a tool for archaeology. The former's results were published in 'La Trace de Rome dans le desert de Syrie',[8] but the latter's had to await 1985 for publication as 'Sir Aurel Stein's Limes report'.[9] Both STEIN and POIDEBARD were looking at areas in Syria and Iraq which have for the most part not been visited by this writer.[10] This paper is concerned mainly with roads located in SE Turkey.

Currently, of course, research on the ground throughout south-east Turkey and northern Syria is not possible, although various surveys are under way in Iraqi Kurdistan on the east side of the *Tigris*. Flights of low-flying aircraft for archaeological research have not been possible since the 1930s – except in Jordan where DAVID KENNEDY has been able to carry out research with a helicopter of the Jordanian air force.[11] But the ready availability of satellite imagery has re-awakened interest in the road network throughout the region. Corona imagery from the 1960s and 1970s is especially helpful in analyzing routes in use before the arrival of modernity (see http://corona.cast.uark.edu).

Thus, the study of the roads beyond the Tigris is now beginning in the context of survey work being conducted in northern Iraq by the universities of Tübingen (Eastern Habur Archaeological Survey) and Udine (Land of Nineveh Archaeological Survey). The whole course of the upper Tigris from Mosul up to Diyarbakır has recently been discussed in COMFORT/MARCIAK 2018. This monograph places particular emphasis on transport and the road network; for south-east Turkey it draws substantially on a survey led by GUILLERMO ALGAZE in the late 1990s.[12] For sites of the Roman period found by this survey, LIGHTFOOT examined several in detail but he did not discuss the

---

7 WILKINSON/TUCKER 1995.
8 POIDEBARD 1934.
9 GREGORY/KENNEDY 1985.
10 In September 2016 I was a member of the Eastern Habur Archaeological Survey run from the University of Tübingen and based at Dohuk in Iraqi Kurdistan. Roads around the upper *Tigris* are a current focus of my research.
11 KENNEDY/BEWLEY 2004.
12 ALGAZE 1989; ALGAZE et al. 1991; ALGAZE/HAMMER 2012.

road network as such, although he did find traces of three pre-modern roads along the Tigris valley near a rock relief sculpture.[13]

The Roads

The physical evidence for Roman roads in the region is often poor, partly because the hard ground often required little construction; there are few extant milestones or written texts concerning roads. However, the Peutinger Table and, for the most western part of Mesopotamia (also known as Osrhoene), the Antonine Itinerary constitute important sources.[14] The historians Ammianus Marcellinus and Procopius of Gaza sometimes refer to trade or to the use of wagons, but infrequently. Bridges are the main type of physical evidence, but in this paper attention is paid especially to some examples of milestones, paving, forts and cisterns.

The paper discusses examples of ancient roads around the northern sections of the rivers *Euphrates* and *Tigris*; my research for a doctoral thesis concerning roads and bridges of the three late Roman provinces of *Euphratesia*, *Osrhoene* and *Mesopotamia* covered a wide area and included the hilly areas north of the Mesopotamian plain as far as Diyarbakır, ancient *Amida*.

The three case studies discussed here have been chosen to illustrate different aspects of the road network east of Antioch. They were investigated in the period 1996 to 2008 when travel was still possible in this region on a tourist visa.[15] In contrast to the experience of early visitors to the region who usually travelled on horseback or on foot, modern researchers have the advantage of access to satellite imagery, GPS and sometimes good modern roads. But against these must be offset the local conditions which make ground research currently impossible and the enormous changes to the landscape resulting from the introduction of modern agriculture and from road construction.

---

13 Lightfoot/Naveh 1991.
14 The Antonine Itinerary (Itin. Anton.) edited by Cuntz 1990 mentions in particular two routes from *Germaniceia* via *Doliche* and *Zeugma* to *Edessa* (numbers 184,1–185,3. 188,7–189,5. 190,2–190,5 and 191,1–191,5 – the two routes appear twice); the second and fourth of these take a northerly line via a station called 'In Medio', probably today Büyükhan, where there is still a large medieval caravanserai and a mound; the cistern shown at Fig.16b below is located on this road. Route 192 of the Itin. Anton. refers to another road from *Hierapolis* (Manbij) to *Edessa* passing through 'Bathnas', probably *Batnae/Anthemusia*, thought to be Suruç. The cistern shown in figure 16e below at Sarımağara is located by a cave with an inscription showing that there used to be an inn also here – probably on this latter route of the Itin. Anton. (Mango 1986). The only other routes of interest in the Itin. Anton. east of the *Euphrates* are 186,1–187,1 (*Germaniceia-Samosata-Edessa*) and 192,4–193,1 (*Carrhae-Hierapolis*). 186,1–186,6 coincides in part with the route from *Doliche* to *Samosata* discussed below, as shown in the Peutinger Table.
15 I also worked on a survey using satellite images around *Zeugma* in the years 1996 to 1999 and in 2002 as a member of the Franco-Turkish team excavating the city.

Milestones and Forts

1) The Roads from A) *Cyrrhus* to *Zeugma* and B) *Doliche* to *Samosata*

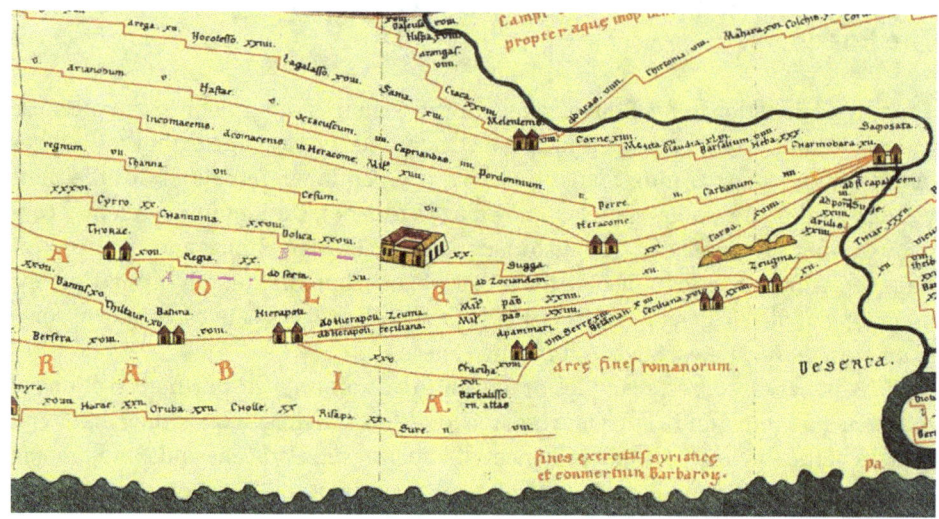

Fig. 1: Extract from the Peutinger Table showing in pink approximate locations of the sections discussed from: https://www.hs-augsburg.de/~harsch/Chronologia/Lspost03/Tabula/tab_pe00.html

The first road was an essential part of the network linking the Euphrates to the Mediterranean. In the Hellenistic period the cities of *Cyrrhus* and *Seleuceia*-on-the-Euphrates (later twinned with Apamea on the east bank and called 'Zeugma') were important links on the road joining together the Syrian provinces of the Seleucid kingdom with Mesopotamia, Iran and the Far East. In the early Roman period Zeugma continued to be the main crossing point of the Euphrates, although after it was sacked by Shapur I in AD 256 it may have lost its pre-eminence as a crossing point to *Ceciliana*, north-east of *Hierapolis* (now Manbij).

A milestone now in the museum of Gaziantep has been identified as dating from the years AD 112–4 and the emperor Trajan.[16] It was found near the village of Kazıklı about 20km north of Kilis (itself 14km east of the important Hellenistic and Roman city of *Cyrrhus*). In 2008 I was able to visit this village and speak to the person who had found it. He showed me the findspot (36°47'34"N, 37°18'13"E) adjacent to a cause-

---

16 BEYAZLAR/CROWTHER 2008, respectively AE 2008, 1522: *Im[p(erator)] / Caesar d[ivi Nervae f(ilius)] / Nerva Tr[aianus Aug(ustus)] / Germ(anicus) D[ac(icus) pont(ifex) max(imus)] / trib(unicia) pot(estate) [--- imp(erator) VI] / co(n)s(ul) VI p(ater) [p(atriae)]*. No distance or placename indicated.

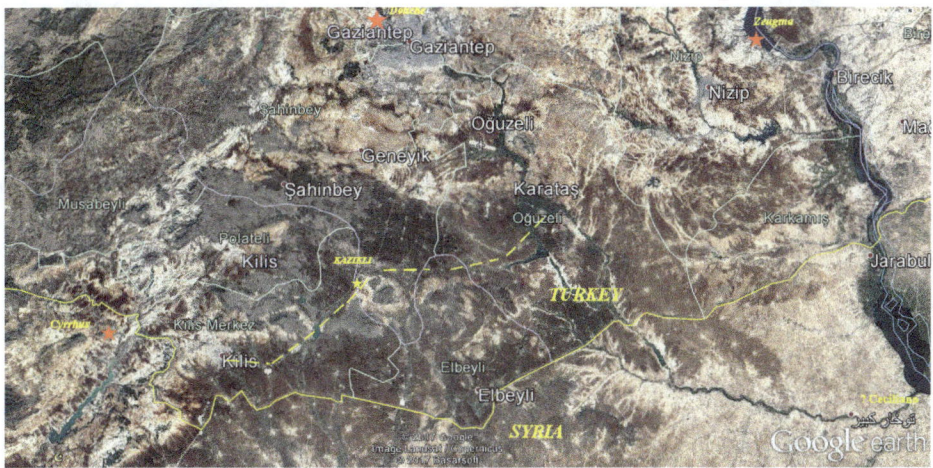

Fig. 2: The road from Kilis to Zeugma GE 25/11/2016 ©2017 DigitalGlobe

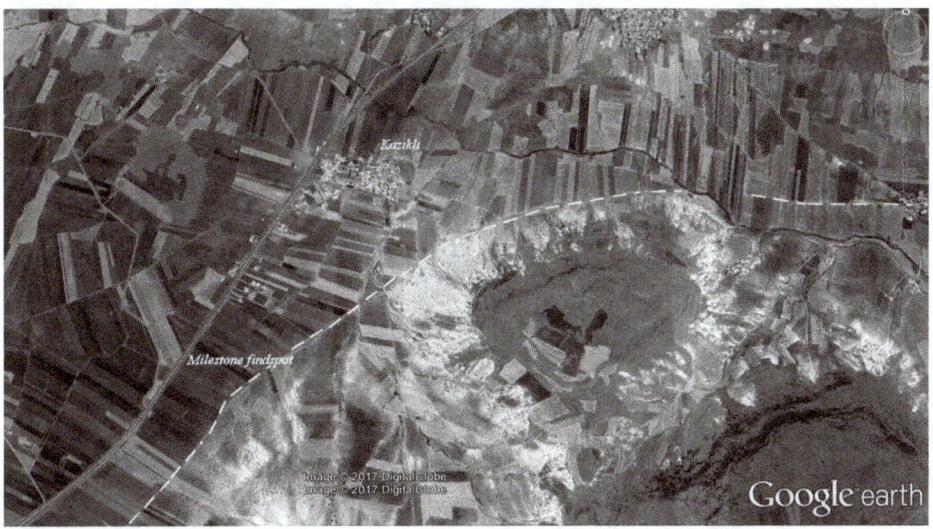

Fig.3a: Kazıklı milestone: situation GE 25/11/2016 ©2017 DigitalGlobe

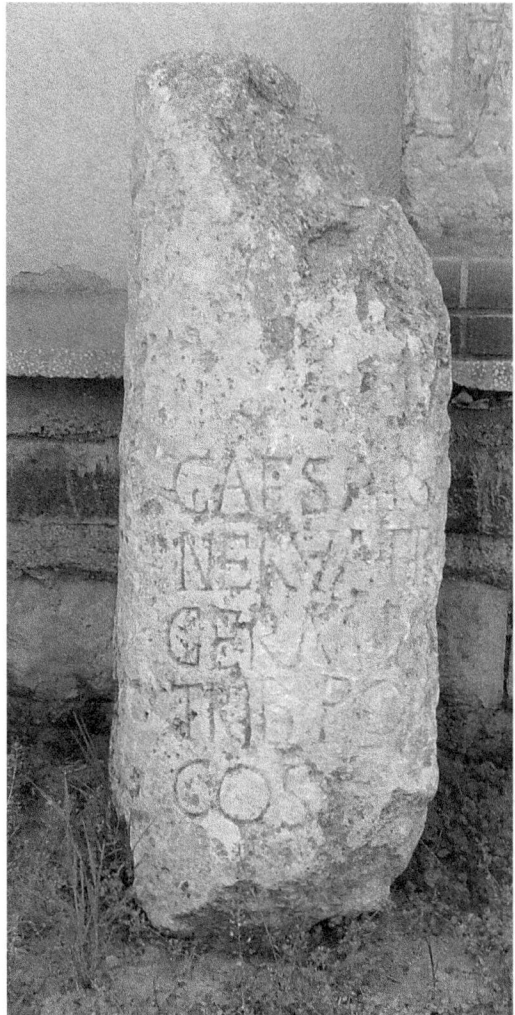

Fig.3b: The milestone in Gaziantep Museum Photo: COMFORT 2008

way still in existence but with a surface of jumbled stone. Possibly paving had been removed by local people for re-use. We also visited this causeway at a point 1.7km to the north-east. The course of the road on the causeway, which is still up to 1m20 above the surrounding fields, is clearly visible on Google Earth and leads north-east towards Tilbeshar, a Bronze Age mound, probably to be identified with one or other of the sites on the Peutinger Table known as 'Regia' or 'Ad Serta' in the Roman period.[17]

---

[17] KEPINSKI 2005; COMFORT 2009, 156–7.

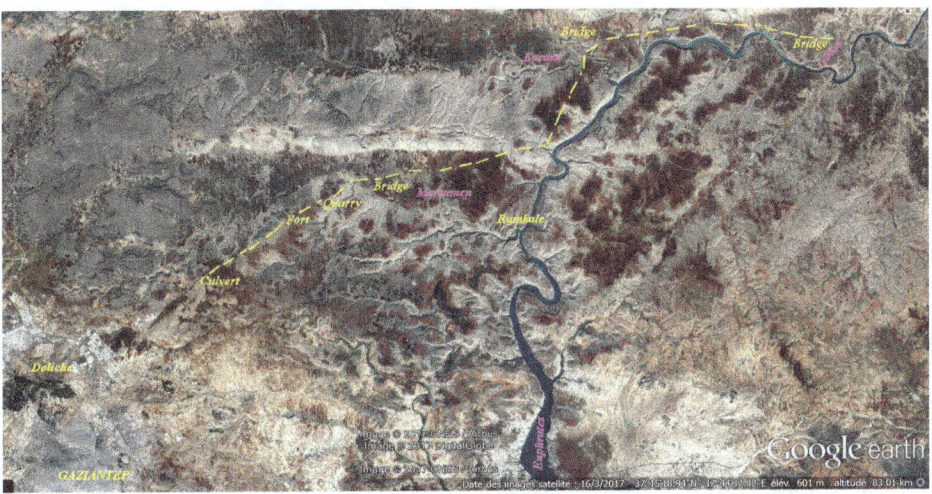

Fig. 4: The road from *Doliche* to *Samosata* (under water of Ataturk Dam) GE 16/3/2017
©2017 DigitalGlobe, CNES/Airbus

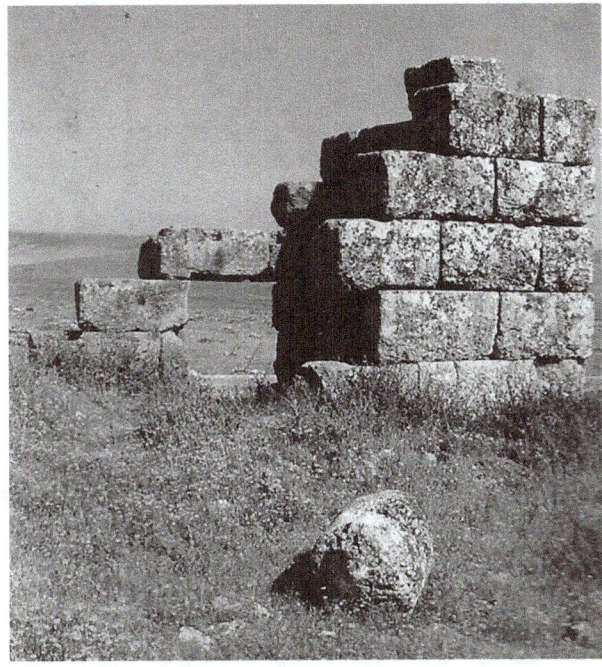

Fig. 5: Milestone and fort Photo: COMFORT 1997

This place was also a Crusader castle in the early Middle Ages, when it was known as Turbessel. The road continued from there to *Zeugma* on the *Euphrates*, but its course is less evident.

Milestones are a rarity in this region. David French had planned a volume of his 'Roman Roads and Milestones of Asia Minor' to be dedicated to northern Syria and Commagene, but this was not completed before his death. Amongst those known to this writer there is another one in the museum of Gaziantep which had been found to the north of the city towards Kahramanmaraş (*Germaniceia*) and near the village of Yiğitler.[18] CROWTHER ascribes it to the year AD 197.

On the Roman road from *Doliche* to *Samosata*, also visible on Google Earth, an anepigraphic milestone was lying adjacent to a small fort, discovered in 1998 during research around *Zeugma* (37°16'02"N, 37°35'20"E).[19] A group of four or five milestones, also anepigraphic, were mentioned in this area by CUMONT near the remarkable funerary monuments at Elif and Hasanoğlu, but seem to have since disappeared.[20]

The course of the Roman road from *Doliche* to *Samosata* is also clearly visible on Google Earth. Apart from the three extant Roman bridges on the Göksu (37°26'46"N, 38°09'50"E), at Süpürgüç (37°25'58"N, 37°53'43"E) and Yarımça (37°18'58"N, 37°40'59"E),[21] there are also remains of a culvert and a strange relief sculpture in a quarry by the road, south-west of the Yarımça bridge.

Although this route does not figure in its entirety in the Antonine Itinerary, there is some overlap in its final section before *Samosata* with route 186/7 of the Itin. Anton.

To the north-west, there are also three milestones in the courtyard of the museum at Kahramanmaraş (*Germaniceia*). These are shortly to be discussed elsewhere by our colleague Mustafa Sayar. Further to the south and outside the area discussed here, POIDEBARD found two milestones on the Strata Diocletiana.[22]

East of the Euphrates milestones are even rarer. Only five have been reported in northern Mesopotamia to my knowledge; on the northern side of the current border between Turkey and Syria I am aware of only the two at Kızılburç (see below), despite the existence of the important road from *Nisibis* to the *Tigris* mentioned by

---

18 BEYAZLAR/CROWTHER 2011: *[Imp(erator) Caes(ar), divi M(arci) Antonini Pii Germ(anici) f(ilius), divi Commodi frat(er), divi Antonini Pii nep(os), divi Hadriani pronep(os), divi Traiani abnep(os), divi] Ner[vae adnep(os) L(ucius) Se] / ptimius Sev [er]us Pius Per[r] / tinax Aug[g[ustus) Arab(icus) Adiab(enicus)] / pont(ifex) max(imus) [trib(unicia) pot(estate) V (?), imp(erator) X (?)] // co(n)s(ul) II, pr[oco(n)]s(ul), p(ater) p(atriae) [et] Im[p(erator) Caes(ar)] / M(arcus) Au[r]elius [A]nt[o]ni[nus] / Au[g(ustus) f(ilius) eius.*
No distance or placename indicated.
19 COMFORT/ABADIE-REYNAL/ERGEÇ 2000: 117–8; see also COMFORT/ERGEÇ 2001.
20 CUMONT 1917, 295.
21 Bridges 17, 18 and 20 in COMFORT 2009.
22 POIDEBARD 1934, Pl XXVI.

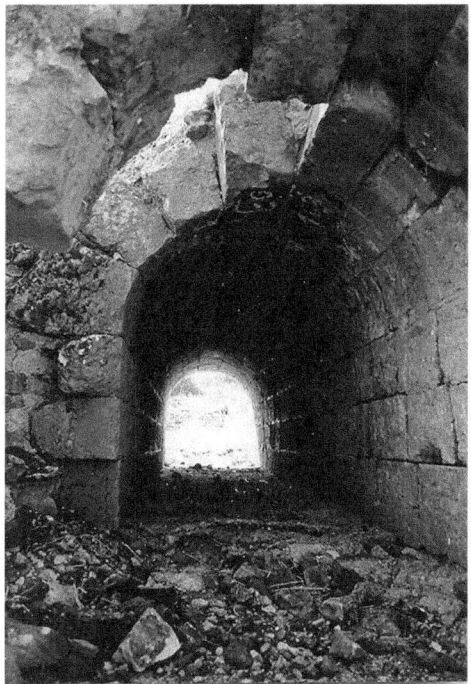

Fig. 6: Culvert Photo: COMFORT 2008

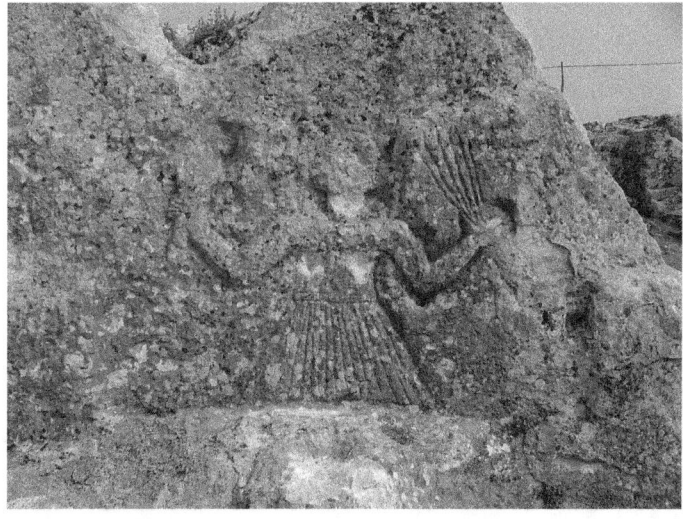

Fig. 7: Relief in quarry Photos: COMFORT 1997

Procopius and the neighbouring fortress of Rhabdion.[23] The five known milestones were located at:
- Kızılburç, west of *Edessa* on the road from *Zeugma*;[24] one records the construction of a road in AD 205, ten years after creation of the Roman province of Osrhoene; a second, found in the same village, was anepigraphic; both are located at a point near where the two routes mentioned in the Antonine itinerary converge (see footnote 12 above),
- Amouda, south of Dara but on the Syrian side of the border and probably on the road from *Edessa* to *Nisibis*, attributed to Caracalla (AD 216/7?);[25]
- possibly at Kursi (also spelt Karsi) in the north centre of Mount Sinjar, dated to AD 116/7;[26]
- and lastly one 5 kms south-west of Sinjar, attributed to Alexander Severus (AD 222–235).[27]

It would seem that after the reign of Diocletian milestones ceased to be erected east of the Euphrates, even if fortresses were still being constructed and traders were still using the road network.

Small roadside forts are apparent today especially along the road from *Doliche* to *Samosata* (see above); none have so far been found along the road from Antioch to *Zeugma*, although several exist in *Osrhoene* on or near the road from *Zeugma* to *Edessa*; one of these, poorly preserved, is linked to the two milestones at Kızılburç

---

23 COMFORT 2017, 181–229.
24 WAGNER 1983, 114 = AE 1984, 920: *Imp(erator) Caes(ar) L(ucius) Septimius / Severus Pius Pertinax / Aug(ustus) Arab(icus) Adiab(enicus) Parth(icus) / max(imus) pont(ifex) max(imus) trib(unicia) pot(estate) / XIII imp(erator) XII co(n)s(ul) III p(ater) p(atriae) / et Imp(erator) Caes(ar) M(arcus) Aurel(ius) / Antoninus Aug(ustus) Augusti / n(ostri) fil(ius) trib(unicia) pot(estate) VIII co(n)s(ul) / II et [[P(ublius) Septimius Geta]] / Caes(ar) co(n)s(ul) fil(ius) et frater / Aug(ustorum) nn(ostrorum) viam ab Euphrate / usque ad fines regni Sept(imi) / Ab(g)ari a novo munierunt / per L(ucium) Aelium Ianuarium / proc(uratorem) Aug(usti) prov(inciae) Osrhoenam(!) / m(ilia) p(assuum) XXXXVIII.*
25 POIDEBARD 1928, 111: *[Imp(eratori) Caes(ari) Marco / [Aurelio Ant]onino / [P(io) F(elicit) Aug(usto) Parth(ico) Bri]tannico (sic) / [Germanico max)imo / p(ontifici) m(aximo) trib(uniciae) pote]statis / [--- imp(eratori) --- co)nsuli --- pro c[o(n)s(uli)] ------.*
26 CAGNAT 1927, respectively AE 1927, 151: *Imp(erator) Caes(ar) [di]vi / Nervae f[i]l(ius) Nerva / Traianus Optimus / Aug(ustus) G[er]manicus / Dacicus [Pa]rthicus / pontif(ex) [max(imus) t]rib(unicia) [potes]/ [tate] ------.* It is uncertain even whether a milestone is involved, but this seems probable. But this milestone's location is doubtful; the main Roman road to Sinjar south-east from *Nisibis* is likely to have followed a route either to the west or the east of the main range and not across the middle via Kursi, which would have involved hair-raising climbs and descents.
27 A brief anonymous report is given in *Sumer* 8, 1952, p.229, respectively AE 1958, 241: *Imp(erator) Caesar / M(arcus) Aurelius / Severus / Alexander / Pius [Fel(ix)] Aug(ustus) / pont(ifex) maxim(us) / trib(unicia) pot(estate) XI / co(n)s(ul) III [p(ater) p(atriae)] proc(onsul) / a Sing(ara) / m(ilia) p(assuum) III.*

mentioned above and a further inscription on a boundary stone.²⁸ The fort is part of a group of such forts in north-western *Osrhoene* discussed by WAGNER; another, dated to the end of the second century AD, but of which almost nothing remains today, was seen and photographed by SAMUEL GUYER at Eski Hisar in 1911.²⁹ The latter apparently guarded a route linking the two legionary bases of *Zeugma* and *Samosata*, but on the east bank of the Euphrates. Two more have been seen at the villages of Yoğunburç and Keciburç west of *Edessa*.³⁰

More forts probably remain to be discovered east of *Edessa*. In his account of a journey to Ressaina, JOHN GEORGE TAYLOR, British Consul in Diyarbakır, recounted that:

> "Nisibin is about 20 hours [on horseback] from [Ras el-Ayn]; Harran and Orfa three days; and the isolated ridge of the Abd al Azeez Mountain eight hours off. An intelligent officer of the Turkish staff corps, Soheyl Bey, attached to the Pasha, had passed along all these routes, and found ruins existing at regular distances throughout; the remains, probably, of ancient military posts or relays connecting the different localities alluded to."³¹

Paving and Bridges

2) The Road from *Amida* (Diyarbakır) to the North-West

Paving is rarely found in the area of the *Euphrates* and the *Tigris*, usually because the hard surfaces do not require it but also because of the removal of flat stone as building material; nevertheless, some examples do exist outside towns. Ufacıklı, an important road junction north of *Doliche* which may be the Sicos Basilisses of the Antonine Itinerary (route 184), has at least one such paved road.³²

Another fine example was found north of *Amida* (Diyarbakır) in 2006. This road is likely to have been a part of the Persian Royal Road from Sardis to Susa;³³ it may also have been an important link between Constantinople, Cappadocia and the eastern frontier during the later Roman Empire, although much traffic is likely to have come from Anatolia and the Mediterranean to Mesopotamia via Cilicia and Antioch. *Amida* was fortified by Constantius II in AD 354, following the increase in the Roman presence in the north of Mesopotamia which resulted from Galerius' victory over Narses in 297.

---

28 WAGNER 1983, 110; COMFORT 2009, 127.
29 GUYER 1939.
30 COMFORT 2009, 127.
31 TAYLOR 1868, 352–3.
32 COMFORT 2009, 159.
33 CHAUMONT 1986; COMFORT 2009, 106–116.

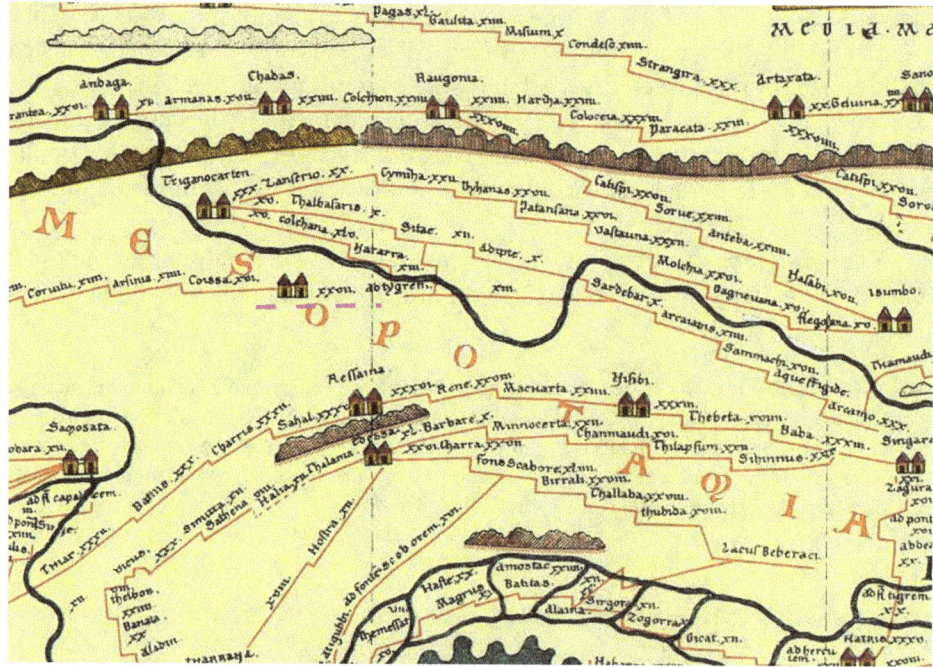

Fig. 8: Extract from Peutinger Table showing in pink approximate location of section discussed from: https://www.hs-augsburg.de/~harsch/Chronologia/Lspost03/Tabula/tab_pe00.html

A search for Roman bridges in this area in 2006 in preparation for a doctoral thesis resulted in the discovery of a Roman bridge, until then unpublished, called Karaköprü on the river Devegeçidi, 19km NNW of *Amida*, near the village of Hantepe (38°04'00"N, 40°08'30"E).[34] To the south the road leading back to *Amida* was paved with large flat stones and still is in some sections. Its route is clearly visible on Google Earth. To the north lies the territory of the Armenian principality of Sophene/Ingilene whose capital was at the nearby fortress of Eğil (probably Carcathiocerta in the ancient world; perhaps the tower symbol shown on this stretch of the Peutinger Table at Fig. 8 above). This territory was not formally incorporated into the Roman Empire until Justinian's reign. Following the division of Armenia in 387 Ingilene remained under Roman protection but its formal status outside the empire may explain why the Roman road to the north-west from *Amida* was paved only as far as this bridge. To the north only tracks are visible, despite the probable long-term importance from antiquity to the present day of the copper mines of Ergani, located about 40km to the north-west.[35]

---

34 Number 1 in COMFORT 2009 and COMFORT 2011.
35 SHEPHERD 1993, 221.

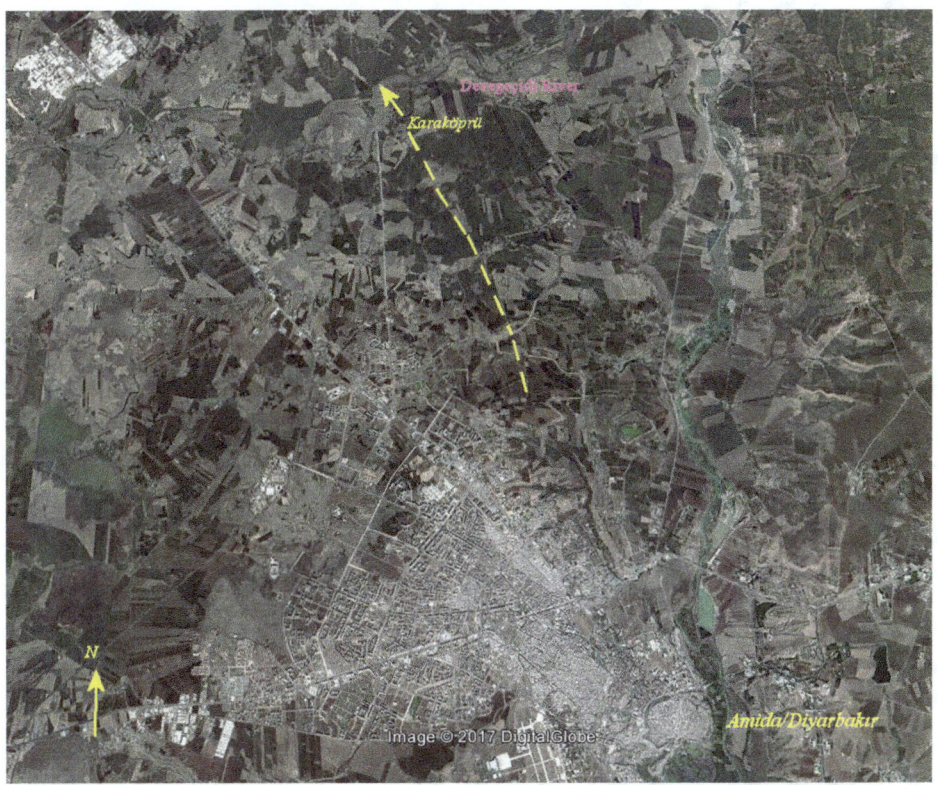

Fig. 9: The road from *Amida* to the Devegeçidi river GE 8/11/2016 © 2017 DigitalGlobe

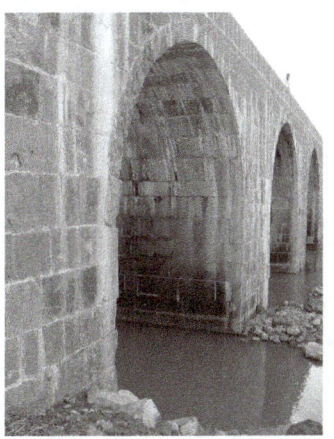 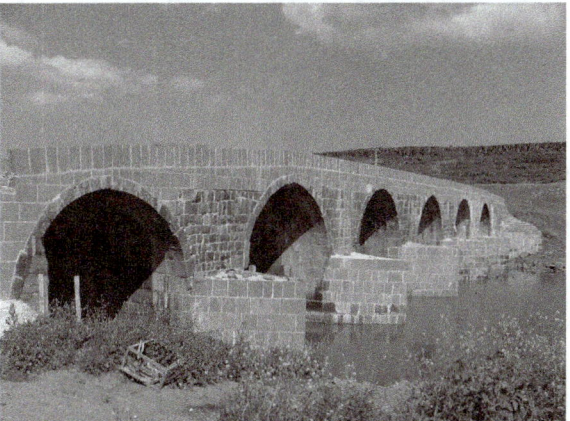

Figs. 10a and b: Bridge on Devegeçidi river, north of *Amida* (Diyarbakır) Photo: COMFORT 2007

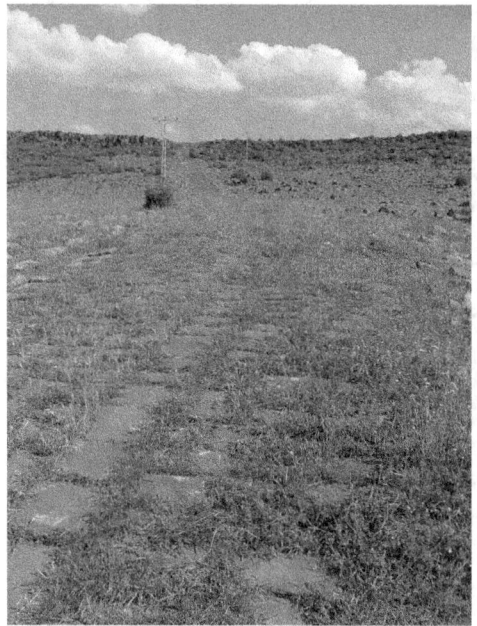

Fig. 11a: Road to south of bridge Photo: COMFORT 2008

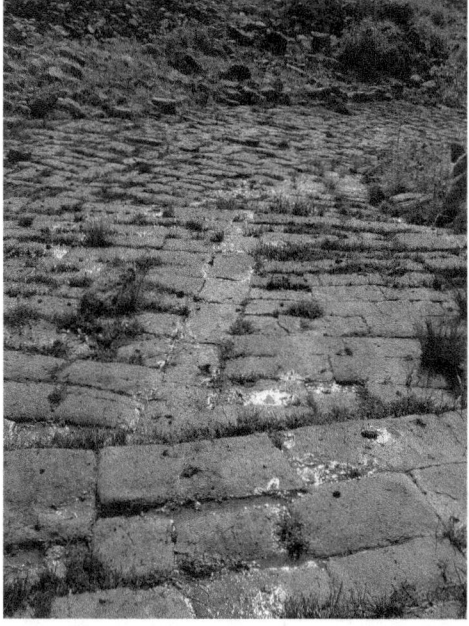

Fig. 11b: Steps in road Photos: COMFORT 2007

South of the bridge the road rises gently 60m to the hillside bordering the river valley from where it continues south on roughly the same level all the way to *Amida*. As it approaches the crest of the hill the road makes a zig-zag and climbs over several low steps. But there are no ruts or evident wear of the road. It seems likely that the road itself may have been abandoned fairly soon after its construction for another unpaved route along the *Tigris*. This later road crosses the Devegeçidi only 1km from the confluence with the *Tigris* by an Artukid bridge called Halil Viran, which then arrives at the medieval caravanserai of Hantepe. The change from paved to unpaved road is an interesting example of the likely abandonment of wheeled vehicles in the course of the sixth century AD.[36] Camels and donkeys do not need paved roads.

In total 24 ancient bridges in the three late Roman provinces of *Euphratesia*, *Osrhoene* and *Mesopotamia* are discussed in Comfort 2009, 55–100 and Comfort 2011.

Cisterns and Military Routes

3) The Road from *Cepha* to *Tilli*

Some roads of the region were clearly constructed by the Romans for military purposes, despite the thriving commercial importance of many routes throughout the region.[37] The roads from *Doliche* to *Samosata* mentioned above and that along the *Euphrates* on the west bank north of *Zeugma* are two such examples of military roads.[38] A third example is a road along the crest north of the river *Tigris* from *Cepha* (now Hasankeyf) to *Tilli* (now Çattepe), a Roman fortress at the confluence of the *Tigris* and Bohtan rivers. This road is not shown on the Peutinger Table.

Cepha was the base of *legio II Parthica*;[39] after the victory of Galerius over Narses in AD 297 it appears to have become for over 60 years the capital of a principality under Roman control called Arzanene, even though this had been traditionally located on the north bank of the *Tigris* while the citadel of *Cepha* was on the south bank (Comfort 2017: 197–8). The current remains of an Artukid bridge across the *Tigris* are therefore likely to have had a Roman predecessor. Until AD 363 when *Nisibis* and fifteen fortresses were surrendered to the Persians following the death of Julian, Rome maintained control of the north bank of the river at least as far as the confluence with the Bohtan, where the fortress of *Tilli*/Çattepe is located.[40] Remains of a Roman bridge

---

36 BULLIET 1975.
37 A paper entitled 'Military highways or silk routes? Roads and bridges on the frontier between Rome and Persia in Late Antiquity' should appear shortly in the proceedings of a conference of the British Institute at Ankara on the topic of 'Pathways of Communication' held in March 2014.
38 Routes 8 and 12 in Chapter 4, 'Roads', of COMFORT 2009.
39 Not. dign. or. 36 Dux Mesopotamiae.
40 COMFORT 2017, 221–2.

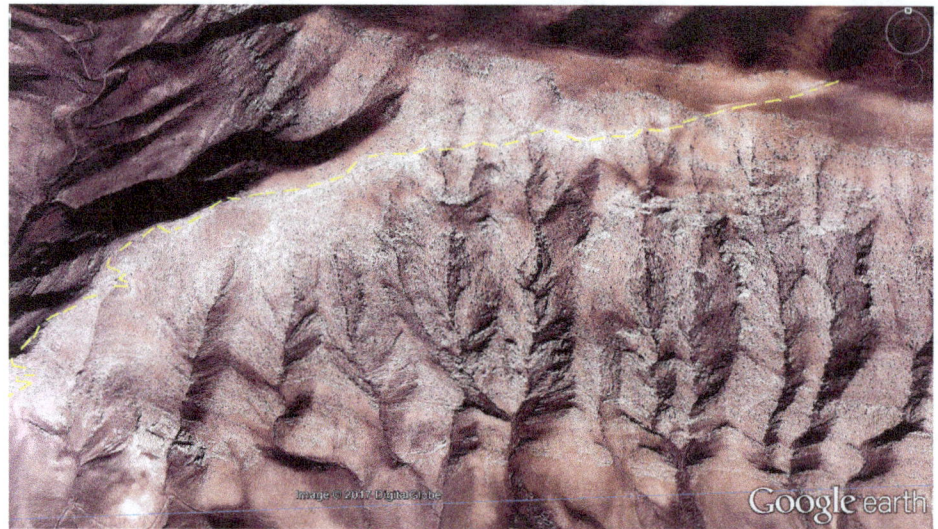

Fig. 12a: The road north of *Cepha* (Hasankeyf – centrepoint: 37°44'43"N, 41°27'05"E) GE 21/11/2010 ©2017 Google, Basarsoft, CNES/Airbus

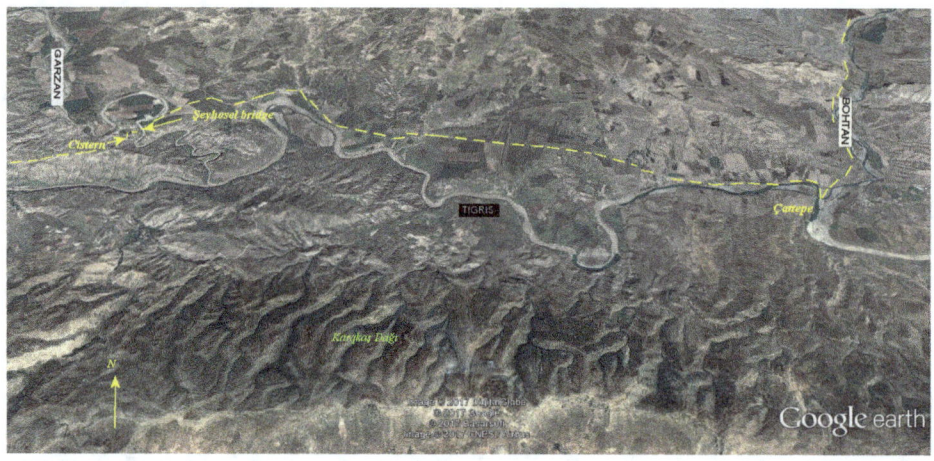

Fig.12b: The road from *Cepha* to *Tilli*/Çattepe (north bank of the *Tigris* – centrepoint: 37°43'26"N, 41°41'17"E) GE 23/06/2010 © Google Earth 2017 Google, DigitalGlobe, Basarsoft, CNES/Airbus

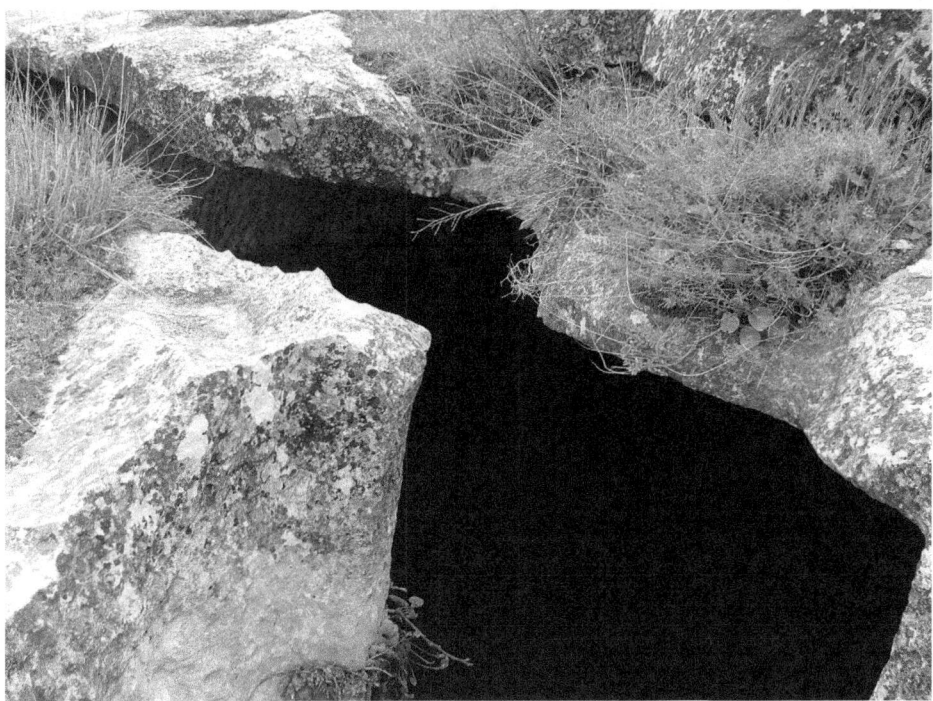

Fig. 13: The hidden cistern above Şeyhosel Photo: COMFORT, 2007

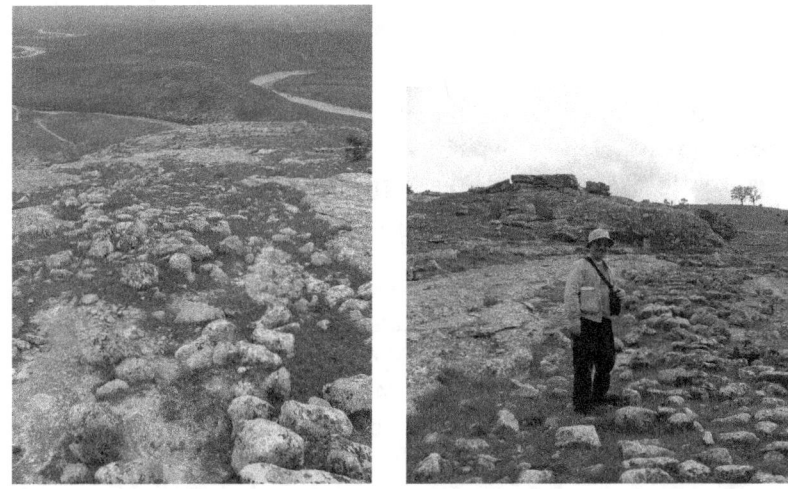

Figs.14a and b: Paving above Şeyhosel Photos: COMFORT 2007

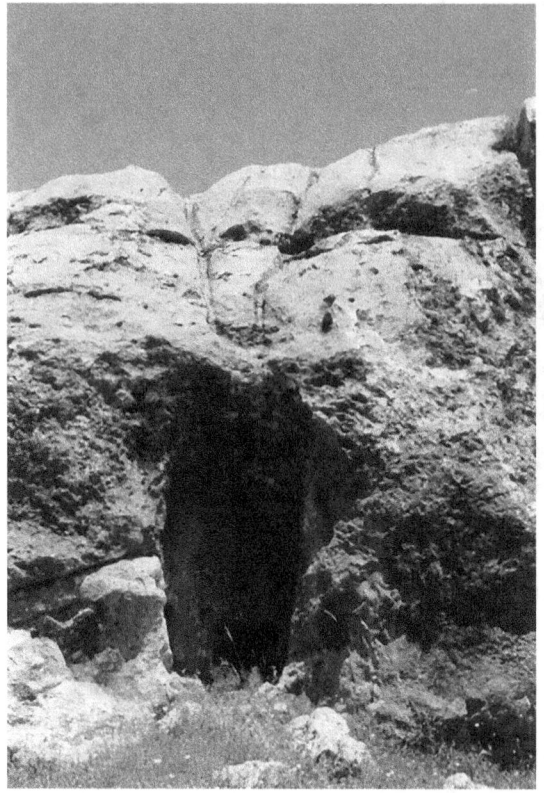

Fig. 15: Cistern on the *Euphrates* west bank south of Rumkale Photo: COMFORT 1998

on the Garzan Su (*Nicephorion*) at Şeyhosel (number 8 in Chapter 3 of COMFORT 2009) and some paving on the steep slopes to its south-west indicate the likely course of the road linking Hasankeyf to *Tilli*. To the west, the steep ascent from *Cepha* to the crest of the mountain is likely to have been by a zig-zag road now badly damaged but of which remains are still visible on the satellite imagery.

One feature of all roads in this region, but especially of the military routes, is the construction of cisterns. Sometimes these are hidden in unlikely places. One such is to be found about 1km south-west of the bridge at Şeyhosel on the way back up to the ridge dominating the *Tigris* at approximately 37º44'40"N, 41º35'06"E. A similarly placed cistern is on the Roman road along the west bank of the *Euphrates* south-east of the village of Köseler and 5km south of Rumkale. Some remains of paving are to be seen near the *Tigris* cistern.

The fortress at *Tilli*/Çattepe is discussed in COMFORT 2017. The road leading to it from *Cepha* was presumably built to provide supplies. But Çattepe is also known to have been an important river port in the Middle Ages (and probably in Late Assyrian times as well). It is likely that the road from *Cepha* continued north from Çattepe towards the Bitlis pass, joining a direct route from *Amida* to *Armenia*.⁴¹ The junction may have been near present-day Ziyaret, north-west of Siirt, but this area needs further investigation.

On commercial highways, cisterns are of course also present. They vary substantially in type: one deep rectangular cistern was found east of *Zeugma*, but others are round and tapering to a small surface outlet. Occcasionally underground cisterns were built with access by steps. No attempt has yet been made to classify and date these different types. Five examples are shown below:

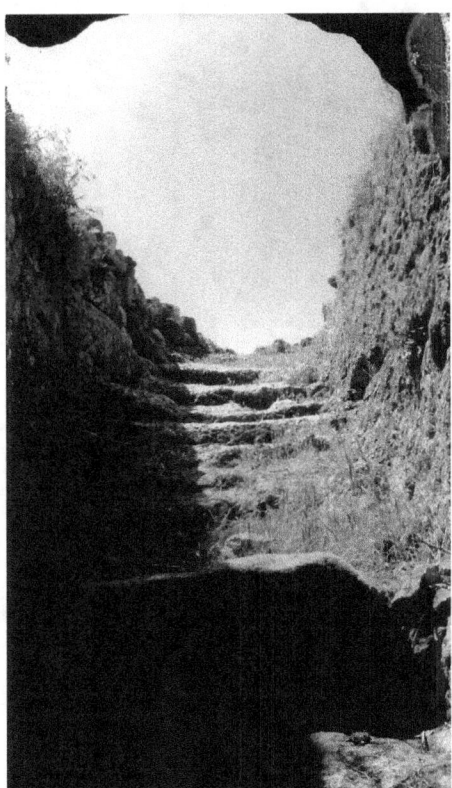

Fig.16a: Cistern at Hacıobası (Beyreli, Gaziantep province) Photo: COMFORT 2008

---

41 See COMFORT 2009, 116–125 (route2).

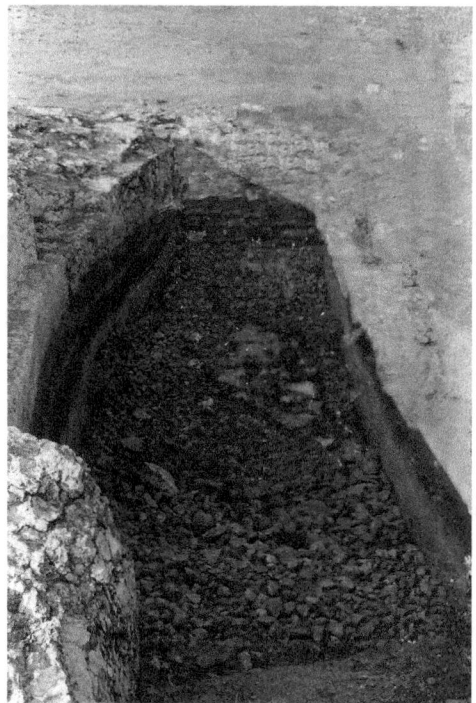

Fig.16b: Cistern near Ekenek (E of *Zeugma*) Photo: COMFORT 2008

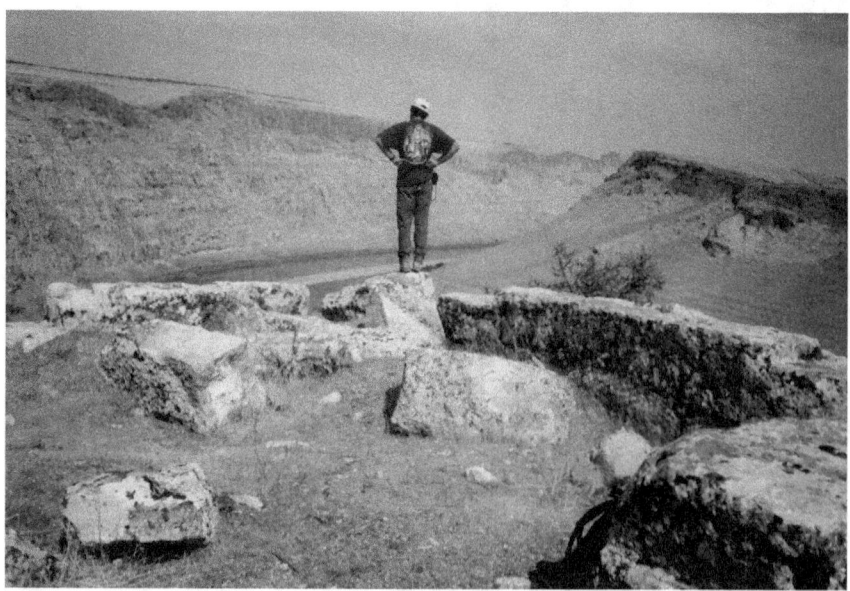

Fig.16c: Cistern opposite Kenk (*Euphrates*, north of Rumkale) Photo: COMFORT 2008

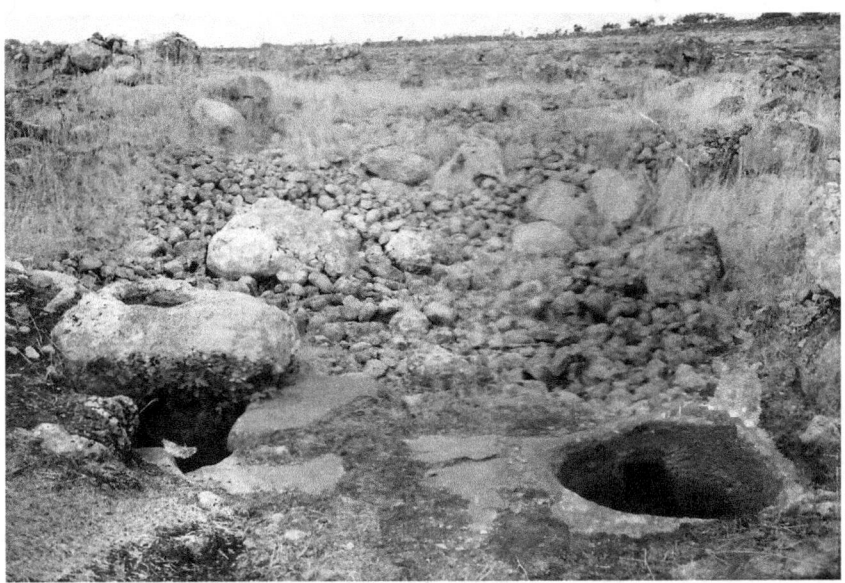

Fig.16d: Cisterns at Hamurkesen (abandoned village on E bank of *Euphrates*, near Gözeli/Ayni) Photo: COMFORT 2008

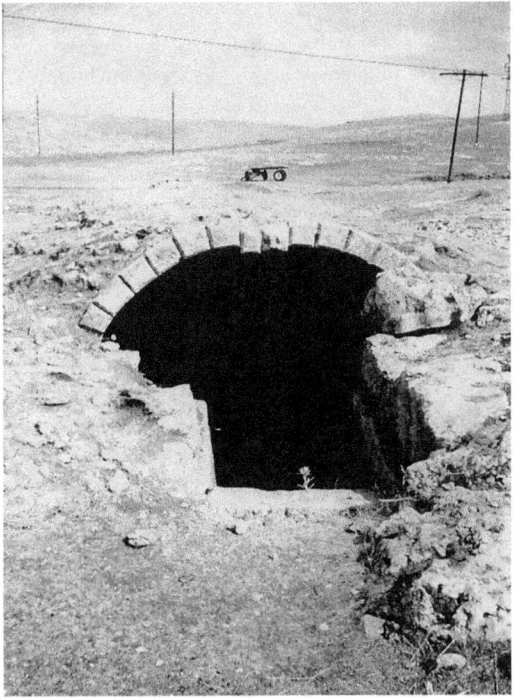

Fig.16e: Cistern at Sarımağara (between Urfa and Suruç) Photo: COMFORT 2008

Bibliography

ALGAZE 1989 = G. ALGAZE, A new frontier: First Results of the Tigris-Euphrates Archaeological Reconnaissance Project 1988, *Journal of Near Eastern Studies,* 48, 1989, 241–281.

ALGAZE et al. 1991 = G. ALGAZE/R. BREUNINGER/C. LIGHTFOOT/M. ROSENBERG, The Tigris-Euphrates Archaeological Reconnaissance Project: A Preliminary Report of the 1989–1990 Seasons, *Anatolica* XVII, 1991, 175–235.

ALGAZE/HAMMER 2012 = G. ALGAZE/E. HAMMER et al., The Tigris-Euphrates Archaeological Reconnaissance Project. Final Report of the Cizre Dam and Cizre-Silopi Plain Survey Areas, *Anatolica,* 38, 2012, 1–115.

BALL 2003 = W. BALL (ed.), Ancient Settlement in the Zammar Region: Excavations by the British School of Archaeological Expedition to Iraq in the Saddam Dam Salbage Project 1985–86, Oxford 2003.

BEYAZLAR/CROWTHER 2008 = A. BEYAZLAR/C. CROWTHER, A New Trajanic Milestone from Kilis, in: E. WINTER (ed.), ΠΑΤΡΙΣ ΠΑΝΤΡΟΦΟΣ ΚΟΜΜΑΓΗΝΗ: Neue Funde und Forschungen zwischen Taurus und Euphrat, Bonn 2008, 257–262.

BEYAZLAR/CROWTHER 2011 = A. BEYAZLAR/C. CROWTHER, A New Severan Milestone in Gaziantep Museum, in: E. WINTER (ed.), Von Kummuḫ nach Telouch: historische und archäologische Untersuchungen in Kommagene, Bonn 2011, 409–416.

BULLIET 1975 = R.W. BULLIET, The Camel and the Wheel, Cambridge/New York 1975.

CAGNAT 1927 = R. CAGNAT, Inscription romaine du Sindjar au nom de Trajan, *Syria* 8, 1927, 53–54.

CHAUMONT 1986 = M. CHAUMONT, L'Arménie et la route royale des Perses, *REArm* 20, 1986, 287–307.

COMFORT 2009 = A. COMFORT, Roads on the Frontier between Rome and Persia, Exeter 2009, http://hdl.handle.net/10036/68213

COMFORT 2011 = A. COMFORT, Roman Bridges of South-East Anatolia, in: H. BRU/G. LABARRE (ed.), L'Anatolie des peuples, des cités et des cultures (IIe millénaire av. J.-C. – Ve siècle ap. J.C.), Besançon 2011, 315–349.

COMFORT 2017 = A. COMFORT, Fortresses of the Tur Abdin and the Confrontation between Rome and Persia, *AS* 67, 2017, 181–229.

COMFORT/ABADIE-REYNAL/ERGEÇ 2000 = A. COMFORT/C. ABADIE-REYNAL/R. ERGEÇ, Crossing the Euphrates in Antiquity: Zeugma Seen from Space, *AS* 50, 2000, 99–126.

COMFORT/ERGEÇ 2001 = A. COMFORT/R. ERGEÇ, Following the Euphrates in Antiquity: North-South Routes around Zeugma, *AS* 51, 2001 19–50.

COMFORT/MARCIAK 2018 = A. COMFORT/M. MARCIAK, How Did the Persian King of Kings Get His Wine? The Upper Tigris in Antiquity (c.700 BCE to 636 CE), Oxford 2018.

CUMONT 1917 = F. CUMONT, Etudes Syriennes, Paris 1917.

CUNTZ 1990 = O. CUNTZ, Itineraria Antonini Augusti et Burdigalense, Itineraria Romana, vol. 1, Editio stereotypa editionis primae 1929, Stuttgart 1990.

DILLEMANN 1962 = L. DILLEMANN, Haute Mésopotamie orientale et pays adjacents, Paris 1962.

GREGORY/KENNEDY 1985 = S. GREGORY/D. KENNEDY, Sir Aurel Stein's Limes Report, Oxford 1985.

GUYER 1939 = S. GUYER, Eski Hissar, ein römisches Lagerkastell im Gebiet von Edessa, in: Académie des inscriptions et belles-lettres (France) (ed.), Mélanges syriens offerts à René Dussaud, Paris 1939, 183–190.

KENNEDY/BEWLEY 2004 = D. KENNEDY/R. BEWLEY, Ancient Jordan from the Air, London 2004.

KEPINSKI 2005 = C. KEPINSKI, Tilbeshar: a Bronze Age City in the Sajur Valley (Southeast Anatolia), *Anatolica* 31, 2005 145–159.

LERICHE 1986–1992 = P. LERICHE (ed.), Doura-Europos. Études I–III (DEE), 'Syria', IFAPO Damascus 1986–1992.

LIGHTFOOT/NAVEH 1991 = C.S. LIGHTFOOT/J. NAVEH, A North Mesopotamian Aramaic Inscription on a Relief in the Tigris Gorge, *ARAM,* 3, 1991 310–337.
MANGO 1986 = C. MANGO, A Late Roman Inn in Eastern Turkey, *OJA* 5, 1986, 223–231.
OATES 1956 = D. OATES, The Roman frontier in Northern Iraq, *GJ* 122, 1956 190–199.
OATES 1968 = D. OATES, Studies in Ancient History of Northern Iraq, London 1968.
OATES/OATES 1990 = D. OATES/J. OATES, Aspects of Hellenistic and Roman Settlement in the Khabur Basin, in: P. MATTHIAE/M.N. VAN LOON/H. WEISS (ed.), Resurrecting the Past, Istanbul 1990, 227–248.
POIDEBARD 1928 = A. POIDEBARD, Milliaire provenant de 'Amouda, *Syria* 9.2, 1928, 110–113.
POIDEBARD 1934 = A. POIDEBARD, La trace de Rome dans le désert de Syrie: le limes de Trajan à la conquête arabe, Paris 1934.
SHEPHERD 1993 = R. SHEPHERD, Ancient Mining, London 1993.
STARK 1966 = F. STARK, Rome on the Euphrates, London 1966.
TAYLOR 1868 = J.G. TAYLOR, Journal of a Tour in Armenia, Kurdistan and Upper Mesopotamia, *GJ* 38, 1868, 281–361.
WAGNER 1975 = J. WAGNER, Die Römer am Euphrat und Tigris in: F. DÖRNER (ed.), Kommagene: Geschichte und Kultur einer antiken Landschaft, *AW* 6, Sondernummer, Küssnacht 1975, 68–82.
WAGNER 1983 = J. WAGNER, Provincia Osrhoenae: New Archaeological Finds Illustrating the Military Organisation under the Severan Dynasty in: S. MITCHELL (ed.), Armies and Frontiers in Roman and Byzantine Anatolia, Oxford, 1983, 103–123.
WIESSNER 1981–1993 = G. WIESSNER, Christliche Kultbauten im Tur Abdin, Göttinger Orientforschungen, vol. 4. 1–4, Wiesbaden 1981–1993.
WILKINSON/TUCKER 1995 = T.J. WILKINSON/D.J. TUCKER, Settlement Development in the North Jazira, Iraq, Baghdad, London 1995.

Chaim Ben David
Milestones near Roman Army Installations in Desert Areas of the Provinces of Palaestina and Arabia

Abstract: A general observation on milestones in the Roman province of Palaestina shows that in the northern and central part of the province some 650 milestones are known along the Roman road system, while in the southern part – the Negev Desert – they are very rare, even along well known and preserved Roman roads. I suggest that all the examples of milestones in the Negev Desert area including those along the incense route were an initiative and labor of local Roman Army units and are not part of the regular Roman road network connecting major cities. A similar phenomenon of erecting milestones near Roman military camps or forts rather than along the entire road is found also east of the *Via Nova Triana* in southern Jordan.

Zusammenfassung: Eine allgemeine Betrachtung von Meilensteinen in der römischen Provinz Palästina zeigt, dass im nördlichen und zentralen Teil der Provinz entlang der römischen Straßen etwa 650 Meilensteine bekannt sind, während sie im südlichen Teil – in der Wüste Negev – sehr selten sind; dies gilt auch für bekannte und gut erhaltene Verbindungen. Ich schlage vor, dass all die Beispiele von Meilensteinen in der Region der Wüste Negev, einschließlich denen entlang der Weihrauchstraße, auf Initiative und Arbeit lokaler römischer Armeeeinheiten errichtet wurden und nicht Teil des regulären römischen Straßennetzes sind, das die bedeutenden Städte miteinander verband. Ein ähnliches Phänomen, bei dem Meilensteine nahe römischer Militärlager oder Militärposten errichtet wurden statt entlang der gesamten Straße, findet sich auch östlich der *Via Nova Traiana* in Südjordanien.

A general observation on milestones in the Roman province of *Judea-Palaestina* shows that in northern and central part of the province some 650 milestones are known along the Roman road system, while in the southern part – the Negev Desert they are very rare.[1] They are missing even along well-known and preserved Roman paved or built roads, such as the roads going down from *Judea* to *Mampsis* or *Zoara*.

In desert areas one would expect a better rate of preservation, had there been milestones there, as is the case along the desert stretches of the *Via Nova Traiana*.[2]

---
[1] The Israel Milestone Committee (IMC) has documented and maintains files on 698 milestones as of August 2017. Basic data on the milestone and Roman roads in the province of Judea/Palaestina can be found at http://milestones.kinneret.ac.il, launched by the Kinneret College on the Sea of Galilee and directed by the author.
[2] GRAF 1995; MACDONALD 1996; BORSTAD 2008.

https://doi.org/10.1515/9783110638332-008

Many milestones are also known from the settled areas in the province of *Arabia*, while in the desert areas, apart from the *Via Nova Traiana* less than 20 milestones have been documented. As in the Negev, even on major Roman roads like the *Catraba*[3] and *Zoar*[4] ascents, where long stretches of well-built Roman roads are still seen, no milestones were found. It seems that milestones, which were also set up for propaganda purposes, were erected predominantly in the settled areas of the country, where large volumes of traffic ensured they would be seen by many.

I would like to propose that all the examples of milestones in the desert areas, including those along the well-known *Petra-Gaza* incense route, were initiated and implemented by local Roman army units and were not part of the regular Roman road network connecting major cities.

The Negev and Wadi 'Arabah

Milestones in the Negev and Wadi 'Arabah are known at the following sites (fig. 1):
1. At the head of the Scorpions ('Aqrabim) Ascent[5]
2. Between *Oboda* and *Haluza*[6]
3. The Nafha Plateau[7]
4. Makhtesh Ramon[8]
5. The area of Yahel in the Arabah[9]
6. A milestone quarry in the southern 'Arava, near Qa'a es-Sa'idiyeen,[10] where five limestone milestones were found. According to the surveyors, the quarry was apparently operated by the garrison of the nearby fort (32 x 21 m) at Qa'a es-Sa'idiyeen,[11] whose building stones were probably taken from that same quarry. Ten km farther south is the Roman fort of *Gharandal* (37 x 37 m).[12] According to DARBY,[13] the building stones of this fort probably derived from that quarry.
7. South of Bir Madhkur.[14]

---

3 MITTMANN 1982.
4 BEN DAVID 2002, 2017.
5 ROLL 1989, 260, no. 101, IMC no. 597.
6 MESHEL/TSAFRIR 1975, 3 n.1, IMC nos. 285, 572–574.
7 MESHEL/TSAFRIR 1975, 3–7, IMC nos. 576–584, 645.
8 MESHEL/TSAFRIR 1975, 7–8, IMC nos. 585–596.
9 ISAAC 1998, 71–75; ROLL/AVNER 2008, IMC nos. 541–568.
10 SMITH 2010, 69.
11 SMITH 2010, 34–36.
12 DARBY/DARBY 2015.
13 DARBY 2015, 471.
14 SMITH 2005, 65–66.

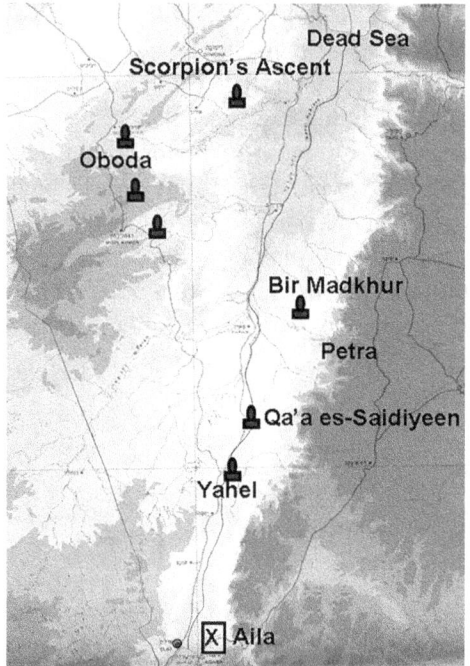

Fig. 1: Milestone clusters in the Negev and Wadi Arabah (Chaim Ben David)

Of all the groups of milestones, only that of Yahel yielded decipherable inscriptions. As will be elaborated below, in my opinion, this group provides the key to our understanding of the presence of milestones in the Negev and Wadi 'Arabah.

In 1994 three clusters of milestones were discovered in the sand dunes south of Kibbutz Yahel in the 'Arabah Valley. There are 8–12 stones in each cluster (fig. 2), approximately one Roman mile apart. Most of the inscriptions that were published by ROLL and AVNER[15] were painted only with red paint, and only a few were engraved. They all mention either Diocletian or Constantine, and they date between 293 and 324 CE. Fortunately the inscriptions bear the name of the *caput viae* – the point of origin from which distances were measured. Finding the milestones in Wadi 'Arabah, 60 km north of *Aila*, a city and the headquarters of the Tenth Legion one would expect *Aila* – or any other major urban center in the area to have been the *caput viae* – but that was not the case. The *caput viae* in the provinces of *Judea-Palaestina* and *Arabia* were usually major cities like *Scythopolis, Caesarea, Eleutheropolis* in *Palaestina*, or in *Arabia, Bostra* and *Esbus*. Looking at the list of all the place names found on mile-

---

15 ROLL/AVNER 2008.

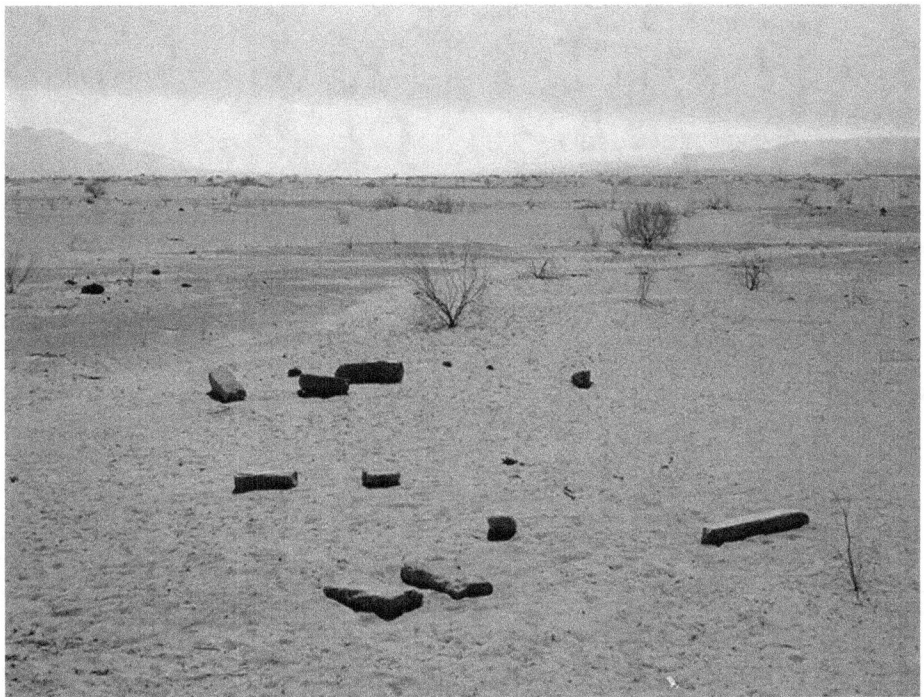

Fig. 2: Yahel milestones, Group I looking south (Uzi Avner)

stones,[16] we can see that they were main urban centers as well as important junctions in the Roman road network.

In the Yahel milestones, all the inscriptions mention *Osia* (fig. 3) as the point of origin from which distances were measured, but only in the middle cluster was the distance clearly legible – 12 miles, the exact distance to the Roman fort at Yotvata.[17] The fort at Yotvata (39 x 39 m)[18] yielded a clear founding inscription,[19] dating its construction to the days of Diocletian. It is not the largest Roman camp in the region; that, of course, was at *Aila*, the headquarters of the Tenth Legion beginning in the late third century CE. Yet the milestones clearly relate to Yotvata and not to *Aila*, suggesting that the custom of erecting milestones was the initiative of a local unit in an area close

---

16 BEN DAVID 2001, 30–31.
17 ROLL/AVNER 2008, 271. On the right, Lower part of a carved inscription, with letters painted in red: *[Dominis nostris / Diocletiano et / Maximiano / Augustis et / Constantio et] / Maximian [o] / nob(ilissimis) Caes(aribus) / ab Osia / mi(lia passuum) XII[I]*. On the left red painted inscription entirely preserved: *D(ominis) n(ostris) / Constantio [et] / Maximian[o] / Aug (ustis) et / Severo et / Maximino / nob(ilissimis) C(ae)s(aribus) / ab Osia / mi(lia passuum) XII*.
18 MESHEL 1989; AVNER/DAVIES/MAGNESS 2004 ; DAVIES/MAGNESS 2008 ; DAVIES/MAGNESS 2015.
19 ROLL 1989.

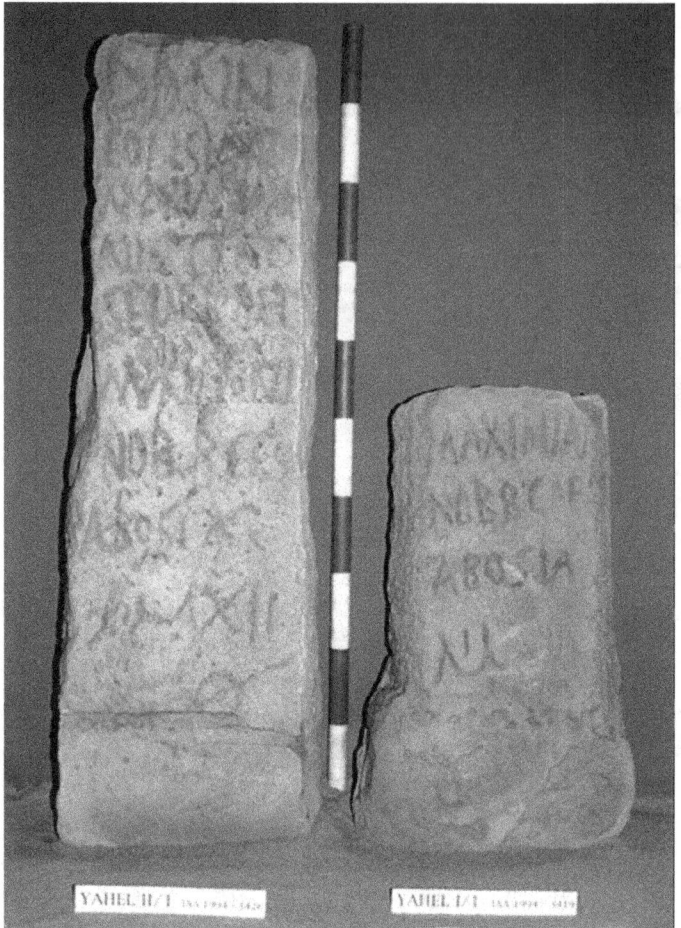

Fig. 3: Yahel milestones, painted inscriptions mentioning the name of Osia (Uzi Avner)

to its base. I therefore suggest that all of the relatively few examples of milestones in the Negev, in Wadi 'Arabah and in southeastern Jordan should be interpreted in this light. This includes the milestone station at the top of the Scorpions ('Aqrabim) Ascent, which should be seen as related to the fort system apparently constructed in the days of Diocletian.[20]

As for the milestone clusters along the Incense Route in the Negev, many scholars have dated this paved section, as well as its milestones, to the Nabataean Kingdom

---

20 COHEN 1993, 1143–1144.

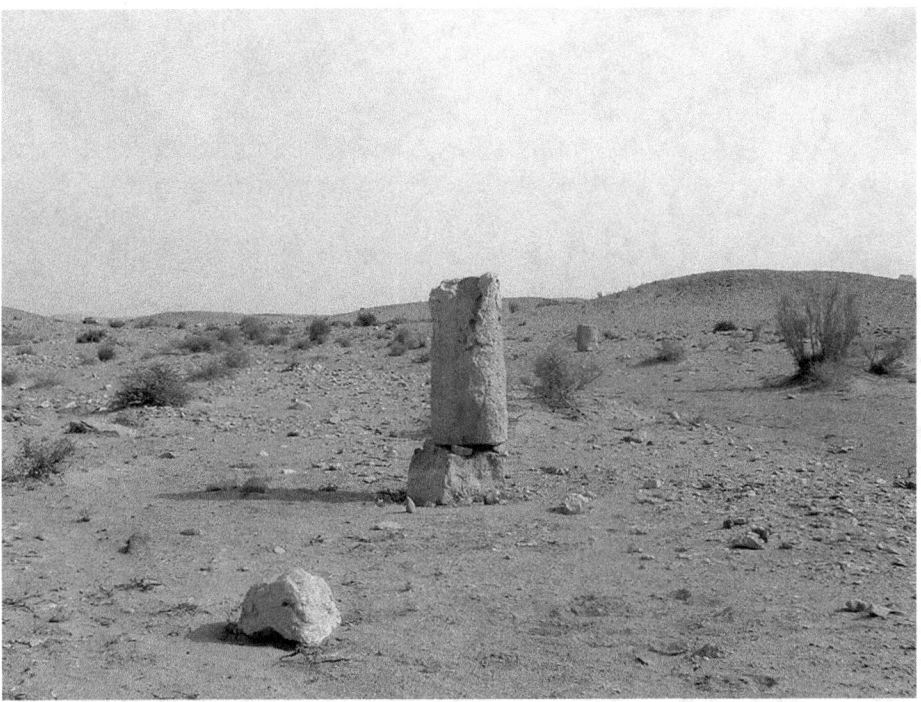

Fig. 4: Makhtesh Ramon milestone station (Chaim Ben David)

period.[21] Others agree with this early date but suggest that the road continued in use during the later Roman period as well.[22]

Apart from this Negev segment, neither paving stones nor milestones were recorded along the spice routes from the Persian Gulf or from Southern Arabia to *Petra*. Furthermore, no more than three milestones in the entire region antedate 106 CE. These and other issues have led me to doubt the likelihood of the suggested Nabataean date for this specific road.[23]

Two sections were studied in remarkable depth by MESHEL and TSAFRIR[24] who noted that the two clusters of milestones between 'Avdat and Sha'ar Ramon counted the miles from different points, rather than the norm of measuring the distance between cities from one of the cities. The cluster of Makhtesh Ramon (fig. 4) relates

---

21 NEGEV 1966; MESHEL/TSAFRIR 1974; MESHEL/TSAFRIR 1975.
22 COHEN 1982.
23 BEN DAVID 2012.
24 MESHEL/TSAFRIR 1975, 3–8.

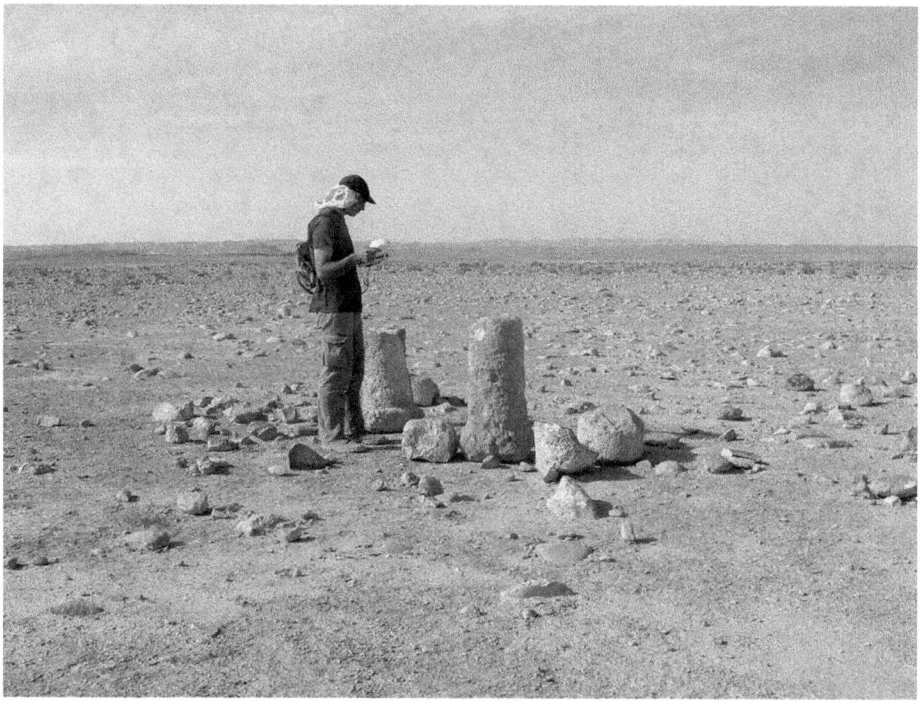

Fig. 5: Nafha plateau milestone station (Chaim Ben David)

to Sha'ar Ramon, where clear evidence of a Roman military presence was found in an inscription mentioning the *cohors* VI *Hispanorum*.[25]

The second cluster, the milestones of the Nafha Plateau (fig. 5) is connected to the military camp at *Oboda*, which was initially dated to the Nabatean period. But now excavations have clearly revealed it to be a Roman camp built after 106 CE. According to PETER FABIAN[26] the camp dates from the reign of Trajan, while TALI ERICKSON-GINI dates it to the reign of Diocletian.[27]

It seems that the paved sections and the milestones in this region were a local Roman initiative following the construction of the Roman camp at *Oboda*. The latest paving efforts and erection of milestones apparently date to the time of Diocletian, while the earliest were probably carried out in the second century CE. These paved roads between *Oboda* and Sha'ar Ramon are 4.0–8.7 m wide and served mainly Roman troops, apparently moving in formations of several soldiers abreast. This section

---

[25] FIGUERAS 1992, 76–179; ISAAC 1998, 157.
[26] FABIAN 2005; HERMON/FABIAN 2002.
[27] ERICKSON-GINI 2002.

was certainly not passable for wheeled vehicles, because at Ma'ale Mahmal, located between the two clusters, the road narrows to a 1-m-wide path.

It is noteworthy that in neither of these two clusters were inscriptions found on the milestones; it stands to reason that the red-painted – not incised – inscriptions were erased over time. At some sites several milestones were found at the same station, indicating prolonged use of the road. More evidence of prolonged use comes from the Nafha Plateau, where two different stretches of the same route were found.

With regard to milestones north of *Oboda*, since the 1970s[28] information about the number of concentrations of milestones has increased but has not been sufficiently published. Below is a list of the milestones discovered in the area over the past few decades.

1. UTM coordinates 6683 4097 – a milestone column, 0.55 m. in height, appears to fit the location of the second mile from *Oboda* (IMC no. 575).
2. UTM coordinates 6677 4130 – four sections of milestones in secondary use were discovered in a terrace, one 0.67 m. in height, with carved inscription painted in red (IMC no. 285). I. ROLL was unable to decipher this inscription. The second milestone is 0.67 m. high and bears a Greek inscription: MI Δ (IMC no. 572), which, according to ROLL should be interpreted as the fourth mile, undoubtedly from *Oboda*. According to ROLL two other sections of milestones (IMC nos. 573–574), measuring 0.65 m and 0.87 m high were left by the surveyors in the field. Their size makes it probable that these are the two milestones on display in the visitor's center at Avdat National Park. The shorter one bears a very indistinct inscription of three to four lines in red paint.
3. UTM coordinates 6683 4144 in a tributary of Nahal Havarim, three sections of milestones (fig. 6), 0.76, 0.77 and 0.93 m high (IMC nos. 569–571) were discovered by Yuval Sela, former director of the Sede Boker field school. This group is the sole concentration still in the field at this time, although they are not in their original position. The probably rolled down the slope from the ancient track that passed above the wadi and were not intentionally transferred from afar to their present location. If we accept this contention, then there was apparently a concentration of milestones 2 km west of the easily negotiated route through Nahal Besor. In my opinion, this concentration of milestones was placed along the road between the Roman army camp at *Oboda* and *Mampsis* and was never part of the main road to Halutza. It should be noted that three Late Roman fortified structures are known along this route, Horvat Haluqim,[29] Mesad Yeruham[30] and Mesad Horvat Bor.[31]

---

28 MESHEL/TSAFRIR 1975, 3 no. 1.
29 COHEN 1976, 47–50.
30 COHEN 1967.
31 ISRAEL/ERICKSON-GINI 2001–2002.

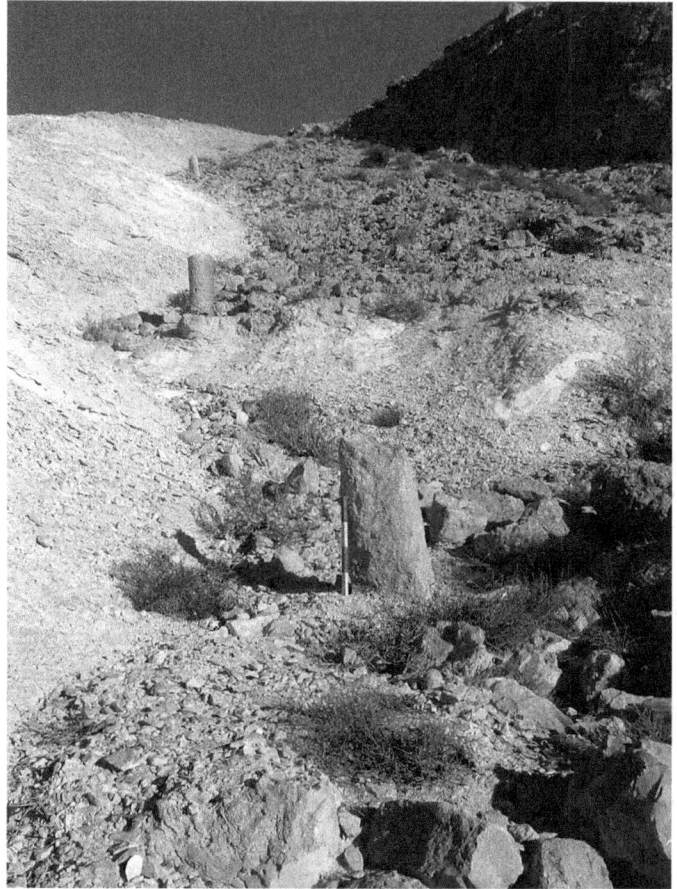

Fig. 6: Nahal Havarim milestone station (Chaim Ben David)

On ROLL's map a milestone is marked on the road to Halutza at UTM coordinates 6665 4197 – on a bank of Nahal Besor (IMC no. 437), but ZEEV MESHEL, who saw this milestone in situ, believed it to be a regular stone column. In any case, in my opinion, the milestones were installed by soldiers belonging to the Roman army unit based at *Oboda*.

As for the milestones found on the Jordanian side of Wadi 'Arabah, those west of Bir Madhkur relate to the Late Roman fort at the site,[32] while those found in the quarry in the southern 'Arabah relate most probably to the Roman fort at Qa'a

---

32 SMITH 2010, 39–42.

es-Sa'idiyeen or *Gharandal* where a Diocletian foundation inscription has recently been found.[33]

Southern Jordan

In their pioneering publication, BRÜNNOW and DOMASZEWSKI noted several milestones east of the *Via Nova Traiana*, especially in southern Jordan.[34] This information was repeated in THOMSEN's monumental paper on milestones,[35] where he suggested that they were part of a continuous road that connected the military installations along the eastern *limes*.

THOMSEN presented the following milestone stations (sometimes comprising several milestones):

No. 176 (THOMSEN's numbering) — about an hour and twenty minutes southeast of Lejjun in Moab (the distance in time according to BRÜNNOW and DOMASZEWSKI).

In his summary of the regional road system east of the Dead Sea, PARKER[36] noted that the milestones found by BRÜNNOW and DOMASZEWSKI near Lejjun were the only attested milestones along the eastern route and that the survey of the *Limes Arabicus* found no trace of milestones in the area.

No. 177, about half an hour south of Qal'at Hasa.

No.178, about an hour north of Jurf ad-Darawish

Nos. 179–181, south of no. 178 at intervals of 17, 12 and 17 minutes.

Nos. 182–184, south of Jurf ad-Darawish at intervals of 10, 17 and 12 minutes.

Nos. 172–173, at intervals of 18 and 34 minutes north of Udhruh.

Except for station no. 177 south of Qal'at Hasa, all other stations are near military camps such as Lejjun or Udhruh, or near the Roman fort at Jurf ad-Darawish (below).

Significantly, all the milestone clusters in the Jurf ad-Darawish area were rediscovered by GEORGE FINDLATER[37] in the course of the archaeological survey of the Dana area (DAS), which still awaits publication. On the 1:400,000 scale map accompanying FINDLATER's article, six milestone stations were marked. FINDLATER notes that his survey identified all five of THOMSEN's clusters, nos. 177–181, some containing up to five milestones.

---

33 DARBY 2015.
34 BRÜNNOW/DOMASZEWSKI 1905.
35 THOMSEN 1917.
36 PARKER 2006, 534.
37 FINDLATER 2002.

South of Jurf ad-Darawish FINDLATER's survey identified THOMSEN's clusters, nos. 182–184, containing two milestones each, and close to some, an 8-m-wide road was found, with stones along the edges. Contrary to the common opinion that the road from Jurf ad-Darawish led to Da'ajaniya and Udhruh, FINDLATER suggests that in fact it led toward Ma'an. Moreover, he believes that there is no unequivocal evidence that Jurf ad-Darawish was a Roman fort at all.[38] Yet in a later survey conducted in the same area in the course of the Tafila-Busayra project (TBAS), MCDONALD et al. noted that Jurf ad-Darawish (MCDONALD's site no. 141[39]) was a Roman fort measuring 38 x 37 m, with walls 3.41–3.58 m wide and a tower in the northwest corner. MCDONALD rightly notes the similarity of the plan to that of the forts at Bshir and Thuraiya. It is interesting that this survey documented only one cluster of milestones. This cluster, at site TBAS 250,[40] UTM coordinates 7732 3981, about 1.5 km from the Jurf ad-Darawish fort, should be identified as the first mile station south and is probably identical with THOMSEN's cluster no. 182.

As for the milestones near Udruh, a new survey of Udruh documented more than 30 sites that show evidence of the ancient road system in that area.[41] A few of them were previously recorded and although some were still visible and traceable for long stretches, the survey recovered no new milestones along any of the roads.

The two milestone stations near Udruh were part of the evidence used by scholars, for example KILLICK[42] and PARKER,[43] to argue that the *Via Nova Triana* bypassed *Petra* heading to Sadaka via Udruh and Ayl. Yet GRAF[44] presented convincing arguments that the *Via Nova Triana* passed near *Petra*, thus concluding that the milestone stations near Udruh were not on the main road.

GRAF noted that the abovementioned milestones are clustered near forts and camps and do not form a continuous line. He suggested that there was no connecting road between the sites and summarized his view by stating that "...the widely separated milestones near Lejjun and Jurf ad-Darawish perhaps only marked the approaches to the military camps for travelers... In any case the finds are insufficient for postulating a continuous road between these distant points."[45] GRAF believed that none were found with inscriptions because the inscriptions were painted and the paint disappeared over the years.

I fully concur with his view. The milestone near Lejjun relates of course to the large Roman camp in Lejjun, and those of Jurf ad-Darawish to the Roman *castellum*

---

38 FINDLATER 2002, 140.
39 MCDONALD et al. 2004, 285.
40 MCDONALD et al. 2004, 385.
41 ABUDANAH 2006, 101.
42 KILLICK 1987, 173–175.
43 PARKER 1986, 87–88.
44 GRAF 1995.
45 GRAF 1997, 280.

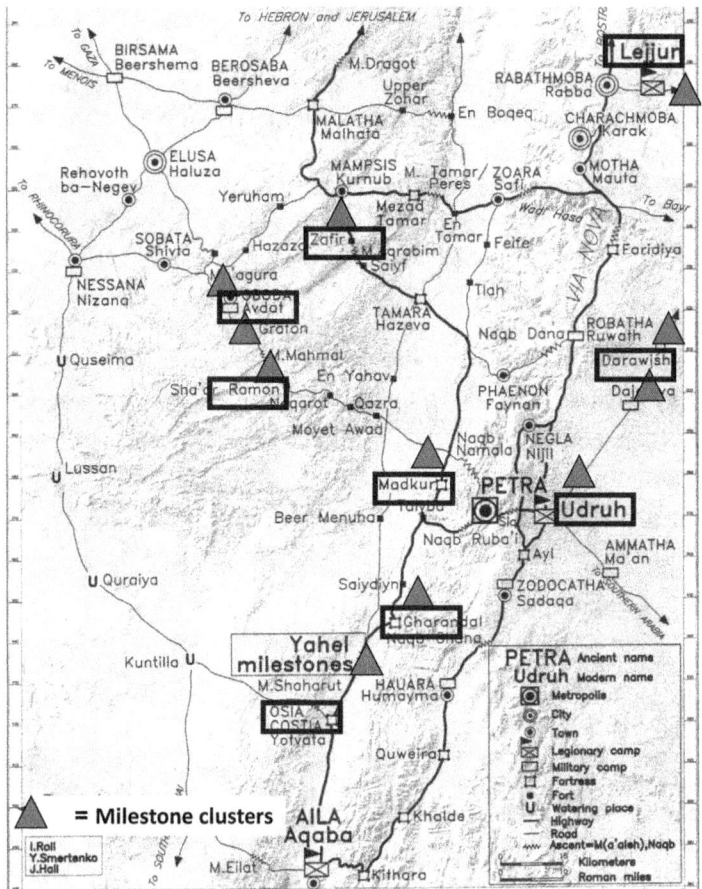

Fig. 7: Milestone clusters in the Negev, Wadi Arabah and southern Jordan with related Roman army installations based on the map in ROLL and AVNER[47]

at the site. The milestones near Udruh relate to the Roman camp where a Diocletian inscription was found and published.[46]

In conclusion, the phenomenon of milestone clusters in the desert areas in *Arabia* and *Palaestina* seems to have been an initiative and labor of local Roman army units (fig.7) – not part of the regular Roman road network connecting major cities. Thus, one must use caution in using these milestone clusters to map a Roman road network.

---

46 KENNEDY/FALAHAT 2008.
47 ROLL/AVNER 2008, 286.

Recent Finds 2018

11 milestones in six milestone stations have been found in the Negev along the incense route in between the two former known groups – the Nafha Plateau to the north and Makhtesh Ramon to the south mentioned above. Two stones have almost full readable inscriptions and another two only few words could be seen. Prof. Benjamin Isaac identified one inscription from the reign of Emperor Pertinax (193–194 CE) mentioning also Publius Aelius Severianus governor of the Roman province of Arabia and another of Septimius Severus (200 CE) mentioning also Marius Perpetuus governor of the Roman province of Arabia. For more information and photos of the milestones see our website http://milestones.kinneret.ac.il – News. The new milestones and inscriptions will be published by Prof. Benjamin Isaac and the author.

Bibliography

ABUDANAH 2006 = F.A. ABUDANAH, Settlement Patterns and Military Organization in the Region of Udruh (Southern Jordan) in the Roman and Byzantine Periods. Unpublished Ph.D. dissertation, Newcastle upon Tyne University.

AVNER/DAVIES/MAGNESS 2004 = U. AVNER/G. DAVIES/J. MAGNESS, The Roman Fort at Yotvata: Interim Report (2003), *JRA* 17, 2004, 405–412.

BEN DAVID 2002 = C. BEN DAVID, The Zoar Ascent – a Newly Discovered Roman Road Connecting Zoar-Safi and the Moabite Plateau, in: P. FREEMAN/J. BENNETT/ Z.T. FIEMA/B. HOFFMANN (ed.), Limes XVIII – Proceedings of the XVIIIth International Congress of Roman Frontier Studies held in Amman, Jordan (September 2000), Oxford 2002, 103–112.

BEN DAVID 2001= C. BEN DAVID, Place Names on Roman Milestones in the Provinces of Palaestina and Arabia, *'Al 'Atar Journal of the Land of Israel Studies* 16, 2001, 27–40 (Hebrew).

BEN DAVID 2012 = C. BEN DAVID, Nabataean or Late Roman? Reconsidering the Date of the Paved Sections and Milestones along the Petra – Gaza Road, in: L. NEHME/L. WADESON (ed.), The Nabataeans in Focus: Current Archaeological Research At Petra, Oxford 2012, 17–26.

BEN DAVID 2017= C. BEN DAVID, The Roads Leading to Zoara in the Roman and Byzantine Periods, in: B. DOLINKA/W. WARD (ed.), The Socio-Economic History and Material Culture of the Roman and Byzantine Near East – Essays in Honor of S. Thomas Parker, Piscataway NJ 2017, 63–87.

BORSTAD 2008 = K.A. BORSTAD, History from Geography: The Initial Route of the Via Nova Traiana in Jordan, *Levant* 40.1, 2008, 55–70.

BRÜNNOW/DOMASZEWSKI 1905 = R.E. BRÜNNOW/A. VON DOMASZEWSKI, Die Provincia Arabia, vol. 2, Straßburg 1905.

COHEN 1967 = R. COHEN, Mesad Yeruham, *IEJ* 17, 1967, 123–124.

COHEN 1976 = R. COHEN, Excavations at Horvat Haluqim, *Atiqot* 11, 1976, 34–50.

COHEN 1982 = R. COHEN, New Light on the Date of the Petra-Gaza Road, *The Biblical Archaeologist* 45, 1982, 240–247.

COHEN 1993 = R. COHEN, Hellenistic, Roman and Byzantine Sites in the Negev Hills, The New Encyclopedia of Archaeological Excavations in the Holy Land, vol. 3, Jerusalem 1993, 1135–1145.

DARBY 2015 = R. DARBY, Aufidius Priscus, the Cohors Secunda Galatarum, and Diocletian's Re-organization of Arabia and Palaestina: the New Tetrarchic Inscription from 'Ayn Gharandal, *JRA* 28, 2015, 471–484.

DARBY/DARBY 2015 = R. DARBY/E. DARBY, The Late Roman Fort at 'Ayn Gharandal, Jordan: Interim Report on the 2009–2014 Field Seasons, *JRA* 28, 2015, 461–470.

DAVIES/MAGNESS 2008 = G. DAVIES/J. MAGNESS, The Roman Fort at Yotvata, 2007, *IEJ* 58.1, 2008, 103–112.

DAVIES/MAGNESS 2015 = G. DAVIES/J. MAGNESS, The 2003–2007 Excavations in the Late Roman Fort at Yotvata. Eisenbrauns, Winona Lake, Indiana 2015.

ERICKSON-GINI 2002 = T. ERICKSON-GINI, Nabataean or Roman? Reconsidering the Date of the Camp at Avdat in Light of Recent Excavations, in: P. FREEMAN/J. BENNETT/Z.T. FIEMA/B. HOFMANN (ed.), Limes XVIII. The Proceedings of the XVIIIth International Congress of Roman Frontier Studies held in Amman, Jordan (September 2000), Oxford 2002, 113–130.

FABIAN 2005 = P. FABIAN, Avdat during the Establishment of Provincia Arabia. Unpublished Ph.D. dissertation, Ben-Gurion University of the Negev, 2005 (Hebrew).

FIGUERAS 1992 = P. FIGUERAS, The Roman Worship of Athena-Allat in the Decapolis and the Negev, *Aram* 4:1, 2, 1992, 173–183.

FINDLATER 2002 = G. FINDLATER, *Limes Arabicus, via militaris* and Resource Control in Southern Jordan, in: P. FREEMAN/J. BENNETT/Z.T. FIEMA/B. HOFMANN (ed.), Limes XVIII. The Proceedings of the XVIIIth International Congress of Roman Frontier Studies held in Amman, Jordan (September 2000), Oxford 2002, 137–152.

GRAF 1995 = D.F. GRAF, The *Via Nova Traiana* in Arabia Petraea, in: J.H. HUMPHREY (ed.), The Roman and Byzantine Near East, vol. 1, Ann Arbor 1995, 141–167.

GRAF 1997 = D.F. GRAF, The Via Militaris in Arabia, *Dumbarton Oak Papers* 51, 1997, 271–281.

HERMON/FABIAN 2002 = S. HERMON/P. FABIAN, Virtual Reconstruction of Archaeological Sites: Some Archaeological Scientific Considerations, in: F. NICCOLUCCI (ed.), Virtual Archaeology, Proceedings of the V.A.S.T. Conference in Arezzo. Italy, Oxford 2002, 103–108.

ISAAC 1998 = B. ISAAC, The Near East Under Roman Rule. Selected Papers, 71–75, New York/Köln 1998.

ISRAEL/ERICKSON-GINI 2001–2002 = Y. ISRAEL/T ERICKSON-GINI, Mesad Horvat Bor, *Bulletin of the Anglo-Israel Society*, 19–20, 2001–2002, 7–17.

KENNEDY/FALAHAT 2008 = D. KENNEDY/H. FALAHAT, Castra Legionis VI Ferratae: A Building Inscription for the Legionary Fortress at Udruh near Petra, *JRA* 21, 2008, 150–169.

KILLICK 1987 = A. KILLICK, Udruh and the Trade Route through Sothern Jordan, in: A. HADIDI (ed.), Studies in the History and Archeology of Jordan, vol. 3, London 1987, 173–179.

MACDONALD 1996 = B. MACDONALD, The Route of the Via Nova Traiana Immediately South of Wadi al Hasa, *PalEQ* 128, 1966, 12–15.

MCDONALD et al. 2004 = B. MCDONALD/L.G. HERR/M.P. NEELEY/T. GAGOS/K. MOUMANI/M. ROCKMAN, The Tafila-Busayra Archaeological Survey 1999–2001, West-Central Jordan, Boston 2004.

MESHEL 1989 = Z. MESHEL, A Fort at Yotvata from the Time of Diocletian, *IEJ* 39, 1989, 228–238.

MESHEL/TSAFRIR 1974 = Z. MESHEL/Y. TSAFRIR, The Nabataean Road from 'Avdat to Sha'ar-Ramon, *PalEQ* 106, 1974, 103–118.

MESHEL/TSAFRIR 1975, 3–8 = Z. MESHEL/Y. TSAFRIR, The Nabataean Road from 'Avdat to Sha'ar-Ramon, *PalEQ* 107, 1975, 3–21.

MITTMANN 1982 = S. MITTMANN, The Ascent of Luhit, in: ed. A. HADIEH (ed.), Amman, Studies in the History and Archeology of Jordan, vol. 1, Amman 1982, 175–180.

NEGEV 1966 = A. NEGEV, The Date of the Petra-Gaza Road, *PalEQ* 88, 1966, 89–98.

PARKER 1986 = S.T. PARKER, Romans and Saracens: A History of the Arabia Frontier, Philadelphia 1986.

PARKER 2006 = S.T. PARKER, The Roman Frontier in Central Jordan, Final Report on the Limes Arabicus Project, 1980–1989, Washington D.C. 2006.

ROLL 1989 = I. ROLL, A Latin Imperial Inscription from the Time of Diocletian Found at Yotvata', *IEJ* 39, 1989, 239–260.

Roll/Avner 2008 = I. Roll/U. Avner, Tetrarchic Milestones found near Yahel in the Southern Aravah, ZPE 165, 2008, 267–286.

Smith 2005 = A.M. Smith II, Bir Madhkur Project: A Preliminary Report on Recent Fieldwork, *BASO* 340, 2005, 57–75.

Smith 2010 = A.M. Smith II, Wadi Araba in Classical and Late Antiquity: An Historical Geography, Oxford 2010.

Thomsen 1917 = P. Thomsen, Die römischen Meilensteine der Provinzen Syria, Arabia, und Palastina, *Zeitschrift des Deutschen Palastina-Vereins* 40, 1917, 1–103.

Mustafa H. Sayar
Römische Straßen und Meilensteine im Ebenen Kilikien

Abstract: The relatively secure dates of the milestones found so far prove that the roads in the Cilician plain were expanded from the middle of the 2nd century onwards. Up until the fall of the Parthian Empire in 224 CE, expansion and maintenance of the road network in Kilikia Pedias were intensified due to the increasing campaigns against the Parthians, because the state of these main routes for the movement of troops to the front were strategically crucial for the fate of the Roman Empire. This construction activity continued after the founding of the Sassanian Empire in the year 224 CE until the raid by the Sassanian king Sapor I. in 260 CE. The road network saw its next phase of renewal only after the devastation of urban life in the first quarter of the 4th century as a result of the increasing military activity against the Sassanians during the first tetrarchy, when Diocletian carried out administrative, economic, political and military reforms throughout the empire.

Zusammenfassung: Die relativ sicheren Datierungen der bisher gefundenen Meilensteine stellen unter Beweis, dass die Straßen im Ebenen Kilikien ab der Mitte des 2. Jhs. ausgebaut worden sind. Ausbau und Erneuerung der Straßen in Kilikia Pedias wurden bis zum Untergang des Partherreiches 224 n. Chr. mit den zunehmenden Feldzügen gegen die Parther wesentlich intensiver durchgeführt, weil der Zustand dieser Hauptverbindungswege für die Truppenverlegungen zum Kriegsgebiet eine entscheidende strategische Rolle für das Schicksal des römischen Reiches spielte. Diese Bautätigkeit wurde nach der Gründung des sassanidischen Reiches im Jahre 224 n. Chr. bis zum Überfall des Sassanidenkönigs Sapor I. im Jahre 260 n. Chr. fortgesetzt. Eine weitere Phase der Erneuerung des Straßennetzes im Ebenen Kilikien erfolgte erst nach der Verwüstung des städtischen Lebens im ersten Viertel des 4. Jhs. infolge der zunehmenden Feldzüge gegen die Sassaniden während der ersten Tetrarchie, als Diocletian administrative, wirtschaftliche, politische und militärische Reformen im gesamten Reich durchführte.

In der Landschaft Kilikiens voller Extreme und Gegensätzlichkeiten entwickelten sich im Laufe der Jahrhunderte Wege,[1] die bestimmt waren vom Gelände und der natürlichen Gliederung der Landschaft.[2] Diese von der Natur vorgezeichneten Wege verban-

---

[1] Zu hethitischen und assyrischen Verbindungswegen JASINK 1991, 253–259; FORLANINI 2013, 1–34.
[2] Zu den geographischen Gegebenheiten Kilikiens SCHAEFFER 1903, 13; HELLENKEMPER/HILD 1990, 22–29.

den die Küste mit dem anatolischen Hochland, führten also zumeist vom Süden nach Norden.³ In den gebirgigen Teilen Kilikiens orientierten sie sich an den Flussläufen.

Die Existenz der Straßenverbindungen an der Küste und über die Pässe wird durch mehrere antike Quellen, die von historisch wichtigen Feldzügen berichten, bezeugt: Die bekanntesten sind die Feldzüge des Kyros⁴, die von Xenophon beschrieben wurden, sowie die Feldzüge Alexanders des Großen. Ferner werden in den Briefen Ciceros, die er während seiner Statthalterschaft verfasste, mehrere Straßen erwähnt. Diese natürlichen Wege und Pässe waren nur in den trockenen Jahreszeiten benutzbar.⁵

ULUĞ BAHADIR ALKIM und HALET ÇAMBEL von der Universität Istanbul untersuchten die römischen und spätantiken Straßenverbindungen und Pässe im nortdöstlichen Ebenen Kilikien nach Kappadokien.⁶ Im Laufe des letzten Viertels des 20. Jhs. forschte DAVID FRENCH, der frühere Direktor des Britisch Archäologischen Instituts, zu römischen Straßen und Meilensteinen Kleinasiens und publizierte neben anderen Regionen auch die Meilensteine aus Kilikien.⁷ Neben FRENCH haben FRIEDRICH HILD von der Akademie der Wissenschaften und HANSGERD HELLENKEMPER, früherer Direktor des Römisch-Germanischen Museums in Köln, Kilikien bereist und publizierten im fünften Band der Publikationsreihe *Tabula Imperii Byzantini*.⁸ Sie haben folgende Hauptverbindungswege im Ebenen Kilikien identifiziert:

1) Die Nordwest-Südost-Verbindung durch die Pylai Kilikiai nach Nordsyrien kann als Hauptverkehrsader verfolgt werden.
2) Die zweite wichtige Straße ist die West-Ost Verbindung entlang der Küste, die von Side in Pamphylien bis Seleukeia Pierias in Nordsyrien führte.
3) Die zahlreichen Nord-Süd-Verbindungen, die die wichtigsten Zentren Lykaoniens und Kappadokiens mit der Mittelmeerküste verbinden; von Westen nach Osten:
   a) Ikonion – Ad fines -Tetrapyrgia – Pompeiopolis.
   b) Kaisareia am Argaios – Rodandos – Baka – Sision – Adana – Mallos.
   c) Von Kaisareia am Argaios – Rodandos – Baka – Sision – Anazarbos – Mopsouhestia – Aigeai.
   d) Kukusos – Flavioupolis – Kastabala – Epiphaneia.
   e) Die an der Nahtstelle von Taurus- und Amanus-Gebirge gelegenen Straßenverbindungen, die Kilikien mit Syrien und Kommagene verbinden.⁹

---

3 HILD/HELLENKEMPER 1990, 128–140.
4 WILLIAMS 1996, 284–314.
5 Während des Bürgerkrieges zwischen Septimius Severus und Pescennius Niger mußten die Truppen Nigers die Besetzung der Pylai Kilikiai wegen des schlechten Wetters vorzeitig räumen Herodian. 3,3,7.
6 ALKIM 1965, 1– 41.
7 RRMAM III 7.
8 HELLENKEMPER/HILD 1986, 87–99. und HELLENKEMPER/HILD 1990, 128–142.
9 Neue Vorschläge zu dieser Strecke, s. KAPLAN 2017, 703–714.

Alle diese Straßen wurden während der Untersuchungen des Verfassers im Ebenen Kilikien zwischen 1990 und 2000 untersucht und ein Vorbericht über die damaligen Ergebnisse wurde im Rahmen eines Kolloquiums der Ernst Kirsten Gesellschaft in Stuttgart 2002 präsentiert.[10]

Im Folgenden werden die Straßenzüge vorgelegt, die durch die neuen Meilensteinfunde der letzten 15 Jahre besser bezeugt sind.

Erst mit der Wiedereinrichtung der Provinz Cilicia unter Vespasian im Jahre 72 n. Chr. wurden die Fernverbindungen zwischen den größeren Städten und damit zwischen Kleinasien und Syrien zu festen Straßen ausgebaut[11]. Durch dieses ganzjährig nutzbare Straßennetz gelang es, die Wirtschaft in der neuen Provinz zu unterstützen. Die römisch-frühbyzantinischen Itinerarien bezeugen zahlreiche *mansiones* und *mutationes*, es gelang jedoch bisher nicht, diese Bauten zu identifizieren.

Die Hauptstraßenverbindung begann in Antiocheia am Orontes und führte durch das Ebene Kilikien über die Kilikische Pforte nach Kappadokien.[12] Der markanteste Punkt dieser Strecke ist zweifellos die Kilikische Pforte, von den antiken Autoren Pylai Kilikiai genannt,[13] heute als Gülek-Pass bekannt.

In mittelalterlichen Quellen wurde die dortige Festung Kuklak oder Guglag genannt, in arabische Quellen ist sie als Hişn Bulas bekannt.[14] Zwei Meilensteine wurden im Norden des Gülek-Passes im kappadokischen Territorium gefunden, die in das Jahr 216 bzw. 217, in die Zeit von Caracalla bzw. Macrinus datiert werden und beweisen, dass diese Strecke *via Tauri* genannt wurde.[15]

Am Gülek-Pass deckt sich der Verlauf der antiken Straße mit der modernen vor 25 Jahren fertiggestellten Autobahn.

---

10 SAYAR 2002, 452–472.
11 Zur Diskussion über die Datierung der ersten Provinzwerdung Kilikiens KREILER 2007, 117–124; zur erneuten Gründung der *provincia Cilicia* VITALE 2012, 291–306.
12 Zur Kilikischen Pforte HILD/HELLENKEMPER 1990, 386; DESTEPHEN 2016, 260–261 und 280; zur Fortsetzung der Hauptverbindungsstraße in Kappadokien BERGES/NOLLÉ 2000, 14–22; zu einer an der kilikischen Pforte gefundenen lateinischen Inschrift über die Heuschreckenplage BERGES/NOLLÉ 2000, 290–292 Nr. 134.
13 Plin. nat. 5,98; Amm. 21,9,13; RAMSAY 1903, 357–410.
14 HELLENKEMPER/HILD 1990, 323 f.
15 RRMAM III 3, 165 (Kırkgeçit 217/8 n. Chr.) = AE 2009, 1527: ... *viam]/ Tauri montis fr[equentissi]/mis inluvionibus [dirutam ac cae]/sis rupibus ac dilat[atis itineri]/bus cum pontibus [institutis]/[restit]utam perfece[runt.] A Pylas ...* ; der zweite Meilenstein wurde nördlich von Podandos (=Pozantı) 15 Meilen nördlich der kilikischen Tore gefunden, dazu BERGES/NOLLÉ 2000, 288–289 Nr. 132; RRMAM III 3, 166 (216/7 n. Chr.) = AE 1969/70, 607: ... *viam Tauri vetustate / [conl]apsam conplanatis monti/[bus e]t caesis rupibus · ac dilata/[tis i]tineribus cum pontibus / institutis restituit. / A Pylas m(ilia) p(assuum) XV.*

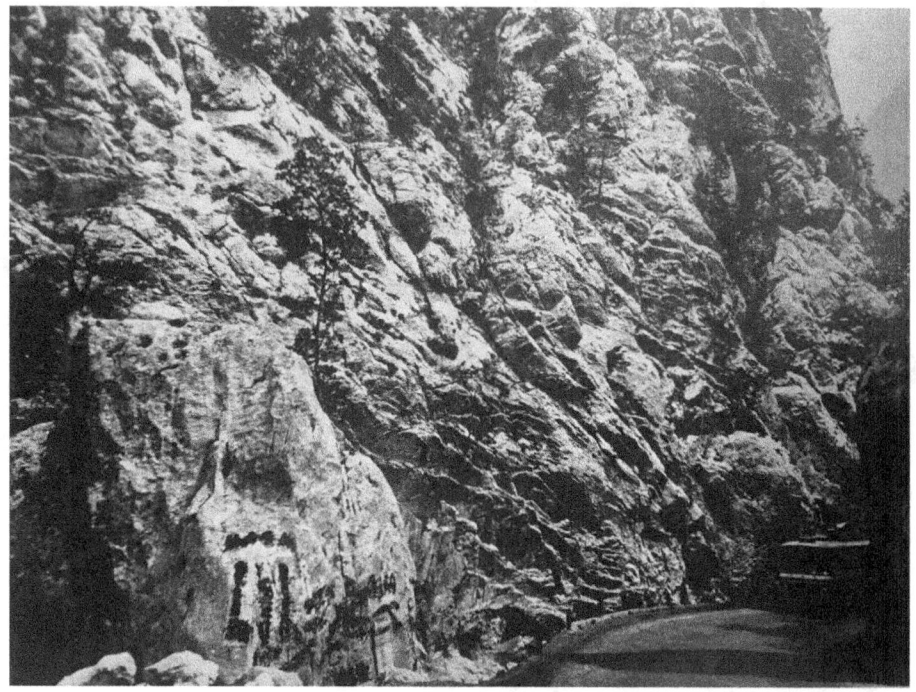

Abb. 1: Kilikische Pforte vor dem Autobahnbau (Foto F. Hild)

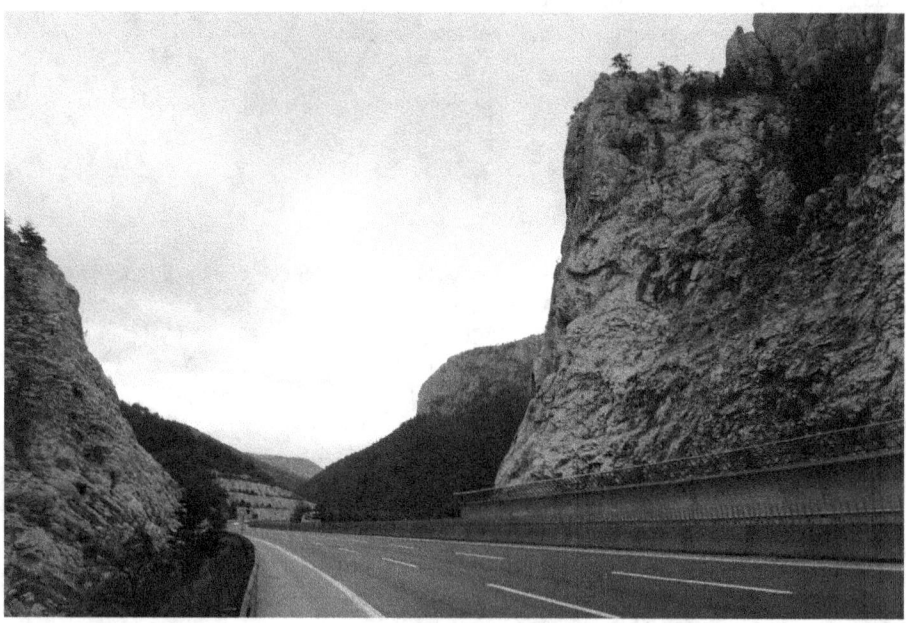

Abb. 2: Ansicht der Kilikischen Pforte nach dem Bau der Autobahn (Foto: Verfasser)

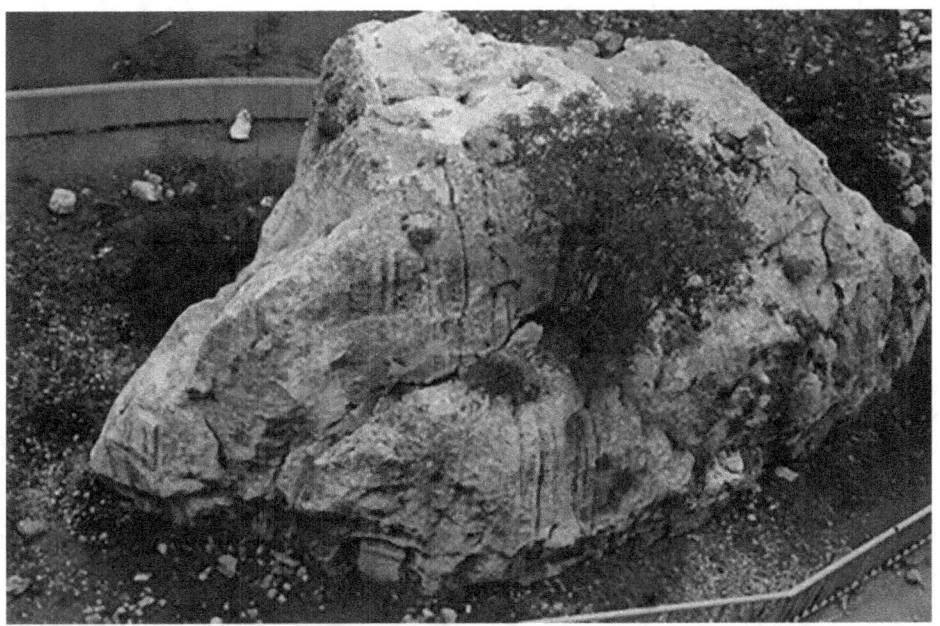

Abb. 3: Felssporn an der engsten Stelle der Kilikischen Pforte (Foto: Verfasser)

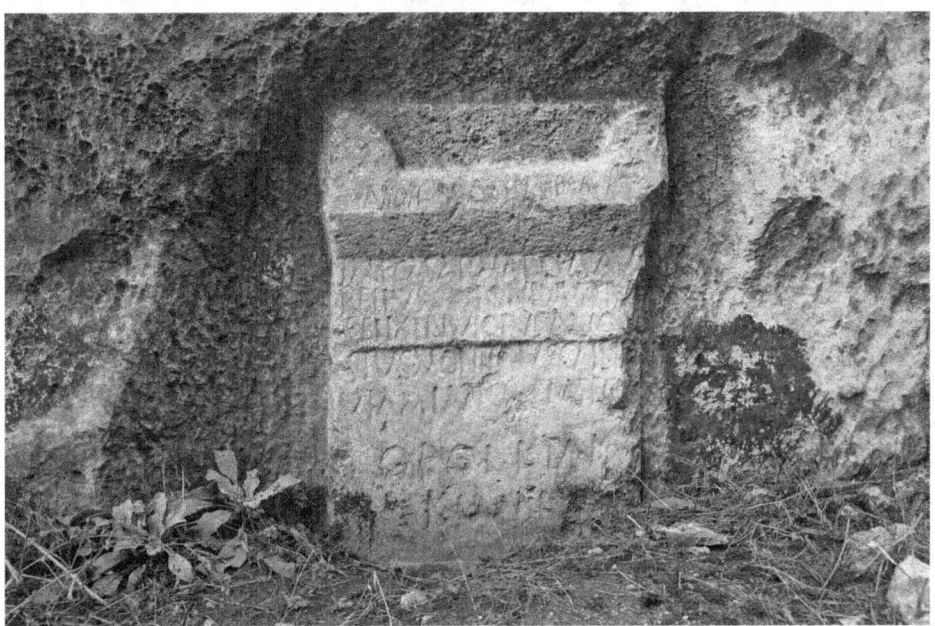

Abb. 4: Felsaltar an der Kilikischen Pforte (Foto: Verfasser)

Die engste Stelle der kilikischen Pforte wurde beim Bau der Autobahn vor etwa 30 Jahren teilweise zerstört. Eine seit 200 Jahren bekannte an der Ostseite der Pforte befindliche Grenzinschrift in griechischer Schrift auf einem Felsaltar ist dank einer Schutzmauer erhalten geblieben.

Auf dem Altar, der heute noch als Alexander-Stein bekannt ist, ist oberhalb der griechischen Grenzinschrift eine lateinische Bauinschrift aus der Zeit des Kaisers Marcus Aurelius Antoninus eingemeißelt, auf der der Name Antoninus eradiert wurde.[16]

Nach früherer Editionen dieser Inschrift handelt es sich bei dem Kaiser Marcus Aurelius Antoninus um Caracalla[17]. Wenn man aber die Tilgung bei dem Kaisernamen als eine Reflektierung der verhängten *damnatio memoriae* betrachtet, so war dies für Caracalla nur beschränkt der Fall. Denn für Caracalla wurde weder eine offizielle *consecratio* beschlossen noch gegen ihn die *damnatio memoriae* verhängt[18]. Trotzdem war sein Name aus den Inschriften teilweise eradiert. Ein anderer Kaiser, der den gleichen Name hatte wie Caracalla, war Elagabal. Als Augustus hieß er allerdings *Marcus Aurelius Antoninus Pius Felix invictus Augustus*, wie auf der Inschrift am Felsaltar eingemeißelt ist, während Caracalla den Titel *invictus* erst 211 n. Chr. erhielt.[19] Über Elagabal wurde nach seiner Ermordung im Jahre 222 n. Chr die *damnatio memoriae* verhängt.[20] Somit dürfte die Inschrift an den Pylai Kilikiai erst unter Elagabal eingemeißelt worden sein.[21] Diese Grenz- bzw. Bauinschrift bezeichnet die Grenze zwischen Kilikien und Kappadokien.[22] Die in den letzten zwei Zeilen angegebene Grenzinschrift in griechischen Buchstaben – ὅροι Κιλίκων – aus der Zeit des Kaisers Marcus Aurelius Antoninus (Elagabal) markiert die Grenze zwischen zwei römischen Provinzen. Nach dieser Inschrift ließ der Kaiser hier den Pass erweitern, um den Durchmarsch der Truppen, die wegen des Partherkrieges zunehmend nach Osten verlegt wurden, zu erleichtern. Eine fast gleich lautende Inschrift, die heute fast völlig verwittert ist, wurde an einer Felswand an der nach Süden führenden antiken Straße eingemeißelt[23]. Aus dem südlichen Bereich der kilikischen

---

16 CIL III 227; CIL I 12118; CIL III 14177[11]; LANGLOIS 1854, 78 Nr. 31; LANGLOIS 1861 ; HARPER 1970, 149–153; HILD 1977, 58 Abb. 24, 25; RRMAM I app. 1; HELLENKEMPER/HILD 1990, 132 f.: *Imp(erator) Cas(ar) (sic!) Marcus Au/relius [[Antoninus]] Pius / Felix invictus Aug/ustus montibus caisis (sic!) / viam latiorem fecit /* ὅροι Κιλίκων.
17 RRMAM I app. 1.
18 Cass. Dio 79,17,2; KIENAST 2017, 157.
19 KIENAST 2017, 157.
20 Cass. Dio 79,3,3; KIENAST 2017, 165.
21 So auch bei BERGES/NOLLÉ 2000, 292–293 Nr. 135; HAYMANN 2014, 255 und Anm. 1680.
22 HELLENKEMPER/HILD 1990, 132.
23 CIL III 228; RRMAM I app. 4. *Imp(erator) Caes(ar) [Ma]rcu[s] Au/relius Pius Fel[i]x Inv[i]ctu[s] / Aug(ustus) montibus caesis / [vi]am latiore[m fecit ---]*; zu CIL III 228 und zur Via Tauri ferner SPANU 2016, 29–56, bes. 36–37 und Abb. 5-6-7, nach der Zeichnung in Abb. 7 ist unterhalb des Altars eine zweizeilige griechische Inschrift lesbar: κωμῶν κυρια[κ]ῶν.

Pforte sind zwei weitere Meilensteininschriften aus der Zeit des Kaisers Severus Alexander bekannt[24].

Darüber hinaus kam während des Autobahnbaus ein weiterer Meilenstein ans Tageslicht, der unter Caracalla errichtet worden war. Die lateinische Inschrift des Meilensteins, in der vom Straßenbau in diesem Bereich die Rede ist, ist in das Jahr 214 n. Chr zu datieren. Nach dieser Inschrift hat Caracalla in diesem unbesiedelten Gebiet eine neue Straße (*via nova*) errichten lassen. Vielleicht wurde auch die Felsinschrift im Zuge der Straßenbauarbeiten im Jahre 214 errichtet. Die Bezeichnug *via nova* für diese Strecke, die sich nach Süden in Richtung Tarsos fortsetzt, findet sich auch auf einem anderen Meilenstein, der nach der Inschrift 23 römische Meilen außhalb der Provinzhauptstadt Tarsos in der Zeit der Samtherrschaft von Antoninus Pius und Marcus Aurelius zwischen 139 und 161 n. Chr. errichtet worden war.[25] Es sieht so aus, dass das Straßennetz im Territorium der Provinzhauptstadt Tarsos zwischen der kilikischen Pforte und Tarsos im Zuge der Vorbereitungen des bevorstehenden Partherfeldzuges ausgebaut worden ist[26]. Dieser Teil wurde als *via nova* bezeichnet, während die Strecke nördlich der kilikischen Pforte auf dem kappadokischen Boden sowohl als *via Tauri* und auch *via nova* genannt worden war[27]. Andere Meilensteine im nördlichen Bereich der Kilikischen Pforte auf dem Kappadokischen Boden sind aus den Regierungszeiten verschiedener römischer Kaiser von Severus Alexander bis Gordian III und sogar bis Licinius und Constantinus Magnus bezeugt.[28]

Alle diese Meilensteine zeigen, dass diese Hauptverbindung über Kappadokien durch die Kilikische Pforte zwischen Podandos (modern Pozantı) und die Kilikische Pforte selbst (Gülek-Pass) nach der Gründung der Provinz Cilicia im Jahre 72 n. Chr. unter Vespasian zunehmend strategische Bedeutung gewann. Es dürfte diese Strecke schon im 2. Jh. n. Chr. unter den Antoninen ausgebaut worden sein, wie der kürzlich gefundene Meilenstein unter Beweis stellt. Der Grund dafür könnten die Vorberei-

---

24 RRMAM I app. 3 und app. 2: *[-------]s viam/ et [ponte]s a Pylis / us[que ad] Alexa[n]dream / ex in[te] gro restituit*; nach BERGES/NOLLÉ 2000, 293–294, Nr. 136: *[Kaiser Severus Alexander] stellte den Weg und die Brücken von den Kilikischen Toren bis nach Alexandreia von neuem wieder her.*
25 Der Ausdruck *via nova* ist auch auf der nördlichen Fortsetzung der Hauptstraße durch zwei Meilensteininschriften bezeugt, die im Territorium der *colonia Archealis* (= Aksaray) in Kappadokien gefunden worden sind. Beide Meilensteine sind zwischen Mai und Juni 217 n. Chr. unter der Samtherrschaft von Macrinus und Diadumenianus errichtet; RRMAM III 3, 159 (Topakkaya/Aksaray) und RRMAM III 3, 161 (Demirci/Aksaray).
26 Zur Bautatigkeit unter Antoninus Pius ECK 2017, 215 bes. 220–228.
27 BERGES/NOLLÉ 2000, 288–289; HAYMANN 2014, 255, Anm. 1678; vgl. auch o. Anm. 23.
28 RRMAM I app. 2–3; RRMAM III 3, 162C Kemerhisar (Severus Alexander). 163B Kavuklu (Severus Alexander). 164 Eminlik (Severus Alexander). 164B (Severus Alexander) und 168 Podandos (Severus Alexander); RRMAM III 3, 162A Kemerhisar (Gordianus III/ Constantinus Magnus und Crispus), 162B Kemerhisar (Constantinus-Constantius-Constans) (333–337 n. Chr.), 163A Kavuklu (Gordianus III), 165 Kırkgeçit Deresi (Macrinus), 166 Pozantı (Caracalla), 167 Pozantı (Licinius und Constantine).

tungen für die bevorstehenden Partherkriege unter Marcus Aurelius sein. Zu Beginn des 3. Jhs. n. Chr., während der Feldzüge gegen die Parther, wurde auch diese Strecke jedenfalls mehrfach erweitert und ausgebaut um den Truppentransport zu erleichtern.[29]

Im weiteren Verlauf der Straße liegt nach dem *Itinerarium Burdigalense* eine Straßenstation, die *Mopsukrene* hieß und nach Entfernungsangaben verschiedener Itineraren etwa 22 km südlich der Kilikischen Pforte lag. (Karte) Die genaue Lokalisation wird zwischen Kırıtlar und Hacıhamzalı vermutet.[30] Zwischen Kırıtlar und Sağlıklı ist ein etwa 5 km langes Straßenstück mit Pflastersteinen sichtbar[31]. Der am besten erhaltene Teil dieser wichtigen Verbindungsstraße ist seit Mitte des 19. Jhs. bekannt. Am südlichen Ende dieser Strecke befindet sich ein Straßentor, das ins 5. oder 6. Jh. n. Chr. datiert wird.

Ungefähr in der Mitte dieser Strecke liegt ein Meilenstein mit einer lateinischen Inschrift. Aus dieser Inschrift geht hervor, dass der Meilenstein während der ersten Tetrarchie in den Jahren 306/307 n. Chr. errichtet wurde.[32]

In der letzten Zeile dieses Meilensteins wird die Entfernung von Tarsos angegeben: 12 Meilen. Diese Angabe stimmt mit der Entfernung von dem Fundort bis zur Provinzhauptstadt Tarsos, nämlich 17 km, ungefähr überein.

Der Kaiser, der auf den Meilensteininschriften auf dieser Strecke am häufigsten genannt wird, ist Severus Alexander, der auch in der Provinzhauptstadt Tarsos mehrfach geehrt wurde.[33]

Nach dem *Itinerarium Burdigalense* verläuft diese Strecke über Tarsos Richtung Adana weiter. Vor einigen Jahren kamen am Bach Çakıt, ca. 5 km östlich von Tarsos, zwei Meilensteinfragmente mit stark zerstörten lateinischen Inschriften zutage, die an der Straße zwischen Tarsos und Adana errichtet worden waren. Nach den erhaltenen Resten der Inschriften wurde einer dieser Meilensteine wahrscheinlich während der Samtherrschaft von Constantinus II., Constantius II. und Constans zwischen 337–340 errichtet. In der letzten Zeile der Inschrift auf dem zweiten Fragment ist die Entfernungsangabe 3 Meilen lesbar, die mit der Entfernung der Fundstelle von Tarsos übereinstimmt.

Der weitere Verlauf dieser Strecke über Adana – Mopsuhestia nach Syrien mit zahlreichen Stationen ist durch mehrere Itinerarien gesichert. Ein Meilenstein aus der

---

29 Sheldon 2010, 54.
30 Hellenkemper/Hild 1990, 359–360.
31 Harada/Cimok 2008, 304.
32 RRMAM III 7, 39 (Bayramlı); Spanu 2016, 38–39.
33 Le Bas/Waddington 1847–1877; Waddington 1883, 281–292, Nr. 2; IGR III 880; OGIS 578; G. Laminger-Pascher 1974, 31–68; Dagron/Feissel 1988, 74 Nr. 30 Taf. XVI; Pilhofer 2015, 159 f.; Sayar 2016, 177–186.

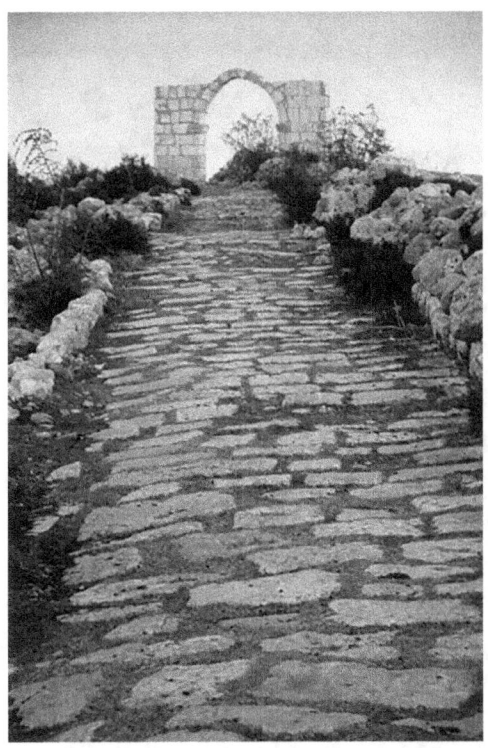

Abb. 5: Straßentor bei Sağlıklı im nördlichen Territorium von Tarsos (Foto: Verfasser)

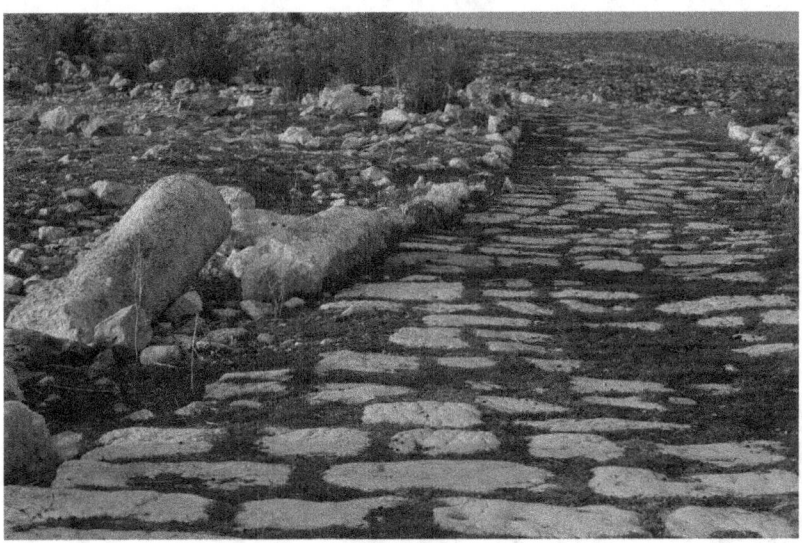

Abb. 6: Römische Straße mit umgestürztem Meilenstein aus der Zeit der zweiten Tetrarchie zwischen Mopsoukrene und Tarsos (Foto: Verfasser)

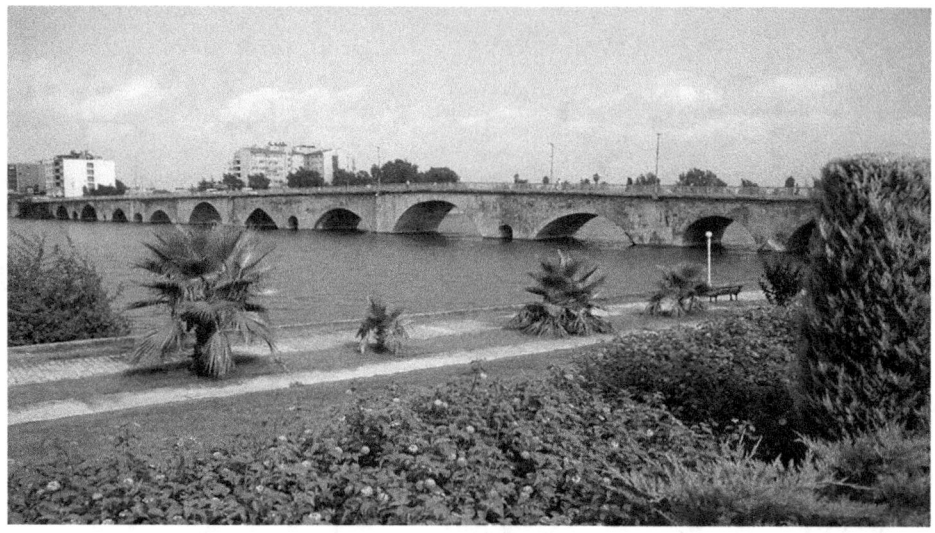

Abb. 7: Brücke bei Adana (Foto: Verfasser)

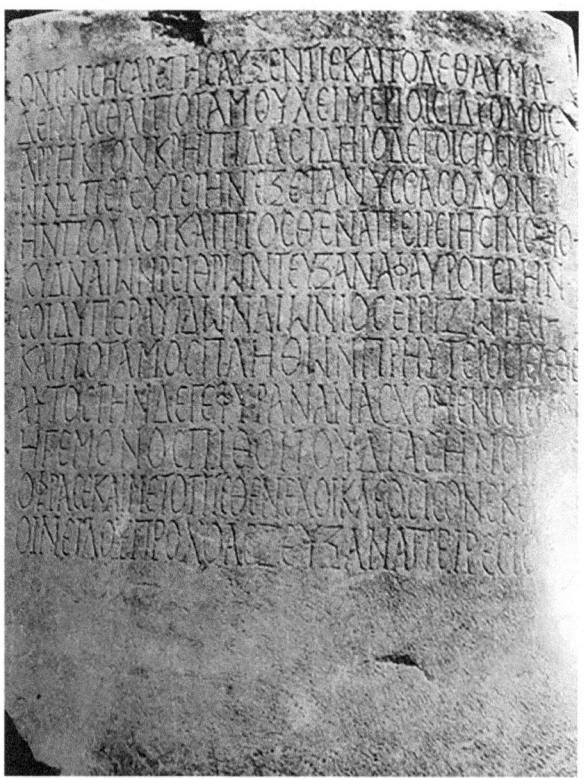

Abb. 8: Brückenbauinschirft aus Adana (CIG III 4440) (Foto: Verfasser)

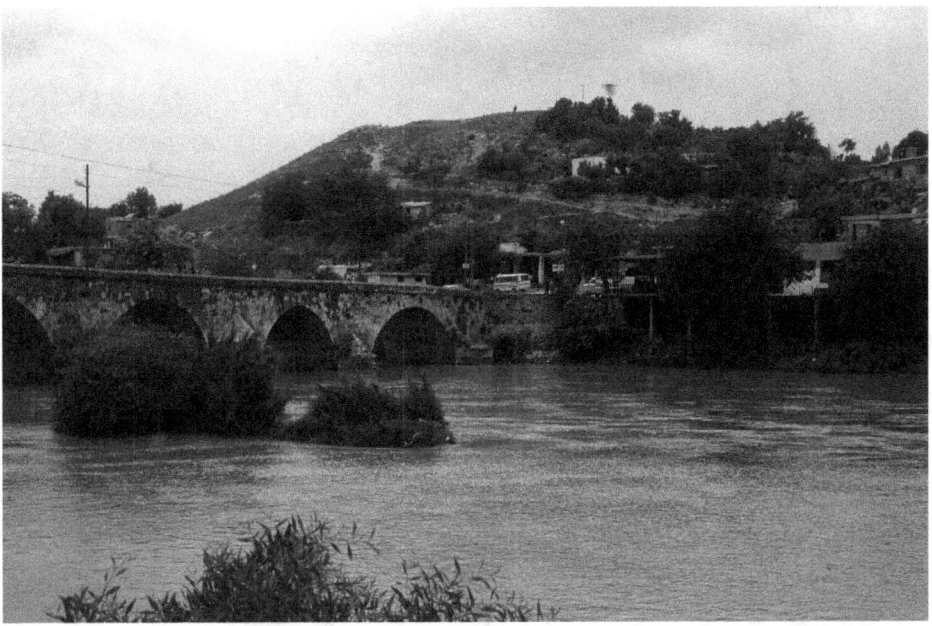

Abb. 9: Brücke über den Pyramos bei Mopsuhestia (Foto: Verfasser)

Gegend von Adana, der unter Kaiser Severus Alexander im Jahre 230/1 n. Chr. errichtet wurde, ist zu Beginn des vergangenen Jahrhunderts bei İncirlik, etwa 2,5 km nordöstlich des antiken Stadtzentrums gefunden worden.[34]

Ein wichtiges archäologisches Zeugnis auf dieser Strecke ist die Brücke, die von Hadrian über den Saros errichtet wurde. Nach etlichen Reparaturen wird diese Brücke noch heute benutzt.

Eine weitere Brücke auf dieser Strecke wurde von Kaiser Valerian für größere Truppentransporte bei Mopsuhestia über den Pyramos errichtet.[35]

Aus Mopsuhestia selbst sind zwei Meilensteine bekannt; einer mit lateinischer Inschrift ist in der Zeit von Severus Alexander im Jahre 223 errichtet worden;[36] ein weiterer, auf dem zwei lateinische Inschriftentexte engemeißelt worden sind, wurde in einem Zeitraum zwischen 367–375 errichtet.[37]

---

34 RRMAM I 64 = RRMAM III 7, 41 (Adana).
35 Zu dieser Brücke Anth. Pal. 9,698: Μόψου τήνδ' ἐσορᾷς κλεινὴν πόλιν, ἥν ποτε μάντις / δείματο τῷ ποταμῷ κάλλος ὑπερκρεμάσας; PÉKARY 1966, 139–141.
36 CIL III 226; CIL III 974; RRMAM I 65 a = RRMAM III 7, 42A.
37 CIL III 13624; RRMAM I 65 b = RRMAM III 7, 42B.

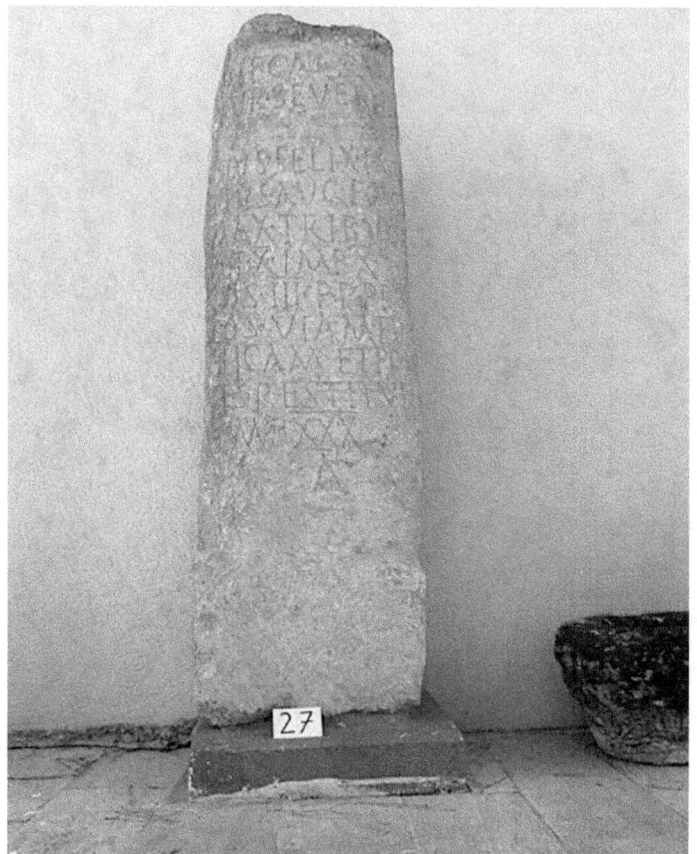

Abb. 10: Meilenstein aus Adana; Errichtet unter Severus Alexander 230/1 n. Chr. (Foto: Verfasser)

Auf beiden Meilensteininschriften ist neben dem Ausbau der Straßen auch von den Reparaturen der Brücken die Rede. Es handelt sich dabei sehr wahrscheinlich um die Brücken über Saros und Pyramos.

Nach Mopsuhestia zweigt eine Straße nach Süden ab und führt zur ostkilikischen Hafenstadt Aigeai.[38]

Ein in den letzten Jahren im südlichen Territorium von Mopsuhestia gefundener Meilenstein aus der Regierungszeit Vespasians liefert einen neuen Beweis für diese Strecke. Die angegebene Entfernungsangabe von 48 Meile stellt unter Beweis, daß die Entfernung von der Provinzhauptstadt Tarsos aus berechnet wurde. Diese Entfernung beträgt etwa 71 km und stimmt ungefähr mit der heutigen Strecke von etwa 70 km zwischen Mopsuhestia und Tarsos überein.

---

38 Hellenkemper/Hild 1990, 160–163; Haymann 2012, 135–141; Haymann 2014.

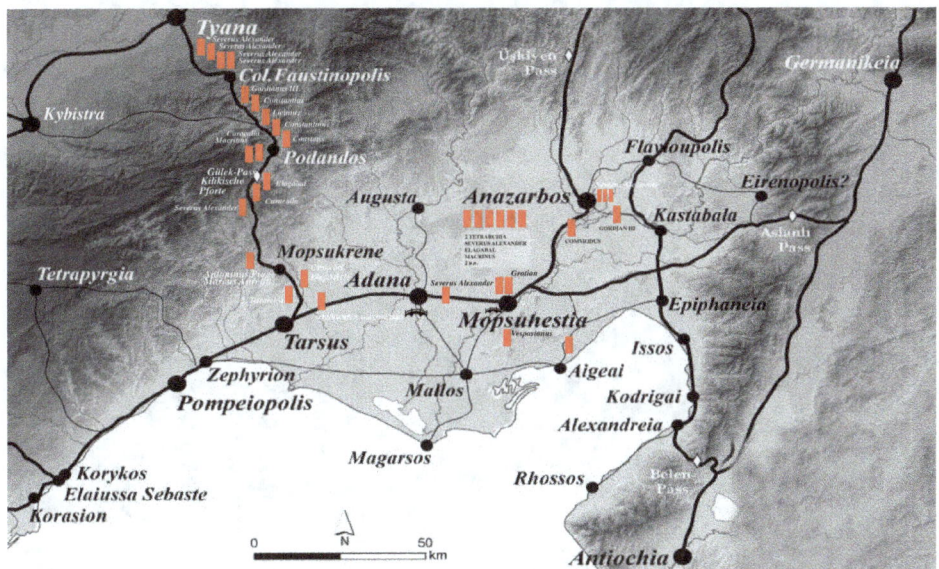

Karte der antiken Straßen im Ebenen Kilikien

Die Hauptstraße verläuft nach Mopsuhestia entlang des linken Ufers des Pyramos nach Osten, wahrscheinlich über den Harami-Pass nach Kurtkulağı, wo die *mansio Tardequeia* lokalisiert wird.[39]

Eine andere Straße, die nach Adana über Mallos zur oben genannten Straße bei Tardequeia führte, ist uns durch die Beschreibung von Arrian bekannt.[40] Nach Arr. an. 2,5,9, überquerte Alexander den Fluss Pyramos bei Mallos[41]. Die Lage der Stadt Mallos wird beim Dorf Kızıltahta vermutet, wo heute noch die Reste einer alten Brücke und eine Wassermühle aus osmanischer Zeit mit Fundamenten aus der römischen Kaiserzeit sichtbar sind.

Diese Straße verlief, nachdem sie bei Kızıltahta den Pyramos überquerte, über Aigeai nach Norden und erreichte über Narlıören die große Verbindungsstraße bei der *mansio Tardequeia*. In Narlıören hat der Verfasser ein Meilensteinfragment mit lateinischer Inschrift gefunden, welche die Reparatur einer bereits bestehenden Straße dokumentiert.

Nach Kurtkulağı führte die Straße über Kızlarkuyusu (auch Kızlarsuyu genannt), wo ein Meilenstein aus der Zeit der ersten Tetrarchie gefunden wurde.[42] Die Entfernungsangabe von 11 Meilen dürfte die Entfernung von Aigeai markiert haben. Diese

---

39 HELLENKEMPER/HILD 1990, 427.
40 HELLENKEMPER/HILD 1990, 337.
41 HAYMANN 2014, 250.
42 RRMAM I 66 = RRMAM III 7, 37.

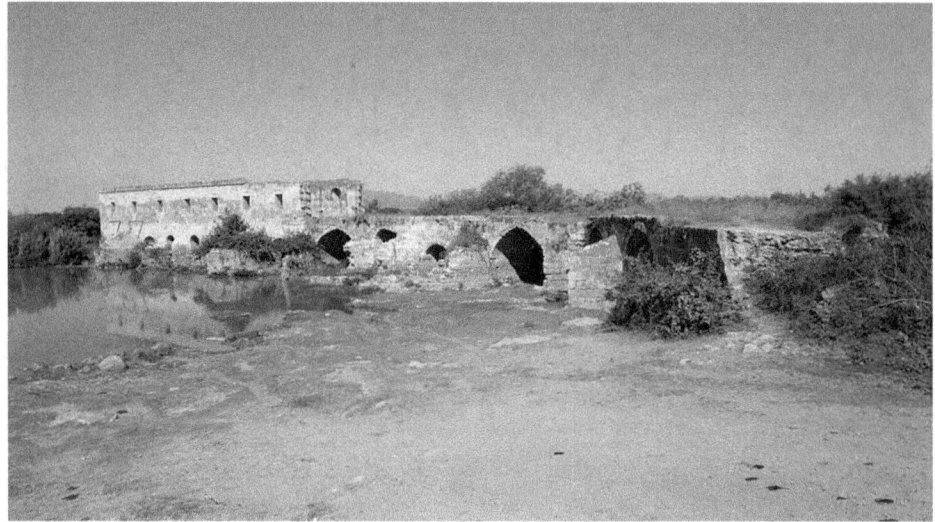

Abb. 11: Reste einer Brücke und Wassermühle am Pyramos bei Kızıltahta (Foto: Verfasser)

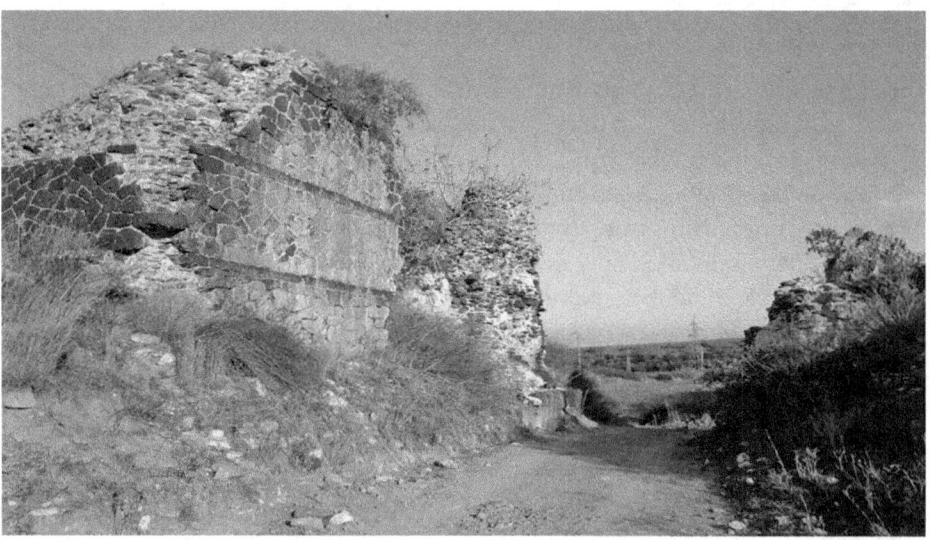

Abb. 12: Karanlıkkapı; (Foto: Verfasser)

Verkehrsverbindung verläuft von Kızlarkuyusu nach Karanlıkkapı, einer Toranlage,[43] und durch diese weiter in Richtung Muttalip Höyük am Golf von Issos, wo die *mansio Catabolo* lokalisiert wird.[44]

Von hier führte die Straße das Nordufer des Issikos Kolpos entlang, südlich der Stadt *Epiphaneia*[45] bei Burnaz Han und Kinet Höyük vorbei.[46] Sie erreichte nach 17 Meilen die *mansio Baiae* (= heute Payaş).[47] Ca. 12 km südlich von *Baiae* lief die Straße am Ufer des Meeres an einem Bogenmonument vorbei.[48] Dieses Denkmal, dessen Fundamenreste noch sichtbar sind, wurde kürzlich als Bogenmonument des Germanicus identifiziert.[49] Nach weiteren 10 km erreicht man *Alexandreia* mit dem Beinamen *kat'Isson* (= heute İskenderun). Nach dem *Itinerarium Burdigalense* beträgt die Entfernung von *Baiae* bis *Alexandreia*[50] 16 Meilen (= 23,76 km).

Zu den weniger bekannten Straßenverbindungen, die sowohl die von Tarsos nach Antiocheia führende Hauptstraße durch die Cilicia Pedias mit den Städten Kappadokiens und des Euphrat-Gebietes als auch die Städte im Einzugsgebiet des Pyramus miteinander verband, gehört die häufig verwendete Strecke, die von Mopsuhestia über Anazarbos, Flaviopolis, bis nach Melitene am Euphrat führte.[51] Eine zweite Straße lief von Anazarbos über Komana nach Kaisareia am Argaios.

Im Bereich dieser beiden Verbindungen spielte Anazarbos eine zentrale Rolle. Die Stadt gewann gegen Ende des 2. und im ersten Viertel des 3. Jhs. wegen der Feldzüge gegen die Parther zunehmend an Bedeutung und bekam schließlich neben anderen Privilegien im 204 n. Chr. auch den Titel *metropolis*.[52] Bisher waren aus der Gegend von Anazarbos einige Meilensteine bekannt, die die antiken Straßenverläufe bezeugen.[53] Östlich von Anazarbos wurden vier Meilensteine gefunden, die an der von Anazarbos nach Kastabala führenden Straße errichtet worden waren.[54] Drei der Meilensteine stammen aus der Zeit von Severus Alexander und enthalten u. a. die diversen Titel der Stadt. Auf einem der Meilensteine ist die Entfernungsangabe von 1 Meile lesbar, während auf einem anderen Meilenstein die Entfernungsangabe von 2 Meilen verzeichnet ist. Ein weiterer Meilenstein aus dem östlichen Teil des Territoriums von

---

43 HELLENKEMPER/HILD 1990, 174; TIB lokalisiert dort die bei Strab. 14,5,18, Strab. 14,2,8 und peripl. m. m. 478 erwähnten *Amanikai Pylai*; HAYMANN 2014, 251–252.
44 HELLENKEMPER/HILD 1990, 361; über *Catabolo* oder *Castabalum* TOBIN 2001, 386 und HAYMANN 2014, 252–253.
45 HELLENKEMPER/HILD 1990, 249–250.
46 HELLENKEMPER/HILD 1990.
47 HELLENKEMPER/HILD 1990, 206.
48 HEBERDEY/WILHELM 1896, 19 Nr. 48; HAYMANN 2014, 254.
49 SCHMITT 1997, 99–131.
50 HELLENKEMPER/HILD 1990, 170–172.
51 ZIEGLER 1985, 13.
52 GOUGH 1952, 143, Nr. 25; HELLENKEMPER/HILD 1990, 178–185; SAYAR 2000.
53 SAYAR 2000, 23–29 Nr. 11–19; RRMAM III 7, 15A-18.
54 RRMAM III 7, 16A-17.

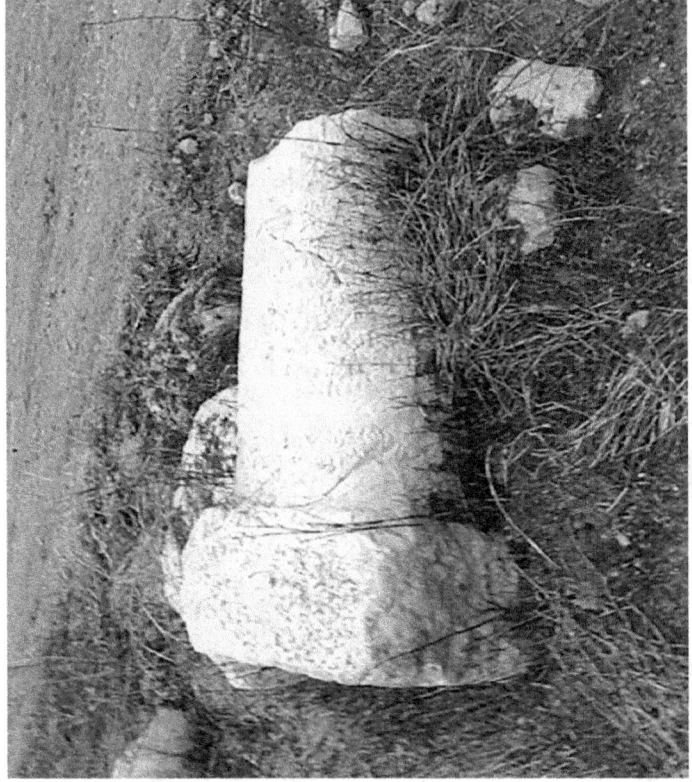

Abb. 13: Meilenstein aus der Zeit Elagabals; gefunden bei Anazarbos; (Foto: Verfasser)

Anazarbos wurde am Pyramos gefunden. Nach der Kaiser Gordian III. gewidmeten griechischen Inschrift wurde der Meilenstein wahrscheinlich während des Durchmarsches Gordians III. auf dem Weg nach Osten durch das Ebene Kilikien, 8 Meilen von Anazarbos entfernt, errichtet.

Auch an der von Anazarbos nach Mopsuhestia führenden Straße kamen einige Meilensteine an ein und derselben Stelle zutage.[55] Einer wurde unter Macrinus (217–218) 1 Meile von der Stadt entfernt errichtet. Ein weiterer Meilenstein, der vor einigen Jahren gefunden wurde, war unter Elagabal (218–222), während der Statthalterschaft von Claudius Nysius, 1 Meile von der Stadt entfernt aufgestellt worden.

An derselben Stelle kam ein weiterer Meilenstein ans Tageslicht, der nur mehr sehr fragmentarisch erhalten ist. Aus den erhaltenen Resten der Inschrift geht jedoch hervor, dass es sich dabei um einen Meilenstein aus der Zeit von Severus Alexander (222–235) handelt. Die Namen des Kaisers und seiner Mutter Iulia Mammea wurden

---

55 RRMAM III 7, 15A-15D.

nach ihrer Ermordung im Jahre 235 eradiert, nachdem die *damnatio memoriae* über sie verhängt worden war.

Alle diese Meilensteininschriften aus der Umgebung von Anazarbos beinhalten neben der Kaisertitulatur auch sämtliche Beinamen der Stadt. Auf einem weiteren Meilenstein waren zwei lateinische Inschriften eingemeißelt worden.[56] Beide Inschriften sind trotz des Fehlens der oberen und unteren Teile weitgehend erhalten geblieben. Nach der einen Inschrift wurde dieser Meilenstein, wie die anderen an dieser Stelle gefundenen Meilensteine, 1 Meile von Anazarbos entfernt unter den Tetrarchen M. Aurelius Valerius Maximianus, Galerius Valerius Maximianus, Maximinus Daia und Constantinus I. zwischen 307–308 errichtet. Im zweiten Text sind die Namen von Licinius, Crispus, Constantinus und seines Sohnes Constantinus zu lesen. Aufgrund der historischen Ereignisse können wir die zweite Inschrift zwischen 317 und 324 datieren.

Wenn man die relativ sicheren Datierungen der bisher vorgelegten Meilensteine zusammenstellt, so stellt man fest, dass die Straßen im Ebenen Kilikien ab der Mitte des 2. Jhs. ausgebaut worden sind. Ausbau und Erneuerung der Straßen in Kilikia Pedias wurden bis zum Untergang des Partherreiches 224 n. Chr. mit den zunehmenden Feldzügen gegen die Parther wesentlich intensiver durchgeführt, weil der Zustand dieser Hauptverbindungswege für die Truppenverlegungen zum Kriegsgebiet eine entscheidende strategische Rolle für das Schicksal des römischen Reiches spielte. Diese Bautätigkeit wurde nach der Gründung des sassanidischen Reiches im Jahre 224 n. Chr. bis zum Überfall des Sassanidenkönigs Sapor I. im Jahre 260 n. Chr. fortgesetzt. Eine weitere Phase der Erneuerung des Straßennetzes im Ebenen Kilikien erfolgte erst nach der Verwüstung des städtischen Lebens im ersten Viertel des 4. Jhs. infolge der zunehmenden Feldzüge gegen die Sassaniden während der ersten Tetrarchie,[57] als Diocletian administrative, wirtschaftliche, politische und militärische Reformen im gesamten Reich durchführte.

Bibliographie:

ALKIM 1959 = U.B. ALKIM, Ein altes Wegenetz im südwestlichen Antitaurus-Gebiet, *Anadolu Araştırmaları* 1,2, 1959, 207–222.

ALKIM 1965 = U.B. ALKIM, The Road from Sam'al to Asitawandawa: Contributions to the Historical Geography of the Amanus Region, *Anadolu Araştırmaları* 2, 1965, 1–41.

BERGES/NOLLÉ 2000 = D. BERGES/J. NOLLÉ, Tyana. Archäologisch-historische Untersuchungen zum südwestlichen Kappadokien. IK 55,1, Bonn 2000.

DAGRON/FEISSEL 1988 = G. DAGRON/D. FEISSEL, Inscriptions de Cilicie, Paris 1988.

DESTEPHEN 2016 = S. DESTEPHEN, Le voyage impérial dans l'Antiquité tardive. Paris 2016.

---

56 RRMAM III 7, 15E.
57 ZIEGLER 1993, 23.

Eck 2017 = W. Eck, Die Städte des Reiches und ihr kaiserlicher „Euerget": Antoninus Pius' Politik gegenüber den Gemeinden des Imperiums, in: C. Michels/P.F. Mittag (Hg.), Jenseits des Narrativs. Antoninus Pius in den nicht-literarischen Quellen, Stuttgart 2017, 215–228.

Forlanini 2013= M. Forlanini, How to Infer Ancient Roads and Itineraries from Heterogenous Hitite Texts: The Case of the Cilician (Kizzuwatnean) Road System, *Kaskal* 10, 2013, 1–34.

Gough 1952 = M. Gough, Anazarbus, *AS* 2, 1952, 85–150.

Harada/Cimok 2008 = T. Harada/F. Cimok, Roads of Ancient Anatolia. Volume I, Istanbul 2008.

Harper 1970 = R.P. Harper, Podandus and the Via Tauri, *AS* 20, 1970, 149–153.

Haymann 2012 = F. Haymann, Aigeai: Eine numismatische Stadtgeschichte, *NNB* 61, 2012, 135–141.

Haymann 2014 = F. Haymann, Untersuchungen zur Geschichte und Identitätskonstruktion von Aigeai im römischen Kilikien (20 v.–260 n. Chr.), Bonn 2014.

Hellenkemper/Hild 1986 = H. Hellenkemper/F. Hild, Neue Forschungen in Isaurien und Kilikien, Wien 1986.

Hellenkemper/Hild 1990 = H. Hellenkemper/F. Hild, Tabula Imperii Byzantini, Bd. 5: Kilikien und Isaurien, Wien 1990.

Hild 1991 = F. Hild, Die Route der Tabula Peutingeriana von Iconium über ad fines und Tetrapyrgia nach Pompeiopolis in Kilikien, *Anatolia Antiqua* 1, 1991, 310–330.

Hild 1998 = F. Hild, Jerpanion und die Probleme der historischen Geographie Kappadokiens: Neue Forschungen und deren Ergebnissé, *MEFRA* 110, 1998, 941–951.

Hild 1977 = F. Hild, Das byzantinische Straßensystem in Kappadokien, Wien 1977.

Jasink 1991 = A.M. Jasink, Hitite and Assyrian Routes to Cilicie, *Anatolia Antiqua* 1, 1991, 253–259.

Kienast 2017 = D. Kienast/W. Eck/M. Heil, Römische Kaisertabelle. Grundzüge einer römischen Kaiserchronologie, Darmstadt 2017[6].

Kaplan 2017 = A. Kaplan, Yukarı Seyhan Havzası bağlantılarını sağlayan antik yol güzergahlarının merkezi: Almadere (Elmadere) Geçidi, *Belleten* 81, 2017, 703–714.

Laminger-Pascher 1974 = G. Laminger-Pascher, Kleine Nachträge zu kilikischen Inschriften, *ZPE* 15, 1974, 31–68.

Langlois 1854 = V. Langlois, V., Inscriptions grecques, romaines, byzantines et armenniennes, Paris 1854.

Langlois 1861 = V. Langlois, Voyage dans la Cilicie et dans les montagnes du Taurus exécuté pendant les années 1852–1853, Paris 1861.

Le Bas/Waddington 1847–1877 = P. Le Bas/W.H. Waddington, Voyage archéologique en Grèce et en Asie Mineure: fait par ordre du gouvernement français pendant les années 1843 et 1844, Bd. 3,2, Paris 1847–1877.

Pilhofer 2015 = S. Pilhofer, Romanisierung in Kilikien. Das Zeugnis der Inchriften, München 2015[2].

Ramsay 1903 = W. M. Ramsay, Tarsus und Cilicia, Tarsus and the Great Taurus Pass, *The Geographical Journal* 22. 4, 357–410.

RRMAM I = D.H. French, Roman Roads and Milestones of Asia Minor, RRMAM, Bd. 1 Oxford 1981.

RRMAM II = D.H. French, Roman Roads and Milestones of Asia Minor, RRMAM, Bd. 2 Oxford 1988.

RRMAM III 3 = D.H. French, Roman Roads and Milestones of Asia Minor Vol. 3: Milestones, Fasc. 3.2: Galatia (BIAA Electronic Monograph 2), London 2012.

RRMAM III 7 = D.H. French, Roman Roads and Milestones of Asia Minor Vol. 3: Milestones, Fasc. 3.7: Cilicia, Isauria et Lycaonia (and South-West Galatia) (BIAA Electronic Monograph 7, London 2014.

Sayar 2000 = M.H. Sayar, Die Inschriften von Anazarbos und Umgebung: Inschriften aus dem Stadtgebiet un der nächsten Umgebung der Stadt 1. IK 56, Bonn 2000.

Sayar 2002 = M.H. Sayar, Antike Straßenverbindungen Kilikiens in der römischen Kaiserzeit, in: E. Olshausen/H. Sonnabend (Hg.), Zu Wasser und zu Land: Verkehrswege in der antiken Welt, Stuttgart 1999, 452–473.

Sayar 2016 = M.H. Sayar, Tarsus und Severus Alexander, *EA* 49, 2016, 177–186.
Schmitt 1997 = T. Schmitt, Die drei Bögen für Germanicus und die römische Politik in frühtiberischer Zeit, *Rivista Storica dell'Antichità* 27, 1997, 99–131.
Sheldon 2010 = S.R.M. Sheldon, Rome's Wars in Parthia: Blood in the Sand, London 2010.
Spanu 2016 =M. Spanu, C.I.L. III, 228 e la Via Tauri in Cilicia, *JAT* 26, 2016, 29–56.
Speidel 2014 = M.A. Speidel, Herrschaft durch Vorsorge und Beweglichkeit. Zu den Infrastrukturen des kaiserzeitlichen römischen Heeres im Reichsinneren, in: A. Kolb (Hg.) Infrastruktur und Herrschaftsorganisation im Imperium Romanum, Berlin 2014, 80–99.
Tobin 2001 = J. Tobin, The Tarcondimotid Dynasty in Smooth Cilicia, in: É. Jean/A. M. Dinçol/S. Durugönül (Hg.), La Cilicie; Espaces et Pouvoirs Locaux (2e millénaire av. J. C. – 4e siècle ap. J. C.). Actes de la Table ronde internationale d'Istanbul, 2–5 novembre 1999, Paris 2001, 382–387.
Waddington 1883 = W.H. Waddington, Inscriptions de Tarse, *BCH* 7, 1883, 281–292.
Williams 1996 = F. Williams, Xenophon's Dana and the Passage of Cyrus'Army over the Taurus Mountains, *Historia* 45, 284–314.
Vitale 2012 = M. Vitale, Eparchie und Koinon in Kleinasien von der ausgehenden Republik bis ins 3. Jh. n. Chr., Bonn 2012.
Ziegler 1985 = R. Ziegler, Städtisches Prestige und kaiserliche Politik: Studien zum Festwesen in Ostkilikien im 2. und 3. Jahrhundert n. Chr, Düsseldorf 1985.
Ziegler 1993 = R. Ziegler, Kaiser, Heer und Städtisches Geld: Untersuchungen zur Münzprägung von Anazarbos und anderer ostkilikischer Städte, Wien 1993.

Hamdi Şahin
CIL XVII, 5, 3: Neue Meilensteine und Straßen aus der *Cilicia Aspera*

Abstract: In Cilicia, the ancient roads for the most part run from south to north, climbing the natural incline of the terrain from the coast to the high country. The majority of Roman roads in the region follow pre-Roman routes, supplemented by long-distance routes that run parallel to the coastline and provide easier access to the region. Over centuries, the landscape of Cilicia therefore developed a road system determined by the terrain and the natural structure of the topography. To the north, the Cilician provinces were further delimited by the Taurus Mountains, with the result that supra-regional road connections into the Anatolian Highlands largely had to pass through valleys and across passes. Written sources and the milestones found by modern research hence reveal both regional and supra-regional building programmes. For the planned volume CIL XVII, 5, 3 Miliaria Provinciarum Lyciae-Pamphyliae et Ciliciae field research was undertaken in Cilicia. As part of this research, new road sections and several milestones were discovered, while a number of old ones were re-discovered and a few previously published milestones re-autopsied. The article published here presents the newly discovered road sections and milestone inscriptions discovered during this fieldwork.

Zusammenfassung: Im kilikischen Raum folgen die antiken Straßen, der Landesnatur gemäß, mehrheitlich der Nord-Süd-Richtung von der Küste in das Hochland. Die römischen Straßen folgen mehrheitlich den vorrömischen Trassen. Zusätzlich erschließen küstenparallele Fernwege in diesen Gebieten den gesamten Raum. In diesen Landschaften entwickelten sich im Laufe der Jahrhunderte Wege, die vom Gelände und der natürlichen Gliederung der Topographie geprägt waren. Die Provinzen wurden im Norden vom Taurusgebirge begrenzt, so dass überregionale Straßenverbindungen zum Anatolischen Hochland in den meisten Fällen durch Täler und Pässe verlaufen mussten. Schriftliche Quellen und die durch die modernen Forschungen gefundenen Meilensteine lassen regionale und überregionale Bauprogramme erkennen. Für den geplanten Band CIL XVII, 5, 3 *Miliaria provinciarum Lyciae-Pamphyliae et Ciliciae* wurden im kilikischen Raum Feldforschungen in Angriff genommen. In diesem Zusammenhang wurden neue Straßenabschnitte und mehrere Meilensteine entdeckt, einige alte widergefunden und einige bereits publizierte Meilensteine einer erneuten Autopsie unterzogen. Der hier publizierte Aufsatz legt die neugefundenen Straßenabschnitte und Meilensteininschriften, die während dieser Feldforschungen entdeckt wurden, vor.

Einleitung

Durch Ausgrabungen und ausgedehnten Feldforschungen nehmen die Inschriftenfunde der griechisch-römischen Welt stetig zu, wodurch die Dringlichkeit zur Zusammenstellung und Veröffentlichung der Inschriften in den Corpora wächst. Dies gilt auch für die Edition aller Meilensteine des Imperium Romanum, die im Corpus Inscriptionum Latinarum XVII *Miliaria Imperii Romani* unternommen wird. Das von Prof. G. WALSER† gegründete Editionsprojekt wird seit dem Jahr 2000 unter der Leitung von Prof. A. KOLB in Zusammenarbeit und mit Unterstützung von Wissenschaftlern aus verschiedenen Ländern weitergeführt.[1] Geplant ist im Rahmen des CIL XVII auch ein Band mit den Meilensteinen der Provinzen *Lycia-Pamphylia* und *Cilicia*. Dafür wurden im kilikischen Raum Feldforschungen in Angriff genommen. In diesem Zusammenhang wurden neue Straßenabschnitte und Meilensteine entdeckt,[2] einige alte widergefunden und einige bereits publizierte Meilensteine einer erneuten Autopsie unterzogen.

Theodor Mommsen publizierte 1873 erstmals im CIL III die Meilensteine aus dem kilikischen Raum[3] und 1902 zusammen mit O. HIRSCHFELD und A. DOMASZEWSKI die Meilensteine aus Pamphylien[4] und Kilikien.[5]

Meilensteine tragen nicht nur Inschriften, mit einem *caput viae*, die die Entfernungen zwischen den antiken Städten und Siedlungen angeben. Sie fungieren darüber hinaus als Inschriftenträger Symbole römischer Herrschaft und Propaganda, da sie Kaiser prominent zur Schau stellen.[6] Ferner bezeugen die Meilensteintexte den Namen des Statthalters, der für den Straßenbau oder Reparaturmaßnahmen zuständig war.[7] Öfter werden auch die Namen antiker Städte und Siedlungen durch Meilensteine und durch antike „Wegweiser" wie das *Stadiasmus Patarensis* gewonnen,[8] was für die Historische Geographie, Archäologie und Epigraphik von unbezahlbarem Wert ist.

Die Gesamtzahl der Meilensteine der römischen Welt wird auf rund 8000 geschätzt. Davon entfallen aller Wahrscheinlichkeit nach 1100 auf den kleinasiatischen Raum.[9] Von den erwähnten rund 8000 Miliarien stammt der überwiegende Teil aus der Kaiserzeit und Spätantike. Wie es für das gesamte *Imperium Romanum* der Fall ist, erreichte

---

1 SCHMIDT 2007, 20; 32. Siehe CIL XVII 2 (*Galliae, Germaniae*); CIL XVII 4,1 (Raetia, Noricum), CIL XVII 4,2 (*Dalmatia*) und CIL XVII 1,1 (*Tarraconensis*).
2 ŞAHIN 2015a, passim; ŞAHIN 2015b, passim. Dieses Projekt wurde durch die Abteilung zur Förderung der wissenschaftlichen Forschungsprojekte der Universität Istanbul (Projekt Nr. 55091) und der Suna-Inan Kıraç Research Center for Mediterranean Civilizations unterstützt.
3 CIL III 226–229.
4 CIL III 13626.
5 Z. B. CIL III 13623–13625. 14177[11-12].
6 ECK 2004, 18; KOLB 2004, 135; MROZEWICZ 2004, 350–351.
7 RATHMANN 2006, 201–202.
8 ŞAHIN/ADAK 2007, passim.
9 KOLB 2004, 137.

die Aufstellung der Meilensteine auch in Kleinasien ihren Höhepunkt während der Spätantike. Kleinasien nimmt quantitativ nach Nordafrika die zweite Stelle bei den Meilensteinfunden ein. Davon sind rund 120 Meilensteine aus Kilikien bis heute bekanntgeworden, von diesen wurden 64 in der *Cilicia Aspera* aufgestellt.

Die durch zahlreiche Institute und Universitäten durchgeführten Feldforschungen und Ausgrabungen in Kleinasien[10] lassen hoffen, dass wir auch in den kommenden Jahren weitere Funde neuer Meilensteine erwarten dürfen. Kleinasien ist zu einem großen Teil epigraphisch noch wenig erschlossen. In der Tat zeigt sich, dass noch eine große Menge von Inschriften neu zu finden sind. Seit über hundert Jahren und auch heute noch werden eingehende Feldforschungen in Kleinasien durchgeführt, durch die gewaltige Mengen von Inschriften, die bereits verschwunden oder in ihrer Existenz gefährdet waren, für die Wissenschaft gerettet wurden und werden.

Geographische Abgrenzung des Gebietes (Karte 1).:
Das südliche Kleinasien umfasste in der römischen Kaiserzeit drei Provinzen. Diese sind von Westen nach Osten: *Lycia*, *Pamphylia* und *Cilcia*. Die Grenze zwischen Pamphylien und Kilikien verlief anscheinend nahe den Orten *Laertes* und *Syedra*.[11] Eine späthellenistische Inschrift aus *Syedra* bezeichnet nämlich deren Bewohner ausdrücklich als „Pamphylier".[12] Im Norden umschließen die Gebirgszüge des *Taurus* und *Amanos* das gesamte kilikische Gebiet von West nach Ost. Das Mittelmeer (*Kilikios Aulon*) bildet im Süden eine natürliche Grenze.

Die in der Forschungsdiskussion geläufige Unterscheidung zwischen *Trakheia* und *Pedias*, also dem Rauhem und Ebenem Kilikien, geht auf diese Strabonpassage zurück. Strabon beschreibt folgende Orte und Flüsse als zu Kilikien gehörig: Im Rauhen Kilikien *Korakesion, Arsinoe, Hamaxia, Laertes, Selinus* (Stadt und Fluß), *Kragos, Charadros, Anemourion, Nagidos, Arsinoe, Melania, Kelenderis, Holmoi*, den Fluß *Kalykadnos, Zephyrion, Seleukeia*, die Insel *Krambousa, Korykos*, den Fluß *Pikron Hydor*, die Insel *Elaiussa/Sebaste*, den Fluß *Lamos, Olympos* (Berg und Festung). Es folgt *Soloi* bzw. *Pompeiopolis* als Grenzstadt zwischen beiden Kilikien. Im Ebenen Kilikien schließt sich ein weiteres *Zephyrion* an, *Anchiale*, die Festung *Kyinda*, der Fluß *Kydnos, Tarsos*, der Fluß *Pyramos, Mallos*, die *Aleion*-Ebene, *Aigeai*, die Amanische Pforte, *Issos*, der Fluß *Pinaros*, der Golf von *Issos* mit *Rhosos, Myriandros, Alexandreia* und *Nikopolis*, sodann noch *Mopsouhestia*, und schließlich die Syrische Pforte, also der Paß über das Amanosgebirge, der die Grenze zu Syrien bildet. *Seleukeia* am

---

10 Zur Zeit über 500; vgl. Proceedings of the International Congress of Excavations, Surveys and Archaeometry, Ankara 1970ff.
11 Da sich in der Kaiserzeit die Grenzen der römischen Provinzen unter den Maßnahmen der römischen Kaiser mehrmals geändert haben, stütze ich mich bei der geographischen Abgrenzung der Gebiete auf die Provinzeinteilung, die in TIB 5 und TIB 8 herangezogen wurde, und die auf der Provinzeinteilung des Hierokles (*Synekdemos*) beruht.
12 AE 1977, 793.

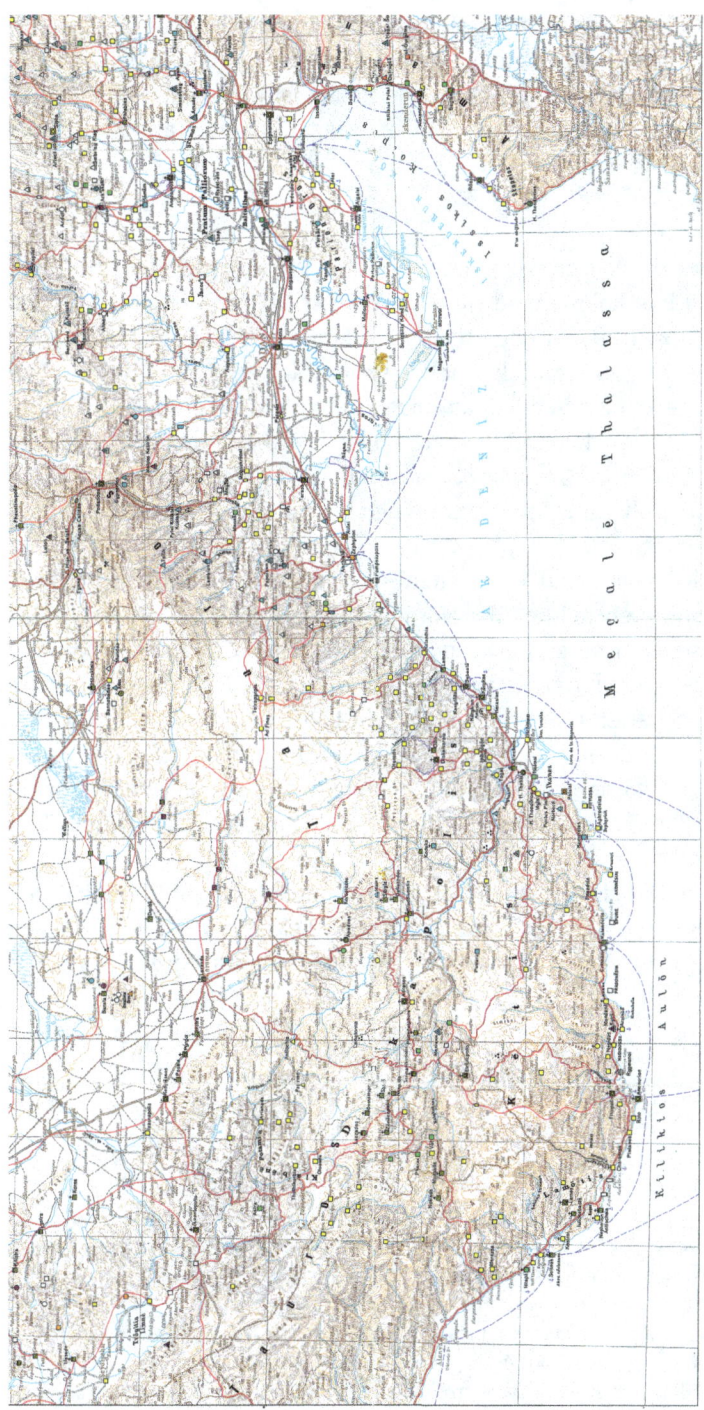

Karte 1: Kilikien (Hild/Hellenkemper 1990)

Orontes liegt dann bereits in Syrien.[13] Die Grenze zwischen den beiden Gebieten ist *Soloi*, (Viranşehir), das nach dem Piratensieg des Pompeius zu *Pompeiopolis* umbenannt wurde.[14] Heute erstreckt sich das kilikische Gebiet teilweise auf sechs Provinzen der Türkei, von West nach Ost: Antalya, Mersin, Konya, Adana, Kahramanmaraş und Hatay.[15]

Die Straßen:
Der römische Einfluss äußerte sich wie auch in anderen Provinzen in der Gründung von Städten und Veteranenkolonien sowie dem Ausbau des Straßennetzes. Damit wurden die südlichen Provinzen zum Durchgangsland für römische Soldaten auf dem Weg in den Orient bzw. von dort zurück. Auch wirtschaftlich erreichte dieses Gebiet von der römischen Kaiserzeit bis in die Spätantike ihre Blüte. Die seit hellenistischer Zeit allgemein gebräuchliche griechische Sprache blieb in diesen Provinzen dominierend, daneben wurden auch zahlreiche anatolische Dialekte gesprochen; lateinisch wurde nur ausnahmsweise benutzt, aber fand seinen Platz auf Ehreninschriften römischer Kaiser und Meilensteinen.[16]

Im lykisch-pamphylischen und kilikischen Raum folgen die antiken Straßen, der Landesnatur gemäß, mehrheitlich der Nord-Süd-Richtung von der Küste in das Hochland.[17] Die römischen Straßen folgen mehrheitlich den vorrömischen Trassen. Zusätzlich erschließen küstenparallele Fernwege in diesen Gebieten den gesamten Raum. In diesen Landschaften entwickelten sich im Laufe der Jahrhunderte Wege, die vom Gelände und der natürlichen Gliederung der Topographie geprägt waren. Die Provinzen wurden im Norden vom Taurusgebirge begrenzt, so dass überregionale Straßenverbindungen zum Anatolischen Hochland in den meisten Fällen durch Täler und Pässe verlaufen mussten.

Seit dem 5. Jahrhundert sind Straßen in Lykien, Pamphylien und Kilikien durch schriftliche Quellen bezeugt. Die bekanntesten sind die Feldzüge des Kyros, die von Ksenophon beschrieben wurden.[18] Alexander der Große zog im Winter 334/333 v.

---

13 Strab. 14,5,4.
14 HILD/HELLENKEMPER 1990, 381–382.
15 HILD/HELLENKEMPER 1990, 17–19.
16 ECK 2004, 6–7.
17 FRENCH 1965, 177.
18 Arr. an. 1,3,2: Ἐντεῦθεν ἐπειρῶντο εἰσβάλλειν εἰς τὴν Κιλικίαν· ἡ δὲ εἰσβολὴ ἦν ὁδὸς ἁμαξιτός, ὀρθία ἰσχυρῶς καὶ ἀμήχανος εἰσελθεῖν στρατεύματι, εἴ τις ἐκώλυεν. Ἐλέγετο δὲ καὶ Συέννεσιν εἶναι ἐπὶ τῶν ἄκρων φυλάττοντα τὴν εἰσβολήν· δι' ὃ ἔμεινεν ἡμέραν ἐν τῷ πεδίῳ. Τῇ δ' ὑστεραίᾳ ἧκεν ἄγγελος λέγων ὅτι λελοιπὼς εἴη Συέννεσις τὰ ἄκρα, ἐπεὶ ᾔσθετο τό τε Μένωνος στράτευμα ὅτι ἤδη ἐν Κιλικίᾳ ἦν εἴσω τῶν ὀρέων καὶ ὅτι τριήρεις ἤκουε περιπλεούσας ἀπ' Ἰωνίας εἰς Κιλικίαν Ταμὼν ἔχοντα τὰς Λακεδαιμονίων καὶ αὐτοῦ Κύρου. Κῦρος δ' οὖν ἀνέβη ἐπὶ τὰ ὄρη οὐδενὸς κωλύοντος καὶ εἶδε τὰς σκηνὰς οὗ ἐφύλαττον οἱ Κίλικες. Ἐντεῦθε κατέβαινεν εἰς πεδίον μέγα καὶ καλὸν καὶ ἐπίρρυτον καὶ δένδρων παντοδαπῶν σύμπλεων καὶ ἀμπέλων· πολὺ δὲ καὶ σήσαμον καὶ μελίνην καὶ κέγχρον καὶ πυροὺς καὶ κριθὰς φέρει. Ὄρος δ' αὐτὸ περιέχει ὀχυρὸν καὶ ὑψηλὸν πάντῃ ἐκ θαλάττης εἰς θάλατταν. Καταβὰς

Chr. durch diese Gebiete.[19] Der Konsul G. M. Vulso führte 189 v. Chr. einen Feldzug durch lykisches und pamphylisch-pisidisches Gebiet gegen die Galater.[20] Nach der Einrichtung der römischen Provinz *Asia* baute Konsul Manius Aquilius 129 -126 n. Chr. die Fernstraße von *Pergamon* nach *Side* aus.[21] Im Kampf gegen die Piraten in Lykien und Pamphylien (78–75 v. Chr) baute P. Servilius Vatia (Isauricus) die erste Straße über den *Taurus*.[22] C. Aquila legte 6 v. Chr. während der Vorbereitung zur Niederwerfung der Homanadenser die *Via Sebaste* an.[23] Der erste Statthalter Lykiens, Q. Veranius, ließ nach der Einrichtung der Provinz (45/46 n. Chr.) die lykischen Strecken vermessen und ein Verzeichnis der Straßen anfertigen. Dieses Verzeichnis wurde 1993 in *Patara* entdeckt und bereits mehrmals publiziert.[24] Weitere Belege zu den lykisch-pamphylischen und kilikischen Straßen geben die *Tabula Peutengeriana*,[25] der Geograph von Ravenna, die *Itineraria Romana*[26] und zahlreiche Meilensteine, die regionale und überregionale Bauprogramme erkennen lassen.[27]

Die „Küstenstraße" dieser Provinzen führte von *Kaunos* in Lykien über *Kalynda*, den *Glaukos Potamos* nach *Telmessos, Patara, Antiphellos, Limyra, Korydalla, Phaselis* in Pamphylien *Olbia, Magydos Perge, Syllaion Aspendos, Side, Kibyra, Korakesion, Syedra* in Kilikien nach *Iotape*, über *Anemourion, Kelenderis Seleukeia (ad Calycadnum), Korykos, Elaiussa/Sebaste, Pompeiopolis Magarsos, Aigaiai* bis *Antiokheia*. Der Verlauf dieser „Küstenstraße" ist durch mehrere Meilensteinfunde belegt, die in oder zwischen diesen oben genannten Städten entdeckt wurden und Bauphasen verschiedener Jahrhunderte bezeugen. Unter diesen sind hier als Basis und Wiederspiegelung der verschiedenen Straßenbaumaßnahmen der Kaiser die folgenden zu nennen (Karte 1).[28]

Die erhaltenen Straßenbauinschriften und Meilensteine lassen zu bestimmten Zeiten übergeordnete Bauprogramme erkennen, da die Reichsverwaltung ein beson-

---

δέ, διὰ τούτου τοῦ πεδίου ἤλασε σταθμοὺς τέτταρας, παρασάγγας πέντε καὶ εἴκοσιν, εἰς Ταρσούς, τῆς Κιλικίας πόλιν μεγάλην καὶ εὐδαίμονα. Ἐνταῦθα ἦσαν τὰ Συεννέσιος βασίλεια τοῦ Κιλίκων βασιλέως· διὰ μέσης δὲ τῆς πόλεως ῥεῖ ποταμὸς Κύδνος ὄνομα, εὖρος δύο πλέθρων. Ταύτην τὴν πόλιν ἐξέλιπον οἱ ἐνοικοῦντες μετὰ Συεννέσιος εἰς χωρίον ὀχυρὸν ἐπὶ τὰ ὄρη, πλὴν οἱ τὰ καπηλεῖα ἔχοντες· ἔμειναν δὲ καὶ οἱ παρὰ τὴν θάλατταν οἰκοῦντες ἐν Σόλοις καὶ ἐν Ἰσσοῖς.

19 Arr. an. 2,4,3. Strab. 7,2,9; Curt. 3,4,1.
20 Pol. 21, 35,1–5; Liv. 38, 15, 1–6.
21 RRMAM III 1, 7; 8; 9a; 9b; 10.
22 Fest. 7.
23 Zu den Meilensteinen RRMAM III 2, 90c; 94b; 95d; 95e; 97a; 97b.
24 ŞAHIN/ADAK 2007, passim; GRASSHOFF 2009, passim.
25 MILLER 1916, 665f; 692; 753; 766.
26 CUNTZ 1929, 93.
27 HILD/HELLENKEMPER 1990, 128–131.
28 FRENCH 1988, 855 (Iulian, Gratian), 852, 185, 192 (Diokletian u. Maximian mit Constantius u. Galerius), 186 (Valentinian I. u. Valens); NOLLÉ 2001, Nr. 177 (Diokletian), Nr. 178 (Diokletian und Maximian, Constantius und Galerius, Severus und Maximinus Daia, 305/306), Nr. 179 (Constans, 333–337); AKYÜREK ŞAHIN/ŞAHIN 2000, 475 (Konstantin I. oder Valens).

deres Interesse an der Erhaltung der Fernstraßen hatte. So sind unter Vespasian, Hadrian, Septimius Severus, Caracalla, Macrinus, Severus Alexander, Maximian, Konstantin sowie Valentinian, Valens und Gratian Straßenbauarbeiten inschriftlich bezeugt.²⁹ Diese Straßenerneuerungen stehen teilweise in Zusammenhang mit den Kriegen an der Ostgrenze des Reiches.³⁰

Die Nord-Süd Hauptverkehrswege im Rauhen Kilikien sind:
1-*Anemourion-Germanikopolis-Leontopolis-Lystra-Ikonion*
2-*Seleukeia-Germanikopolis-Leontopolis-Lystra-Ikonion*
3-*Seleukeia-Klaudiopolis-Laranda-Ikonion*
4-*Seleukeia-Diokaisareia-Karanda-Ikonion*
5-*Pompeiopolis-Tetrapyrgia-Ikonion*

Eine weitere Nord-Süd Verbindung zum Hochland belegt eigentlich noch ein bereits mehrmals publizierter Meilenstein ca. 5 km nördlich von *Elaiussa/Sebaste*.³¹ Laut dem Bericht von RUDOLPH HEBERDEY und ADOLF WILHELM haben die beiden Gelehrten, diesen Meilenstein" auf dem Weg von *Kanytella* nach *Elaiussa/Sebaste* und "eine halbe Stunde von der Küste entfernt' entdeckt.³²

Es handelt sich dabei um einen Meilenstein aus Kalkstein mit einer 10 zeiligen lateinischen Inschrift.³³ Die Inschrift wurde nach der *tribunicia potestas* des Hadrian zwischen die Jahre 119 und 120 datiert. DAVID FRENCH vermutete ohne weitere Argumente, dass dieser Meilenstein die Küstenstrasse von *Seleukeia* nach *Tarsos* bezeugt.³⁴ Seine Vermutung wurde in der Literatur ohne weitere bedenken oftmals zitiert.³⁵ Doch zieht man die Worte der beiden Gelehrten genauer an, scheint dies unmöglich zu sein. Dieser Meilenstein kann nur die Strecke zwischen der an der Küste liegenden Stadt *Elaiussa/Sebaste* und dem Hochland bezeugen. Die verwitterten Meilensteinfragmente³⁶ bei *Esenpınar* (=Güvere),³⁷ ca. 7 km weiter nördlich von dem antiken Dorf *Kanytella*, sowie auch eine ca. 18 Meter lange und 3,30 Meter breite römische Brücke bei *Efrenk*,³⁸ die die Abhänge des Lamas-Tals verbinden, und sich ca. 6 km weiter nördlich

---

29 Vespasian: FRENCH 1988, 461; Hadrian: FRENCH 1988, 407–408; 631.
30 HILD/HELLENKEMPER 1990, 130.
31 Zu Elaiussa/Sebaste HILD/HELLENKEMPER 1990, 400–401; SCHNEIDER 1999; 2003; 2010.
32 HEBERDEY/WILHELM 1896, 51, Nr. 118; CIL III 13625; AE 1898, 408; HAGEL/TOMASCHITZ 1998, Kan 26; ŞAHIN 2009, 134, Nr. 21; RRMAM III 7, 11; SAYAR 2015, 113–114, Nr. 4.
33 *Imp(erator) Caesar / divi Traiani / Parthici f(ilius) divi / Nervae nepos / Traianus Hadria/nus Aug(ustus) pont(ifex) max(imus) / tr(ibunicia) pot(estate) IIII co(n)s(ul) III p(ater) p(atriae) p[e]r / Iu<l>(ium) <C>a<s>tum <l>e<g>(atum) / <Au>g(usti) pr(o) pr(aetore) / m(ilia) p(assuum) XXI.*
34 RRMAM III 7, 11.
35 SAYAR 2015, 114.
36 SAYAR 2002, 468.
37 HILD/HELLENKEMPER 1990, 264.
38 HILD/HELLENKEMPER 1990, 244.

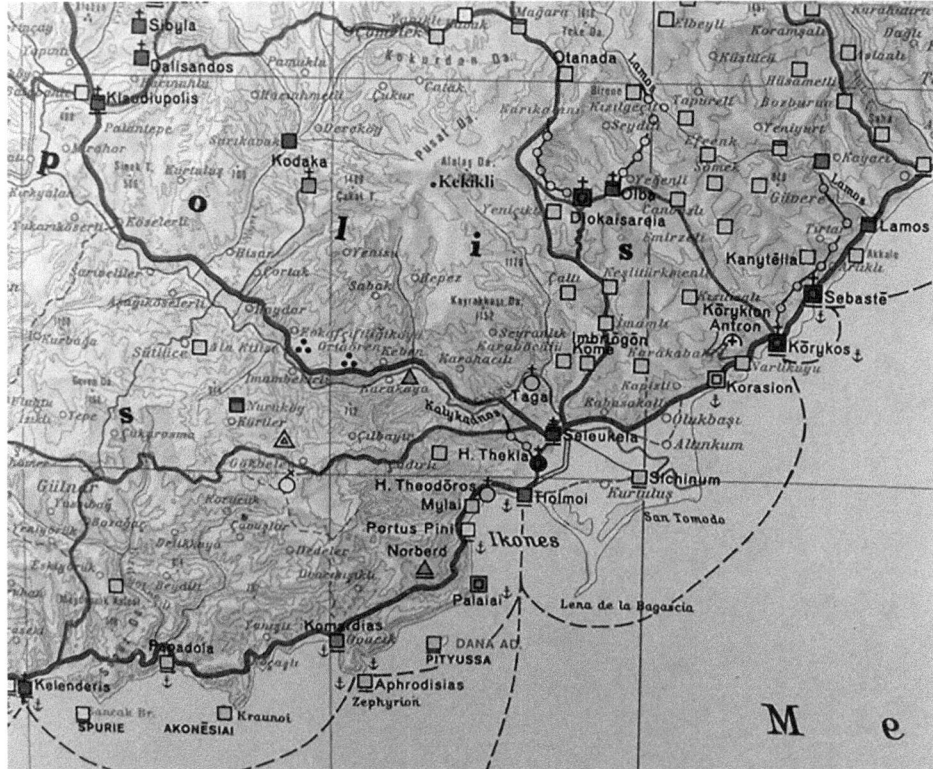

Karte 2: Fundort des Meilensteins aus der Flur Kekikli (HILD/HELLENKEMPER 1990)

der genannten Meilensteine befindet, bezeugen, dass der Straßenverlauf sich weiter in nördlicher Richtung ausstreckt. Deshalb kann der von FRENCH publizierte Meilenstein nur als Beweis für die von *Elaiussa/Sebaste* über *Kanytella-Sömek*-Efrenk-*Tapureli* und Elbeyli weiter nach Norden führenden Straße angesehen werden.

Während den historisch-geographischen und epigraphischen Forschungen im Rauhen Kilikien[39] 2009 wurde ca. 8 km nordwestlich von Yeniçıktı, (Flur Kekikli), ca. 25 km nordwestlich von Silifke und ca. 11 km nordwestlich von *Diokaisareia* (Uzuncaburç) (Karte 2), ein neuer Meilenstein aus der Zeit Diokletians entdeckt.[40]

---

39 Mein Dank gilt dem Fond der Universität İstanbul (İstanbul Üniversitesi Bilimsel Araştırma Projeleri Başkanlığı) (Projekt Nr. 3498) und der Suna-İnan Stiftung, Institut für Mediterrane Forschungen (Suna-İnan Kıraç Vakfı, Akdeniz Medeniyetlerini Araştırma Enstitüsü), die unsere Feldforschungen gefördert haben.
40 ŞAHIN 2009, 131–132: Αὐτοκράτορι | vac. Καίσαρι vac. | Γαΐῳ Οὐαλερίῳ |Διοκλετιανῷ Εὐσεβεῖ Εὐτυχεῖ ||[5] [Σεβαστῷ ca. 5] | [---.

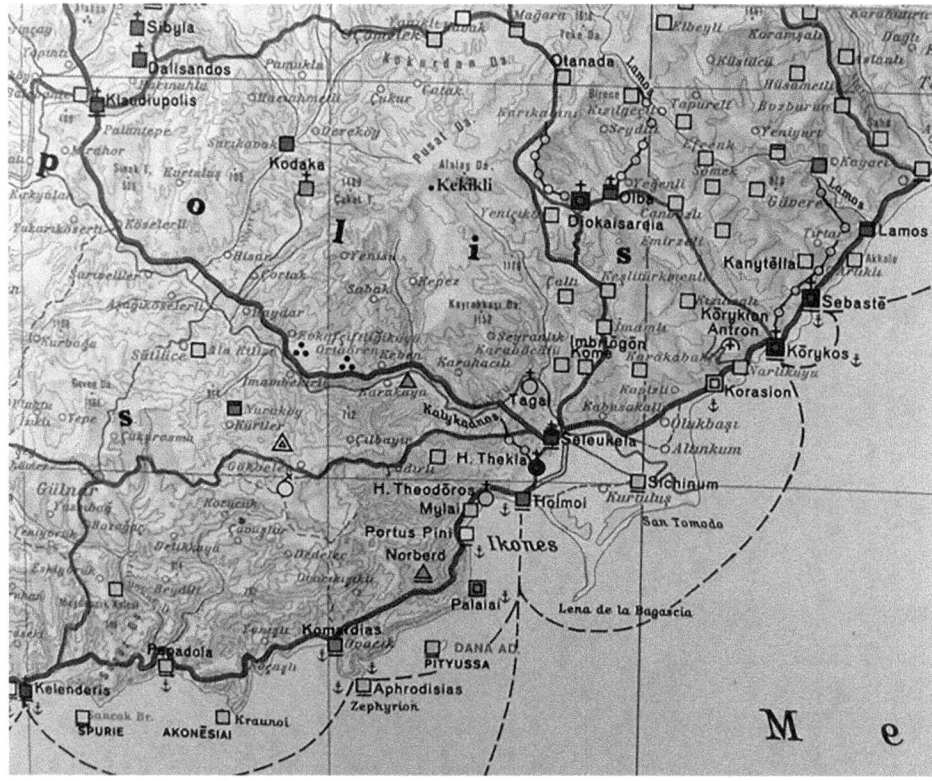

Karte 3: Strecke zwischen *Klaudiopolis* und *Seleukeia* (HILD/HELLENKEMPER 1990)

Im östlichen Rauhen Kilikien, zwischen den Flüssen *Lamos* (Limonlu) und *Kalykadnos* (Göksu), sind mehrere Strecken in nordsüdlicher Richtung vorhanden, die die Küstenstädte ins Landesinnere und weiter nach *Laranda* und *Iconium* verbinden. Die westlichste Strecke führt von *Laranda* über *Klaudiopolis* nach *Seleukeia*. Durch eine Abzweigung in *Klaudiopolis* nach Osten, ist es möglich über *Mara* (Kırobası) nach *Diokaisareia* zu gelangen. Die zweite Strecke führt Südlich von Kırobası über einen weiten Paß nach *Otanada* (Hotamış), folgt mehrere Kilometer der antiken Wasserleitung nach *Diokaisareia* und wendet sich bei Yeniçıktı nach Osten ab, um nach *Diokaisareia* aufzusteigen. Von hier aus ist es möglich über *Olba* (Uğuralanı) in die Küstenstadt *Korykos* (Kızkalesi) zu gelangen. Durch eine Abbiegung in südwestlicher Richtung bei Yeniçıktı, besteht die Möglichkeit über Keşlitürkmenli und *Imbriogon Kome* (Demircili), *Seleukeia* (pros to Kalykadno) zu erreichen (Karte 3).[41]

---

41 HILD/HELLENKEMPER 1990, 402–406.

Da der Meilenstein in einer Entfernung von ca. 10 km von der antiken Straße entdeckt wurde ist zu vermuten, dass dieser entweder von den Dorfbewohnern verschleppt wurde oder dass es sich hier um eine neue, bislang unbekannte Strecke handelt. Eine Antwort auf diese Frage konnte erst im Jahr 2014 gefunden werden. Während der Untersuchungen wurde ca. 4 km westlich des Meilensteines aus Kekikli, ein neuer Stein entdeckt (Abb. 1):

1) Meilenstein aus der Zeit des Kaisers Diokletian von der Flur Memedöldü

Die Inschrift ist oben, unten und auf der rechten Seite stark verwittert.

		Maße:		
Höhe:		Durchmesser:	Buchstabenhöhe:	Datierung:
Nr. 1	121 cm	60 cm	4,5–5 cm	295–305 n. Chr.

Der nur spärlich lesbare Text der Inschrift lautet:

ΑΝΩ
    ΕΠΙΦΑΝΕΣΤΑΤΩ
ΚΑΙΣΑΡΙ
    ΕΩΝΗΠΟΛΙΣ

Der Text kann folgendermaßen rekonstruieren werden:

    [Αὐτοκράτορι Καίσαρι Οὐαλ(ερίῳ)
    Διοκλητιανῷ εὐσεβεῖ εὐτυχεῖ
    Σεβ(αστῷ) καὶ Αὐτοκράτορι Καίσαρι
    Μάρ(κῳ) Αὐρ(ηλίῳ)
5   Μαξιμιανῷ Σεβ(αστῷ) καὶ
    Φλα(ουίῳ) Οὐαλ(ερίῳ) Κωσταντίῳ
    ἐπιφανεστάτῳ Καίσαρι καὶ Γαλερίῳ
    Μαξιμι]ανῷ
    ἐπιφανεστάτῳ Καίσαρι
10   [Διοκαισαρ]έων ἡ πόλις.

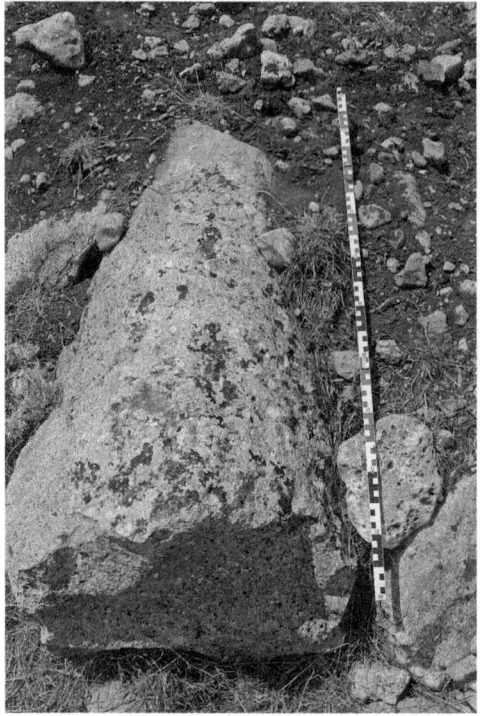

Abb. 1: Meilenstein aus Memedöldü

Da es im römischen Kaiserreich seit dem Ende des julisch-claudischen Dynastie üblich war, dass die Thronerben als Zeichen ihrer Anwartschaft die Bezeichnung Caesar mit oder ohne das Ehrenprädikat *nobilissimus* = ἐπιφανέστατος verliehen bekamen,[42] sind in den mittleren verschollenen Zeilen der Inschrift der Name oder die Namen von Caesaren zu erwarten. Es könnte sich hier ebenfalls um einen Meilenstein aus der Zeit Diocletians und seiner Mitregenten handeln, der zusammen unter demselben Bauprogramm mit dem Meilenstein aus Kekikli aufgestellt wurde. Diese beiden Meilensteine bezeugen ferner eine neue Strecke, die sich früherer als die bekannte Straße nach Nord-Nordwesten wendet. Somit wurde vermutlich eine viel kürzere, strategische Straße gebaut, wie es auch die letzte Zeile der Inschrift bezeugt, um vom *caput viae Diokaisareia* über Yeniçıktı, Memedöldü und *Kodaka*, *Klaudiopolis* zu erreichen (Karte 2).

Die wichtigste Nord-Süd Strecke im östlichen Rauhen Kilikien ist freilich die von der Küste gelegenen Handelsstadt *Korykos* über das Hochland nach *Iconium* führende Straße. Sie ist aus mehreren Publikationen bekannt,[43] wurde aber bisher nicht syste-

---

42 MITTHOF 1993, 97ff.
43 Zu den Strassen HILD/HELLENKEMPER 1990, 128ff; SAYAR 2002, 468f.

matisch dokumentiert. Auf dieser Strecke sind bereits 58 beschriftete und anepigraphische Meilensteine bekannt. Während der Feldforschungen im Jahr 2015 wurden weitere 22 neue Meilensteine entdeckt, die ca. 130 km lange antike Straße mit GPS vermessen und dokumentiert.

2) Meilensteine aus der Flur Tol bei Hüseyinler

Mit der Vermessung wurde ca. 8. Nördlich des Dorfes Hüseyinler bei der Flur Tol angefangen. Hier wurden vier neue Meilensteine aus Kalkstein entdeckt, die inmitten der antiken Straße mit den beschrifteten Flächen nach unten vergraben waren.[44] (Abb. 2)

		Maße:
	Höhe:	Durchmesser:
Nr. 1	235 cm	65 cm
Nr. 2	240 cm	70 cm
Nr. 3	173 cm	65 cm
Nr. 4	180 cm	65 cm

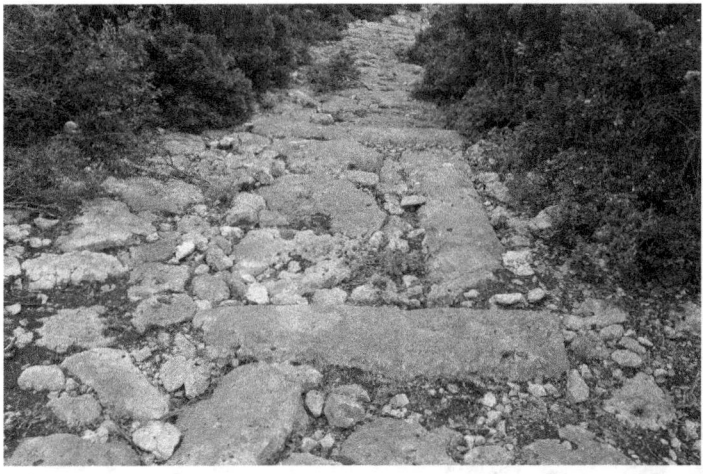

Abb. 2: Meilensteine aus der Flur Tol bei Hüseyinler

---

44 ŞAHIN/KÜÇÜKOĞLU 2016, 183.

3) Meilensteine aus dem Karyağdı-Tal

4 km nordwestlich von Hüseyinler im Karyağdı-Tal hatten wir die Gelegenheit, die schon durch die ältere Literatur bekannten vier Meilensteine mit deren Publikationen[45] zu vergleichen. Ca. 150 m nördlich von diesen wurden weitere fünf neue Meilensteine entdeckt.[46]

Meilenstein aus grauem Kalkstein. Vollständig erhalten. Die achtzeilige Inschrift an mehreren Stellen stark verwittert (Abb. 3).

	Maße:			
Höhe:		Durchmesser:	Buchstabenhöhe:	Datierung:
Nr. 1	240 cm	56 cm	3–6 cm	306–307 n. Chr.

```
    DD(ominis) nn(ostris)
    Maxi[m]ian[o]
    [et] [M]aximian[o]
    [in]victi[s] [A]u[gg](ustis)
5   [et] Maximino
    [e]t Constantino
    [n]obilissimis
    vac. [C]aess(aribus) vac. m(ilia) p(assuum) X[--
```

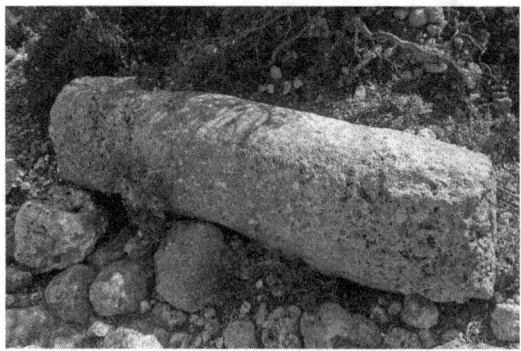

Abb. 3: Meilenstein mit Sockel aus dem Karyağdı-Tal

---

45 Sayar 1995, 118.
46 Şahin/Küçükoğlu 2016, 184.

Aus derselben Zeit stammt auch der Meilenstein aus dem ca. 4 km weiter nordwestlich gelegenen Yeğenli[47] und drei weitere Exemplare aus der Kilikia Pedias.[48]

Ca. 50 m südlich dieses Fundes wurden zwei weitere Miliarien aus demselben grauen Kalkstein entdeckt, die höchstwahrscheinlich auch in die Zeit der Tetrarchie zu datieren sind.[49]

Meilenstein aus grauem Kalkstein mit Sockel. Vollständig erhalten. Nur noch einige Buchstaben der letzten Zeile erhalten (Abb. 4).

Höhe:	Maße: Durchmesser:	Buchstabenhöhe:	Datierung:
Nr. 2 183 cm	59 cm	3,5–4 cm	295–305 n. Chr.?

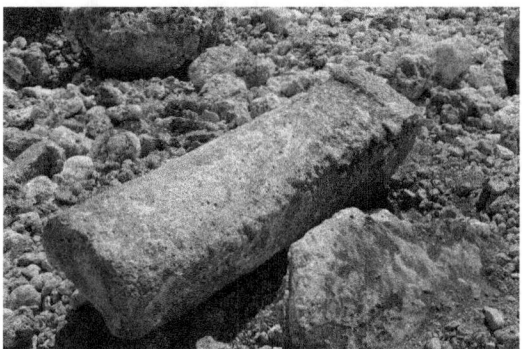

Abb. 4: Meilenstein mit Sockel aus dem Karyağdı-Tal

- - - - -

Διοκαισα]ρέων ἡ π[όλις].

---

47 RRMAM III 7, 31B: *DD(ominis) nn(ostris) | Maximiano [et] | Maximiano | invictis Augg(ustis) | et Maximino |/⁵ et Constantino | [no]bilissimis | [Ca]es[ar]ibus| m(ilia) p(assuum) II |]MA[- – –] | imp(erator) X[- – –] ||¹⁰ co(n)s(ul) p(ater) p(atriae) [- – -*
48 RRMAM III 7, 15E (Yeşildam): *DD(ominis) nn(ostris) Maximiano et | Maximiano inv(ictis) Augustis [et] | Maximino et | Constantino | nobiliss(imis) Caess(aribus) |m(ilia) I ||⁵ DD(ominis) nn(ostris) | Crispo et |Licinio et | Constantino | n[obili]ss(imis) Caess(aribus).; 38 (Bayramlı, Tarsus): DD(ominis) nn(ostris) | [[[Maximiano et]]] | Maximiano | invictis Augg(ustis) et | [[[Maximino et]]] ||⁵ Constantino | nobilissimis Caess(aribus) |mil(ia) | [XII].* Sayar 2000, Nr. 19: *D(ominis) n(ostris) Maximiano et | Maximiano Inv(ictis) Augustis [et] | Maximino et | Constantino | nobilis(simis) Caes(aribus) | m(ilia) I ||⁵ D(ominis) n(ostris) | Crispo et | Licin{n}io et| / Constatino| / n[obili]s(simis) Caes(aribus).*
49 Die Meilensteine werden zur Publikation vorbereitet.

Meilenstein aus grauem Kalkstein. Oben und unten abgebrochen. Inschrift stark verwittert (Abb. 5).

Höhe:	Maße: Durchmesser:	Buchstabenhöhe:	Datierung:
Nr. 3	75 cm	50 cm	2, 5–5 cm	–

```
       [- - - - - -
       [- - - - - -
       [- - - - - -
       [- - - - - -TON- - - - - -
 5     [- - - - - -
      -[- - - - - -Γ
       [- - - - - -ΦΛ- - - - - -
       [- - - - - -ΚΩΝ- - - - - -
       [- - - - - -ΝΕΙ – Η - - -
10     [- - - - - -ΝΟ- - - - - -
```

Z. 4: Σεβαστὸν?
Z. 7: Φλαβίῳ?
Z. 8: Κωσταντείνῳ?

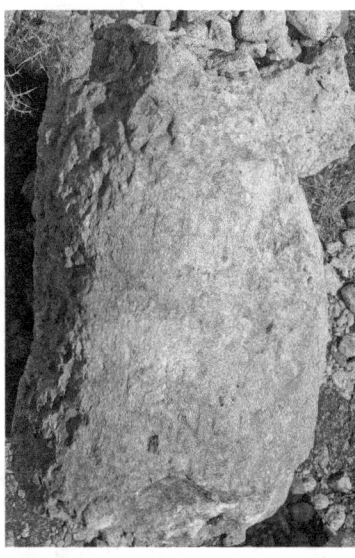

Abb. 5: Meilensteinfragment aus dem Karyağdı-Tal

Meilenstein aus grauem Kalkstein mit zwei Inschriften (A-B). Inschrift B, rechts von der Inschrift A. Der Stein ist unten abgebrochen. Inschriften strak verwittert (Abb. 6).

	Maße:			
Höhe:		Durchmesser:	Buchstabenhöhe:	Datierung:
Nr. 4	150 cm	45 cm	2,5–5, 5cm	306–307 n. Chr.

Inschrift A: Inschrift B:

    [DD(omini) nn(ostris)]   [– - – - – -
    [Maximiano]   [– - – - – -
    [et Maximiano]   [– - – - – -
    [invictis Augg(ustis)]   [– - – - – -
5   [et Maximino]   [– - – - – -NOS
    et Con[stan]tino   [– - – - – – IOS
    no[b]ilissim[is]   [- – - - – - -
    Caess(aribus)   [C - - - - –
    C ˋR ˋV ˋP ˋI ˋL ˋO ˋ   [CAE
    Milia [- – -

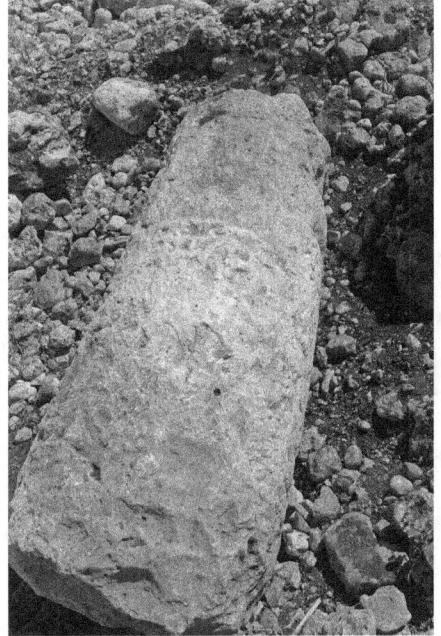

Abb. 6: Meilenstein aus dem Karyağdı-Tal

Meilenstein aus grauem Kalkstein mit Sockel. Inschrift stark verwittert. Am Anfang der achten Zeile Reste griechischer Buchstaben.

		Maße:		
Höhe:		Durchmesser:	Buchstabenhöhe:	Datierung:
Nr. 5	166 cm	60 cm	3–5 cm	306–307 n. Chr.

```
    DD(ominis) nn(ostris)
    [[Maximiano]]
    [et] Maximiano
    invicti[s] Augg(ustis)
5   [et] M[aximino]
    et Constantino
    [nobil]issimis
    θ  vac.  C[ae]ss[a]ri[bus]
```

4) Meilenstein aus der Flur Dikenlialan

Nach dem Karyagdı-Tal führt die Straße ca. 6 km weiter nach Norden, wo sie östlich der Stadt Olba nach Westen in Richtung *Diokaisareia* und Dikenlialan abbiegt. Wegen des Baus der modernen Landstraße war es nicht möglich den Straßenabschnitt zwischen diesen beiden Orten zu verfolgen. Ca. 200 m weiter nördlich von Dikenlialan sind die Reste der antiken Trassenführung wieder zu sehen (Abb. 7). Direkt neben der Straße wurde ein neuer Meilenstein aus Kalkstein entdeckt. Dieser ist oben und unten abgebrochen und anepigraph (Abb. 8).[50] Vermutlich war der Text aufgemalt, was keineswegs selten war.

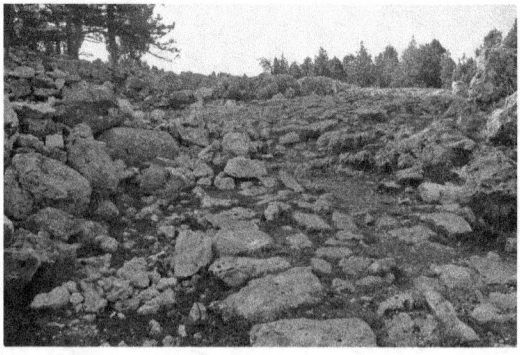

Abb. 7: Dikenlialan: Reste der Antiken Straße

---

50 ŞAHIN/KÜÇÜKOĞLU 2016, 185.

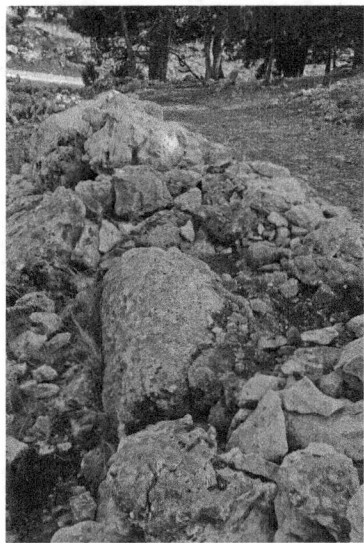

Abb. 8: Meilensteinfragment aus der Flur Dikenlialan

	Maße:	
	Höhe:	Durchmesser:
Nr. 1	115 cm	63 cm

5) Meilenstein aus der Flur Bozağaç

Die Straße führt von Dikenlialan für ca. 2 km weiter in nordwestlicher Richtung. In der Flur Bozağaç wurde ein weiterer Meilenstein aus grauem Kalkstein entdeckt, der in drei Teile gebrochen ist (Abb. 9).[51]

	Maße:	
	Höhe:	Durchmesser:
Nr. 1	104 cm	60 cm

---

51 ŞAHIN/KÜÇÜKOĞLU 2016, 185.

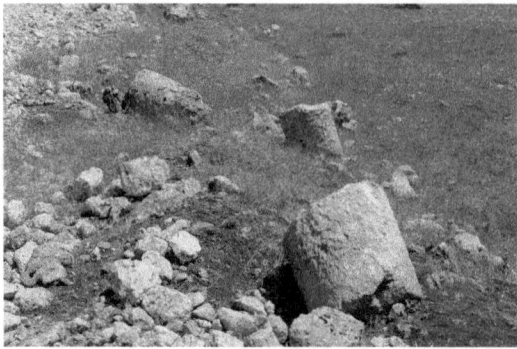

Abb. 9: Meilensteinfragmente aus der Flur Bozağaç

Die Inschrift befindet sich auf dem mittleren Steinstück und ist bis zur Unkenntlichkeit verwittert. Jedoch zeigt dieser Fund, dass die Strecke nach den Orten *Diokaisareia*-Dikenlialan-Bozağaç weiterhin nach Norden, in Richtung *Laranda* führt. Dieser Teil der Straße führt bis nach Hotamış, dem antiken *Otanada*, und gabelt sich hier. Der nach Westen führende Zweig endet bei dem Dorf *Mara* (Kırobası). Während unseren Feldforschungen im Jahr 2015 entdeckten wir bei dem Dorf Kocaoluk einen neuen Straßenabschnitt, der sich 7 km nach *Otanada*, weiter in Richtung Norden wendet. Dieser Teil der Straße ist bis zum 4 km nördlich gelegenen Saraydın weiter verfolgbar. Reste der antiken Trasse in der Flur Ayaştürkmenli bezeugen, dass die Straße ab Saraydın weiter nach Norden führt. Hier beträgt die Breite der Fahrbahn ca. 4.5 m. Auch Spurrillen von Pferdewagen sind sichtbar.

6) Meilenstein aus dem Söğüt-Tal

Im ca. 10 km weiter nördlich gelegenen Söğüt-Tal (Abb. 10) wurden weitere Reste der gut gepflasterten Straße entdeckt, deren Breite 4,5 m beträgt. Ca. 10 m. rechts der Fahrbahn liegt ein Meilenstein der auch mit der Inschriftenfläche nach unten begraben ist (Abb. 11).

	Maße:	
	Höhe:	Durchmesser:
Nr. 1	170 cm	50 cm

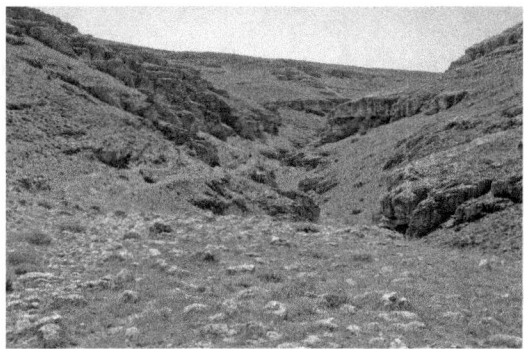

Abb. 10: Straßenverlauf durch das Söğüt-Tal

7) Meilensteine aus der Flur Borcakesiği

Vom Söğüt-Tal aus ist der Verlauf der Straße für gut 2 km zu verfolgen. 4 km weiter nördlich, bei Alanboğsak trafen wir wieder auf ihre Spuren. Von hier aus ist die Trasse bis zu dem sechs km nördlich gelegenen Ort Borcacekiği zu verfolgen. Direkt neben der ca. 4 m breiten Fahrbahn bei Borcakesiği (Abb. 12) wurden drei weitere Meilensteine entdeckt. Zwei dieser Meilensteine sind erneut anepigraphisch.[52] Auf dem dritten sind sehr leichte rote Farbspuren zu erkennen, die Zeugnis für die grundsätzliche Existenz von aufgemalten Inschriftentexten ablegen. Leider sind nur wenige Buchstaben der Inschrift zu lesen, die zudem keinerlei Hinweise zur Datierung geben (Abb. 13).

	Maße:	
Höhe:	Durchmesser:	Buchstabenhöhe:
Nr. 1	193 cm	54 cm	–
Nr. 2	95 cm	53 cm	–
Nr. 3	147 cm	53 cm	3,5 cm

---

52 ŞAHIN/KÜÇÜKOĞLU 2016, 187.

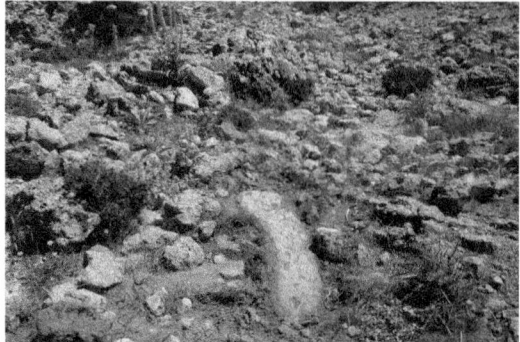

Abb. 11: Antike Straße und Meilenstein aus dem Söğüt-Tal

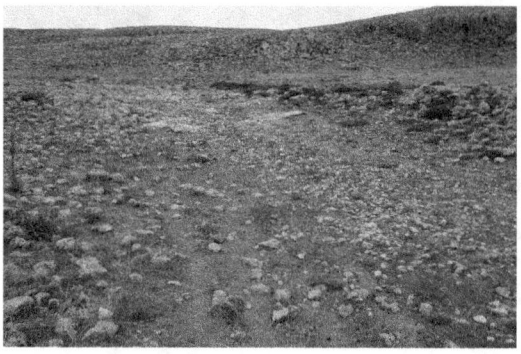

Abb. 12: Antike Straßenreste bei Borcakesiği

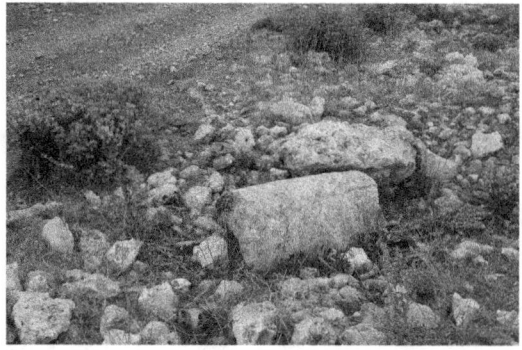

Abb. 13: Meilensteinfragment aus der Flur Borcakesiği

8) Meilenstein aus der Flur Kazanpınar

Ca. 3 km weiter nördlich von Borcakesiği trafen wir bei Kazanpınar wieder auf die antike Straße. 1,5 km nördlich hiervon wurde ein weiterer neuer Meilenstein gefunden, der Zeugnis vom weiteren Trassenverlauf nach Norden gibt. Der Meilenstein ist in mehrere Stücke gebrochen (Abb. 14). Auf einem der Stücke sind einige Spuren von lateinischen Buchstaben erkennbar.

	Maße:	
	Höhe:	Durchmesser:
Nr. 1	111 cm	59 cm

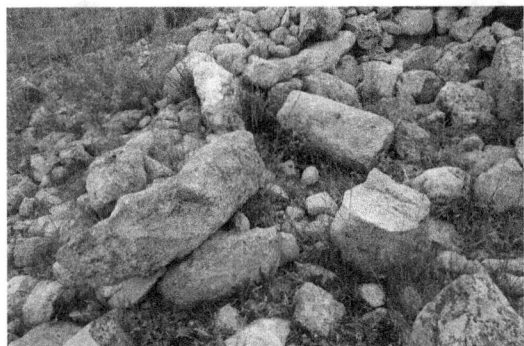

Abb. 14: Meilensteinfragmente aus der Flur Kazanpınar

9) Meilensteine aus der Flur Yılanlıkeben

Reste der antiken Straße (Abb. 15) und zwei weitere anepigraphische Meilensteinfunde bei der Flur Yılanlıkeben (Abb. 16), ca. 5 km nordwestlich von Borcakesiği, bezeugen weiterhin den Streckenverlauf nach Norden.[53] Die antike Straße führt von Gölyeri über den Belveren-Pass und zwischen den Bergen Aldan und Kızıl nach *Laranda*.

	Maße:	
	Höhe:	Durchmesser:
Nr. 1	165 cm	36 cm
Nr. 2	164 cm	49 cm

---

53 ŞAHIN/KÜÇÜKOĞLU 2016, 188.

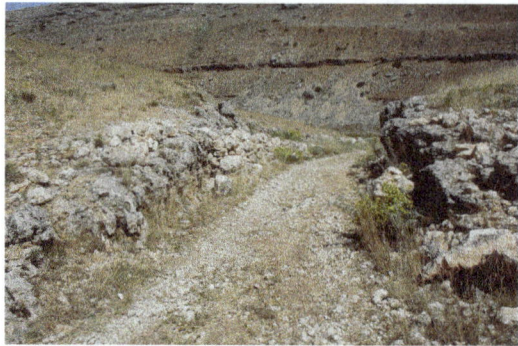
Abb. 15: Reste der antiken Straße bei Yılanlıkeben

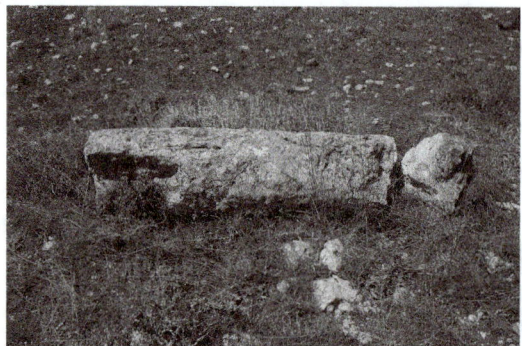
Abb. 16: Meilenstein aus der Flur Yılanlıken

Durch die oben angeführten Meilensteininschriften sind im Rauhen Kilikien vier Phasen des Ausbaues und der Renovierung der Straßen zwischen dem 1. und 4 Jahrhundert n. Chr. zu erkennen. Die frühesten Zeugnisse in diesem Gebiet stammen aus der Zeit Vespasians und seines Sohnes. Die zweite Phase fällt in die Regierungszeit Hadrians, welche die Meilensteininschriften aus Charadros und Kırkkuyu im Westen der Provinz belegen. Die dritte Phase fällt in den Zeitraum der Samtherrschaft von Septimius Severus und Caracalla, wie weitere Meilensteine aus Kırkkuyu, *Korakesion*, *Syedra* und *Antiokheia* ad *Cragum* sowie aus *Diokaisareia*, aus dem östlichen Teil des Gebiets bezeugen. Die vierte Phase belegen die Inschriften aus der Zeit der Tetrarchie aus dem Karyağdı Tal, Kekikli, Memedöldü und die neuen Meilensteine aus der Strecke Korykos-Laranda.

Bibliographie

AKYÜREK ŞAHIN/ŞAHIN 2000 = N.E. AKYÜREK ŞAHIN/S. ŞAHIN, Ein Meilenstein aus Tlos, *Klio* 98/2, 2000, 475–482.
CUNTZ 1929 = O. CUNTZ, Itineraria Antonini Augusti et Burdigalense, Itineraria Romana, Bd. 1, Leipzig 1929.
ECK 2004 = W. ECK, Lateinisch, Griechisch, Germanisch...? Wie sprach Rom mit seinen Untertanen?, in: L. DE LIGT/E.A. HEMELRIJK/H.W. SINGOR (Hg.) Roman rule and civic life: Local and regional perspectives, Proceedings of the Fourth Workshop of the International Network, Impact of Empire (Roman Empire, c. 200 B. C.–A. D. 476), Leiden, June 25–28, 2003, Leiden 2004, 3–19.
FRENCH 1965 = D.H. FRENCH, Prehistoric Sites in the Göksu Valley, *AS* 15, 1965, 177–201.
FRENCH 1988 = D.H. FRENCH, Roman Roads and Milestones of Asia Minor, Fasc. 2: An Interim Catalogue of Milestones 1,2, BAR, Oxford 1988.
GRASSHOFF 2009 = G. GRASSHOFF, Untersuchungen zum Stadiasmos von Patara: Modellierung und Analyse eines antiken geographischen Streckennetzes, Bern 2009.
HAGEL/TOMASCHITZ 1998 = S. HAGEL/K. TOMASCHITZ, Repertorium der westkilikischen Inschriften, Wien 1998.
HEBERDEY/WILHELM 1896 = R. HEBERDEY/A. WILHELM, Reisen in Kilikien. Ausgeführt 1891 und 1892 im Auftrage der kaiserlichen Akademie der Wissenschaften, Wien 1896.
HILD/HELLENKEMPER 1990 = F. HILD/H. HELLENKEMPER, Tabula Imperii Byzantini, Bd. 5: Kilikien und Isaurien, Wien 1990.
KOLB 2004 = A. KOLB, Römische Meilensteine: Stand der Forschung, in: R. FREI-STOLBA (Hg.), Siedlung und Verkehr im römischen Reich, Bern 2004, 135–155.
MILLER 1916 = K. MILLER, Itineraria Romana. Römische Reisewege an der Hand der Tabula Peutingeriana, Stuttgart 1916.
MITTHOF 1993 = F. MITTHOF, Vom ἱερώτατος Καῖσαρ zum ἐπιφανέστατος Καῖσαρ. Die Ehrenprädikate in der Titulatur der Thronfolger des 3. Jh. n. Chr. nach den Papyri, *ZPE* 99, 1993, 97–111.
MROZEWICZ 2004, = L. MROZEWICZ, Via et imperium. Strassenbau und Herrschaft in römischer Welt, in: R. FREI-STOLBA (Hg.), Siedlung und Verkehr im römischen Reich, Bern 2004, 345–359.
NOLLÉ 2001 = J. NOLLÉ, Side im Altertum, Geschichte und Zeugnisse, Bd. 2, Bonn 2001.
RATHMANN 2006 = M. RATHMANN, Der Statthalter und die Verwaltung der Reichsstraßen, in: A. KOLB (Hg.), Herrschaftsstrukturen und Herrschaftspraxis, Berlin 2006, 201–259.
RRMAM III = D.H. FRENCH, Roman Roads and Milestones of Asia Minor Vol. 3: Milestones, Fasc. 3.7: Cilicia, Isauria et Lycaonia (and South-West Galatia) (BIAA Electronic Monograph 7, London 2014.
ŞAHIN 2009 = H. ŞAHIN, Ein neuer Meilenstein Diokletians aus dem östlichen rauhen Kilikien, *Gephyra* 6, 2009 131–135.
ŞAHIN 2014 = H. ŞAHIN, Corpus Inscriptionum Latinarum XVII/5-3 Miliaria Provinciarum Lyciae-Pamphyliae et Ciliciae Project 2013 Studies, Anmed, *News of Archaeology from Anatolias Mediterranean Areas* 2014-12, 184–188.
ŞAHIN 2015a = H. ŞAHIN, Zwei neue Meilensteine aus dem Rauhen Kilikien –Vorarbeiten zum Band Corpus Inscriptionum Latinarum XVII/5, 3, Miliaria Provinciarum Lyciae-Pamphyliae et Ciliciae, *MDAI(I)* 65, 2015, 293–304.
ŞAHIN 2015b = H. ŞAHIN, Work of the Corpus Inscriptionum Latinarum XVII/5-3 Miliaria Provinciarum Lyciae-Pamphyliae et Ciliciae Project, Anmed, *News of Archaeology from Anatolias Mediterranean Areas* 2015-13, 180–184.
ŞAHIN/KÜÇÜKOĞLU 2016 = H. ŞAHIN/S. KÜÇÜKOĞLU, Corpus Inscriptionum Latinarum XVII/5-3 Miliaria Provinciarum Lyciae-Pamphyliae et Ciliciae Project 2015 Studies, Anmed, *News of Archaelogy from Anatolias Mediterranean Areas* 14, 2016, 183–189.

Şahın/Adak 2007 = S. Şahın/M. Adak, Stadiasmus Patarensis, Istanbul 2007.
Sayar 1995 = M.H. Sayar, Kilikia'da Epigrafi ve Tarihi Coğrafya Araştırmaları 1995, *Araştırma Sonuçları Toplantısı* 14.1, 1995, 115–122.
Sayar 2000 = M.H. Sayar Die Inschriften von Anabarzos und Umgebung (IK56,1), Bonn 2000.
Sayar 2002 = M.H. Sayar, Antike Straßenverbindungen Kilikiens in der römischen Kaiserzeit, in: E. Olshausen/H. Sonnabend (Hg.), Zu Wasser und zu Land: Verkehrswege in der antiken Welt, Stuttgarter Kolloquium zur historischen Geographie des Altertums, Bd. 7, Stuttgart 2002, 452–473.
Sayar 2015 = M.H. Sayar, Kanytellis Yazıtlar, in: Ü. Aydınoğlu (Hg.), Kanytellis. Dağlık Kilikia'da Bir Kırsal Yerleşimin Arkeolojisi, İstanbul 2015, 113–130.
Schmidt 2007 = M.G. Schmidt, Corpus Inscriptionum Latinarum, Berlin 2007.
Schneider 1999 = E.E. Schneider (Hg.), Elaiussa Sebaste. Campagne di scavo 1995–1997, Rom 1999.
Schneider 2003 = E.E. Schneider (Hg.), Elaiussa Sebaste II. Un porto tra Oriente e Occidente, Rom 2003
Schneider 2010 = E.E. Schneider (Hg.), Elaiussa Sebaste III. L´Agora Romana, Istanbul 2010.

Stefan Groh – Helga Sedlmayer
Via publica vel militaris: Die Bernsteinstraße in spätantoninischer und severischer Zeit

Abstract: The amber road was primarily a *via publica*, maintained by colonies as well as *municipia*, which were each subject to different rights of intervention by the governor and thus the imperial house in questions of infrastructure. It was a *via militaris* only where it passed through territory with a special military status, so for example at the time of the Marcomannic Wars in the passport area between the Regio X and Noricum, and during the first two centuries CE in the area of Strebersdorf *metalla*.

Zusammenfassung: Die Bernsteinstraße war primär *via publica*, instand gehalten von Kolonien wie auch Munizipien, für die ein jeweils unterschiedliches Durchgriffsrecht des Statthalters und somit des Kaiserhauses in Fragen der Infrastruktur bestand. *Via militaris* war sie nur dort, wo ein Sonderstatus in Form eines Militärterritoriums vorlag, so beispielsweise zur Zeit der Markomannenkriege im Bereich der Passpassage zwischen der Regio X und *Noricum*, und zudem während der ersten beiden Jahrhunderte n. Chr. im Bereich der *metalla* von Strebersdorf.

Die Funktion der aus der Regio X nach Nordosten führende Bernsteinstraße (Abb. 1) als *via militaris* hat eine lange Tradition und reicht in der Zeit des frühen Prinzipats zurück. Mit der spätaugusteischen Gründung des Legionslagers *Poetovio*-Ptuj (*legio VIII Augusta*)[1] erfolgte eine zügige Erschließung der nördlich angrenzenden Gebiete in tiberisch-claudischer Zeit durch die – bislang archäologisch gesicherten – befestigten militärischen Stützpunkte in *Salla*-Zalalövő[2] und Strebersdorf/Burgenland[3].

Archäologische Zeugnisse eines Legionslagers sind in Poetovio nicht vorhanden; es wird vermutet, dass sich dieses südlich der Drau in Spodnja Hajdina erstreckte und durch eine Verlagerung des Flussbetts der Drau zerstört wurde[4]. In *Salla*-Zalalövő und Strebersdorf (Abb. 1, 4) hingegen sind Befunde römischer Holz-Erde-Lager dokumentiert; die Errichtung des Quinquenaria-Lagers I von Strebersdorf wird in augusteisch-frühtiberische Zeit datiert[5].

Unter Claudius I. wurde schließlich ein zusätzlicher Legionsstandort an der Donau, in *Carnuntum*-Bad Deutsch-Altenburg[6], mit der Stationierung der *legio XV*

---

1 VOMER GOJKOVIČ 2005, 49.
2 REDŐ 2003, 202–204; REDŐ 2005, 133–142.
3 GROH 2009a, 180–182; GROH 2009b, 61.
4 VOMER GOJKOVIČ 2005, 50.
5 GROH 2009a, 180–182; GROH 2009b, 61.
6 GUGL 2007, 197–201, 203.

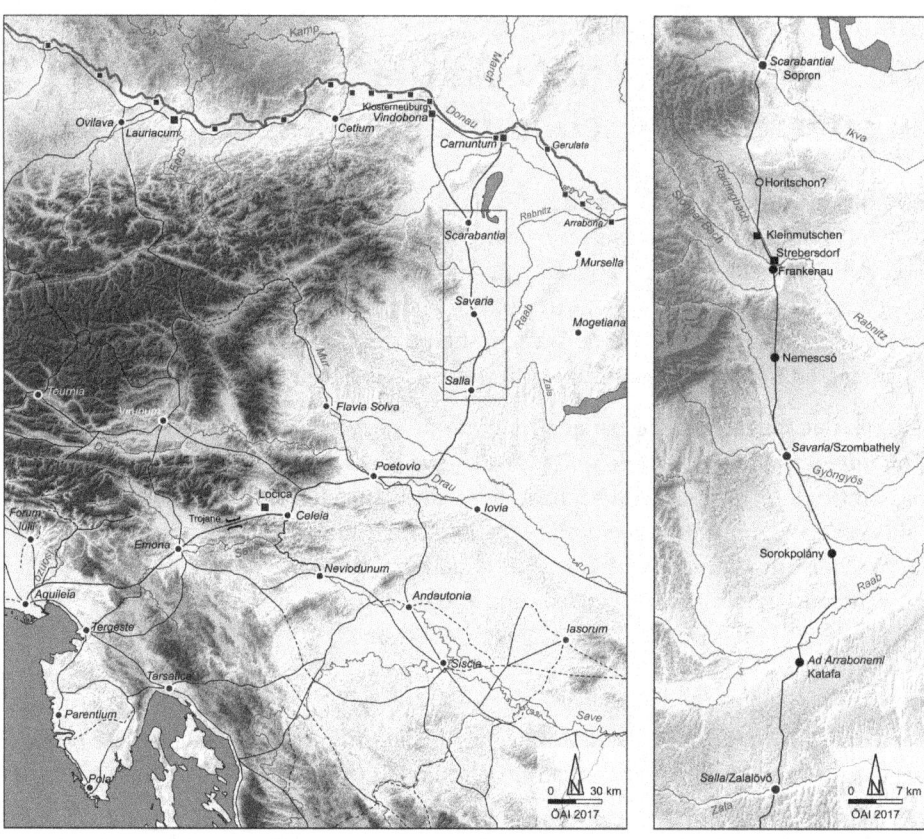

Abb. 1: Verlauf der Bernsteinstraße zwischen *Aquileia* und dem Donaulimes (Graphik ÖAW/ÖAI)

Apollinaris geschaffen und die Veteranenkolonie *Savaria*-Szombathely gegründet[7], die spätestens in traianischer Zeit eine Befestigung erhielt[8].

Die Bernsteinstraße hatte zeitweilig im frühen 2. Jh. n. Chr. als militärische Aufmarschroute ihre Bedeutung gegenüber dem Donaulimes eingebüßt. Ein Wechsel von militärischer zu ziviler Verantwortlichkeit ist für den Raum zwischen *Poetovio* und *Salla* zu dokumentieren. Bereits unter Traianus (vor 102 n. Chr.) wurde die in *Poetovio* stationierte Legion (*XIII Gemina*) nach *Vindobona*-Wien abgezogen und die Ansiedlung zur *colonia*[9]. Das Kastell in *Salla* bestand nur im 1. Jh. n. Chr., die verbleibende Zivilsiedlung wurde unter Hadrianus zum Munizipium[10]. In Strebersdorf ist

---

7 SCHERRER 2003, 53.
8 GABLER 2002, 130.
9 MOSSER 2010, 29.
10 REDŐ 2005, 142.

die Errichtung des Lagers II in der zweiten Hälfte des 1. Jhs. n. Chr. anzusetzen, die Zeitstellung des jüngsten Kleinkastells III bleibt noch zu klären[11].

Zum *exercitus Pannonicus* an der Bernsteinstraße zur Zeit der Markomannenkriege

Im Falle eines feindlichen Übergriffs waren somit während der mittleren Kaiserzeit durchgreifende operative Maßnahmen im Einzugsgebiet der Bernsteinstraße ausschließlich durch die am Donaulimes stationierten Truppen möglich, die aus den Legionsstandorten *Vindobona* und *Carnuntum* sowie aus den mit Auxilien belegten Kastellen *Carnuntum*-Petronell und *Gerulata*-Rusovce die Einfallsroute nach Italien auf schnellstem Wege sichern konnten (Abb. 1)[12].

Truppenangehörige des *exercitus pannonicus* sind unter Marcus Aurelius entlang der Bernsteinstraße – südlich der Militärplätze am Donaulimes – nur in *Poetovio* epigraphisch erfasst. Die diesbezügliche Quellenlage ist allerdings sehr eingeschränkt: Laut B. LŐRINCZ könnte für eine Reaktivierung eines militärischen Standplatzes in *Poetovio* zur Zeit der Markomannenkriege der Nachweis eines Soldaten der neu aufgestellten *cohors II Aurelia Dacorum milliaria equitata* sprechen[13].

Mangels aussagekräftiger epigraphischer wie archäologischer Quellen sind demnach kaum Schlüsse auf ein militärisches Vorgehen seitens der Römer am pannonischen Abschnitt der Bernsteinstraße südlich von Carnuntum zur Zeit der Markomannenkriege möglich. In Hinblick auf die inschriftlichen Testimonia ist für Oberpannonien zudem hervorzuheben, dass für die Zeit des Marcus Aurelius kein einziges vorliegt, das Militärs einer *expeditio Germanica* nennt[14].

---

11 GROH 2009a, 180.
12 Das gesamte oberpannonische Heer setzte sich zur Zeit der Markomannenkriege aus drei Legionen und durchschnittlich 17 Auxiliareinheiten (circa 30.000 Mann) zusammen.
13 LŐRINCZ 2001, 92–93, 245, Nr. 293. Unter den Severern ist diese Kohorte durch Ziegelstempel im Kastell *Cornacum*-Sotin am unterpannonischen Limes nachgewiesen (LŐRINCZ 2001, 93, 98, 246, Nr. 294), rund 25 km südlich der Einmündung des Flusses Drau in die Donau; der zitierte *optio* könnte somit auch einfach *Poetovio* passiert haben, um *Cornacum* zu erreichen.
14 Die noch in ROSENBERGER 1992, 104, Anm. 81 als Beleg für eine Nennung einer *expeditio Germanica* zitierte bruchstückhafte Weihung aus *Carnuntum* (AE 1982, 778) wird heute völlig anders ergänzt und interpretiert: AEA 1982, 19 und Korrektur in: EHD-001223.

Gründung eines Legionslagers am Fuß des Trojanerpasses *extra Italiam* 169/170

Ein einschneidender Wechsel in der Zuständigkeit von der zivilen Verwaltung zu einer militärischen lässt sich an der Grenzpassage der Bernsteinstraße Richtung Italien dokumentieren. Hier ist – im Vergleich zum oben Gesagten – ein militärisches Operieren seitens der Römer in deutlich stärkerem Ausmaß zu erfassen. Zwischen der Regio X einerseits und der Provinz *Noricum* andererseits wurde als Gegenreaktion auf die feindlichen Übergriffe eine verwaltungstechnische Neuorganisation an der Bernsteinstraße von Marcus Aurelius durchgesetzt[15]. Mit der Schaffung einer *praetentura Italiae et Alpium* wurde die Möglichkeit eingeräumt, das Gebiet der prokuratorischen *provincia inermis* Noricum zu beschneiden, eine Legion (*legio II*) in Ločica zu stationieren, und somit den Streckenabschnitt der Bernsteinstraße über den Trojanerpass Richtung Italien als *via militaris* zu kontrollieren. Dass es sich hierbei um eine temporäre Lösung im Rahmen der *expeditio Germanica* handelte, dokumentiert die Quellenlage zu dieser Praetentur, die nur ein einziges Mal auf einer Ehreninschrift für den zuständigen kaiserlichen Legaten überliefert ist[16]: *[Q(uinto) Antistio Advento] / Q(uinti) f(ilio) Quir(ina) Postumio A[q]u[i]/lino co(n)s(uli) sacerdoti fetia/li leg(ato) Aug(usti) pr(o) pr(aetore) provinc(iae) Ger/maniae inferioris leg(ato) Aug(usti) / at praetenturam Italiae et / Alpium expeditione Germa/nica cura(tori) operum locorum-q(ue) / publicorum* usw.

Q. Antistius Adventus war spätestens ab 174 n. Chr. Praetor von Niedergermanien. Sein Auftrag für die *praetentura Italiae et Alpium* datiert früher. Laut J. Šašel bietet „einen terminus post quem für den Beginn des Auftrages ... die Prokuratel *operum publicorum* in den Jahren 168/169"[17]. Als *consularis* war der Legat der *praetentura*, Q. Antistius Adventus, für mindestens zwei Legionen verantwortlich[18], und zwar für die Truppenkörper der *legio II Pia* und *legio III Concordia*.

Es wird davon ausgegangen, dass die *praetentura Italiae et Alpium* nach dem Angriff auf Italien im Jahre 169 oder 170 eingerichtet wurde[19]. Dieses Datum wird bekräftigt durch den konkret 169/170 n. Chr. datierbaren gemeinsamen Einsatz von Vexillationen beider Truppenkörper, *legio II Pia* als auch *III Concordia*, beim Mauerbau von *Salona*-Solin[20].

Für die Sicherung der Grenzpassage nach Italien und im Zuge der *expeditio Germanica* wurde mit dem Bau der an der Bernsteinstraße, am Fuß des Trojanerpasses *extra Italiam* gelegenen *castra* von Ločica durch die *legio II Italica* zwar begonnen,

---

15 Šašel 1992, 388.
16 AE 1893, 88: gefunden in *Annouona*-Thibilis, Numidien.
17 Šašel 1992, 392.
18 Fitz 1968, 46, 50.
19 Fitz 1968, 43–44; Strobel 2001, 119.
20 CIL III 857.

jedoch eine Fertigstellung nie erreicht; so verblieb die Wehranlage ohne vorgelagerten Graben[21]. Die Bautätigkeit der zweiten Legion ist ebenda durch zahlreiche Ziegelstempel belegt ist. Auf der für das Legionslager Ločica bestimmten Baukeramik scheint neben dem nunmehr gängigen Beinamen *Italica* fallweise auch das ältere, in *Salona* dokumentierte Attribut *Pia* auf. Diese Ehrenbezeichnung ist in der Ziegelproduktionsstätte von Vransko dokumentiert, die vom Baudetachement der *legio II* nahe Ločica betrieben wurde, und zwar durch zwei unterschiedliche Stempelformulare: *[Leg(ionis) II] Ital(icae) P(iae) F(idelis)*[22] sowie *Leg(ionis) II Ital(icae) Pat(riae) P(iae)*[23].

Die *Legio II Italica* tug nach dem vorzeitigen Abbruch der Baumaßnahmen in Ločica[24] das Qualitativ *Pia* auch in dem am Donaulimes bezogenen Standlager in *Lauriacum*; dies ist dokumentiert anhand von Ziegelstempeln mit der alleinigen Kombination *Italica Pia* als auch in der Variante *Italica Pia Fidelis*[25].

Über ein Aufgebot von Allem was noch zum Schutz von Italien und Illyricum zur Verfügung stand durch die beiden Kaiser Lucius Verus und Marcus Aurelius wird kurz vor dem Tod des Lucius Verus im Frühjahr 169 in der *Historia Augusta* berichtet: *denique transcensis Alpibus longius processerunt composueruntque omnia, quae ad munimen Italiae atque Illyrici pertinebant*[26]. Zudem wird hier für die Zeit nach dem Tode des Lucius Verus nachdrücklich betont, dass Marcus Aurelius den Status von Provinzen aufgrund der Bedürfnisse des Krieges verändern musste, eine Tatsache, die in besonderem Maß *Noricum* im Zuge der erstmaligen dauerhaften Stationierung einer Legion (*II Italica*) betraf: *Provincias ex proconsularibus consulares aut ex consularibus proconsulares aut praetorias pro belli necessitate fecit*[27].

Die Situation unter Marcus Aurelius an der Bernsteinstraße zwischen Trojane und Ločica steht exemplarisch für die abschnittsweise verwaltungstechnische Umstrukturierung einer *via publica* in eine *via militaris*, verbunden mit einem zeitweiligen territorialen Verlust eines zivilen städtischen Zentrums.

---

21 GROH 2018, 33–35; 94–95.
22 LAZAR 2006, 36, Abb. 76/8.
23 LAZAR 2006, 35–36, Abb. 74, 75/1; SEDLMAYER 2018, 159–160 (Vransko). Zur Formel *Patriae Piae*: CIL X 5826 (Ferentino, 213 n. Chr.).
24 GROH 2018, 94–95.
25 RUZICKA 1919, 92–94, Abb. 22/15.17–20; DERINGER 1953, 79, Abb. 36/4; PETROVITSCH 2006, 335; SEDLMAYER 2018, 159–162.
26 HA Aur. 14,6; s. Kommentar FITZ 1968, 44–45.
27 HA Aur. 22,9.

Infrastruktur der Bernsteinstraße bis zur Periode der Markomannenkriege: Fallbeispiele des Abschnitts zwischen *Salla* und *Scarabantia*

Tab. 1: Distanzen der Straßentrasse zwischen Siedlungen, militärischen Einrichtungen Stationen an der Bernsteinstraße zwischen *Salla*-Zalalövő im Süden und *Scarabantia*-Sopron im Norden

Siedlungen/Stationen und Wachtürme an der Bernsteinstraße	Straße/Befund	*Itinerarium Antonini* 261,6–261,8	*Itinerarium Antonini* 262,5–262,7
Munizipium *Scarabantia*-Sopron ▲	16,2 km / 10,9 mp	Mpm XXXIIII	Mpm XXXIIII
Station(?) Horitschon ▲	7 km / 4,7 mp		
Wachturm/Station Kleinmutschen ▲	3,9 km / 2,6 mp		
Vicus Frankenau/Auxiliarkastell Strebersdorf ▲	12,2 km / 8,2 mp		
Wachturm/Station Nemescsó ▲	13 km / 8,8 mp		
Colonia Savaria-Szombathely ▲	13,7 km / 9,2 mp	Mpm XX	Mpm XXXI
Station Sorokpolány ▲	16 km / 10,8 mp		
Kleinkastell/Station *Ad Arrabonem*-Katafa ▲	17,7 km / 11,9 mp	–	
Munizipium *Salla*-Zalalövő			

Die Anrainer der *viae publicae* waren für Leistungen im Spanndienst und für die Beherbergung von Reisenden im staatlichen Auftrag verantwortlich, somit war der Erhalt der Straßeninfrastruktur Teil der *munera* der städtischen Verwaltungszentren eines Territoriums[28]. Im mittleren Abschnitt des pannonischen Verlaufs der Bernsteinstraße betraf dies die Munizipien *Salla* und *Scarabantia* einerseits sowie die *Colonia Savaria* andererseits. Der Ausbau des *cursus publicus* entlang der Bernsteinstraße mit einem dichten Netz untergeordneter Straßenstationen ist kaum vor traianischer Zeit anzunehmen. Bevorzugter Anlaufpunkt der Reisenden waren sicherlich die städtischen Zentren, die über eine Distanz von 47,4 km (*Salla – Savaria*) und 52,3 km (*Savaria – Scarabantia*) allerdings nur von Berittenen oder bei einem Wechsel der Transportmittel innerhalb einer Tagesetappe erreichbar waren[29]. Fraglich ist,

---

28 KOLB 2000, 123–136; SPEIDEL 2009, 508–511.
29 KOLB 2000, 312–314.

welcher Natur die von der zivilen Administration unterhaltenen Stationen außerhalb der Städte waren. Im Vicus von Frankenau könnte ein unmittelbar an einer Bachfurt errichtetes und an der Grenze eines städtischen und eines militärischen Territoriums situiertes Gebäude eventuell in diesem Sinn gedeutet werden, mit einem an den streifenförmigen Bau im Süden angrenzenden Hof mit möglichen Stellplätzen (Abb. 4)[30]. Allein schon die strategische Position nächst der naturräumlichen Trennlinie in Form des Bachs und die eventuell aus einem feindlichen Übergriff resultierende Brandzerstörung könnten Hinweise für einen speziellen Status dieser Baustruktur sein (s. unten zu Frankenau).

Da wie einleitend ausgeführt, die Bernsteinstraße seit Beginn der römischen Okkupation auch eine wichtige Funktion als *via militaris* erfüllte, ist prinzipiell davon auszugehen, dass, trotz der den Zivilisten auferlegten Beherbergungspflicht von *militantes*, eine eigenständige militärische Infrastruktur unabhängig von zivilen Einrichtungen für die abschnittsweise Kontrolle der wichtigen Fernverkehrsroute durch Benefiziarier und für eine kurzfristige Stationierung kleinster Detachements bestand. Solche durch das Militär betriebenen Stützpunkte sind insofern zu postulieren, als die in Form von Holzfachwerkbauten während der traianischen bis antoninschen Zeit entlang des hier behandelten Abschnitts der Bernsteinstraße bestehenden relativ kleinflächigen Strukturen als typisches Charakteristikum jeweils eine räumliche Begrenzung durch eine umgebende *fossa* oder Palisade aufweisen. Beispiele hierfür finden sich an der durch den Fluss Raab definierten Trennlinie zwischen den Territorien von *Salla* und *Savaria* in *Ad Arrabonem*-Katafa, zudem in Nemescsó/Periode 1 und in Kleinmutschen, 3,8 km nördlich des Standplatzes der einleitend genannten fühkaiserzeitlichen Militärlager von Strebersdorf (Abb. 2/1–3). Allen diesen Anlagen militärischen Charakters gemeinsam ist die Einhegung durch einen Graben bzw. eine Palisade. Diese sind als Annäherungshindernisse ebenso zu verstehen wie als territoriale Abgrenzung einer militärischen Einrichtung gegenüber dem zivil verwalteten Gebiet der Städte.

Die in Holzständerbauweise in der Periode vor den Markomannenkriegen errichteten militärischen Posten bestanden bis in spätantoninsche Zeit. Dann wurde der Standort entweder gewechselt, wie beispielsweise im Falle der Station von *Ad Arrabonem*-Katafa, oder aufgegeben, wie im Falle des Wachturms von Kleinmutschen, oder aber dieser diente in weiterer Folge während der frühseverischen Zeit zur Errichtung von Steinfundamentbauten mit Risalitarchitektur, ohne umgebende *fossa* (s.unten zu severischen Reformen, mit dem Beispiel von Nemescsó/Periode 2).

Von den oben genannten Gebäuden, die als Militärarchitektur konzipiert waren, unterscheiden sich die tabernenartigen Bauten ohne Begrenzung durch einen Graben, deren Existenz bereits in vorseverische Zeit nachzuweisen ist. Die vermutlich während der Markomannenkriege durch Brand zerstörte ältere Gebäudestruktur von Winden

---

30 Vgl. *Ambrussum*: FICHES 2003, 51–52, Abb. 4.

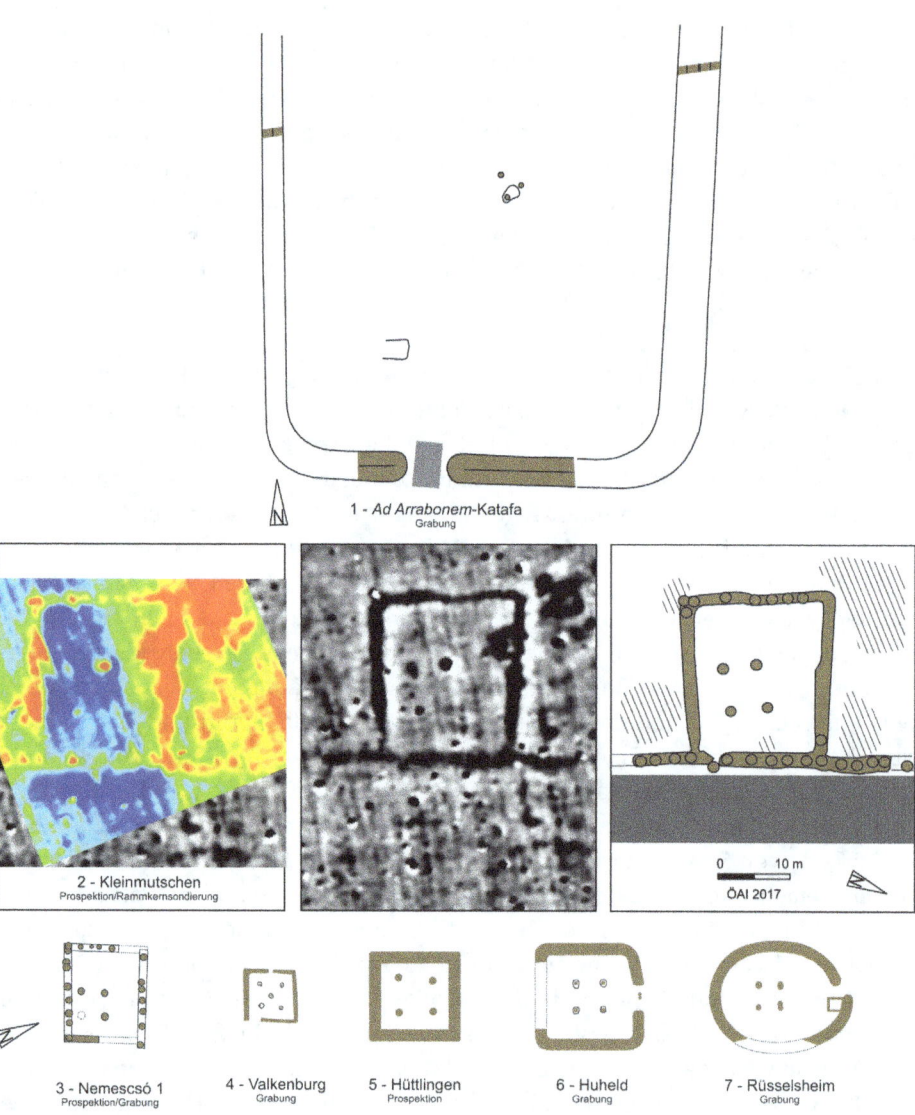

Abb. 2: Infrastruktur der Bernsteinstraße bis zur Periode der Markomannenkriege (1–3) und Vergleichsbefunde (4–7) (Graphik ÖAW/ÖAI, auf Basis von BENDER 2012, Abb.; CSERMÉNYI/TÓTH 1979–80, Abb. 10; FABRICIUS 1936, Taf. 13; HAALEBOS 2006, Abb. 455; SCHALLMAYER 2006, Abb. 421)

am See könnte an der Bernsteinstraße einen solchen Bautypus repräsentieren[31] und des Weiteren, im Einzugsgebiet dieser Haupttransitroute, die Station von Biedermannsdorf knapp vor *Vindobona*-Wien[32].

Der in Tabelle 1 definierte, rund 100 km lange Abschnitt der Bernsteinstraße zwischen den Munizipien von *Salla* und *Scarabantia* war in den letzten Jahren Teil eines vom Österreichischen Archäologischen Institut getragenen Forschungsprojekts zu den infrastrukturellen Einrichtungen der Fernhandelsroute abseits der städtischen Zentren. Seit einer 1980 vorgelegten Publikation zum Kleinkastell von *Ad Arrabonem* (Abb. 2/1)[33] im Territorium von *Salla* war es ein Desiderat, weitere Evidenzen zur militärischen oder zivilen Organisation in diesem Gebiet zu erfassen. Als erste sensationelle Ergebnisse konnten im Verwaltungsbezirk der *Colonia Savaria* die beiden *stabula* von Sorokpólany und Nemescsó (Abb. 3) vorgelegt werden, die in gleichförmiger baulicher Konzeption als Eckrisalitgebäude in annähernd übereinstimmender Distanz zum städtischen Zentrum *Savaria* während der frühseverischen Zeit umgesetzt wurden[34]. Mittels dieser Befunde konnte gezeigt werden, dass zwischen *Salla* im Süden und dem Vicus von Frankenau (Abb. 4) am nördlichsten Rand des Territoriums von *Savaria* die Bernsteinstraße circa alle 10 mp durch Stationen erschlossen war. Über die Infrastruktur nördlich des Militärplatzes von Strebersdorf hingegen lagen bislang keinerlei Informationen vor. Umfangreiche geophysikalische Prospektionen[35] auf einem Streckenabschnitt von 15 km Länge nördlich der Militärlager von Strebersdorf brachten in Hinblick auf die Infrastruktur der Fernverkehrsstraße neue Erkenntnisse. Erstmalig liegen Informationen zu einem Wachturm (Abb. 2/2) vor, der unfern der *castra* prospektiert und mittels Rammkernsondierungen am Fundplatz Kleinmutschen untersucht werden konnte. Zudem ist anhand der kombinierten Auswertung von Geophysik- und Luftbilddaten ersichtlich, dass die Trasse der Bernsteinstraße nicht, wie ursprünglich angenommen, von hier aus in Richtung Raiding ihre Fortsetzung fand, sondern vielmehr bereits auf der Höhe von Großwarasdorf einen deutlich kürzeren Verlauf in Richtung Horitschon nahm. Auf Basis älterer und jüngerer Forschungsergebnisse werden im Folgenden die in die Periode bis zu den Markomannenkriegen datierten Stationen in den Territorien von *Salla* und *Savaria* sowie jenem des *castrum* von Strebersdorf im Detail vorgestellt.

***Ad Arrabonem*-Katafa:** Der *ager* des Munizipiums *Salla* war im Norden durch den Fluss Raab von jenem der *Colonia Savaria* getrennt (Abb. 1)[36]. Der Flussübergang wurde durch das Kleinkastell *Ad Arrabonem*-Katafa am Rande des Territoriums von

---

31 SARIA 1951, 9–12, 14.
32 GROH 2013, 175, Abb. 92, Gebäude C, 2. Jh. n. Chr.
33 CSERMÉNYI/TÓTH 1979–80, 186–187, Abb. 2.
34 GROH 2013, 138–139, Abb. 11, 76.
35 GROH/FREITAG 2015.
36 REDŐ 2003, 193–194.

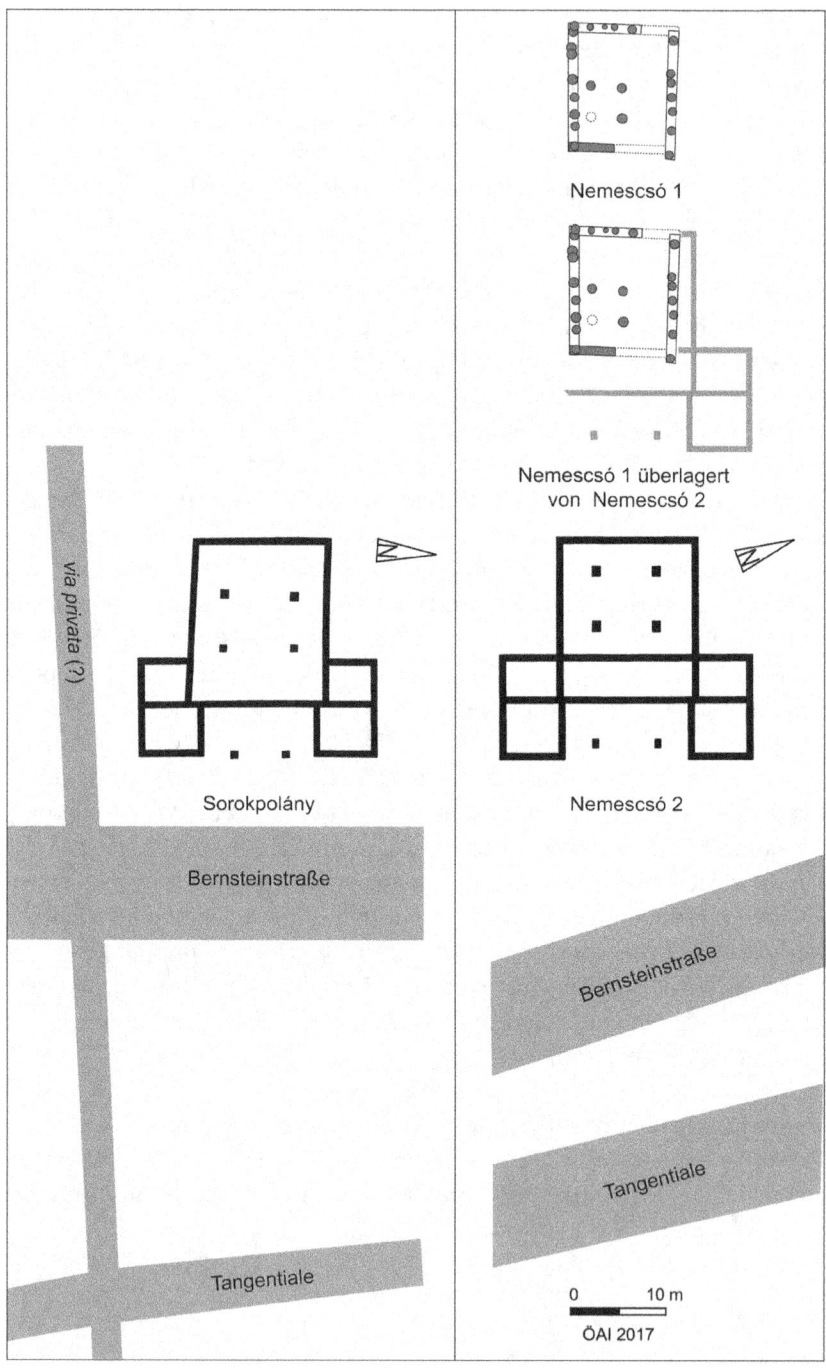

Abb. 3: Infrastruktur der Bernsteinstraße im Territorium von *Savaria* während der severischen Periode (Graphik ÖAW/ÖAI)

Salla gelegen, kontrolliert³⁷, das – befestigt durch eine Grabenanlage (42×34 m=1428 m²) – das Tal in Spornlage überragte (Abb. 2/1). Über die Innenverbauung liegen abgesehen von der Dokumentation einzelner Pfostengruben keine Informationen vor. Die Umwehrung war unterschiedlich konzipiert, im Detail untersucht wurde ein breiter Sohlgraben (Breite 1,6 m, Tiefe 1,0 m) an der West-, und ein parallel zur Straßentrasse ausgerichteter Doppelspitzgraben (max. Breite 5,8 m, Tiefe 2,0 m) an der Ostflanke³⁸. Entlang des Flusses Raab offerierte sich ein direkter Verbindungsweg zum Donaulimes über das Auxiliarlager *Arrabona*-Győr. Das Kleinkastell lag 11,7 mp nördlich des Munizipiums *Salla* und 76 mp südwestlich des Kastells *Arrabona*-Győr am Donaulimes (Abb. 1). Die im Verhältnis zur Periode 1 der Station von Nemescsó (Abb. 1/3) deutlich größer konzipierte befestigte Anlage von *Ad Arrabonem*-Katafa trug dieser besonderen strategischen Position Rechnung. Das Mündungsgebiet der Raab in die Donau war abseits der Militärkonzentration Klosterneuburg/*Vindobona*-Wien und *Carnuntum*/*Gerulata*-Rusovce nur durch kleinere Auxiliarlager bis *Arrabona*-Győr bewacht und somit durchlässiger. Zur Zeit der Markomannenkriege wurde diese leichter passierbare Einfallsroute gegen Süden durch die Aggressoren beschritten. Im Mündungsgebiet des Flusses Raab in die Donau liegen im Kastellstandort *Arrabona*-Győr Befunde eines Zerstörungshorizonts der Markomannenkriege vor³⁹. Die Stoßrichtung von diesem Abschnitt der Donau über das Raabtal bis zur Bernsteinstraße und dem hier befindlichen ersten städtischen Zentrum *Salla*-Zalalövő ist anhand einer Kette von Befunden zwischen *Arrabona*-Győr (Brandschicht), *Ad Arrabonem*-Katafa (Münzschatz) und schließlich *Salla*-Zalalövő (weitläufige Zerstörungshorizonte)⁴⁰ aufzuzeigen.

Für das Kleinkastell von *Ad Arrabonem*-Katafa wird aufgrund eines Hortfunds ein Hiat in der Zeit der Markomannenkriege postuliert und festgestellt, dass nach dieser Kriesenzeit keine neuerliche Nutzung erfolgte. Ein Münzschatz mit 18 *Aurei* liefert den *t.p.q.* 167 n. Chr.⁴¹. Apetlon II, ein Münzschatz 110 km nördlich von *Ad Arrabonem* aufgefunden, datiert ebenfalls in diesen Zeitraum, bis 166/167 n. Chr.⁴².

Da die Verbindung zum Limes entlang der Raab von hoher strategischer Bedeutung war und eine mögliche Einfallsroute darstellen konnte, ist nach dem Verlassen des erhöht, auf einem Sporn situierten Kleinkastells von Katafa eine neue Standortwahl am Flussübergang, näher zur Trasse der Bernsteinstraße wahrscheinlich. Der weitere Bestand einer Infrastruktur ist durch den Eintrag von *Arrabone* 20 röm. Meilen von *Sabaria* (=*Savaria*-Szombathely) im *Itinerarium Antonini* klar ersichtlich⁴³.

---

37 CSERMÉNYI/TÓTH 1979–80, 186–187, Abb. 2, 8, 10.
38 CSERMÉNYI/TÓTH 1979–80, 186, Abb. 12–13.
39 GABLER 1971, 53, Abb. 26–28; GABLER 2017, 23–24.
40 REDŐ 2003, 212.
41 SCHACHINGER 2013, 167–171, Abb. 89.
42 SCHACHINGER 2008, 848.
43 Itin. Anton. 262,8.

Nemescsó/Periode 1: 13 km nördlich der *Colonia Savaria* befindet sich der Standort einer mehrperiodigen infrastrukturellen Einrichtung der Bernsteinstraße. Unter dem in severischer Zeit in Form eines Eckrisalitgebäudes errichteten Stationsgebäude liegen ältere Holz-Erde-Befunde (Abb. 3), die darauf schließen lassen, dass bereits bis in das zweite Drittel des 2. Jhs. n. Chr. an Ort und Stelle eine Infrastruktur bestand. In einer Neuinterpretation der Magnetik-Geophysikdaten des Jahres 2009 ist ersichtlich, dass zwei parallel ausgerichteten Gräben als Teil einer kleinen rechteckigen Palisade von rund 11×14 m zu interpretieren sind, in deren Inneren sich während der Periode 1 ein Turm in Ständerkonstruktion von 4,2×4,4 m Größe befand (Abb. 2/3). Teile der Konstruktion, insbesondere die West- und Ostflanke der Palisade, wurden in Periode 2 von dem mittels Steinfundament errichteten Stationsgebäude überlagert[44].

Frankenau/Strebersdorf: Der Vicus von Frankenau und Strebersdorf stellt eine Besonderheit an diesem mittleren Abschnitt der Bernsteinstraße dar, zumal das Straßendorf durch einen Bacheinschnitt geteilt ist. Wie bereits einleitend ausgeführt war der Bereich von Strebersdorf, also der Fundplatz nördlich des Stoober-Baches, geprägt durch die sich superponierenden Militärlager I–III. Diese lagen östlich einer nach Nordwesten zielenden Biegung der Bernsteinstraße, deren geradlinige Trasse südlich der kleinen *castra* beiderseits von Vicus-Architektur gesäumt war (Abb. 4). In diesem Areal sind zahlreiche archäologische Strukturen der Eisenverarbeitung in den geophysikalischen Messbildern dokumentiert und anhand der Auswertung von Oberflächenfunden verifiziert.

Eine Trennlinie zwischen diesem Siedlungsteil in Strebersdorf, entstanden unter militärischer Kontrolle, und der Fortsetzung des Straßendorfes in Frankenau südlich davon bildete das querende Bachbett. Da sich die Fundstelle Frankenau/Strebersdorf circa auf halbem Weg zwischen der *Colonia Savaria* und dem Munizipium *Scarabantia* erstreckte, wurde lange davon ausgegangen, dass hier die Grenze dieser beiden städtischen Verwaltungsbezirke verlief, umso mehr als ein spezielles Bleisiegel angetroffen wurde. Es liegt eine Bleibulle mit der Darstellung der Fortuna vor, deren Aufschrift am Revers sich auf *Savaria*-Szombathely beziehen dürfte, nimmt man an, dass die Transkription des dreizeiligen Texts *For/tuna / [S]aba(riae)* lautet[45]. Nach der Entdeckung der Militärlager von Strebersdorf ist von einer anderen Form der verwaltungstechnischen Organisation auszugehen, zumal sich nördlich der naturräumlichen, durch den Stoober-Bach definierten Demarkationslinie ein militärisches Territorium zwischen den genannten zivilen von *Savaria* und *Scarabantia* wahrscheinlich während des 1. wie auch des 2. Jhs. n. Chr. erstreckte.

Bei der Untersuchung einer unmittelbar südlich der natürlichen Trennlinie des Stoober-Baches liegenden großflächigen streifenförmigen Baustruktur des Vicus von

---

44 Vgl. GROH 2013, 27, Abb. 76.
45 Fundort Strebersdorf: DEMBSKI 1975, 50, 59, Nr. 21, Taf. 8/21.

Via publica vel militaris: Die Bernsteinstraße in spätantoninischer und severischer Zeit — **203**

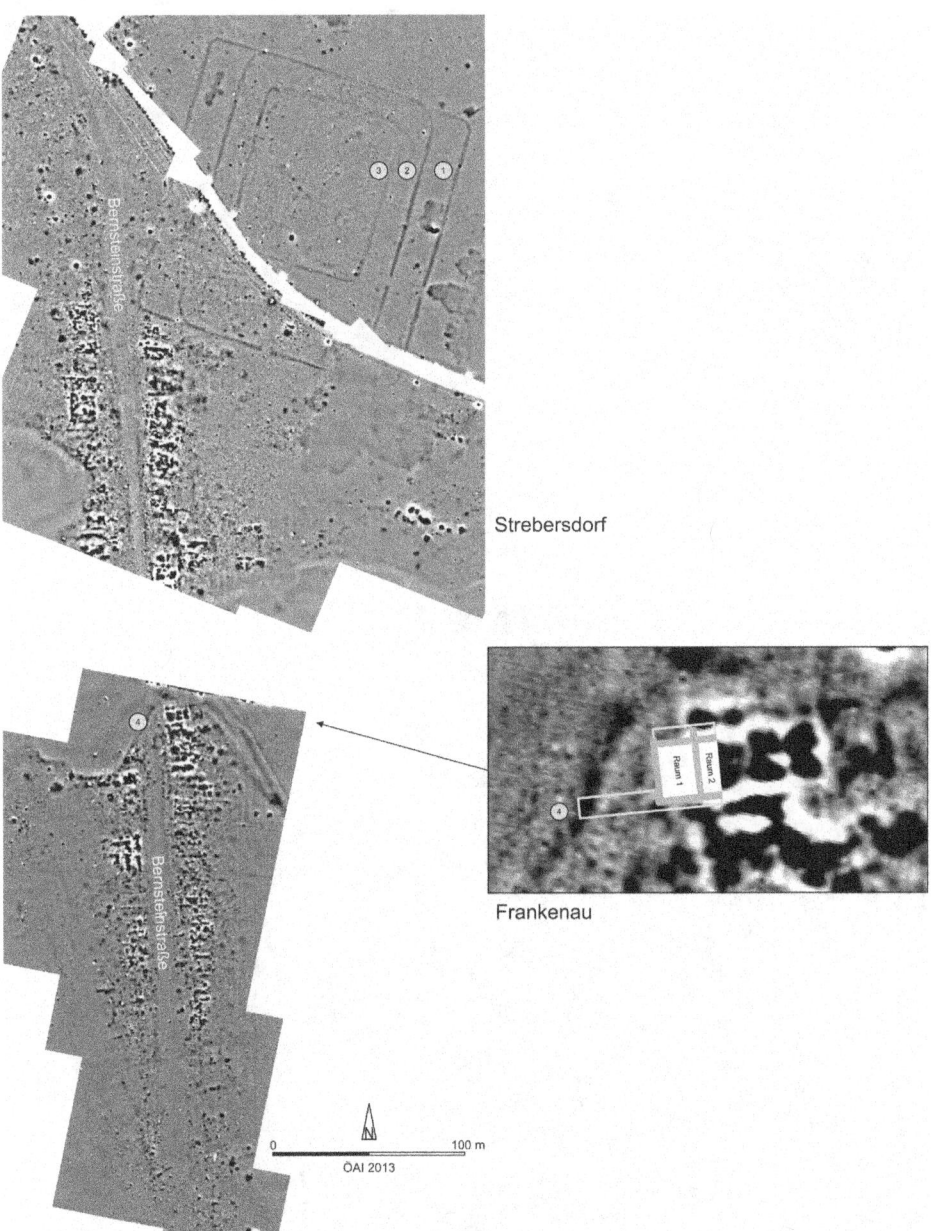

Abb. 4: Militärlager von Strebersdorf und Vicus von Frankenau an der Bernsteinstraße. Strebersdorf: 1 –Lager I. 2 – Lager II. 3 – Lager III. Frankenau: 4 – Grabungsschnitt (Daten und Graphik ÖAW/ÖAI)

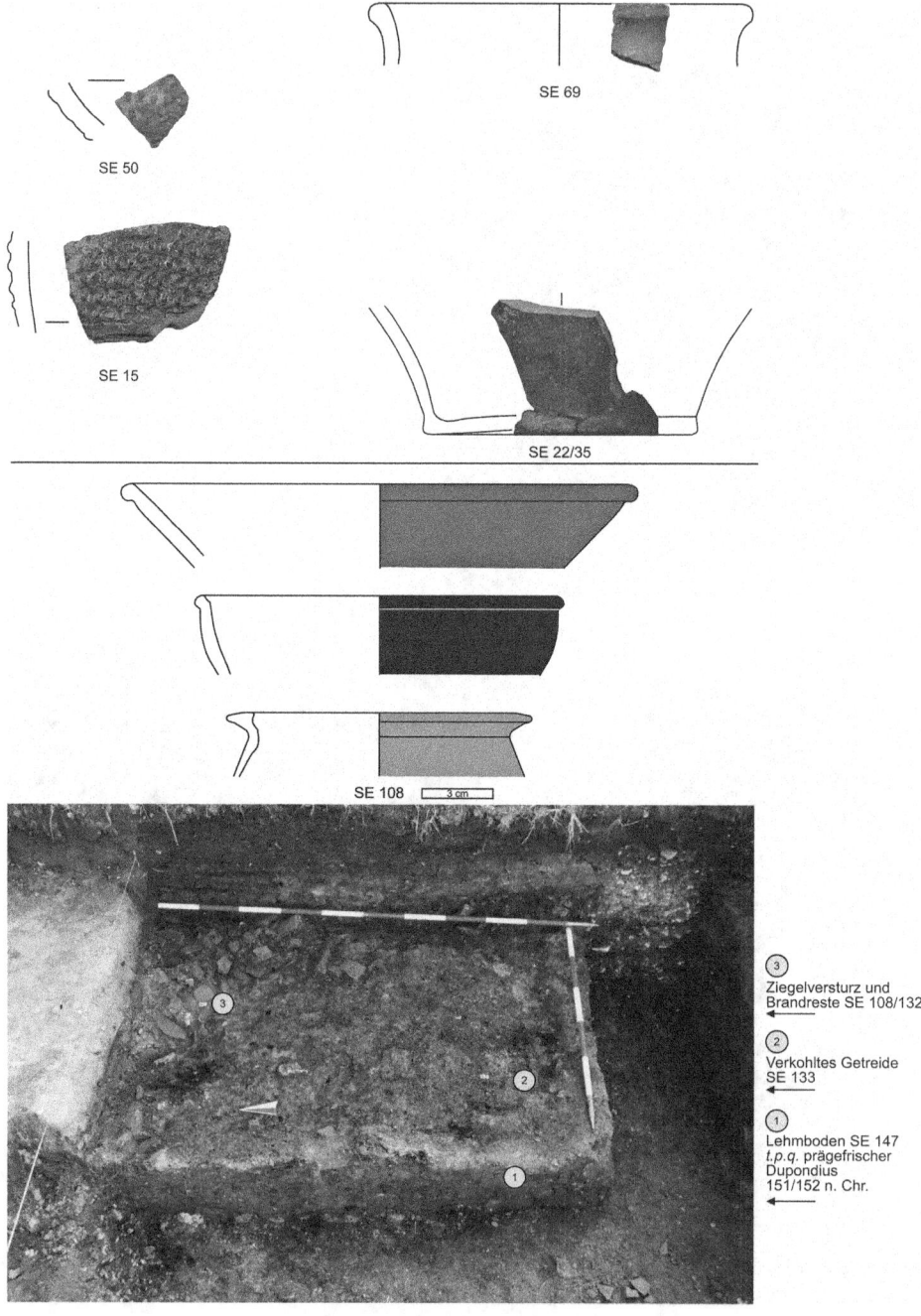

Abb. 5: Vicus von Frankenau. Befundsituation im Raum 1 des untersuchten Gebäudes. Oben: Germanische Gefäßkeramik aus dem Aufgabehorizont (SE 15, 50, 22/35, 69). Mitte: Funde aus dem Versturz (SE 108). Unten: Befundsituation (Daten und Graphik ÖAW/ÖAI)

Frankenau konnte hinsichtlich einer markomannenkriegszeitlichen Zerstörung der Siedlung an der Bernsteinstraße ein möglicher erster Hinweis erfasst werden[46]. Das mehrräumige Streifenhaus mit vorgelagertem Laubengang maß insgesamt circa 140 m² (Abb. 4). In einem kleinen Tiefschnitt von 2,4 m² konnte eine flächige Brandschicht im Inneren des Gebäudes (Raum 1) untersucht werden. Der Lehmboden des Raums 1 ist durch einen darin gefundenen prägefrischen Dupondius der Jahre 151/152 n. Chr. *t.p.q.* datiert (Abb. 5/1). Auf dem Boden erstreckte sich ein In-situ-Befund einer verstürzten Holzfachwerkkonstruktion (Abb. 5/3). Unter der Versturzsituation wurde eine ursprünglich in organischem Behältnis aufbewahrte Ration Getreide (Abb. 5/2) direkt auf dem Boden angetroffen. Keramische Funde waren wenige vorhanden, mit dem Gebrauchskeramiktopf (Abb. 4/SE 108) ist eine Datierung in die Zeit der Markomannenkriege vorzuschlagen; Vergleichsfunde desselben liegen aus Iža und vom Mušov vor[47].

Das Radiokarbondatum des hier festgestellten verkohlten Getreides aus Frankenau (Tab. 2/4) definiert mit weiteren Proben aus Befunden der Zeit der Markomannenkriege nach Erstellung einer Kombinationskalibration einen recht eindeutigen '*fingerprint*' mit einer BP-Datierung von 1867±10 (Tab. 2)[48].

Tab. 2: Radiokarbondatierungen: 1 – *Flavia Solva*-Wagna, 2 – *Carnuntum*-Petronell, 3a/b – Charvátská Nová Ves, 4 – Frankenau und 5 – Hulín-Pravčice. BP (1950).

	Fundort	t.p.q.	BP (1950)	68,2%	95,4%
1	*Flavia Solva*-**Wagna** Periode II				
	UBA-25749	166	1862±26 BP	88–212 AD	81–225 AD
	UBA-25750		1891±26 BP	77–130 AD	58–179 AD (93,9%)
					187–213 AD (6,1%)
2	*Carnuntum*-**Petronell** Latrine, SE 955				
	UBA-25752	161/176	1898±28 BP	74–128 AD	32–36 AD (0,6%)
					52–178 AD (94,7%)
					188–212 AD (4,7%)
3a	**Charvátská Nová Ves** Grubenverfüllung				
	CHNV 2013_078		1805±30 BP	140–197 AD	129–259 AD
3b	**Charvátská Nová Ves** Verfüllung Lagergraben				
	CHNV 2013_039		1860±30 BP	123–180 AD	80–231 AD

---

46 GROH 2009a, 184.
47 RAJTÁR 1992, 162, Abb. 17/5; DROBERJAR 1993, 61, Taf. 12/H5.
48 GROH 2015, 180–184, Tab. 14, Abb. 124.

Tab. 2 (fortgesetzt)

	Fundort	t.p.q.	BP (1950)	68,2%	95,4%
4	Frankenau Verkohlter Getreidefund UBA-25748	151/152	1860±31 BP	89–214 AD	79–232 AD
5	Hulín-Pravčice Verfüllung Lagergraben VERA 4112		1890±35 BP	60–140 AD (62,1%) 150–170 AD (1,8%) 190–210 AD (4,3%)	20–40 AD (1,2%) 50–230 AD (94,2%)

Wie bereits oben angemerkt könnte das streifenförmige Gebäude aufgrund seiner strategischen Situation an einer naturräumlichen Trennlinie durch den Bachlauf eine besondere Funktion an der *via publica* erfüllt haben. Interessant ist die weitere Geschichte des Standortes in Frankenau, zumal festgestellt werden konnte, dass das Gebäude nach der Brandkatastrophe keine Rekonstruktion erfuhr. Für den Vicus von Frankenau, der sich am Randes des Territoriums von *Savaria* befand und dessen Existenz abhängig vom Bestand des Militärlagers von Strebersdorf als Wirtschaftsfaktor war, ist eine stark regressive Entwicklung nach den Markomannenkriegen zu erfassen, ganz ähnlich der Situation im Munizipium *Salla* (s. unten).

Den *t.a.q.* der Zerstörung durch Feuer liefert im oben besprochenen Befund von Frankenau das archäologische Material aus Ausrissgräben der Fundamentmauern. Dieses datiert zwischen dem letzten Drittel des 2. und dem 1. Jahrzehnt des 3. Jhs. n. Chr. Neben dem Steinraub wurde offenkundig auch eine Bergung sonstigen, (wahrscheinlich) primär keramischen Baumaterials in der Ruine vorgenommen, worauf zahlreiche Gruben deuten[49]. Bemerkenswert in diesen archäologischen Strukturen des Aufgabehorizonts sind – in Anbetracht der geringen Größe der Grabungsfläche und der Entfernung des Fundplatzes vom Donaulimes (83 km=56 mp) – die Nachweise mehrerer germanischer Gefäße (Abb. 5/SE 15, 50, 69 +/- 22/35) der Stufe B2/C1[50].

Germanische Funde, die typisch für den markomannenkriegszeitlichen Horizont sind, fanden sich im näheren Umfeld der Bernsteinstraße bis auf Höhe von *Poetovio* (Abb. 6), davon Reitersporen (Knopfsporen Typ E1 und E7[51]) in der unmittelbaren

---

49 Solche Anzeichen einer regressiven Entwicklung lassen sich gleicherweise auch an der Nachnutzung der Brandstätten in *Salla* aufzeigen: REDŐ 2003, 209, Abb. 20.
50 Vgl. TEJRAL 1999, 142, Abb. 6/8, 7/5, 12/15.
51 Zum Typ: GINALSKI 1991, 59–61, 63–64, Abb. 12.

Via publica vel militaris: Die Bernsteinstraße in spätantoninischer und severischer Zeit —— 207

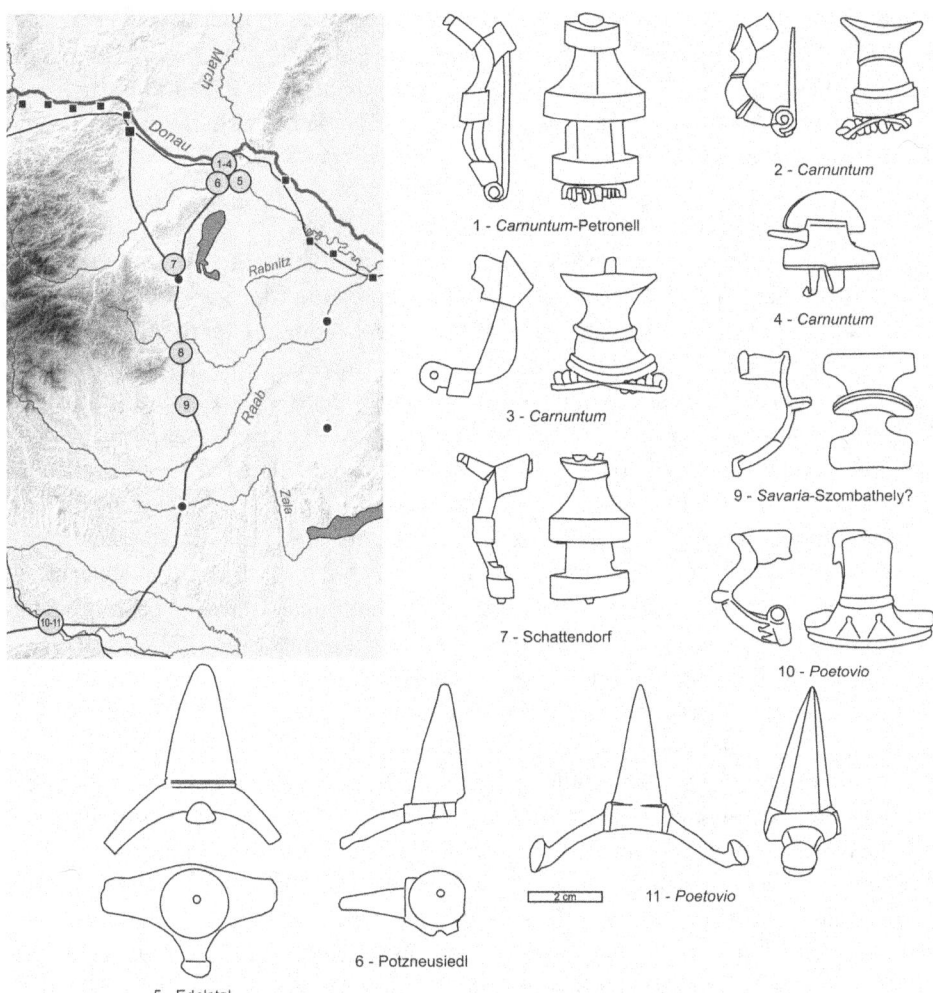

Abb. 6: Germanische Funde an der Bernsteinstraße zwischen *Carnuntum* und *Poetovio*. 1–4 Carnuntum, 5 Edelstal, 6 Potzneusiedl, 7 Schattendorf, 8 Frankenau, 9 Verwahrort Szombathely, 10–11 Poetovio (Graphik ÖAW/ÖAI, auf Basis von Buora/Jobst 2002, Abb. IId.6; Fundberichte aus Österreich 21, 1982, Abb. 686; Fundberichte aus Österreich 24–25, 1985–1986, Abb. 515, 524; Fundberichte aus Österreich 30, 1991, Abb. 937; Horvat 1982, Taf. 1/6; Jobst 1992, 493, mit Abb. Nr. 27; Patek 1942, Taf. 23/14; Preložnik/Nestorović 2015, Abb. 2; Tejral 2004, Abb. 29/11)

Donaulimesregion (Edelstal, Potzneusiedl[52]) sowie singulär in Ptuj[53], Fibeln der Frauentracht (Dreisprossenfibel Almgren 95, Einsprossenfibel Almgren 128, Rollenkappenfibel Almgren 41 und Almgren 43) hingegen weitläufiger im Hinterland wiederum bis *Poetovio*[54]. Zu ergänzen sind die hier vorgestellten keramischen Funde aus dem Vicus von Frankenau (Abb. 5).

Kleinmutschen: Bildeten die Siedlungsbefunde von Frankenau die nördlichste zivile Infrastruktur im Territorium von *Savaria*, so lag unmittelbar nördlich davon, innerhalb naturräumlicher Grenzen (Stoober-, Raidingbach) ein Militärterritorium während der ersten beiden Jahrhunderte n. Chr. Ausgehend von dem Standort der *castra* in Strebersdorf (Abb. 4) wurden in den Jahren 2015–2016 großräumige geophysikalische Prospektionen (mehr als 85 ha) initiiert[55], mit dem Ziel, den weiteren Verlauf der Bernsteinstraße in dieser Militärzone gegen Norden und deren Infrastruktur zu erfassen: Ein Teilstück von 15 km Länge konnte so dokumentiert werden und als weitere infrastrukturelle Einrichtung ein Wachturm bei Kleinmutschen. Bemerkenswert ist, dass innerhalb des von Stoober- und Raidingbach eingegrenzten Gebiets keinerlei zivile ländliche Baustrukturen prospektiert wurden, vielmehr dürfte dieses durch die in Strebersdorf stationierte Militäreinheit kontrollierte Gebiet weiträumig für den Abbau und die Verhüttung von Eisen genutzt worden sein. Der Wachturm von Kleinmutschen (Abb. 2/2) liegt in nächster Nähe einer Biegung der Bernsteinstraße und markiert im Nordosten den Eintritt in dieses Militärterritorium. Östlich davon und somit abseits des in diesem Bereich militärisch organisierten Straßenabschnitts ist aufgrund der Luftbildauswertung eine Tangentiale der Hauptverkehrsroute zu postulieren, die als *via publica*, die Militärzone umging. Eine solche Ausbildung von Tangentialen ist zudem für die *Colonia Savaria* zu beobachten, wo eine Gabelung der Bernsteinstraße auch eine von Benefiziariern kontrollierte Passage westlich außerhalb des Mauerrings der *colonia* erlaubte (s. unten).

Die Metalldetektorprospektionen indizieren aufgrund dreier Münzfunde eine Nutzung des Turms von Kleinmutschen in den mittleren Jahrzehnten des 2. Jhs. n. Chr.: As des Hadrianus (125/128 n. Chr.), verbrannter As des Antoninus Pius für Marcus Aurelius (140/161 n. Chr.) und Sesterz des Marcus Aurelius (161/180 n. Chr.)[56]. Die leicht trapezförmige, im Osten zur Bernsteinstraße etwas schmälere Anlage mit Palisadenumwehrung (Abb. 2/2) misst 18–20,5×22,5–24 m (470 m²), die Innenfläche beträgt 340 m². Der Wachposten setzte sich aus einem im Grundriss rechteckigen Holzturm und einem U-förmigen Palisadengraben zusammen, der an eine parallel zur Straßentrasse verlaufende Palisade angefügt war. Laut den Ergebnissen der Ramm-

---

52 Tejral 1999, 162–163, Abb. 22, 23/5.
53 Preložnik/Nestorović 2015, 288, Abb. 1–2.
54 Horvat 1982, 41–42, Taf. 1/6; Rajtár 2002, 355, 360; Tejral 1999, 160, Abb. 16; Tejral 2004, 345, 347, Abb. 30.
55 Groh/Freitag 2015.
56 Bestimmung: Ursula Schachinger, Obersdorf.

kernsondierungen beträgt die Tiefe des Grabens im Norden und Süden noch 0,4 m, im Osten und Westen lediglich 0,2 m, die Breite 1,6–2,1 m. Die Konstruktion des 24,5 m² großen Holzturmes kann aufgrund von vier Punktfundamenten als Ständerbau angesprochen werden. Der Abstand zwischen den bis zu 0,2 m tief erhaltenen Pfostengruben beträgt 4,5 m in nordsüdlicher und 5,5 m in ostwestlicher Richtung. Mörtelreste in einer Grubensohle indizieren Stabilisierungsmaßnahmen der Fundamente dieser leicht in Hanglage situierten Holzkonstruktion.

Die Grundfläche des Turms entspricht mit 24,5 m² vergleichbaren Konstruktionen in Holzbautechnik am obergermanischen-raetischen Limes. In Hüttlingen wurde ein hölzerner Wachturm prospektiert, der größenmäßig und proportional vergleichbar ist, ebenfalls mit einer leicht aus der Flucht springenden Pfostenstellung, dessen umgebender Graben allerdings mit 13×13 m viel enger dimensioniert ist (Abb. 2/5)[57]. Dieses proportionale Größenverhältnis von Turm und Graben ist auch bei einer insgesamt deutlich kleiner dimensionierten Anlage in Valkenburg (Abb. 2/4) zu beobachten[58], wohingegen ein Befund aus Huheld in den räumlichen Dimensionen nicht so eng bemessen ist (Abb. 2/6)[59]. Gleichfalls an einer Straßentrasse, von Hofheim in Richtung Groß-Gerau, wurde ein bis gegen die Mitte des 2. Jhs. n. Chr. genutzter Holzturm in Rüsselsheim (Abb. 2/7) angetroffen[60]. Dieser ist ganz ähnlich dem hier behandelten Befund von Kleinmutschen in einen umfriedeten Hof gesetzt, der in Relation zu den Gesamtproportionen geräumiger ist als bei den Türmen der Limeszone[61]. Die vergleichsweise weitläufige Einhegung von Kleinmutschen dürfte dafür sprechen, dass neben dem Turm auch eine Rangierfläche eingeplant war. Mit 0,047 ha repräsentiert die Struktur von Kleinmutschen einen im Vergleich zu sonstigen Feldwachen relativ großdimensionierten Wachtposten, der aber nicht an die Ausmaße von Kleinkastellen (>1 ha) heranreicht[62].

Reformen im Betrieb der Straßenstationen am oberpannonischen Abschnitt der Bernsteinstraße unter Septimius Severus

Wie durch viele Quellen belegt, bemühte sich Septimius Severus nach Erlangung der Kaiserwürde in Oberpannonien besonders um diese für ihn strategisch bedeutsamste Provinz. Beim infrastrukturellen Ausbau der Bernsteinstraße wird allerding auch

---

57 BENDER 2012, 13–14, mit Abb. Diese räumliche Beschränkung ist auch am norischen Limes anhand der in Stein errichteten Wachtürme von Maria Ponsee aufzuzeigen, deren Grabenanlage dokumentiert ist: PLOYER 2013, 78, Abb. 50.
58 HAALEBOS 2006, 403, Abb. 455, Turm: 3×3 m, Graben: 7,5×7,5 m.
59 FABRICIUS 1936, 49–54, mit weiteren Beispielen von Türmen in Holz, die häufig von solchen mit Steinfundament abgelöst wurden; zu Huheld: FABRICIUS 1936, 99–100, Taf. 13, Turm: 4,5×4,6 m, Graben: 14,7×14,6 m.
60 ROTH 1965–66, 89–95.
61 SCHALLMAYER 2006, 376, Abb. 421, Turm: 2,8×3 m, Graben: 19×15 m
62 BAATZ 2007, 10, Abb. 3.

unter Septimius Severus, wie in allen übrigen Perioden des 1.-3. Jhs. n. Chr., die verwaltungstechnische Differenzierung von Finanzflüssen im Gebiet der *coloniae* einerseits und der Munizipien andererseits deutlich. In allen Verwaltungsdistrikten von Kolonien, sei es nun *Aquileia* in der Regio X oder aber *Poetovio*, *Savaria* und *Carnuntum* in Oberpannonien ist das völlige Fehlen von Meilensteinen, die ein Formular mit Titulatur des Kaisers im Nominativ aufweisen, augenfällig, ebenso wie die in keinem Fall nachzuweisende nominell hervorgehobene Kuratorenschaft des Statthalters[63].

Ganz anders zeigt sich hier die Quellenlage im Territorium des Munizipiums *Celeia*, wo zahlreiche Miliarien mit dem direkten Bezug auf Statthalter und Kaiser (Septimius Severus wie auch Caracalla) deren Durchgriffsrecht dokumentieren[64].

In Hinblick auf die Finanzierung des Straßenerhalts ist generell von einem *munus publicum* auszugehen, der die *possessores*, also die unmittelbaren Anlieger, zum Erhalt verpflichtete[65]. Ein Fehlen der Quellen im Verwaltungsdistrikt von *Savaria* könnte also dahingehend gedeutet werden, dass die Finanzkraft der Kolonie ausreichte, die Infrastrukturmaßnahmen zu bestreiten, und ein Einschreiten des Statthalters nicht erforderlich war. Die nur in severischer Zeit erfolgten expliziten Nennungen des Statthalters auf Meilensteinen ausschließlich im Gebiet von Munizipien entlang der Bernsteinstraße sind so zu interpretieren, dass kaiserliche Interessen in Hinblick auf Bau bzw. Instandhaltung der Trasse ausschließlich in diesen Verwaltungseinheiten durch die direkten Anweisungen an den Statthalter durchgeführt wurden[66].

Dies mag auch mit einer allgemeinen wirtschaftlichen Schwächung der Munizipien als Folgeerscheinung der Markomannenkriege in Zusammenhang stehen. Die *Colonia Savaria* war innerhalb der Stadtmauern offenbar von keinen feindlichen Übergriffen während der Kriegsereignisse betroffen[67]. Nach den durch einen Münzschatz mit *t.p.q.* 176/177 indizierten unsicheren Zeiten[68], dürfte sich die *colonia* schnell konsolidiert haben.

Die Entwicklung des benachbarten Munizipiums *Salla* stagnierte hingegen nach weitreichenden Brandzerstörungen spätantoninischer Zeit völlig und die Stadt dürfte ab dem zweiten Drittel des 3. Jhs. n. Chr. in großen Teilen aufgegeben worden sein[69]. Dieser Niedergang des Munizipiums bei gleichzeitigem weiteren Betrieb einer im *Itinerarium Antonini* als *Arrabone*[70] bezeichneten Station (s. oben) dürfte eng verbunden gewesen sein mit deren kriegstechnischer Bedeutung. Der Standort *Ad Arrabonem* am

---

63 SEDLMAYER 2013, 191–192.
64 SEDLMAYER 2013, 191–192, 198–201.
65 RATHMANN 2003, 142.
66 RATHMANN 2003, 90.
67 GABLER 2002, 130.
68 BIRÓNE SEY 1960, 75–89.
69 REDŐ 2003, 209, 231–233: Die Siedlungsdichte von *Salla* war stark rückläufig, bis im 4. Jh. n. Chr. ein letzter Aufschwung mit dem Ausbau einer '*villa publica*' an der Bernsteinstraße festzustellen ist.
70 Itin. Anton. 262,8.

Übergang des auf kurzem Weg zum Donaulimes führenden Flusses Raab war aus militärischer Sicht ein Hotspot, wohingegen jener des Munizipiums *Salla* an dem Richtung *Lacus Pelso*-Balaton und somit ausschließlich in das zentrale Gebiet von Pannonien entwässernden Flusses *Salla*-Zala niederrangig in der strategischen Wertigkeit war.

Der besondere Bezug der Bewohner der *Colonia Savaria* zu der – letztlich – sinnstiftenden Hauptverkehrsroute der Bernsteinstraße, die den Ort einerseits durchquerte, andererseits aber auch über eine Tangentiale nur am westlichen Rand berührte und dort durch eine Zollstation gewinnbringende Einnahmequelle war[71], bezeugen Weihungen in Form zweier Altäre. Diese sind den ausschließlich in *Savaria* belegten Göttern *Itunus* und *Ituna* sowie den *Dii Itinerarii* gewidmet und waren an der Grenze der Kolonie aufgestellt gewesen, wahrscheinlich direkt an der dort in die südlichen Stadtquartiere einmündenden Bernsteinstraße[72]. Die loyale Hinwendung der Kolonie zum severischen Kaiserhaus dokumentieren nicht zuletzt zwei fragmentarisch erhaltene Weiheinschriften aus der Stadt, datiert in die Jahre zwischen 195/198 und 211 n. Chr.[73].

Das Fehlen der als propagandistische Repräsentation verstandenen Meilensteine[74] im Territorium der *Colonia Savaria* beruhte, wie im Falle aller anderen Kolonien entlang der Bernsteinstraße, also nicht so sehr auf einer eigenmächtigen, gar oppositionellen Politik der städtischen Verwaltungen, sondern vielmehr auf unterschiedlichen Geldflüssen. Für die *coloniae* waren wahrscheinlich zufolge der oben beschriebenen Quellenlage keine Direktfinanzierungen seitens des Kaiserhauses in den Erhalt des Straßensystems erfolgt.

Ein Indiz hierfür bieten auch die im Territorium von *Savaria* in frühseverischer Zeit entstandenen, bereits mehrfach erwähnten Straßenstationen von Sorokpolány und Nemescsó (Abb. 3). Diese wurden in annähernd übereinstimmender Distanz zum städtischen Zentrum *Savaria* von 16 bzw. 13 km (Tab. 1) unter Verfolgung eines einheitlichen Bauprogramms als Eckrisalitbauten umgesetzt: Sorokpolány, 25×27 m=520 m². Nemescsó/Periode 2, 23,5×26 m=470 m². Abgesehen von der deutlich massiveren Bauweise der beiden Strukturen (etwa im Vergleich mit dem Turm der Periode 1 von Nemescsó) ist insbesondere das Fehlen einer Einfriedung ein typisches Charakteristikum dieser Stationsgebäude severischer Zeit. Mit diesem speziellen Merkmal, nämlich der nicht vorhandenen Notwendigkeit einer räumlichen Abgrenzung, sind sie als zum

---

71 CSAPLÁROS/MLADONICZKI/SOSZTARITS 2010, 121–123, Abb. 1. Westlich, außerhalb der Stadt befand sich eine Einrichtung für Zollorgane wie auch Benefiziarier, Kontrolleure, die entlang der Bernsteinstraße häufig in Kombination überliefert sind: SEDLMAYER 2013, 193, 196–197.
72 Das Formular des an die *Dii Itinerarii* geweihten Altars dürfte laut der Transkription nach BORHY/SOSZTARITS 1996–97, 116 zudem einen Bezug zu einer Zweiteilung dieser Hauptverkehrsroute südlich von Savaria herstellen; es sei aber angemerkt, dass die Lesung der entscheidenden Textpassage *utriusque [viae]* nur auf einer hypothetischen Ergänzung des Formulars beruht, zumal der Inschriftenträger rechts von *utriusque* nicht erhalten ist (s. Ubi-erat-lupa ID 7905).
73 TÓTH 2011, 62–63, Nr. 6; BALLA 1971, 97, Nr. 78–79.
74 Hierauf deuten in severischer Zeit speziell die unter Caracalla vorgenommenen Eradierungen: SEDLMAYER 2013, 191.

städtischen Territorium gehörig gekennzeichnet, anders als die zuvor behandelten Befunde von *Ad Arrabonem*, Nemescsó/Periode 1 und Kleinmutschen. Die kurze Betriebszeit bis maximal in das zweite Drittel des 3. Jhs. n. Chr. lässt darauf schließen, dass die *munera* zum Erhalt der Infrastruktur nur in den Jahren des severischen Aufschwungs seitens der Kolonie zu leisten bzw. leistbar waren.

Literatur

BAATZ 2007 = D. BAATZ, Zur Funktion der Kleinkastelle am obergermanisch-raetischen Limes, in: Forschungen zur Funktion des Limes, Stuttgart 2007, 9–24.

BALLA et al. 1971 = L. BALLA/T.B. BUOCZ/Z. KÁDÁR/A. MÓCSY/T. SZENTLÉLEKY, Die römischen Steindenkmale von Savaria, Budapest 1971.

BENDER 2012 = S. BENDER, Neue Einblicke am raetischen Limes bei Hüttlingen, *Der Limes* 6.2, 2012, 12–15.

BIRÓNE SEY 1960 = K. BIRÓNE SEY, A szombathelyi korascsászárkori denárlelet (Ein Denarfund aus der frühen Kaiserzeit in Szombathely), *Folia Archaeologica* 12, 1960, 75–89.

BORHY/SOSZTARITS 1996–97 = L. BORHY/O. SOSZTARITS, Dii Itinerarii, *Itunus* és *Ituna* – Az utazás istenei savariában (*Dii Itinerarii*: *Itunus* und *Ituna* – unbekannte Götter der Römer aus *Savaria*/Szombathely, Ungarn), *Savaria* 23/3, 1996–1997 (1998) 115–132.

BORHY/ZSIDI 2005 = L. BORHY/P. ZSIDI, Die norisch-pannonischen Städte und das römische Heer im Lichte der neuesten archäologischen Forschungen. II. Internationale Konferenz über norisch-pannonische Städte, Budapest-Aquincum, 11.-14. 9. 2002, Budapest 2005.

BUORA/JOBST 2002 = M. BUORA/W. JOBST, Roma sul Danubio, Cataloghi e Monografie Archeologiche dei Civici Musei di Udine, Rom 2002.

CSAPLÁROS/MLADONICZKI/SOSZTARITS 2010 = A. CSAPLÁROS/R. MLADONICZKI/O. SOSZTARITS, Ein topographischer Überblick der Bernsteinstraße zwischen Salla und Scarbantia, in: G. GRABHERR/B. KAINRATH (Hg.), *Conquiescamus! longum iter fecimus*. Römische Raststationen und Straßeninfrastruktur im Ostalpenraum, Akten des Kolloquiums zur Forschungslage zu römischen Straßenstationen, Innsbruck, 4.–5. Juni 2009, Innsbruck 2010, 111–131.

CSERMÉNYI/TÓTH 1979–80 = V. CSERMÉNYI/E. TÓTH, Eine römische Straßenstation und die Straßenstrecke zwischen Salla und Arrabona, *Savaria* 13–14, 1979–80, 171–201.

DEMBSKI 1975 = G. DEMBSKI, Römische Bleisiegel aus Österreich (Eine Materialvorlage), *RÖ* 3, 1975, 49–64.

DERINGER 1953 = H. DERINGER, Neues aus dem Ennser Museum, in: Die Versuchsgrabung des Jahres 1951. Forschungsberichte 1950–1951, Linz 1953, 76–80.

DROBERJAR 1993 = E. DROBERJAR, Die römische Keramik vom Burgstall bei Mušov, Mähren, *Archaeologia Austriaca* 77, 1993, 39–87.

FABRICIUS 1936 = E. FABRICIUS, Strecke I. Der Limes vom Rhein bis zur Lahn nach den Untersuchungen der Streckenkommissare, in: G. LOESCHCKE/O. DAHM/W. SOLDAN (Hg.), Der obergermanisch-raetische Limes des Römerreiches A/I, Berlin/Leipzig 1936, 11–172.

FICHES 2003 = J.-L. FICHES, L'apport des fouilles récentes (1993–2000) à la connaissance de la station routière d'Ambrussum, Montpellier 2003, 49–58.

FITZ 1968 = J. FITZ, Zu der Geschichte der *praetentura Italiae et Alpium* im Laufe der Markomannenkriege, *Arheološki Vestnik* 19, 1968, 43–51.

GABLER 1971 = D. GABLER, Kutatások Arrabona canabaejában (Research in the canabae of Arrabona), *Arrabona* 13, 1971, 5–54.

GABLER 2002 = D. GABLER, Savaria városfalának építési ideje a terra sigilláták tükrében (Die Bauzeit der Stadtmauer von Savaria im Spiegel der Terra Sigillata), in: T. BUÓCZ/D. GABLER (Hg.), Savariai városfal, Sárvár 2002, 61–163.

GABLER 2017 = D. GABLER, Die archäologischen Evidenzen der markomannisch-sarmatischen Kriege (166–180 n. Chr.) in den Donauprovinzen, *Študnijné zvesti archeologického ústavu SAV* 61, 2017, 21–40.

GINALSKI 1991 = J. GINALSKI, Ostrogi kabłąkowe kultury przeworskiej (Bügelsporen der Przeworskkultur), *Przegląd Archeologiczny* 38, 1991, 53–84.

GROH 2009a = S. GROH, Neue Forschungen an der Bernsteinstraße in Nordwestpannonien – Die römischen Militärlager und der Vicus von Strebersdorf und Frankenau/Frakanava (Mittelburgenland, Österreich), in: S. BÍRÓ (Hg.), Ex officina ... Festschrift Dénes Gabler, Győr 2009, 175–188.

GROH 2009b = S. GROH, Neue Forschungen an der Bernsteinstraße in Nordwestpannonien. Die römischen Militärlager von Strebersdorf und der Vicus von Strebersdorf-Frankenau/Frakanava (Mittelburgenland), *Archäologie Österreich* 20/2, 2009, 59–64.

GROH 2013 = S. GROH, Straßenstation von Nemescsó: Grabungen, geophysikalische Prospektionen und Surveys 2009–2012. Bautypologie der Straßenstationen von Nemescsó und Sorokpolány, in: GROH/SEDLMAYER/ZALKA 2013, 21–52; 137–142.

GROH 2015 = S. GROH, Römische Feldlager in der March-Thaya-Region, in: S. GROH/H. SEDLMAYER, Expeditiones barbaricae. Forschungen zu den römischen Feldlagern von Engelhartstetten, Kollbrunn und Ruhhof, Niederösterreich, Krems 2015, 154–184.

GROH 2018 = S. GROH, Im Spannungsfeld von Macht und Strategie. Die *legio II Italica* und ihre *castra* von Ločica (Slowenien), Lauriacum/Enns und Albing (Österreich), Linz 2018.

GROH/FREITAG 2015 = S. GROH/K. FREITAG, KG Kleinmutschen, Nebersdorf; Gem. Frankenau-Unterpullendorf, Großwarasdorf; VB Oberpullendorf, Bundesland Burgenland, *Fundberichte aus Österreich* 54, 2015.

GROH/SEDLMAYER/ZALKA 2013 = S. GROH/H. SEDLMAYER/C. V. ZALKA, Die Straßenstationen von Nemescsó und Sorokpolány an der Bernsteinstraße (Pannonien, Ungarn), Wien 2013.

GUGL 2007 = C. GUGL, Stratifizierte Fundkontexte des 1.-3. Jahrhunderts, in: C. GUGL/R. KASTLER (Hg.), Legionslager Carnuntum, Wien 2007, 159–230.

HAALEBOS 2006 = J.K. HAALEBOS, Valkenburg aan den Rijn. Praetorium Agrippinae, in: REDDÉ et al. 2006, 397–403.

HORVAT 1982 = M. HORVAT, K rimskim fibulam iz Rabelčje vasi v Ptuj (Zu römischen Fibeln aus Rabelčja vas in Ptuj), *Arheološki Vestnik* 33, 1982, 47–56.

JOBST 1992 = W. JOBST, Römische und germanische Fibeln, in: W. JOBST (Hg.), Carnuntum. Das Erbe Roms an der Donau, Bad Deutsch-Altenburg 1992, 489–506.

KOLB 2000 = A. KOLB, Transport und Nachrichtentransfer im Römischen Reich, Berlin 2000.

LAZAR 2006 = I. LAZAR, Ilovica pri Vranskem. Zbirka Arheologija na avtocestah Slovenije, Ljubljana 2006.

LŐRINCZ 2001 = B. LŐRINCZ, Die römischen Hilfstruppen in Pannonien während der Prinzipatszeit. Teil 1: Die Inschriften, Wien 2001.

MOSSER 2010 = M. MOSSER, Der Wiener Judenplatz und das Legionslager Vindobona, in: M. MOSSER et al. (Hg.), Die römischen Kasernen im Legionslager Vindobona, Wien 2010, 13–39.

PATEK 1942 = E. PATEK, A pannoniai fibulatípusok elterjedése és eredete (Verbreitung und Herkunft der römischen Fibeltypen von Pannonien), Budapest 1942.

PETROVITSCH 2006 = H. PETROVITSCH, Legio II Italica, Linz 2006.

PLOYER 2013 = R. PLOYER, Der norische Limes in Österreich, Wien 2013.

PRELOŽNIK/NESTOROVIĆ 2015 = A. PRELOŽNIK/A. NESTOROVIĆ, Germanic spur from Ptuj. Germanska ostroga s Ptuja, in: J. ISTENIC/B. LAHARNAR/J. HORVAT (Hg.), Evidence of the Roman army in Slovenia. Sledovi riimske vojske na Slovenskem, Ljubljana 2015, 285–296.

RAJTÁR 1992 = J. RAJTÁR, Das Holz-Erde-Lager aus der Zeit der Markomannenkriege in Iža, in: K. GODLOWSKI/R. MADYDA-LEGUTKO (Hg.), Probleme der relativen und absoluten Chronologie ab Latènezeit bis zum Frühmittelalter, Kraków 1992, 151–170.

RAJTÁR 2002 = J. RAJTÁR, Zur Verbreitung der Fibeln Almgren 43 im Mitteldonaugebiet, in: K. KUZMOVÁ/K. PIETA/J. RAJTÁR (Hg.), Zwischen Rom und dem Barbaricum, Festschrift Titus Kolník, Nitra 2002, 355–364.

RATHMANN 2003 = M. RATHMANN, Untersuchungen zu den Reichsstraßen in den westlichen Provinzen des Imperium Romanum, Bonn 2003.

REDDÉ et al. 2006 = M. REDDÉ/R. BRULET/R. FELLMANN/J. HAALEBOS/S. VON SCHNURBEIN (Hg.), Les fortifications militaires, Paris 2006.

REDŐ 2003 = F. REDŐ, Municipium Aelium Salla, in: ŠAŠEL KOS/SCHERRER 2003, 191–235.

REDŐ 2005 = F. REDŐ, Strategical significante of Salla and its effect on the development of the inner-pannonian municipium, in: BORHY/ZSIDI 2005, 133–144.

ROSENBERGER 1992 = V. ROSENBERGER, Bella et expeditiones, Stuttgart 1992.

ROTH 1965–66 = S. ROTH, Der römische Wachtturm bei Rüsselsheim, Kr. Groß-Gerau, in der Flur Haßlocher Tanne, *Fundberichte aus Hessen* 5/6, 1965–66, 89–95.

RUZICKA 1919 = F. RUZICKA, Ziegel aus Lauriacum mit Schrift, in: Der römische Limes in Österreich, Bd. 13, Wien 1919, 85–116.

SARIA 1951 = B. SARIA, Der römische Gutshof von Winden am See, Eisenstadt 1951.

ŠAŠEL 1992 = J. ŠAŠEL, Über Umfang und Dauer der Militärzone Praetentura Italiae et Alpium zur Zeit Mark Aurels, in: J. ŠAŠEL, Opera selecta, Situla, Bd. 30, Ljubljana 1992, 388–396.

ŠAŠEL KOS/SCHERRER 2003 = M. ŠAŠEL KOS/P. SCHERRER (Hg.), The autonomous towns of Noricum and Pannonia/Die autonomen Städte in Noricum und Pannonien. Pannonia I, Ljubljana 2003.

SCHACHINGER 2008 = U. SCHACHINGER, Der römerzeitliche Geldverkehr im norisch-pannonischen Gebiet, in: C. FRANEK/S. LAMM/T. NEUHAUSER/B. POROD/K. ZÖHRER (Hg.): Thiasos. Festschrift Erwin Pochmarski, Wien 2008, 843–872.

SCHACHINGER 2013 = U. SCHACHINGER, Die Fundmünzen eines Oberflächensurveys 2012 im Nordteil der Straßenstation von Nemescsó, in: GROH/SEDLMAYER/ZALKA 2013, 159–172.

SCHALLMAYER 2006 = E. SCHALLMAYER, Rüsselsheim, in: REDDÉ et al. 2006, 376.

SCHERRER 2003 = P. SCHERRER, Savaria, in: ŠAŠEL KOS/SCHERRER 2003, 53–80.

SEDLMAYER 2013 = H. SEDLMAYER, Epigraphische Quellen zur Entwicklung der verkehrstechnischen Infrastruktur an der Bernsteinstraße, in: GROH/SEDLMAYER/ZALKA 2013, 185–206.

SEDLMAYER 2018 = H. SEDLMAYER, Extra muros. Lebenswelt der consistentes ad legionem von Lauriacum, Linz. 2018.

SPEIDEL 2009 = M.A. SPEIDEL, Heer und Straßen – militares viae, in: M.A. SPEIDEL, Heer und Herrschaft im römischen Reich der hohen Kaiserzeit, Stuttgart 2009, 501–513.

STROBEL 2001 = K. STROBEL, Die „Markomannenkriege" und die neuen Provinzen Marc Aurels: Ein Modellfall für die Verflechtung von Innen- und Außenpolitik des Römischen Reiches, in: F.W. LEITNER (Hg.): Carinthia romana und die römische Welt. Festschrift Gernot Piccottini, Klagenfurt 2001, 103–124.

TEJRAL 1999 = J. TEJRAL, Die Völkerwanderungen des 2. und 3. Jh.s und ihr Niederschlag im archäologischen Befund des Mitteldonauraumes, in: J. TEJRAL (Hg.): Das mitteleuropäische Barbaricum und die Krise des römischen Weltreiches im 3. Jahrhundert, Brünn 1999, 137–213.

TEJRAL 2004 = J. TEJRAL, Mušov und Czarnówko – Bemerkungen zu weiträumigen Verbindungen zwischen germanischen Herrschaftszentren, in: H. FREISINGER/A. STUPPNER (Hg.): Zentrum und Peripherie – Gesellschaftliche Phänomene in der Frühgeschichte, Wien 2004, 327–387.

TÓTH 2011 = E. TÓTH, Lapidarium Savariense, Szombathely 2011.

VOMER GOJKOVIČ 2005 = M. VOMER GOJKOVIČ, Verbindungen des römischen Heeres mit dem Leben in Poetovio, in: BORHY/ZSIDI 2005, 49–64.

Florin-Gheorghe Fodorean
The Peutinger Map, the Roman Army and the First Military Roads in Dacia

Abstract: Until the moment when Trajan conquered Dacia, the regions to the north of the Danube were basically unknown. This situation changed after the conquest of Dacia in 106 A.D. To understand the role of the Roman army in the geographical knowledge of the Dacian territories, the contribution tries to reveal the fact that the very first roads built in Dacia were the military lines used by the Roman army during the Dacian conquest. These roads were afterwards depicted in the Peutinger map.

Zusammenfassung: Bis zu dem Augenblick, in dem Trajan Dakien einnahm, waren die Regionen nördlich der Donau im Grunde unbekannt. Diese Situation änderte sich nach der Einnahme Dakiens 106 n. Chr. Um die Rolle der römischen Armee für die geographische Kenntnis des dakischen Geländes zu verstehen, versucht dieser Beitrag deutlich zu machen, dass die allerersten Strassen, die in Dakien gebaut wurden, die militärischen Linien waren, welche die römische Armee während der Einnahme Dakiens benutzt hatte. Diese Strassen wurden später in die *Tabula Peutingeriana* eingezeichnet.

1 Premises

What determined the Romans to conquer a new territory? How much did they know, geographically speaking, about an area? Were they capable of understanding the economic value of a certain territory? If so, from where did they get information? During the conquest of a new area, how did they organize the army?

For quite a long time, general works on Roman Dacia emphasized the idea that the Romans decided to conquer the north-danubian territories because of several reasons. Among these, almost always the first reason supposed by the historians was the wealth of these areas, including a list of assets, like the gold, the salt, the stone quarries, and other metals like iron and silver. Since the moment I started to study the Roman roads, I questioned myself if the Romans were actually conscious about these economic advantages of Dacia, or such assumption is, more or less, a modern vision, a contemporary way of thinking, based on the fact that today we know about all the resources of Dacia. Therefore, searching for some answers, I ended to conceive this study, which is focused on some essential aspects: 1. Which was the level of knowledge about the north-danubian territories before the Roman conquest? 2. Which were the real reasons for the conquest of Dacia? 3. How this conquest was prepared? 4. During the conquest, which was the role of the Roman army beside the war episodes? Which roads did they build? Where? Why? 5. How can cartographic sources, like the famous Peutinger map, offer new data regarding the building of roads and the creation of the first itineraries in the new province?

All in all, I try to offer a detailed story of one movie: the discovery, the exploration, the organization, the road building and the creation of the first cartographic documents regarding the infrastructure network of Roman Dacia.

2 *Terra incognita*: Descriptions of the North-Danubian Territories Before the Roman Conquest

Until the moment when Trajan conquered Dacia, the regions to the north of the Danube were basically unknown. Most of the ancient authors mentioned the 'legendary' *Scythicum frigus*,[1] the drunkenness of the barbarians, and their awkward, savage way of life. Exiled by Augustus to Tomis, Publius Ovidius Naso complained about the coldness of the weather, the savageness of the barbarians and their strange, wild customs.[2] Even Strabo provides only a general description of the land of the Dacians,[3] mentioning, in very general lines, the courses of the rivers Marisus and Danubius (Strab. 7,3,13). Pliny the Elder had also little knowledge of the territory under discussion.[4] The name *Daci* is mentioned only once, at the end of Book 6 (Plin. nat. 6,219). It is obvious that Pliny had a vague idea about these lands and that his writing style, in this case and in others, was linear.[5] This means that he tried to inform the reader using geographic and topographic details, but he did not provide proper 'spatial descriptions', but rather a linear construction of his discourse.[6]

The geography of Dacia remained a mystery until the reign of Domitian. This was the first moment when the Romans, i. e. the military troops, took notice of the north-Danubian territory.[7] Domitian's war against the Dacians and its political and military consequences have been the subject of numerous debates.[8] In Moesia the Dacians unleashed a devastating attack[9] in the winter of 85/86 or already in the spring or summer of 85 A.D. The causes of this attack emerged because the Dacians were dissatisfied with the Roman measure of reducing the subsidies and because they really wanted to regain control over the north-Danubian territories supervised by the Romans. Cornelius Fuscus (*praefectus praetorio*) succeeded in driving the Dacians

---

1 Ov. trist. 3,10,14. 10,25; NEMETI 2009, 411–427.
2 POPA-LISSEANU 2006, 30, 46.
3 Strab. 7,1,1.
4 MATTERN 1999, 209.
5 McQUIGGAN 2006/7, 80–81.
6 WHITTAKER 2004, 68.
7 More details in FODOREAN 2016, 23–24.
8 STROBEL 1989; JONES 1992; STEFAN 2005; NEMETH 2007, 144.
9 Iord. Get. 76.

across the Danube. Then, in 86 A.D. he invaded the Dacian territory, but was defeated at Tapae (the Transylvanian Iron Gates, close to the capital of the Dacian kingdom). Domitian returned to Moesia. In 87, Tettius Iulianus was designated to prepare and lead an expedition into Dacia; this proved successful. In 88 he managed to defeat the Dacians in the same place where his predecessor died, at Tapae. Then, moving towards Pannonia, the Roman troops took the shortest route from the Dacian war sites.[10] One inscription shows that some of them had to march through Dacia[11] and then northwards through the Hungarian Plain. Therefore, this episode might be considered the first moment when the Roman soldiers were really in the position to see some of the areas which were later to form Trajan's Dacia.

3 Trajan and the Conquest of Dacia. Real Reasons

Generally, the main motifs of the conquest of Dacia were considered to be the following: 1. Its gold resources; 2. The second motive was strategic: the separation of the Sarmatians Iazyges and Roxolanii;[12] 3. Trajan's plan was to create a province north of the Danube to avoid further attacks on Moesia Superior.

Nevertheless, some historians have described the process of the conquest of Dacia and the reasons for this action in other terms. WHITTAKER perceived the annexation of Dacia in totally different terms.[13] Unfortunately, many of his arguments are unsustainable. Trajan had enough time to prepare the conquest of Dacia. The construction of the road along the right bank of the Danube was finished in 100 A.D., as the building inscription, the so called *Tabula Traiana* (CIL III 1699) proves. Trajan used a huge number of soldiers from Pannonia and Moesia.[14] It should be noted that the first military campaign started in March 101 A.D. After one year, the Banat region was

---

10 MÓCSY 1974, 84.
11 ILS 9200: [...] *et bel | lo Marcommannorum Quadorum | Sarmatarum adversus quos expedi | tionem fecit per regnum Decibali* [...].
12 BĂRBULESCU 2001, 74.
13 WHITTAKER 2004, 34–35: 'Or, to take another prominent example, much has been made of Trajan's motives for war and his supposed strategy in annexing Dacia in the early second century AD. Trajan's aims are ascribed by Roman authors, some of them contemporaries, to revenge or desire for gold and glory, but never elevated to a grand, strategic aim for the defence of the Balkans. The results, if we are meant to believe Trajan had secretly planned some wider, strategic aim behind closed doors, are hardly convincing. Trajan had no time to organize the defence of Dacia before rushing off to Parthia. [...] If the annexation of Dacia was really strategically determined, why on earth did the province not include a frontier across the Hungarian plain, which would have shortened the defences of the middle Danube by some 500 km? In fact, the action does not appear to have been based on any geo-political assessment of the military viability of the annexations. That is what Hadrian, Trajan's successor, realized, although he could not reverse the decision, according to Dio.'
14 FODOREAN 2016, 25.

already under Roman control. Longinus was designated, before the creation of Dacia, as commander in chief of the military troops left by the Romans in Dacia. In two years' time, the Romans built the longest bridge ever known in their Empire, at Drobeta. The second campaign lasted for one year (105 to the summer of 106 A.D). Dacia was conquered quickly and efficiently.

The first glance at a map of the Roman Empire shows the awkward position of Dacia. LUTTWAK noticed that in fact, on a map, the new province presented a classic profile of vulnerability.[15] Possibly Trajan, among the reasons mentioned above, wanted to reach the Northern Ocean. Pliny records that Agrippa, referring to the north-danubian area, approximated the distance from the Danube to the sea to 396 miles.[16]

It is not certain that the Romans already possessed relevant information about the Dacian gold, located during the Roman period and extracted in Alburnus Maior. In fact, I think they found out about it only after the creation of the new province when exploring this new territory. Therefore, I would suggest that it was only after the second military campaign and the annexation of Dacia that the Romans became aware of this region's huge potential.[17]

Trajan did not hesitate to use a large number of soldiers in his two military campaigns against Dacia. In the first campaign Trajan relied on nine legions (from a total of 30) available at that time in the Roman Empire and already stationed along the front. No less than 90 auxiliary troops were camped along the Ister at this date.[18] In the second campaign, Trajan used an even larger army. He even ordered the creation of two new legions, the *II Traiana fortis* and *XXX Ulpia victrix*.[19]

If Trajan gathered such an army, the costs of the annexation of Dacia were high. Obviously, the Romans did not follow a strategy of cost–benefit analysis before annexation.[20] Trajan or his staff did not act like good economists, calculating the ratio cost-benefits, or the costs of the war against the Dacians. Strabo or Pliny the Elder, they both were unconscious of Dacia's resources, because, as we saw above,

---

15 LUTTWAK 1976, 100.
16 Plin. nat. 4,12,80–81: "*Agrippa totum eum tractum ab Histro ad oceanum bis ad decies centenum millium passuum in longitudinem, quattuor milibus minus CCCC in latitudinem, ad flumen Vistlam a desertis Sarmatiae prodidit*"; english translation is RACKMAN 1947, 179–181: "Agrippa describes the whole of this area from the Danube to the sea as being 1200 miles in length by 396 in breadth, as far as the river Vistula in the direction of the Sarmatian desert"; MATTERN 1999, 61; a detailed debate based on data from other ancient literary sources regarding the area north of the Danube in NEMETI 2011, 37–49; NEMETI 2014, 23–42.
17 One argument is that during the first campaign the Romans did not penetrate so deep into the Dacian territory. Alburnus Maior (today Roşia Montană) is located in the heart of the Apuseni Mountains. In 102 A.D the Romans only occupied the south-western region (Banat).
18 BENNETT 1997, 91; POPESCU/ŢENTEA 2006, 75–120.
19 BENNETT 1997, 101.
20 WHITTAKER 2004, 35.

this region did not enjoy a reputation for wealth. On the contrary, the ancient authors described Dacia as a cold and infertile region, inhabited by drunken, savage barbarians. They never referred any riches to be found there. In the case of Britain, the situation was perceived differently. Strabo believed that Britain was very rich in gold and silver.[21] Therefore, information about Dacia or about other territories was often far from the truth.

No matter the costs, the benefits of the annexation of Dacia were discovered after the conquest. Besides gold, other natural resources could be exploited by the Romans in Dacia: iron, copper and silver from the Banat, marble from Bucova (close to Sarmizegetusa) and Ampoița (close to Apulum). Salt was extracted in numerous places in Dacia (Ocna Dejului, Jelna, Domnești, Sic, Cojocna, Pata, *Potaissa*, *Salinae*, Mărtiniș, Sânpaul, Ocna Sibiului, Ocnele Mari), thermal waters were available at *Germisara* (today Geoagiu-Băi), and there was a great number of stone quarries.[22]

Before the conquest, during Trajan's reign, precisely in 100 A.D., the construction of the road on the right bank of the Danube, which started during the reign of Tiberius, was now finished. One should notice the importance of this piece of infrastructure: it was a road, but also a frontier.[23] Of course, the navigation conditions in this particular area were also improved.[24]

The rock-carved inscription discovered in Ogradena[25] clearly proves the tremendous efforts made by the soldiers from *legio IIII Flavia Felix* and *legio VII Claudia*[26] to enlarge the surface of this road, which was suspended over the Danube waters using an efficient system and creating a sort of wooden bridge.

---

21 Strab. 4,5,2. Strabo provided reasons against conquering more of Britain (Scotland). See for this BREEZE 1988, 10.
22 BĂRBULESCU et al. 2005, map XVII (mineral resources).
23 MIRKOVIĆ 2007, 27.
24 An inscription dated 101 A.D. discovered at Karataš attests the efforts for the rehabilitation of the Danube course, in order to make it easily navigable ILJug 2, 468: *ob periculum cataractarum derivato flumine tutam Danuvi navigationem fecit*; see NEMETH 2007, 148; ŠAŠEL 1973, 80–85; TIMOC 2001, 97–116.
25 CIL III 1699: *Imp(erator) Caesar Divi Nervae f(ilius) / Nerva Traianus Aug(ustus) Germ(anicus) / pontif(ex) maximus trib(unicia) pot(estate) IIII /pater patriae co(n)s(ul) III / montibus excisi[s] anco[ni]bus / sublat[i]s via[m r]e[fecit]*; PETROVIĆ 1986, 41; ROSSI 1968, 41–46; BECATTI 1982, 566; LE ROUX 1998, 73.
26 PETROVIĆ 1986, 52.

4 Trajan and Balbus. Measuring the Land, Building the Roads. The First Military Campaign in Dacia (101–102 A.D.) and the Creation of the First *itineraria*

Using two lines of advance, one starting from Lederata (today Ram in Serbia) to Tibiscum (today Jupa in Caraș-Severin County), and the other one from Dierna (today Orșova in Mehedinți County) to the same Tibiscum, the Romans penetrated into the new territory (through the region known today as Banat) and concomitantly they built the future roads of the province. These two branches became part of the main imperial road.

To understand the role of the Roman army in the geographical knowledge of the Dacian territories we must focus on the following aspects. During the advance into the new territory, Trajan wrote a 'book': *De bello Dacico*. Of all content, only one sentence has survived: *inde Berzobim, deinde Aizi processimus* ('from there we advanced to Berzobis, and then to Aizis').[27] We can easily notice the style of Trajan's book: concise information, basically a text where the emperor provided data about the settlements encountered along his advance, and maybe the distance between these settlements. If such supposition seems reasonable, then we can sustain that Trajan's book became, in fact, a written *itinerarium*,[28] even if this was not the purpose of the work. We can suppose that the first painted *itineraria* were created based on Trajan's information from his book.

But how Trajan accomplished such difficult task? Obviously, with the help of the most experienced surveyor of his time, namely Balbus.[29] Though information about his life is almost inexistent, at least his work can be dated, because fragments from his book, entitled *Expositio et ratio omnium formarum* (*Description and explanation of all figures*) have survived. This book was dedicated to Celsus, the famous mathematician from Alexandria in Egypt. Some historians are skeptical in associating the activity of Balbus with Trajan. For example, WHITTAKER thinks that Balbus' work was written during Domitian's campaign and it is not connected with activities regarding terrain surveying.[30]

We should emphasize some aspects regarding these statements. First, Domitian's campaign and its events, shortly presented in this study, did not imply such a large amount of infrastructure tasks. Even the number of the troops which attacked Dacia

---

[27] The sentence survived in the Latin grammar work by Priscian, *Institutiones grammaticae* 6.13 (HRR II 117, F 1 Peter); an extended debate upon the toponym *Berzovia* in DANA/NEMETI 2016, 68–74.
[28] BĂRBULESCU 1999, 34.
[29] Balbus gromaticus, Expositio et ratio omnium formarum, in: KARL LACHMANN (ed.), *Gromatici veteres*, Berlin 1848, p. 99, 14–102.16. Some data about his work in LEWIS 2001, 66–67.
[30] WHITTAKER 2004, 69: 'The document called *expositio et ratio omnium formarum*, which was possible written by Domitian's military surveyor, Balbus, has nothing to do with a general survey map, despite its title, and there is nothing in it to suggest that Balbus did any surveying for that purpose.'

was inferior to the tremendous number of soldiers used by Trajan to conquer Dacia. Second, surveying operation in the terrain were, of course, not only useful for the creation of the 'maps', but based on such measurements and other data the Romans were capable of producing written or painted itineraries. And these documents were first created and used by the army.

The text below was included by Balbus right at the beginning of his work, describing the surveying techniques he used during the military campaigns of Trajan in Dacia:

> At postquam primum hosticam terram intravimus, statim, Celse, Caesaris nostri opera mensurarum rationem exigere coeperunt. Erant dandi interveniente certo itineris spatio duo rigores ordinati, quibus in tutelam commeandi ingens vallorum adsurgeret molis: hos invento tuo operis decisa ad aciem parte ferramenti usus explicuit. Nam quod ad synopsim pontium pertinet, fluminum latitudines dicere, etiam si hostis infestare voluisset, ex proxima ripa poteramus. Expugnandorum deinde montium altitudines ut sciremus, venerabilis diis ratio monstrabat. Quam ego quasi in omnibus templis adoratam post magnarum rerum experimenta, quibus interveni, religiosius colere coepi, et ad consummandum hunc librum velut ad vota reddenda properavi. Postquam ergo maximus imperator victoria Daciam proxime reseravit, statim ut e septentrionali plaga annua vice transire permisit, ego ad studium meum tamquam ad otium sum reversus, et multa velut scripta foliis et sparsa artis ordini inlaturus recollegi.[31]

The text is very interesting. It shows Balbus in action, tracing the lines of the future roads (*rigores*), using topographic instruments (*ferramentum*), and establishing the location of the future forts in Dacia. What really matters, beside this important text, is that Balbus spent one year after the Roman conquest of Dacia in 106 A.D., together with Trajan, organizing, topographically, the new province. This effort is illustrated by the careful location of the legions which remained in Dacia after 106 A.D.: The *legio XIII Gemina* was garrisoned in Apulum (today Alba Iulia, Alba County) and the *legio IIII Flavia Felix* was garrisoned in Berzobis (today Berzovia in Banat). Both were strategically located on Dacia's main Roman road, exactly 72 Roman miles south and north of the Dacian capital, Ulpia Traiana Sarmizegetusa. This shows that very precise, accurate measurements along roads were made from the beginning of the Roman presence in Dacia. These data were grouped into written or painted *itineraria*, first used by the army.

---

31 Text after CRIȘAN/TIMOC 2004/5, 157–170. A very accurate translation is to be found in ROBY 2014, 34–35: "After we entered enemy territory for the first time, Celsus, the operations of our emperor immediately began to require surveying skill. Two aligned straight lines (*rigores*) had to be established, with a defined width for the roadway between them … Through your invention the use of the *ferramentum* revealed these (lines), when part of the work had been brought into the line of sight. In respect of the survey of bridges, we were able to work out from the adjacent bank the width of rivers, even if the enemy wished to launch repeated attacks. Furthermore, that skill venerated by the gods showed us how to work out the height of mountains that had to be stormed. After it had been tested in the great events in which I had participated, I began to cultivate this skill more devoutly, as if it were worshipped in all the temples, and hastened to complete this book as if I were fulfilling a vow."

Obviously, we should assume that Balbus was not the only *mensor* who participated the this huge task of organization. In their advancement into Dacia, the Romans used *exploratores*, which were cavalry units used for the reconnaissance of the terrain. The most famous in this context was *Tiberius Claudius Maximus* (ca. 65–117), the decurion who followed Decebalus sometime after September 2nd 106 A.D., after his withdrawal from the Dacian capital. His entire career is known because his tombstone was found, by chance, at Grammeni, in Macedonia.[32]

Unlike the *speculatores*, the *exploratores* acted mostly with their troops, sometimes identifying the position of the enemy, or, in other situations, offering logistic information. Such troops are attested by the literary sources: *exploratores Batavi, Divitienses, Germanici, Nemaningenses, Sciopenses* (in Germania), *Bremenienses* (in Britannia), and *Pomarienses* (in Africa). They are also mentioned for the armies of the Danubian provinces.[33] Numerous inscriptions were found in Germania.

Another important troop with an essential role during the Dacian conquest was *numerus Germanorum (Germanicianorum) Exploratorum*, attested in Dacia[34] at Orăștioara de Sus, on stamped tiles[35] and on a funerary stela dedicated for *Iulius Secundus* by his heirs.[36]

Though each cohors from a legion had its own *mensor*, in Dacia only three *mensores* are attested, on which two from military units and one civilian. The civilian one is mentioned in an inscription found in the amphitheatre of Ulpia Traiana Sarmizegetusa.[37] Another *mensor* is attested at *Potaissa*, in the *legio V Macedonica*. His name is *Aurelius Castor*. He calls himself *mens(or) leg(ionis) V Mac(edonicae) p(iae)*. The third inscription, discovered in Apulum, mentions another *mensor*, *Aurel(ius) Maximilia(nus)*. He was a soldier of the *XIII Gemina* legion.[38]

Serving in many branches of the Roman army, *mensores* played an essential role in geographical expeditions and military campaigns. Every legion had around 10 *mensores*, one for each *cohors*. An interesting study on this topic was published in 1974 by

---

32 See FODOREAN 2016, 31, note 41, with a detailed bibliography, references and the text of the inscription.
33 Details in FODOREAN 2016, 31, note 43.
34 For the history of the unit, see: SPEIDEL 1983, 63–78.
35 AE 1972, 487 (*Apulum/Alba Iulia*); AE 1974, 548 (Orăștioara de Sus).
36 AE 1974, 546; IDR III/3, 263. Also AUSTIN/RANKOV 1995, 191.
37 ALICU/PAKI 1985–1986, 469–479 = AE 1987, 837 On a grid stone placed at the entrance of a room accessed from the arena the archaeologists could read the inscription *loc(us) menso[ris]*. The editors advanced two possible explanations for this inscription. The first one outlines the fact that it could make reference to a member of the technical stuff of the arena. The second one, more plausible, is that the inscription reffers to a *mensor frumentarius*. The inscription discovered at Ulpia Traiana is probably related to activities regarding the distribution of *alimenta*.
38 FODOREAN 2016, 33.

ROBERT K. SHERK.[39] In numerous cases, the surveyors are mentioned in inscriptions on funerary monuments. For example, in Viminacium 11 *mensores* are attested in one inscription.[40] At Lambaesis, 9 *mensores* are attested in *legio III Augusta*.[41] In *legio I Italica* garrisoned in Novae (Moesia Inferior) a *mensor*, Aurelius Mucianus, is attested on a funerary stela.[42] Another one is attested in *legio XI Claudia*, garrisoned in Durostorum: Aurelius Epictetus.[43] Rarely *mensores* are attested in auxiliary troops.[44] Papyri mention some *mensores* on duty in the *cohors XX Palmyrenorum* in the middle of the third century A.D.[45]

The Roman surveyors, especially those parts of legions, were in charge of establishing the location of the future forts, and the survey and the construction of the roads. Such aspects were essential after the conquest of Dacia, or of any other province. Trajan understood really well this, that is why Dacia was efficiently and rapidly organized, immediately after the existence of it as a province.

Therefore we should outline that before the conquest, information about Dacia was extremely general. During and after the conquest, the Romans began to explore the geography of the regions situated north of the Danube. This confirms Pliny the Elder's observation that one cannot expect to know anything about a region where the Roman army had never been before. The army played the main role in expanding such geographical knowledge.[46]

5 After the Conquest: *Dacia Augusti Provincia*, the First Military Roads and the Milestone from Aiton

The new province created north of the Danube in 106 A.D. included, at the beginning of its existence, Transylvania (without its south-eastern corner), the region of Banat and western Oltenia. *Dacia Augusti Provincia* was constituted based on an imperial decree (*lex provinciae*), promulgated by Trajan before his return to Rome. *Legio XIII Gemina* was garrisoned at Apulum (today Alba Iulia, Alba County), and *legio IIII Flavia Felix* was garrisoned at Berzobis (today Berzovia, Caraș-Severin County). The map of the Roman roads and forts in Dacia **(Fig. 1)** clearly illustrates the location of these two

---

39 SHERK 1974, 534–562. Few *mensores* are recorded in the auxiliary units. See also BAATZ 1984, 315–325. *Mensores* among the auxilia (CIL III 6358), as SPEIDEL 1987, 143–144 observed, are recorded as *mensores frumenti*, i.e. supply officers rather than surveyors.
40 CIL III 8312.
41 AE 1904, 72
42 MATEI-POPESCU 2010, 112.
43 MATEI-POPESCU 2010, 156.
44 See CIL XIII 6538, from Mainhardt in Upper Germany, mentioning a Maximus Dasantis *mensor co(ortis) [I?] Asturum*.
45 SHERK 1974, 546–551. See also for more general aspects NICOLET 1991, 151–157.
46 NICOLET 1991, 85–94; SHERK 1974, 534–562; MATTERN 1999, 24–80.

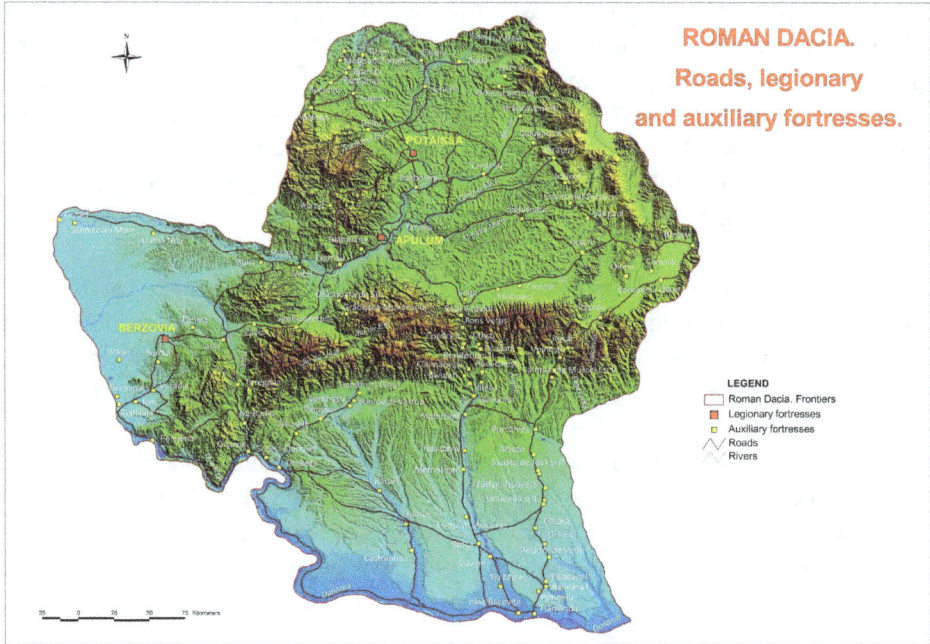

Fig. 1: Map of Roman Dacia, showing the roads, the legionary fortresses and the auxiliary forts (FODOREAN 2013, fig. 22).

forts along the main imperial road, which begins from the Danube line and ends at Porolissum (today Moigrad, Sălaj County), the northernmost point of Dacia.

How rapidly was built this road? The answer to this is provided by the milestone discovered during the XVIIIth century in a small village located between Potaissa (today Turda) and Napoca (today Cluj-Napoca, Cluj County), called Aiton (Fig. 2, Fig. 3).[47]

Aiton is located exactly 10 miles (14,785 km) North of *Potaissa,* which is actually the distance mentioned in the text:[48]

> *Imp(erator) / Caesar Nerva / Traianus Aug(ustus) / Germ(anicus) Dacicus / pontif(ex) maxim(us), / (tribunicia) pot(estate) XII, co(n)s(ul) V (sic), / imp(erator) VI, p(ater) p(atriae) fecit / per coh(ortem) I Fl(avia) Vlp(ia) / Hisp(anorum) mil(liaria) c(ivium) R(omanorum) eq(uitata) / a Potaissa Napocae / m(illia) p(assuum) X.*

---

47 More details about this settlement and the archaeological discoveries identified within the territory of this village in FODOREAN 2015, 217–232; regarding the milestone, data about it in NEIGEBAUR 1851, 221–222; TORMA 1864, 30; ACKNER/MÜLLER 1865, 149; GOOSS 1876, 64; MARŢIAN 1920, 6; WINKLER 1982, 80–84
48 CIL III 1627.

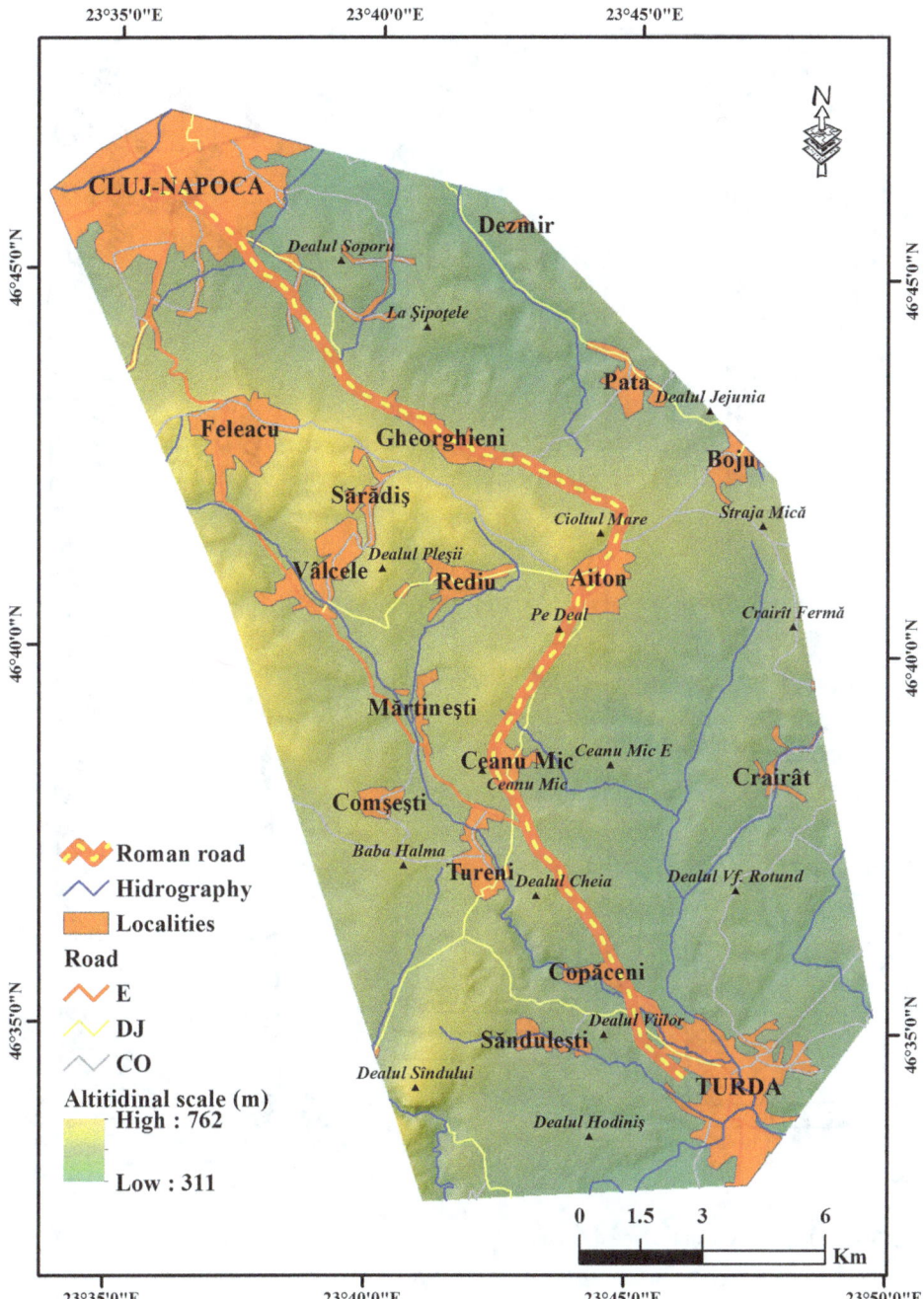

Fig. 2: Digital elevation model of the Roman road between Potaissa and Napoca (FODOREAN 2015, 224, fig. 6).

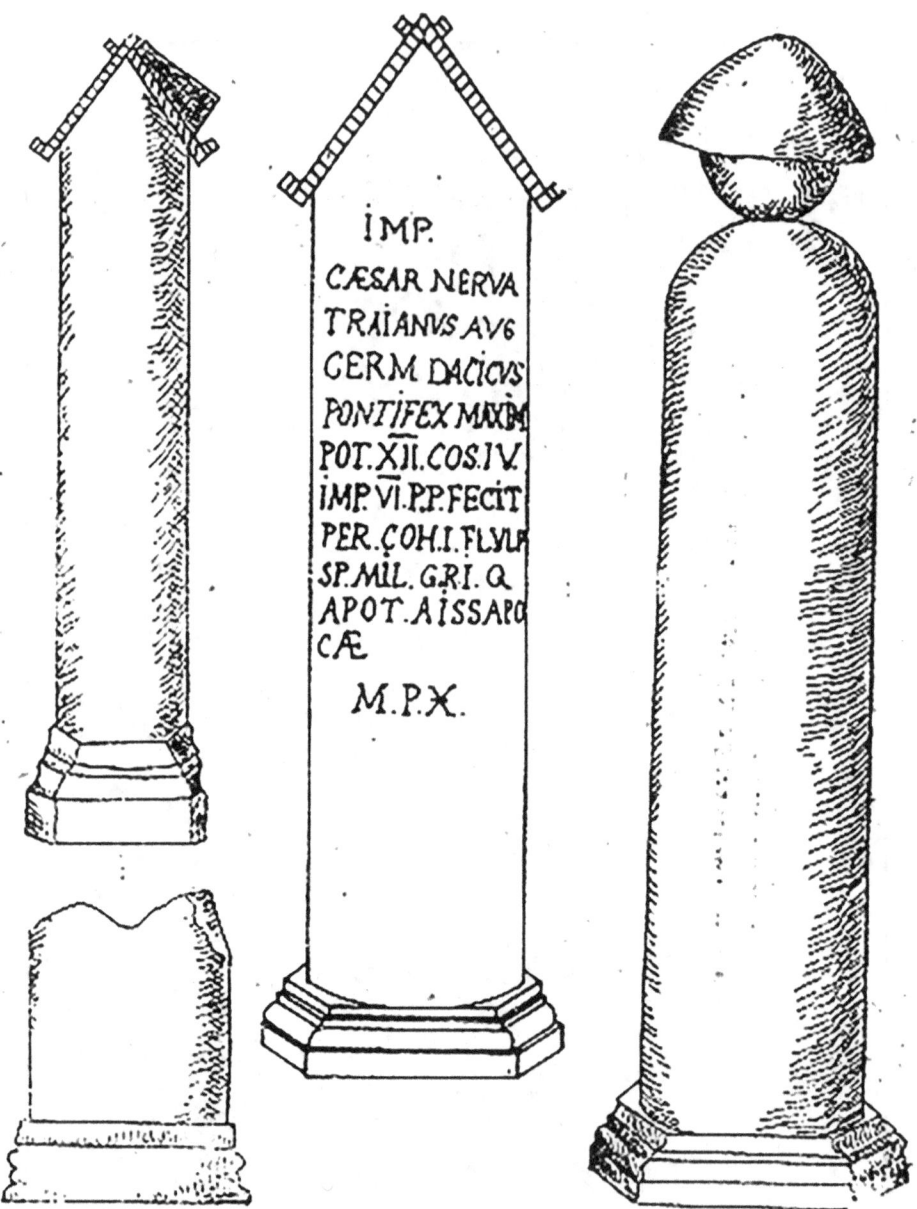

Fig. 3: Drawing with the milestone discovered in 1758 in Aiton (Winkler 1982, 83).

This monument is important for the history of Roman Dacia and implicitly for the road system of the province because of several reasons.[49] First, in the formula *a Potaissa Napocae* we find the first epigraphic evidence of *Potaissa* and *Napoca*. Second, this road sector was built by *cohors I Flavia Ulpia Hispanorum milliaria civium Romanorum equitata*, which is mentioned among the military forces used by Trajan in the war against the Dacians. After 106 A.D., it was garrisoned at Orheiul Bistriței, along the northeastern frontier.[50]

Between Potaissa and Napoca this road measures 36 kilometers, i.e. 24 Roman miles, which is the same distance as the one recorded in the Peutinger map between the same settlements. Potaissa was the most important military settlement from the Northern part of Dacia. With an estimated population of 20.000 inhabitants, the settlement was the headquarters of the *legio V Macedonica*, which arrived here after 168 A.D., during the Marcomannic wars. Its fortress (573 x 408 m) was positioned on the Cetate Hill, in the Western part of the city.

The entire sector between these two settlements was identified in the terrain, surveyed and mapped.[51] Close to the area of the current village of Ceanu Mic, the road was identified in 2005 due to some preventive archaeological excavations.

Some data about the topography of Aiton during the Roman period are also known from different publications. In 1913, MÁRTON ROSKA excavated the remains of a building with five rooms, in the northern part of the village, in a point named "Podul de piatră".[52] The building has the shape of the letter "L". More recently, during the 80' of the last century, the Roman road was identified and excavated in several locations within the territory of the village, together with several other spots with Roman artifacts, like ceramic fragments, tiles, bricks, and stone foundations.[53] Mapping all these discoveries in an accurate way, combining data from modern cartographic maps, using data from local gazetteers, and expanding our research in the terrain, to identify these remains, we succeeded to establish a comprehensive image about the topography of this site.

An area with discoveries is located north of the village, right in the vicinity of the Roman road. The building excavated by ROSKA in 1913, together with other archaeological excavations carried out in this area, leaded us to the conclusion that these wall substructions and the materials discovered here indicate the existence, during the Roman period, of a *mansio*. As we have noted before, the discoveries are very consistent: foundations of stone walls, fragments of inscriptions, fragments of monuments, fragments of columns, coins, heating installations of hypocaust etc. But the most important and the essential argument is, in fact, the location of these discover-

---

49 FODOREAN 2006, 65–68; FODOREAN 2013, 34.
50 PROTASE 2008.
51 WINKLER/BLĂJAN/CERGHI 1980, 63–73; WINKLER 1982a, 587–589.
52 ROSKA 1915, 48–50.
53 STOIA 1976, 273; BLĂJAN/TATAI-BALTĂ 1978, 33; BLĂJAN/CERGHI 1978, 131–147.

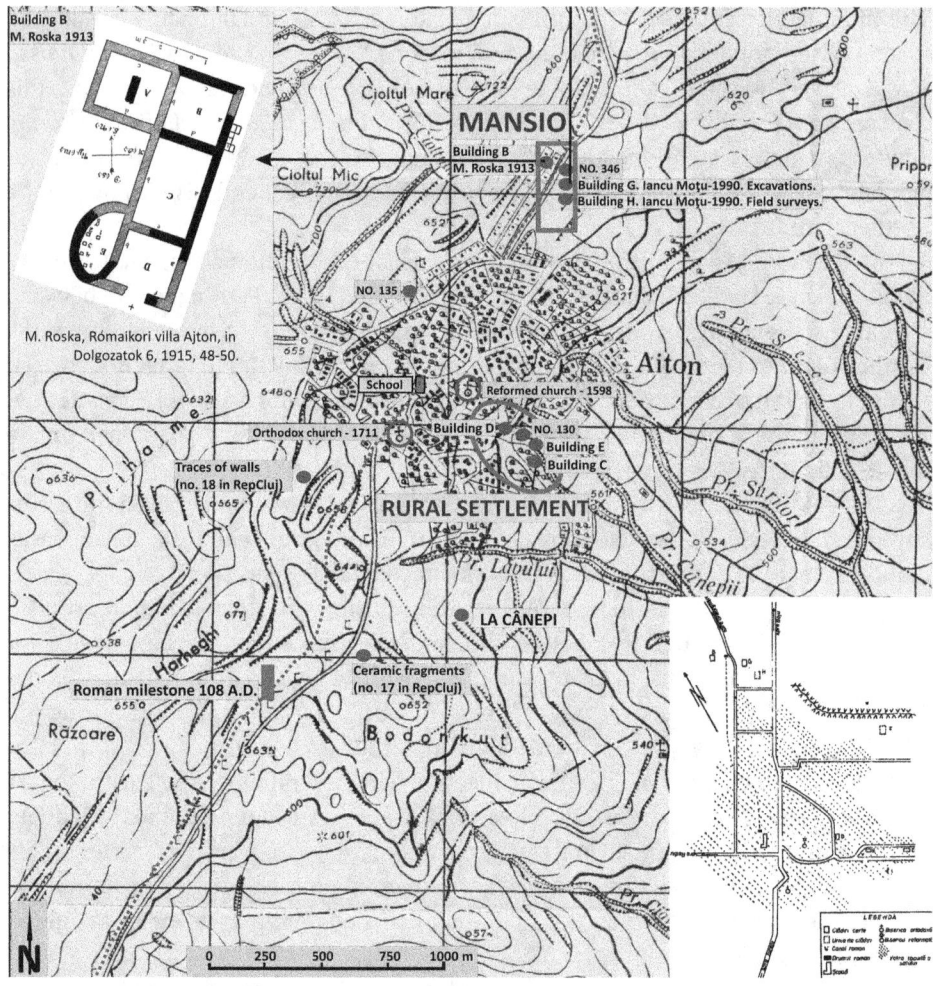

Fig. 4: The topography of Aiton, indicating the location of the *mansio* and the rural settlement (adapted after FODOREAN 2015, 230, fig. 10).

ies, very close to the main imperial Roman road. All the other discoveries are grouped in the eastern part of the village, indicating the area where the rural settlement was established. Useful for our topographical analyze were the analogies from Britannia, where the majority of the *mansiones* discussed in 1995 by E.W. BLACK are located close to the roads, indicating, obviously, a logical pattern regarding the location of these structures.[54]

---

54 BLACK 1995.

6 *Tabula Peutingeriana* and Dacia

Over the last century, historians have published a large amount of data about the Peutinger map.[55] Some of these contributions focused on different aspects concerning this document, such as its content, and especially the authorship and the date of the lost original. We have already pointed out some of these attempts.[56] R. CHEVALLIER considered the original a 'compilation tardive'.[57] ANNALINA AND MARIO LEVI agreed that the document was created in the third century and then completed with other data in the fourth and fifth centuries.[58] V.W. VON HAGEN dated the original around 250 A.D.[59] E. MANNI supposed that the document was created after 260 A.D.[60] R.J.A. TALBERT recently concluded that the original can be dated during Diocletian's Tetrarchy (around 300).[61] K. MILLER dated the document in 365–366 A.D.[62] E. WEBER considered that the document was created in 435 A.D.[63] B. SALWAY dated it in the fourth or the fifth century A.D.[64] E. ALBU dated the original in the early ninth century A.D.[65] In the most recent book on the Peutinger map, M. RATHMANN offered a valuable and interesting approach of the document, including a very plausible scheme which illustrates the chronological frames of the document starting with its archetype, considered to be of Hellenistic period.[66]

These attempts were based on the content of the map, the inclusion of certain cities and settlements (Rome, Constantinople, Antioch[67] – personified vignettes; Ravenna, Aquileia, Nicaea, Nicomedia, Tessalonicae, Ancyra? – vignettes of the 'cities surrounded by walls' type), certain landscape details (*silva Vosagus*: 2A2–3, *silva Marciana*: 2a4–3a1), the presence/absence of certain roads, the representation/non-representation of vignettes of the 'double-tower' type, or the meaning of special vignettes/drawings (Ad Sanctum Petrum, the temple of Apollo in Antioch). Suppositions about the map's author, place of production, method of creation, dimensions,

---

[55] To quote only few of these contributions: MILLER 1916; LEVI/LEVI 1967; WEBER 1976; BOSIO 1983; TALBERT 2010; ALBU 2014; RATHMANN 2016 (I am grateful to my colleague and friend Michael, who offered me a copy of his book). More details in FODOREAN 2016, 41, especially note 7.
[56] FODOREAN 2016, 41–43.
[57] CHEVALLIER 1997, 53–56.
[58] LEVI/LEVI 1967.
[59] VON HAGEN 1978, 14.
[60] MANNI 1949, 30–31.
[61] TALBERT 2010, 136, 153; a review-article of this book, with details regarding the topography of Dacia, in FODOREAN 2011, 9–19.
[62] MILLER 1916, XXX. BOSIO 1983 has agreed with this date.
[63] WEBER 1989, 113–117.
[64] SALWAY 2005, 131.
[65] ALBU 2005, 136–148; ALBU 2008, 111–119.
[66] RATHMANN 2016, 20, fig. 18.
[67] LEYLEK 1993, 203–206.

purpose, role, and sources used were also made. The map was assumed to have served as a road map,[68] reflecting the official transportation system (*cursus publicus*),[69] or as a propaganda map, depicting, at the time of the Tetrarchy, the former glory, power and geographical extent of the Roman Empire.[70] The distances written in between settlements are sometimes correct, but at times they are not, and the vignettes represent important cities, or stopping places along the routes (*mansiones*).[71] The map was ordered by a private citizen or by an emperor (Septimius Severus,[72] Theodosius II)[73] and it stood as a parchment scroll in a library or was displayed on a wall in Diocletian's palace in Split (Spalatum).[74] The author of the original was either Castorius, or an anonymous, or a team. Peutinger's map mentions Pompeii, Roman Dacia, Constantinople, Antioch, old St. Peter's church in Rome, and regional names such as *Francia*, *Suevia* and *Allamania*.

In our opinion, the document is an *itinerarium pictum* which reflects the Roman linear perception of space.

Dacia is represented in the segments VI and VII,[75] where three roads are represented: Lederata-Tibiscum, Dierna-Tibiscum-Sarmizegetusa-Apulum-Napoca-Porolissum and Drobeta-Romula-Caput Stenarum-Apulum. The settlements Sarmizegetusa and Aquae are not connected to any road, albeit after the name of the first locality the distance to the next one (XIIII MP) is marked. Five settlements are represented by double-tower vignettes: *Tivisco, Sarmategte, Apula, Napoca* and *Porolisso*. Ad Aquas is marked by a special vignette, indicating spas or thermal constructions.[76] The other settlements, villages or *mansiones* are marked only by their names and the distance between them.

The distances and settlements indicated in Dacia are:
1. *Segmentum* VI 2: the road between Lederata and Tibiscum: Lederata-XII (Roman miles); apo Fl.-XII; Arcidava-XII; Centū Putea-XII; Bersovia-XII; Azizis-III; Caput bubali-X; Tivisco (depicted by a vignette). Eight settlements are mentioned as well as a total distance of 73 Roman miles.
2. *Segmenta* VI 3 and VII 1: the road between Tierva and Porolisso: Tierva-XI (Roman miles); Admediā-XIIII; Pretorio-IX; Ad Pannonios-IX; Gaganis-XI; Masclianis-XI-III; Tivisco-XIIII; Agnavie-VIII; Ponte Augusti-XV; Sarmategte-XIIII; Ad Aquas-XIII;

---

[68] Most researchers agree with this.
[69] Levi/Levi 1967.
[70] Talbert 2010, 133–157.
[71] See recent information in Klee 2010.
[72] Levi/Levi 1967.
[73] Weber 1989, 113–117.
[74] Talbert 2010, 149.
[75] I have already mentioned (Fodorean 2016, 83, note 2) that I agree with Weber's system of counting only the 11 existing segments. Miller's reconstruction, with one added segment, remains only a supposition.
[76] More details about these vignettes in Fodorean 2004, 51–58.

Petris-VIIII; Germizera-VIIII; Blandiana-VIII; Apula-XII; Brucla-XII; Salinis-XII; Patavissa-XXIIII; Napoca-XVI; Optatiana-X; Largiana-XVII; Cersie-IIII; Porolisso. Twenty-four settlements are indicated as well as a total distance of 270 Roman miles.

3. *Segmenta* VI 4, VI 5 and VII 1: the road between Drubetis and Apulum, via Romula: Drubetis-XXXVI (Roman miles); Amutria-XXXV; Pelendova-XX; Castris novis-LXX; Romula-XIII; Acidava-XXIIII; Rusidava-XIIII; Ponte Aluti-XIII; Burridava-XII; Castra tragana-VIIII; Arutela-XV; Pretorio-VIIII; Ponte vetere-XLIIII; Stenarum-XII; Cedonie-XXIIII; Acidava-XV; Apula. Seventeen settlements are mentioned and a total distance of 379 Roman miles.

To sum up, three roads are indicated in Dacia along with 48 settlements and a total distance of 703 Roman miles (1039.385 km).

Some of these distances are correct. Others are mistakenly written, but it is difficult to establish if such mistakes belonged to the original creator/creators or they are mistakes made by the medieval copyist/copyists of the document. We have detailed these aspects recently.[77] What is more important for our demonstration here is the fact that these three roads represent the basis road system of Dacia, with Apulum as the main crossroads and with the first legionary fortresses located along the main imperial road.

7 Final Observations. Dacia and *itineraria*

We think that the military roads indicated on the Peutinger map represent the lines of advance taken by the Roman marching columns during the Dacian wars. The forts and stations built immediately after the conquest replaced the provisory ones built by the army during the military campaigns. In many cases, the distance between the stopping points is 12 miles (sometimes 13, 11 or 9, indicating a *iustum iter*). During the conquest of the Dacian territories, the Romans applied an efficient strategy, using at least five marching columns to attack the north-danubian territories. These columns usually marched for three days, covering an average of 12 miles per day. A column, led by Trajan, started from Viminacium and advanced into Dacian territory along the Lederata-Tibiscum road. Another one entered Dacia at Dierna and then advanced along the Timiș and Cerna valleys. A third column used the most direct route to the Dacian capital, starting from Drobeta, through the Vâlcan Pass, up to the Depression of Hațeg. The soldiers part of the troops from Moesia Inferior marched along the river Alutus (Olt). The Pannonian legions advanced from Lugio to Partiscum and along the river Mureș towards Apulum.

---

[77] FODOREAN 2016, 83–100 (ch. 6).

Therefore, we agree that these marching routes were turned into the first functional roads immediately after the conquest. Two of them are not depicted on the Peutinger map: the Drobeta – Vâlcan Pass – Ulpia Traiana Sarmizegetusa road and the road along the Mureş valley. But, as we have stated before, the Peutinger map was a document of spatial limits and precise dimensions.[78] There was not enough space to represent all the roads, such as might have been the case with other local itineraries created after these campaigns. To conclude, our believe is that the sources used to create the map of Dacia were military itineraries from the early times of the province.

Bibliography and References

ACKNER/MÜLLER 1865 = M.J. ACKNER/F. MÜLLER, Die römischen Inschriften in Dacien, Wien 1865.

ALBU 2005 = E. ALBU, Imperial Geography and the Medieval Peutinger Map, *Imago Mundi* 57, 2005, 136–148.

ALBU 2008 = E. ALBU, Rethinking the Peutinger Map, in: R.J.A. TALBERT/R.W. UNGER (ed.), Cartography in Antiquity and Middle Ages: Fresh Perspectives, New Methods, Leiden 2008, 111–119.

ALBU 2014 = E. ALBU, The Medieval Peutinger Map: Imperial Roman Revival in a German Empire, Cambridge 2014.

ALICU/PAKI 1985–1986 = D. ALICU/A. PAKI, O inscripţie inedită din amfiteatrul roman de la Ulpia Traiana Sarmizegetusa, *Acta Musei Napocensis* 22–23, 1985–1986, 469–479.

AUSTIN/RANKOV 1995 = N.J.E. AUSTIN/N.B. RANKOV, Exploratio: Military and political intelligence in the Roman world from the Second Punic War to the battle of Adrianople, London/New York 1995.

BĂRBULESCU 1999 = M. BĂRBULESCU, Traian şi descoperirea Daciei, in: D. PROTASE/D. BRUDAŞCU (ed.), Napoca. 1880 de ani de la începutul vieţii urbane, Cluj-Napoca 1999, 32–38.

BĂRBULESCU 2001 = M. BĂRBULESCU, Istoria politică, in: D. PROTASE/A. SUCEVEANU, Istoria Românilor: Daco-romani, romanici, alogeni, vol. 2, Bucharest 2001, 73–98.

BĂRBULESCU et al. 2005 = M. BĂRBULESCU/C. BĂRBULESCU/I. FODOREAN/F. FODOREAN/A. HUSAR/ C. MIHĂILĂ/E. NEMETH/I. NEMETI/S. NEMETI/M. PÎSLARU/M. SĂLĂŞAN/V. ZOTIC, Atlas-dicţionar al Daciei romane, Cluj-Napoca 2005.

BAATZ 1984 = D. BAATZ, Quellen zur Bauplanung römischer Militärlager, in: DEUTSCHES ARCHÄOLOGISCHES INSTITUT/ARCHITEKTURREFERAT (ed.), Bauplanung und Bautheorie der Antike, Berlin 1984, 315–325.

BECATTI 1982 = G. BECATTI, La Colonna Traiana, espressione somma del rilievo storico romano, ANRW II 12.1, 1982, 536–578.

BLACK 1995 = E.W. BLACK, Cursus Publicus: The Infrastructure of Government in Roman Britain, Oxford 1995.

BLĂJAN/CERGHI 1978 = M. BLĂJAN/T. CERGHI, Descoperiri romane şi postromane la Aiton (jud. Cluj), *Potaissa. Studii şi comunicări* 1, 1978, 21–27.

BLĂJAN/TATAI-BALTĂ 1978 = M. BLĂJAN/C. TATAI-BALTĂ, Descoperiri din epoca neolitică şi perioada de tranziţie spre epoca bronzului în judeţele Sibiu, Alba şi Cluj (I), *Apulum* 16, 1978, 9–38.

---

[78] FODOREAN 2016, 95.

Bennett 1997 = J. Bennett, Trajan, Optimus Princeps: A Life and Times, London/New York 1997.
Bosio 1983 = L. Bosio, La Tabula Peutingeriana: una descrizione pittorica del mondo antico, Rimini Maggioli 1983.
Breeze 1988 = D.J. Breeze, Why Did the Romans Fail to Conquer Britain?, *Proceedings of the Society of Antiquaries of Scotland* 118, 1988, 3–22.
Chevallier 1997 = R. Chevallier, Les voies romaines, Paris 1997².
Crişan/Timoc 2004/5 = D.S. Crişan/C. Timoc, Inginerii împăratului Traian (I). Mensorul Balbus. Die Ingenieure Kaisers Trajan (I). Balbus der Mensor, *Analele Banatului* 12–13, 2004/5, 157–170.
Dana/Nemeti 2016 = D. Dana/S. Nemeti, Ptolémée et la toponymie de la Dacie (VI–IX), *Classica et Christiana* 11, 2016, 67–94.
Fodorean 2004 = F. Fodorean, Tabula Peutingeriana and the Province of Dacia, *ActaMN* 39–40, 1, 2002–2003 (2004), 51–58.
Fodorean 2006 = F. Fodorean, Drumurile din Dacia romană, Cluj-Napoca 2006.
Fodorean 2011 = F. Fodorean, review to R.J.A. Talbert, Rome's World: The Peutinger Map Reconsidered, Cambridge 2010, *Plekos* 13, 2011, 9–19.
Fodorean 2013 = F. Fodorean, The Topography and the Landscape of Roman Dacia, Oxford 2013.
Fodorean 2015 = F. Fodorean, A Potaissa Napocae MP X. Trajan's Imperial Road and the Mansio from Aiton (Cluj County), *AArchHung* 66,1, 2015, 217–232.
Fodorean 2016 = F. Fodorean, Pannonia, Dacia and Moesia in the Ancient Geographical Sources, Stuttgart 2016.
Gooss 1876 = C. Gooss, Chronik der archaologischen Funde Siebenbürgens, Hermannstadt 1876.
Jones 1992 = B.W. Jones, The Emperor Domitian, London/New York 1992.
Klee 2010 = M. Klee, Lebensadern des Imperiums. Strassen im Römischen Weltreich, Stuttgart 2010.
Le Roux 1998 = P. Le Roux, Le Haut-Empire romain en Occident d'Auguste aux Sévères: 31 av. J.-C.-235 apr. J.-C., Paris 1998.
Levi/Levi 1967 = A. Levi/M. Levi, Itineraria picta: Contributo allo studio della Tabula Peutingeriana, Rome 1967.
Leylek 1993 = H. Leylek, La vignetta di Antiochia e la datazione della Tabula Peutingeriana, *Journal of Ancient Topography* 3, 1993, 203–206.
Lewis 2001 = M.J.T. Lewis, Surveying Instruments of Greece and Rome, Cambridge 2001.
Luttwak 1976 = E. Luttwak, The Grand Strategy of the Roman Empire from the First Century A.D. to the Third, Baltimore 1976.
Manni 1949 = E. Manni, L'impero di Gallieno, Rome 1949.
Marţian 1920 = I. Marţian, Repertoriu arheologic pentru Ardeal, Bistriţa 1920.
Matei-Popescu 2010 = F. Matei-Popescu, The Roman Army in Moesia Inferior, Bucharest 2010.
Mattern 1999 = S. Mattern, Rome and the Enemy: Imperial Strategy in the Principate, California 1999.
McQuiggan 2006/7 = R. McQuiggan, Roman Geography and Spatial Perception in the Republic, *Hirundo. The McGill Journal of Classical Studies* 5, 2006/7, 77–98.
Miller 1916 = K. Miller, Itineraria romana. Römische Reisewege an der Hand der Tabula Peutingeriana dargestellt, Stuttgart 1916.
Mirković 2007 = M. Mirković, Moesia Superior. Eine Provinz an Der Mittleren Donau, Mainz 2007.
Mócsy 1974 = A. Mócsy, Pannonia and Upper Moesia. A History of the Middle Danube Provinces of the Roman Empire. London/Boston 1974.
Neigebaur 1851 = J.F. Neigebaur, Dacien: Aus den Ueberresten des klassischen Alterhums. Mit besonderer Rücksicht auf Siebenbürgen, Braşov 1851.

NEMETH 2007 = E. NEMETH, Politische und militärische Beziehungen zwischen Pannonien und Dakien in der Römerzeit: Relaţii politice şi militare între Pannonia şi Dacia în epoca romană, Cluj-Napoca 2007.

NEMETI 2009 = S. NEMETI, Scythicum frigus. Repères pour une histoire du climat au Bas-Danube (Ier siècle apr. J.-C.), in: E. HERMON (ed.), Société et climats dans l'Empire romain. Pour une perspective historique et systémique de la gestion des ressources en eau dans l'Empire romain, Napoli 2009, 411–427.

NEMETI 2014 = S. NEMETI, In circuitu tenuit...Dacia and Roman Geographical Knowledge, *Ephemeris Napocensis* 21, 2011, 37–49.

NEMETI 2014 = S. NEMETI, Finding Arcobadara. Essay on the Geography and Administration of Roman Dacia, Cluj-Napoca 2014.

NICOLET 1991 = C. NICOLET, Space, Geography, and Politics in the Early Roman Empire, Michigan 1991.

POPA-LISSEANU 2006 = G. POPA-LISSEANU, Dacia în autorii clasici, Bucharest 2006.

POPESCU/ȚENTEA 2006 = F.M. POPESCU/O. ȚENTEA, Participarea trupelor auxiliare din Moesia Superior şi Moesia Inferior la cucerirea Daciei, in: E.S. TEODOR/O. ȚENTEA (ed.), Dacia Augusti Provincia. Crearea provinciei. Actele simpozionului desfăşurat în 13–14 octombrie 2006 la Muzeul Naţional de Istorie a României, Bucharest 2006, 75–120.

PROTASE 2008 = D. PROTASE, Castrul roman de la Orheiul Bistriţei. Das Römische Kastell von Orheiu Bistriţei, Cluj-Napoca 2008.

RATHMANN 2016 = M. RATHMANN, Tabula Peutingeriana: Die einzige Weltkarte aus der Antike, Darmstadt 2016.

ROBY 2014 = C. ROBY, Experiencing Geometry in Roman Surveyors' Texts, *Nuncius* 29, 2014, 9–52.

ROSKA 1915 = M. ROSKA, Rómaikori villa Ajton (Kolozs vm.) határában, *Dolgozatok* 6, 1915, 48–50.

ROSSI 1968 = L. ROSSI, The Representation on Trajan's Column of Trajan's Rock-cut Road in Upper Moesia, *AntJ* 68, 1968, 41–46.

SALWAY 2005 = B. SALWAY, The Nature and Genesis of the Peutinger Map, *Imago Mundi* 57, 2005, 119–135.

ŠAŠEL 1973 = J. ŠAŠEL, Trajan's Canal at the Iron Gate, *JRS* 6, 1973, 80–85.

SHERK 1974 = R.K. SHERK, Roman Geographical Exploration and Military Maps, ANRW II 1, 1974, 534–562.

SPEIDEL 1983 = M.P. SPEIDEL, Exploratores. Mobile Elit Units of Roman Germany, *Epigraphische Studien* 13, 1983, 63–78.

SPEIDEL 1987 = M.P. SPEIDEL, A Building Inscription from the Fort of Numerus Germanicianorum at Orăştioara de Sus in Upper Dacia, *Apulum* 24, 1987, 143–144.

STEFAN 2005 = A.S. STEFAN, Les guerres daciques de Domitien et de Trajan: architecture militaire, topographie, images et histoire, Rome 2005.

STOIA 1976 = A. STOIA, Les fouilles archaeologiques en Roumanie, *Dacia* 20, 1976, 273–286.

STROBEL 1989 = K. STROBEL, Die Donaukriege Domitians, Bonn 1989.

TALBERT 2010 = R. TALBERT, Rome's World: the Peutinger Map Reconsidered, Cambridge 2010.

TIMOC 2001 = C. TIMOC, Despre dirijarea navigaţiei fluviale în zona Porţilor de fier ale Dunării în epoca romană, in: D. BENEA (ed.), In memoriam Dumitru Tudor, Timişoara 2001, 97–116.

TORMA 1864 = K. TORMA, Adalék észak-nyugati Dacia föld-és helyiratához, Pesta 1864.

VON HAGEN 1978 = V.W. VON HAGEN, Le grande strade di Roma nel mondo, Rome 1978.

WEBER 1976 = E. WEBER, Tabula Peutingeriana: Codex Vindobonensis 324, Graz 1976.

WEBER 1989 = E. WEBER, Zur Datierung der Tabula Peutingeriana, in: H. HERZIG/R. FREI-STOLBA (ed.), Labor omnibus unus: Festschrift für Gerold Walser, Stuttgart 1989, 113–117.

WHITTAKER 2004 = C. WHITTAKER, Rome and Its Frontiers: the Dynamics of Empire, London/New York 2004.

Winkler 1982 = I. Winkler, Date noi despre CIL III, 1627, cea dintâi atestare epigrafică a Potaissei, *Potaissa. Studii şi comunicări* 3, 1982, 80–84.

Winkler 1982a = I. Winkler, Drumul roman Napoca-Potaissa II, *ActaMN* 19, 1982, 587–589.

Winkler/Blăjan/Cerghi 1980 = I. Winkler/M. Blăjan/T. Cerghi, Drumul roman Napoca-Potaissa I, *Potaissa. Studii şi comunicări* 2, 1980, 63–73.

Miroslava Mirković
Roman Roads in *Moesia Superior* at Six Points

Abstract: The earliest communication between the Roman world and the central Balkan region started from the south, from the Roman province of *Macedonia*. Following the line of the Vardar and Južna Morava valleys it reached the central Balkan region and the lower Danube at the time the Romans were endeavoring to come to the Danube in order to subdue the tribes in *Thracia*. The communication with Italy and the West began during the time when the Roman politics was turning toward the Balkans, in the first century BC. The Roman efforts to connect the military camps in Illyricum with their bases on the lower Danube, divided by the Danube canyon and the cliffs in Djerdap, began after the new province of *Moesia* was organized. The first steps were made under Tiberius and Claudius and continued under Domitian. The main communication from Italy to the East passed through *Pannonia* and reached the Danube at *Singidunum*, on the confluence of the Sava River. It was not until after the time of Domitian that Roman politics became offensive and the legionary camp was established in *Viminacium*. The roads from *Viminacium* went in two main directions: east of the camp, along the Danube and south in the direction towards *Dardania* and *Naissus*. From the main *Naissus – Lissus* communication the road to *Scupi* branched off at the station of *Hammeo*, parallel to the old communication along the Južna Morava valley, now neglected because it had become useless in the new Roman politics. From *Naissus* the communication led to the Danube in the north, passing from *Naissus* through *Timacum Minus* to *Ratiaria*; and the other one led through *Remesiana* and *Turres* to Thrace and further on to Asia Minor.

Zusammenfassung: Der erste Verkehr zwischen der römischen Welt und dem Gebiet des zentralen Balkan ging vom Süden aus, von der römischen Provinz *Macedonia*. Indem er der Linie der Vardar und Južna Morava Täler folgte, erreichte er das Gebiet des zentralen Balkan und die untere Donau zu der Zeit, als die Römer sich bemühten, zur Donau zu gelangen, um die Stämme in Thrakien zu unterwerfen. Der Verkehr mit Italien und dem Westen begann während der Zeit, als die Römische Politik sich zum Balkan wandte im ersten Jahrhundert v. Chr. Die römischen Bemühungen, die Militärlager in Illyricum mit ihren Lagern an der unteren Donau zu verbinden, die durch die Donauschlucht und die Felsen in Djerdap voneinander getrennt wurden, begannen, nachdem die Provinz *Moesia* eingerichtet worden war. Die ersten Schritte wurden unter Tiberius und Claudius unternommen und wurden unter Domitian fortgeführt. Der Hauptverkehr von Italien in den Osten durchlief Pannonien und erreichte die Donau bei *Singidunum*, beim Zusammenfluss des Flusses Sava in die Donau. Erst nach Domitian wurde die römische Politik offensiv und das Legionslager in *Viminacium* errichtet. Die Straßen *Viminacium*s verliefen in zwei Richtungen: östlich des Lagers, entlang der Donau und südlich in Richtung *Dardania* und *Naissus*. Vom Hauptverkehrsweg *Naissus–Lissus* zweigte die Straße nach *Scupi* an der *statio Hammeo* ab, parallel zur alten Verkehrsroute entlang dem Južna Morava Tal, die nun aufgegeben wurde, da sie für die neue römische Politik nutzlos geworden war. Von *Naissus* aus führte die Verkehrsroute an die Donau im Norden, wobei sie von *Naissus* durch *Timacum Minus* nach *Ratiaria* führte. Der andere Verkehrsweg führte durch *Remesiana* und *Turres* nach Thrakien und weiter nach *Asia Minor*.

There were two important intersections in the province of *Moesia Superior*: *Viminacium*, the big legionary camp on the Danube, and *Naissus* in *Dardania*, in the geographic center of the province. The main communication which came from Italy bifurcated in *Viminacium* in two directions: one leading to the East along the Danube; the other following the south direction to *Dardania*, starting from this point. The road from *Viminacium* to the south branched off from *Naissus* in four ways: one leading to *Thracia* in the East, another to the Danube following the Timok valley in the North, and a third was directed towards *Lissus* in the West from which the road to *Scupi* diverged; *Scupi* was also connected with *Naissus* by a road which followed the course of the river Južna Morava. Considering the Roman strategic aims and the time of their construction, discussion about communications in *Moesia Superior* could be summarized in six points:

I. Along the Danube: terrestrial roads and a fluvial way
II. After crossing the Danube: the roads in the big plain of Banat
III. A *compendium* from *Viminacium* to *Dardania* and IMS II 50
IV. South of *Naissus*: new discoveries of the road along the Južna Morava valley and missing stations.
V. Southwest of *Naissus*: the main road to *Lissus* and the bifurcation from *Hammeo* to *Scupi* and from *Scupi* to *Stobi*.
VI. East of *Naissus*: new discoveries of the Roman road and mile stones found in Bela Palanka.

I Along the Danube

A description of the road network: the main intersections: 1. *Viminacium*: a) to *Lederata*, b) to *Pincum, Novae, Scrofulae, Taliata*; 2 *Taliata*: a) To *Dierna*, b) To *Egeta*; 3. *Egeta*: a) to *Drobeta*. b) to *Ratiaria*,

Starting from the confluence of the Sava and the Danube, Tab. Peut. seg. 6–7, enumerates East of *Pannonia* stations *Singiduno* – XIIII – *Tricornio* – XII – *Monte Aureo* -XIIII – *Margum fl.* – X – *Viminatio*; X – *Lederata* – XIII – *Punicum* and further

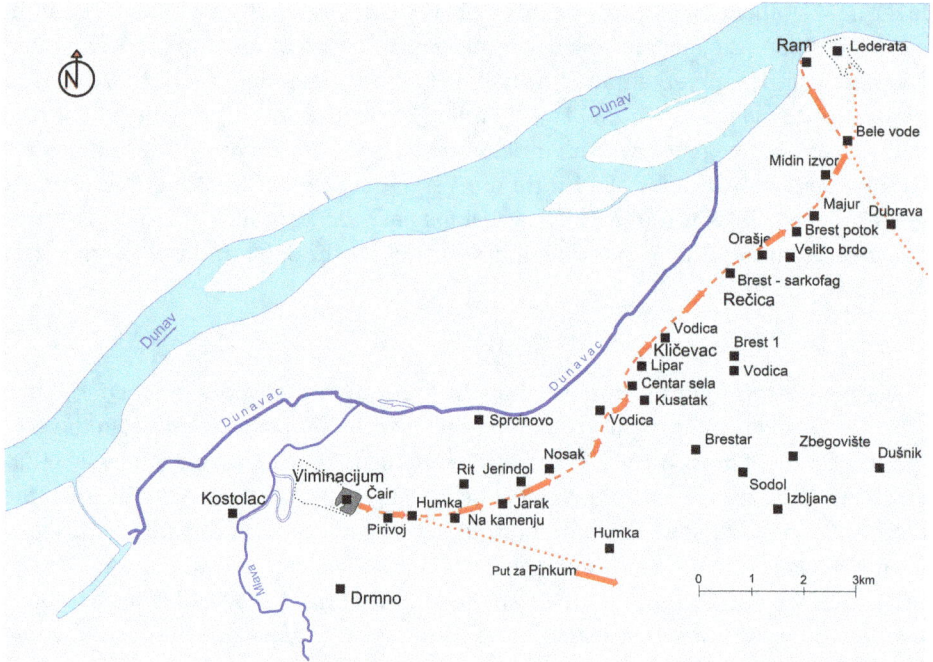

Fig. 1: From *Viminacium* to *Lederata*: road and the canal Dunavac? (D. Spasić-Djurić and D. Jacanović)

along the Danube after XI miles *Vico Cuppe* – XII – *Ad Novas* -X – *Ad Scrofulas* –XV – to *Taliata*, the station between two Danube canyons.[1]

Ten miles east of *Viminacium*, a big military camp on the Danube, the road branches off in two directions, a) to *Lederata* XIII and b) to *Pincum* XI miles. The road to *Lederata* followed the same direction as the Danube canal, the so called Dunavac (a small Danube). Its almost parallel course with the road could point to its artificial construction as a canal. Both the canal and the road followed a parallel route and ended in Ram, opposite *Lederata* on the left Danube bank, where the crossing of the Danube is marked in the *tabula*. The road which is archaeologically prospected,[2] continued to the *Apo fluvius*, to the North of the Danube. The inscription of the centurion from the *VII Claudia* legion, engraved in the rock on the right Danube bank in Ram probably commemorates the crossing of the army in the Domitian Dacian expeditions or in Trajan's first Dacian war.[3]

---

[1] Marsili 1726, 81 ff.; Kanitz 1892, 25–54; Swoboda 1939; Mirković 2003, 8–27; Mirković 2007, 25–45; Mirković 2015, 40–50.
[2] Spasić-Djurić/Jacanović 2007, 123–164.
[3] IMS II 293 = Mirković 2015, no. 11, with photo. On the archaeological investigations on the island Sapaja between Ram on the right Danube bank and Lederata on the left see Dimitrijević 1984, 29–62.

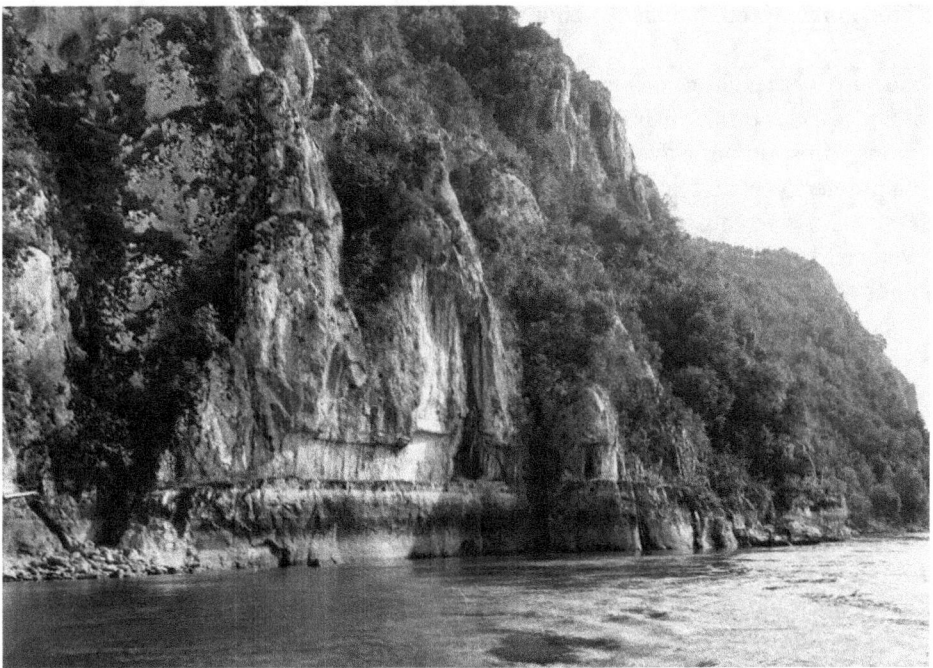

Fig. 2: Trajan's inscription and road in the Lower Canyon (M.Mirković)

The most intriguing part of the network is that through the Iron Gates, the big canyons of the Danube's Djerdap. At about 150 km long, the Djerdap Canyon (Iron Gates) begins after Novae, with cliffs on the right bank which spring up vertically several hundreds of meters from the river, leaving no place for a road. The road had to be cut in the rocks. The remains of such a road have been discovered only in the cliff of Gospodjin vir in the first narrow passage, not far from the station of *Ad Scrophulas*. Taliata, between two of the Djerdap canyons, was an important fluvial harbor and road intersection. From this point the road branched off in three directions, only one of which was terrestrial. At a distance of XV miles upstream from *Taliata* is recorded *Tierna* (*Dierna*) on the left Danube bank in *tabula*. The road crossed the Danube at that point and continued on the left Danube bank reaching the first station of *Ad Media* after a further XI miles of *Dierna* on the left bank. Another road started from *Taliata*, which left the Danube bank and following the shortest distance over the mountain, and reached the Danube again at *Egeta* after fourteen miles (after VIII – *Gerulatis* –VI – *Unam)*; from *Egeta* the road bifurcated again and followed the Danube upstream to the station of *Drobeta* (XXI – *Drubetis*), continuing on the other side to the East toward *Ratiaria*, VIII– *Clevora* – VIIII – *Ad Aquas* – XXIII – *Dortico* –XXV – *Ad Malum* – XIII – *Ratiaria*.

Three Problems on the Danube Line

The purpose of building communications in *Moesia Superior*, as well as in other Balkan provinces, was primarily military and strategic. Roads were built in order to make the troops' transport possible. For the Romans, after the province of *Moesia* was founded, the problem was first how to connect the military camps on the Danube in Illyricum (*Pannonia*) with those on the lower Danube, in the new province of *Moesia*, and to overcome the difficulties of navigation through the Danube canyon in Djerdap. Later, in the expeditions against the Dacian state, which were organized by Domitian and Trajan, great military strength was engaged. A consular army usually took part in the expeditions in Dacia under Domitian, which meant no fewer than two legions; Trajan took 12 legions with him and a considerable number of auxiliaries. It is assumed that the main transport was carried out by ships on the Danube, but the fluvial communication between Illyricum and the lower Danube was broken by the big Djerdap Canyon and by cataracts near present-day Sip, between *Dierna* and *Drobeta*. If the transport was done by ship, it was necessary to overcome the difficulties in navigation in the narrow passages of the Danube in Djerdap, and to avoid the cataracts at the exit of Djerdap. The terrestrial transport of two legions in the first case, and twelve in Trajan's wars, would have been dangerous and time-consuming, considering the narrowness of the road which had to be cut in the rock. First, the Gospodjin vir cliff in the upper gorge, about 200 m long, which scales more than 15 meters in the Danube and breaks off any communication. It could only be surpassed by dragging ships.

a. Dragging Ships

There are no mile stones on the route along the Danube. Instead the imperial inscriptions were engraved in the rocks of the canyons in order to commemorate the work on cutting the road. No distance is mentioned.

The imperial inscriptions of Tiberius, Claudius and Domitian carved in the rock of Gospodjin vir[4] testify to the construction of the road. The road is mentioned in Domitian's inscription from 93 AD: *iter vetu[s]tate [e]t incursu Danubi(i) c[or]ruptum operibu[s i]teratis [reparavit.*[5] Similar work was done by Trajan in the lower canyon. His inscription briefly describes the method of construction: *montibus excisi[s] anconibus sublat[i]s via[m refecit.*[6] But the remains of the road as described by KANITZ and

---

[4] CIL III 1698 = 13813b = ILS 2281: MIRKOVIĆ 2003, 12–18; MIRKOVIĆ 2010, 176–186 ; MIRKOVIĆ 2015, 55–68 (Tiberius); VULIĆ 1942, 1–2; MIRKOVIĆ 2010, 181–182; MIRKOVIĆ, 2015, 59–60, no. 3 (Claudius).
[5] Domitian's inscription; VULIĆ 1942, no.3; MIRKOVIĆ 2010, 183–184; MIRKOVIĆ 2015, 62–63, nos. 4 and 5.
[6] Trajan's inscription: CIL III 1699 = 8267 = ILS 5863; MIRKOVIĆ 2003, no.6; MIRKOVIĆ 2011, 6; MIRKOVIĆ 2015, 64–65 no. 6

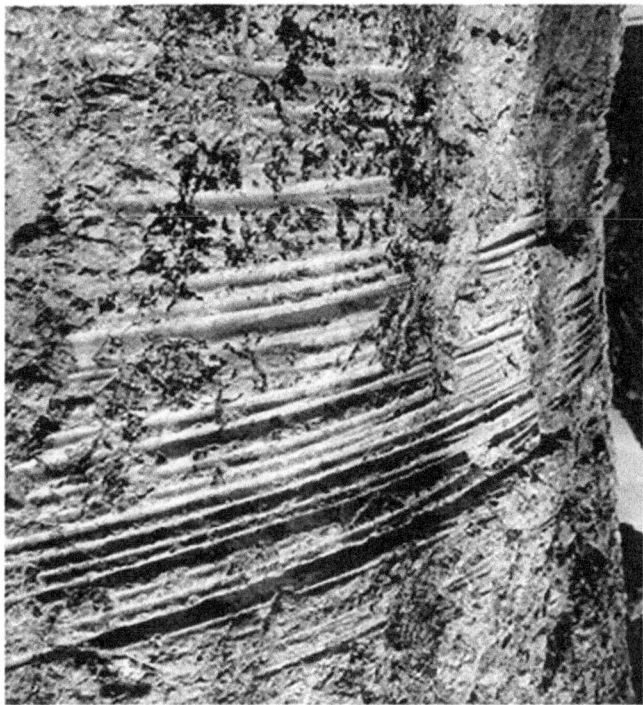

Fig. 3: Vestiges of the ropes in the rock not far from the *Tabula Traiana* (Republički Zavod za zaštitu spomenika kulrure Srbije)

SWOBODA, could not have served to transport the army. SWOBODA reports that he was unable to find remains of a road more than 4–5 m long and 3 m wide.[7] He also reports than after Golubac, which means after the entrance to the narrows, no vestiges of a roman road have been discovered. This leads to the conclusion that the main communication along the Danube in the Iron Gates was not terrestrial, but fluvial. If so, the road cut into the rock of Gospodjin vir, as well as that in the lower canyon near Ogradina, too narrow even when enlarged by wooden support, was probably not destined to transport large numbers of troops and mounted units, but rather for those who dragged the ships through the whirls in Djerdap. That is why no mile stones have been found on the road following the Danube course.

The next station after *Taliata* in the *tabula* was *Dierna* on the left Danube bank, accessible only by water. Transfer from the right to the left bank was done by ferry boat. Vestiges of ropes are preserved in the rock on the right bank not far from *Tabula Traiana* (Fig. 3).

---

7 SWOBODA 1939, 64; KANITZ 1892.

Two navies were engaged on the middle and lower Danube: the *Classis Flavia Pannonica* and *Classis Moesica*. The navigation was protected by a series of forts on the right Danube bank, discovered in Saldum, Bosman, Velike Livadice, Boljetin, Ravna, forts in the bay of *Taliata* at the mouth of the Porečka reka, and in Golubinje in the lower canyon, *Transdierna*, Sip, Karataš and *Pontes*. If so, *Scrofulae*, *Taliata* and *Egeta* on the right, and *Dierna* and *Drobeta* on the left Danube bank, were not mansions or mutations on the terrestrial route, but harbors serving to embark the army on ships.[8]

b. Cataracts and the Canal

The connection along the Danube, as described by *tabula*, was broken at two points: between *Taliata* and *Egeta* and between *Dierna* and *Drobeta*. No station is recorded between *Taliata* and *Egeta* in Itin. Anton. 217,5–219,3 either: *Item per ripam a Viminacio Nicomediam m.p.m. XILXII sic: Cuppe m.p.m. XXIIII Novas m.p.m. XXIIII Talia m.p.m. XII Egeta m.p.m. XXI Aquis m.p.m. XVI Dortico m.p.m. X Bononia m.p.m. XVII Ratiaria leg. XIIII gemina m.p.m. XVIII*. The next station after *Taliata* along the Danube was *Dierna* on the left bank; the first station from *Egeta* to the north was *Drobeta*, also a station on the left Danube bank.

The cataracts between *Dierna* and *Drobeta*, not far from the village of present-day Sip, represented a further obstacle for the navigation. At the exit of Djerdap the Danube splits, releasing a huge number of rocks which appear on the river surface thus making navigation difficult even in modern times.[9] The cataracts were the reason for breaking the line of navigation between *Dierna* and Drobeta, as is reflected in the itineraries. No connection is marked between these two places either in the *tabula* or in the Itinerarium Antonini. Maps like these served as a guide to the emperor and his army and had to reflect existing communications. From *Dierna* and *Drobeta*, the roads continued to the Dacian land.[10]

Trajan solved the difficulties in navigation between *Dierna* and *Drobeta* caused by the cataracts by digging the canal whose remains were discovered not far from present-day Sip. As it is formulated in the inscription found not far from the *statio Diana*, he let the river deviate because of the danger caused by the cataracts and thus made navigation on the Danube safe, *ob periculum cataractarum derivato flumine*

---

[8] Results of the archaeological investigation from 1968–1970 on the Serbian part of the Danube limes are summarised by several contributions in *Starinar* 33–34, 1982–83 [1984]; Cf. e.g. BOŠKOVIĆ 1984, 18–28.
[9] Cataract on the Danube: MARSILI 1726, 17 (descriptio cataractae maioris) and 2 tab 7.
[10] On the road from on the left Danube bank toward Sarmizegetusa see the well documented article by Florin FODOREAN in this preceedings.

tutam Danubii navigationem fecit.¹¹ By navigating through the canal the connection between *Dierna* and *Drobeta* was established.

Judging from the Roman itineraries, the terrestrial roads *Taliata – Dierna* and *Dierna – Drobeta* did not exist. The road near the *Tabula Traiana* cut from the rock served those who dragged the ships.

c. Crossing the Danube

Trajans's army crossed the Danube at three points. All three are denoted in the *tabula*: in the first war the Ram – *Lederata* crossing, opposite *Apo fluvius* was used, the second was via Dierna; and to these two the bridge in *Drobeta*, constructed between 102 and 105, was added as the third. Legions and cavalry were brought to these points not only from *Viminacium* – the camp was not big enough to accommodate an army numbering many legions and auxiliary troops – but also from other camps along the Danube and in the interior of the province. Ten miles east of *Viminacium* the army was divided. One part was brought to Ram by both terrestrial road and ships, which used the Dunavac canal. Other troops marched further on to *Pincum* and to *Novae* and *Cuppae* and other harbors on the right Danube bank, such as *Taliata* and *Egeta*. From there the army was transported further to *Dierna*, *Drobeta* and then to the Dacian land. *Taliata*, between two Danube canyons, on the confluence of the river Porečka and the Danube, was of great importance for the transport of troops. It must have been a big harbor protected by the forts in the surrounding hills and by the walls on both sides of the river. A *cohors* was camped here in 79 AD.

Before Trajan's second expedition against Decebalus a bridge was constructed across the Danube between Kostol (*Pontes*) and Turn Severin (*Drobeta*), which connected the two banks at the point which was closer to the Dacian capital. The troops were transported upstream to *Drobeta* from *Egeta*, the harbor which was connected with the forts in Lower *Moesia*. A harbor was discovered in Pontes during systematic archaeological research as well as a fort at the entrance to the bridge. The corresponding fort was built at *Drobeta*, on the other side of the bridge.¹²

Trajan must have attacked the Dacian state from no fewer than two directions, one coming from *Dierna*, to which another which started at *Lederata* was joined. Ships brought the army to these two harbors in Ram, to *Taliata*, and to Pontes on the right Danube bank. Troops set off from *Transdrobeta* (*Pontes*) on the right bank where a plastered platform for landing troops was discovered in the excavations. Some of the

---

11 MIRKOVIĆ 2003, 18; MIRKOVIĆ 2011, no. 3; MIRKOVIĆ 2015, 66, no. 9
12 MARSILI 1726, 25–32, fig. 33, tab. 15; KANITZ 1892, 45–48; new archaeological researches: GARAŠANIN/VASIĆ 1980, 35–41; GARAŠANIN/VASIĆ 1984, 55–85.

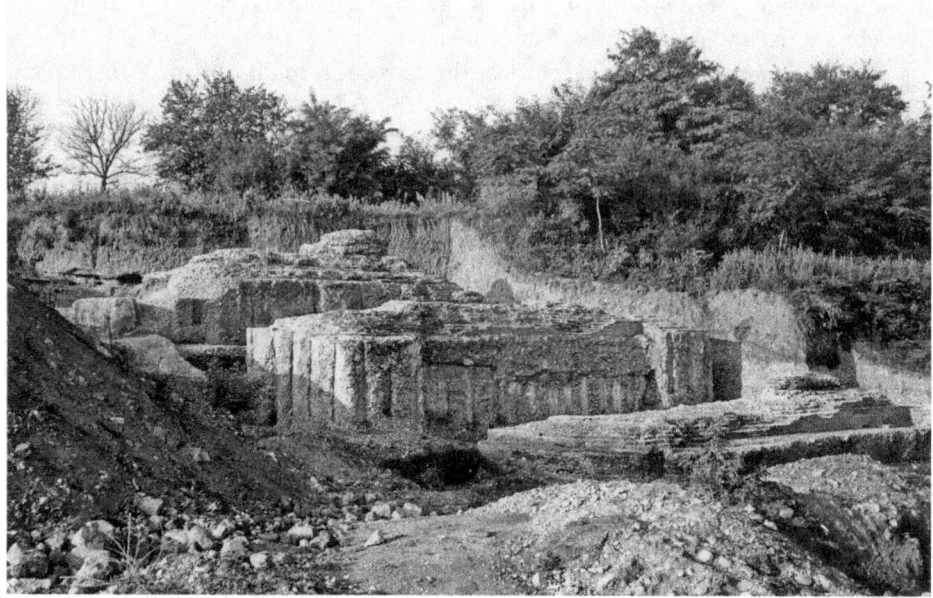

Fig. 4: The substruction of the Roman bridge in Kostol (GARAŠANIN/VASIĆ 1984)

troops must have been transported from *Taliata* across the mountain to *Egeta* and from *Egeta* upstream to *Pontes*.

II Communications in the Banat

Through the big plain Banat north of the Danube pass many Roman transversal roads, from the south to the north and from the west to the East. Their construction was not caused by the same reason nor are to be dated in the same time. Two main causes brought about their construction: the transport of troops in the time of Trajan's expedition and second, the control of the plain inhabited by Sarmatian tribes after the subjugation of Dacia.[13]

The eldest Roman roads in Banat are constructed in preparation for the Trajan's Dacian expedition. One connected the forts on the left Danube side garrisoned with troops under the command of the governor of Upper *Moesia*. Three routes lead to Dacia as continuation of those on the right Danube side. They begin at the points of crossing the river, at *Lederata*, *Dierna* and *Drobeta*. After crossing the Danube, Roman roads continue on the left Danube side, following routes leading to the Dacian land, one as the continuation of the road from *Lederata* to *Apo fluvius* (2), the second from

---

[13] The reconstruction of the road in Banat by MIRKOVIĆ 2002, 757–764.

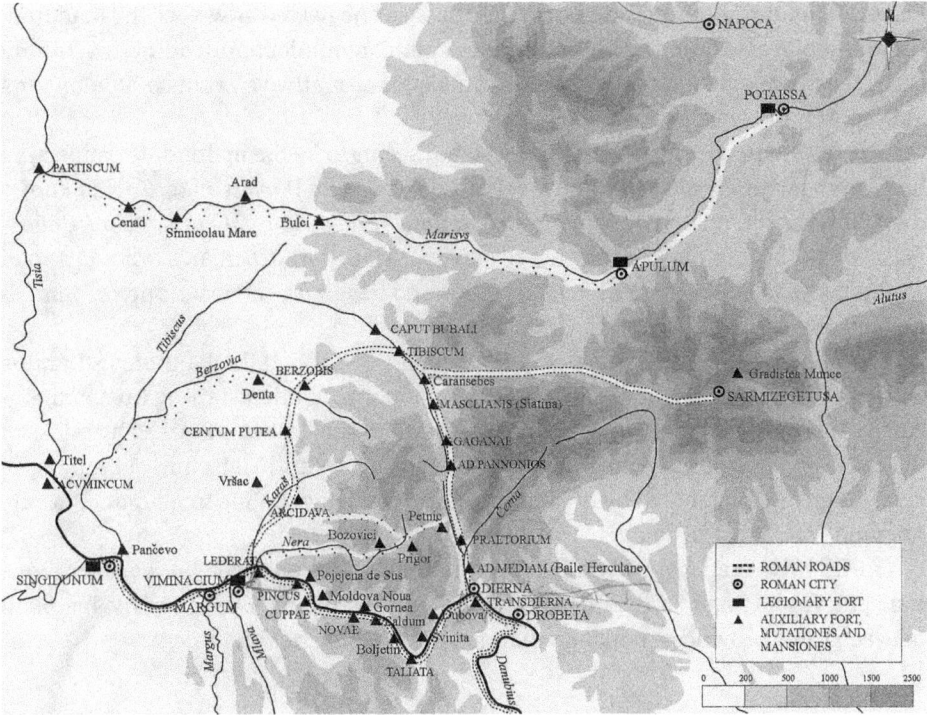

Fig. 5: Communication lines in Banat, on the left Danube bank (V.Ivanišević)

Dierna to *Tibiscum* (3), third was directed from *Drobeta* to the north and the Dacian capital *Sarmizegethusa* in the second expedition (4), after the Danube bank were connected by bridge; two roads cross transversal the Banat, along the valleys of Mares (*Partiscum – Potaisa*) and Bersobis (*Acumincum – Bersobis*).

(1) The line along the left Danube bank is marqued by bricks and monuments of the *cohors V Callica* and the legions *IV Flavia* and *VII Claudia* found in the forts in Banatska Palanka, Pojejena, Gornea, Sviniţa, Dubova and Moldava. Significant is the productions of bricks in Banatska Palanka, opposite to Lederata, bearing stemps of the units which took part in the Trajan's Dacian wars, *ala II Pannoniorum, cohors I Cretum, cohors II Hispanorum* and two Upper Moesian legions *IV Flavia* and *VII Claudia*. Some of the latter belong to the II century before Hadrian, some to the Later Roman empire. These forts had to protect the navigation on the Danube, together with those on the opposite bank

(2) From Lederata two routes opened, one along the Karas valley and another following the Nera river to Berzobis. Along Karas on the road leading to Tibiscum *tabula* notes the stations Arcidava, Centum putei, Bersobis. It must have been constructed in the time of the first Trajan's Dacian expedition. From Tibiscum opens the way to Sarmizegetusa, located middle in the Carpats. The fort in Berzobis was built by the *IV*

Flavia legion. After conquering Dacia this road was neglected as well as the road from Lederata to Praetorium (Mehadia) on the main communication leading north from Dierna. It is not noted in *tabula* but the connection is marked by ruins of Roman forts in Dalboset, Bozovic, Petnic and Prigor.

(3) The communication north from *Dierna* seems to be the main route connecting the Danube with *Tibiscum* and further with the centre of Dacian state. *Tabula* knows the following station on it: *Dierna – Ad Mediam – Praetorio – Ad Pannonios – Gaga – Masclianus – Tibiscum*. Constructed to serve for transport of Trajan's army this road was in use also later, under Marcus Aurelius and Severi, as the inscriptions found in Ad Mediam testify.

Two further communications in Banat connect transfers the Pannonian Danube with Dacia, one along Maros from Partissus to Apulum, another starting from Acumincum at Tisa mouth in the Danube, reached Tibiscus. The former is marked by bricks of the *XIII Gemina* legion; on the line between Acumincum and Tibiscum, at Denta have been found bricks stamped by IV Flavia legion. Roman inscription in Acumincum date from the time of Caracala.

At first the road have been used in the time of Trajan's Dacian war for troops transport from *Pannonia Inferior* to *Dacia*; later it served for controlling the big plain between three provinces, *Pannonia Inferior, Moesia Superior* and *Dacia*.

III A Shorter Way, a *compendium* from *Viminacium* to *Dardania*

was established under Hadrian, as testifies the inscription IMS II 50 from *Viminacium*, preserved broken in many pieces, which could be reconstructed as the following text:

> [Imp(erator) Caes]ar divi Tr[ainani Parthici f(ilius)] di[vi Nervae n]epos Tr[aianus Hadrianus Aug(ustus) pont(ifex) max(imus) trib(unicia) pot(estate) --- c]o(n)s(ul) III p(ater) [p(atriae) per ---- leg(atum) Aug(usti) pr(o) pr(aetore) viam] novam qua[e coepta a divo patre suo Traia]no compen[dio facto per m(ilia) p(assuum) --- ad ---] in Dadania [direxit et munivit ut vehiculis commeare [---] fecit.[14]

If the reconstruction of the text is right, Trajan began the construction of the road. Communication with the interior of the province was necessary because of supplying the army. There is evidence preserved in Hunt's Pridianum (papyrus) that the cohors *I Hispanorum*, garrisoned in Nicopolis in about AD 100 sent a detachment to *Margus* with the task of providing horses.[15]

This road was used as shorter, instead of the, elder but longer, leading from *Naissus* along the Timok valley to the lower Danube Tab. Peut. seg. 6 notes the fol-

---

[14] MIRKOVIĆ 1980, 745–755 and IMS II 50.
[15] HUNT's pridianum (Brit. Libr. inv. 2851): Rom.Mil.Rec. no. 63, col. 2, l. 20–21 and note ad l. 20.

lowing stations on the line *Viminacium – Naissus*: *Viminacio xviii – Municipio x – Jovis pago- xii – Idimo–xvi – Horeo Margi – xvii – Preaesidio Dasmini – xv – Praesidio Pompei – xii – Gramrianis – xii- Naissi*. In Idimum the mansion was discovered.[16]

IV South of *Naissus*; New Discoveries of the Road Along the Južna Morava Valley and Missing Stations

During the archaeological investigation of protection caused by the construction of the modern highway corridor 10 in the south of Serbia, a large settlement was discovered along with the remains of the Roman road between *Naissus* and Vranje, near the present-day village of Mala Kopašnica, known before as the site of the necropolis of the "Mala Kopašnica – Sase" type, 47 km south of *Naissus* and in Davidovac on the same line, 152 km from *Naissus*. The discovered segment of the road in Kopašnica is 25 m long and 4 m wide, in Davidovac 12 m long and 7.70 m wide. The road connected *Naissus* along the river Južna Morava with Scupi. The discovered remains of the road near Mala Kopasnica was dated by Ivanisević as belonging to the first half of the 2nd century on the basis of the coin of Antoninus Pius found in the road subtraction;[17] the road near Davidovac shows two chronologically distinctive layers, dated preliminary by S. Petković in the period of time from the beginning of the 2nd until the 5th century AD.[18] A big flood dated by her in the 5th, or 6th century, destroyed the later Roman settlement and covered the road with 1 and 1.5 m thick alluvium.

The line which follows the shortest route from *Naissus* to the south, the same as the modern corridor 10, is noted neither on *tabula* nor in the other Roman itineraries.[19] This natural corridor to the north of Macedonia, which was used for the transport of troops during the early Roman wars against the tribes on the lower Danube, lost its importance after Macedonia gained *inermis* after 31 AD. The Roman emperors in the first and second centuries followed another route leading from Brundisium or Tarent to the Balkans and the Via Egnatia for transporting troops to the East. In their expeditions to the East, Trajan and the emperors in the second and third centuries followed the route which led from the north of Italy along the river Sava to *Singidunum* and *Viminacium* in order to collect troops in the camps in *Pannonia* and *Moesia*; from *Viminacium* they used the compendium to *Naissus* and from *Naissus* they travelled on to *Thracia*.

---

16 Vasić/Milošević 2000.
17 Ivanišević/Stamenkovič/Jović 2016, 47–70.
18 Petković 2016, 101–151.
19 On roads in the region of *Scupi* see IMS VI 18–20. 195–206.

V Southwest of *Naissus*: the Main Road to *Lissus* and the Bifurcation from *Hammeo* to *Scupi* and from *Scupi* to *Stobi*

The *Naissus–Scupi* route along the river Južna Morava was replaced by another which branched off from the main communication leading from *Naissus* to *Lissus* at the *Hammeo* station, 20 miles from *Naissus*.[20] The *tabula* gives no stations or miles numbers between *Hammeo* and *Scupi*, but between *Scupi* and *Stobi* there follows a series of stations: at XXI miles from *Scupi* there is a vignette of a large building, without any name, and from it follows *Anausaro* at the XIIth mile, *Ad fines* at XXV miles – the southern border of *Dardania*? -*Ad Herculem* at the next VIIII- *Praesidium* at a further VIIII – *Ad Cefalon XIII- Curbita VIII – Stobi*.

All of the enumerated stations between *Scupi* and *Stobi* together with the corresponding miles cannot have belonged to this line.[21] The distance *Naissus–Scupi*, following the west line to *Lissus* and turning to the south at *Hammeo* is ca. 190 km, in the *tabula* the distance from *Scupi* to *Stobi* is 95 miles, or ca. 150 km, and in reality 79 km following the modern Skoplje – Gradsko highway. The *tabula* notes more stations with distance numbers which makes the distance longer that it actually is. A reasonable explanation would be that some of the stations in the *tabula* or even most of them, belonged to another relation. The stations after XXV miles partly, or even all, are not from the *Scupi–Stobi* line, but belong to the *Naissus–Scupi* line leading through the Južna Morava valley. *Scupi* could be reached from *Naissus* by two directions, via the Južna Morava, or passing Kosovo, as modern roads today. It could be assumed that both were not contemporary.

VI East of *Naissus*

The remains of the Roman road near Dimitrovgrad, discovered in the archaeological investigations when the modern road was being built, correspond to the direction of the Roman road leading from *Naissus* to *Thracia*, as it is described in the *tabula* and itineraries: *Naissso XXXIV – Remesiana XXV – Turribus*, in Itin. Hieros: *civitas Naisso XII – mutatio Redicibus VII – mutatio Ulmo VIIII – mansio Romansiana VIIII – mutatio Latina VIIII – mansio Turribus*.[22]

---

[20] The road from *Naissus* to *Lissus* see MILLER 1916, Strecke 78, 553–555, for via leading from Ulpiana to Novi Pazar and futher on the west, see CIL XVII/4, 552–572b.
[21] VULIĆ 1925, 1–22 proposes the following outposts between *Naissus* and *Scupi*: *Naisso XIII – Ad Herculem vIII – Ad fines XXXII – Anausaro – XII – Aquas VIIII –Praesidio – VIIII Ad Cephalum – XIII – Curbita – VIII – Stobis*. See also MIRKOVIĆ 1960, 249–257.
[22] IMS IV 20–29.

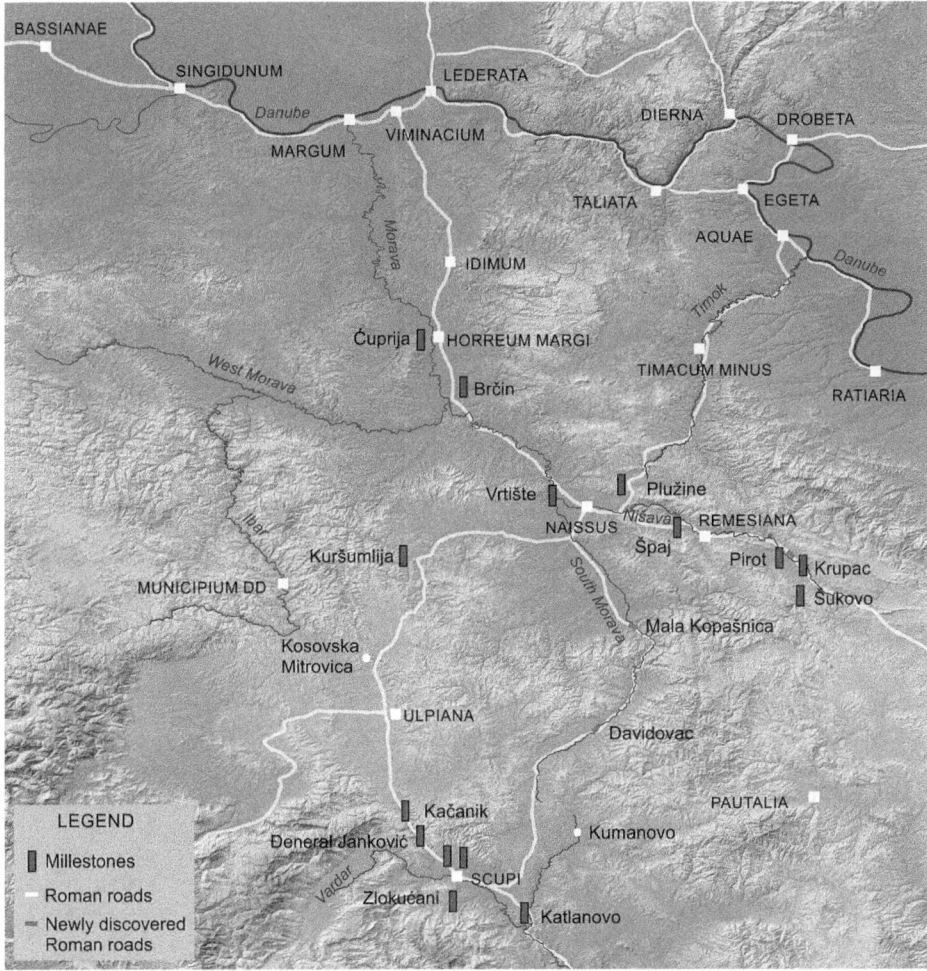

Fig. 6: Roads and milestones in *Moesia Superior* (V. Ivanišević)

During the excavations two milestones were found near Remesiana, in the modern village of Spaj, one from the time of Alexander Severus, another unepigraphic. Other milestones from this line are known, one found in Pirot,[23] and another in the village of Krupac.[24]

---

[23] Milestones from the line *Naissus* – Turribus, IMS IV 123. 124. 125. 126. 127. 128, from Bela Palanka MIRKOVIĆ 2017, 293–294. On Roman politics in the constructions and repair of the road in this part of the Balkans under Maximinus Thrax and Gordianus III see BARTELS 2014, 222–245.
[24] BRNBOLIĆ/MITIĆ/LAZAREVIĆ 2013, 62.

Bibliography

Bartels 2014 = J. Bartels, Meilensteine und Barbaren, Die Straßenbaupolitik auf dem Balkan unter Maximinus Thrax und Gordian, in: A. Kolb (ed.), Infrastruktur und Herrschaftsorganisation im Imperium Romanum, Herrschaftsstrukturen und Herrschaftspraxis III, Akten der Tagung in Zürich 19.-20. 10. 2012, Berlin 2014, 222–245.

Boškovic 1984 = D. Boškovic, Recherches archéologiques aux Portes des Fer 1956–1970, *Starinar* 33–34, 1982-83 [1984], 18–28.

Brnbolić/Mitić/Lazarević 2013 = M.Brnbolić/Z.Mitić/K. Lazarević, Antički miljokazi iz ikoline Remesijane, *Glasnik društva konzervatora Srbije* 37, 2013, 38–62.

CIL XVII/4 = A. Kolb/G. Walsert (ed.), Corpus Inscriptionum Latinarum, Volumen decimum septimum, Miliaria imperii Romani. Pars quarta, Illyricum et provinciae Europae graecae. Fasciculus secundus: Miliaria provinciae Dalmatiae, CIL XVII/4, Berlin/New York 2012.

Dimitrijević 1984 = D. Dimitrijević, Sapaja, rimsko i sredjovekovno utvrdjenje na ostrvu kod Stare Palanke, *Starinar* 33–34, 1982-83 [1984], 29–62.

Garašanin/Vasić 1980 = M. Garašanin/M. Vasić, Le pont de Trajan et le castellum Pontes, *Djerdapske sveske [Cahiers de Portes de Fer]* 1, 1980, 35–41.

Garašanin/Vasić 1984 = M. Garašanin/M. Vasić, Pontes: camp et pont de Trajan, *Djerdapske sveske [Cahiers de Portes de Fer]* 2, 1984, 55–85.

IMS I = M. Mirković, Singidunum et le Nord-Ouest de la province, Inscriptions de la Mésie Supérieure, vol. I, Beograd 1976.

IMS II = M. Mirković, Viminacium et Margum, Inscriptions de la Mésie Supérieure, vol. II, Beograd 1986.

IMS IV = P. Petrović, Naissus, Remesiana, Horreum Margi, Inscriptions de la Mésie Supérieure, vol. IV, Beograd 1979.

IMS VI = B. Dragojević-Josifovska, Scupi et la région de Kumanovo, Inscriptions de la Mésie Supérieure, vol. VI, Beograd 1982.

Ivanišević/Stamenkovič/Jović 2016 = V.Ivanišević/S.Stamenkovič/S.Jović, Rimsko naselje i zanatski centar u Maloj Kopašnici [A Roman settlement and workshop center at Mala Kopašnica], in: S. Perić/A. Bulatović (ed.), Arheološka istraživanja na putu E 75 [Archaeological investigations along the highway route E 75] 2011–2014, Beograd 2016, 47–70.

Kanitz 1892 = F. Kanitz, Römische Studien in Serbien: Der Donau-Grenzwall, das Straßennetz, die Städte, Castelle, Denkmale, Thermen und Bergwerke zur Römerzeit im Königreiche Serbien, Wien 1892.

Marsili 1726 = L.F. Marsili, Danubius pannonico-mysicus observationibus geographicis, astronomicis, hydrographicis, historicis, physicis perlustratus, vol. II, Hagae 1726.

Miller 1916 = K. Miller, Itineraria Romana: Römische Reisewege an der Hand der Tabula Peutingeriana dargestellt, Stuttgart 1916.

Mirković 1960 = M. Mirković, Rimski put Naissus-Scupi i stanicce Ad Fines, *Živa antika* 10, 1960, 249–257.

Mirković 1980 = M. Mirković, Vom obermösischen Limes nach dem Süden: *via nova* von Viminacium nach Dardanien, in: W.S. Hanson (ed.), Roman Frontier Studies 1979, Oxford 1980, 745–755.

Mirković 2002 = M. Mirković, Deserted forts: the Moesian *limes* after the conquest of Dacia, in: F.Freeman/J. Benett/Z.T. Fiema/B. Hoffmannm (ed.), Limes XVIII, Proceedings of the XVIIIth International Congress of Roman Frontier Studies held in Amman, Jordan, September 2000, Oxford 2002, 757–764.

Mirković 2003 = M. Mirković, Römer an der mittleren Donau, Römische Straßen und Festungen von Singidunum bis Aquae, Beograd 2003.

Mirković 2007 = M. Mirković, Moesia Superior: eine Provinz an der mittleren Donau, Mainz 2007.
Mirković 2010 = M. Mirković, Les inscriptions de Djerdap et la politique romaine sur le Danube de Tibère à Hadrian, in: L. Zerbini (ed.), Roma e le province del Danubio, Convegno intern. Ferrara-Cento 15–17 ott. 2009, Ferrara 2010, 176–186.
Mirković 2011= M. Mirković, Djerdap pages, Beograd 2011.
Mirković 2015 = M. Mirković, Rimljani na Djerdapu, istorija i natpisi, Zaječar 2015.
Mirković, 2017 = M. Mirković, Kurze Bemerkungen zu den Inschriften aus dem mösisch-thrakischen Gebiet, *ZPE* 202, 2017, 292–296.
Petković 2016 = S. Petković, Zaštitna arheološka istraživanja na lokalitetu Davidovac: Gradište, preliminarni rezultati, in: S. Perić/A. Bulatović (ed.), Arheološka istraživanja na putu E 75 [Archaeological investigations along the highway route E 75] 2011–2014, Beograd 2016, 101–151.
Rom.Mil.Rec. = R. Fink, Roman Military Records on Papyrus, Cleveland 1971.
Spasić-Đurić/Jacanović 2007 = D. Spasić-Đurić/D. Jacanović, Trasa puta Viminacium – Lederata, rezultati mikrorekognosciranja 2003–2004 godine, *Viminacium* 15, 2007, 123–164.
Swoboda 1939 = E.V. Swoboda, Forschungen am obermösischen Limes, Wien/Leipzig 1939.
Vasić/Milošević 2000 = M.Vasić/G. Milošević, Mansio Idimum, Beograd 2000.
Vulić 1925 = N. Vulić, Teritorija rimskog Skoplja, *Glasnik skopskog naučnog društva [Bulletin de la Société scientifique de Skoplje]* 1, 1925, 1–22.
Vulić 1942 = N. Vulić, Kaiserinschriften an der serbischen Donau, *Klio* 35, 1942, 178–181.

Vladimir P. Petrović
Some Considerations about the Roman Road Network in Central Balkan Provinces

Abstract: The strategic position of the region of Central Balkans between East and West of the Roman Empire and its well known wealth in mineral sources (ores), gave the most favorable preconditions for the construction and establishment of the large scale of Roman terrestrial and fluvial communication lines of the different character and chronology as well, as for the particular urbanization system. Some recent developments concerning the scientific research in this territory tend to broaden our previous knowledge and to revise the persisting conclusions.

Zusammenfassung: Die strategische Position der Region des zentralen Balkans zwischen dem Osten und dem Westen des römischen Imperium und ihr wohl bekannter Reichtum an Mineralvorkommen, sorgten für äusserst günstige Bedingungen sowohl für die Errichtung und Einrichtung der römischen Verkehrsrouten zu Land und zu Wasser mit unterschiedlicher Beschaffenheit und zeitlicher Abfolge in grossem Umfang als auch für das spezifische System der Urbanisierung.

Introduction

The territory of Central Balkans which is the geographical framework of this study covers the large area of modern Serbia south of the rivers Danube and Sava as well as the parts of some neighboring countries like the north of the North Macedonia, western and northwestern parts of Bulgaria, the eastern part of Bosnia and Herzegovina (Republic of Srpska) and the eastern segment of Montenegro. This wide territory in Roman times was covered by full range of the province of Upper Moesia (*Moesia Superior*), western part of Thrace (*Thracia*) and eastern part of Dalmatia.[1]

This region has long been regarded as an area difficult to cross, due to many mountains covered with dense forests. However, the river valleys of the Sava and the Danube as well as of smaller rivers like Morava, Vardar, Toplica, Nišava, Timok, Drim, etc., cut this space and create very often the narrow gorges in the rocks, connecting

---

Article note: This article is the result of the project of the Institute for Balkan Studies of the Serbian Academy of Sciences and Arts: Society, material and spiritual culture and communication lines in prehistory and protohistory of the Balkans (project n° 177012).

---

1 WILKES 1969, PETROVIĆ 2015, 23–27 (Dalmatia); PETROVIĆ 2015, 34–36 (Pannonia); MÓCSY 1974; PETROVIĆ 2015, 42–44 (Moesia Superior); PETROVIĆ/GRBIĆ 2015, 23–32 (Thrace).

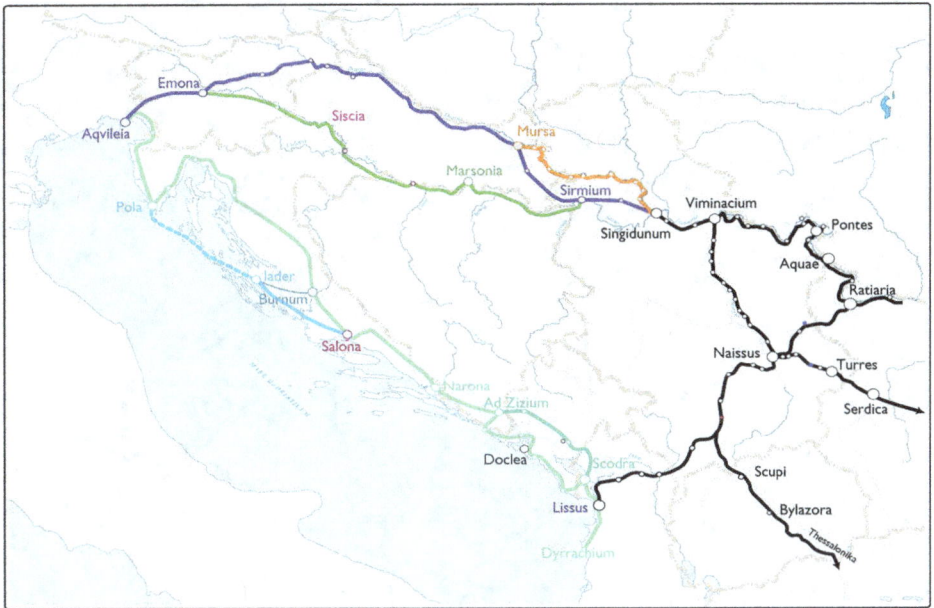

Fig. 0: Map of Major Roman Roads in Central and Western Balkans (map by Vladimir Petrović)

spacious and fertile valleys that have always attracted different human communities. The massifs and mountain tops bordering these basins often abounded in mineral resources provided a good source of raw materials for the development of metallurgy and the stimulation of trade. The strategic position of the region of Central Balkans between East and West of the Roman Empire and its well-known wealth in mineral sources (ores), gave the most favorable preconditions for the construction and establishment of the large scale of Roman terrestrial and fluvial communication lines of different character and chronology.[2]

A well developed road network contributed to the prosperity and economic progress of the region.[3] The evidences obtained from the Roman itineraries testify of the main travel routes on the territory, their importance and the character of the settlements connected by them, and occasionally of certain significant characteristics of the landscape.[4] The routes we deal with are the following: 1) **Danube Limes Road**, which

---

[2] On mining activities in Central Balkans in Roman times, see Dušanić 1977a; Dušanić 1977b; Dušanić 1995; Dušanić 2000 and Dušanić 2004.

[3] Talbert 2000, 286–309 (Map 20: *Pannonia-Dalmatia*); 310–332 (Map 21: *Dacia-Moesia*); 749–760 (Map 49: *Illyricum*); TIR, K–34, Naissus.

[4] Kubitschek 1916, 2308–2363; Miller 1916; Bosio 1983, 156 (Tab. Peut.); Geyer 1898 (Itin. Burdig.); Reed 1978 (Itin. Anton.); Funaioli 1914, 305–310; Schillinger-Häfele 1963 (Geogr. Rav.); Herrmann 2007, 179–182.

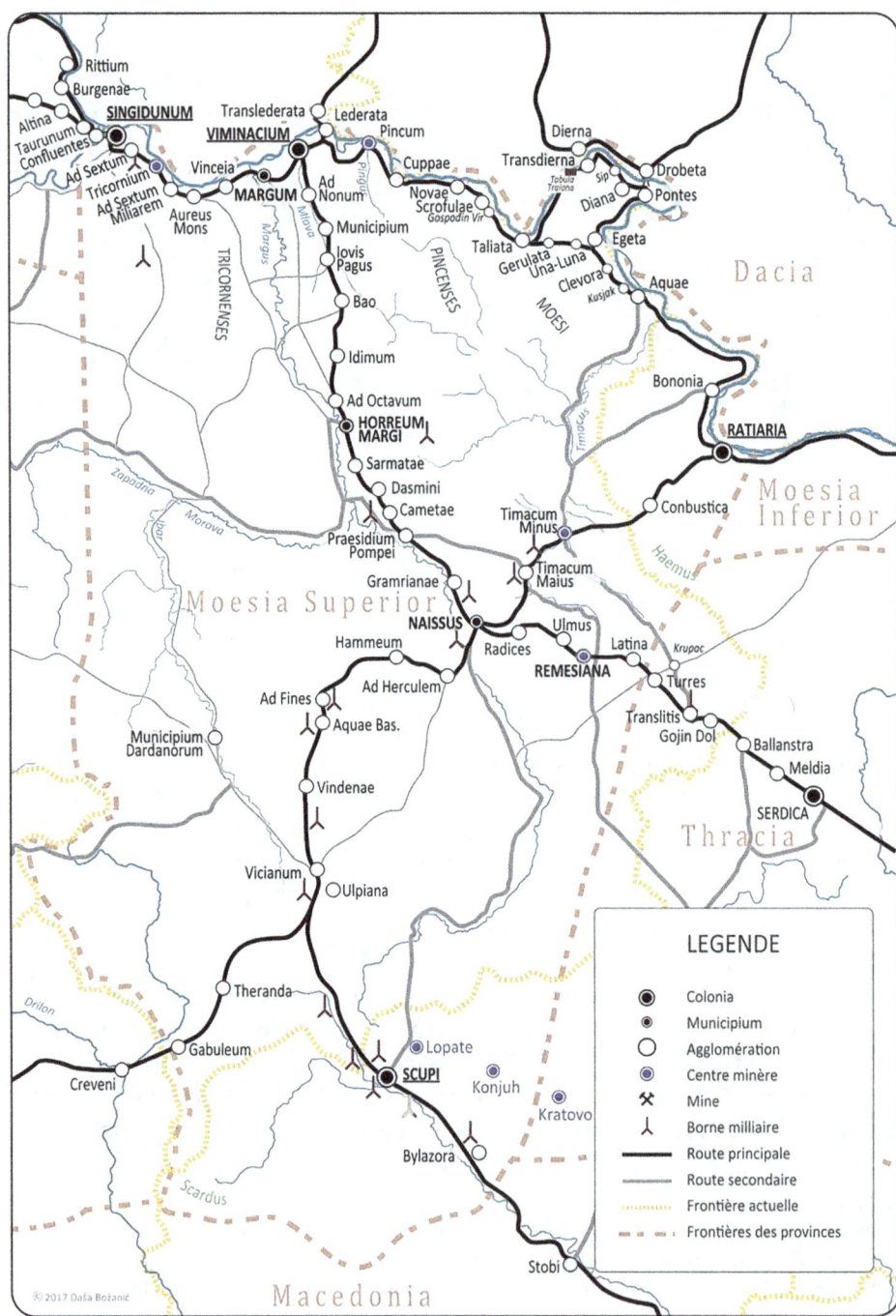

Fig. 1: Map of Central Balkans in Roman Times (map by Vladimir Petrović)

went along the right bank of the Danube from Belgrade (*Singidunum*)[5] and *Viminacium* (Stari Kostolac – Drmno),[6] as the legionary centers, to Trajan's colony *Ratiaria* – (Artchar)[7] and continued up to the confluence of the river Cibrica into the Danube on the territory of Lower Moesia (*Moesia Inferior*), all the way to the Black Sea;[8] 2) the well-known **Constantinople (*Byzantium*) or Military Road** (*via militaris*), *Singidunum* — *Naissus* — *Remesiana* — *Turres* (Beograd – Niš – Bela Palanka – Pirot), which went farther to the East across the territory of Thrace towards Sofia (*Serdica*), Plovdiv (*Philippopolis*) and Constantinople (*Constantinopolis*), was a back bone of the transbalkanic communication system;[9] 3) The road *Lissus* — *Naissus* — *Ratiaria* was significantly important as it connected the Adriatic Coast *Lissus* (Lezhë), Central Balkans with the city of *Naissus* and the Trajanic colony *Ratiaria* situated on the Danube. 4) From the road of *Lissus* — *Naissus*, which was presumably located in the vicinity of *Vicianum* (Ugljare, Čaglavica), as prof. Mirković concluded by the milestone from Kačanik that notes the distance of 200 miles presumably to *Viminacium*,[10] a separate road led to *Scupi* (Skopje),[11] and *Thessalonica* (Θεσσαλονίκη), i.e. the Aegean Sea.[12] It seems worthfull to include in this text a brief overview about the recent developments regarding the research of two secondary but very significant communication lines. There are mainly epigraphical (milestones) but also the archaeological data about those Roman roads of interprovincial character, which were not mentioned in the known Roman itineraries. Between Upper Moesia and Thrace existed at least one local road: *Timacum Minus* (Ravna by Knjaževac) – *Pautalia* (Kyustendil). On the other hand, the south of Upper Moesia and Dalmatia were also connected by the secondary road *Vicianum* – *Municipium Splonum* (Komini-Kolovrat) that further branched westward into at least three separate directions to the Adriatic coast: to *Narona* (Vid near Metković), to *Risinium* (Risan) and both to *Scodra* (Shkodër) and *Lissus*.

Obviously, the major intersection of the itinerary land roads in Moesia Superior and Central Balkans was located in *Naissus*,[13] but there where also some very important intersections such us: *Singidunum, Viminacium, Lederata, Egeta, Timacum Minus, Timacum Maius, Hammeum* (or *Vicianum*), etc.[14] But *Naissus* was at the cross-

---

[5] TIR L–34, 102; IMS I 23–42; Bikić/Ivanišević 1996, 260–261; Bojović 1996; Popović 1997, 1–20; Popović 2006.
[6] TIR L–34, 119; IMS II 21–59; Spasić-Djurić 2015, 1–223; Vojvoda/Mrdjić 2015; Golubović 2008, 1–255; Korać/Golubović 2009, 1–562; online, visited on 10th October 2017: http://viminacium.org.rs/
[7] Luka 2014, 50–64.
[8] For the Roman road in the Iron Gates: Kanitz 1892, 4–59; Petrović 1986, 41–52; Petrović/Vasić 1996, 19–20; Petrović 2011, 404–414; Petrović 2019, in print.
[9] AE 1999, 1397: *tabernas et pr[aetoria] / per vias [militares] / [fieri iussit]*; Petrović 2007, 65–81.
[10] CIL III 8270, 6; Mirković 1960, 249 sqq.
[11] TIR K–34, 112.
[12] Mirković 1960, 249 sqq.; Petrović 2008, 31–40.
[13] Petrović 1979; Petrović 2015, 45–46.
[14] Petrović 2015.

roads of about all transbalkanic land communications, wherefrom the routes lead also into five other directions: towards the north to *Viminacium* and *Singidunum*, towards the northeast to *Ratiaria*, towards the west to *Lissus* and the Adriatic coast, towards the south to *Thessalonica* and the Aegean sea, and towards the east to *Serdica* and *Constantinopolis*.[15]

In the wider range, the contacts were established by the large system of Roman roads with distant and important centers like *Aquileia, Salona, Narona, Lissus, Dyrrachium* and *Appolonia, Thessalonica, Constantinople,* Adriatic, Aegean and Black sea coast or by the fluvial communications of the Danube and the Sava with *Aquincum, Carnuntum, Siscia,* etc. The well-developed road network also allowed trade, closely connected with Italy and the western and eastern provinces. Fine pottery, glass, vine and olive oil arrived from the north of Italy and Istria and from Gaul and the Rhine area. Luxurious goods, such as expensive fabrics and jewellery, were mainly imported from the eastern provinces. On the other hand the raw materials, such as various ores were transported from the inland of the Balkans to the closest sea ports and more further to Italy and the Mediterranean Sea, by terrestrial and fluvial communications.

The Roman urban centers are here a matter of special concern because they represented not only the seminaries of Roman influence and culture among the local population but also the military, economic, administrative and religious centers of the wide regions. Important fortifications, residences, temples and administrative or economic buildings are witnesses of the great significance and heterogeneous character of the territories in the Central Balkans, especially of its strategic and economic meaning.

Regarding the urbanization of Upper Moesia, only four cities were ranked as colonies: *Scupi,* located in the far south of the province near the Macedonian border, established during the reign of Domitian,[16] and three cities situated on the right bank of the Danube, on the *limes*: *Ratiaria* from the epoch of the emperor Trajan, and *Viminacium* and *Singidunum*, granted with the status of a colony at the time of Gordian III. Five cities had been approved as *municipia* as far as we know: *Ulpiana* (Gračanica),[17] *Naissus* (Niš), *Horreum Margi* (Ćuprija),[18] *Margum* (Dubravica – Orašje)[19] and the *Municipium Dardanorum* (Sočanica),[20] whereas there is no clear evidence in literary or epigraphic materials concerning other important urban centers, like *Remesiana* (Bela

---

15 Petrović 1979; Petrović 2015, 137; Petrović 2018.
16 Mirković 1968, 63; Mócsy 1970, 67 sq.; cf. Dragojević-Josifovska 1982, 25 sq.; Dušanić 1996, 41–51.
17 TIR, K–34, Naissus, 129; Čerškov 1969, 42–43.
18 TIR, K–34, Naissus, 63; Vasić/Petković 2010, 9–25.
19 TIR, L–34, 77–78; Ivanišević/Bugarski 2012, 239–255.
20 TIR, K–34, Naissus, 89; Čerškov 1965; Čerškov 1969.

Palanka) or *Timacum Minus* (Ravna), for instance.²¹ The urbanization of Upper Moesia provided favorable conditions for the growth of the economy in the province, based primarily on the rich mineral resources. Plentiful precious metal and other ore deposits were concentrated in the south and north of the province. The most important mines were in the south of the province in the uppermoesian mining district of Dardania (*metalli Dardanici*) with its administrative centers *Ulpiana, Municipium Dardanorum, Remesiana, Timacum Minus* etc., connected with the Kopaonik and Balkan mountains. Gold, silver, lead and zinc were extracted from these mines. The most important mines in the north of Upper Moesia (*ripa Danuvii*) were rich of lead ores that contained silver, and possibly copper and gold mines from the mountains of Kosmaj, Rudnik and Kučajske mountains. There were also mines rich in gold, silver, copper, lead and iron in the basins of the rivers of Mlava and Pek and the Timok Rivers. The administrative centers of *Ripa Danuvii* were in *Tricornium* (Ritopek), *Pincum* (Veliko Gradište) and *Aquae* (Prahovo).²²

As regards urbanization in the province of Dalmatia, we have to consider this province as divided in two distinctive parts: coastal and continental.²³ The settlements ranked as colonies and *municipia* were more numerous in the littoral belt of Dalmatia by the Adriatic coast and they were older compared to the settlements in the eastern, continental part of the province. The following cities of Dalmatia had been granted the status of colonies ever since the Julio-Claudian epoch: *Iader* (Zadar), *Salona* (Solin), *Narona* (Vid near Metković), *Aequum* (Čitluk), *Senia* (Senj), *Epidaurum* (Cavtat), *Risinium* (Risan), and *Scodra* (Shkodra).²⁴ *Domavia* (Gradina near Srebrenica) was the only colony in the east of the province.²⁵ Around thirty settlements on the Adriatic coast and less in the inland were ranked as *municipia*. So the number of Roman settlements in Dalmatia with the rank of *colonia* or *municipium* gradually falls from the west to the east of the province.²⁶ The east of Dalmatia was as well as it is the case with Upper Moesia abundant of metal deposits and divided into several mining districts: In the north were silver mines (*argentariae Dalmaticae*) around *Argentaria* (Srebrenica), a *vicus metalli* ?, and the settlement of *Domavia* with the rank of Roman colony and in the south around the *municipia Malve(n)siatium* (Skelani)²⁷ and *Splonum* (Komini near Pljevlje) with the supposed *vicus metalli* in Kolovrat.²⁸

---

21 TIR, K–34, Naissus, 108, IMS IV 51–57, Petrović 2000, 346–359, (*Remesiana*); TIR, K–34, Naissus, 125; IMS III/2 37–50, (*Timacum Minus*).
22 Dušanić 2004; Petrović 2015; Petrović 2018.
23 Wilkes 1969.
24 CIL III 12695 = ILS 7159: *in co<l>(onia) / Sc<o>dr(a)* ; AE 2014, 1031: *coloniae Scodr/anorum*.
25 Pašalić 1966, 230–236; Bojanovski 1988, 200; Petrović 2015, 120–123.
26 Petrović 2015, 23–27.
27 Loma 2010; Gavrilović/Popović 2015, 197–220.
28 Dušanić 2004, 247–270.

Recent Developments in Research of Roman Roads in Central Balkans

Under Trajan, who founded *Ratiaria* as the easternmost colony in Upper Moesia (*Colonia Ulpia Ratiaria*), comprehensive preparations for the defense of the Danubian limes zone were started, especially in the Iron Gates region on the eve of Dacian wars. Old auxiliary camps were restored and new ones were constructed.[29] Special attention was paid to road infrastructure. The road along the right bank of the Danube, the **Danube Limes Road**, connecting the legionary camps and smaller forts along the limes, had a vital importance and represented indeed an infrastructural masterpiece. Trajan renovated and extended the road along the Danube, partially carved into the slopes, the construction of which had started as early as the reigns of Tiberius, Claudius and Domitianus.[30] The built road, commemorated in the so called *Tabula Traiana*, made the movement of troops and vessels along the Danube faster and easier.[31] The Traianic construction works comprise also the digging of a navigation channel in the Danubian river bed as well as the building of the large river port close to *Aquae* (Prahovo) in Kusjak, which is all attested by archaeological researches and in commemorative inscriptions.[32] The most famous infrastructure object that was built during the Trajan's epoch is the bridge over the Danube, constructed by Apollodorus of Damascus that linked two *castra*: *Pontes* (Kostol, Serbia) and *Drobeta* (Turnu Severin, Romania).[33]

Although almost all the archeological remains are now located under the artificial lake that was caused by the construction of the hydro power plant complex of Djerdap I and II in the Iron Gates during the communist rule in ex-Yugoslavia and Romania, there still exists a large number of important testimonies of the Roman works in the Iron

---

29 PETROVIĆ/VASIĆ, 1996, 15–27.
30 CIL III 1698 = 13813b = ILJug I 57 = 60 = IMS I 162 = AE 1910, 176 (*Tiberius*); ILJug I 56 = AE 1944, 70 (*Claudius*); CIL III 13813c = ILJug I 58 = AE 1896, 17 = 1944, 71a et CIL III 13813a = 13813d = ILS 9373 = ILJug I 55 = AE 1896, 18 = 71b (*Domitianus*): *Imp(erator) Caesar divi / Vespasiani f(ilius) Domi/[tianus] Aug(ustus) Germ(anicus) pont(ifex) / maximus trib(unicia) pot(estate) XII / imp(erator) XXII co(n)s(ul) XVI censor / perpetuus p(ater) p(atriae) i[t]er Scor/fularum vetu[s]tate [e]t / incursu Danuvi c[or]/ruptum operibu[s i]/teratis O[--- per] / leg(atum?) ------*.
31 CIL III 1699 = 8267 = ILS 5863 = ILJug I 63 = AE 1978, 474: *Imp(erator) Caesar divi Nervae f(ilius) / Nerva Traianus Aug(ustus) Germ(anicus) / pontif(ex) maximus trib(unicia) pot(estate) IIII / pater patriae co(n)s(ul) III / montibus excisi[s] anco[ni]bus / sublat[i]s via[m r]e[fecit]*.
32 ILJug II 468 = AE 1973, 475: *Imp(erator) Caesar divi Nervae f(ilius) / Nerva Traianus Aug(ustus) Germ(anicus) / pontif(ex) max(imus) trib(unicia) pot(estate) V p(ater) p(atriae) co(n)s(ul) IIII / ob periculum cataractarum / derivato flumine tutam Da/nuvi navigationem fecit*. Roman navigation channel was by the village of Sip: PETROVIĆ 1972, 31–40, KANITZ 1892, 50; KANITZ 1904–1914, 494. For *Statio Cataractarum Diana*: AE 2003, 1531 = AE 2013, 1318; For *Aquae* port by the village of Kusjak, PETROVIĆ 1991, 212–215. Inscription: CIL III 1642 = ILJug III 1362 (*Aquae* port).
33 For the bridge over Danube: KANITZ 1892, 45; KANITZ 1904–1914, 483; PETROVIĆ 1997, 67–68; ŠERBAN 2009, 1–12.

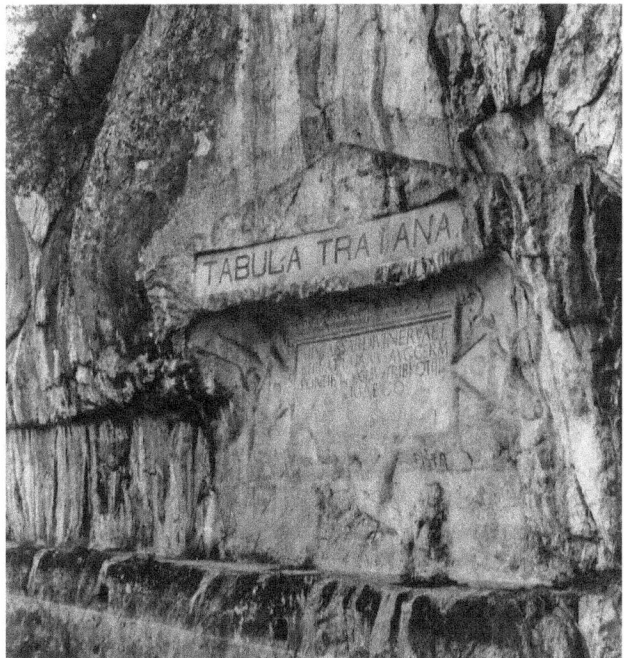

Fig. 2: *Tabula Traiana* (private documentation of Vladimir Petrović)

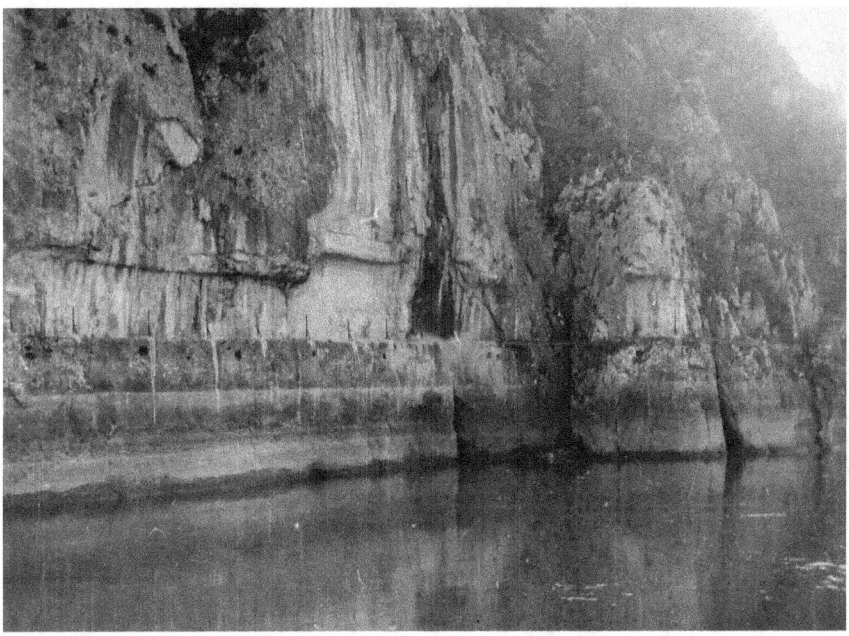

Fig. 3: Roman Road in the Iron Gate (private documentation of Vladimir Petrović)

Gate (*Tabula Traina*, Roman *castra* such as *Lederata* – Ram, *Taliata* – Donji Milanovac, *Statio Catharactarum Diana* – Karataš, *Pontes* with the remains of the bridge at Kostol, *Aquae* – Kusjak and Prahovo, etc.). Recently, during the reconstruction works of the medieval fortress in Golubac (Roman *Cuppae*) we found the only remaining segment of the Roman Iron Gate road that survived the recent developments.[34]

The **Roman Military Road**, *via militaris*, as already stated, was of major importance for the economic life in the province as back bone of the transbalkanic transport. The road began at *Singidunum* and *Viminacium*, continued southward through the valley of the *Margus* river (Velika Morava) and led to *Byzantium* (Constantinople), on the shore of the Bosphorus, via *Naissus* and *Serdica*. It followed the path of an earlier trade route linking Italy and the Central Balkans with Asia Minor. One of the best-preserved sections, approximately 140 paces long, is located at the exit of *Serdica*. The road was built in the first half of the 1st century AD, definitely prior to AD 61, when, according to one inscription, the *tabernae* and *praetoria* were erected along the section between *Naissus* and *Serdica*.[35] The importance of the section of the road *Viminacium* – *Naissus* is also indicated by the fact that it was repaired and renovated several times, which is attested by the milestones from the time of Philip the Arab (244–249), Trajan Decius (249–251) and Gallienus (253–268).[36]

In 2012 a completely preserved Roman milestone with a Latin inscription,[37] was discovered during construction work on the highway E75 (corridor X), which largely coincides with the route of ancient *via militaris*. The monument is unearthed in the environs of the village Špaj, on 7 km to the west of Bela Palanka (*Remesiana*) in the direction of Niš. The spot lies on the eastern leg of the E75 highway, in the section Crvena reka – Čiflik of the future highway E 80. The text of the milestone is:

> *Imp(eratori) C(a)esari di[vi] Ṣẹ[veri] / nepoti Antonini / Magni Pio filio Mar[co] / Aur(elio) Severo [[Alexan[⁵dro]] Pio Felici Aug(usto) po[n]tifici maximo tribu/nicie (sic) potestati(s) VIIII co(n)s(uli) ter pater (sic) patrie (sic) m(ilia) p(assuum) / vac. XXII.*[38]

Milestones served to communicate the direction and distances between places. They were often set up on the occasion of the (re)constructions of the road, but milestones

---

34 About the Roman works in the Iron Gate, Petrović 2015, 290–297. The remains of the Roman road will be exposed after the renovation works of the medieval fort in Golubac, conduct by the Institute for the Protection of Monuments of the Republic of Serbia.
35 AE 1999, 1397: *tabernas et pr[aetoria] / per vias [militares] / [fieri iussit]*.
36 AE 1980, 792; AE 1976, 605; CIL III 8268.
37 The emphasis on the language of the inscription is important. The route of the Roman road left the territory of the Latinophone province of *Moesia Superior* and crossed into the area of the Hellenophone province of Thrace, somewhere near *mutatio* with the eloquent name *Latina* (Itin. Burdig. 566, 7), a station between *Remesiana* and *Turres* (Pirot), distanced 9 miles from the former. In *Turres* (Pirot), milestones are already set up in Greek, indicating *Pautalia* as *caput viae*, cf. AE 1913, 175 = ILJug III 1459.
38 AE 2013, 1323.

were also set up for other reasons. This type of monuments may also have had honorific character and served the purposes of imperial propaganda, without having any connection to the actual road-building or repairs, especially in the 3rd and 4th century. Their erection may have coincided with imperial visits. However, the fact that the distance of 22 miles to the *caput viae* (*Naissus*) is indicated in our inscription, testifies to its practical function. The milestone may have been erected in the course of repairs of the roadway. Dating of the inscription sheds some light on the circumstances in which the monument was erected and provides a broader context: it is in connection with the Persian campaign of Severus Alexander.[39]

Based on the number of consulships (*consul tertium*) and the number of the tribunician power (*VIIII*), the inscription from *Remesiana* can be dated in the period of the 10th of December 229–11th of December 230 AD, when Severus Alexander held the consulship with Cassius Dio, *consul bis*.[40]

In order to compare the evidences from the Roman itineraries with the data obtained from the new milestone, let us show the entries from different itineraries relating to the section *Naissus – Remesiana* in the Central Balkans:

Tab. Peut., segm. VI: *Naisso* XXIIII *Romesiana*;
Itin. Anton. 134–135.4: *Naisso* XXV *Remisiana*;
Itin. Burdig. 565.1–566.8: *civitas Naisso* XII *mutatio Redicibus* VII *mut. Ulmo* VIII *mansio Romansiana*;
Geogr. Rav. 4,7: *Naison Romessiana*.

It is obvious that the data from the itineraries differ in a number of elements. The distance in Roman miles between the road stations in different itineraries varies considerably as well as the tradition of ancient toponyms. Let us take the total distance between *Naissus* and *Remesiana* (Bela Palanka). According to Tab. Peut. it is 24 Roman miles, Itin. Anton. records the distance of 25 miles and Itin. Burdig. 27 miles. Geogr. Rav. registers only the names of stations but not the distance between them. Explaining such differences between itineraries is not simple and it requires a broader analysis, which is beyond the scope of this article. Clearly, not all of them were assembled at the same time, with equal motives and purpose. Furthermore, not all survived in an equal number of copies and equal quality of transcript. Measuring of distances on the same section of the Roman road could vary due to different circumstances. It is difficult to interpret whether these divergences occur as a result of copyist's error, or differently calibrated measuring instruments, the choice of starting and ending points of measurement, or variability of the path of the old or new road, even to a lesser degree.[41]

---

39 Petrović/Grbić 2014, 95–106.
40 Cass. Dio 80,5,1.
41 Petrović/Grbić 2014, 103–104.

The shortest modern road Niš – Niška Banja – Bela Palanka largely coincides with the path of the Roman road between *Naissus* and *Remesiana*. The section is about 41 km long, which equals 27 Roman miles. It appears that the record in the Itin. Burdig. of 27 Roman miles fits best the actual distance between the two cities. The milestone that was recently found *in situ* during the construction of a modern highway was located by the route of the Roman road from *Remesiana* to the west, in the direction of *Naissus* in the area of the modern village of Špaj. However, the distance of XXII miles (32.5 km) indicated on this milestone, clearly represents the distance from the first large city (*civitas*) which has to be *Naissus*, and not one of the intermediate stations, *mutatio Ulmus* and *mutatio Radices*, mentioned only in the *Itinerarium Hierosolymitanum*, also known as *Itinerarium Burdigalense*. The distance that we read on the milestone corresponds to the path that could be passed during the daylight. Judging from the position of its finding spot, the milestone appears to have been set approximately 5 miles from the centre of the Roman *Remesiana* in the direction to *Naissus*.[42]

Comparing the data on mileage indicated in the itineraries with the distance recorded on the milestone and also taking into account the actual distance between *Remesiana* and *Naissus* as *caput viae*, it could be concluded that the data from the Itin. Burdig. are the most accurate and that they correspond with the text of the new milestone. To this may point the relatively late date of Itin. Burdig. It is the earliest itinerary in connection with Christian pilgrims travelling to the Holy Land, from today's Bordeaux (*Burdigala*) in Aquitania, dated in 333 AD, in the year of the consulship of Flavius Dalmatius and Domitius Zenofilus.[43] Besides the relative accuracy in mileage, testified by our new milestone, too, this itinerary reflects the path of the road as it was in the Late Roman period. It surely differed to some extent from the original path of the road which was built in the 1st century AD, when the Roman government in the Central Balkans was established. Itin. Burdig is characteristic not only for its high accuracy in communicating the character of the stations on the Roman road (*civitas*, *mansio*, *mutatio*) and their mutual distances, it is evidently the most exhaustive itinerary; it registers many places and their names which are not documented in other itineraries.[44]

The new milestone furthermore confirms that the Roman road *Singidunum – Viminacium – Naissus – Serdica – Constantinopolis*, the *via militaris*, represented a suitable choice when travelling between the Central Balkans and *Constantinopolis*. An alternate link with *Constantinopolis* would go to the south from *Naissus* through *Scupi* and through the province of Macedonia, via *Stobi* to *Thessalonica* and further on the famous *via Egnatia*. However, this communication would have been significantly longer than a *via militaris*.

---

[42] Petrović/Grbić 2014, 104.
[43] Herrmann 2007, 176.
[44] Herrmann 2007, 175.

The recent archaeological researches at the site of Gojindolsko Kale exposed also some new findings concerning the *via militaris*. This was actually the late antique and early Byzantine fortification erected probably in the fourth century and renewed in the sixth century under the emperor Justinian.[45] The fortification had an important role in controlling the Roman communications and quite probably served as a *refugium* in Late Antiquity. It is positioned on the right bank of Nišava River in the environs of the village Gojin Dol, on a hilltop that dominates the area. The latest archaeological researches conducted during the construction of the modern highway have revealed that this place was an important intersection of Roman roads.

At this place, the *via militaris* or the Constantinople Road, the key trans-Balkan Roman communication that was the main artery of the traffic in the Balkans, namely its section *Turres — Serdica*, crossed paths with a smaller vicinal communication. This vicinal communication should without doubt be identified as the road between *Timacum Minus* and *Pautalia*, which is approved by the positions of the large amount of late antique fortresses built along the road and milestones that point to *Pautalia*, as *caput viae*.[46]

The course of the Constantinople Road on the territory of the modern village Gojin Dol passed to the right bank of the Nišava River, and after the intersection with the vicinal road, continued towards Dimitrovgrad and nowadays Bulgaria.[47]

The transbalkan communication artery between Adriatic and Danube, the **Lissus – Naissus – Ratiaria road** dates back to the first decades of the first century AD. This was partly a *compendium* (shortcut), especially the section *Vicianum – Lissus*, as we learn from an interesting Hadrianic inscription about the *via nova* (*Viminacium – Naissus – Scupi*) and its *compendium* (*Vicianum – Lissus*).[48] Its function could be, on the one hand, to enable the army to move as fast as possible between the Adriatic coast and the Danubian border and, on the other hand to facilitate the conditions for the transport of metals to Rome. The Roman road followed the course of an earlier pre-Roman road, so after the Roman conquest we have a continuation of traffic on this axis. The early dating of the road construction could be explained by the great strategic importance of this terrestrial communication. Many legions used the *Lissus – Naissus – Ratiaria* road at the time when Rome was consolidating its authority in the Central Balkans and at the time when the Empire established its frontier on the banks of the Danube. The fact that some important cities in Upper Moesia such as the *municipium Dardanorum* (Sočanica) and *Ulpiana* (Gračanica) are separated from this route and that they are not mentioned in the roman itineraries testifies to the oldness of the road. These cities were erected after the construction of the main axis of circulation. At the same time, the emergence of new centers meant that, during the 2nd and

---

45 Petrović 2017, 140–142.
46 Petrović/Grbić 2015, 23–32; Milestones: AE 1913, 175; IGBulg IV 2041.
47 Petrović 2017, 140–141.
48 AE 1980, 786 = AE 1984, 792.

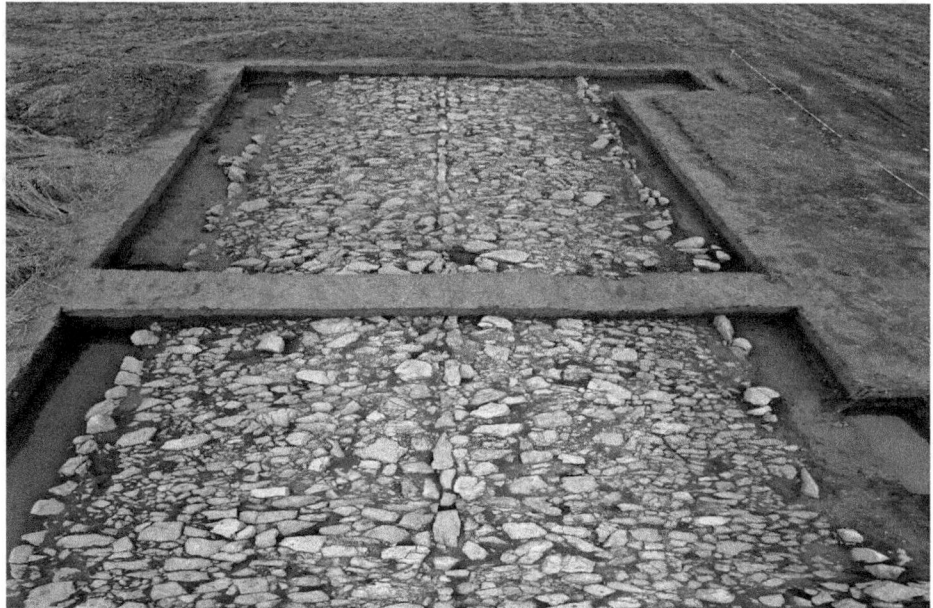

Fig. 4: Remains of *via militaris* by Gojin Dol (private documentation of Vladimir Petrović)

3rd centuries AD, the communication route lost its essentially military character from the 1st century AD to play a major economic role.[49] The vicinity of certain areas rich in mineral sources imposed the creation of an entire network of secondary roads to allow the transport of raw materials. In this regard, the presence of troops becomes indispensable, as the case of *cohortes Aureliae Dardanorum*, I in *Naissus* and II in *Timacum Minus*. This type of local militia protected the roads from robbers, the *latrones*, who plundered convoys and merchants.[50]

Based on the knowledge of the archaeological and epigraphic situation I would like to indicate the problematic with certain data from the Tab. Peut. concerning the Roman *Lissus – Naissus – Ratiaria* road. For the section between *Lissus* and *Naissus*, the Table of Peutinger reveals the following stations: *Lissum* XXX *Ad Picaria* XXX *Creveni* XVII *Gabuleo* XXX *Theranda* XXV *Viciano* XIX *Vindenis* XX *Ad Fines* XX *Hammeo* VI *Ad Herculem* XIV *Naisso*. Close to the station *Ad Fines* (modern Kuršumlija), one milestone was recently found and published in the scientific literature, among other archaeological finds.[51] This milestone was discovered *in situ* at Kuršumlijska banja – Kuršumlijska Spa (*Aquae Bas.*), along the path of the Roman road on the

---

49 Petrović 2008, 31–40.
50 About the *latrones Dardaniae*, see Mócsy 1968 and Dušanić 2000, 347–352.
51 Petrović 2006, 367–376.

Lissus – Naissus section. Kuršumlijska Spa is not specifically indicated in the Roman itinerary, but it is now clear that the road passed through it. On the other hand on the following section to the south *Scupi* (Skopje) – *Stobi* it exists a representation (image) of a Spa whose name is not specified, as well as a number of stations which considerably extend the actual distance between these two cities. Unlike this section, there are no specified road stations between *Hammeum* (Prokuplje) or (*Vicianum*, scientifically proofed)[52] and *Scupi*, where, according to Tab. Peut. the *Lissus – Naissus* and *Scupi – Naissus* paths intersected and took the same way to *Naissus*. It is possible that there was an error of the copyist due to a lack of space so the abovementioned Spa as well as other stations were moved from one road to another, from *Naissus – Scupi* to *Scupi – Stobi*. Although the *Lissus – Naissus* and *Scupi –Naissus* pathways, according to Tab. Peut. intersected in *Hammeum* (Prokuplje), according to the scientific literature, geographical, archaeological and epigraphic data it is more likely that the junction of the two lines was at *Vicianum* (Ugljare or Čaglavica)[53] the station 59 miles away from *Hammeum* and thus Kuršumlijska Spa could be located on the common section of the two roads, from *Lissus* and from *Scupi*. Perhaps the vignette (image) of the Spa indicated on the *Scupi –Stobi* road could be linked to Kuršumlijska Spa if the excess of *Scupi – Stobi* road stations is transferred to the *Naissus – Scupi* road as already proposed in the scientific literature. In this case the restitution and correction of the data from the itinerary for the *Naissus – Scupi* road would be as follows: *Naisso* XIIII *Ad Herculem* VI *Hammeo* XX **Ad Fines** IX **Aquae Bas. [Spa]** XI *Vindenis* XIX *Viciano* **XII Anausaro XXXV Ad Fines VIII Ad Herculem VIIII** *Scupis*.[54]

As regards oldness of the road to *Naissus – Scupi*, it is clearly elaborated by the milestones from the vicinity of *Scupi* and Djeneral Janković, which all date back to reigns of Hadrian, Antoninus Pius and Marcus Aurelius.[55]

---

52 Mirković 1960, 249–257.
53 Mirković 1960, 249–257.
54 Petrović 2018.
55 CIL III 8272 = IMS VI 199 (*Scupi*): *Imp(eratori) Caesari | divi Traiani Parth(ici) f(ilio) | divi Nervae [n] epoti| Traiano H[adr]iano |⁵ Aug(usto) p(ontifici) m(aximo) tri[b(unicia) pot(estate) --- co(n)s(uli) ---] | ICIIIOR[---] | [---]COI[---] | m(ilia) p(assuum) I ------* ; IMS VI 200: *Imp(erator) Caesar | T(itus) Aelius H[a]dria|nus Anto[ni]nus | Aug(ustus) Pius d[i]vi H[a]|⁵driani f[i]l(ius) divi | Traiani nepos | divi Nerv[a]e | pronepos pont(ifex) |maxim(us) trib(unicia) |¹⁰ pot(estate) II co(n)s(ul) II [---] | m(ilia) p(assuum) II*; IMS VI 195 (Đeneral Janković/*Scupi*): *Imp(eratori) Caesari | divi Traiani Parthici f(ilio) | divi Nervae nepoti | Traiano Hadriano |⁵ Aug(usto) p(ontifici) m(aximo) trib(unicia) pot(estate) IIII | co(n)s(uli) III L(ucio) Coelio Rufo | leg(ato) Aug(usti) pr(o) pr(aetore) col(onia) Scupin(orum) | m(ilia) p(assuum) VIIII*; IMS VI 196: *Imp(erator) Caes(ar) | divi Hadri/[a]ni fil(ius) divi | [T]raiani nepos |⁵ divi Nervae | pronepos | Antoninus | Aug(ustus) Piu(s) | [res]tituit |¹⁰ m(ilia) p(assuum) VIIII]*; CIL III 8271 = IMS VI 197 = ILJug III 1432: *Imp(erator) C[ae]s(ar) [divi Ant]onini | f(ilius) divi [Veri] P[art]hici max(imi) | frate(r) div[i Had]riani nepos | divi Tra[iani Pa]rthici pro|⁵ nepos diviN[er]vae abnepos | M(arcus) Aurel(ius) Anto[nin]us Aug(ustus) Germa|nic(us) Sarmatic(us) [p]ontif(ex) ma[x(imus)] trib(unicia) | [p]otest(ate) XXXI imp(erator) VIII co(n)s(ul) | III p(ater) p(atriae) |¹⁰Con]sstantin[us] | [--- maximus] victor | [--- Im]per(ator) Aug(ustus) | [---]ILXII [----]*.

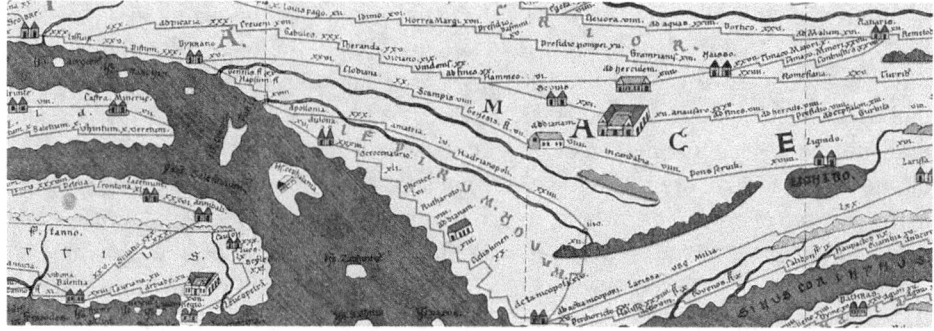

Fig. 5: Tabula Peutingeriana, *segm.* VI (Roman Roads around *Scupi*) (MILLER 1916)

Although there are no evidences in ancient sources and itineraries, there is the assumption that at the station *Vicianum*, on the common section of the *Lissus – Naissus* and *Scupi –Naissus* roads, one secondary road went to the *municipim Splonum* and further to *Narona*, *Risinum* and *Scodra*, as already mentioned above. This road connected the southern part of Upper Moesia, its southern mining district of *Dardania* with the strategic ports along the Adriatic coastline. The pathway of this road went to the north of *Vicianum* in the direction of the Kopaonik Mountain, by the valley of the river Ibar. It passed through the nowadays region of Novi Pazar and went further to Prijepolje, Mileševa, Kolovrat and Pljevlja where the *municipium Splonum*, one of the administrative centers of the Roman mines in the east of Dalmatia, was situated close to the village of Komini. From the *municipium Splonum* the Roman road branched into three or maybe more separate sections in the direction of the Adriatic Sea. This important Roman road had a large significance in the mining activities, especially in the terrestrial transport from the Central Balkans' inland to the nearest see ports and it was certainly the alternative way to the itinerary road *Lissus – Naissus*, constructed in the first decades of Roman rule in these territories. The large network of secondary roads like *Vicianum – Municipium Splonum* –Adriatic Sea was, like the *via metallica*, built predominantly in the later epoch when roman roads had mainly an economic significance. The hypotheses of the existence of the *Vicianum – Municipium Splonum –* Adriatic Sea road are supported by numerous archeological findings and the considerable number of milestones as epigraphical testimonies.[56] In the 17th century existed the trade road Dubrovnik – Foča – Pljevlja – Prijepolje – Novi Pazar (*via Ragusa*) that passed almost by the same pathway like these earlier Roman roads.[57]

On the section of the *Lissus – Naissus – Ratiaria* road, now between *Naissus* and *Ratiaria*, the Tab. Peut. reveals the following stations: *Naisso* XXVII *Timaco Maiori* X

---

56 MIRKOVIĆ 1960, 253; Milestones (Prijepolje): CIL XVII/4, 571, 572, 572a, 572b.
57 BOJANOVSKI 1987, 64–65.

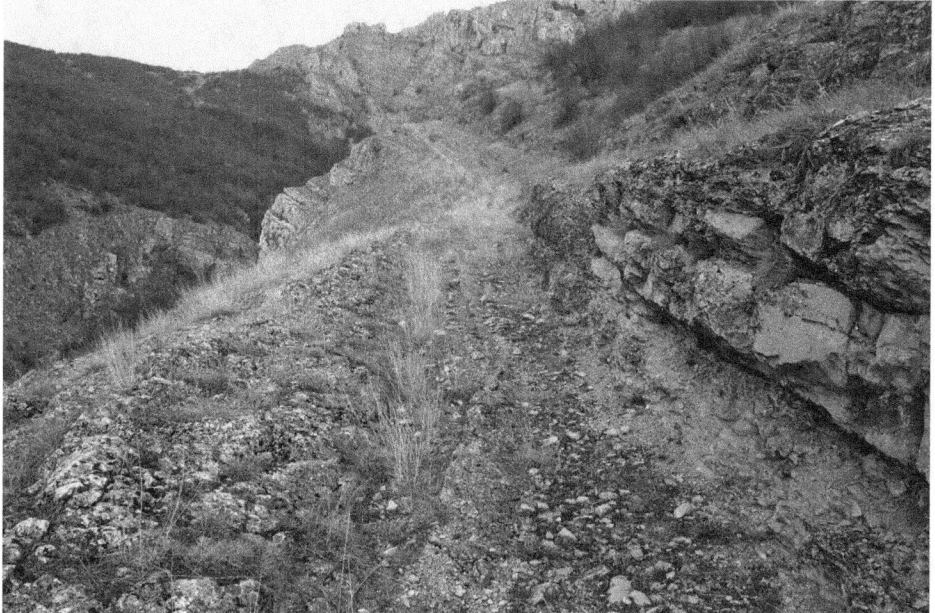

Fig. 6: Remains of the Roman road to Ratiaria in the vicinity of *Timacum Maius* (Niševac) (photo by Vladimir Petrović)

Timaco Minori XXVII *Conbustica* XXVII *Ratiaris*. The geographical and archaeological situation does not correspond to the data from the Tab. Peut.[58] The location of the first two stations *Timacum Maius* (Niševac by Svrljig) and *Timacum Minus* (Ravna by Knjaževac) would involve a change of distances between *Naissus* and *Timacum Maius*, as well as between *Timacum Maius* and *Timacum Minus*.[59] It is actually a 10-mile transfer from *Naissus* – *Timacum Maius* section to *Timacum Maius* and *Timacum Minus*. The revised data from Tab. Peut. would have the following shape: *Naisso* XVII *Timaco Maiori* **XX** *Timaco Minori* XXVII *Conbustica* XXVII *Ratiaris*. In this way the data from the Roman itinerary would correspond to the reality on the terrain: *Timacum Maius* would be XVII miles (about 25 km) distant from of *Naissus*, while the distance between *Timacum Maius* and *Timacum Minus* would be XX Roman miles. The archaeological findings at the locality of Niševac by Svrljig in the Svrljiški Timok river valley in eastern Serbia (*Timacum Maius*), and that from Ravna by Knjaževac (*Timacum Minus*), justify the correction of data from the Tab. Peut.[60]

---

58 Petrović/Filipović/Milivojević 2012, 90–92.
59 Petrović/Filipović/Milivojević 2012, 92.
60 Petrović 2015, 152–153.

Conclusion

At the end of this paper, in relation to the importance and complexity of the subject, we should add a few final remarks. The Central Balkans well positioned geographically and strategically, had been the outstanding territory of transit and residence for a very long time. In Roman times as well as today, it was the crossroad of several axes of communication, linking the capital of the Empire, Italy and the western provinces with territories of the east, rich, advanced and of strategic importance. On the other hand, roads from the Aegean Sea and the Greek cities to the Danubian basin led through the Central Balkan region. The north of the Central Balkans was also an important part of Roman *limes* from the first decades of the first century A.D. onwards, when a huge amount of construction works started that comprise the somewhat particular terrestrial road in the Iron Gates, in order to prepare the Dacian campaigns under Trajan. All those facts left without doubt significant consequences on the territory of Central Balkans in various aspects.

The new scientific developments concerning Roman Roads and Settlements in the Central Balkans are somewhat motivated by the large modern infrastructure works. On the other hand the important inscriptions supported with the archaeological remains enable a partial reconstruction of the secondary road network, which was used extensively especially for trade but not specifically mentioned in the Roman itineraries. Before making conclusions, the scientists have to be aware of two important facts. We learn information about the main communication lines, toponymy, character of settlements and distances between them while reading the data of precious Roman itineraries we have today. The scientific interpretation of the itineraries have to be conducted with a necessary scientific and critical approach to the data they provide us and have to take into account the important results of both archaeological research and epigraphic sources. It is also important to be aware of archeological remains and epigraphical testimonies in order to complete the image of the Roman communication network, which was certainly more developed as it is indicated by the ancient itineraries and which included a significant number of secondary roads. In this way it will be possible to reconstruct with a certain precision a complex and multi-faceted picture of the Roman settlements and roads in the territory of the Central Balkans.

Bibliography

Bosio 1983 = L. Bosio, La Tabula peutingeriana. A Description of the Ancient World, Rimini 1983.
Bojanovski 1987 = I. Bojanovski, Prilozi za topografiju rimskih i predrimskih komunikacija i naselja u rimskoj provinciji Dalmaciji V: Gornje Podrinje u sistemu rimskih komunikacija [Contributions à la topogaphie des communications et des agglomerations romaines et préromaines dans la province romaine de Dalmatie V: Gornje Podrinje dans le système des communications romaines], *Godišnjak* 25, 1987, 63–174.
Bojanovski 1988 = I. Bojanovski, Bosna i Hercegivina u antičko doba, Sarajevo 1988.

ČERŠKOV 1965 = E. ČERŠKOV, Municipium D.D. kod Sočanice, Beograd 1965.
ČERŠKOV 1969 = E. ČERŠKOV, Rimljani na Kosovu i Metohiji, Beograd 1969.
DUŠANIĆ 1977a = S. DUŠANIĆ, Aspects of Roman Mining in Noricum, Pannonia, Dalmatia and Moesia Superior, ANRW II 6, 1977, 52–94.
DUŠANIĆ 1977b = S. DUŠANIĆ, Iz istorije rimskog rudarstva u Gornjoj Meziji, AArchSlov 28, 1977, 163–179.
DUŠANIĆ 1995 = S. DUŠANIĆ, Late Roman Mining in Illyricum: Historical Observations, Ancient Mining, in: B. JOVANOVIĆ/P. PETROVIĆ/S. ĐURĐEKANOVIĆ (ed.), Southeast Europe, International Symposium, Donji Milanovac 1990, Belgrade 1995, 219–225.
DUŠANIĆ 1996 = S. DUŠANIĆ, The Frontier and the Hinterland: the Role of Scupi in Domitian's Wars on the Danube, in: P. PETROVIĆ (ed.), Roman Limes on the Middle and Lower Danube, Belgrade 1996, 41–52.
DUŠANIĆ 2000 = S. DUŠANIĆ, Army and Mining in Moesia Superior, in: G. ALFÖLDY/W. ECK/B. DOBSON (ed.), Kaiser, Heer und Gesellschaft in der römischen Kaiserzeit, Stuttgart 2000, 343–363.
DUŠANIĆ 2004 = S. DUŠANIĆ, Roman Mining in Illyricum: Historical Aspects, in: G. URSO (ed.), Dall' Adriatico al Danubio: L'Illirico nell'eta greca e romana, Cividale del Friuli, Pisa 2004, 247–270.
FUNAIOLI 1914 = G. FUNAIOLI, Ravennas Geographus, RE I A 1, 1914, 205–310.
GAVRILOVIĆ/POPOVIĆ 2015 = N. GAVRILOVIĆ/B. POPOVIĆ, Kasnoantički domus u Skelanima (Municipium Malvesiatium), Starinar 65, 2015, 197–220.
GOLUBOVIĆ 2008 = S. GOLUBOVIĆ, Grobovi u obliku bunara sa nekropola Viminacijuma [Well Graves in the Roman Cemeteries at Viminacium], Beograd 2008.
GEYER 1898 = P. GEYER, Itinera Hierosolymitana saeculi IIII–VIII (Itinerarium Burdigalense), Wien 1898.
HERRMANN 2007 = P. HERRMANN, Itinéraires des voies romaines de l'Antiquité au Moyen Age, Paris 2007.
IGBulg = G. Mihailov (ed.), Inscriptiones Graecae in Bulgaria repertae, Vol I^2-V, Serdicae 1958–1997.
ILJug I = A. ŠAŠEL/J. ŠAŠEL, Inscriptiones Latinae quae in Iugoslavia inter annos MCMXL et MCMLX repertae et editae sunt, Ljubljana 1963.
ILJug II = A. ŠAŠEL/J. ŠAŠEL, Inscriptiones Latinae quae in Iugoslavia inter annos MCMLX et MCMLXX repertae et editae sunt, Ljubljana 1978.
ILJug III = A. ŠAŠEL/J. ŠAŠEL, Inscriptiones Latinae quae in Iugoslavia inter annos MCMII et MCMXL repertae et editae sunt, Ljubljana 1986.
IMS I = M. MIRKOVIĆ/S. DUŠANIĆ, Singidunum et le Nord-Ouest de la province, Inscriptions de la Mésie Supérieure, vol. I, Beograd 1976.
IMS II = M. MIRKOVIĆ, Viminacium et Margum, Inscriptions de la Mésie Supérieure, vol. II, Beograd 1986.
IMS III/2 = P. PETROVIĆ, Timacum Minus et la vallée du Timok, Inscriptions de la Mésie Supérieure, vol. III/2, Beograd 1995.
IMS IV = P. PETROVIĆ, Naissus, Remesiana, Horreum Margi, Inscriptions de la Mésie Supérieure, vol. IV, Beograd 1979.
IMS VI = B. DRAGOJEVIĆ-JOSIFOVSKA, Scupi et la région de Kumanovo, Inscriptions de la Mésie Supérieure, vol. VI, Beograd 1982.
IVANIŠEVIĆ/BUGARSKI 2012 = V. IVANIŠEVIĆ/I. BUGARSKI, Primena LiDAR tehnologije u analizi topografije Marguma/Morave i Kuliča, Starinar 62, 2012, 239–255.
KANITZ 1892 = F. KANITZ, Römische Studien in Serbien 1–2, Wien 1892.
KANITZ 1904–1914 = F. KANITZ, Das Königreich Serbien und das Serbenvolk von der Römerzeit zur Gegenwart, vol. 1–3, Leipzig/Berlin 1904–1914.

Korać/Golubović 2009 = M. Korać/S. Golubović, *Viminacium*: Više Grobalja, vol. 2, Beograd 2009.
Kubitschek 1916 = W. Kubitschek, Itinerarien, RE IX 2, 1916, 2308–2363.
Loma 2010 = S. Loma, Klaudije Gal i Severovi novi senatori – istraživanja iz epigrafike, prosopografije i rimske političke istorije devedesetih godina II veka, Beograd 2010.
Luka 2014 = K. Luka, Colonia Ulpia Traiana: Rediscovering of the Ancient City, in: R. Ivanov (ed.), Ratiaria and its territory researches, Sofia 2014, 50–64.
Miller 1916 = K. Miller, *Itineraria Romana*. Römische Reisewege an der Hand der Tabula Peutingeriana, Stuttgart 1916, reprint Rom 1964.
Mirković 1960 = M. Mirković, Rimski put Naissus–Scupi i stanica Ad Fines, *ZAnt* 10, 1960, 249–257.
Mirković 1968 = M. Mirković, Rimski gradovi na Dunavu u Gornjoj Meziji, Beograd 1968.
Mócsy 1968 = A. Mócsy, Latrones Dardaniae, *AAntHung* 16, 1968, 351–354.
Mócsy 1970 = A. Mócsy, Gesellschaft und Romanisation in der römischen Provinz Moesia Superior, Budapest 1970.
Mócsy 1974 = A. Mócsy, Pannonia and Upper Moesia. A History of Middle Danube Provinces, London/Boston 1974.
Pašalić 1966 = E. Pašalić, Antička naselja i komunikacije u Bosni i Hercegovini, Sarajevo 1966.
Petrović 1972 = P. Petrović, Nova Trajanova tabla u Đerdapu [Nouvelle table de Trajan dans le Đerdap], *Starinar* 21, [1970] 1972, 31–39.
Petrović 1979a = P. Petrović, Ponišavlje u antičko doba, *Pirotski zbornik* 8–9, 1979, 177–184.
Petrović 1986 = P. Petrović, Rimski put u Đerdapu [La voie romaine dans les Portes de Fer], *Starinar* 37, 1986, 41–52.
Petrović 1991 = P. Petrović, Classis Flavia Moesica na Dunavu i Gornjoj Meziji [Classis Flavia Moesica on the Danube in Upper Moesia], *Starinar* 40–41, 1991, 207–216.
Petrović 1997 = P. Petrović, Le limes romain, *Les Dossiers d'Archéologie* 220, 1997, 60–72.
Petrović/Vasić 1996 = P. Petrović/M. Vasić, The Roman Frontier in Upper Moesia: Archeological Investigations in the Iron Gate Area – Main Results, in: P. Petrović (ed.), Roman Limes on the Middle and Lower Danube, Belgrade 1996, 15–27.
Petrović 2000 = V. Petrović, Une inscription romaine tardive païenne de Remesiana (Province de Dacia Mediterranea), *Phoinix* 6, 2000, 346–359.
Petrović 2006 = V. Petrović, Une nouvelle borne milliaire découverte sur la voie romaine Naissus–Lissus, *Starinar* 56, 2006, 367–376.
Petrović 2007 = V. Petrović, Dardanija u rimskim itinerarima : gradovi i naselja [Dardanie dans les itinéraires romaines], Belgrade 2007.
Petrović 2008 = V. Petrović, The Roman Road Naissus–Lissus: The Shortest Connection between Rome and the Danubian Limes, *Archaeologia Bulgarica* 12,1, 31–40.
Petrović 2011 = V. Petrović, Les voies de communication en Mésie supérieure, L`homme et son environnement dans le Sud-Est européen, Paris 2011, 404–414.
Petrović 2015 = V. Petrović, *Римска насеља и комуникације од Јадрана до Дунава (I – IV век)* [Roman Settlements and Communication Lines between the Adriatic and the Danube (First to Fourth Centuries)], Niš/Beograd 2015.
Petrović 2017 = V. Petrović, La voie romaine Timacum Minus – Pautalia: les contacts entre la Mésie supérieure et la Thrace d'après les recherches archéologiques et les sources écrites, in: S. Zanni (ed.), La route antique et médiévale : nouvelles approches, nouveaux outils, Bordeaux 2017, 133–144.
Petrović 2019 = V. Petrović, Les voies et agglomérations romaines au coeur des Balkans – le cas de la Serbie, Scripta Antiqua numéro 120, Bordeaux, 2019, in print.
Petrović/Grbić 2014 = V. Petrović/D. Grbić, Ancient Remesiana: a New Milestone from the Times of Severus Alexander, *Journal of Ancient Topography: Rivista di Topographia Antica* 23, 2013, 95–106.

Petrović/Grbić 2015 = V. Petrović/D. Grbić, The Roman Roads between Upper Moesia and Thrace: Archaeological and Epigraphic evidence, *Journal of Ancient Topography: Rivista di Topographia Antica* 24, 2014, 23–32.
Petrović/Filipović/Milivojević 2012 = V. P. Petrović/V. Filipović/S. Milivojević, Svrljiška oblast u praictoriji: antici srednjem veku [La région de Svrljig en Serbie orientale: préhistoire, antiquité et moyen age], Belgrade 2012.
Popović 1997 = M. Popović, Antički Singidunum: dosadašnja otkrića i mogućnost daljih istraživanja, *Singidunum* 1, 1997, 1–20.
Popović 2006 = M. Popović, *Beogradska tvrđava* [The Fortress of Belgrade], Beograd 2006.
Reed 1978 = N. Reed, Pattern and Purpose in the Antonine Itinerary, *AJPh* 99, 1978, 228–251.
Spasić-Djurić 2015 = D. Spasić–Djurić, *Viminacium*, the Capital of the Roman Province of Upper Moesia, Požarevac 2015.
Schillinger-Häfele 1963 = U. Schillinger-Häfele, Beobachtungen zum Quellenproblem der Kosmographie von Ravenna, *BJ* 163, 1963, 238–251.
Šerban 2009 = M. Šerban, Trajan`s Bridge over the Danube, *IJNA* 38,2, 2009, 331–342.
TIR K-34 = J. Sašel/G. Alexandrov/R. Chevallier, Naissus: Dyrrachion – Scupi – Serdica – Thessalonice, Tabula Imperii Romani, vol. K 34, Ljubljana 1968.
TIR L-34 = S. Soproni, Budapest: Aquincum – Sarmizegetusa – Sirmium, Tabula Imperii Romani, vol. L 34, Amsterdam 1968.
Talbert 2000 = R.J.A. Talbert, Barrington Atlas of the Greek and Roman World, Princeton 2000.
Vasić/Petković 2010 = M. Vasić/S. Petković, Rezultati istraživanja višeslojnog nalazišta Horreum Margi – Ravno – Ćuprija u 1990. godini [The Results of Multilayer Site Horreum Margi – Ravno – Ćuprija in 1990], *Vesnik Vojnog muzeja* 37, 2010, 9–25.
Vojvoda/Mrdjić 2015 = M. Vojvoda/N. Mrđić, Coin Finds from Viminacium Necropolis Više grobalja and their Role in Funeral Ritual, Beograd 2015.
Wilkes 1969 = J.J. Wilkes, Dalmatia, London 1969.

François Mottas
Du premier milliaire au dernier palimpseste: cinq siècles et demi de présence romaine en Grèce

Abstract: First erected along the Via Egnatia, built shortly after 146 B.C. to connect Rome to the East, milestones accompanied the main repairs of the road followed by the Trajan's or Severans' legions fighting against Parthians. South of Macedonia, milestones appeared later, due to administrative changes (Thessaly) or by the effect of generosity of emperors like Trajan (Achaia), or Hadrian traveling in Greece. Thereafter milestones were widely reused, sometimes up to 6 or 7 times, to display allegiance of the cities to emperors who quickly succeeded each other. Last milestones followed the barbaric incursions and ravages.

Zusammenfassung: Die ersten Meilensteine wurden entlang der Via Egnatia aufgestellt, die kurz nach 146 v. Chr. erbaut worden war, um Rom mit dem Osten zu verbinden. Meilensteine begleiteten die grossen Wellen an Straßenausbesserungen, die den Kämpfen gegen die Parther unter Trajan oder den Severern folgten. Südlich von Makedonien kommen Meilensteine erst später vor. Sie stehen dort im Zusammenhang mit administrativen Veränderungen (Thessalien), den Folgen der Großzügigkeit von Kaisern (wie von Trajan) oder den Reisen Hadrians in Griechenland. Später wurden Meilensteine in großem Umfang wiederverwendet, gelegentlich bis zu sechs- oder siebenmal, um die Loyalität der Städte zu Kaisern zur Schau zu stellen, die schnell aufeinander folgten. Die letzten Meilensteine folgten auf die Barbareneinfälle und Verwüstungen.

Quelles sont les diverses circonstances qui suscitent l'érection de milliaires le long des voies romaines ? C'est à cette question que je vais tenter de répondre en centrant mon propos sur les provinces romaines du Sud des Balkans: Epire, Macédoine, Thrace, Thessalie et Achaïe. Ces provinces, dont l'organisation administrative s'est modifiée au cours des temps, ont occupé une aire géographique d'une relative homogénéité: la péninsule sud-balkanique, ou péninsule grecque, entre mers Ionienne et Adriatique à l'ouest, et mer Egée à l'est. Marquée par un relief accidenté, les chaînes et massifs montagneux ne laissant que peu de place aux paysages plus ouverts – plaines littorales ou bassins intérieurs – la région présente des conditions de communication difficiles, qui ont souvent favorisé le trafic maritime au détriment du trafic routier. Pour illustrer cette réalité, il suffira de rappeler la tentative avortée de Néron, en 67–68 apr. J.-C., de percer l'Isthme de Corinthe par un canal permettant d'éviter le fastidieux, et souvent dangereux, contournement du Péloponnèse[1].

---

[1] Suet. Nero 19; Ps.-Lukian. Nero 78.

Cnaeus Egnatius et la Via Egnatia

Le plus ancien milliaire (fig. 1)[2] de la péninsule grecque a été mis au jour en 1972 dans les alluvions de la rivière Gallikos, à une dizaine de kilomètres à l'ouest de Thessalonique.

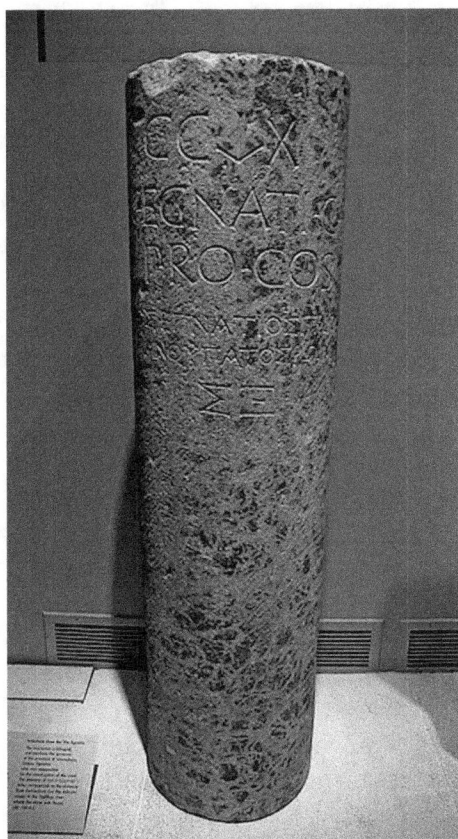

Fig. 1: Milliaire d'Egnatius. Sindos. © Photo Jona Lendering, Livius.org.

Indiquant le 260ᵉ mille, il a été découvert tout près de son emplacement d'origine. Nous savons en effet par Strabon, citant Polybe, que la distance séparant Apollonia, sur l'Adriatique, de Thessalonique était de 267 mille pas[3]. Le milliaire se dressait au bord de la Via Egnatia et son inscription, mentionnant en latin et en grec le nom du proconsul Cnaeus Egnatius, est venue confirmer l'hypothèse que la voie romaine

---

2 Romiopoulou 1974, 813–816 = ILGR 246. Cf. Collart 1976, 197, n° 1.
3 Strab. 7,7,4 C 323.

devait son nom au gouverneur responsable de son aménagement et de la pose des milliaires dressés sur son parcours. Cette vaste opération se situe nécessairement à une date antérieure à la mort de Polybe (vers 120 av. J.-C.), dont le passage cité par Strabon[4] montre qu'il connaissait non seulement l'existence de la route mais aussi ses points extrêmes et la distance les séparant: «D'Apollonia en Macédoine, l'Egnatia est une route vers l'orient, mesurée mille par mille et jalonnée de milliaires (‹ stèles ›) jusqu'à Kypsela et au cours de l'Hèbros, sur une distance de 535 milles.»

La date du proconsulat d'Egnatius fait encore l'objet de débats, la liste des proconsuls entre 146, date de création de la province de Macédoine, et 120 av. J.-C. restant incomplète. L'opinion majoritaire tend néanmoins à placer le proconsulat d'Egnatius dans les premières années d'existence de la province[5].

Ni le texte du milliaire, conforme aux formules de son temps, ni le passage de Polybe ne mentionnent explicitement la construction de la Via Egnatia. La «création» de la voie romaine semble s'être davantage apparentée à un aménagement des cheminements existants qu'à une construction *ex nihilo*[6]. On sait par Tite-Live que la route menant de Macédoine en Thrace était déjà pourvue de ponts et qu'une bonne viabilité y était assurée à l'époque de Philippe V (190 av. J.-C.: passage de Ti. Sempronius Gracchus)[7]. Un certain nombre de bornes bordaient la route dès le 4ᵉ siècle, certaines indiquant même, aux siècles suivants, des distances calculées en stades. Il se pourrait donc que l'essentiel de l'action proconsulaire ait concerné la pose des milliaires, ce qui représente déjà une opération d'une grande envergure, soulignée par la découverte d'un second milliaire d'Egnatius sur le tronçon oriental de la Via Egnatia, entre Philippes et son port de Néapolis (Kavala)[8]. Quoi qu'il en soit, la pose de milliaires et l'aménagement d'une grande route transversale assurant la communication entre la mer Adriatique et l'Italie d'un côté, l'Hellespont et l'Orient de l'autre, figurent assurément parmi les actes constitutifs de la nouvelle province. Le parallèle éclairant du milliaire de Cn. Domitius Ahenobarbus[9] (119–117 av. J.-C.), trouvé sur la Via Domitia à vingt milles de Narbonne, illustre la volonté de la République romaine de doter de milliaires les grandes voies traversant ses nouveaux territoires, peu après leur annexion, notamment si ces axes vitaux ont pour fonction de relier Rome aux provinces-frontières, l'Espagne (*Hispania*) pour la Via Domitia, l'Asie mineure (*Asia*) pour la Via Egnatia. A ce rôle de nature plutôt civile et administrative s'ajoute une évidente

---

[4] Strab. 7,7,4 C 322: Ἐκ δὲ τῆς Ἀπολλωνίας εἰς Μακεδονίαν ἡ Ἐγνατία ἐστὶν ὁδὸς πρὸς ἕω, βεβηματισμένη κατὰ μίλιον καὶ κατεστηλωμένη μέχρι Κυψέλων καὶ Ἕβρου ποταμοῦ · μιλίων δ'ἐστὶ πεντακοσίων τριάκοντα πέντε.
[5] Vers 143 av. J.-C.: MRR 1986, 84; 145 av. J.-C.: WALBANK 1985, 203. VANDERSPOEL 2010, 265, vu les conditions à réunir pour une véritable construction de la voie, penche pour une date un peu plus tardive (140–135 av. J.-C.).
[6] Cf. KOLB 2012, 59.
[7] Liv. 37,7,8–15.
[8] SAMARTZIDOU 1990, 559–578.
[9] KÖNIG 1970, 65–66, 275, n° 256 = CIL XVII/2, 294.

dimension stratégique, soulignée par l'expression utilisée par Cicéron pour qualifier la Via Egnatia au 1ᵉʳ siècle av. J.-C.: *via illa nostra ... militaris*[10].

Auguste et la province d'Achaïe

Dans l'ordre chronologique, le prochain milliaire de la péninsule grecque (fig. 2), trouvé à Larissa (Thessalie), est gravé d'une titulature d'Auguste[11].

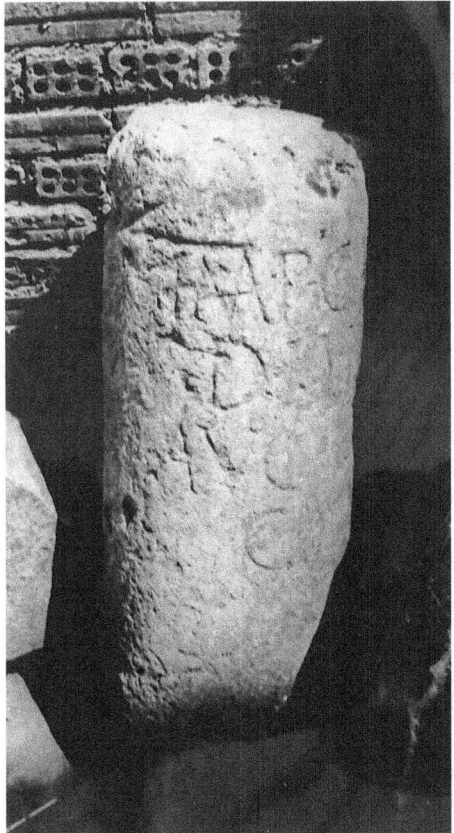

Fig. 2: Milliaire d'Auguste. Larissa. © Photo F. Mottas.

---

10 Cic. prov. 2,4.
11 MOTTAS/DECOURT 1997, 348, n° 2: *Imp(erator) Caesar | divi f(ilius) | Aug[u]stus | (milia passuum) CXIII*. Sur les circonstances, MOTTAS/DECOURT 1997, 315 et 322.

L'empereur y porte le nouveau nom que le Sénat lui a accordé le 16 janvier 27, *Augustus*, accompagné de la filiation au divin César. La même année, Auguste est élu stratège de la Confédération thessalienne et, toujours en 27 av. J.-C., il détache la Thessalie de la Macédoine pour l'intégrer à la toute nouvelle province d'Achaïe (*Achaia*). L'an 27 s'impose donc avec évidence comme la date d'érection du milliaire, et la circonstance qui l'explique est un changement administratif, le rattachement de la Thessalie à la province d'Achaïe, vécu, semble-t-il, comme un bienfait d'Auguste.

La titulature impériale est suivie d'une indication de distance, 113 mille pas, sans mention du *caput viae*. Nous avons pu montrer que la seule ville susceptible d'être le point de départ ou d'arrivée du calcul des milles, dans un rayon de 167 km autour de Larissa, était Thessalonique; quant à l'ellipse du *caput viae*, elle ne peut s'expliquer que si la position du milliaire rendait la mention superflue, par exemple si le milliaire se dressait au sortir de Larissa, au départ d'une route ne pouvant mener qu'à Thessalonique. Ces considérations font douter de l'existence d'un jalonnement systématique, mille après mille, le long de cette voie; l'unicité du milliaire parle plutôt en faveur d'un jeu réduit d'indicateurs de distance placés aux portes des grandes villes, très différent du balisage systématique que suggère la brève description que Polybe consacre à la Via Egnatia.

Claude et Néron: la province de Thrace

En 46 apr. J.-C., l'empereur Claude pacifie la Thrace et y crée une nouvelle province. Le littoral égéen de la Thrace, entre les confins orientaux de la colonie de Philippes, à l'ouest du Nestos, et le fleuve Hèbros, est détaché de la Macédoine et intégré à la nouvelle province. Périnthe est choisie comme capitale en raison de sa situation de nœud des communications maritimes et terrestres, avec des couloirs qui la relient à Byzance (est), Hadrianopolis (nord) et Kypsela (ouest), terme de la Via Egnatia au 2e siècle av. J.-C. Entre Kypsela et Périnthe, une colonie est installée à Apri/Apros, peuplée notamment de colons venus de Philippes.

Les premiers milliaires de la nouvelle province n'apparaissent pas avant le règne de Néron. Ils s'inscrivent dans un programme général d'installation ou de réfection des voies militaires. Mis en œuvre par le procurateur T. Iulius Ustus dans les années 61 à 63 apr. J.-C., il comprend l'établissement de *tabernae* et de *praetoria*[12], infrastructures nécessaires aux déplacements des légions et au bon fonctionnement du *cursus publicus*, ainsi que la pose de milliaires.

---

12 CIL III 6123 = 14207[34] = ILS 231; Filov 1912/13, 17, n° 13 = AE 1912, 193. Adams 1989, 31–32, met les travaux sur la voie intérieure de la Thrace (vallée de la Maritza) en relation avec les préparatifs de la seconde phase de la guerre parthique, associée à la nomination de Corbulon comme gouverneur de Syrie et aux mouvements de troupes et d'approvisionnement en direction du Pont et de la Cappadoce.

En publiant le premier milliaire de Néron[13], mis au jour près de Pherai (Grèce), sur la rive droite de l'Hèbros, je restituais dans l'une des nombreuses lacunes d'un monument brisé en multiples morceaux la formule courante *[vias facien]das cura[vit]*, conjecturant une entreprise générale de construction routière dans la nouvelle province. Le nouveau milliaire de Néron découvert récemment à Komotini et publié dans les présents actes par Chryssa Karadima, où se lit la formule *vias derigendas curavit*, oblige à modifier la restitution proposée et oriente l'interprétation dans une autre direction. Il ne s'agit plus ici de travaux de construction routière à partir de zéro, mais d'une opération consistant à corriger les tracés existants, à les rectifier et redresser pour gommer sinuosités et détours inutiles[14]. Le fait que les deux milliaires retrouvés à ce jour l'ont été sur le parcours de la Via Egnatia ne permet pas d'étendre la conclusion à l'ensemble de la province de Thrace, où l'aménagement de nouvelles routes était sans doute nécessaire, notamment pour relier son chef-lieu, Périnthe, à la Via Egnatia et aux destinations plus lointaines (Byzance et Thrace intérieure); mais la situation de la Thrace égéenne, où préexiste une grande artère transversale, la Via Egnatia, a, semble-t-il, limité l'intervention à modifier et corriger le tracé de la *via militaris* en lui donnant une ligne plus directe, nécessitant en corollaire la pose d'une série de milliaires jalonnant le nouveau tracé. On ne manquera pas d'observer, détail piquant, qu'au 2ᵉ siècle av. J.-C., Philippe V s'était au contraire appliqué à détendre le tracé de l'ancêtre de la Via Egnatia, l'antique voie royale perse, dans sa traversée de la région de Komotini (la Paroreia, le «Piémont» de Thrace) et à l'infléchir en direction du littoral afin d'annexer terres et villes dépendant alors de Maronée[15].

Trajan

On doit à COLLART le mérite d'avoir mis en lumière le rôle capital joué par Trajan dans l'entretien et la restauration de la Via Egnatia[16]. Deux milliaires, mis au jour l'un dans les faubourgs de Thessalonique, l'autre dans un village à l'ouest de Philippes (fig. 3), nous font connaître les travaux entrepris sous l'ordre de Trajan.

---

13 MOTTAS 1989, 98 = AE 1991, 1407.
14 On se gardera de minimiser l'ampleur de ces travaux de correction dans la mesure où ils impliquent en général l'adoption de nouveaux tracés et la construction à neuf de tronçons entiers, ce dont témoigne ici ou là l'utilisation du verbe *derigere* associé à *viam novam* («aménager une nouvelle route en ligne directe»): cf. MAMA VII 193: *Imp(erator) Caesar / divi Nervae f(ilius) / Nerva Traianus Au/g(ustus) ... viam [n]ovam derexit...* (milliaire de Trajan, Aksehir – Philomelion). La rectitude ainsi obtenue est évoquée, sous le stylet du poète, par l'image du Méandre qui aurait miraculeusement perdu ses sinuosités: *Maeander derexit aquas*, «le Méandre aligna ses eaux» (Lucan. 6,437).
15 Liv. 39,27: *Q. Fabium Labeonem, cum in regione ea fuisset, derexisse finem Philippo veterem viam regiam, quae ad Thraciae Paroreian subeat, nusquam ad mare declinantem: Philippum novam postea deflexisse viam, qua Maronitarum urbes agrosque amplectatur* (discours des ambassadeurs de Maronée).
16 COLLART 1935, 395–411. pl. XXVI = AE 1936, 51–52.

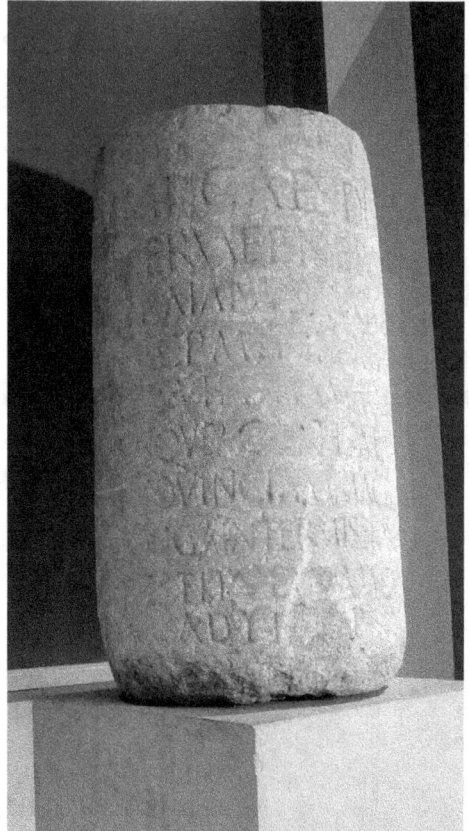

Fig. 3: Milliaire de Trajan. Agios Athanasios. © Photo F. Mottas

Une réfection générale de la voie était devenue indispensable, car elle avait été trop longtemps laissée à l'abandon, ce dont témoigne le texte des milliaires: *viam a Dyrrachio ... per provinciam Macedoniam longa intermissione neglectam restituendam curavit*, «à partir de Dyrrachium, il fit réparer à travers la province de Macédoine la route dont l'entretien avait été trop longtemps négligé». Le terme des travaux est Néapolis (Kavala), le port de Philippes (milliaire de Thessalonique), ou Acontisma, à 8 mille pas de là, sur la frontière est de la Macédoine (milliaire d'Agios Athanasios). La date d'érection du second milliaire, la seule à être assurée, est 112 apr. J.-C.[17]

---

[17] Le milliaire de Thessalonique comporte une incohérence dans la numérotation des «magistratures» impériales. Adams 1989, 32–36, rejette avec de bons arguments la correction proposée par Collart, qui daterait ce milliaire de 107 apr. J.-C., soit une époque où Trajan ne songeait pas encore à la campagne parthique.

Les circonstances qui entourent les travaux entrepris par Trajan ont été clairement analysées par COLLART[18]. La réfection de la Via Egnatia s'inscrit dans le prolongement des réparations et constructions nouvelles réalisées en Italie sur la Via Appia et la Via Traiana, aboutissant toutes deux à Brindes. Du port apulien, la traversée s'effectue dans les conditions les plus favorables en direction de Dyrrachium, promu désormais au rang de principal *caput viae* de la Via Egnatia. L'objectif de Trajan est d'assurer, par une voie transmacédonienne remise à neuf, la communication la meilleure et la plus rapide possible avec l'Orient, dans la perspective, notamment, de la grande expédition parthique, qui débutera en 114 ap. J.-C.

La découverte d'un milliaire à Epitalio (fig. 4)[19], non loin d'Olympie, a montré que la sollicitude de Trajan ne s'était pas limitée à la Via Egnatia. Le contexte est ici différent, car l'inscription ne mentionne pas de réparations, mais, dans une formulation rare, commémore la mise en place de milliaires après une opération de mensuration des routes: *mensuris viarum actis poni iussit*. Le pluriel *viarum* suggère une programme d'envergure, confirmé par la découverte d'autres milliaires présentant le même énoncé. Tous datent de la même année (114–115 apr. J.-C.), et le fait qu'ils aient été retrouvés dans plusieurs régions de la Grèce méridionale – Péloponnèse, Etolie (en face de Patras, sur le territoire de cette colonie)[20], Béotie[21] – démontre une entreprise étendue à l'ensemble de la province d'Achaïe.

La mention explicite de la mensuration des routes[22], clairement associée à la pose des milliaires, semble démontrer que l'action de Trajan est ici présentée comme un fait digne d'être souligné, un fait nouveau, voire un bienfait. L'importance qui lui est accordée dans la rédaction du texte qui s'offrait au regard des passants suggère même qu'il n'existait pas de milliaires dans la province d'Achaïe avant l'intervention de Trajan[23], qui serait le premier empereur à prendre l'initiative et, sans doute, à assumer tout ou partie des frais pour améliorer un réseau préexistant, en procédant à un bornage systématique des principaux chemins de la province, promus désormais au rang de *viae publicae*, comme le suggère KOLB[24].

---

18 COLLART 1935, 411–414.
19 AE 1969/70, 589 = ILGR 156. Epitalio se situe sur la côte ouest du Péloponnèse.
20 AXIOTI 1980, 186–187, n° 1.
21 KALLIONTZIS 2010/13, 309–313, n° 1–2 = AE 2013, 1423–24.
22 Il s'agit d'un cas unique dans le paysage routier romain et l'épigraphie des milliaires. Pratiquée par les *agrimensores* et autres spécialistes, la mesure des routes ne devait pas se limiter à calculer les distances et les intervalles séparant les milliaires, mais, dans le cadre de travaux, s'intéresser aussi à d'autres éléments mesurables tels que la largeur, la pente, la rectitude ou le rayon de courbure des chaussées.
23 On objectera à mon hypothèse l'existence du milliaire d'Auguste à Larissa. Je crois avoir montré plus haut qu'il représente un cas isolé et ne fait pas partie d'une série, comme les milliaires de Trajan mis au jour dans la province d'Achaïe.
24 KOLB 2013, 117.

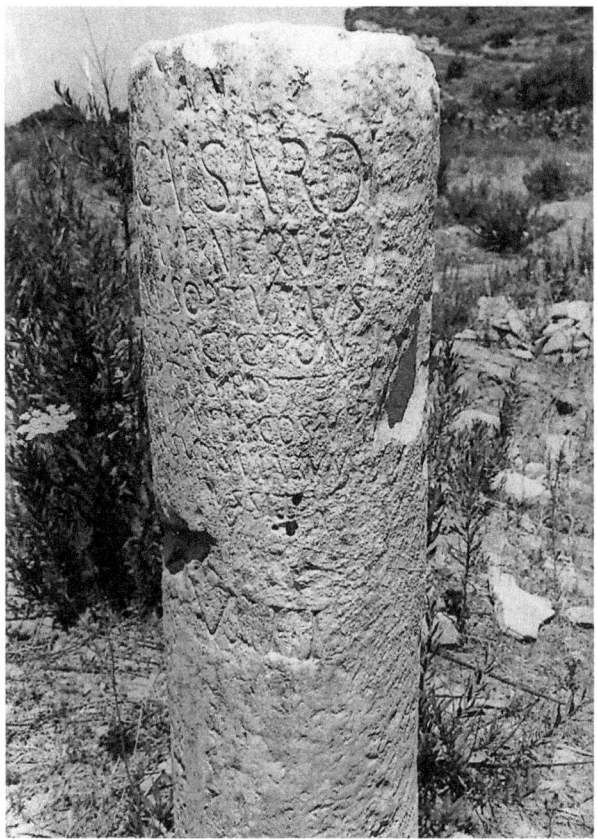

Fig. 4: Milliaire de Trajan. Epitalio. © Photo F. Mottas.

Faut-il alors, en raison de la coïncidence des dates (114 apr. J.-C.), mettre en relation les travaux effectués dans la partie méridionale de la péninsule grecque avec la campagne parthique de Trajan ? L'explication est possible, mais elle ne rend pas compte de l'ampleur de l'opération à l'échelle provinciale, qui touchait aussi et surtout des routes sans vocation stratégique et sans véritable lien avec l'Orient. Dans ce cas, l'œuvre de Trajan paraît répondre davantage à des buts civils et administratifs, peut-être dans une intention évergétique dont la raison nous échappe.

Hadrien et le voyage de Grèce

L'époque d'Hadrien voit fleurir les milliaires dans les provinces grecques. La raison de cet élan nouveau est connue: le voyage de neuf mois que l'empereur entreprend dans la péninsule grecque à son retour d'Asie, en 125 apr. J.-C.[25]. Les milliaires surgissent dans les pas de l'empereur ou précèdent son arrivée annoncée. La plupart sont rédigés en latin, et au nominatif, ce qui semble montrer qu'ils font suite à un ordre émis par l'empereur dans le cadre de la préparation de son voyage.

Les milliaires hadrianiques de Thessalie, datés de 125 apr. J.-C., se distinguent de ceux de Macédoine (124 apr. J.-C.) par une particularité: la mention du *caput viae* y est anonyme (*a civitate*), se référant sans la nommer à la cité la plus proche du milliaire. Ce détail, combiné à la date de 125 et à la formulation identique de la titulature impériale, permet de regrouper les sept milliaires d'Hadrien retrouvés en Thessalie dans une série homogène.

Cette situation mérite une explication, notamment quand on se remémore la série des milliaires d'Achaïe érigés sur l'ordre de Trajan. Jusqu'à ce jour, on n'a pas retrouvé de milliaire de Trajan en Thessalie. Tout se passe comme si les travaux qu'il a entrepris n'ont pas touché la Thessalie. Or, à l'époque de Trajan, la Thessalie était redevenue macédonienne, un transfert que BOWERSOCK[26] attribue à Néron, au moment où il accorde la liberté et l'immunité aux cités de Grèce. Ne doit-on pas dès lors imaginer qu'à l'occasion de son passage en Thessalie – ou dans le cadre de la préparation de son voyage – Hadrien a ordonné une campagne générale de pose de milliaires analogue à celle menée quelque dix ans auparavant par Trajan dans la province d'Achaïe[27] ?

Au sud de la Thessalie, la Béotie, la Mégaride et l'Attique ont livré des milliaires d'Hadrien très différents. A Pétra (Béotie), l'inscription, en grec, émane d'une kômè, un village dont le nom n'est pas mentionné (fig. 5)[28]: . | Αὐτοκράτο|ρος Τραϊανοῦ | Ἀδριανοῦ Καί|σαρος μείλι|ον ἀπὸ Ἀλκο|μεναίου ἀ|νέστησεν | ἡ κώμη.

Selon toute probabilité, le bourg en question n'est autre qu'Alalkoménai, l'inscription précisant qu'il a érigé un milliaire sur la route venant de l'Alalkomenaion (abrégé en Alkomenaion), important sanctuaire panbéotien dédié à Athéna. Le nom de l'empereur est au génitif, cas rarement employé sur les milliaires du Haut-Empire. Plutôt que de le supposer, comme le fait sous toute réserve BIZARD, précédé d'un [Ὑπὲρ σωτηρίας (?)], choix impossible faute de place, la solution la plus simple est d'en faire le complément du nom *meilion* (μείλιον), «milliaire d'Hadrien»[29]. Quant au bas de haste que l'on distingue à la première ligne, parfaitement isolé et centré par rapport aux lignes suivantes, il ne peut que transcrire l'indication de distance,

---

25 Cf. HALFMANN 1986.
26 BOWERSOCK 1965, 282–288. D'autres savants considèrent que la Thessalie fut rendue à la Macédoine au moment où Vespasien révoqua les privilèges accordés aux Grecs par Néron: cf. MÜLLER 2014, 24.
27 MOTTAS/DECOURT 1997, 322.
28 BIZARD 1905, 99–101 = AE 2013, 1425. Cf. KNOEPFLER 2008b, 624 n° 231.
29 On se rappellera que, en grec, le nom *meilion* (μείλιον) est ambigu, signifiant aussi bien mille que milliaire.

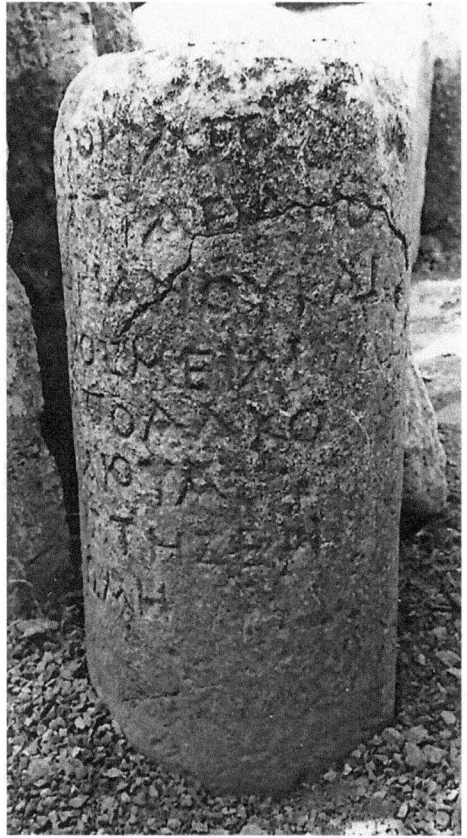

Fig. 5: Milliaire d'Hadrien. Petra. © Photo F. Mottas.

sans qu'on puisse savoir s'il correspond à un *I* latin ou à une lettre grecque comme un gamma (*Γ*), pour ne citer que cette possibilité. Il reste à se demander pour quelle raison c'est une kômè qui est responsable de l'érection d'un milliaire. Serait-ce parce que l'Alalkomenaion, ainsi que le bourg voisin, jouissait d'une forme d'exterritorialité et ne dépendait d'aucune cité, selon l'hypothèse de Knoepfler[30] ?

Découvert il y a 150 ans dans une tour médiévale de l'acropole de Mégare, le fragment de colonne de marbre (fig. 6) gravé au nom d'Hadrien (125 apr. J.-C.)[31] n'a été que tardivement mis en relation avec les travaux entrepris par l'empereur pour améliorer la viabilité de la route côtière menant de Mégare à Corinthe[32].

---

30 Knoepfler 2008b, 624, n° 231; Knoepfler 2008a, 651.
31 IG VII 69.
32 Mottas/Decourt 1997, 323, n. 71.

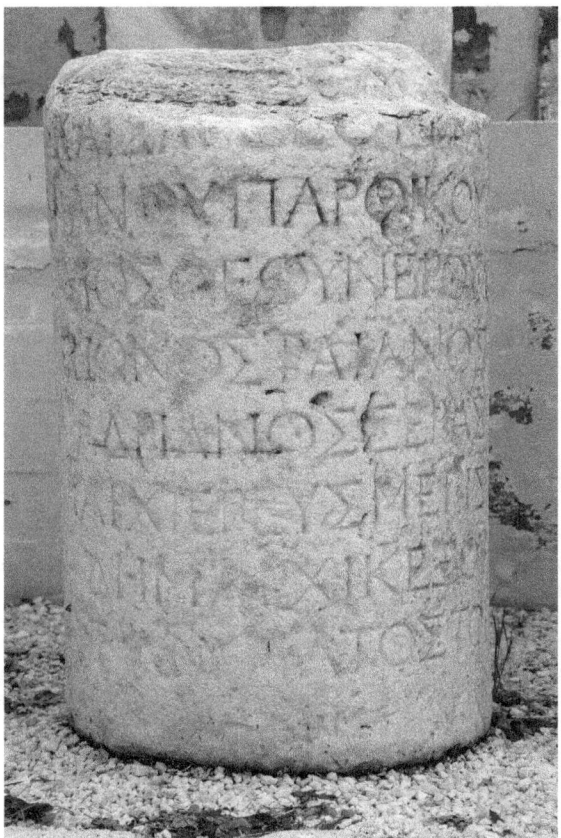

Fig. 6: Milliaire d'Hadrien. Mégare. © Photo Carole Raddato (Frankfurt), Wikimedia.

Ces travaux sont connus par un texte de Pausanias[33]: «Le chemin [de Mégare à Corinthe] porte encore aujourd'hui un nom dérivé de Skiron, ce Skiron qui, alors qu'il était polémarque des Mégariens, fut le premier, disent-ils, à avoir rendu le chemin praticable aux hommes sans équipage[34]. De son côté, l'empereur Hadrien le fit élargir et aménager afin que même les chars puissent s'y croiser.» C'est l'absence d'une indication de distance qui a longtemps fait douter, malgré le nominatif impliquant une intervention directe de l'empereur, qu'il s'agisse d'un milliaire, sans doute la borne qui marquait le départ de la route et commémorait, à Mégare même, son aménagement.

---

33 Paus. 1,44,10.
34 Pour les non-Mégariens, Athéniens notamment, Skiron était ce trop fameux brigand qui, installé sur la corniche la plus étroite du chemin, s'amusait à précipiter les voyageurs dans le vide. Le mythe illustre à merveille les difficultés d'un défilé scabreux, dont les cités voisines se disputaient le contrôle.

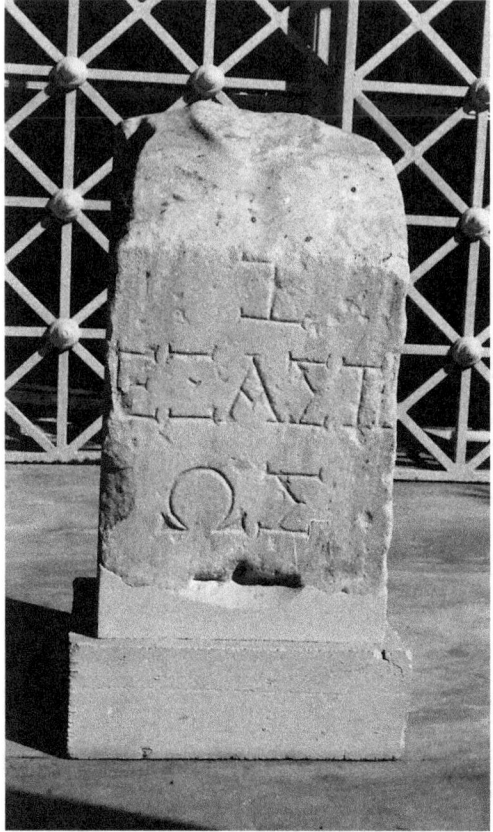

Fig. 7: Hermès-milliaire. Daphni. © Photo F. Mottas.

L'élargissement de la route des Roches Skironiennes ne fut pas la seule construction routière liée au séjour d'Hadrien en Grèce. Cependant le pont de 4 arches qu'il fit jeter sur le Céphise éleusinien témoigne davantage de motivations religieuses. Il est à mettre en relation avec l'initiation d'Hadrien aux Mystères d'Eleusis lors de sa première visite à Athènes, en 124 apr. J.-C. Il est vraisemblable que les hermès-milliaires retrouvés le long de la Voie Sacrée menant d'Athènes au sanctuaire éleusinien lui sont aussi attribuables. Son nom n'y figure pas, sans doute par respect du caractère sacré de ces monuments et de leur contexte. Découvert à Daphni, l'hermès[35] signalant le 7ᵉ mille à partir de la ville d'Athènes, l'ἄστυ, jalonnait la Voie Sacrée dans son premier tronçon, commun avec la route de Corinthe (fig. 7).

---

35 IG II² 5182.

Les Sévères et les guerres parthiques

La grande entreprise du règne des Sévères, les campagnes contre les Parthes, eut un impact certain sur la Via Egnatia, voie essentielle pour l'acheminement et le retour des troupes engagées sur le front oriental de l'empire romain. En témoignent plusieurs milliaires érigés le long de la voie en deux périodes distinctes, d'abord sous Septime Sévère et ses fils, puis sous le règne de Caracalla.

Trouvé à Kavala (Néapolis), sur le territoire de la colonie de Philippes, un milliaire de Septime Sévère et Caracalla Augustes, rédigé en latin, semble en relation directe avec la première campagne parthique (197–201), qui coïncide avec la date d'érection du milliaire (entre 198 et 201)[36]. Malheureusement, le bloc étant mutilé, la fin de l'inscription manque, ce qui empêche de savoir si elle mentionnait des travaux de réparation. Ceux-ci sont des plus vraisemblables, puisqu'un autre tronçon, plus oriental, de la Via Egnatia, sur le territoire de Traianoupolis (province de Thrace), a fait l'objet d'une réfection générale en 202 apr. J.-C.[37]

Les recherches de Papazoglou[38] ont permis d'établir que la Via Egnatia était l'itinéraire prévu pour le retour de Septime Sévère d'Orient en 202 ap. J.-C. L'empereur le suivit-il effectivement, comme le pense Papazoglou? Cela reste une question débattue[39]. Aux travaux réalisés en Thrace et au témoignage des privilèges accordés à certaines des cités traversées (Héraclée des Lyncestes, notamment) s'ajoute néanmoins celui des inscriptions des milliaires de la Via Egnatia rédigées sous forme de dédicace honorifique, en grec et au datif, par les cités d'Amphipolis et d'Allantè, entre 201 et 209[40]. S'il faut se garder de mettre toutes les dédicaces de milliaires en relation avec le passage ou la présence des empereurs honorés[41], l'existence conjointe dans deux cités voisines d'un milliaire latin au nominatif (Philippes) et de milliaires à dédicace grecque (Amphipolis) parle en faveur d'un souci commun d'honorer les Sévères à l'occasion de leur retour victorieux d'Orient, qu'ils aient ou non emprunté l'itinéraire prévu.

---

36 Salac 1923, 80–83, n. 1 = ILGR 244: *Imp(erator) Caes(ar) L(ucius) Septi|mius Severus Pius | Pe{p}rtinacis Aug(ustus) Ar(abicus) | Adiab(enicus) Part(hicus) Max(imus) pont(ifex) | max(imus) imp(erator) XI trib(unicia) pot(estate) V[- - -] | co(n)s(ul) II p(ater) p(atriae) et Imp(erator) C[aes(ar)] L(ucii) Sept(imii)] | Severi Pi(i) Pert[- - -]*.
37 Sur cette réfection, effectuée mille par mille par chacune des *komai* de la cité de Traianoupolis, voir Mottas 1989, 101–104.
38 Papazoglou 1961, 162–175.
39 Gounaropoulou/Hatzopoulos 1985, 56 et n. 2.
40 Amphipolis: Perdrizet 1895, 111, n. 1 = Munro 1896, 315–316 (Paléokomi); Otatzis 1997, 187–190 = AE 1997, 1363 (Akrogiali); Gounaropoulou/Hatzopoulos 1985, 54–61 = SEG 35, 753 (Allantè).
41 Gounaropoulou/Hatzopoulos 1985, 72–73 soulignent fort justement le parfum d'adulation et de propagande que dégagent de telles dédicaces.

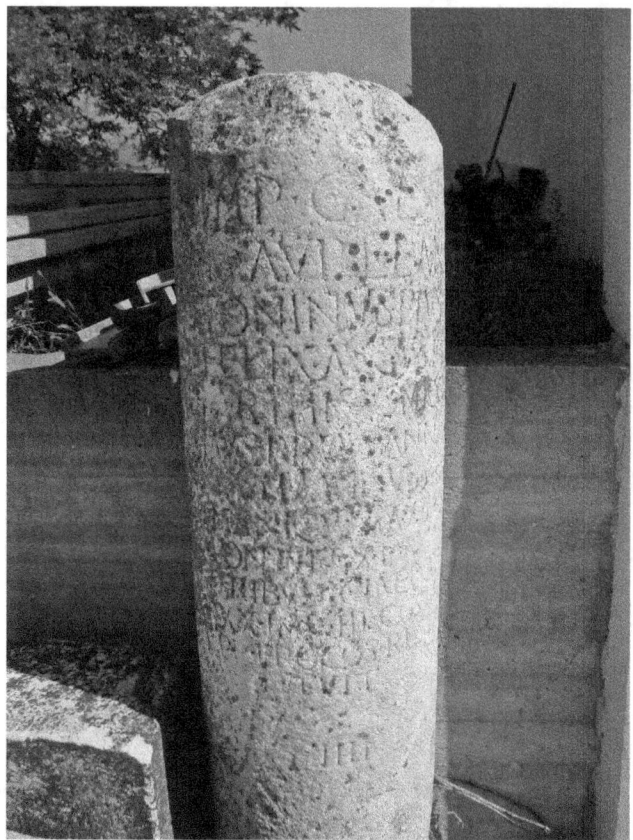

Fig. 8: Milliaire de Caracalla. Chrysoupolis. © Photo F. Mottas.

Le milliaire de Caracalla (fig. 8)[42] trouvé dans la muraille de Chrysoupolis, cité byzantine qui succéda à Eion, le port d'Amphipolis, ne laisse quant à lui aucun doute.

Mentionnant une réfection de la route entre le 10 décembre 216 et le 8 avril 217 apr. J.-C., date indiquée par la dernière puissance tribunitienne de l'empereur – la 20ᵉ –, il s'inscrit dans une série de milliaires de la Via Egnatia, tous datés de la même période[43]. La réparation effectuée, d'une ampleur qu'on n'avait plus connue depuis

---

42 Otatzis 1993, 117, n. 21 = AE 1999, 1441. Lecture revue et corrigée sur la pierre: *Imp(erator) Caes(ar) | M(arcus) Aurel(ius) An/toninus Pius | Felix Augustus | Parthicus maxi/mus Brittani/[c]us maximus Ger/m[a]nicus maximus | pontifex maximus | tribuniciae pot(estatis) | XX imp(erator) III co(n)sul IIII | p(ater) p(atriae) proco(ns(ul) resti/tuit | (milia passuum) IIII.*

43 Liste et texte des milliaires de 216–217 chez Collart 1976, 199, n° 7–10. S'y ajoutent aujourd'hui les milliaires de Chrysoupolis (*supra*, n. 42) et d'Akrogiali (Otatzis 1997, 192–195 = AE 1997, 1365).

l'époque de Trajan, préparait le retour à Rome des légions d'Orient; Caracalla lui-même n'entreprit jamais ce voyage, car il mourut assassiné le 8 avril 217.

L'âge des empereurs-soldats: les milliaires honorifiques

Le milieu du 3ᵉ siècle apr. J.-C., époque des empereurs-soldats, est marqué par un changement radical dans la configuration des milliaires et la composition des textes. Les règnes souvent très courts ne laissent guère le temps aux détenteurs du pouvoir de se lancer dans des entreprises de construction ou de réfection routière d'une certaine envergure. Les inscriptions des milliaires reflètent cette situation nouvelle et précaire. La grande majorité prennent la forme de dédicaces et d'hommages rendus par les cités aux empereurs. C'est l'époque où prolifèrent les milliaires honorifiques. Quant aux supports des inscriptions, ils présentent de moins en moins la forme canonique des milliaires des siècles précédents, le recours à des colonnes ou colonnettes en remploi se faisant de plus en plus fréquent.

Pour illustrer cette évolution, je ne prendrai qu'un seul exemple, dans la province de Thrace. L'accession au pouvoir d'un empereur né en Thrace fait fleurir dans cette province les milliaires rendant hommage à Maximin le Thrace et à son fils Maxime.

Trouvée en 1983 près du village de Xerias (province de Kavala), cette colonne de marbre blanc à la surface très érodée (fig. 9) présente sur le devant une inscription de 16 lignes[44]:

    Α[ὐ]τ ο κ.[ράτ]ορι
    Καίσαρ[ι Γ]αίῳ ['Ιουλίῳ?]
    [[Οὐήρ[ῳ Μαξε]ι[μί-]]]
4   νῳ Εὐ[σεβ]εῖ Ε ὐ-
    τυχεῖ Σεβ(αστῷ) [Γ]ερ-
    μανικῷ Μ ε-
    γ.[ί]στῳ, αὐτο-
8   κράτορι τὸ Δ´,
    δημα[ρχ]ικῆς
    ἐξουσίας τὸ Γ´,
    καὶ Γαίῳ 'Ιουλίῳ

---

[44] Dimensions: 147x28 cm, hauteur des lettres: 3–3,5 cm. Sigma, epsilon et omega de forme lunaire, ligature H+P (l. 3 & 12). Nom de Maximin martelé. Mes remerciements les plus chaleureux vont à M. l'Ephore Bonias, qui m'a permis d'étudier ce milliaire, et à Angelos Zannis, qui n'a pas ménagé ses efforts pour tirer clichés et estampages dans des conditions des plus précaires.

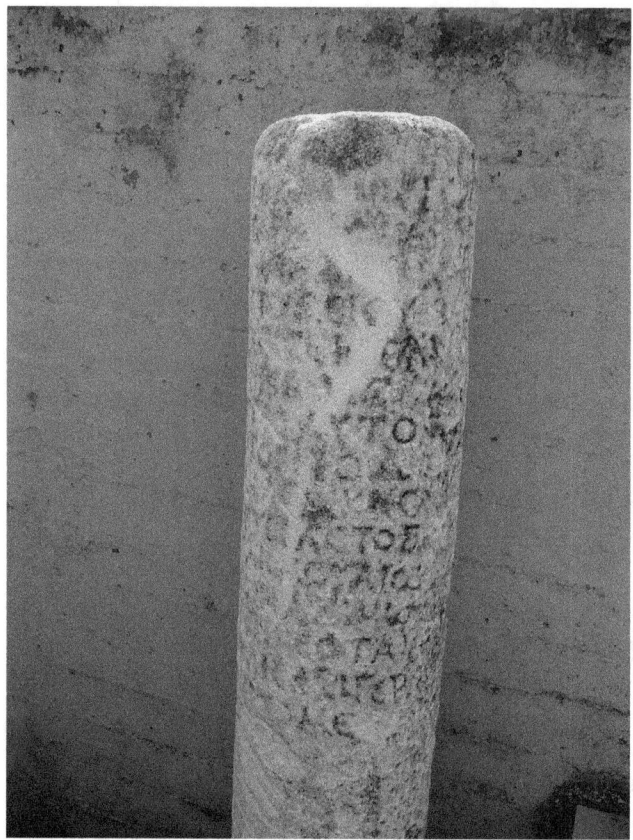

Fig. 9: Milliaire de Maximin et Maxime. Xerias. © Photo F. Mottas.

12 Ο(ὐ)ήρῳ Μαξίμῳ
    τῷ (ἐ)π[ιφ]ανεστά-
    τῳ Καίσαρι Γερ-
    [μ]ανικῷ Μεγ.(ίστῳ)
16 ἡ πόλις ἡ [Τοπει]ρι[τ]ῶν.

L'inscription a été gravée entre le 10 décembre 236, date à laquelle Maximin entre dans sa 3e puissance tribunitienne, et l'an 237, au cours duquel il est salué *imperator* pour la 5e fois. Le dédicant est sans doute la cité de Topeiros (Topiros), dans la province de Thrace. La présence de Maximin en Thrace est attestée par Aurelius Victor[45]: c'est là qu'il apprit, en 237, la sédition de Gordien et la décision du Sénat de le déclarer, lui et son fils, ennemis publics. Au delà de l'adulation convenue ou de la propagande

---

45 Aur. Vict. Caes. 27,3.

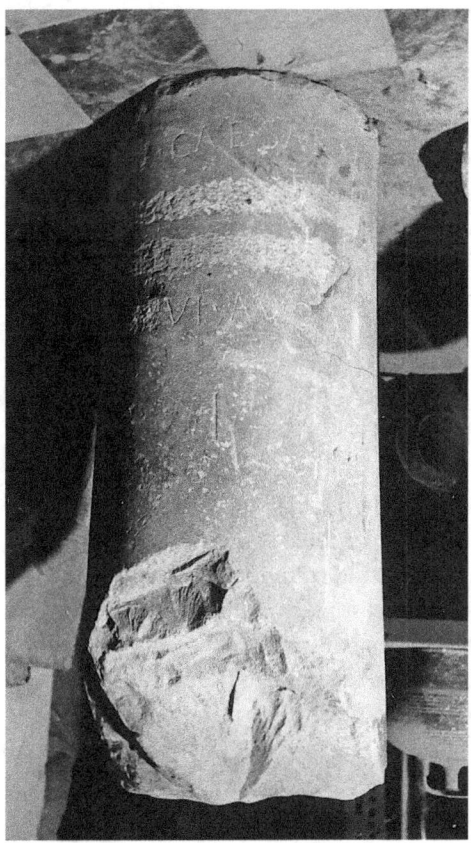

Fig. 10: Milliaire de Probus. Patras. © Photo F. Mottas.

assumée, l'inscription semble aussi refléter l'attachement et la fidélité de la Thrace aux empereurs originaires de la province. Quant au martelage du nom de Maximin, il fera suite à la *damnatio memoriae* de l'empereur, assassiné par ses soldats et décapité afin que sa tête, ramenée à Rome avec celle son fils, servît de preuve de sa disparition définitive.

On retrouve la *damnatio memoriae* à l'origine des modifications apportées aux inscriptions des milliaires sur une colonnette de Patras: gravure et regravures s'y succèdent dans un intervalle de temps assez court, suffisamment court pour qu'on reconnaisse la main d'un même lapicide dans les trois textes qui couvrent les surfaces antérieure et postérieure de la pierre. L'inscription primitive[46], au nominatif, ce qui peut faire

---

46 RIZAKIS 1998, 111, 30b et pl. VI. Malgré le martèlement, je lis encore: *[[Imp(erator)]] Caesar | [[M(arcus) Aureli[u]s]] | [[Probus P(ius) F(elix)]] | [[in]]vi(ctus) Aug(ustus). | (Mille passus) I.*

penser qu'elle émane d'un ordre impérial, lié peut-être à un aménagement routier (construction, réparation ou pose de milliaire), date du règne de Probus, entre 276 et 282 (fig. 10).

Par la suite, elle a été soigneusement martelée pour effacer le souvenir d'un empereur pourtant encensé par les textes qui nous sont parvenus. La *damnatio memoriae* de Probus n'est en effet attestée que par des témoignages épigraphiques[47]. Le milliaire de Patras ne laisse aucun doute sur la volonté affichée de faire disparaître le souvenir de Probus et de n'en garder que l'image d'un vaincu, ce que souligne cyniquement le martelage du préfixe négatif (*in*) du titre élogieux porté par l'empereur déchu – *invictus Augustus*[48]. Quant à son «vainqueur» et successeur, Carus, associé à son fils, le César Carin, son accession au pouvoir à l'automne 282 est célébrée, au datif cette fois-ci, au revers du milliaire[49]. Enfin, quelques semaines ou mois plus tard (fin 282-début 283), le second fils de Carus, Numérien, est à son tour honoré, sans doute au moment où il reçoit le titre de César.

La succession rapide des inscriptions illustre la nouvelle tendance d'utiliser les milliaires, monuments officiels et publics, lisibles par tous, comme supports permettant aux autorités provinciales ou municipales – ici la colonie de Patras – d'afficher leur allégeance aux nouveaux empereurs au fur et à mesure des changements à la tête de l'empire. Collant à l'actualité, les inscriptions des milliaires sont en majorité honorifiques (au datif latin, ou à l'accusatif ou datif grecs), et il devient de plus en plus difficile et hasardeux de les associer à des travaux effectifs de construction ou de restauration du réseau routier.

Dioclétien et le régime tétrarchique

L'arrivée au pouvoir de Dioclétien et son action, tant sur le plan politique, avec l'instauration progressive du régime tétrarchique, qu'administratif, avec la réorganisation des provinces, ont eu une incidence démontrable sur le développement de certaines voies romaines des provinces grecques et son corollaire, l'installation de nouveaux milliaires.

C'est en Thessalie qu'on peut le mieux appréhender les changements intervenus. Promue au rang de province au sein du diocèse des Mésies, la Thessalie voit son réseau routier réorganisé en étoile autour de son chef-lieu, Larissa[50]. Un axe transversal relie

---

47 La liste en a été dressée par LAUBRY/POCCARDI 2009, 78. L'inscription de Patras vient s'ajouter à cette liste, ainsi qu'un milliaire, encore inédit, récemment découvert près d'Amphipolis.
48 Sur l'assassinat et la *damnatio memoriae* de Probus, cf. COTTON/ECK 2004.
49 RIZAKIS 1998, 111, 30a, qui inverse l'ordre chronologique: *Imp(eratori) Caes(ari) M(arco) | Aur(elio) Caro P(io) F(elici) A(ugusto) | et M(arco) Aur(elio) Carino | nobil(issimo) Caes(ari). | [[Mille passus I]] et M(arco) Aurelio | Numeriano nobil(issimo) | Caes(ari). | (Mille passus) I.*
50 Cf. MOTTAS/DECOURT 1997, 323–327.

directement Larissa au tronçon occidental de la Via Egnatia à travers les monts Cambouniens, et se prolonge au sud-est en direction des ports égéens comme Thèbes de Phthiotide (Pyrasos). Cet itinéraire principal est jalonné de milliaires qui appartiennent à une même série, même si leur pose s'étend sur une dizaine d'années, entre 297 et 307 après J.-C., sous la première puis la seconde Tétrarchie. Plusieurs points communs confèrent à ce groupe de milliaires son homogénéité: toutes les inscriptions sont gravées sur des blocs de remploi, colonnes ou colonnettes récupérées, semble-t-il, sur des édifices en ruine; toutes les inscriptions sont en latin; tous les formulaires sont au génitif; tous se concluent sur une même abréviation – MIL – qui remplace le sigle habituellement utilisé pour introduire l'indication de distance: MP, *m(ilia) p(assuum)*. L'emploi du latin dans une région où il n'y a pas de colonie romaine, dans un milieu thessalien hellénophone, marque l'intervention directe de l'autorité impériale, alors que le génitif remplit une double fonction, indiquant d'abord l'appropriation des blocs transformés en milliaires, et complétant aussi et surtout le terme final, dans lequel nous avons proposé de lire *mil(liarium)*.

A l'époque où sont réalisés en Thessalie des travaux d'aménagement routier et érigés de nouveaux milliaires, un regain d'activité semble également toucher la Via Egnatia. On peut y observer une plus grande concentration de milliaires nouvellement installés sur le tronçon de la voie situé entre Héraclée des Lyncestes et Edesse[51]. Ce tronçon s'inscrit exactement dans le prolongement de la route partant de Larissa et franchissant le massif montagneux qui sépare la Thessalie (Perrhébie) de la Macédoine (Eordée). Il est tentant d'intégrer les cinq milliaires mis au jour en Eordée – et le milliaire du Lyncos – dans le même programme d'aménagement routier observé en Thessalie: l'époque correspond, les six milliaires concernés portant une inscription de la deuxième Tétrarchie, et l'utilisation de blocs en remploi rappelle le mode de faire utilisé en Thessalie.

Ici s'arrête cependant la ressemblance entre les deux groupes de milliaires: les remplois macédoniens sont constitués de colonnes coupées en deux dans le sens de la longueur, l'inscription prenant place sur la tranche plate dégagée par la coupe (fig. 11); les inscriptions de la 2e Tétrarchie sont en grec, et le nom et les titres des Augustes et des Césars à l'accusatif. Il s'agit donc clairement de dédicaces honorifiques, précédées de l'adresse à la Bonne Fortune (Ἀγαθῇ Τύχῃ) et suivies de la mention anonyme de la cité dédicante (ἡ πόλις), accompagnée d'une formule de souhait (Εὐτυχῶς).

Ajoutant aux milliaires d'Eordée et du Lyncos un milliaire de Thessalonique[52], COLLART voit dans cette concentration «la preuve d'une nouvelle réfection générale de la route»[53]. A l'appui de sa thèse, on pourrait alléguer les quelques inscriptions de la

---

51 GOUNAROPOULOU/HATZOPOULOS 1985, 12–48.
52 *Infra*, n. 53.
53 COLLART 1976, 196.

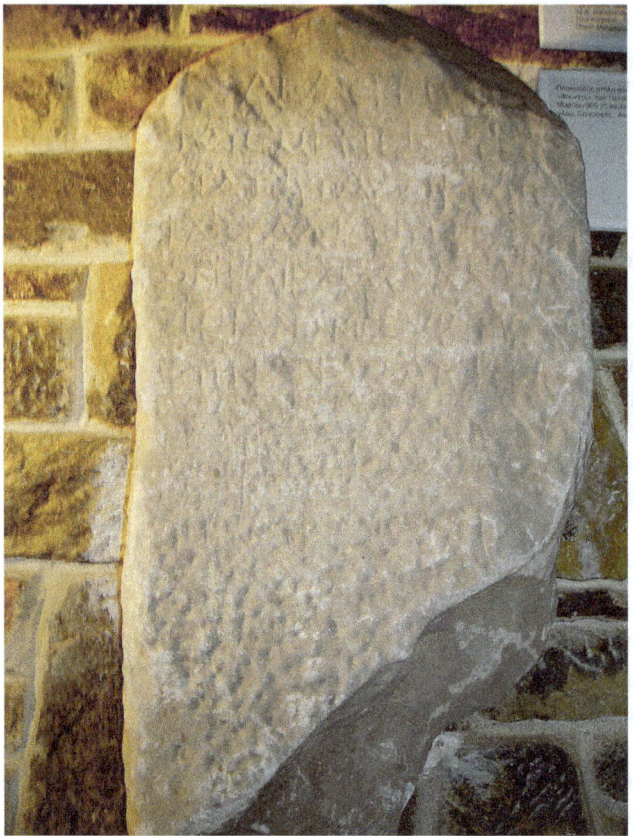

Fig. 11: Milliaire de la 2ᵉ Tétrarchie. Petres. © Photo F. Mottas.

seconde Tétrarchie nouvellement découvertes ou déchiffrées le long du tracé de la Via Egnatia, entre Edesse et Thessalonique (4), et au-delà de cette dernière ville (1)[54]. GOUNAROPOULOU et HATZOPOULOS mettent en garde contre cette interprétation: aucune de ces dédicaces, dont ils soulignent l'exécution souvent négligée, ne mentionne explicitement des travaux de réfection routière[55], et toutes semblent «servir de simples buts d'adulation ou de propagande[56]». Le contexte historique se prête particulièrement bien au foisonnement de marques d'honneur, puisque Galère, alors qu'il n'est encore

---

54 GOUNAROPOULOU/HATZOPOULOS 1985, 43, VII = ILGR 243 (Edesse); 44, VIII (Edesse); 47, IX (Edesse); 64, XIII (Héraclée de Mygdonie) = SEG 35, 737–38. 754; AE 1999, 1439b (Amphipolis).
55 Au contraire d'un milliaire de Galère Auguste jalonnant la route de Larisa à Thessalonique, où le verbe ἀποκατέστησεν («il a fait réparer, il a remis en état») suit le nom et les titres de l'empereur, au nominatif: MOTTAS/DECOURT 1997, 351, n°21 = AE 1997, 1344.
56 GOUNAROPOULOU/HATZOPOULOS 1985, 73.

que César, a élu résidence à Thessalonique, où il célèbre en 298 ap. J.-C. sa victoire sur les Perses en faisant ériger un arc monumental, un tétrapyle élevé au croisement du *decumanus maximus* et de l'avenue menant de son palais à son (futur) tombeau.

Durant la plus grande partie du 4e siècle apr. J.-C., le souci des cités sera d'éviter un impair qui les exposerait à la vindicte des empereurs régnants. Il s'agit d'adapter constamment les textes des milliaires à l'actualité politique. La regravure des inscriptions existantes permet de le faire à moindres frais, en utilisant toute la surface de pierre à disposition. Je me contenterai de citer l'exemple d'un milliaire de Thessalonique[57] où se succèdent les dédicaces, mêlant sans logique apparente datif, nominatif et accusatif grecs: sur une inscription primitive dont ne subsistent après martelage que le début (Ἀγαθῇ Τύχῃ) et la fin (Θεσσαλονικέων ἡ πόλις / (μείλιον) Α΄) se superpose le nom de Dioclétien seul (284–285) avec ses titres, bientôt effacés pour lui associer Maximien (285–286), puis complété par celui des Césars Constance et Galère (293), avant que ceux-ci ne soient promus Augustes et associés à deux nouveaux Césars, Sévère et Maximin (305). Le graveur, ou plutôt son commanditaire, a suivi pas à pas l'édification du régime tétrarchique, de la monarchie de Dioclétien à la seconde Tétrarchie, en passant par une courte période de dyarchie (Dioclétien et Maximien), suivie de la constitution de la première Tétrarchie, avec ses deux Augustes et ses deux Césars, puis de la seconde Tétrarchie, après le retrait des deux fondateurs du régime.

La période constantinienne

Si l'époque de la Tétrarchie a multiplié martelages et regravures pour suivre au plus près l'évolution politique, rendant utopique toute tentative d'interprétation historique des inscriptions de milliaires, et notamment leur mise en relation avec des entreprises de construction ou de réfection du réseau routier, la période suivante, avec l'accession au pouvoir de Constantin, n'est pas moins agitée. Reflétant les soubresauts de l'histoire, l'épigraphie des milliaires constantiniens offre cependant quelques possibilités nouvelles d'interprétation historique.

Un milliaire (fig. 12) trouvé le long de la route menant de Bérée (Beroia/Veria) à Thessalonique présente un intérêt particulier pour l'étude de cette période[58].
Si je laisse de côté l'inscription primitive, presque totalement effacée, et l'inscription la plus récente, dédiée à Valentinien et Valens (364–367 ap. J.-C.)[59], la partie centrale de la pierre est gravée d'un texte où les noms de Constantin et Licinius appa-

---

[57] MAKARONAS 1951 = IG X, II 1009.
[58] EKM I 482. Le lieu de découverte exact est décrit par PETSAS 1964, 359.
[59] EKM I 482 : *Dd(ominis) nn(ostris) / Valentiniano et / Valente Augg(ustis)*.

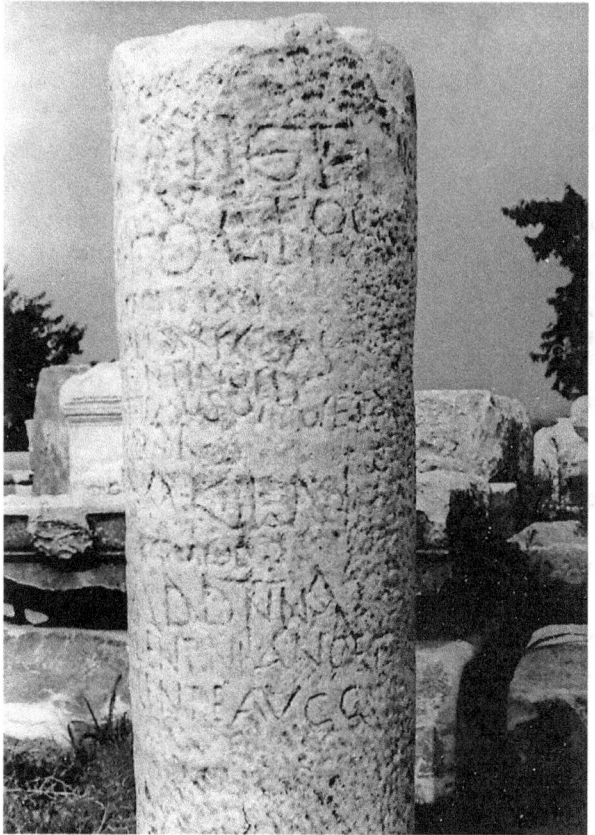

Fig. 12: Milliaire de Constantin et Licinius, puis de Constant. Alexandria. © Photo F. Mottas.

raissent au nominatif latin, entre l'adresse à la Bonne Fortune (Ἀγαθῇ Τύχῃ) et la formule de souhait (Εὐτυχῶς), toutes deux en grec[60].

Ἀγαθῇ τύχῃ.
Imp(erator) Cae[s]ar Fl(avius) Va[l(erius)]
Constantinus P(ius) F(elix)
Inv(i)ctus Augustus et

---

60 Contre l'opinion du premier éditeur, Touratsoglou 1969, 320–321, n° 3, le mélange des langues conduit Gounaropoulou et Hatzopoulos, dans EKM I 482, à conjecturer, sous le texte de Constantin et Licinius, une dédicace en grec honorant Constance et Galère, qui aurait été effacée. Outre le fait qu'on n'en voit aucune trace sur la pierre, il n'est guère plausible que Constantin ait fait effacer le nom de son père pour mettre le sien à sa place.

5   *[[[Imp(erator)]]] Caesar [[[Licini(anus)]]]*
    [[[Licinius P(ius) F(elix) Inv(ictus) Aug(ustus).]]]
    Εὐτυχῶς.

Dans une cité grecque comme Bérée, il ne convient pas d'attacher au nominatif latin une importance particulière. Les formules grecques qui l'entourent assimilent l'inscription à une dédicace, les «auteurs» du texte se contentant de transcrire la titulature officielle dans sa langue d'origine, sans modifier le cas de la source dont ils s'inspirent. L'inscription peut être datée entre l'an 314, qui voit se rétablir la concorde entre Constantin et Licinius, et 317 apr. J.-C., année où Crispus, Constantin le Jeune et Licinius le Jeune sont faits Césars. Mais, après 320, le nom et les titres de Licinius seront martelés, le conflit entre les deux empereurs s'étant rouvert, jusqu'à la défaite de Licinius en 324.

Autour de l'inscription constantinienne, au-dessus et au-dessous, est gravé ensuite un texte en gros caractères très irréguliers, le graveur prenant néanmoins grand soin de ne pas altérer le nom et les titres de Constantin le Grand (ni même la formule de souhait!), alors qu'il s'efforce par ailleurs d'anéantir toute trace du nom et des titres de Licinius.

[Ὁ] κ[ύρ]ιο[ς ἡμῶν]
[ὁ ε]ὐανθέ[στ]ατος
Αὔγουστος
Ἀγαθῇ τύχῃ.
Imp(erator) Cae[s]ar Fl(avius) Va[l(erius)]
Constantinus P(ius) F(elix)
Inv(i)ctus Augustus et
Caesar
Φλ(άβιος) Βα(λέριος) Κων-
Ε_τυχες.
σταντας.

Honorant l'un des fils de Constantin, Constant[61], l'inscription semble avoir été gravée en deux temps, d'abord lorsqu'il est devenu César, en 333, comme l'indique le fait que le graveur a conservé le titre de César de Licinius afin de le réutiliser pour Constant. Puis, en 337, son accession à l'Augustat[62] est célébrée en même temps qu'il reçoit l'administration de la Thrace et de la Macédoine, après la mort de Delmatius. L'espérance

---

61 Le nominatif Κώνσταντας n'est pas à considérer comme un solécisme; il est simplement reformé sur l'accusatif Κώνσταντα, comme πατέρας, formé sur πατέρα, remplace progressivement le grec classique πατήρ.
62 On remarquera que le nouvel Auguste remplace son propre gentilice, Iulius, par Valerius, gentilice de son père Constantin, décédé quelques mois auparavant.

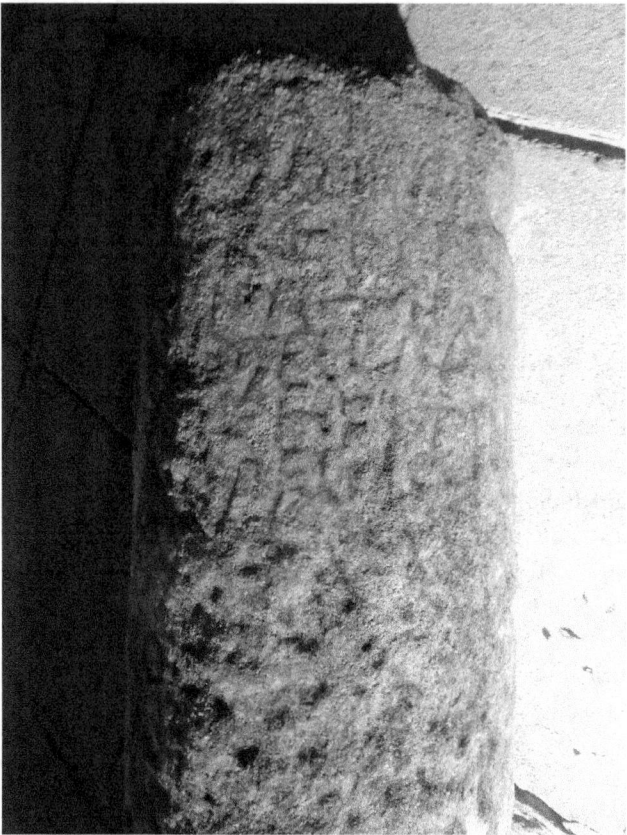

Fig. 13: Inscription de Constantin et de ses fils. Xerias. © Photo A. Zannis.

placée dans le jeune Auguste, âgé alors de 14 ans, est exprimée par une épithète assez rare sur les milliaires, εὐανθέστατος, équivalent du latin *florentissimus*.

Trouvé aux confins de la Macédoine et de la Thrace, sur la Via Egnatia, le milliaire de Maximin et Maxime, étudié quelques pages plus haut, présente un autre cas de remploi intensif à partir du règne de Dioclétien jusqu'à celui de Valens, Gratien et Valentinien II. Toute la surface disponible au dos de la pierre a été exploitée pour graver 5 textes successifs (fig. 13); la deuxième inscription revêt un intérêt particulier pour notre propos[63].

---

[63] L'inscription est encore bien visible sous les textes postérieurs grâce à son alignement précis, à la petite taille des lettres (2,5 cm; U = V) et à la répétition superposée du nom Flavius, abrégé en FL. Un grand merci à ANGELOS ZANNIS pour les photos de la pierre et des estampages, qui confirment la lecture.

> [- - -]
> [C]oṇ[st]aṇ[t]ino Ạu[gus]ṭ[o]
> et Fl(avio) Iul(io) C[ri]spo
> [e]ṭ Fl(avio) Cl(audio) Coṇ[stan]ṭin[o]
> ẹt Fl(avio) Cl(audio) Con[s]ṭ[ant]io
> 5 ṇobbb(ilissimis) Ç[ae]ṣṣ[s(aribus)].

Dédiée à Constantin Auguste et à ses fils Crispus, Contantin II et Constance II Césars, l'inscription a été gravée après l'élévation de Constance le Jeune au Césarat, le 8 novembre 324, et avant la mort de Crispus, en 326. La date mérite qu'on s'y arrête: elle coïncide avec des événements historiques qui ont touché de près la Macédoine orientale et la Thrace en 324 apr. J.-C., événements avec lesquels l'inscription est certainement en relation directe. Car la région se trouve au cœur des opérations militaires qui mèneront à la double défaite de Licinius devant Andrinople et dans l'Hellespont. Ces opérations, à la fois terrestres et maritimes, sont menées conjointement par Constantin, parti de Thessalonique par la Via Egnatia, et par Crispus, commandant la flotte stationnée au Pirée et appelée à croiser au large des côtes macédoniennes et thraces avant de rejoindre l'Hellespont, où elle infligera à la flotte de Licinius une cuisante défaite. L'inscription de Xerias est liée à la présence des deux empereurs dans les parages, qu'elle prépare leur passage ou le suive de peu.

Les invasions barbares

A partir du milieu de 4ᵉ siècle apr. J.-C. et jusqu'au règne d'Arcadius et d'Honorius, il semble que, du moins dans l'état actuel de nos connaissances, plus aucun milliaire nouveau n'ait été érigé sur sol grec. Les inscriptions en l'honneur de Julien, Jovien, Valentinien, Valens et Gratien sont toutes venues s'ajouter à des textes préexistants, sur des milliaires déjà en place. La seule exception est une colonne lue au 15ᵉ siècle par Cyriaque d'Ancone sur la muraille de Patras[64]: les noms de Valentinien et Valens y sont au génitif grec, sans indication du nombre de milles, mais l'on ignore si l'ensemble de la colonne, aujourd'hui perdue, était visible, avec, le cas échéant, d'autres inscriptions dissimulées au regard de l'observateur. Le génitif, sur un monument en forme de colonne, est néanmoins un indice en faveur d'un milliaire, sinon nouveau, du moins réutilisant un matériau disponible.

Il faut attendre les dernières années du 4ᵉ siècle et les incursions barbares en Grèce, notamment les ravages exercés par Alaric et les Goths dans la région d'Athènes et les villes du Péloponnèse, pour que les autorités romaines réagissent et se préoccupent

---

64 CIG I 1558 = Rizakis 1998, 105–106, n° 26.

de restaurer les installations mises à mal. Tandis que Stilicon règle la question sur le plan militaire, les autorités civiles prennent les mesures de restauration nécessaires. Un certain nombre de milliaires témoignent des efforts entrepris, notamment autour de Patras et d'Athènes, où le proconsul Eusèbe (396–397?) restaure d'anciens milliaires ou en fait ériger de nouveaux. Plusieurs milliaires d'Arcadius et Honorius trouvés le long de la Voie Sacrée menant à Eleusis se révèlent être des blocs de récupération, comme des stèles gravées de textes grecs d'époque classique ou hellénistique. Il revient à PERDRIZET[65] le mérite d'avoir mis ces monuments en relation avec un rescrit impérial envoyé au Comte d'Orient Asterius le 1er novembre 397[66]: «Puisque tu nous as signalé que les routes et les ponts fréquentés par le trafic, ainsi que les aqueducs et les murailles, nécessitent l'engagement de moyens financiers, nous pensons que tous les matériaux adéquats provenant de la démolition des temples doivent être affectés aux besoins mentionnés.»

Avec le règne commun d'Arcadius, Honorius et Théodose II (402–408 ap. J.-C.) s'achève l'histoire des milliaires dans les provinces de la péninsule grecque: une dernière série d'inscriptions, gravées sur d'anciens milliaires de la Via Egnatia, y honore les trois Augustes, sans doute peu après la naissance de Théodose, le plus jeune empereur à avoir reçu le titre suprême, quelques mois seulement après avoir vu le jour[67]. Le génitif latin y marque la réutilisation et la réappropriation de milliaires plus anciens, de Caracalla dans le cas étudié (fig. 14).

   [Ddd(ominorum) nnn(ostrorum)]
   [Arcadi et] Ono-
   [ri et T]heodo-
   [si s]s[s]e(m)ppp(iternorum) Au[ggg(ustorum).]

Si l'on revient, en conclusion, sur la question posée au début de cette étude, la pose des milliaires a obéi à des impératifs qui ont beaucoup évolué au cours des cinq siècles et demi de présence romaine dans la péninsule grecque. Les premiers milliaires sont installés peu après la création de la première province et sont liés à l'aménagement de la Via Egnatia reliant Rome à l'Orient à travers la Macédoine. Par la suite, la grande voie militaire, quelque temps négligée, retrouve toute son importance lors des campagnes parthiques: elle est restaurée sur toute son étendue – et pourvue de nouveaux milliaires – une première fois sous Trajan, puis sous Septime-Sévère et Caracalla,

---

65 PERDRIZET 1897, 573.
66 Cod. Theod. 15,1,36.
67 Inscriptions visibles sur deux milliaires du territoire de Philippes, l'un encore inédit (Argyroupolis), l'autre publié par KOUKOULI-CHRYSANTHAKI 1972, 474–485 & fig. 1–2 (provenance: Lefki/Nea Karvali) = AE 1974, 590. L'autopsie de la pierre m'a permis de reconstituer l'inscription, dont les lettres encore visibles ne laissent aucun doute sur les destinataires.

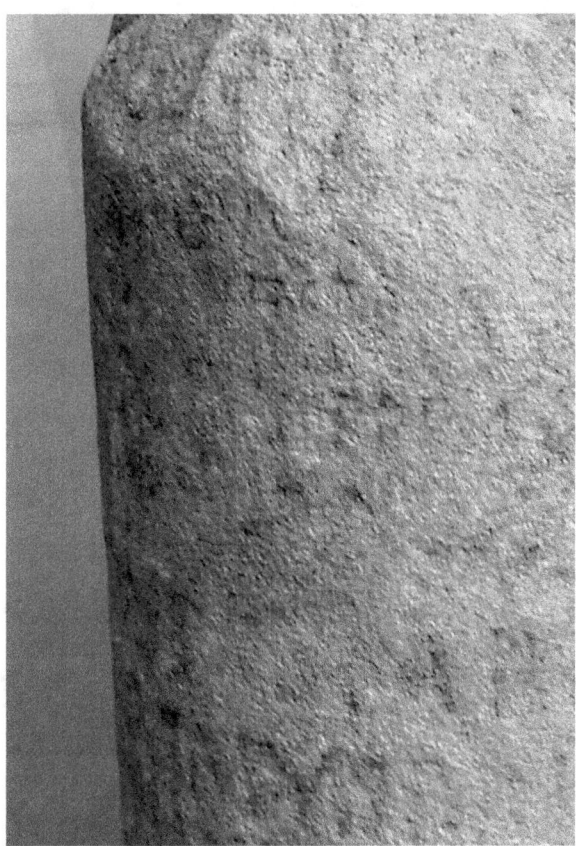
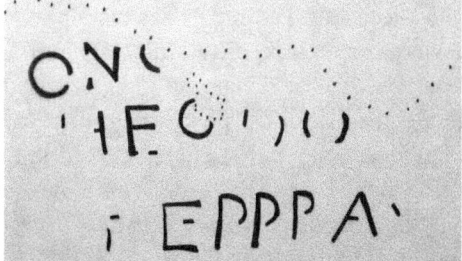

Fig. 14: Inscription d'Arcadius, Honorius et Théodose II. Lefki. © Photo F. Mottas.

après que son tronçon oriental eut été corrigé et complété peu après la création de la province de Thrace.

Les autres routes de la péninsule grecque, sans véritable vocation stratégique, n'intéressent les empereurs que lors de changements administratifs: un milliaire isolé, indicateur de distance plus que jalon routier, est installé sous Auguste aux portes de Larissa au moment où la Thessalie quitte la Macédoine pour entrer dans la province d'Achaïe. Plus au sud, l'Achaïe, restée à l'écart des grands travaux, doit à la sollicitude de Trajan d'être pourvue de milliaires après une opération générale de mensuration des routes existantes. Absente de ce programme, la Thessalie attendra la venue d'Hadrien en Grèce pour recevoir à son tour une série de milliaires. Le voyage d'Hadrien représente pour la péninsule grecque une occasion qui ne se renouvellera pas d'améliorer les conditions de communication par des travaux d'une certaine envergure: élargissement de la route en corniche Mégare-Corinthe, aménagement de la Voie Sacrée Athènes-Eleusis (avec construction d'un pont) et pose des milliaires accompagnant ces travaux. Après cette embellie, les interventions impériales se font plus rares: quelques milliaires où le nom des empereurs apparaît au nominatif témoignent peut-être de travaux – rarement mentionnés explicitement par les inscriptions – aux abords des villes.

Phénomène nouveau, apparu au 2e siècle de notre ère, les inscriptions de milliaires rédigées au génitif (latin ou grec) ont retenu notre attention. La plupart sont gravées sur des colonnes ou colonnettes en remploi, et le génitif y marque entre autres l'appropriation et le passage dans le domaine public d'un bloc qui n'en faisait pas partie auparavant. C'est le cas notamment des milliaires installés par Dioclétien et les Tétrarques en Thessalie: leur pose coïncide avec la création d'une nouvelle province autonome et avec le remaniement du réseau routier autour de Larissa, sa capitale. On retrouve le même génitif «possessif» sur une certain nombre de milliaires installés sous le règne d'Arcadius et Honorius, en conformité avec le rescrit autorisant la réutilisation de blocs tirés des temples païens pour la réfection des routes endommagées par les incursions barbares.

Dès le 3e siècle apr. J.-C., la configuration des milliaires n'a cessé d'évoluer: la colonne en remploi remplace le milliaire classique (cube et cylindre), l'inscription au nominatif cède la place au texte au datif ou à l'accusatif. La plupart des inscriptions sont désormais de type honorifique, hommages des cités aux souverain(s) régnant(s). Le milliaire est devenu un media public permettant d'afficher son allégeance au pouvoir en place ou de véhiculer sa propagande. Il est de ce fait plus difficile de saisir les circonstances de son érection, sauf lorsqu'on est aidé par le contexte historique ou une coïcidence chronologique: présence de Maximin le Thrace dans sa province natale, opérations militaires de Constantin et de Crispus en Thrace égéenne, accession de Constant à l'Augustat avec autorité sur la province de Macédoine.

Le phénomène du remploi atteint son paroxysme au 4e siècle: il n'est pas rare de trouver, sur d'anciens milliaires réutilisés, jusqu'à 6, 7 voire 8 inscriptions superposées, toute la surface de la pierre étant mise à profit, au besoin en la retournant sens dessus dessous. L'instabilité politique qui se développe au 3e siècle, la succession rapide des empereurs et les luttes incessantes pour le pouvoir qui se poursuivent au 4e siècle ont pour effet cette prolifération d'inscriptions gravées à la hâte sur la même pierre. Il est vain dès lors de s'interroger sur les circonstances qui entourent ces inscriptions, puisque le milliaire a complètement perdu sa fonction première pour se métamorphoser en palimpseste, jusqu'à en devenir parfaitement illisible.

Bibliographie

ADAMS 1989 = J.P. ADAMS, Trajan and Macedonian Highways, in: Ancient Macedonia V. Papers Read at the Fifth International Symposium Held in Thessaloniki, October 10–15, 1989, Thessaloniki 1993, 29–39.
ΑΧΙΟΤΙ 1980 = Κ. ΑΧΙΟΤΙ, Ρωμαϊκοί δρόμοι της Αιτωλοακαρνανίας, AD 35, 1980, 186–205.
BIZARD 1905 = L. BIZARD, Inscriptions de Béotie, BCH 29, 1905, 99–104.
BOWERSOCK 1965 = G.W. BOWERSOCK, Zur Geschichte des römischen Thessaliens, RhM 108, 1965, 277–289.
COLLART 1935 = P. COLLART, Une réfection de la «Via Egnatia» sous Trajan, BCH 59, 1935, 395–415.
COLLART 1976 = P. COLLART, Les milliaires de la Via Egnatia, BCH 100, 1976, 177–200.
COTTON/ECK 2004 = H.M. COTTON/W. ECK, Lateinische Inschriften aus der Ustinov Collection in Oslo und ein opistograph mit der *damnatio memoriae* des Kaisers Probus, in: L. RUSCU et al. (ed.), Orbis antiquus. Studia in honorem Ioannis Pisonis, Cluj-Napoca 2004, 48–57.
EKM I = L. GOUNAROPOULOU/M.B. HATZOPOULOS, Ἐπιγραφὲς Βεροίας, Ἐπιγραφὲς Κάτω Μακεδονίας [Inscriptions de Basse Macédoine], vol. I, Athènes 1998.
FILOV 1912/13 = B.D. FILOV, Антични паметници въ Народния музей, BullSocArchBulg 3, 1912/1913, 1–52.
GOUNAROPOULOU/HATZOPOULOS 1985 = L. GOUNAROPOULOU/M.B. HATZOPOULOS, Les milliaires de la Voie Egnatienne entre Héraclée des Lyncestes et Thessalonique, Athènes 1985.
HALFMANN 1986 = H. HALFMANN, Itinera Principum, Stuttgart 1986.
ILGR = M. ŠAŠEL KOS, Inscriptiones Latinae in Graecia repertae. Additamenta ad CIL III, Faenza 1979.
KALLIONTZIS 2010/13 = Y. KALLIONTZIS, Επιγραφές Βοιωτίας, Horos 22–25, 2010/2013, 309–326.
KNOEPFLER 2008a = D. KNOEPFLER, Épigraphie et histoire des cités grecques, ACF 107, 2006/2007 [2008], 637–662.
KNOEPFLER 2008b = D. KNOEPFLER, Bulletin épigraphique, Béotie. Eubée, REG 121, 2008, 613–668.
KOLB 2012 = A. KOLB, The Conception and Practice of Roman Rule: The Example of Transport Infrastructure, Geographia antica 20–21, 2011/2012, 53–70.
KOLB 2013 = A. KOLB, Die Erfassung und Vermessung der Welt bei den Römern, in: K. GEUS/ M. RATHMANN (ed.), Vermessung der Oikumene, Berlin 2013, 107–188.
KÖNIG 1970 = I. KÖNIG, Die Meilensteine der Gallia Narbonensis, Bern 1970.
KOUKOULI-CHRYSANTHAKI 1972 = C. KOUKOULI-CHRYSANTHAKI, Via Egnatia-Akontisma, AthAnArch 5, 1972, 474–485.
LAUBRY/POCCARDI 2009 = N. LAUBRY/G. POCCARDI, Une dédicace inédite à l'empereur Probus provenant des thermes de la porte Marina à Ostie, ArchCl 60, 2009, 275–305.
MAKARONAS 1951 = C. MAKARONAS, Via Egnatia and Thessalonike, in: G.E. MYLONAS (ed.), Studies Presented to David Moore Robinson, vol. 1, Washington 1951, 380–388.
MOTTAS 1989 = F. MOTTAS, Les voies de communication antiques dans la Thrace égéenne, in: H.E. HERZIG/R. FREI-STOLBA (ed.), Labor omnibus unus. Gerold Walser zum 70. Geburtstag dargebracht von Freunden, Kollegen und Schülern, Stuttgart 1989, 82–104
MOTTAS/DECOURT 1997 = F. MOTTAS/J.-C. DECOURT, Voies et milliaires romains de Thessalie, BCH 121, 1997, 311–354
MRR 1986 = T.R.S. BROUGHTON, The Magistrates of the Roman Republic, 3 (Supplement), 1986.
MÜLLER 2014 = C. MÜLLER, Les Romains et la Grèce égéenne du 1er s. av. J.-C. au 1er s. apr. J.-C.: un monde en transition ?, Pallas 96, 2014, 193–216.
MUNRO 1896 = J.A.R. MUNRO, Epigraphic Notes from Eastern Macedonia and Thrace, JHS 16, 1896, 313–322.
ΟΤΑΤΖΙS 1993 = Μ. ΟΤΑΤΖΙS [Οτατζής], Οι Σέρρες και η περιοχή τους από την αρχαία στη μεταβυζαντινή κοινωνία (διεθνές συνέδριο), Serres 1993 [Thessaloniki 1998], 113–136 = Μ. ΟΤΑΤΖΙS, Εγνατία οδός: Από την Αμφίπολη στους Φιλίππους, Kavala 1996, 9–59.

Otatzis 1997 = M. Otatzis [Οτατζής], Μιλιάρια της Εγνατίας Οδού από τα Κερδύλλια Σερρών, in: P. Adám-Veléni et al. (ed.), Μνήμη Μανόλη Ανδρόνικου, Thessaloniki 1997, 187–198.

Papazoglou 1961 = F. Papazoglou, Septimia Aurelia Heraclea, *BCH* 85, 1961, 162–175.

Perdrizet 1895 = P.F. Perdrizet, Voyage dans la Macédoine première I. Inscriptions de la région strymonique (suite), *BCH* 19, 1895, 109–112.

Perdrizet 1897 = P. Perdrizet, Nouvelles et correspondance, *BCH* 21, 1897, 572–573.

Petsas 1964 = P.M. Petsas, ΑΡΧΑΙΟΤΗΤΕΣ ΚΑΙ ΜΝΗΜΕΙΑ ΔΥΤ. ΜΑΚΕΔΟΝΙΑΣ, *AD* 19, 1964, 350–423.

Rizakis 1998 = A.D. Rizakis, Achaïe II. La cité de Patras: épigraphie et histoire, Athènes 1998.

Romiopoulou 1974 = C. Romiopoulou, Un nouveau milliaire de la Via Egnatia, *BCH* 98, 1974, 813–816.

Salac 1923 = A. Salac, Inscriptions du Pangée, de la région Drama-Cavalla et de Philippes, *BCH* 47, 1923, 49–96.

Samartzidou 1990 = S. Samartzidou (Σαμαρτζίδου), Εγνατία οδός: Από τους Φιλίππους στη Νεάπολη, in: Μνήμη Δ. Λαζαρίδη: Πόλις και χώρα στην αρχαία Μακεδονία και Θράκη, Actes du Congrès archéologique de Kavala, vol. 1986, Ελληνογαλλικές Έρευνες, vol. 1, Thessaloniki 1986 [1990], 559–579.

Touratsoglou 1969 = I. Touratsoglou, Μιλιάρια τοῦ μουσείου Βεροίας [Milliaires du Musée de Veroia], *Makedonika* 9, 1969, 317–322.

Vanderspoel 2010 = J. Vanderspoel, Provincia Macedonia, in: J. Roisman/I. Worthington (ed.), A Companion to Ancient Macedonia, Oxford 2010, 264–267.

Walbank 1985 = F.W. Walbank, Via illa nostra militaris: some thoughts on the Via Egnatia, in: F.W. Walbank, Selected Papers: Studies in Greek and Roman History and Historiography, Cambridge 1985, 193–209.

Michael Rathmann
Miliaria in der Provinz *Lusitania*

Abstract: The article outlines the scope and content of the edition of the milestones of the Roman province of Lusitania planned as part of CIL XVII. So far, 266 milestones have been recorded in a database, collecting material that is currently scattered across numerous publications. This has shown certain peculiarities with regard to their time of origin, their distribution, and the imperial titulatures inscribed on them: There are no republican and relatively few late-antique examples; most of them are from the 1st and 2nd century. The inscriptions on the miliaria are consistently shorter than comparable texts from other provinces of the West; only rarely are cities epigraphically named as *capita viae*. Around 80% of the milestones come from one single road, the Camino de la Plata.

Zusammenfassung: Der Beitrag umreißt Umfang und Inhalt der geplanten Edition der Meilensteine der römischen Provinz *Lusitania* im Rahmen CIL XVII-Reihe. Bislang wurden 266 Meilensteine in einer Datenbank erfasst, die verstreut in der Fachliteratur publiziert sind. Dabei zeigen sich hinsichtlich der Entstehungszeit, der Kaisertitulaturen und der Fundverteilung einige Besonderheiten: Es gibt keine republikanischen und relativ wenig spätantike Stücke; die meisten stammen aus dem 1. und 2. Jahrhundert. Die Inschriften auf den Milarien sind durchgängig kürzer als Vergleichstexte aus anderen Provinzen des Westens; nur selten sind die Stadtnamen als *caput viae* epigraphisch belegt. Rund 80 % der Meilensteine stammen von einer einzigen Straße, dem Camino de la Plata.

1 Einleitung

Ohne eine leistungsfähige Verkehrsinfrastruktur hätte das Imperium Romanum nicht zu einer weltgeschichtlichen Größe werden können. Auch in der Eroberungsphase war Rom rund um das Mittelmeer auf ein bereits existierendes Wegenetz angewiesen. Hierbei handelte es sich pikanterweise stets um das Wege- und Straßensystem des politischen Gebildes, das gerade von Rom niedergeworfen und in dessen Herrschaftsraum implementiert wurde. Folglich können wir heute beobachten, dass die Zeitspanne zwischen der militärischen Eroberung und der administrativ-wirtschaftlichen Durchdringung eines Raums nicht zuletzt von der Entwicklungsstufe des vorgefundenen Straßennetzes abhing.

Mit Blick auf die iberische Halbinsel sehen wir, dass die von Keltiberern und Karthagern infrastrukturell erschlossenen Räume nicht zuletzt deshalb rascher von Rom erobert werden konnten, weil bereits ein qualitätvolles Wege- und Straßennetz existierte. Die offenbar schlechter erschlossene kastilische Hochebene, Galizien oder

Lusitanien gerieten jedoch erst später unter römische Herrschaft. Gemessen daran und vor dem Hintergrund der Blütephase Iberiens in der Hohen Kaiserzeit überrascht es, dass eine zusammenfassende Studie zur Genese der iberischen Verkehrsinfrastruktur bislang nicht vorliegt.[1] Gerade die Korrelation von Annexion und römischem Wegebau oder Straßenausbau scheint unter mehreren Gesichtspunkten ein lohnenswertes Forschungsvorhaben zu sein, um die Prozesse der eigentlichen Eroberung des iberischen Raums, seiner anschließenden wirtschaftlichen und administrativen Erfassung samt der territorialen Verteilung der Koloniegründungen[2] sowie den individuellen Grad der Romanisierung besser verstehen zu können.

Die Basis jeder Erforschung des römischen Straßenwesens ist eine wissenschaftliche Edition der Miliarien im Kontext aller weiteren infrastrukturell relevanten Quellen. Dabei fällt mit Blick auf Iberien ein deutliches regionales Ungleichgewicht auf: Die Römerstraßen des heutigen Andalusien sind 1990 durch PIERRE SILLIÈRES umfassend aufgearbeitet worden.[3] 1992 legte JOAQUÍN LOSTAL PROS eine fundierte Edition der tarraconensischen Meilensteine (ohne Galizien) vor, der 2015 der CIL-Band XVII/1 der Herausgeber MANFRED SCHMIDT und CAMILLA CAMPEDELLI zum gleichen Raum folgte.[4] Schließlich legten ANTONIO RODRÍGUEZ COLMENERO, SANTIAGO FERRER SIERRA und RUBÉN D. ÁLVAREZ ASOREY 2004 eine Ausgabe der galizischen Miliarien vor.[5] Für die *Lusitania* muss man allerdings auf das CIL II von 1869 mit dem Nachtrag von 1892 zurückgreifen. HÜBNER hatte seinerzeit öfters Material nur aus zweiter Hand übernommen und einen Teil der Steine schon aufgrund der damaligen Reise- und Kommunikationsmöglichkeiten nicht persönlich in Augenschein nehmen können. Lediglich für den Camino de la Plata, also die Verbindung von *Emerita Augusta* (Mérida) über *Salmantica* (Salamanca) nach *Ocelum Duri* (Zamora), liegen mit den Arbeiten von JOSÉ MANUEL ROLDÁN HERVÀS und CARMEN PUERTA TORRES zwei neuere Darstellungen vor.[6]

Wer sich einen quantitativen Überblick über die Miliarien der *Lusitania* verschaffen möchte, ist auf die Epigraphik-Datenbank CLAUSS/SLABY (EDCS) angewiesen.[7] So findet man dort zwar aktuell 212 Meilensteine, sieht sich aber unter anderem mit dem Problem konfrontiert, dass diese nicht systematisch nach Straßen geordnet sind. Zudem sind die Miliarien nicht in den Kontext weiterer relevanter Quellen zum Straßenwesen eingebunden, etwa Bauinschriften, Itinerare oder archäologische Zeug-

---

[1] Vgl. den Beitrag von NÜNNERICH-ASMUS 1993, der erkennbar an den fehlenden Vorarbeiten zum römischen Straßenwesen gescheitert ist.
[2] GALSTERER 1971.
[3] SILLIÈRES 1990.
[4] CIL XVII/1,1.
[5] RODRIGUEZ COLMENERO et al. 2004. Ihr Werk ist jedoch nicht frei von strukturellen Mängeln. Vgl. Rez. von KOLB 2007. Ein hilfreiches Arbeitsinstrument für den Nordosten Iberiens bietet ALBALADEJO 2012.
[6] ROLDAN 1971; PUERTA 1995; vgl. JIMÉNEZ/RUPIDERA. Zur Straße Mérida – Braga sei noch auf BELO 1960 verwiesen.
[7] http://db.edcs.eu/epigr/epi.php?s_sprache=de (8. 3. 2018)

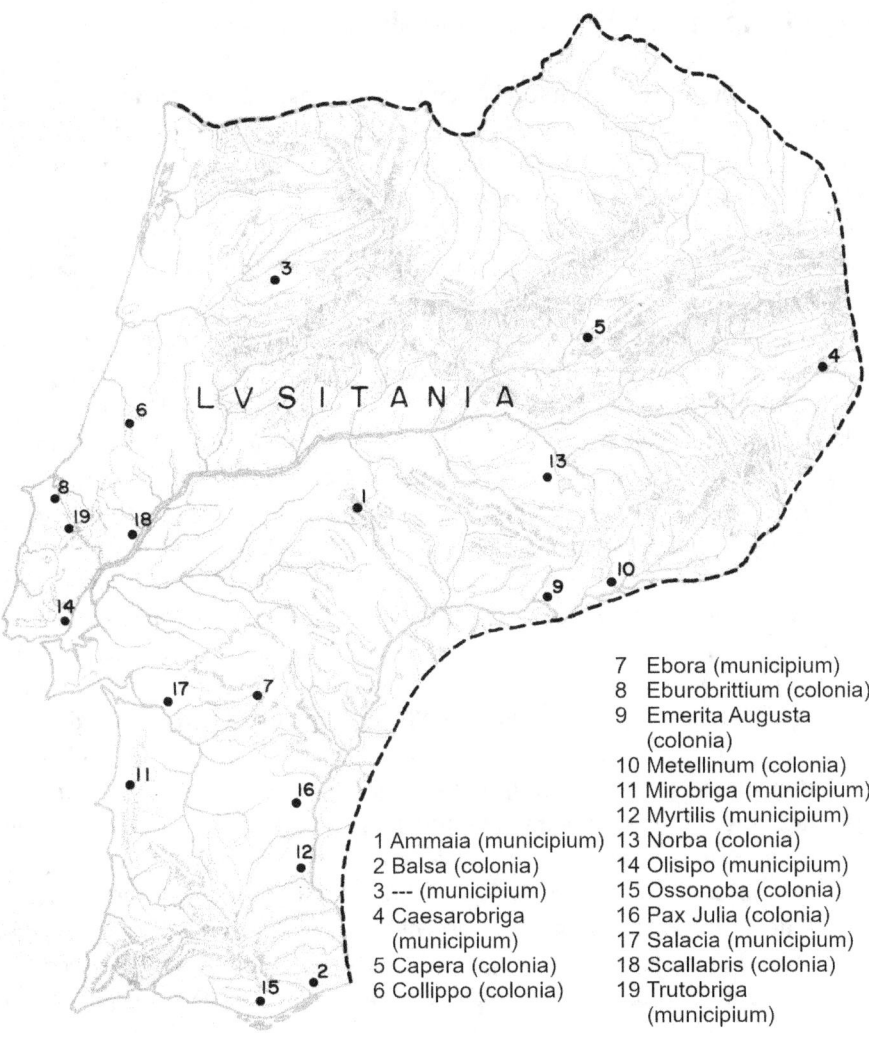

Fig. 1: Die Städte der Lusitania (nach Galsterer) © M. Rathmann/K. Hamacher

nisse wie *mansiones*, römische Brücken oder weitere straßenbegleitende Bauten.[8] Auf lange Sicht ist es daher erforderlich, im Rahmen von CIL XVII einen Faszikel mit den Miliarien der Provinz Lusitanien vorzulegen. Die folgenden Ausführungen sollen knapp den Rahmen der geplanten Arbeiten abstecken.

---

8 Zum römischen Straßenwesen in Lusitanien SAA 1956–1967; GIL 2012. Die Untersuchung konzentriert sich auf archäologische Aspekte und ordnet die Römerstraßen in den allgemeinen kulturgeschichtlichen Kontext ein. Bei der Erforschung der lusitanischen Reichsstraßen muss zudem TIR K 29 (mit der unverständlichen Auslassung der portugiesischen Region), TIR J-29, TIR K-30 sowie TIR J-30 herangezogen werden.

2 Anmerkungen zum Straßenwesen der *Lusitania*

Die *Lusitania* gehört im Reigen der römischen Verwaltungseinheiten zu den kleineren, weniger bedeutenden Provinzen.[9] Im Gegensatz zu ähnlich kleinen Provinzen, wie beispielsweise der *Germania inferior* oder der *Moesia inferior*, verfügte sie niemals über eine dort stationierte Legion und war demnach unter militärischen Gesichtspunkten von nachgeordneter Bedeutung. Zudem liegt sie geostrategisch am Rande des Imperiums[10], hat folglich nie durchziehende Heeresverbände erlebt und war kein Ziel kaiserlicher Inspektionsreisen.[11]

Ein etwas anderes Bild bietet sich hingegen auf der Ebene der Städte (s. Abb. 1).[12] Im Gegensatz zu den bereits erwähnten Provinzen mit Militär (*Germania inferior, Moesia inferior*) verfügte die *Lusitania* über eine beachtliche Zahl an römischen Städten: *Ammaia* (*municipium*), *Balsa* (*colonia*), [---] (*municipium*)[13], *Caesarobriga* (*municipium*), *Capera* (*colonia*), *Collippo* (*colonia*), *Ebora* (*municipium*), *Eburobrittium* (*colonia*), *Emerita Augusta* (*colonia*), *Metellinum* (*colonia*), *Mirobriga* (*municipium*), *Myrtilis* (*municipium*), *Norba* (*colonia*), *Olisipo* (*municipium*), *Ossonoba* (*colonia*), *Pax Julia* (*colonia*), *Salacia* (*municipium*), *Salmantica* (*municipium* ?)[14], *Scallabris* (*colonia*) und *Trutobriga* (*municipium*). Diese auf den ersten Blick beeindruckende Liste an städtischen Siedlungen sollte aber nicht darüber hinwegtäuschen, dass viele der genannten Orte bestenfalls Klein- oder Kleinststädte waren, die keinen überregional relevanten Handel oder eine entsprechende Wirtschaftskraft entfaltet haben dürften. Es ist also nicht davon auszugehen, dass die lusitanischen Städte die treibende Kraft bei der Entwicklung der Verkehrsinfrastruktur gewesen sind. Auch lässt sich kein einziger Statthalter der *Lusitania* im Zusammenhang mit dem Bau, Ausbau oder der Verwaltung von Reichsstraßen literarisch oder epigraphisch belegen.[15]

Eine Edition der Miliarien muss demnach stark auf archäologische Überreste setzen, gerade bei der Bestimmung der Trassenführung. Dies birgt jedoch das methodische Problem, dass gekieste oder gepflasterte Straßen nicht ohne weiteres als römisch zu erkennen sind. Selbst im positiven Falle – beispielsweise durch identifi-

---

9 NONY 2001; CARVALHO 2016.
10 Dies bezeugt beispielsweise die Statthalterschaft Othos (Suet. Otho 3,2). Er sollte, so legt es Sueton nahe, nach seiner Entfernung vom Hofe ‚ans Ende der Welt' geschickt werden. Und das war in seinem Fall und anders als bei Ovid eben Lusitanien.
11 Lediglich Augustus hat mit einiger Wahrscheinlichkeit einmal Lusitanien besucht; HALFMANN 1986, 160.
12 GALSTERER 1971, 68f. mit Karte im Anhang.
13 CIL II 401 = AE 2003, 864.
14 TOVAR 1976, 245. Für den Rechtsstatus der Stadt lassen sich m.E. keine Quellen beibringen.
15 RATHMANN 2003, 202, Taf. 2; vgl. RATHMANN 2006. Nicht einmal eine so bedeutende Figur wie Otho findet sich als Statthalter auf den Miliarien, obwohl allem Anschein nach unter seiner Ägide in der Provinz umfangreicher an den Reichsstraßen gearbeitet wurde; vgl. S. 313.

zierbare straßennahe Bauten wie *mansiones*[16] – hilft diese Bestimmung bei der Datierung der Straße oder der Bestimmung der Bauherrn nicht wirklich weiter. Bedauerlich ist zudem, dass der iberische Teil der Tabula Peutingeriana[17] nicht überliefert ist und auch die einschlägigen Kulturgeographen, wie beispielsweise Strabon[18], oder die entsprechenden Plinius-Passagen[19], keine straßenrelevanten Informationen bereithalten. Unter den literarisch verwertbaren Quellen bleiben somit nur das Itinerarium Antonini[20] sowie die Cosmographia des sog. Ravennaten[21] mit den dort eingetragenen Straßen.[22] Von diesen ist das Itinerarium Antonini hilfreich bei der Definition der diversen Routen, denen die Miliarien zugewiesen werden können.

3 Die Miliarien der *Lusitania*

Der nachweisbare römische Straßenbau in Lusitanien setzte mit Augustus erst recht spät ein. Dies ist wenig überraschend, da auch in anderen Provinzen des Westens erst seit Augustus ein Schub im Ausbau der Verkehrsinfrastruktur ausgemacht werden kann. Mit dem Einsetzen des Prinzipats vollzog sich nach unserem Kenntnisstand ein grundsätzlicher Paradigmenwechsel im Umgang Roms mit den Provinzen im Westen, so dass DIETMAR KIENAST in diesem Zusammenhang zu Recht vom „Werden einer Reichseinheit" spricht.[23]

Zu den markanten Impulsen in der *Hispania ulterior* gehört die Deduktion der *colonia Emerita Augusta*[24] im Jahr 25 v. Chr., die verkehrstechnisch Richtung *Baetica* und *Salmantica* vernetzt wurde. Augustus und seine Nachfolger konnten durch die Ansiedlung von Veteranen in den Provinzen eines der zentralen sozialen Probleme der späten Republik beheben und zugleich mit der stärkeren administrativen Durchdringung der außeritalischen Räume durch Stadtgründungen die Wertabschöpfung zugunsten Roms verbessern. War die Motivation zum Ausbau des Verkehrsnetzes administrativ-wirtschaftlich geprägt, so war die neue prinzipale Praxis des regel-

---

16 Vgl. ROLDÁN 1971, 75–108.
17 MILLER 1916, 149–186; ebd. Abb. 41 mit der oft zitierten Rekonstruktionszeichnung einer möglichen Darstellung der iberischen Halbinsel auf der Tabula. ROLDÁN 1975, 106–110 (mit Taf. X).
18 Vgl. Strab. 3,3,1–7.
19 Plin. nat. 4,113–118.
20 Itin. Anton. 416,4–418,5; 418,7–419,6; 419,7–420,7; 420,8–421,7; 425,6–427,3; 431,4–7; 433,1–434,4; 438,2–6; zu den Routen ROLDÁN 1975, 63–67, 77–79, 81–83, 86. Allg. s. ROLDÁN 1975, 19–101 (mit Taf. II & III); einige Ausführungen (z.B. S. 24) entsprechen nicht mehr dem Stand der Forschung. Vgl. ferner GIL 2012, 113–229.
21 ROLDÁN 1975, 111–142 (mit Taf. XII). Vgl. GIL 2012, 113–229.
22 Klaudios Ptolemaios (Ptol. 2,5,1–10) gibt zwar keine Informationen zum Straßennetz, hilft aber gelegentlich beim Verständnis der antiken Topographie.
23 KIENAST 2009, 499–515.
24 Zur Deduktion Cass. Dio 53,26,1; Isid. orig. 15,1,69; TOVAR 1976, 223.

mäßigen Aufstellens von Meilensteinen einem propagandistischen Zweck geschuldet. Denn die Miliarien, eine Sonderform der Bauinschriften, waren ein hervorragendes Medium, um den Reichsbewohnern buchstäblich auf Schritt und Tritt vorzuführen, wer in Rom Herrscher war.[25]

Betrachtet man die Quantitäten in verschiedenen Publikationen und online-Portalen, so ergibt sich folgende Übersicht:

CIL II	72	Miliarien[26]
EDCS	212	Miliarien
ROLDAN 1971	103	Miliarien (10 „falsae")
PUERTA 1995	147	Miliarien (76 anepigraph)
HURTADO 1977	6	Miliarien
ENCARNAÇÃO 1984	18	Miliarien
HERNÁNDEZ 2001	20	Miliarien (5 anepigraph)

Vom Autor des Beitrags konnten bislang in einer Datenbank 266 Meilensteine gesammelt werden. Diese Daten wurden ausschließlich aus der einschlägigen Literatur zusammengetragen.[27] Eine Edition der lusitanischen Miliarien ist also ein Desiderat der Forschung. Soweit ersichtlich, sind die Steine überwiegend noch existent, also nicht nur literarisch überliefert.[28] Interessant ist ferner, dass sich nach den bisherigen Recherchen eine nicht unerhebliche Menge an Meilensteinen in Privatbesitz befindet.

Die regionale Verteilung der zuweisbaren Miliarien, geordnet nach den Straßenangaben im Itinerarium Antonini, zeigt folgendes Bild:[29]

1) *de Esuri Pace Iulia*[30]	7	Miliarien
2) *ab Olisippone Bracam Augustam*[31]	3	Miliarien
3) *ab Olisippone Emeritam* (Nordroute)[32]	10	Miliarien
4) *ab Olisippone Emeritam* (Südroute)[33]	9	Miliarien
5) *ab Emerita Caesaraugusta* (Camino de la Plata)[34]	217	Miliarien

---

25 ALFÖLDY 1991, 322–324 spricht zutreffend von der „Geburt der imperialen Epigraphik".
26 CIL II listet zudem 12 weitere Steine unter „falsae vel alianae" auf. Wie CIL II 435* = ENCARNAÇÃO 1984, Nr. 663 zeigt (s.u.), ist auch diese Gruppe einer erneuten Prüfung zu unterziehen.
27 In der Zahl der 266 Miliarien sind folgende Arbeiten noch nicht berücksicht: ALONSO/CRESPO 1999; ALONSO/CRESPO 2000; GARCÍA 1973.
28 Vgl. WALSER 1981, 385–388.
29 Vgl. GIL 2012, 113–229; MILLER 1916, 149–186.
30 Itin. Anton. 425,6–427,3; 431,4–7; vgl. ROLDÁN 1975, 77–79.
31 Itin. Anton. 420,8–421,7; vgl. ROLDÁN 1975, 67f.
32 Itin. Anton. 418,7–419,6; 419,7–420,7; vgl. ROLDÁN 1975, 65–67.
33 Itin. Anton. 416,4–418,5; vgl. ROLDÁN 1975, 63f.
34 Itin. Anton. 433,1–434,4; 438,2–6; vgl. ROLDÁN 1975, 81–83, 86.

Miliaria in der Provinz *Lusitania* — 309

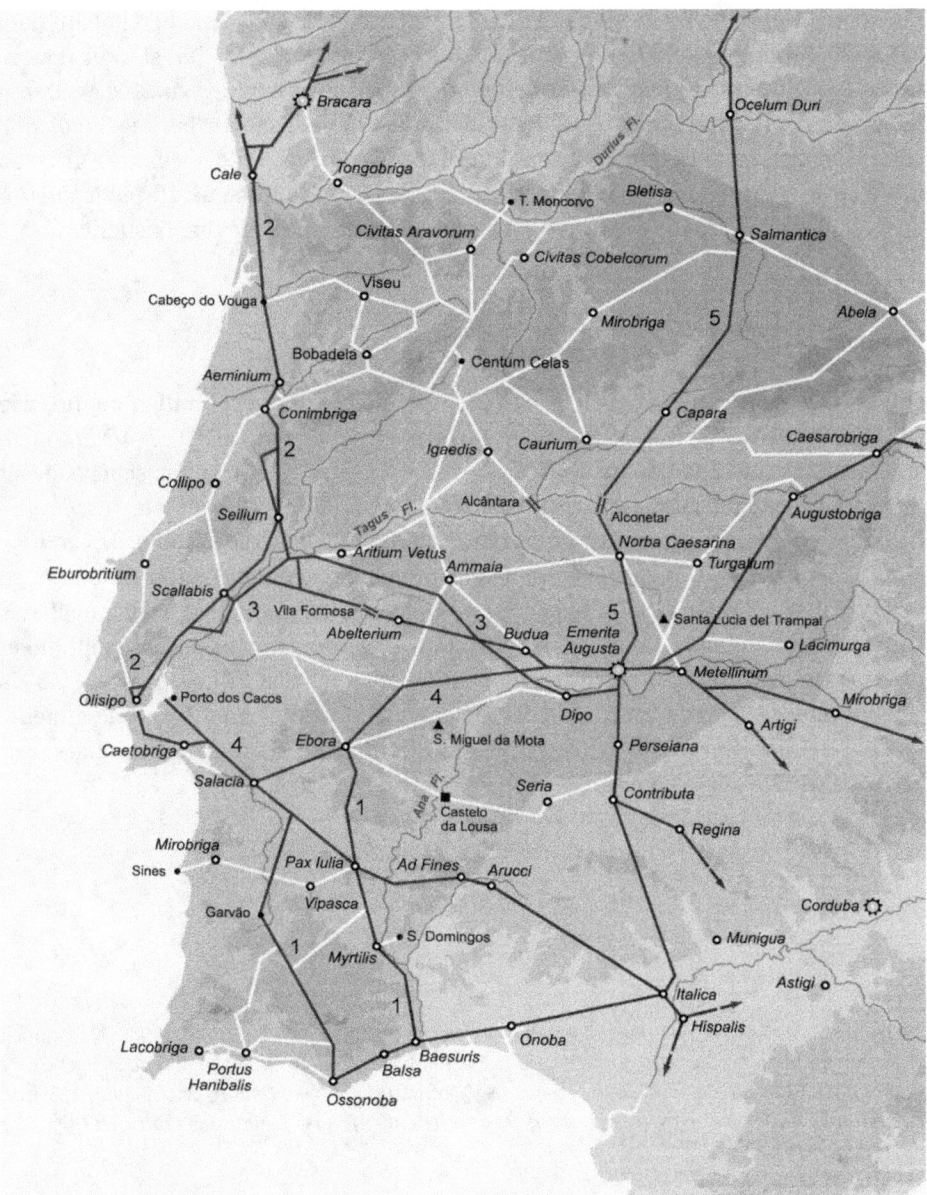

Fig. 2: Das römische Straßennetz der Provinz Lusitanien © M. Rathmann/K. Hamacher

Eine chronologische Einordnung der bislang erfassten Meilensteine bereitet auf dem aktuellen Stand der Arbeiten Probleme. So lassen mehrere zum Teil stark fragmentierte Inschriftentexte keine oder keine eindeutige Bestimmung zu. Des Weiteren liefern die diversen Arbeiten bisweilen widersprüchliche Lesungen bei angeblich gleichen Meilensteinen. Dennoch lassen sich einige für die *Lusitania* relevante Aussagen treffen. Nach aktuellem Stand können republikanische Miliarien für *Hispania citerior* ausgeschlossen werden. Der bislang älteste Meilenstein der Provinz Lusitanien trägt ein augusteisches Formular:

> *Imp(erator) Caesar / Augustus / (milia passuum) LIX.*[35]

Selbst für einen frühen augusteischen Stein ist der Text ungewöhnlich knapp, wie die Parallelen aus dem Nordosten der *Tarraconensis* oder aus der *Gallia Narbonensis* zeigen.[36] So fehlen der Zusatz *divi filius*, die Angabe einer tribunizischen Gewalt oder des Konsulats. Zu datieren ist dieser Stein vom Camino de la Plata ausschließlich durch sein nicht genanntes *caput viae*: Emerita Augusta. Die Kolonie, das heutige Mérida, wurde 25 v. Chr. für Veteranen der fünften und zehnten Legion deduziert, so dass wir hiermit einen *terminus post quem* besitzen.[37] *Terminus ante* ist demnach das Todesjahr des Augustus (14 n.Chr.). Die formale Gestaltung der Inschrift im republikanischen Duktus spricht meines Erachtens für eine möglichst frühe Datierung, so als sei die „imperiale Epigraphik" (ALFÖLDY) noch nicht wirklich zum Zuge gekommen.

Der zeitlich jüngste Meilenstein wurde offenbar für den letzten Gesamtkaiser Theodosius (379–395) aufgestellt:

> *DD(omini) nn(ostri) / Fla(vius) / The<o>/dosius / perpe/[tuus Aug(ustus).*[38]

---

[35] HURTADO 1977, Nr. 677 = PUERTA 1995, Nr. 74 = ESTEBAN 2007, Nr. 193 = ROLDÁN 1971, Nr. 25. Noch zwei weitere lusitanische Miliarien sind für Augustus belegt; AE 2012, 729: *(milia passuum) CXX / Imp(erator) / Caesar / divi f(ilius) / Augustus / co(n)s(ul) XI / imp(erator) X*; AE 1967, 185: *[Ab Emer?]i[ta?] / CX[X ad ---] / Im[p(erator)] / Caesa[r] / divi f(ilius) / Augustus c[o](n)s(ul) XII[I] / imp(erator) X[VI?].*
[36] CIL XVII/1 p. 247; XVII/2 p. 265.
[37] TOVAR 1976, 223.
[38] AE 2014, 579. Erhalten ist nur der obere Teil der Steinsäule. Es ist aufgrund des geringen Durchmessers dennoch unwahrscheinlich, dass die Säule ursprünglich so viel höher gewesen sein sollte, dass sie die Titulatur eines weiteren Augustus getragen haben könnte. Theoretisch wäre für Theodosius eine Doppelherrschaft mit Gratian (375–383) oder Valentian II. (375–392) in Frage gekommen, also die Zeit von 379 bis 392. Jedoch war Theodosius vor 392 lediglich Herrscher im Osten. Warum hätte dieser im Westen für die betreffende Zeit einer Doppelspitze vor dem Herrscher des Westens auf dem Stein genannt werden sollen? Daher sollte der Stein trotz des Plurals (DD NN) in die Phase der Alleinherrschaft des Theodosius zwischen 392 und 395 datiert werden.

Auch wenn nicht klar ist, warum die einleitende Devotionsadresse im Plural gestaltet ist, entspricht das kaiserliche Formular mit seiner Kürze dem typischen Duktus der Spätantike. Der Stein hat augenscheinlich seine ursprüngliche Funktion als Bauinschrift trotz des Nominativs, der den Kaiser ja eigentlich als handelnden Akteur ausweisen sollte, eingebüßt. Das charakteristische Schlagwort der Zeit lautet: *perpetuus Augustus*. Für die Provinzialen war die Doppelung der Reichsspitze mit einem Augustus im Westen und einem im Osten derartig vertraut, dass die politische Realität nicht mehr von Belang war und das DD NN vom Steinmetz wohl eher routinemäßig eingesetzt wurde. So ist am besten die ideologische Kluft zwischen einem alleinigen Flavius Theodosius Augustus an der Spitze und der doppelten Devotionsadresse zu Beginn des Textes zu erklären.

Unter den Meilensteinen des 1. Jahrhunderts fallen die Exemplare des Caligula und Nero auf. Beide Principes sind bislang im Imperium Romanum selten auf Miliarien bezeugt. Auffällig an einem Caligula-Meilenstein ist der Umstand, dass der Name des Princeps im Dativ genannt wird:

CIL II 4639 & p. 991: *[C(aio)] Caesari divi / Aug(usti) pron(epoti) Aug(usto) / [p]ont(ifici) max(imo) [trib(unicia) / po]t(estate) III co(n)s(uli) des(ignato) / [IIII] p(atri) p(atriae) / m(ilia passuum) IIII.*

Damit hätten wir aus der *Lusitania* den frühesten Beleg eines Miliarium mit einem Dativformular im Westen des Reiches.[39] Ob aus dem Kasus zwangsläufig auf eine Dedikation ohne tatsächliche Bautätigkeit geschlossen werden kann, ist nicht sicher. Erst zeitlich nahestehende Meilensteine vom gleichen Straßenabschnitt (Nr. 2: *ab Olisippone Bracaram Augustam*) würden CIL II 4639 zu einer Dedikation machen. Von dem betreffenden Straßenstück sind jedoch keine älteren Meilensteine bekannt, aus denen zu schließen wäre, dass dieser Caligula-Stein keinen Bezug zu tatsächlich durchgeführten Bautätigkeiten hat. Des Weiteren ist das Exemplar laut Datierung des Formulars auch nicht mit dem Herrschaftsantritt oder besonderen Ereignissen des Princeps in Verbindung zu bringen – bekanntlich beliebte Anlässe für Dedikationen. Festzuhalten bleibt aber dennoch, dass wir zumindest den Beginn eines Mentalitätswandels (Nominativ-Formular → Dativ-Formular) konstatieren dürfen.

Seit Augustus war der jeweilige Princeps als oberster *curator viarum* auch in den Provinzen *de iure* für den Straßenbau verantwortlich und erscheint folglich auf den Meilensteinen auch mit einer Nominativ-Titulatur, d.h. als Bauherr der Straße.[40] Jedoch änderte dies wenig an der provinzialen Realität vor Ort. Hier waren vor allem

---

39 Der Caligula-Stein bietet keinen Anhaltspunkt für eine Eradierung. Zur *damnatio* des Caligula s. Suet. Claud. 11,3; Cass. Dio 60,4,5. Vgl. KÖNIG 1973; RATHMANN 2003, 121. Ein zweiter Stein für Caligula ist mit einem Nominativ-Formular versehen; CIL II 4640 & p. 991: *[--- Cae]sar divi / [p]ron(epos) Aug(ustus) / max(imus) trib(unicia) / pot(estate)] co(n)s(ul) desi(gnatus) / p(ater) p(atriae) / (milia passuum) XII.*
40 Vgl. zu den diversen Teilaspekten RATHMANN 2003, 47–53, 56–61, 120–134.

lokale Kräfte wie Städte oder *civitates* für den Bau und Unterhalt von Straßen verantwortlich. Dass diese womöglich die eigene Rolle etwas stärker betont sehen wollten, indem sie den Kaiser „nur" in den Dativ setzten, überrascht also nicht. Mit Blick auf die gut zu beobachtenden Verhältnisse in Nordafrika wäre auch in der *Lusitania* erwartbar gewesen, dass sich parallel zum sukzessiven Kasus-Wechsel des kaiserlichen Formulars vom Nominativ zum Dativ die betreffenden Städte auch in der *caput-viae*-Zeile etwas stärker exponiert hätten. Aber dieses Phänomen ist, wie unten noch zu zeigen sein wird, in Lusitanien nicht festzustellen.

Interessant sind noch die bereits erwähnten neronischen Steine. So ist festzuhalten, dass wir entgegen dem sonst üblichen Befund im Westen des Reiches eine recht hohe Zahl von Nero-Meilensteinen besitzen, von denen keiner Spuren einer *damnatio memoriae* zeigt.[41] Diese passen zudem, wie die folgenden Beispiele aus dem Jahr 59 belegen, in das klassische Schema der iulisch-claudischen Miliarien.

> CIL II 4652 = Roldán 1971, Nr. 32 = Hurtado 1977, Nr. 682 = Puerta 1995, Nr. 89 = Esteban 2007, Nr. 209: *Nero Claudius / Caesar Aug(ustus) / Germanicus / pontif(ex) max(imus) / trib(unicia) potest(ate) V / imp(erator) IIII / (milia passuum) LXII.*

> CIL II 4683 (p. LXXX) = Alonso / Crespo 1999, Nr. 259 = Hernández 2001, Nr. 228 = Puerta 1995, Nr. 181 = Roldán 1971, Nr. 98: *Nero Claudius Caesar / Aug(ustus) Germ(anicus) pont(ifex)*

---

[41] a) Nero mit Nominativ-Titulatur: CIL II 4652 = Roldán 1971, Nr. 32 = Puerta 1995, Nr. 89 = Hurtado 1977, Nr. 682 = Esteban 2007, Nr. 209 (Text s.o.); CIL II 4683 & p. LXXX = Alonso/Crespo 1999, Nr. 259 = Hernández 2001, Nr. 228 = Puerta 1995, Nr. 181 = Roldán 1971, Nr. 98 (Text s.o.); CIL II 4657 = Puerta 1995, Nr. 100: *Nero Claudius Caes(ar) / Aug(ustus) pont(ifex) maxim(us) / trib(unicia) pot(estate) V imp(erator) III p(ater) p(atriae) / (milia passuum) CII*; AE 1967,198 = Puerta 1995, Nr. 109 = Esteban 2013, Nr. 1075 = Roldán 1971, Nr. 52: *Nero Cl[audius] / Caesar [Aug(ustus) Germ(anicus?)] / [po]ntifex max(imus) / [trib(unicia)] potest(ate) V [co(n)s(ul) III] / imp(erator) III p(ater) p(atriae) / (milia passuum) CX*; Puerta 1995, Nr. 173: *Nero Claudius [Caesar] / Aug(ustus) Germ(anicus) pont(ifex) m[ax(imus) trib(unicia) pot(estate)] V co(n)s(ul) III imp(erator) [III p(ater) p(atriae)] / (milia passuum) CLIIX*.
b) Nero mit Dativ-Titulatur: Puerta 1995, Nr. 1 (Text s. S. 313).
c) Kasus nicht bestimmbar oder generell unsicher in der Zuweisung an Nero: HEp 1, 1989, 163 = Esteban 2007, Nr. 186 = Puerta 1995, Nr. 34: *[Nero Claudius / Caesar Aug(ustus) Germ(anicus) / pont]if(ex) max(imus) / [tri]b[u]nic[ia] / potes[t(ate) III / im]p(erator) II p(ater) p(atriae) / m(ilia) p(assuum) / [XXIX]*; Esteban 2007, Nr. 187 = Puerta 1995, Nr. 40: *[Nero C]lau[dius divi] / [Claudi] f(ilius) Germ[anici] / [Caes(aris) nep(os) T]i(beri) Caes(aris) pr[onep(os)] / [divi Aug(usti)] abnep(os) Ca[es(sar)] / [Aug(ustus) G]er(manicus) p(ontifex) m(aximus) t[rib(unicia)] / [pot(estate) III i]mp(erator) II c(onsul) / (milia passuum) XXXII*.
Mit Emerita Augusta als Zählpunkt, aber vermutlich nicht mehr aus der Lusitania stammt folgender Stein HEp 2, 1990, 734 = HEp 4, 1994, 946 = AE 1987, 612 = Puerta 1995, Nr. 188 = Lostal 1992, Nr. 57: *Nero Claudius divi C[laudi Aug(usti) f(ilius)] / Germanici Caeseris [Aug(usti) nepos] / Ti(beri) Caeseris Aug(usti) [p]ro[nepos] / divi Aug(usti) abnepos / Caeser Aug(ustus) Germa[nicus] / pont(ifex) max(imus) tri(bunicia) potesta[te V] / imp(erator) V co(n)s(ul) [III] / (milia passuum) CCLIX*. Ein solcher Fall ist m.E. nicht einzigartig; zum Problem von *caput viae* und Provinzgrenzen Rathmann 2003, 113f. besonders mit Anm. 671; allg. Kolb 2013, 111–118.

max(imus) trib(unicia) / pot(estate) V co(n)s(ul) III imp(erator) IIII p(ater) p(atriae) / (milia passuum) CLXIIX.

Freilich können erst nach einer vollständigen Aufnahme aller lusitanischen Meilensteine zuverlässige Aussagen über Straßenbauaktivitäten getroffen werden. Aber dennoch verlangt der ungewöhnliche Befund der neronischen Steine schon jetzt eine Erklärung. Ausgang des Erklärungsmodells ist, dass wir im Westen seit Augustus regionale Wellen im Ausbau der Verkehrsinfrastruktur ausmachen können. So hatte beispielsweise der erste Kaiser einige *viae publicae* in Italien (z.B. die *via Flaminia*) sowie die Reichsstraßen durch Südfrankreich (*via Domitia*) und weiter bis nach Gades (*via Augusta*) ertüchtigt. Claudius hat diesbezüglich in Gallien gewirkt.[42] Und vermutlich ist unter Nero in Lusitanien das Netz an Reichsstraßen weiter ausgebaut worden. Leider fehlen Hintergrundinformationen, die Auskünfte über die Initiatoren dieses Unternehmens liefern könnten.[43]

Daneben fällt auch auf, dass einer der uns bekannten Nero-Steine aus dem Jahr 62 ein Dativformular trägt. Er stammt vom Camino de la Plata und stand unmittelbar vor den Toren der *colonia Emerita Augusta*:

PUERTA 1995, Nr. 1: *[N]eron[i Claudio] / [Cae]sari Aug(usto) [Germ(anico)] / [p]ontif(ici) ma[x(imo)] / [trib(unicia) pot]est(ate) VIII im[p(eratori) ---] / (milia passuum) II.*

Da wir an dieser Straße aufgrund der Koloniegründung und aufgrund der Meilensteinsetzungen seit augusteischer Zeit regelmäßig Bautätigkeiten vermuten dürfen, dieser Stein zudem unmittelbar vor der Stadt stand und wir keinen weiteren Nero-Stein dieses Streckenabschnitts mit einem Dativformular kennen, spricht vieles für eine Dedikation. Vielleicht wollte sich die *colonia* aufgrund der Krise im Kaiserhaus nach der Ermordung der Octavia sowie der Heirat mit Poppaea Sabina mit vertretbarem Aufwand, aber gut sichtbar, loyal zeigen.

Neben den iulisch-claudischen Steinen deutet sich eine zweite Fundhäufung in traianisch-hadrianischer Zeit an. Dies lässt sich damit erklären, dass nach Traians Agieren im Süden der Halbinsel auch Hadrian seiner iberischen Heimatregion verstärkte Aufmerksamkeit zukommen ließ und vermutlich traianische Unternehmungen abschließen wollte. In dieses Bild passt es, dass die hadrianischen Steine in der *Lusitania* häufiger ein bis dahin in dieser Provinz unübliches Bau- oder Reparaturverb nennen.

---

42 Vgl. KOLB 2013, 117 mit einer vergleichbaren These zu traianischen Aktivitäten in der Achaia.
43 Vielleicht darf man diese Straßenbauaktivitäten (oder auch nur die Meilensteinsetzungen) mit dem späteren Princeps Otho in Verbindung bringen (Suet. Otho 3,2), der ab 58 als *legatus Augusti pro praetore* in der Provinz war.

CIL II 4682 = ALONSO/CRESPO 1999, Nr. 47 = HERNÁNDEZ 2001, Nr. 220 = PUERTA 1995, Nr. 169: *Imp(erator) Caesar divi Traiani Par/thici f(ilius) divi Nervae nepos / (H)adrianus Aug(ustus) pont(ifex) max(imus) / trib(unicia) pot(estate) V co(n)s(ul) III resti/tuit / CXLIX.*

CIL II 4633: *Imp(erator) Caes(ar) / divi Traiani Parthici f(ilius) di/vi Nervae nepos Traianus / Hadrianus Aug(ustus) pont(ifex) max(imus) / trib(unicia) pot(estate) XVIIII co(n)s(ul) III p(ater) p(atriae) / refecit.*

Die meisten Steine stammen jedenfalls vom Camino de la Plata und legen die Vermutung nahe, Hadrian habe den infrastrukturellen Anschluss Méridas Richtung Norden weiter ausbauen wollen. Das Reparaturverb ist eventuell ein Indiz für eine zweite Ausbaustufe. Zudem lässt der Stein (CIL II 4633) aus der Nähe von Lissabon darauf schließen, dass der Princeps in Lusitanien weitere infrastrukturelle Impulse setzen wollte.

Hinsichtlich des gesamten Römischen Reiches zeichnet sich im 3. Jahrhundert eine immer stärkere ‚Barockisierung' der Meilensteintexte ab, also der Gebrauch immer weiter ausufernder kaiserlicher Titulaturen mit einem Mehr an Filiationen, Siegerbeinamen, potentiellen Thronfolgern, Kaisergattinnen usw.[44] Dieser Trend ist besonders gut in Nordafrika und in Kleinasien zu beobachten; Meilensteininschriften mit bis zu 20 Zeilen sind dort nicht selten. Im Vergleich dazu fällt für die Formulare in der *Lusitania* auf, dass diese nicht zur Länge neigen: Akklamationen, Siegerbeinamen oder sonstige Epitheta finden sich im Verhältnis zur angesprochenen Referenzmenge seltener oder zumindest in durchgängig kürzerer Form. Der mit Abstand längste lusitanische Text nennt Maximinus Thrax und seinen Sohn Maximus (a. 238) und ist nur auf einem Exemplar belegt:

CIL II 4649 = 6201 = HURTADO 1977, Nr. 673 = PUERTA 1995, Nr. 49: *[Im]p(erator) Caes(ar) C(aius) Iulius V[erus] / Maximinus Pius / Felix Invictus Aug(ustus) / [pon]tif(ex) max(imus) p(ater) p(atriae) trib(unicia) pot(estate) V / [imp(erator)] VII co(n)s(ul) Germ(anicus) max(imus) / Dacic(us) max(imus) Sarm(aticus) max(imus) [et] / [C(aius) I]ul(i)us Verus Max(imus) / [nob]ilissimus C[aesar] / p[ri]nceps iuven[tutis] / [Germ(anicus)] max(imus) Dacic(us) max(imus) [f(ilius)] / d(omini) n(ostri) Imp(eratoris) C(ai) Iuli Ve[ri] / [Ma]ximini Pii Felicis [Germ(anici)] / maxi(mi) Dacic(i) m[ax(imi) Sarm(atici)] / [m]ax(imi) fortissi[mi et]/ no[bi]lissimi prin[c(ipes)] / refecerunt / XXXIIX.*

Dieses Formular stellt im Umfeld der lusitanischen Miliarien gewissermaßen die Ausnahme von der Regel dar. Die Mehrzahl der Texte ist kurz oder im Verhältnis zu diversen Zeitströmungen in anderen Regionen des Imperium Romanum durchgängig kürzer.

Noch auf einer weiteren Ebene ist eine spezifische Besonderheit dieser Provinz zu registrieren: Für gewöhnlich findet sich ein Peak an Funden in der Zeit Diokletians und Constantins.[45] In der *Lusitania* hingegen sucht man eine solche Materialdichte

---

44 Vgl. WALSER 1981, 391.
45 Vgl. LOSTAL 1992, 365.

vergeblich. Vielmehr deutet es sich an, dass nur wenige Exemplare aus der Tetrarchie und der Spätantike existieren. Dies lässt sich eventuell wie folgt erklären: Das Straßennetz war bereits im 2. Jahrhundert so weit entwickelt und mit Meilensteinen zur praktischen Orientierung am Straßenrand ausgestattet, dass es sich die Städte am westlichen Rande des Imperiums leisten konnten, bei dem im 3. Jahrhundert einsetzenden Dedikationswettlauf an Reichsstraßen nicht teilzunehmen. Für diese Annahme spricht u.a. der Umstand, dass die Kaiser und ihre Feldherren in der Spätantike in anderen Regionen des Reiches gebunden waren und folglich als reale Empfänger von Devotionsadressen ausfielen. Falls Straßenbau oder Reparaturen an Reichsstraßen durchgeführt wurden, konnten sich die bauausführenden Gemeinden folglich die Zusatzkosten für die Aufstellung immer weiterer und im Grunde nicht benötigter Meilensteine sparen. In dieser Praxis zeigt sich das besondere Selbstverständnis der lusitanischen Städte. Im Grunde waren diese ihrer Zeit voraus, denn der Trend sollte sich in den anderen Reichsteilen im 5. Jahrhundert auch einstellen: Man hörte auf, Meilensteine aufzustellen – selbst wenn Straßenbau durchgeführt wurde oder ein neuer Kaiser an die Macht kam.[46]

Innerhalb der Gruppe der spätantiken Steine gibt es noch zwei Besonderheiten anzuzeigen. Die erste ist ein Meilenstein für Crispus (317–326). Dieser verfiel nach seiner Ermordung im März 326 einer *damnatio memoriae* und ist im ganzen Imperium auf Miliarien nur selten belegt. An dem einzigen lusitanischen Exemplar sind die Zeitläufte offenbar vorbeigegangen, denn es zeigt keine Spuren von Umarbeitung oder Eradierung:

>   HURTADO 1977, Nr. 711 = ESTEBAN 2013, Nr. 1112 = AE 1977, 436 = 1985, 542: *D(omino) n(ostro) Fla/vio Iuli/o Crispo / nob(ilissimo) Caes(ari) / (milia passuum) CX*.

Vor dem Hintergrund der relativ geringen Menge an spätantiken Miliarien fällt als zweite Besonderheit auf, dass Usurpatoren – hier Magnentius (350–353) – ganz selten erscheinen:

>   ESTEBAN 2013, Nr. 930 = HEp 2005, 81: *[--- / d(omino) n(ostro) ---] / Magnen/tio vic/tori sem/per Augu/sto bono / [rei] publi/[cae nato / ---]*.

Offenbar haben die lusitanischen Städte, die Meilensteine aufstellten, sich mit Absicht auch dieser Mode entzogen, jedem neuen Teilherrscher im Westen ihre Ergebenheit bekunden zu müssen. Die geostrategische Randlage macht es ihnen freilich auch leichter.

---

46 Formulierungen wie das bereits erwähnte *semper Augustus* zeigen an, dass sich das Medium Meilenstein als Propagandainstrument überlebt hatte (Beispiele: AE 1914, 165; CIL III 204 mit p. 973; CIL V 8071; CIL XVII/2, 157). Lange kaiserliche Formulare mit Litaneien an Siegertitulaturen und sonstigen Epitheta wurden auf ein kompaktes *semper Augustus* komprimiert.

4 *caput viae* und Reparaturverben

Wie bereits festgehalten, waren gerade die Städte die Instanzen, die maßgeblich für den Bau und Ausbau beziehungsweise für die Instandhaltung von Reichstraßen in den Provinzen verantwortlich waren.[47] Häufig versuchten diese im Laufe des 1. und 2. Jahrhunderts, ihre Rolle auf dem Sektor der Verkehrsinfrastruktur durch die Kaisertitulatur im Dativ herauszustellen: Nicht mehr der Kaiser ist der formalrechtlich oberste Akteur, sondern die lokalen Kräfte ehren ihn durch den Straßenbau. Demselben Zweck diente die stärkere Akzentuierung ihrer Stellung durch eine ausführliche Betonung des *caput viae*. Für die *Lusitania* zeigt sich hierzu folgendes Bild:

Zunächst einmal findet sich außer der Provinzhauptstadt *Emerita Augusta* (Mérida) und *Ebora* (Evora)[48] keine einzige Stadt epigraphisch auf einem Meilenstein belegt. Selbst bei *Emerita Augusta* sind die Quantitäten außerordentlich dünn:

HEp 2006, 505 = AE 1967, 185: *[Ab Emer?]i[ta?] / CX[X ad ---] / Im[p(erator)] / Caesa[r] / divi f(ilius) / Augustus c[o](n)s(ul) XII[I] / imp(erator) (milia passuum) X[VI?].*

PUERTA 1995, Nr. 177: *[Imp(erator) Caes(ar) divi] / [Nervae f(ilius) Ner]/va Tra[ia]/[nus] Aug(ustus) [Germ(anicus)] / [p]o[nt(ifex)] max(imus) / co(n)s(ul) II / [trib(unicia)] pot(estate) III / [p(ater) p(atriae) pro]co(n)[s(ul) ---] / ab E[merita Augusta] / (milia passuum) CLXV.*

Die Provinzhauptstadt ist zwar auf allen Miliarien des Camino de la Plata bis unmittelbar vor die Tore Salamancas *caput viae*, erscheint aber abgesehen von diesen beiden Beispielen nicht namentlich. Das ist ungewöhnlich.[49] Vielleicht fühlten sich die Bewohner im Rahmen ihrer Unterhaltsverpflichtung (*munus publicum*)[50] oder die jeweiligen Bautrupps weitab von der Provinzhauptstadt nicht verpflichtet, den Namen Emeritas nennen zu müssen, da das assignierte Territorium der *colonia* offenbar sehr groß war.

Das zweite namentlich belegte *caput viae* wird lediglich auf einem Stein genannt; er trägt das Formular Elagabals aus dem Jahr 219:

CIL II 435* = ENCARNAÇÃO 1984, Nr. 663: *Imp(eratori) Caes(ari) divi Antoni/ni Pii Magni fil(io) / divi Septimi Severi / Pii nepoti M(arco) Aure/lio Antonino / P(io) Fel(ici) Aug(usto) pont(ifici) max(imo) / trib(unicia) pot(estate) II co(n)s(uli) II / proc(onsuli) p(atri) p(atriae) / fortissimo felicissi/moque principi / [Eb]ora m(ilia) p(assuum) / XXII.*

Dieser im Dörfchen Barbacena bei Elvas (Portugal) gefundene Meilenstein gehört vermutlich zur Strecke 4 „*ab Olisippone Emeritam*" (s. Karte). Ungewöhnlich ist die For-

---

47 Vgl. RATHMANN 2003, 102–134; RATHMANN 2004 (mit weiterer Lit.).
48 TOVAR 1976, 217f.
49 RATHMANN 2003, 113f.; RATHMANN 2004, 195, Anm. 196.
50 KISSEL 2002.

mulierung *fortissimo felicissimoque principi* für einen Augustus.[51] Da der Stein nicht aus der Phase unmittelbar nach dem Herrschaftsantritt von Elagabal stammt, in der man in den Provinzen womöglich noch nicht über die korrekte Titulatur des neuen Princeps informiert war, erstaunt die Wortwahl.

In der Summe überrascht die geringe Zahl epigraphisch bezeugter Zählpunkte vor dem Hintergrund des eingangs genannten Kanons an lusitanischen Städten doch. Obwohl wir auf zahllosen Meilensteinen Distanzangaben lesen können, erscheinen die Städte namentlich als *caput viae* nur sehr selten. Gerade im Vergleich mit anderen Provinzen, in denen das *caput viae* im 3. Jahrhundert bisweilen zwei Zeilen füllen konnte, ist die Befundlage ein bemerkenswertes Charakteristikum der *Lusitania*. Brevitas scheint auch dabei ein Faktor gewesen zu sein.

Da Meilensteine zur Gattung der Bauinschriften zählen, soll ein abschließender Blick den unmittelbar für den Straßenbau relevanten Bauverben *fecit*, *refecit* oder *reparavit* gelten. Auch hier scheint sich die Provinz ihrer zurückhaltenden Art bei der Ausformulierung vom Meilensteintexten treu geblieben zu sein; dazu folgende Auswahl:

CIL II 4644 = Puerta 1995, Nr. 3: *[Ti(berius)] Claudius / Drusi f(ilius) Caesar / Aug(ustus) Germ(anicus) / pont(ifex) max(imus) trib(unicia) / pot(estate) X co(n)s(ul) IIII imp(erator) / XXI iter / reparavit / (milia passuum) VI.*

CIL II 4667 & p. LXXX = Hurtado 1977, Nr. 709 = Puerta 1995, Nr. 121 = Esteban 2013, Nr. 1153:[52] *Impe[rator Caesar] / divi Nervae filius / Nerva Traianus / Augustus Germa/nicus pontifex ma/ximus tribunicia / potestate consul / iterum restituit / (milia passuum) CXVI.*

Puerta 1995, Nr. 155: *Imp(erator) Ca[e]sar divi / Nervae [f]ilius Ner/va Traianus Augus/tus Ge[r]manicus / ponti[fex] maxi[m]us / [tr]ibun[icia po]tes[tate] / co(n)s(ul) [--- pr]ocon(sul) / p(ater) p(atriae) viam restituit / (milia passuum) CXL.*

CIL II 4660 & p. 712 = Hurtado 1977, Nr. 694 = Puerta 1995, Nr. 103 = Esteban 2013, Nr. 956: *Imp(erator) Caes(ar) / M(arcus) Aurel(ius) / Severus [[Alex/ander]] Pius / Felix Aug(ustus) pon/tifex maximus / trib(unicia) potest(ate) p(ater) p(atriae) / co(n)s(ul) proc(onsul) / fecit / (milia passuum) CIII.*

Esteban 2013 Nr. 1124: *[--- Titulatur des Domitian ---]a tri[b(unicia)] / [pot]est(ate) II p(ater) p(atriae) / imp(erator) XIIII censo[r] / perpetuus / co(n)s(ul) XIIII vias / corruptas et / pontes restituit / CIII.*

---

51 Diese Formulierung gibt es noch auf Meilensteinen bei Braga (Galizien): CIL II 4766–4768, 4805; HEp 13, 821.
52 Vgl. CIL II 4677 = Alonso/Crespo 1999, Nr. 264 = Hernández 2001, Nr. 204 = Puerta 1995, Nr. 154; CIL II 4679 = Alonso/Crespo 1999, Nr. 175 = Hernández 2001, Nr. 205 = Puerta 1995, Nr. 162; CIL II 4680 = Alonso/Crespo 1999, Nr. 201 = Hernández 2001, Nr. 207 = Puerta 1995, Nr. 163; CIL II 6206 = Puerta 1995, Nr. 184; Esteban 2013, Nr. 1127 = HEp 2006, 102; Puerta 1995, Nr. 144.

Die vier ersten Miliarien liefern die in der *Lusitania* geläufigen Bauverben: *reparavit*, *restituit*[53] und *fecit*. Lediglich ein Stein für Domitian aus dem Jahr 85, in der Provinz ohne Parallele, fällt aus dem Rahmen und ähnelt entsprechenden Reparaturmitteilungen auf baetischen Exemplaren.[54] Von den in benachbarten Provinzen bisweilen anzutreffenden ausführlichen Formulierungen ist also in der Regel wenig zu sehen.[55] Bis auf den zitierten Domitian-Stein zeigen die lusitanischen Miliarien auch hier ein eher schlankes Formular.

Lediglich der Terminus *iter* überrascht und bedarf der Erklärung. Während die kaiserzeitlichen Rechtstexte für gewöhnlich von *via publica* sprechen, gibt es in den Digesten einige Zitate spätrepublikanischer Juristen, die neben diesem Terminus technicus auch den Begriff des *iter publicum* kennen.[56] Ausgehend von der Annahme, dass der Ausbau der Reichsstraßen in der *Lusitania* nach römischen Qualitätskriterien erst mit Augustus einsetzte, passt es ins Bild, dass unter den weiteren iulisch-claudischen Principes jenseits des Camino de la Plata weitere Wege und Straßen ertüchtigt wurden. Angesichts der Qualitätsabstufung zwischen *iter* (= ungepflasterter Weg) und *via* (= befestigte/gepflasterte Straße) passt ein claudischer Stein, der noch von *iter* spricht, gut ins Bild, das wir auch aus anderen Provinzen kennen.[57] Im Zuge einer schrittweisen Qualitätssteigerung wurde aus dem keltiberisch-republikanischen Weg (*iter*) im Laufe der Zeit eine römische *via*, vermutlich mit einer gewissen Breite, einem kompakt gekiesten oder gepflasterten Fahrbahnkörper, Entwässerungsgräben zu beiden Seiten, angrenzenden Viehtriften und eben Meilensteinen zur besseren Orientierung. Daher taucht der Terminus *iter* nach der Mitte des 1. Jahrhundert auf Miliarien auch nicht mehr auf.

5 Die Brücke von Alcántara

Abschließend soll noch ein Blick auf die Brücken der *Lusitania* geworfen werden.[58] Zu keiner der bislang bekannten Brücken gibt es im Rahmen der Verkehrsinfrastruktur interpretierbare Inschriften, bis auf eine, in der Literatur immer wieder zitierte Aus-

---

53 Eine alternative Formulierung ist *iterum restituit* (z.B. CIL II 4667 & p. LXXX = PUERTA 1995, Nr. 121; zu ergänzen auf CIL II 4655 = HURTADO 1977, Nr. 688 = PUERTA 1995, Nr. 94). Damit soll offenbar die erneute Wiederherstellung angezeigt werden.
54 Die baetischen Miliarien Domitians bieten die Formulierung *ab arcu unde incipit Baetica viam Augustam militarem vestuste corruptam restituit* (CIL II 4722 = SILLIÈRES 1990, Nr. 36, SILLIÈRES 1990, Nr. 41, vgl. CIL II 4721 = ILS 269).
55 RATHMANN 2003, 204–209 mit einer Zusammenstellung der geläufigen Bau- und Reparaturmitteilungen auf Miliarien.
56 RATHMANN 2003, 11f.
57 Vgl. RATHMANN 2003, 20–22 mit der Diskussion zu den Termini *iter* und *via* in den Rechtstexten.
58 Bedeutend ist ferner die Brücke von Alconétar am Camino de la Plata. Epigraphische Zeugnisse zu dieser Brücke sind nicht bekannt; GALLIAZZO 1994, 358–361, Nr. 755.

nahme: die berühmte Brücke von Alcántara. Dieses Meisterwerk römischer Ingenieurtechnik erstreckt sich mit ihren sechs unterschiedlich weiten Bögen über eine Länge von rund 182 Metern. Sie überspannt den Tagus (Tajo) und weist eine Gesamthöhe von etwas über 70 Metern auf.[59] Bemerkenswert ist, dass die zugehörige Straße zu keiner der großen antiken *viae* gehört, die durch Meilensteine belegt sind oder in einem der Itinerare genannt werden. In der Mitte der Brücke befindet sich ein Traian-Bogen, der eine zweite, ebenfalls vorgeblich antike Inschrift trägt. Diese nennt die den Bau finanzierenden Munizipien:

> CIL II 759 = ILS 287: *Imp(eratori) Caesari divi Nervae f(ilio) Nervae / Traiano Aug(usto) Germ(anico) Dacico pontif(ici) max(imo) / trib(unicia) potes(tate) VIII imp(eratori) V co(n)s(uli) V p(atri) p(atriae).*

> CIL II 760 = ILS 287: *Municipia / provinciae / Lusitaniae stipe / conlata quae opus / pontis perfecerunt / Igaeditani / Lancienses Oppidani / Talori / Interamnienses / Colarni / Lancienses / Transcudani / Aravi / Meidubrigenses / Arabrigenses / Banienses / Paesures.*

Außerdem wurde an der Südostseite ein kleiner, dem divinisierten Princeps dedizierter Tempel errichtet. Dieser enthält die Grablege des Erbauers der Brücke, Caius Iulius Lacer.[60] Vermutlich war er ein römischer Militäringenieur:

> CIL II 761 = ILS 287b: *Imp(eratori) Nervae Traiano Caesari Augusto Germanico Dacico sacrum // templum in rupe Tagi superis et Caesare plenum / ars ubi materia vincitur ips{s}a sua / avis quali dederit voto fortasse requiret / cura viatorum quos nova fama iuvat / ingentem vasta pontem qui mole peregit / sacra lituro fecit honore Lacer / qui pontem fecit Lacer et nova templa dicavit / scilicet et superis munera sola litan(t) / pontem perpetui mansurum in saecula mundi / fecit divina nobilis arte Lacer / idem Romuleis templum cum Caesare divis / constituit felix utraque causa sacri // C(aius) Iulius Lacer d(e) d(ecurionum) s(ententia) f(ecit) et dedicavit amico Curio Lacone Igeditano.*

Diesen Stand bietet die Forschung[61] und generell wären diese drei Texte für uns auch interessant. Leider wird jedoch dem Umstand, dass alle drei Inschriften nicht im Original überliefert sind, immer noch zu wenig Bedeutung beigemessen.[62] Denn schon HARTMUT GALSTERER hat in seiner Untersuchung zum römischen Städtewesen auf der Iberischen Halbinsel 1971 nachgewiesen, dass die für uns besonders interessante Inschrift CIL II 760 = ILS 287 aus inhaltlichen Gründen eine Fälschung sein muss.[63]

---

59 GALLIAZZO 1994, 353–358, Nr. 754; RICHTER 2011; GIL 2012, 235–241 (mit weiterer Literatur).
60 GEMENO 1995.
61 Vgl. TOVAR 1976, 249f.
62 Auch die traianische Widmungsinschrift auf dem Bogen ist m.E. sicher nicht antik, wie u.a. die fehlerhafte Angabe von *IMP V* und *TRIB POT VIII* deutlich macht. Die Inschrift dürfte aller Wahrscheinlichkeit nach mit den neuzeitlichen Inschriften und Überarbeitungen an Brücke und Tempel zusammenhängen.
63 GALSTERER 1971, 62–64.

Jüngst hat HANS RICHTER erneut auf den Umstand hingewiesen, dass dieser Text auf einer arabischen Überlieferung basiert, die ins Jahr 931 zurückverfolgt werden kann.[64] Bemerkenswert ist des Weiteren, dass auch die Inschrift mit dem Namen des Architekten Lacer nicht unproblematisch ist. Die Inschrift wird zwar schon im 10. Jahrhundert literarisch erwähnt, Lacer erscheint jedoch erstmalig im 14. Jahrhundert. Ohne die Diskussion über die Echtheit der Inschrift erneut weiter auszuführen, können wir festhalten, dass auch CIL II 761 = ILS 287b, bestehend aus elegischen Distichen, für uns als Quelle leider ausfällt.

Im Resultat bedeutet dies, dass wir mit den Brücken von Alconéta und Alcántara zwar zwei beeindruckende Brücken in der *Lusitania* haben – aber gerade die Inschriften, die für die Brücke von Alcántara bislang in der Forschung stets unter diversen Aspekten herangezogen wurden, fallen für die Interpretation des lusitanischen Straßenbaus als nichtantike Dokumente aus. Alle bislang in der Literatur anzutreffenden Thesen rund um eine mögliche traianische Erbauung beider Brücken kommen daher über das Stadium einer Spekulation nicht hinaus.

6 Fazit

Grundsätzlich liegt eine beachtliche Anzahl an Miliarien aus der Provinz *Lusitania* vor, die einen eigenen Faszikel im Rahmen von CIL XVII rechtfertigen. Die epigraphische Datenbank CLAUSS/SLABY (EDCS) bietet einstweilen eine Basis, mit der sich arbeiten lässt. Die Autopsie wird zeigen müssen, ob alle bisher in der Literatur vorliegenden Lesungen tatsächlich Bestand haben. Vergleiche von publizierten Texten mahnen zu großer Vorsicht, da bisweilen beachtliche Abweichungen auszumachen sind.

Die Texte selbst, so wie sie sich uns aktuell präsentieren, sind überraschend schlicht und scheinen somit diversen Trends, die wir beispielsweise aus anderen westlichen Provinzen des Reiches kennen, nicht zu entsprechen. Damit deutet sich an, dass Lusitanien mit seinen Miliarien hinsichtlich der regionalen Verteilung, der Textlänge und der genannten Kaiser durchaus eine eigenständige Position einnimmt. Des Weiteren kann festgehalten werden, dass die überwiegende Anzahl an Meilensteinen vom Camino de la Plata stammt, also der Verbindung von der Provinzhauptstadt *Emerita Augusta* nach Norden. Daneben sind durch das Itinerarium Antonini noch drei weitere Reichsstraßen auszumachen, von denen jedoch deutlich weniger Meilensteine bekannt sind.

In der nun folgenden Arbeit vor Ort, der Durchsicht der Fundberichte und regionalgeschichtlichen sowie provinzialarchäologischen Publikationen wird sich nicht zuletzt zeigen müssen, ob die Zuweisung der Stücke zu den einzelnen Reichsstraßen zu halten ist. Zudem stellt sich die Frage, ob das Netz an Reichsstraßen laut Itinera-

---

64 RICHTER 2011, 20–31 (mit weiterer Literatur).

rium Antonini Bestand hat oder ob eventuell weitere Routen benannt werden müssen, die neben den Miliarien ausschließlich durch archäologische Anhaltspunkte zu definieren sind.

Bibliographie

ALBALADEJO 2012 = M. ALBALADEJO VIVERO, Léxico de Topónimos y Etnónimos del Noreste de la Península Ibérica en la Antigüedad, Madrid 2012.
ALFÖLDY 1991 = G. ALFÖLDY, Augustus und die Inschriften: Tradition und Innovation, *Gymnasium* 98, 1991, 289–324.
ALONSO/CRESPO 1999 = Á. ALONSO ÁVILA/S. CRESPO ORTIZ DE ZÁRATE (Hg.), Corpus de inscripciones romanas de la provincia de Salamanca, Valladolid 1999.
ALONSO/CRESPO 2000 = Á. ALONSO ÁVILA/S. CRESPO ORTIZ DE ZÁRATE (Hg.), Auctarium a los corpora de epigrafía romana del territorio de Castilla y León, Valladolid 2000.
BELO 1960 = A.R. BELO, Nótulas sobre cinco marcos miliários da via militar romana Mérida-Viseu-Braga, encontrados nas proximidades da Torre *Centum Callae* de Belmonte, *Revista de Guimarâes* 70, 1960, 27–50.
CARVALHO 2016 = A. CARVALHO, Lusitânia romana, Lissabon 2016.
ENCARNAÇÃO 1984 = J. D'ENCARNAÇÃO, Inscrições romanas do Conventus Pacensis, Coimbra 1984.
ESTEBAN 2007 = J. ESTEBAN ORTEGA, Corpus de inscripciones latinas de Cáceres, Bd. 1: Norba, Cáceres 2007.
ESTEBAN 2013 = J. ESTEBAN ORTEGA, Corpus de inscripciones latinas de Cáceres, Bd, 3: Capera, Cáceres 2013.
GALLIAZZO 1994 = V. GALLIAZZO, I ponti romani, Bd. 2: Catalogo generale, Treviso 1994.
GALSTERER 1971 = H. GALSTERER, Untersuchungen zum römischen Städtewesen auf der Iberischen Halbinsel, Berlin 1971.
GARCÍA 1973 = L. GARCÍA IGLESIAS, Epigrafia romana de Augusta Emerita, Madrid 1973.
GEMENO 1995 = H. GEMENO PASCUAL, La inscripión del dintel del templo de Alcántara (CIL II 761): una perspectiva diferente, *Epigraphica* 57, 1995, 87–145.
GIL 2012 = V. GIL MANTAS, As vias romanas da Lusitânia, Mérida 2012.
HALFMANN 1986 = H. HALFMANN, Itinera principum. Geschichte und Typologie der Kaiserreisen im Römischen Reich, Stuttgart 1986.
HERNÁNDEZ 2001 = L. HERNÁNDEZ GUERRA, Epigrafía de época romana de la provincia de Salamanca, Valladolid 2001.
HURTADO 1977 = R. HURTADO DE SAN ANTONIO, Corpus provincial de inscripciones latinas, Cáceres 1977.
JIMÉNEZ/RUPIDERA = M. C. JIMÉNEZ GONZÁLEZ/A. RUPIDERA GIRALDO, La Vía de la Plata a su paso por la Provincia de Salamanca (http://www.jcyl.es/jcyl/patrimoniocultural/miliarios/assets/la-v%C3%ADa-de-la-plata-a-su-paso--por-la-provincia-de-salamanca.pdf [8. 3. 2018])
KIENAST 2009 = D. KIENAST, Augustus. Prinzeps und Monarch, Darmstadt 2009[4].
KISSEL 2002 = T. KISSEL, Roadbuilding as a *munus publicum*, in: P. ERDKAMP (Hg.), The Roman Army and the Economy, Amsterdam 2002, 127–160.
KOLB 2007 = A. KOLB, Rez. zu Antonio Rodríguez Colmenero – Santiago Ferrer Sierra – Rubén D. Alvarez Asorey, Miliarios e outras Inscricións viarias romanas do noroeste Hispánico (conventos bracarense, lucense e asturicense). Consello da Cultura Galega, Sección de Patrimonio Histórico, Santiago de Compostela 2004, *JRA* 19, 2006 [2007], 577–582.

Kolb 2013 = A. Kolb, Die Erfassung und Vermessung der Welt bei den Römern, in: K. Geus/M. Rathmann (Hg.), Vermessung der Oikumene, Berlin 2013, 107–118.

König 1973 = I. König, Zur Dedikation römischer Meilensteine. Digesta 43,7,2; 50,10,3,4, *Chiron* 3, 1973, 419–427.

Lostal 1992 = J. Lostal Pros (Hg.), Los miliarios de la Provincia Tarraconense. Conventos Tarraconense, Cesaraugusto, Cluniense y Cartaginense, Zaragoza 1992.

Miller 1916 = K. Miller, Itineraria Romana. Römische Reisewege an der Hand der Tabula Peutingeriana dargestellt, Stuttgart 1916 (ND 1988).

Nony 2001 = D. Nony, Die spanischen Provinzen, in: C. Leppeley (Hg.), Rom und das Reich, Bd. II: Die Regionen des Reiches, [dt.] München/Leipzig 2001, 121–150.

Nünnerich-Asmus 1993 = A. Nünnerich-Asmus, Straßen und Brücken als Zeichen römischen Herrschaftsanspruchs, in: W. Trillmich et al. (Hg.), Hispania Antiqua. Denkmäler der Römerzeit, Mainz 1993, 121–157.

Puerta 1995 = C. Puerta Torres, Los miliarios romanos de la vía de la plata, Madrid 1995 (online publiziert: http://eprints.ucm.es/2439/1/T20210.pdf [8. 3. 2018]).

Rathmann 2003 = M. Rathmann, Untersuchungen zu den Reichsstraßen in den westlichen Provinzen des Imperium Romanum, Mainz 2003.

Rathmann 2004 = M. Rathmann, Städte und die Verwaltung der Reichsstraßen, in: R. Frei-Stolba (Hg.), Siedlung und Verkehr im römischen Reich. Römerstraßen zwischen Herrschaftssicherung und Landschaftsprägung, Bern u.a. 2004, 163–226.

Rathmann 2006 = M. Rathmann, Der Statthalter und die Verwaltung der Reichsstraßen in der Kaiserzeit, in: A. Kolb (Hg.), Herrschaftsstrukturen und Herrschaftspraxis. Konzepte, Prinzipien und Strategien der Administration im römischen Kaiserreich, Berlin 2006, 201–259.

Richter 2011 = H. Richter, Die Brücke des Baumeisters Lacer und sein Baustil. Ein Beitrag zur Baugeschichte römischer Keilsteinbrücken in der Provinz Lusitania, Petersberg 2011.

Rodriguez Colmenero et al. 2004 = A. Rodríguez Colmenero/S. Ferrer Sierra/R.D. Álvarez Asorey (Hg.), Miliarios e outras Inscricións viarias romanas do nordoeste Hispánico, Santiago de Compostela 2004.

Roldán 1971 = J. M. Roldán Hervás, Iter ab Emerita Asturicam. El Camino de la Plata, Salamanca 1971.

Roldán 1975 = J. M. Roldán Hervás, Itineraria Hispana. Fuentes antiguas para el estudio de las vías romanas en la península ibérica, Madrid 1975.

Saa 1956–1967 = M. Saa, As grandes vias da Lusitania, 6 Bde., Lissabon 1956–1967.

Sillières 1990 = P. Sillières, Les voies de communication de l´Hispanie méridionale, Paris 1990.

TIR J-29 = J. de Alarcão et al. (Hg.), Tabula Imperii Romani J-29, Lisboa, Madrid 1995.

TIR J-30 = J. M. Álvarez Martínez et al. (Hg.), Tabula Imperii Romani J-30: Valencia, Madrid 2002.

TIR K-29 = A. Balil Illana et al. (Hg.), Tabula Imperii Romani K-29: Porto, Madrid 1991.

TIR K-30 = G. Fatás Cabeza et al. (Hg.), Tabula Imperii Romani K-30: Madrid, Madrid 1991.

Tovar 1976 = A. Tovar, Iberische Landeskunde, 2. Teil: Die Völker und die Städte des antiken Hispanien, Bd. 2: Lusitanien, Baden Baden 1976.

Walser 1981 = G. Walser, Bemerkungen zu den gallisch-germanischen Meilensteinen, *ZPE* 43, 1981, 385–402.

Stéphanie Guédon
Road Network and Roman Frontier in Numidia: the Region of Tobna

Abstract: The area of Tobna is considered as one of the best kept southern borders in Roman Africa. This idea was deduced from the important remains discovered in this zone, from which the testimonies of road network. These were interpreted as part of the defence of the provincial frontier. The present study proposes to take up the data concerning the roads in the area of Tobna, in order to better understand their relation with the notion of border.

Zusammenfassung: Die Gegend von Tobna wird als eine der besterhaltenen südlichen Grenzen im römischen Afrika angesehen. Diese Idee wurde von den bedeutenden Überresten abgeleitet, die in dieser Zone entdeckt wurden, unter diesen die Zeugnisse des Straßennetzwerkes. Diese wurden als Teil der Verteidigungsanlage der Provinzgrenze gedeutet. Die vorliegende Studie schlägt vor, das Datenmaterial, welches die Straßen in der Gegend von Tobna betrifft, aufzunehmen, um dessen Zusammenhang mit dem Grenzbegriff besser zu verstehen.

The city of Tobna is located between the Chott el Hodna and the Jbel Metlili (western Aurès).[1] This area was often perceived as a depressed zone, landlocked in a margin outside the Roman Empire, which would have been largely dedicated to pastoral nomadism.[2] The prejudices that have long persisted on the pre-desert and desert areas of the Maghreb explain in particular the marginal place that the history of central Maghreb at ancient and medieval times has occupied for a long time in the current research.[3]

Tobna is mentioned by Pliny the Elder and Ptolemy.[4] The city seems to have been a *municipium*, at an unknown date.[5] The epigraphy only states the duumvirate in an inscription of the reign of Septimius Severus.[6] Concerning religious matters, Tobna

---

Article note: I thank ANTHONY COMFORT who re-read this text, and FABRICE DELRIEUX who is the author of the Fig. 1.

---

1 See Fig. 1.
2 PICARD 1947, 49–66.
3 For medieval time: MEOUAK 2006, and MEOUAK 2009.
4 Plin. nat. 5,37 (*Tuben oppidum*); Ptol. 4,2,7.
5 CIL VIII 4486 and BCTH 1900, 175. See GASCOU 1972, 204.
6 CIL VIII 18634 (= 4482).

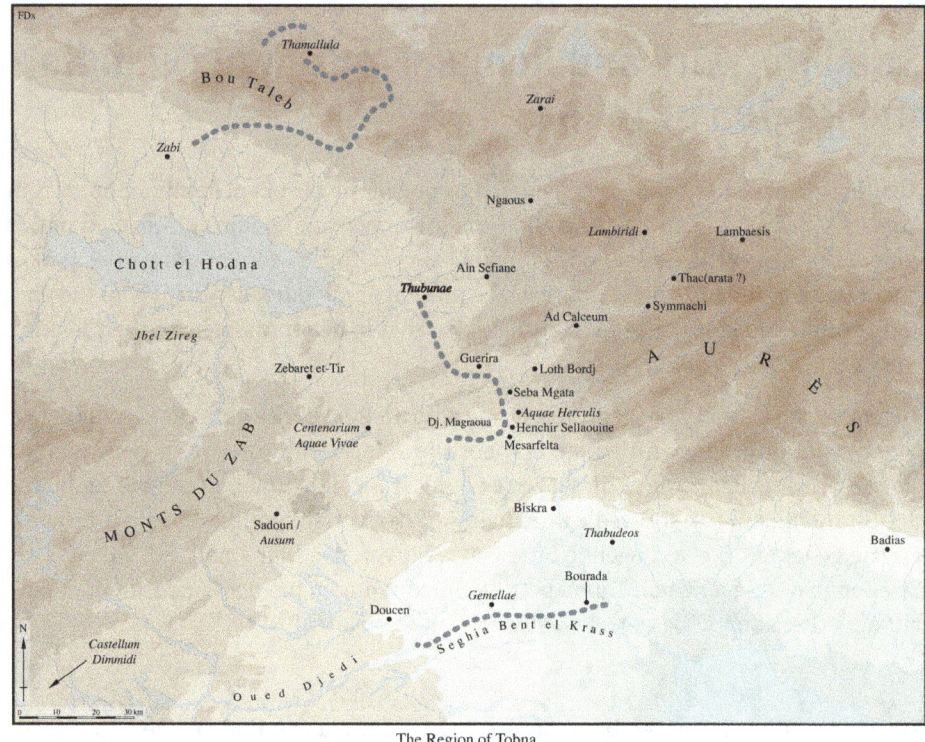

The Region of Tobna
in Late Antiquity

Fig. 1: The Region of Tobna in Late Antiquity, Copyright: Fabrice Delrieux.

was already the seat of a bishopric in 256.[7] The city is quoted by the Tabula Peutingeriana[8], and in Late Antiquity the Notitia Dignitatum makes it the chief town of a military district, the *limes Tubuniensis* mentioned among the sixteen *praepositi limitis* placed under the orders of the *comes Africae*.[9] The military vocation of Tobna is evoked at the same period by the correspondence of Augustine of Hippo who makes the travel to Tobna to meet the future count Boniface, then military tribune, possibly towards 421, in order to dissuade him from becoming a monk.[10]

---

[7] Cyprianus, Sententiae episcoporum LXXXVII de hereticis baptizandis 5 (council of Carthage, in 256: CSEL 3/1, 435–461).
[8] Tab. Peut. 2,2.
[9] Not. dign. occ. 25,21–36. For the discussion about the *limes Tubuniensis*: GUÉDON 2018.
[10] Aug. epist. 220,3 (CSEL 57, 432–433) and 220,12 (CSEL 57, 440–441). Concerning Boniface: MANDOUZE 1982, 152–155. The dating proposal for the travel of Augustine to Tobna: PERLER/MAIER 1969, 367–368.

The site of Tobna, and more widely the region of the Hodna, unfortunately remain poorly studied and documented from an archaeological point of view.[11] The surveys carried out by JEAN BARADEZ in Southern Algeria and published in 1949 gave for the first time an aerial view of the remains of the region of Tobna, in particular those of its fortress, attributed to the reign of Justinian[12], and the linear work of Tobna to the Jbel Magraoua – called *fossatum* –[13], whose dating and nature remain very controversial.[14] For JEAN BARADEZ, these remains were the proof of the necessary military fortification of this region at the border of Roman Africa.[15] YVES MODÉRAN used his analysis of the archaeological data to consider the region of Tobna as one of the best kept southern borders in Africa, because of a constant nomadic threat under the Roman Empire, emanating from the south of Roman Africa.[16] The defensive purpose of the remains identified in the area of Tobna would have been based on a set of roads developed around this place. This network would have been used for military aims, to protect the cultivated grounds with which the area of Tobna and its *fossatum* would have marked the boundary, at the same time as the border of the Roman province.[17] It must be noted, however, that the road network around Tobna is still badly known: the documentation is very scattered and results in large part from the work of JEAN BARADEZ in the 1950s. The hypothesis of a constant nomadic threat under the Roman Empire, originating from the Sahara and justifying the construction of a *fossatum*, is besides questioned.[18]

The present study does not aim to verify the hypotheses of routes formulated by JEAN BARADEZ from his aerial surveys, nor to give a new reading of the epigraphic corpus, which is impossible in the present state of documentation and the conditions for field research. This present study proposes to take up all the data in order to better understand the extension of the Roman presence, its ambitions and its implications in this region of the African borders. To do this, it is necessary to present at first the road network involving the place of Tobna, before considering the question of the interpretation of this data in relation to the notion of border.

---

[11] GRANGE 1902; GSELL 1911, Feuille n°37, 10 and *ad*.
[12] BARADEZ 1949, 293; PRINGLE 2001, 274–276.
[13] BARADEZ 1949, 35–84.
[14] NAPOLI 1997, 64–66, 98–99 and 412–423.
[15] BARADEZ 1949, 148.
[16] MODÉRAN 2003, 395; MODÉRAN 2008, 104.
[17] VAN BERCHEM 1952, 45; NAPOLI 1997, 98–99.
[18] SHAW 1982, 42; TROUSSET 2004.

The Road Network of Tobna

The name of Tobna appears only exceptionally in inscriptions[19], so it is through consideration of the distances reported by the milestones and their location that the role of road station played by Tobna can be recognized. The milestones discovered in the area of Tobna seem to point to four principal roads. The earliest evidence, dating from the reign of Commodus, relates to the road which led to Seba Mgata.[20] Nearby this place milestones dating back to Pertinax were discovered, attributed to a route between *Ad Calceum Herculis* and Tobna, passing by Seba Mgata.[21] North of Seba Mgata, after Guerira[22], a road seems to have branched off towards *Ausum* and El Gahra, where a milestone dating to the reign of Severus Alexander was discovered.[23]

In the field, the course of the Roman road between Tobna and Seba Mgata is not easy to follow, and JEAN BARADEZ admitted that he had difficulty in identifying it through his aerial surveys.[24] Nevertheless, the road was formerly recognized by a dozen kilometers in the northwest of Seba Mgata, and followed for 26 kilometers until Tobna.[25] It apparently continued beyond the Daya plain, crossed the Teniet El Ouasta pass, from which it then emerged into the basin of the Hodna. Between Tobna and the pass itself several milestones were discovered, among those one dates back to the reign of Commodus and was dedicated to the Emperor and his legate, M. Valerius Maximianus;[26] the distance, on milestones quoting the stations VIII, IX, X, XI and XII, was counted from Tobna[27]. It seems to have been towards Guerira, or at the crossroads located at the southwest extremity of the Jbel Gueraat el Guétoul, that the numbering of the miles on the milestones was changed: from the east westward, the distance mentioned on milestones IX, X, XI and XII, was counted from *Ad Calceum*.[28] This might suggest that the territorial jurisdiction of Tobna, which appears as the *caput viae*, extended up to that point, the change of numbering relying on the boundary of the city.[29] The road segment between Tobna and Seba Mgata was finally

---

19 Only one milestone, belonging to the road between Tobna and *Nicivibus*, seems to mention the name of Tobna (*[a Tu]bonis*): CIL VIII 22535.
20 GSELL 1901b, 448, n°1. Concerning this road: GSELL 1911, Feuille n°37, 10, 12, 13, 14.
21 LESCHI 1947, 207; LESCHI 1946–1949; BARADEZ 1949, 60–66.
22 BARADEZ 1949, 60, n. 2, proposed to correct the hypothesis of S. GSELL followed by A. ALBERTINI, locating at Seba Mgata the crossing of the road leading to Tobna and the road towards El Gahra.
23 CARCOPINO 1925, 45–47.
24 BARADEZ 1949, 65.
25 GSELL 1911, Feuille n°37, 10; ALBERTINI 1931b, 252–253.
26 THOMASSON 1996, 164–166, n°43.
27 GSELL 1901a, 316, and GSELL 1901b, 447–450; GSELL 1911, Feuille n°37, 12, 13 and 14; ALBERTINI 1931a, 368; ALBERTINI 1931b, 253–254.
28 BARADEZ 1949, 72.
29 Concerning the link between the territorial boundary of a city, and milestones: SALAMA 1980, 118; JACQUES 1992, 129–130 about Timgad; DUPUIS 1999.

by Jean Baradez associated with the course of the *fossatum* spotted during his aerial surveys, which seems to have gone along the road built, according to him, in a previous period.[30]

Towards the southwest, a road seems to have connected Tobna with *Aqua Viva*, as suggested by some vestiges and a milestone discovered one mile southwest of Tobna.[31] Towards the northeast, a road led from Tobna to *Nicivibus*, 37 kilometers away: this road is attested by milestones, and among these one dates back to the year 214 of the reign of Caracalla.[32] Towards the east, in the direction of Sefiane, not less than 15 milestones were discovered at the 4th mile from Ain Sefiane where some vestiges are quoted, at about 16 miles from Tobna, going back to the reigns of Maximinus Thrax and Gordian III. It seems that the distance was calculated from Ain Sefiane to Tobna.[33]

It has also been supposed that another road, north of *Ad Calceum*, connected Tobna with *Lambaesis*. Various milestones were discovered in the region of *Thac(arata ?)* (Ain Touta, former Mac Mahon); Jean Baradez suggested a crossing of the road Tobna-*Lambaesis*, with that of *Lambaesis* to *Ad Calceum*, at about ten kilometers northeast from *Thac(arata ?)*.[34] In addition, following the aerial surveys that he carried out in the area, Jean Baradez was convinced that Tobna was connected with the road from *Lambaesis* to *Ad Calceum* not only by this first branch, but also by a section leading directly to *Symmachi* that he located on the same road, south of *Thac(arata ?)*.[35]

The data concerning the road network of Tobna show in a concrete way the impressive density of roads identified by Jean Baradez in the south of Numidia, and the major problem posed by this: as remarked by Pierre Salama on the work carried out by Jean Baradez, « seules les datations au sol permettent de discriminer, dans un écheveau routier 'total', les phases successives d'utilisation des voies romaines ou mêmes d'itinéraires plus tardifs. L'entreprise est souvent impossible ».[36]

---

30 Baradez 1949, 66–72, 78–84, and 218 (map).
31 Gsell 1901a, 316, n°18; Grange 1902, 52; Gsell 1911, Feuille n°37, 10. The emperor's names were hammered.
32 CIL VIII 22531 (milestone of Constantine); CIL VIII 22532 (milestone of Julian); CIL VIII 22533 (milestone of Philip the Arab); CIL VIII 22534 (milestone of Caracalla); CIL VIII 22535; CIL VIII 22536 (milestone of Severus Alexander); Gsell 1901a, 316, n°19 (milestone of Philip the Arab); BCTH 1902, 141–142 (milestone dedicated to Diocletian, Maximian, Constantius I and Galerius); Gsell 1902, 516–518 (milestone of Severus Alexander (?); milestone of Maximinus Thrax); Grange 1902, 49–52; Gsell 1911, Feuille n°37, 10; Albertini 1931b, n°67, 258–259 (milestone of Constantius II); Marcillet-Jaubert 1980, 181–182, n°35 (milestone of Claudius Gothicus).
33 Gsell 1902, 506–513; Gsell 1911, Feuille n°37, 10 and 11.
34 Baradez 1953, 162–165.
35 Baradez 1949, 213 (map); Baradez 1953, 160–161.
36 Salama 1980, 103, n. 1.

The routes that would have connected *Lambaesis* with Tobna according to JEAN BARADEZ[37] shared an axis common to the one described by the Tabula Peutingeriana: one that passed by *Lambaesis, Symmachi, Ad Calceum* and *Mesarfelta*.[38] The Tabula Peutingeriana mentions Tobna at sharp corner with roads pointing in two directions. The station is placed on the one hand at the end of a route leading to *Zarai* in the northeast, then connected to *Lambiridi* and *Lambaesis*.[39] On the other hand, Tobna constituted westward the head of a route passing south of the Chott el Hodna, called "*Salinae Nubonenenses*" in the Tabula Peutingeriana, and leading apparently into Caesarian Mauretania.[40]

The Traditional Interpretation of the Road Network of Tobna

The word "*limes*" used by the moderns is commonly seen as an area of military boundaries located at the provincial border, relying first on strategic routes allowing the circulation of the troops and facilitating trade, and thereafter on a hierarchical organization of military posts and outposts, in connection with linear works.[41] This model of a military border served more particularly to interpret the vestiges located in the aera of Tobna, where the remains of the linear work called "*fossatum Africae*" were considered as the materialization of the "*limes Tubuniensis*" mentioned by the Notitia Dignitatum[42], and the border of the Roman province.[43] The region of Tobna would have been a part of the "système défensif aurasien" defined by YANN LE BOHEC[44], who proposed to confer to the road network of Tobna a military origin and a defensive role.[45] His analysis is founded on the mention of the *legatus Augusti pro praetore* in the road epigraphy. However, the mention of the legate is not enough to deduce an exclusive military purpose of the road concerned.[46] Furthermore, YANN LE BOHEC recognizes that the enemy who would have come from the Sahara remains unknown. Besides, the word "*limes*" used to mention in the Notitia Dignitatum the "*limes Tubuniensis*" evokes at first a military district[47], and not specifically the military border. Then, we must recognize that we don't know with precision what were the limits of this district. In addition, the nature and the dating of the linear construc-

---

37 BARADEZ 1949, 335; BARADEZ 1953, 160–165.
38 Tab. Peut. 3,2–4,1. About this road: MORIZOT 1998.
39 Tab. Peut. 2,2–3,2.
40 Tab. Peut. 1,5–2,2.
41 TROUSSET 2004, 60.
42 Not. dign. occ. 25,25.
43 VAN BERCHEM 1952, 48; NAPOLI 1997, 96–99.
44 LE BOHEC 1995.
45 LE BOHEC 2008.
46 See CHRISTOL 2012, about another road context.
47 REDDÉ 2015.

tion called *"fossatum"* remain uncertain and controversial, and its defensive purpose is contested.[48]

According to Jean Baradez, there existed since the beginning of the second century (from de reign of Trajan or that of Hadrian) a route for patrols, passing by *Zarai* and Tobna in the direction of *Mesarfelta* from where it was possible to go to *Lambaesis*.[49] This hypothesis is based on the measures undertaken under the reign of Trajan south of the Aurès with the foundation of the camp of *Ad Maiores* into 104 or 105[50] and the road works carried out in the same period between *Ad Maiores* and *Badias*, on the way to *Thabudeos*.[51] These measures would have aimed at isolating the Aurès which would have constituted a zone of endemic rebellion.[52] In this hypothesis, the encirclement of the Aurès would have led from this period to the development of a south-north road, leading to *Zarai* by Tobna, consequently isolating the Metlili massif from the Hodna mounts. Thus would from the first half of the 2nd century onwards have been established "une grande voie de rocade du *limes* de Trajan", from the Tunisian chotts down to *Zarai* by *Ad Maiores*, *Thabudeos* and Tobna.[53] According to Jean Baradez, from the reign of Trajan on, a road led to *Thabudeos* from *Lambaesis*, by passing through the Aurès and connecting the headquarter of the African garrison to the provincial border.[54] This view fitted fully in the historiographical current for which the mountain was traditionally seen in Africa as a hostile zone for the Roman authority. This thesis was widely criticized and questioned in particular within the framework of the Aurès.[55] The existence of a defensive system around the Aurès, explaining the rough shape of the road network in the area of Tobna[56], remains also very hypothetical.

The reign of Gordian III would have constituted a fundamental step in the defense of the border. Jean Baradez allotted to this emperor, in a preferential way, the construction of the *fossatum*, that would explain the multiplication of milestones in the area in this period, caused by the intensification of traffic.[57] According to Jean Baradez, Gordian III would have proceeded to a massive recourse of *limitanei*

---

48 Van Berchem 1952, 44–45; Trousset 1984, 388–391; Napoli 1997, 64–66, 98–99 and 412–413.
49 Baradez 1949, 353.
50 CIL VIII 2478–2479 (= 17969–17971). See Le Bohec 1989, 430–433; Trousset 1991; Lenoir 2011, 181–182. The camp was founded by the legate of the *legio III Augusta*, L. Minicius Natalis: about him, see Thomasson 1996, 140, n°17.
51 CIL VIII 22348 and 22349. See Gsell 1911, Feuille n°50, 51 and 54; Trousset 1991a; Laporte/Dupuis 2009, 93–94.
52 Cagnat 1913, 575 and 592; Courtois 1955, 118–126; Bénabou 1976, 117–118; Trousset 1980, 150–151.
53 Baradez 1949, 153.
54 Baradez 1959, 29.
55 Janon 1973, 197–199; Janon 1977; Leveau 1977; Morizot 1979; Leveau 1990; Morizot 1997, 268–269.
56 Guédon 2018.
57 The hypothesis of the reorganization of the Numidian border under the reign of Gordian III was advanced by Carcopino 1925, 138–144. The opinion of Fentress 1979, 117, is more reserved.

assigned to the construction and defense of the *fossatum*, in order to mitigate the effects of the dissolution of the *Legio III Augusta*.[58] This hypothesis is based on an erroneous interpretation of a passage of the biography of Severus Alexander in the *Historia Augusta*. The use of the adjective *limitaneus*, which is only used to specify in the text the geographical location of soldiers, resulted in the erroneous conclusion that the emperor had installed peasant soldiers in the border area.[59] Their presence was then presumed in Africa during the 3rd century.[60] Following the work of BENJAMIN ISAAC, the notion of peasant soldiers is no longer viable.[61]

A Road Network with an Exclusively Military Vocation?

From a chronological point of view, considering the epigraphic documentation which at present offers the only data that permit to date the roads in the area, the first intervention of the Roman State goes back to Commodus, on the road which led to Seba Mgata;[62] there is no evidence before this. It can be related to the creation of the *burgus speculatorius* built *inter duas vias* under Commodus, mentioned by an epigraphical testimony in the northeast of Seba Mgata:[63] the isolated stone, whose context of discovery remains uncertain and discussed, does not make it possible however to establish the precise location of the garrison involved in the inscription.[64] At least it points out the importance of the circulation in the area at this time, and a road effort continued under Pertinax attested by milestones of the emperor and his legate Naevius Quadratianus.[65]

The epigraphic data show thereafter a relatively significant number of milestones dating back to the reign of Caracalla, not only on the roads implying Tobna, but more largely on the roads of South-Western Numidia[66], as well as in Tripolitania.[67] The effort made by the heirs of Septimius Severus on the road network fits then in the continuity of the major works carried out in Mauritania under Septimius Severus into 201, with

---

58 BARADEZ 1949, 156–158.
59 HA Alex. 58,4: *Sola, quae de hostibus capta sunt, limitaneis ducibus et militibus donauit...* See REBUFFAT 1980, 118–119; ISAAC 1988.
60 TROUSSET 1974, 150.
61 JANNIARD 2015.
62 GSELL 1901b, 448, n°1.
63 CIL VIII 2495.
64 GSELL 1911, Feuille n°37, 54; BARADEZ 1949, 239.
65 Milestone discovered at the foot of the Jbel Selloum, near the presumed location of the *burgus* of Commodus: ALBERTINI 1931a, 365. Milestone discovered at Seba Mgata: CIL VIII 10238.
66 BARADEZ 1953, 165, n. 15.
67 The majority of milestones discovered in Tripolitania dates from the reign of Caracalla: MATTINGLY 1995, 61.

the establishment of the *nova praetentura* which associates military foundations with road works facilitating circulation between these garrisons.[68]

The period following the reign of Gordian III is also marked by a dense activity as regards milestones, and some of those are particularly concentrated at certain places on the roads involving Tobna. Such is the case at Seba Mgata, at the IXth mile from *Ad Calceum*, where eight milestones were discovered, dated between the reign of Pertinax and the reign of Aurelian.[69] At the Xth mile, twelve milestones were discovered, set up between the reign of Elegabal and that of Magnus Maximus and Flavius Victor in 384–388.[70] In addition, fifteen milestones were found at the IVth mile of the road between Ain Sefiane and Tobna: the inscriptions that could be read are dedicated to Maximinus Thrax, Gordian III, Philip the Arab, Valerian and Gallienus, Aurelian, Constantius Chlorus, Constantius Chlorus and Galerius, Magnus Maximus with his son Victor.[71] It is quite remarkable that, in North Africa, Numidia presents the most important accumulations of milestones in the same station; those relate particularly to the road network of Tobna.[72]

From the middle of the 3rd century onwards, any mention of road activity disappears in a general way on the African milestones.[73] Then, for PIERRE SALAMA the milestones became essentially honorary from the 3rd century in all the African provinces.[74] Such is the case for two milestones discovered on the way between *Lambaesis* and Tobna by *Ad Calceum*, one near Ksar Sidi el Hadj[75], the other a little further north[76], at the confluence of the wadis Fedhala and Maafa. These inscriptions belong to a series of Numidian milestones dating from the end of the reign of Aurelian (in 274 and 275), exalting the *Victoria* or the *Gloria* of the emperor and his *Indulgentia*, and testifying apparently the attachment of the local population to the emperor.[77] Such is also the case for a milestone discovered on the way between *Lambaesis* and Tobna[78], dedicated to the deified emperor Aurelian to whom is also dedicated a milestone at Djemila.[79] Other milestones were dedicated to the divine Constantius: one was found two kilometers north of Tobna.[80] The use of the possessive *noster* on milestones ded-

---

[68] TROUSSET 1980, 151–152; BENSEDDIK 1999.
[69] ALBERTINI 1931a; ALBERTINI 1931b, 242–248; BARADEZ 1949, 65.
[70] LESCHI 1946–1949; BARADEZ 1949, 65.
[71] GSELL 1902, 506–508; GSELL 1911, Feuille n°37, 10 and 11.
[72] SALAMA 2002, 100, n. 51.
[73] SALAMA 1959, 349.
[74] SALAMA 1951, 267; SALAMA 1959; SALAMA 1987; SALAMA 2002, 100–104. For Tripolitania: MATTINGLY 1995, 61 and 223, n. 32.
[75] ALBERTINI 1931b, 241, n°52. See DAGUET 1992.
[76] MORIZOT 1991, 343.
[77] SALAMA 1951, 235–236; DAGUET 1992; DUPUIS 1992, 241.
[78] BARADEZ 1953, 163–164.
[79] SALAMA 1951, 236–237.
[80] CIL VIII 4484. Another milestone: CIL VIII 22212, Sigus. See SALAMA 1987, 113–114.

icated to Philip the Younger and to the emperors Valerian and Gallian discovered at Seba Mgata also confirms the honorific character of the inscriptions.[81]

It must be stressed however that milestones had always constituted elements of imperial propaganda as implied by the recall of the name of the emperor and his titulature, in comparison with which the counting in miles is sometimes secondary.[82] Is it also necessary to distinguish, like PIERRE SALAMA, between milestones written for most part in the dative by the 3rd century and interpreted as imperial dedications emanating from local communities[83], and the few inscriptions in the nominative that could indicate a substantial road restoration? This distinction is not always clear. Such is the case for example for a milestone dating from the reign of Diocletian and written in the nominative, discovered at the Xth mile on the road between *Ad Calceum Herculis* and Tobna.[84] Another milestone, apparently from Diocletian and in the dative, was discovered at the same station.[85] It's therefore difficult to establish, on the basis of the forms adopted, their relationship with possible road works in this area.

The concentration of milestones in a particular place contributed at least to some monumentalization of the route concerned. The grouping of milestones in the Xth mile of the route between *Ad Calceum Herculis* and Tobna gives evidence of it: they were arranged on both sides of the way, in two parallel lines about ten meters apart and are generally aligned in chronological order.[86] The questions persist, who had done this, when and in what purpose. Does this concentration serve to monumentalize the limit of the city? The hypothesis seems to be excluded insofar as milestones have been discovered recording the XIIth mile from Tobna to *Ad Calceum*, and the XIIth mile from *Ad Calceum* to Tobna.

In fact, we know poorly the history of the city. The place of Tobna (*Thuben*), like those of Biskra (*Vescera*) and *Thabudeos* (*Tabudium*), was reached by the armies of Cornelius Balbus in 21 or 20 a.C.[87]. Pliny the Elder, who reports the triumph of Balbus, describes Tobna as an *oppidum*. All those places are located in Caesarian Mauretania by Ptolemy, whose documentation is prior to 110 p.C. This fact suggests that they could have belonged before to the former Gaetulian territories left to Juba II., under the supe-

---

[81] ALBERTINI 1931a, 366.
[82] ISAAC 1990, 305.
[83] SALAMA 1987, 59.
[84] LESCHI 1949, 59: *[Imp(erator) Caesar --- Va]lerius [Diocle]tianus Aug(ustus) Germanicus pontif(ex) maximus p(ater) p(atriae) co(n)s(ul) ---*
[85] LESCHI 1949, 60–61: *Imp(eratori) C(a)es(ari) D[iocl]eti(ano) Victori ac [perpe]tuo semper Aug(usto).*
[86] LESCHI 1949, 58–62: on the left of the road leading to Tobna, a milestone of Elagabal was followed by a milestone of Alexander Severus, and a milestone of Diocletian in the nominative; on the right, in the opposite direction, a milestone of Licinianus, a milestone of Constantius Chlorus, a milestone of Galerius, a milestone without the name of the emperor, then a milestone of Constantine, one of Diocletian, one of Gratian, one of Constantius and one of Maximus and Flavius Victor.
[87] Plin. nat. 5,37. See DESANGES 1980, 400.

rior authority of Rome.⁸⁸ Their integration in the province of *Africa Proconsularis* was perhaps carried out under the reign of Trajan: the construction of the fortress of *Ad Maiores* and the road works on the way to *Thabudeos* would have given a favourable context for the displacement of this interprovincial border between Caesarian Mauretania and *Africa Proconsularis*, westward.⁸⁹ The importance of road traffic in the area during the 2ⁿᵈ century and its consideration by the provincial authorities are attested by the local measures decided under the reign of Commodus, both in terms of surveillance and intervention on the road network as testified by milestones. The role of junction's roadway played by Tobna and attested from this period is confirmed by the Tabula Peutingeriana, which original picture dates perhaps from the tetrarchic period.⁹⁰

Should we then systematically perceive the main roads involving Tobna in terms of military function, linked to the border and its defense as argued since JEAN BARADEZ?⁹¹ This interpretation remains very significant within the framework of the connection between Tobna and *Ad Calceum* leading to *Lambaesis* or the road between *Badias*, *Thabudeos*, Tobna and *Zarai*, both of them considered as "road border".⁹² POL TROUSSET, who subscribed to the interpretation of the road network of Tobna proposed by JEAN BARADEZ, recognizes however that the military function of the "roads of the *limes*" of Numidia should not be overestimated and quotes their trade function which was probably very ancient.⁹³ In a more radical perspective MICHEL JANON did not hesitate to doubt the defensive role of the official measures concerning this area of the Numidian border: indeed, this role would have been turned towards one external enemy, who remains however to identify.⁹⁴

The epigraphic documentation of the Severian period brings some significant evidence of human occupation and circulation in the area of Tobna. The inscription engraved between 198 and 201 on the north face of the Jbel Zireg, south of the Chott el Hodna, mentions an assignment of public lands (*agri*, *pascua* and *fontes*), to civilian or military settlers.⁹⁵ Less than twenty kilometers further south, the area of Aïn Soltane, where an inscription dedicated to Alexander Severus was discovered,⁹⁶

---

88 Ptol. 4,2,7. See DESANGES 1964, 38–47; DESANGES 1999, 31–34.
89 DESANGES 1964; DESANGES 2006, 56.
90 TALBERT 2010, 133–136.
91 BARADEZ 1949, 148–149.
92 TROUSSET 1980, 152; TROUSSET 2003, 366.
93 TROUSSET 1980, 154.
94 JANON 1977, 477–479.
95 AE 1946, 38: *Ex auctoritate Imppp(eratorum) / Caes(arum) L(uci) Septimi Severi et / M(arci) Aurelii Antonini et P(ubli) Sep/timi Getae Auggg(ustorum) agri et / pascua et fontes adsi/gnata [[sunt ---ma]] / [[---]] curantibus Epag/atho et Manilio Caeci/liano corniculario / praef(ecti) iussu Anici Fa/usti leg(ati) co(n)s(ularis) per M(arcum) Gennium / Felicem evocatum / leg(ionis) III Aug(ustae)*. See LESCHI 1948. Concerning the discussion about the interpretation of this inscription: FAURE/LEVEAU 2015, 137–138.
96 CIL VIII 8781 and 18017.

shows notable evidences of centuriation.[97] The aera of Tobna seems to have benefited from a remarkable development during the Severan dynasty, as confirmed in addition by the famous "*Zarai* tariff",[98] written in 202 and which may have described a trade route leading from the oases of the Jerid to Tobna and then *Zarai* by the south of the Aurès.[99] This route evokes singularly the descriptions provided later by the Arab geographers,[100] locating Tobna at the main road towards the Libyan desert eastward, and at the mouth of a road coming from the oasis of Ouargla, in the south. According to AL-BAKRĪ, Tobna was the most important city between Kairouan and Sijilmassa, and for AL-MALĪKĪ the city represented the western border of Ifriqiya.[101]

To conclude, the data concerning the roads involving Tobna at different periods during the Roman Empire invite to consider not only the presumed military purpose, but the importance played locally by the city and its area in terms of road traffic and commercial exchanges, that could explain the number of milestones discovered around Tobna. On the other hand, if the road network in the region of Tobna was related to the Roman frontier in Numidia, where was the Roman border, and what was the Roman border? The answer is more complex than the limit regularly given to extension of the Roman Empire in this region by the maps towards nowadays, reducing the *limes Tubuniensis* to a single line.

Bibliography

ALBERTINI 1931a = E. ALBERTINI, Le réseau routier de la Numidie méridionale, *CRAI* 1931, 363–370.
ALBERTINI 1931b = E. ALBERTINI, Inscriptions d'El Kantara et de la région, *Revue africaine* 72, 1931, 193–261.
BARADEZ 1949 = J. BARADEZ, *Fossatum Africae*: Recherches aériennes sur l'organisation des confins sahariens à l'époque romaine, Paris 1949.
BARADEZ 1953 = J. BARADEZ, Inscriptions de la région du Limes de Numidie de Biskra à Tobna, *Libyca* 1, 1953, 151–165.
BARADEZ 1959 = J. BARADEZ, Réseau routier de commandement, d'administration et d'exploitation de la zone arrière du limes de Numidie, in: Limes-Studien. Vorträge des 3. Internationalen Limes-Kongresses in Rheinfelden/Basel 1957, Basel 1959, 19–30.
BENABBÈS 2005 = A. BENABBÈS, Les premiers raids arabes en Numidie byzantine: questions toponymiques, in: C. BRIAND-PONSART (ed.), Identités et culture dans l'Algérie antique, Rouen 2005, 459–492.

---

97 SOYER 1976, 142.
98 CIL VIII 4508.
99 TROUSSET 2003, 366; GUÉDON 2014, 118–120.
100 The road leading from the Jerid to the south of the Aurès is mentioned by Ibn Ḥawḳal, who precised that it followed a route used in Antiquity: IBN ḤAWḲAL, *Configuration de la terre*, 85 (trad. KRAMERS/WIET 2001, t. 1, 85); also AL-BAKRĪ, *Description de l'Afrique septentrionale* (MAC GUCKIN DE SLANE 1859, 175). Concerning this road, see VANACKER 1973, 664. The road between the Aurès and the tunisian chotts, towards Ouargla, is evoked by IBN KHALDŪN (MAC GUCKIN DE SLANE 1856, 201).
101 BENABBÈS 2005, 483.

BÉNABOU 1976 = M. BÉNABOU, La résistance africaine à la romanisation, Paris 1976.
BENSEDDIK 1999 = N. BENSEDDIK, Septime Sévère, P. Aelius Peregrinus Rogatus et le *limes* de Maurétanie Césarienne, in: C. LEPELLEY/X. DUPUIS (ed.), Frontières et limites géographiques de l'Afrique du Nord antique: Hommage à Pierre Salama, Paris 1999, 89–110.
CAGNAT 1913 = R. CAGNAT, L'armée romaine d'Afrique et l'occupation militaire de l'Afrique sous les empereurs, Paris 1913 [New York 1975].
CARCOPINO 1925 = J. CARCOPINO, Le limes de Numidie et sa garde syrienne, *Syria* 6, 1925, 30–57 and 118–149.
CHRISTOL 2012 = M. CHRISTOL, L'empereur et les cités: la construction de la *via nova* de Cirta vers Rusicade sous Hadrien, *Epigraphica* 74, 2012, 185–200.
COURTOIS 1955 = C. COURTOIS, Les Vandales et l'Afrique, Paris 1955.
CSEL = Corpus Scriptorum Ecclesiasticorum Latinorum.
DAGUET 1992 = A. DAGUET, L. Domitius Aurelianus, *perpetuus imperator*, *AntAfr* 28, 1992, 173–186.
DESANGES 1964 = J. DESANGES, Les territoires gétules de Juba II, *REA* 66, 1964, 33–47.
DESANGES 1980 = J. DESANGES, Pline l'Ancien. Histoire naturelle, livre 5, 1–46. 1ère partie (L'Afrique du Nord), Paris 1980.
DESANGES 1999 = J. DESANGES, Réflexions sur l'organisation de l'espace selon la latitude dans l'Afrique du Nord antique, in: C. LEPELLEY/X. DUPUIS (ed.), Frontières et limites géographiques de l'Afrique du Nord antique: Hommage à Pierre Salama, Paris 1999, 27–41.
DESANGES 2006 = J. DESANGES, Aperçu sur les sources classiques relatives à la Numidie méridionale, *Aouras* 3, 2006, 53–63.
DUPUIS 1992 = X. DUPUIS, Constructions publiques et vie municipale en Afrique de 244 à 276, *MEFRA* 104.1, 1992, 233–280.
DUPUIS 1999 = X. DUPUIS, Cuicul, la Confédération Cirtéenne et les Suburbures: des limites ambiguës, in: C. LEPELLEY/X. DUPUIS (ed.), Frontières et limites géographiques de l'Afrique du Nord antique: Hommage à Pierre Salama, Paris 1999, 129–138.
FENTRESS 1979 = E. FENTRESS, Numidia and the Roman Army: Social, Military and Economic Aspects of the Frontier Zone, Oxford 1979.
FAURE/LEVEAU 2015 = P. FAURE/P. LEVEAU, Les marges de la Numidie romaine à la lumière d'une nouvelle inscription des Monts des Ouled Naïl, *AntAfr* 51, 2015, 119–142.
GASCOU 1972 = J. GASCOU, La politique municipale de l'Empire romain en Afrique proconsulaire de Trajan à Septime Sévère, Rome 1972.
GRANGE 1902 = R. GRANGE, Monographie de Tobna (*Thubunae*), Recueil des notices et mémoires de la Société Archéologique du Département de Constantine 35, 1901 [1902], 1–96.
GSELL 1901a = S. GSELL, Notes d'archéologie algérienne, *BCTH* 1901, 308–323.
GSELL 1901b = S. GSELL, Note sur des antiquités découvertes à Tobna et à Mustapha, *BCTH* 1901, 447- 451.
GSELL 1902 = S. GSELL, Notes d'archéologie algérienne, *BCTH* 1902, 506–532.
GSELL 1911 = S. GSELL, Atlas archéologique de l'Algérie, Alger-Paris 1911.
GUÉDON 2014 = S. GUÉDON, La *lex uestis peregrinae* dans le tarif de Zaraï, *AntAfr* 50, 2014, 111–123.
GUÉDON 2018 = S. GUÉDON, La frontière de l'Afrique romaine à l'époque tardive: Le cas emblématique de Tobna et du *limes Tubuniensis* (*Notitia Dignitatum, Occ.*, 25.25), *Historia* 67.3, 2018 im Druck.
ISAAC 1988 = B. ISAAC, The Meaning of the Terms Limes and Limitanei, *JRS* 78, 1988, 125–147.
ISAAC 1990 = B. ISAAC, The Limits of Empire: The Roman Army in the East, Oxford 1990.
JACQUES 1992 = F. JACQUES, Propriétés impériales et cités en Numidie méridionale, *CCG* 3, 1992, 123–139.
JANNIARD 2015 = S. JANNIARD, Limitanei, in: Y. LE BOHEC (ed.), The Encyclopedia of the Roman Army, vol. 2, Chichester 2015, 587–589.

Janon 1973 = M. Janon, Recherches à Lambèse, I et II, *AntAfr* 7, 1973, 193–254.
Janon 1977 = M. Janon, Lambèse et l'occupation militaire de la Numidie méridionale, in: D. Haupt/H.G. Horn (ed.), Studien zu den Militärgrenzen Roms 2: Vorträge des 10. Internationalen Limeskongresses in der Germania Inferior in Xanten 1974, Bonn 1977, 473–485.
Kramers/Wiet 2001 = J.H. Kramers/G. Wiet, Ibn Hawqal: La Configuration de la Terre (Kitab surat al-ard), Paris 2001.
Laporte/Dupuis 2009 = J.-P. Laporte/X. Dupuis, De *Nigrenses Maiores* à Négrine, *AntAfr* 45, 2009, 51–102.
Le Bohec 1989 = Y. Le Bohec, La Troisième Légion Auguste, Paris 1989.
Le Bohec 1995 = Y. Le Bohec, La « frontière militaire » de la Numidie, de Trajan à 238, in: A. Rousselle (ed.), Frontières terrestres, frontières célestes dans l'Antiquité, Perpignan 1995, 119–142.
Le Bohec 2008 = Y. Le Bohec, Routes et armées dans l'épigraphie de l'Afrique romaine, *CCG* 20, 2008, 185–197.
Lenoir 2011 = M. Lenoir, Le camp romain, Proche-Orient et Afrique du Nord, Rome 2011.
Leschi 1947 = L. Leschi, Nouvelles recherches aériennes sur le « limes » d'Afrique, *Revue africaine* 91, 1947, 201–212.
Leschi 1949 = L. Leschi, Nouveaux milliaires du « limes » d'Afrique », *BCTH*, 1946/1949, 397–407.
Leschi 1948 = L. Leschi, Une assignation de terres en Afrique sous Septime Sévère, *Revue de Constantine* 66, 1948, 103–116.
Leveau 1977 = P. Leveau, L'opposition de la montagne et de la plaine dans l'historiographie de l'Afrique du Nord antique, *Annales de Géographie* 86, 1977, 201–205.
Leveau 1990 = P. Leveau, L'Aurès dans l'Antiquité, *Encyclopédie berbère* 8, 1990, 1097–1103.
Mac Guckin de Slane 1856 = W. Mac Guckin de Slane, Ibn Khaldūn, Histoire des Berbères et des dynasties musulmanes de l'Afrique septentrionale, t. 3, Alger 1856.
Mac Guckin de Slane 1859 = W. Mac Guckin de Slane, Al-Bakrī, Description de l'Afrique septentrionale, Paris 1859.
Mandouze 1982 = A. Mandouze (ed), Prosopographie chrétienne du Bas-Empire 1: Prosopographie de l'Afrique chrétienne (303–533), Paris 1982.
Marcillet-Jaubert 1980 = J. Marcillet-Jaubert, Bornes milliaires de Numidie, *AntAfr* 16, 1980, 161–184.
Mattingly 1995 = D.J. Mattingly, Tripolitania, Londres 1995.
Meouak 2006 = M. Meouak, Fortifications, habitats et peuplement entre Bougie et la Qal'a des Banū Ḥammād. Les données du géographe al-Idrīsī (c.493/1100-c.560/1165), *MCV* 36.1, 2006, 173–193.
Meouak 2009 = M. Meouak, Le Hodna occidental entre régions méditerranéennes et plaines désertiques: organisation des terroirs, communautés rurales et productions agricoles au Moyen Âge, *REMM* 126, 2009, 117–139.
Modéran 2003 = Y. Modéran, Les Maures et l'Afrique romaine (IVe-VIIe siècle), Rome 2003.
Modéran 2008 = Y. Modéran, Des Maures aux Berbères: identité et ethnicité en Afrique du Nord dans l'Antiquité tardive, in: V. Gazeau/P. Bauduin/Y. Modéran (ed.), Identité et Ethnicité. Concepts, débats historiographiques, exemples (IIIe-XIIe siècle), Caen 2008, 91–134.
Morizot 1979 = P. Morizot, Vues nouvelles sur l'Aurès antique, *CRAI* 1979, 309–337.
Morizot 1991 = P. Morizot, Les stations de la Table de Peutinger entre Lambèse et *Ad Calceum Herculis*, in: V. Maxfield/M. Dobson (ed.), Roman Frontier Studies 1989. Proceedings of the XVth International Congress of Roman Frontier Studies, Exeter 1991, 337–346.
Morizot 1997 = P. Morizot, Archéologie aérienne de l'Aurès, Paris 1997.
Morizot 1998 = P. Morizot, Les voies romaines de Lambèse à *Calceus Herculis* (El Kantara, Algérie), *AntAfr* 34, 1998, 149–155.

Napoli 1997 = J. Napoli, Recherches sur les fortifications linéaires romaines, Rome 1997.
Perler/Maier 1969 = O. Perler/J.-L. Maier, Les voyages de saint Augustin, Paris 1969.
Picard 1947 = G. Picard, Castellum Dimmidi, Alger/Paris 1947.
Pringle 2001 = D. Pringle, The Defence of Byzantine Africa from Justinian to the Arab Conquest: An Account of the Military History and Archaeology of the African Provinces in the Sixth and Seventh Centuries, Oxford ²2001.
Rebuffat 1980 = R. Rebuffat, À propos du « Limes tripolitanus », *Revue archéologique* 1, 1980, 105–124.
Reddé 2015 = M. Reddé, Limes, in: Y. Le Bohec (ed.), The Encyclopedia of the Roman Army, vol. 2, Chichester 2015, 586–587.
Salama 1951 = P. Salama, Les bornes milliaires de Djemila-Cuicul et leur intérêt pour l'histoire de la ville, *Revue africaine* 95, 1951, 213–272.
Salama 1959 = P. Salama, Bornes milliaires et problèmes stratégiques du Bas-Empire en Maurétanie, *CRAI* 1959, 346–354.
Salama 1980 = P. Salama, Les voies romaines de Sitifis à Igilgili: Un exemple de politique routière approfondie, *AntAfr* 16, 1980, 101–133.
Salama 1987 = P. Salama, Bornes milliaires d'Afrique Proconsulaire: Un panorama historique du Bas Empire romain, Rome 1987.
Salama 2002 = P. Salama, Les bornes milliaires du territoire de Tipasa (Maurétanie Césarienne), Rome 2002.
Shaw 1982 = B.D. Shaw, Fear and loathing: the nomad menace and Roman Africa, in: C.M. Wells (ed.), Roman Africa / L'Afrique romaine. The 1980 Governor-General Vanier Lectures, Revue de l'Université d'Ottawa, Ottawa 1982, 25–46.
Soyer 1976 = J. Soyer, Les centurations romaines en Algérie orientale, *AntAfr* 10, 1976, 107–180.
Talbert 2010 = R.J.A. Talbert, Rome's World. The Peutinger Map Reconsidered, Cambridge 2010.
Thomasson 1996 = B.E. Thomasson, *Fasti Africani*: Senatorische und ritterliche Amtsträger in den römischen Provinzen Nordafrikas von Augustus bis Diokletian, Stockholm 1996.
Trousset 1974 = P. Trousset, Recherches sur le *limes Tripolitanus* du Chott-el-Djerid à la frontière tuniso-libyenne, Paris 1974.
Trousset 1980 = P. Trousset, Les milliaires de Chebika, *AntAfr* 15, 1980, 135–154.
Trousset 1984 = P. Trousset, Note sur un type d'ouvrage linéaire du *limes* d'Afrique, BCTH n. s. 17B, 1984, 383–398.
Trousset 1991 = P. Trousset, Besseriani (Ad Maiores), *Encyclopédie berbère* 10, 1991, 1478–1480.
Trousset 1991a = P. Trousset, Badias (Badîs, Badès), *Encyclopédie berbère* 9, 1991, 1299–1302.
Trousset 2003 = P. Trousset, Le tarif de Zarai: essai sur les circuits commerciaux dans la zone présaharienne, *AntAfr* 38–39, 2002/2003, 355–373.
Trousset 2004 = P. Trousset, Pénétration romaine et organisation de la zone frontière dans le prédésert tunisien, *L'Africa romana* 15.1, 2004, 59–88.
Van Berchem 1952 = D. Van Berchem, L'armée de Dioclétien et la réforme constantinienne, Paris 1952.
Vanacker 1973 = C. Vanacker, Géographie économique de l'Afrique du Nord selon les auteurs arabes du IXe siècle au milieu du XIIe siècle, *Annales. Économies, Sociétés, Civilisations* 28.3, 1973, 659–680.

Mariette de Vos Raaijmakers
Twin Roads: the Road Carthage-Theveste and the *via nova Rusicadensis*; some Observations and Questions

Abstract: This paper will give some updated information about two roads connecting the Mediterranean coast to the inland of *Africa proconsularis* and *Numidia*. As far as the first road is concerned – from Carthage to Theveste – its use in the Byzantine period will be discussed. Of the second road – from *Rusicade* to *Cirta* – an overview will be presented. At first they were a sort of twin roads: the first one, in *Proconsularis*, was built by Hadrian and his *legatus pro praetore* Publius Metilius Secundus. Before the first road was completed, Hadrian and Sex. Iulius Maior started to build the second one, in *Numidia*, but under different conditions. Both roads were necessary for the army and also for transporting the *onus fiscale* to the ports and ship it to Rome, where the grain distributions were a *conditio sine qua non*: the emperor could not reign without them. In the Appendix three Hadrianic milestones of the road Carthage-Theveste are rediscussed and four milestones of the *via nova Rusicadensis* are illustrated.

Zusammenfassung: Dieser Beitrag wird einige aktualisierte Informationen über zwei Straßen darlegen, die die Mittelmeerküste mit dem Inland der *Africa proconsularis* und der *Numidia* verbinden. Im Bezug auf die erste Straße – von Karthago nach Theveste – wird ihr Gebrauch in byzantinischer Zeit diskutiert werden. Zur zweiten Straße – von *Rusicade* nach *Cirta* – wird ein Überblick präsentiert. Anfangs waren die beiden Straßen eine Art Zwillingsstraße: die erste, in der *Proconsularis*, wurde unter Hadrian und seinem *legatus pro praetore* Publius Metilius Secundus gebaut. Bevor die erste Straße fertiggestellt worden war, begannen Hadrian und Sex. Iulius Maior, die zweite, in *Numidia*, zu bauen, aber unter anderen Konditionen. Beide Straßen waren notwendig für die Armee und um das *onus fiscale* zu den Häfen zu transportieren und es nach Rom zu verschiffen, wo die Kornverteilungen eine *conditio sine qua non* war: der Kaiser konnte ohne sie nicht herrschen. Im Appendix werden drei hadrianische Meilensteine der Straße Karthago-Theveste erneut diskutiert und vier Meilensteine der *via nova Rusicadensis* erläutert.

Article note: I thank ANNE KOLB for the generous invitation to participate at this colloquium, her observations improved this paper consistently; I am grateful to MARINA DE FRANCESCHINI for editing the English text, to ALESSANDRO BATTISTI for 3D modeling and cartography, and to RMN for permission to publish the photos Fig. 11a, 15b-c and 16a-c. The Ministero degli Affari Esteri e della Cooperazione Internazionale and the University of Trento financed the scientific mission in Algeria.

https://doi.org/10.1515/9783110638332-018

Road Carthage-Theveste (Table 1, Fig. 1, 3; App. 1–3, Fig. 10–12)

Three years ago we published the ancient road network of Map 33 (Téboursouk). The Map covers 640 square km of the *Carte des Sites Archéologiques et des Monuments Historiques de Tunisie*.[1] The survey for this map was conducted between 1994 and 2014 by the University of Trento (Italy) in cooperation with the *Institut National du Patrimoine de Tunisie*. In the rural landscape 800 sites have been found and mapped in detail; their density per square km is close to the one of the surroundings of Rome. Complete raw data of this survey are available in: http://rusafricum.org/en/thuggasurvey/home/

Table 1: road Carthage-Theveste,[2] 191.74 miles long = 284 km. Today 320 milestones are known and partially preserved.

Author	year	topography	nr. milestones
Pierre Salama	1987	caput-finis viae	246–1 =245 known
Nabil Kallala	2006, 2012	Sicca Veneria	016 new
Zeïneb Benzina Abdallah, Leïla Ladjimi Sebaï	2011	MP 110	03 new, possibly pertaining
Uwe Bigalke	2005	MP 20–98	020 new
Mariette de Vos/Redha Attoui	2015	Thugga survey	019 new
Moheddine Chaouali	2016	Thurris-Laribus	004 new
Ahmed Boujarra/Lotfi Naddari	2010, 2016	MP 158–162, Ammaedara	016 new
Total			320

26 of the 192 miles of the ancient road between Carthage and Theveste figure on the mentioned Map 33, from the 63rd to the 89th mile; all milestones are numbered starting from Carthage (Fig. 1). The road was built under the supervision of P. Metilius Secundus, who was the imperial *legatus pro praetore* during Hadrian's 7th *tribunicia potestas*, as mentioned on the milestones along the road. In the *lapidarium* of the fortress of Teboursouk the upper part of the 82nd milestone was recently identified (App. 1) and a photograph of the 85th, since the 19th c. at Paris, corrects Letronne's observations of 1844 and unifies CIL VIII 10048 with 10081 = 22071 (App. 2); it stimulated also a re-examination of the distance number on CIL VIII 22063, which came probably from Musti (App. 3).

Metilius probably started the works during Hadrian's 5th *tribunicia potestas*, on December 10th of 121 AD. On July 1st of 123, P. Metilius Secundus was replaced by Sex. Iulius Maior, as we know from the inscription on the bridge on Wadi Naguess, 4 km E

---

[1] de Vos/Attoui 2015 with map.
[2] I thank Hélène Cuvigny who during the congress observed that *a Karthagine Thevestem* is not a hodonym, but part of a phrase graved on the milestones, see Cuvigny 2018, VII. Accordingly, I changed the title of my paper.

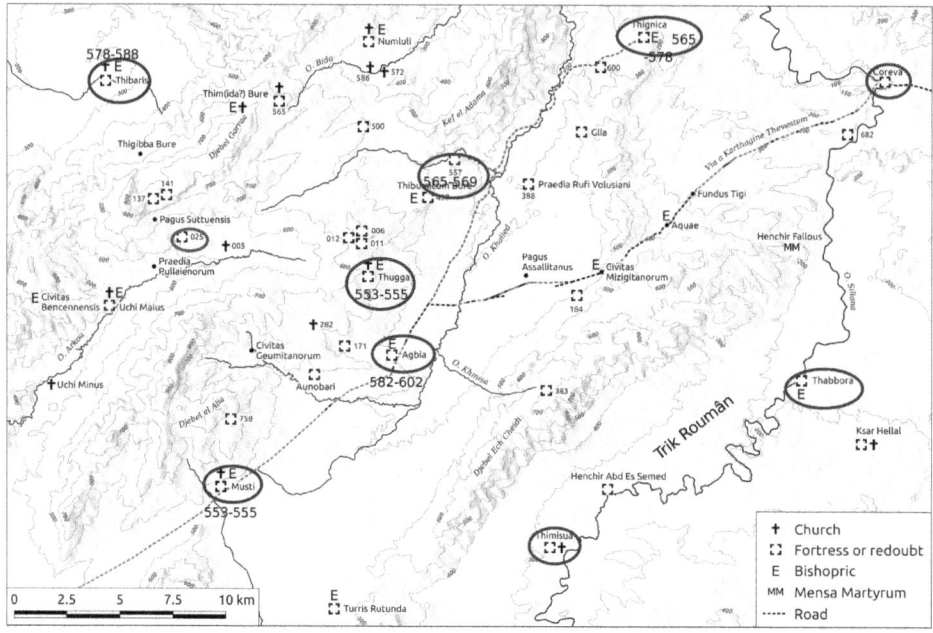

Fig. 1: Thugga survey: map of the main roads and the main Byzantine fortresses (encircled) with building period. Site 25: Farm of Ain Wassel built or enlarged around 600, abandoned shortly after 700. Cartography A. Battisti.

of Ammaedara.[3] On July 1st, the *proconsul* of the proconsular province of Africa was replaced and probably also the *legatus Augusti pro praetore* was replaced. Therefore Metilius must have built the road and related structures in one year and a half (about 560 days) covering a span of 258,5 km: this means building 500 m (half a km) each day. He also built at least 37 bridges[4] and other structures, and left 191 milestones. Metilius' name is preserved on 20 milestones,[5] and also on the final inscription of a stele found in Theveste, the only one where he is called *consul designatus* (CIL VIII 22173).

---

[3] BENZINA BEN ABDALLAH 1995; BOUJARRA/NADDARI, 2010, 113–114, 122 and Tableau 2, Fig. 1, 3, Photos 5- 7; NADDARI 2016, 79, 80, 83–84, Fig. 4, 6,7; GRIRA 2016, 120; RATHMANN 2003, 172, note 933 considers December 9th of 123 as end date of Metilius' road building activities, according to Hadrian's 7th *tribunicia potestas*.

[4] GRIRA 2016.

[5] From the 21 milestones of LE BOHEC 1989, 376, note 87 bis, BENZINA BEN ABDALLAH 1995, 98 and CHAOUALI 2016b, 87, note 10, one has to be cancelled: CIL VIII 10081 = 22071, because identical to 10048, s. App. 2. RATHMANN 2003, 172, 178–181 counts 27 milestones including also the fragmentary where Metilius' name is lacking; his 72nd milestone is based on a wrong bibliographic reference of LE BOHEC 1989, 584 to CARTON 1895, p. 3, viz. p. 7 n. 3: not LXXII, but LXIIII, fragment containing only these numerals, no text, so not datable to 123.

The name *Legio III Augusta* also appears on the milestones, proving that the army was involved in the construction of the road.⁶ The *Legio III Augusta* never had more than 10.000 men.⁷ Hadrian became emperor on August 11ᵗʰ of 117, therefore Metilius or his predecessor probably started to build the road from that date. Anyway, even a period of five years would be a record: working 300 days per year means that in only 1500 days 9000 men were able to build 258 kilometers of roads, an average of 170 meters per day.

The course of the roads was planned by the *gromatici*, and the leveling was verified with *chorobates* by the military *libratores* or *mensores*, in cooperation with *mechanici* and *architecti*. Different teams of soldiers and *possessores* were engaged together for digging the bed of the road (*fossa*) down to the bed rock, for quarrying, and for transporting sand, gravel, rough stones and ashlar for bridges and substructures. The *fossa* was filled with several layers of packed earth, stone and gravel, which formed the *agger* or *dorsum*; then the builders paved the surface and created a drainage system. The upper layer had the shape of a turtle shell, so that the water would flow away, and was topped with gravel (*glarea*); also slabs (*saxo* or *lapide quadrato*) were used, but only inside the cities. The Hadrianic milestones of the *via a Karthagine Thevestem* prove the intervention of the *Legio III* that *stravit viam*, without mentioning how it was paved, since there were different kinds of paving: *glareata* (graveled) and *saxo/lapide quadrato* or *silice* (with squared or irregular stones), or only surfaced. In general, all Roman roads outside the cities were paved with gravel; only inside and near the cities the roads were paved with slabs, as at the entrance of Ammaedara and in its surroundings.⁸ Near the above mentioned bridge of Wadi Naguess, the slabs were joined with dovetail mortises and metal tenons. The road was still very well preserved in the 19ᵗʰ c. between Sidi Abd-er-Rebou and Sidi bou Atila (*i.e.* NE of Musti between the 89ᵗʰ and 85ᵗʰ mile from Carthage): during his trip in 1833–34 Temple observed that the road was not paved with polygon blocks like the Roman roads in Italy, but with materials that resemble those used in London and Paris. Tissot during his exploration from 1–15 October 1876 wrote: 'La voie romaine est parfaitement reconnaissable entre Hedja (Agbia) et Henchir Mest (Musti); sur plusieurs points elle a conservé les dalles bombées de sa *summa crusta*, ainsi que les *gomphi* disposés de distance en distance sur les bas côtés'.⁹ In 1895 ca. Carton sectioned the road near Thugga, S of the 81ˢᵗ

---

6 Drew-Bear/Eck 1976, 294–295.
7 Le Bohec 1989, 542.
8 Boujarra/Naddari 2010, 112–114, Photos 2–4, and 7; discussion of *stravit*: 115–116; cf. Chaouali 2016b, 87–88. According to Galliazzo 1994 I, 477–478 *via strata* has a neutral meaning of *manto stradale* covered with any type of protecting material. Quilici 2008, 567–568: offers a detailed overview of roads in central Italy.
9 Temple 1835, 282; Tissot 1888, 348, see p. XVI of Reinach's Préface. Traces are visible even today to the E of the modern one: de Vos/Attoui 2015, 108–109, Fig. 143–144 (from the upper right to the lower left corner).

milestone, and published a drawing of the surface made with irregular stones.[10] Near Coreva and in many other places on map 33 is documented the *glarea*, that still exists and is in use.[11] Local communities and *possessores* who lived along the roads are supposed to have supplied the building materials. The high quality building technique and the ability of the workmen is proven by the water overflow (*vadum*) at Aquae, between the 72nd and 73rd milestone, where a retaining wall still protects the road passing through the stream of Wadi Kebir, on the slope of Djebel Kechrid. No modern structure in such a position would last for 18 centuries as this one. The workmen left 203 stonecutter marks (*notae lapicidinarum*) on the protruding and unpolished surface of the rough ashlar blocks. The distribution of different groups of marks gives information about the organization for finishing the ashlar blocks.[12] The blocks were cut in the quarry by the *exemptores* (Plin. nat. 36,125), and once they reached the building site they were finished with edges, in order to fit together in regular courses. The marks of the *notae* are rather irregular, because of the rough surface of the stone and also because they were not incised by *scriptores* (CIL VI 9557). They have large, shallow and round incisions, instead of the deep triangular ones that we see in public and private inscriptions of N Africa. These last were more sophisticated, because of the use of shading, i.e. thicker or thinner strokes. The stonecutters simply had to mark the number of stones that they cut and/or drafted, for military, civilian or private accountability; the *notae* were meant for internal use, and when the wall was finished they were not supposed to be seen or read.

In the Ebro valley in Hispania, on a similar but larger dam, the *Legio IIII* marked only one single block in the Augustan age, with the abbreviated *tria nomina* of a person whose role in the construction was not assessed.[13] Another Augustan hydraulic work in Hispania, the Roman bridge of Martorell, has marks of three different Legions.[14] On the other hand, among the many mason's marks of the aqueduct Zaghuan-Carthage there are no legionary marks;[15] nor has them the wall at Aquae, which was built at the same time and has a gravel road passing over its top.

We have imperial patronage for three major bridges: the first one, on the road between Carthage and *Hippo Regius* (Wadi Zerga), was built by Tiberius and was new

---

10 CARTON 1895, 35–36, Fig. 17; DE VOS/ATTOUI 2015, 86–88. Cf. DE BOSREDON 1878, 423 who sectioned the road near Theveste. SALAMA 1951, 7 and LE BOHEC 1989, 368, repeat the above cited 19th c. autoptic descriptions.
11 DE VOS/ATTOUI 2015, Coreva: 30–33; hr. Baghla 35, 42–44; Ain Younès 53–54; to the W of Ain Younès 66–67; near the bridge and 75th milestone: 73; Khalled valley, Wadi Lahmar, 83 and section 84; Wadi Rmel: 108–109; see also KALLALA 2012, 206, 214 Fig. 8 at the 108th mile.
12 DE VOS/ATTOUI 2015, 51–65, Fig. 63, map of the wall Fig. 31–32; section of the slope Fig. 33; http://rusafricum.org/en/thuggasurvey/DU576/gallery/epigrafi/
13 URIBE et al. 2012, 341–344, Fig. 9.
14 GURT/RODA 2005.
15 RÖDER 1974; the aqueduct was probably built around the second quarter of the II sec. For chronology related problems see WILSON 1998, 79–81.

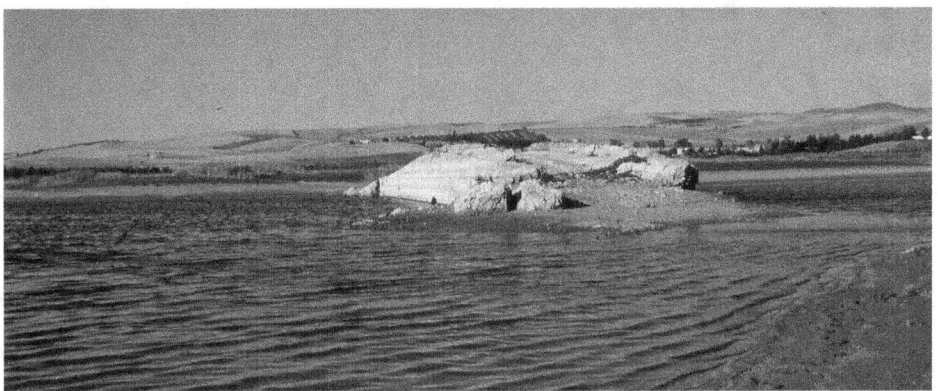

Fig. 2: *Pons Traiani*, Medjerda river, Sidi Salem dam, Photo M. de Vos 1993.

(*pontem novam*) (Fig. 2). The second one, on the road Thabraca – Simitthus – Ammaedara, was built by Trajan with the *Legio III Augusta*.[16] The third one, near Ammaedara (mentioned above),[17] was built by Hadrian in 123 with the *Legio III Augusta*, and is mentioned by an inscription on a slab of the fence (CIL VIII 14386, 10117 and AE 1995, 1652). The emperors eagerly emphasized their euergetism in bridge building.

The most recent milestone of the road Carthage-Theveste dates back to 387–88, at the time of Maximus and Flavius Victor *Augusti*; after that date there is no other information about the road. The law of Constantine, sent in 319 AD to Proculus, *proconsul Africae* (Cod. Theod. 15,3,1), stated that the emphyteutic possessors had to repair the roads. The law of Iulianus, sent in 363 AD to Avitianus, *vicarius Africae* (Cod. Theod. 15,3,2) insisted that nobody could be exempted from roadbuilding, reminding that this concerned an old law: *iuxta morem priscum*. In the following centuries, conservation and maintenance of the road was not as it used to be, as proven by the presence of dromedaries only in that period. During the excavation of the Ain Wassel farm, we found 3 skulls of dromedaries and only one of a donkey and one of a horse. Some African ceramists of the 4th and 5th centuries represented how oil and water were transported by those marvelous animals. In Tunisia local ceramic is transported with animals even today.[18]

The map of the surveyed region (Fig. 1) shows the late antique period, with churches, episcopates and Byzantine fortresses. The fortresses were built starting from the mid 6th century until the end of this century.[19] Their function was to protect the cities, agriculture (Fig. 3) and also the lead and salt mines. The monumental for-

---

16 GALLIAZZO 1994 II, cat. n° 902, 437–438; n° 916, 442–443.
17 BENZINA BEN ABDALLAH 1995.
18 DE VOS 2000, Fig. 9.5.
19 DE VOS/ATTOUI 2011, 68, Cartina 4.

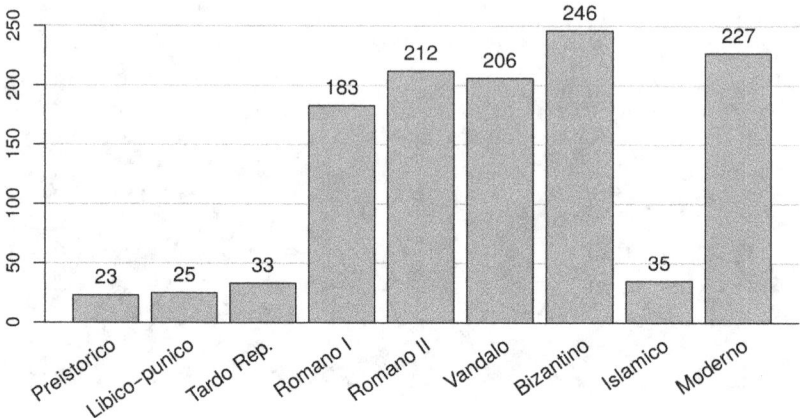

Fig. 3: Thugga survey: chronology sites based on surface pottery and inscriptions. Elaboration A. Battisti.

tresses were all located along the main roads, therefore the roads were probably still in use (Fig. 1).

Thanks to the Roman roads, the great general Belisarius could conquer N Africa defeating the Vandals in few months (from September 14th 533 to March of 534). One century and a half later, the same can be said of the Arab conquest.

Part of the farm of Ain Wassel (site 25 on map 33, here Fig. 1), was excavated to find evidence *inter alia* of the living and working conditions of the Severan *coloni* who had asked the application of the *lex Hadriana* on sharecropping; in 1891, a copy of this *lex* was found there by LOUIS CARTON. However, stratigraphy, building technique, pottery and a coin of the Byzantine emperor Mauritius proved that this part of the farm was built around 600 AD, and abandoned shortly after 700 AD. The decision to build or to enlarge the farm was probably linked to the presence of the fortifications of Thibaris '*Thiberia*' (578–588)[20] and Agbia (582–602):[21] Ain Wassel is located in between. A certain amount of the African Red Slip Ware D found in the pre-byzantine and byzantine stratigraphy came from the high quality ateliers of El Mahrine, 76 km to the N, and some items from Sidi Marzouk Tounsi, 90 km. to the S. This pottery was probably transported along the rivers Siliana and Medjerda until Tichilla, now Testour,[22] and further on along the road, on the *diverticulum* of the road Carthage-Theveste. Two 115 cm high amphorae arrived from the coast region near Nabeul, 150 km from Ain Wassel, by road transport only. The surplus of oil, wine and grain produced by the

---

20 dated by a dedication to Tiberius alone: DUVAL 1983, 199, Fig. 17.
21 PRINGLE 1981, 253–255, 527, Pl. LVIIIa-LXb suggests a date in the period of Mauritius because general layout, size, masonry and design are similar to those of the Maurician fort at Limisa, whose date is indicated by an epigraph (CIL VIII 12035).
22 DE VOS/ATTOUI 2015, 21.

farms was also transported elsewhere, in regional markets and to the coast for seaborne trade. On their way back from the ports of the coast or the river, the caravans of carts and animals could bring home fish and pottery. In most of the other 250 rural settlements on map 33 that we surveyed, an important amount of Byzantine pottery sherds was found. The settlement density and its *longue durée* are linked to intense farming and breeding and also to the lead mines and salt outcroppings which are found all around the surveyed area; it is at the center of the NE Maghreb salt province, one of the largest of the world. This salt province was recently investigated by a team of Tunisian geologists.[23]

The road from Carthage to Theveste enters in map 33 near the Byzantine fortress of Coreva.[24] The city was built inside a bight of the Siliana river, which was a natural defense, and fortified during the Byzantine period. Near the Siliana bridge 6 milestones were discovered; the bridge was destroyed by the river, but the continuous line on the map indicates the remains of the gravel road which resisted erosion until today.

Via nova Rusicadensis (Tables 2–5, Fig. 4–9, Appendix 4–7, Fig. 13–16)

The *via nova* from *Rusicade* to *Cirta* (now Skikda and Constantine) has been built in *Numidia* immediately after the first road in *Africa proconsularis* and in a different way, as if the previous road building experience in *Africa proconsularis* had changed the approach of road and bridge building in *Numidia*. Construction and maintenance of the road were particularly difficult, because it crosses the mountains in the Western part of the *Alpes Numidicae*. For this reason it had to be financed by the *r. p. Cirtensium* and the *possessores territori(i) Cirtensium*, as we know from two milestones, a marble one at the 6th mile N of *Cirta*, and another at 11 km S of *Rusicade*.[25] The bridges were paid by the Cirtan *res publica*, a kind of confederation with the cities of Chullu, *Rusicade* and *Milevum*. The text of the last patronage was inscribed on a marble slab of the fence of a bridge crossing a ravine near Wadi el Hadjar, 12 km to the N of Constantine (Fig. 7–8),[26] as the imperial patronage that was mentioned on the above cited inscriptions of three bridges in Tunisia. The form of the letters on the fence seemed

---

23 Distribution map of Byzantine pottery: DE VOS 2013, Table 6.4, 166; salt: MASROUHI et al. 2005, fig. 8, MASROUHI et al. 2014, 3.
24 DE VOS/ATTOUI 2015, 29–33: Coreva; other preserved parts near Baghla 34–35 and NE of Aquae 42–44.
25 CIL VIII 22370 and 10322: *Ex auctoritate / Imp(eratoris) Caesaris Traiani / Hadriani Aug(usti) / via nova / a Cirta Rusicadem / strata per / possessores / territori(i) / Cirtensium* (Fig. 4).
26 CIL VIII 10296: *Ex auctoritate / Imp(eratoris) Caesaris / Traiani Hadri/an(i) Aug(usti) pontes / viae novae Rusi/cadensis r(es) p(ublica) Cir/tensium sua pec/unia fecit Sex(to) Iulio / Maiore leg(ato) Aug(usti) / leg(ionis) III Aug(ustae) pr(o) pr(aetore)*; on the findspot: GUYON 1852, 57; DE MARCILLY 1853b, 33; CREULLY 1853, 47–48.

to CREULLY rather late antique than Hadrianic, as can be seen in DELAMARE'S copy; the writing style contrasts indeed with that of the nice inscription of the Ammaedara bridge.[27] The difference in quality may depend of whom commissioned the building of the bridge and the graving of the text in stone, and/or of the availability of an expert *scriptor*.

The three inscriptions regarding the *Via nova Rusicadensis* start with *ex auctoritate* of emperor Hadrian. The interpretation of *ex auctoritate* is discussed by CHRISTOL, who suggests 'on command' in accordance with RATHMANN, who explained it in this way: Hadrian directly contacted local communities, by means of Sextus Iulius Maior, commander of the *legio III*, mentioned at the end of the inscription: he was the supervisor and middleman in charge of resolving disputes on cost sharing among the four cities of the Cirtan *res publica*, the *possessores* and the emperor.[28] DE ROMANIS translates it 'by imperial impulse',[29] referring to the good relations between Cirta's elites and Roman Emperors, which appear in the senatorial career of many Cirtensians, in particular of M. Cornelius Fronto, trilingual Λίβυς (Berber or Amazigh):[30] at Rome he was such a successful advocate and orator that Antoninus Pius chose him as preceptor of Marcus Aurelius and Lucius Verus.

The mountain road was precarious, as proven by the inscriptions of 17 out of 37/39 milestones, which mention road and bridge repairs due to *imbribus* (rain damage) and to collapses caused by its *vetustas* (old age) (Table 2). These 17 milestones date back to the 3rd century and bear the name of the emperor in the nominative, all except the one of Carinus (App. 6, Fig. 15a-c). They are concentrated in four sites, two at the 4th mile, six at the 14th mile, five at the 27th/28th miles, plus two at the 29th mile (measured from Cirta). One was found at the 33rd mile and one 11 km S of *Rusicade*. Given their concentration, they could be related with the most troubled sections of the road.[31] The provenance of three of them is unknown, while for another one SALAMA suggests a provenance from the *Cirta*-Milev road, for three reasons: another similar milestone of Caracalla was found along this road, there is a similar reuse of Valens, and there are no other milestones of Caracalla along the *Cirta-Rusicade* road.[32] The opposite theory points out that – according to RENIER 1858 – the milestone was transported

---

27 CREULLY 1853, 47–48; BENZINA BEN ABDALLAH 1995, Fig. 2.
28 CHRISTOL 2012, 193, without quoting RATHMANN 2003, 79–80, 98, 103, who considers the inscription incised on the *End-* or *Schlussstein* at Cirta, but its position was amidst the estates of the *possessores* of Cirta's confederation (Fig. 7).
29 DE ROMANIS 2003, 707.
30 Fronto ep. 2,3,24 ed. VAN DEN HOUT 1988; CLAASSEN 2009, 50: 'Nubian, or Black African' seems to confuse Numidian with Nubian, cf. *ibid.* 61:'the Numidian ('Nubian') Julius Celsinus, mentioned by Gellius 19,10,1'. VAN DEN HOUT 1999, 460–461: gives a list of the numerous Cirtensians at Rome at the time of Fronto, with high percentages of senators of Numidian and esp. Cirtan origin during the 2nd c.
31 Cf. RATHMANN 2003, note 745.
32 CIL VIII 10305 – 10306: SALAMA 1956, 131–132 and notes 1–7. Pl. I a-b; SALAMA 2005, 835 note 1, 840 note 23, Fig. 9–10.

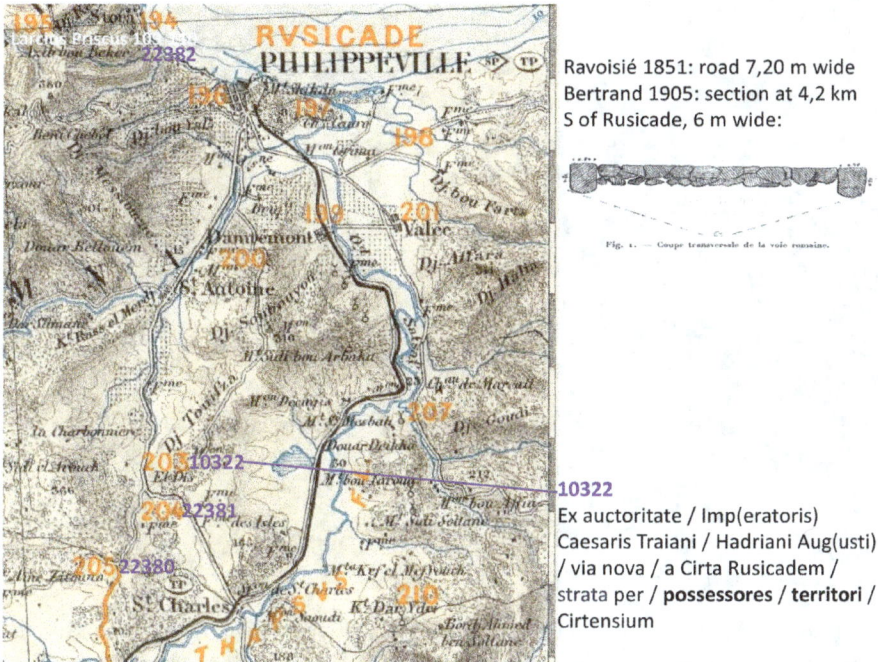

Fig. 4: *Via nova Rusicadensis*, final stretch of the road, AAA 8; the numbers refer to milestones published in CIL VIII 10322, 22380–22382.

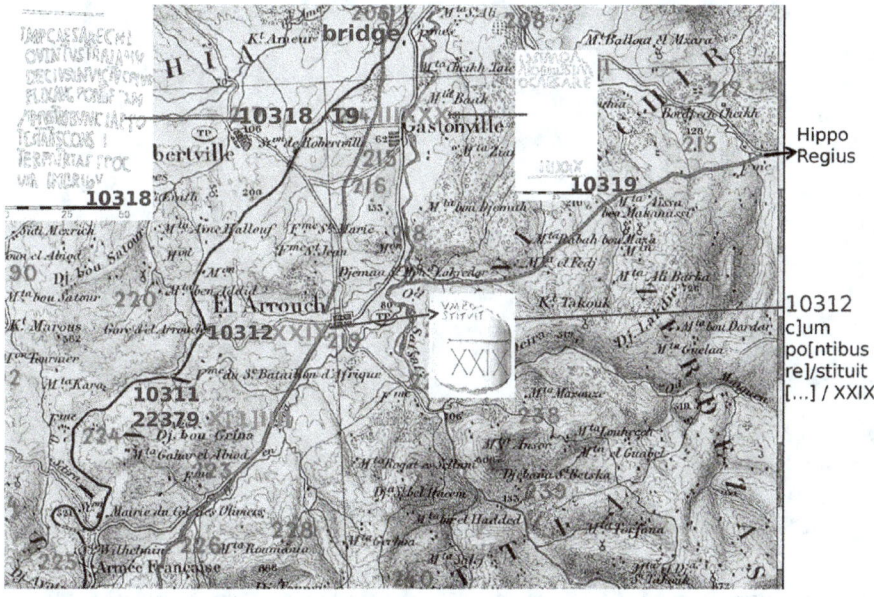

Fig. 5: *Via nova Rusicadensis*, AAA 17, milestones CIL VIII 10311–10312, 10318–10319, 22379.

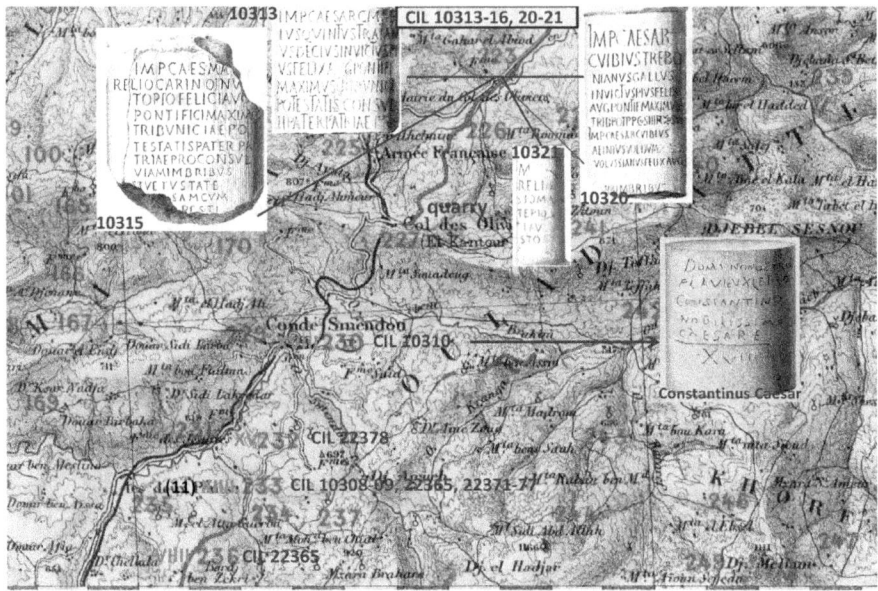

Fig. 6: *Via nova Rusicadensis*, AAA 17 and Delamare 1850, milestones CIL VIII 10308–10310, 10313–10316, 10320–10321, 22365, 22371–22377. Site 17.227: Fedj Kentoures, limestone quarry on the NNE slope used for building material of the Roman road (Fournel 1850, 151–152).

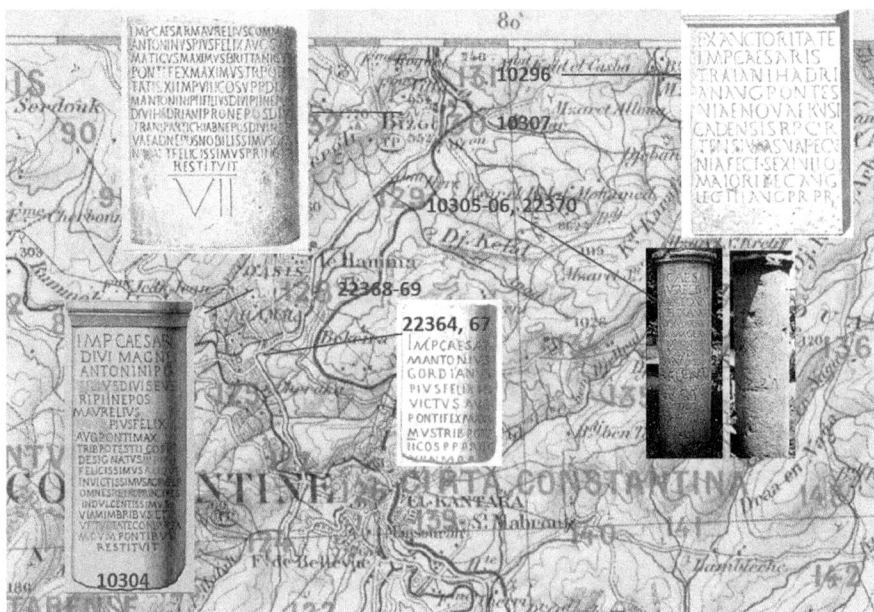

Fig. 7: *Via nova Rusicadensis*, AAA 17, Delamare 1850 and Salama 1956, Cirta *caput viae*: CIL VIII 10304–10307, 10296, 22364, 22368–22370.

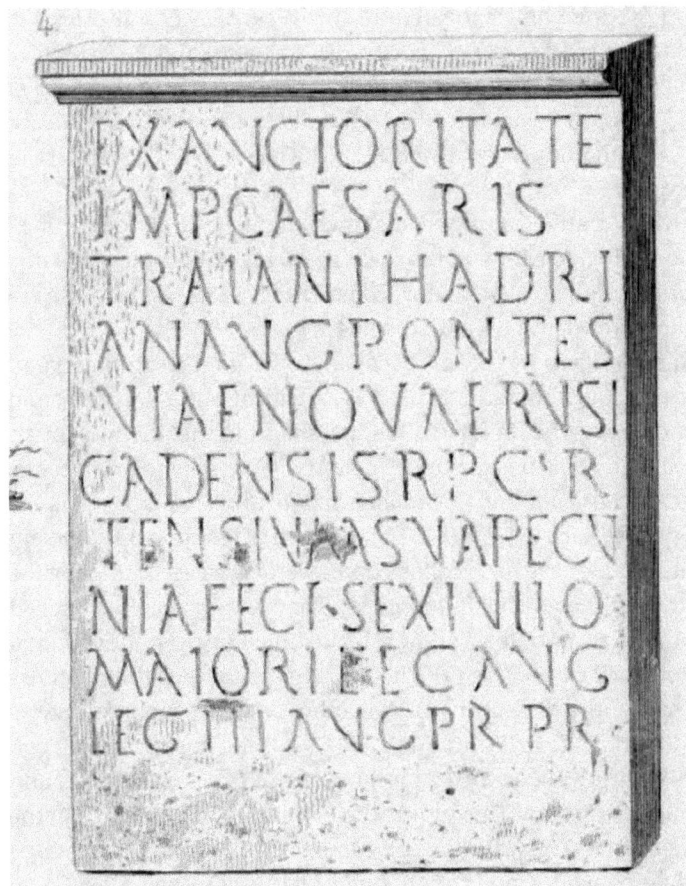

Fig. 8: *Via nova Rusicadensis*, fence of the bridge bearing the inscription CIL VIII 10296: *ex auctoritate ... Hadriani*. DELAMARE 1850 Pl. 49.4.

from Hamma to Constantine, and this is why Gsell ascribes it to the 6th mile of the road *Cirta-Rusicade*;[33] and secondly the *horrea* built at the 4th km N of *Rusicade* by Valentinianus and Valens (364–373)[34] made it compulsory for the road to be in good condition.

The oronym *Alpes Numidicae* is attested on the milestones of 152 AD along the *Hippo Regius-Calama* road, in the Eastern part of the mountain;[35] the road was restored by the *legatus* M. Valerius Etruscus. The road did not join the *Cirta-Rusicade* road near El Arrouch, as BRIAND-PONSART believes; it went further S, to *Calama*, as proven by

---

[33] RENIER 1858, GSELL AAA 17.129.
[34] See below note 67.
[35] ILAlg I 3875 and 3876; BRIAND-PONSART 2016, 273–276: discussion of the oronym, without considering AAA map 9 or Barrington Atlas map 31.

remains of the road and by three milestones found in sites AAA 9.77 and 9.85. Via *Aquae Thibilitanae* it arrived at Cirta: AAA 9.59.15 (p. 10: 4° route) and AAA 9.37, 46, 63. El Arrouch was reached by a road coming from *Hippo Regius*, which passed S of Lac Fetzara (AAA 9.59.15 p. 10, 3rd route and 9.63, 46), and Jemmapes (AAA 9.37–38), and along the left bank of Wadi Haddaratz (AAA 8.231). The recent E-W UMA highroad traces the same itinerary.

A sandstone stele with rounded top and distance number XXIX found at El Arrouch refers to road building activities of the *legio III Augusta* after the mid-1st c. under the imperial *legatus* C. Velleius Paterculus, consul in 60 AD.[36] Maybe these are at the origin of the predicate *nova* in the Hadrianic hodonym?

The road *Cirta – Rusicade* was important because of the *annona* shipments of products coming from the whole Numidia province. Two dedications at *Rusicade* and one at *Stora* refer to the *annona*. The first one – to the *Genius* of Puteoli – was found near the quay and *horrea,* and dates back to the 2nd century.[37] The second one – to the *Genius* of the *colonia Veneria Rusicade* and the *Annona Sacrae Urbis* – was found in the ruins of the theatre[38] and dates back to 225 AD.[39] On the beach of Philippeville (ancient *Rusicade*) hundreds of lead seals have been collected in several occasions, proving the payment of custom duties for the goods of *Rusicade*.[40] They were probably attached to packages in or near the port. Two items show a female bust or personification of the city, with the inscription *Rusicade* (Fig. 9). The headdress of one of them follows the fashion of the first half of the III century AD; the other seals are more recent. As stated by the *Novella Valentiniani* III 18,1,1 of 445 AD, 5% of the custom duties collected by *Rusicade* and Chullu were divided as follows: two fifths for the cities and three fifths for the *sacrae largitiones*.[41] This proves the continuity of commerce in the port of *Rusicade* and its connections with the large and rich hinterland of the high plain,[42] thanks to the road network via *Cirta*. At *Lambiridi* (Aurès) – some 265 km to the S of Rusicade – the *mensurae publicae frumentarie* mention the weight of corn that

---

36 CHRISTOL 2013 with Salama's photo of the stele, which disappeared in 1955.
37 CIL VIII 7959; VARS 1896, 57–58: vastes entrepôts, 19 x 7,9 m, Place de la Marine, AAA 8.196.12; CLARAC 1847, 1315–1316, n°105, Pl. LXXXV; DUCROUX 1975, III, 3 n° 9; CAMODECA 1994, 115: 2nd century AD; STEUERNAGEL 1999, 173. In 1845 Delamare moved it and other finds to Paris to save them from the builders of barracks and bridges: DONDIN-PAYRE 1994, 21–26, Pl. 25 Fig. 2: Delamare's aquarelle of the inscription and personification of the *Genius* with *cornucopia,* similar to his double at Pozzuoli: DEMMA 2007, 150–151.
38 DELAMARE 1859, 134 and not in the amphitheatre as referred by VARS 1896, 2–3, 75 who confuses moreover amphitheatre with *circus,* locating the dedication on the presumed *spina* of the *circus.*
39 CIL VIII 7960; AAA 8.196.24; DE ROMANIS 2003, 708; BRIAND-PONSART 2007, 85, n. 2: about 225 AD.
40 DOUBLET 1890, 54; DOUBLET/GAUCKLER 1892, 49–51; GSELL/BERTRAND 1898, 75; ROSTOVTZEFF 1900, 20, 31, 32, 162.
41 DELMAIRE 1989, 279–280.
42 Historical and agronomic analysis of the High Plains: CÔTE 1979.

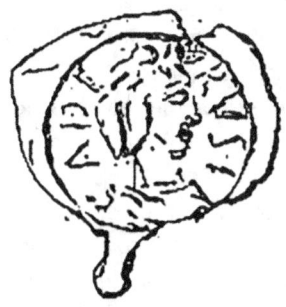 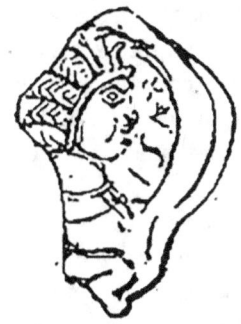

Fig. 9: Skikda, beach, lead seals with personification of Rusicade, Rostovtseff 1900.

belonged to *Rusicade*.[43] Archaeological research in the 19th until the end of the 20th centuries unfortunately ignored pottery, whose study would have greatly improved the chronological record.

The road was still in use during the Middle Ages, as witnessed by Leo Africanus and Gramaye.[44] When the French Army arrived there in 1832 the road needed only some repairs to be viable even to the artillery.[45] The role of the French Army in restoration is equated to that of Emperor Hadrian and his *legatus* Sextus Iulius Maior: below the above cited inscription on the bridge CIL VIII 10296 '1er Régiment du Génie / 1er Juin 1838' was engraved. The original aquarelle of this inscription by Capitan Delamare shows also the modern inscription, which was ignored in the 1850 publication of the engraving.[46] Bertrand described and published a section of the road, 4.2 km S of *Rusicade*: it was 6 m wide, with edges of sandstone ashlar 40/50 cm wide, 50–80 cm long, 65–85 cm high (here Fig. 4).[47] The inner core was made of quartzite and mica schist rubble, coming from the nearby mountain Koudiat Messionène. This description more or less coincides with the observations of Ravoisié: the road was 7,2 m wide, and had borders of large stones connected by chains or sleepers every 8 or 10 meters, each gap was carefully filled with rubble.[48] As far as the preservation of the road is concerned, architect Ravoisié criticizes the optimism of non-experts: 'These Roman roads are far from being so well preserved as it is generally believed. In many places, portions of the roadway still remain, it is true, but nowhere these fragments are in a

---

43 Albertini 1921.
44 Leo Africanus 1550, V, VIII, p. 116 the way is paved '*con pietre negre*' as seen in some places of Italy, being called 'Le strade Romane'; Gramaye 1622, VII, 47: *Sucaicade portus unde ad duas leucas via lapide strata ducit*, the toponym Sucaicade combines Stora and Rusicade.
45 Different sources in the army archives at Vincennes cited by Greenhalgh 2014, 31, 187–188, 192–193.
46 Dondin-Payre 1994, 138–140, Pl. 16 Fig. 2 and 3.
47 Bertrand 1905, 366–367.
48 Ravoisié 1846, 7, and 4 for the next quote.

perfect state of preservation, as has been repeated so many times'. Despite RAVOISIÉ's remark, DE MARCILLY could not suppress his admiration some 7 years later: 'Dans toutes les parties où j'ai reconnu cette voie, elle était large de 3 à 4 mètres, et formée de très gros cailloux ronds, encaissés entre deux lignes parallèles de pierres de taille. La partie la mieux conservée est située au Nord du bois d'oliviers de Gastonville: on la dirait achevée d'hier.'[49]

Also the port of *Stora* – 4 km N of *Rusicade* – was relatively well preserved. In 1832 Colonel Prétot wrote: 'Stora peut revenir en peu de temps ce qu'il étoit sous les Romains'.[50] In 1843, its *castellum aquae*, pipeline and cisterns (with a capacity of 3500 cubic meters) only needed some repair and enlargements to be reused; DELAMARE mapped and described them in detail.[51] *Rusicade* had several major cisterns: three were in the center of the city,[52] other two were on the Bou Yala hills. These last were connected and contained 9000 and 11.000 cubic meters; they too were restored and reused.[53]

Recent research reconstructed the geographic and administrative network of the *Annona* in Numidia, showing the escalation of Numidia's agricultural exploitation between the reigns of Trajan and Hadrian, at the time of Trajan's Parthian campaign (114–117).[54] Part of the Egyptian wheat had to be used for the soldiers engaged in this campaign; Africa had to increase its crop production. To guarantee the corn supply and transport to Rome administrators were appointed, such as the *curator frumenti comparandi in annonam Urbis*. This was one of the functions of T. Flavius Macer, who also was *procurator* of the *Hippo Regius* and *Theveste* imperial estates at the beginning of Hadrian's reign, i.e. in the period when the *via nova Rusicadensis* was built. The citizens of *Calama* offered him a dedication mentioning his *cursus honorum* (CIL VIII 5351). In the Severian period, M. Herennius Victor of *Thibilis* was in charge of the grain collection of the Roman people scattered in the two parts of *Numidia* and was *praefectus iure dicundo* (official of the legal magistracy) at *Rusicade*.[55] Between 198 and 211 AD, L. Iulius Victor Modianus was honoured at Zama Regia as *tractus Numidiae a frumentis* and at *Cirta* by his assistants, the imperial *liberti adiutores tabularii fusae*.[56] Moreover, in his long career A. Vitellius Honoratus was in charge of the grain collec-

---

49 DE MARCILLY 1853b, 35–36. CREULLY 1853 describes the road in detail, but without any cartography or visual documentation.
50 GREENHALGH 2014, 145 and note 271.
51 DELAMARE 1850, Pl. 43–45; DELAMARE 1859, 176–180; a succinct description in DELAMARE/GSELL 1912, 43–47.
52 DE MARCILLY 1853a, 26–28; GSELL 1901, 274.
53 DELAMARE 1850, Pl. 34–36; measures verified by surveyor Jules Chabassière, VARS 1896, 68 and note 2; DE MARCILLY 1853a, 26–27; GSELL 1901, 272–274.
54 CHRISTOL 1994; DE ROMANIS 2003, 705–709; PAPI/MARTORELLA 2007, 183; CARRE 2011, 25–27; BRIAND-PONSART 2012.
55 CIL VIII 18909 and ILAlg II/2.4690 *ad fusa frumenti et res populi per tractum utriusque Numidiae.*
56 Zama: ILTun 575, AE 1942–1943, 105. Cirta: CIL VIII 7053.

tion in the imperial estates in Numidia, *at fusa per Numidiam,* and under Gallienus (260–268) was honoured by Thugga, his city.[57]

In 1845 DELAMARE was excellent in documenting the road: 12 of its 37/39 milestones (Fig. 5–7), the bridge fence (Fig. 8), and even the reuse of three of these milestones in some houses of Constantine. He drew all the objects he saw – even the most modest and fragmentary ones-, within their context or in the landscape, with modern surveying methods, and for this reason he was criticized in his time. Some of his aquarelles have been published only recently.[58]

HENRY FOURNEL, mining engineer and survey pioneer in Algeria from 1843 to 1846 observed the Roman limestone quarry on the W slope of one of the two Toummiettes (Twin hills, S of site AAA 8.226, here Fig. 6). The quarry had delivered much material to the Roman road well preserved along the NNE slope of the Kentoures pass, site AAA8.227, 800 m above sea level; here the road enters in the Saf-saf valley. 'The quarry marks are so neat, they look as if they were made only yesterday'.[59]

According to CHRISTOL the milestone of Aulus Larcius Priscus, *legatus* of Trajan (106–110), belonged to the track which preceded the *via nova Rusicadensis*.[60] The inscription, however, has been found ca. 2 km to the N of *Rusicade*, along the road to *Stora*, in the estate of Ing. JOSEPH GEORGES LESUEUR, sénateur de Constantine.[61] The road is entirely mapped by DELAMARE and by Ravoisié.[62] It runs halfway up along the steep mountain slopes (because there is no space along the sea), passing above three bridges. The nearest one, on the way to *Stora*, was still in use after some restorations when DE MARCILLY described it in 1853[63]; it also appears in the lower part of a landscape drawing by DELAMARE.[64] According to SALAMA the road *Rusicade-Stora* was built in AD 110 by *Legio III*.[65] The port of *Stora* – 4 km to the NW of *Rusicade* – is sheltered from the W and NW winds, and was therefore preferable to *Rusicade*; a pier connected *Stora* to the Île des Singes. It featured large sophisticated cisterns,

---

[57] CIL VIII 26582, MAURIN 2000, 182–186.
[58] DELAMARE 1850 Pl. 47, 49, 125, 126; DONDIN-PAYRE 1994, for the critics: 42, 83.
[59] FOURNEL 1849, 152.
[60] CHRISTOL 2012, 191 note 25.
[61] POULLE 1879, 332–333 n. 9.
[62] DELAMARE 1850, Pl. 15; RAVOISIÉ 1851, Pl. 45.
[63] DE MARCILLY 1853b, 38; GSELL 1901, 11 note 2, linked a Hadrianic inscription mentioning *pontes viae novae Rusicadensis* – similar to CIL VIII 10296 – to one of the bridges, according to an unpublished note of Delamare. BERTRAND 1907, 460 attributed CIL VIII 10296 (found eight miles N of Constantine) as belonging to the first bridge counting from Rusicade. It is improbable that DELAMARE 1859 in his detailed description of the road and its bridges should not have mentioned the inscription, if he really had designed it. This bridge on Wadi Beni Melek is visible in the landscape of DELAMARE 1850 Pl. 40 upper part.
[64] DELAMARE 1850 Pl. 40.
[65] SALAMA 2010, 40.

documented in detail by DELAMARE;[66] it also had *horrea* that we know only from a founding inscription of the governor of the *provincia Numidia Constantina*, with the above mentioned dedication to emperors Valentinianus and Valens (364–367).[67] The *horrea* were built in short time 'for the safety of the population of Rome and in equal measure for the local people'.

The amazing surveying work of DELAMARE around mid-19th century – highlighted by DONDIN-PAYRE[68]– makes it possible to visualize context and details of the *Rusicade-Cirta* road, in a more complete way than for many other roads, whose relics were and are disappearing faster and faster.

Appendix

1–3 Road Carthage-Theveste, 82nd, 85th, 90th Hadrianic Milestones, AD 123

1. upper part of the 82nd milestone, Téboursouk, *lapidarium* in the Byzantine fortress.

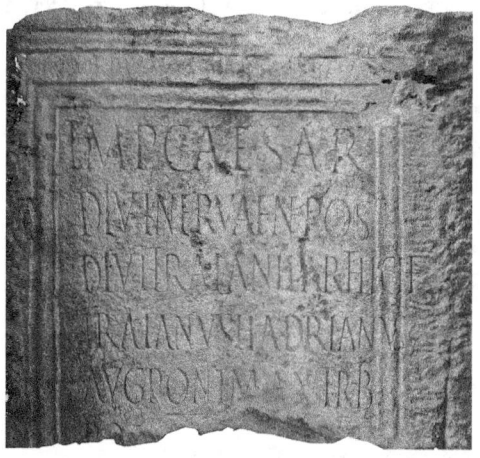 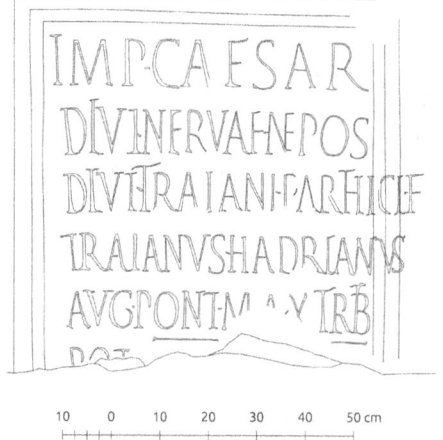

Fig. 10a–b: Road Carthage-Theveste, 82nd Hadrianic milestone, upper part, stored in the fortress of Teboursouk. The lower part with Metilius' name was discovered around 1885. Photo M. de Vos; 3D modeling and digitalization A. Battisti.

---

66 DELAMARE 1850, Pl. 44–45, with erroneous caption.
67 CIL VIII 19852: *Pro magnificentia temporum / principum maximorum domi/norum orb[i]s Valentiniani et / Valenti[s] semper Augg(ustorum) horrea / ad securitatem populi Romani / pariter ac provincialium con/structa omni maturitate / dedicavit Publilius C{a}eionius / Caec[i]na Albinus v(ir) c(larissimus) cons(ularis) / sexf(ascalis) p(rovinciae) N(umidiae) Cons(tantinae).*
68 DONDIN-PAYRE 1994 and 1998.

Imp(erator) – Caesar / divi – Nervae – 'ne'pos /divi – Traiani – p̣art'th'ici – f(ilius) / Traianus – Hadrianus / Aug(ustus) · pont(ifex) – m̨ax(imus) tr'ib' / p̣ọṭ [VII̅ co[n]s[ul] I̅I̅I̅]

Dimensions: cylinder H 95 cm, diameter 53 cm. Epigraphic field: W 67 cm x H 71cm (preserved). H letters: l 1: 10.2–10.3; l 2: 9.2–9.3; l 3: 8.2–8.1 cm.

Letters: cut with deep V-shaped grooves; monumental, elegant, shaded, regular, serifed; some I and T are *longae*; T with curved horizontal bar; the bottom serif of I is larger than the upper one; open P. *Nexus*: l. 2 NE, l. 3 TH, l. 5 IB. L. 4 VS overwritten. L. 6 only the bar over the numerals is preserved.

Lay out: a moulding frames the inscription; the text is lined up to the left; the left margin gradually widens down the epigraphic field, by consequence lines 3 and 4 continue across the frame at the right, but not so much as in the 90th Hadrianic milestone CIL VIII 22063 (App. 3).[69]

Punctuation: words separated by dashes.

Provenance: Chaouali discovered its provenance, unknown to me. For this reason our copy Fig. 10b, was not published in 2015; the lower part was found in site 072, Henchir Sidi-Mohammed-bel-Kassem, CIL VIII 22050.[70]

2. 85th milestone, lower part, Paris, Louvre Museum, Inv. MND 1589, MA 4123, Dépôt du Cabinet des Médailles, Ducroux 1975, n. 88. Left and central side on two pictures in http://rusafricum.org/en/thuggasurvey/DU574/DU574MS009

------ / [Tr]ạịạ[nus Had]r̞ịạ[nus] / Aug(ustus) · poṇt(ifex) · [m]ax(imus) · tr'ib'(unicia) / pot(estate) · VII̅ · co(n)ṣ(ul) · I[II] / ỵịạm · a Ḳạr'th'ag[in(e)] / Thevestem strạ[v(it)] / per · leg(ionem) I̅I̅I̅ Aụg(ustam) / [P(ublio)] Metilio · Secundo / leg(ato) · Aug(usti) · pr(o) pr(aetore) / LXXXV

Ximénez 1720, Shaw 1757, 156	Falbe *apud* Letronne 1844, 825	CIL VIII 10081=22071 Letronne, Hirschfeld
IMP. CAESAR	IMP. CAESAR	
DIVI. NERVAE. NEPOS	DIVI. NERVAE. [NEPOS]	
DIVI TRAIANI PARTHICI. F.	[DIVI. TRAIANI. PARTHICI. F.	------ /
TRAIANVS HADRIANVS	TRAIANVS. HADRIANVS]	[T]raia[nus Had]ria[nus] /
AVG. PONT. MAX. TRIB.	AVG. PONT. MAX(TRIB)	Aug(ustus) · pont(ifex) · max(i-
POT. VII. COS. III.	POT. VII COS III	mus) · tr'ib'(unicia) /
VIAM A CAR'TH'AGINE	VIAM. A. KARTHAGINE	pot(estate) · VII · co(n)s(ul) · III /
THEVESTEN STRAVIT	THEVESTEM STRAVIT	viam · a Kar'th'agin(e) / The-

---

69 de Vos/Attoui 2015, 98–100, Pl. IVa; http://rusafricum.org/en/thuggasurvey/DU574/DU574MS001/
70 Chaouali 2016b, 85–88: 'selon certains témoins... découverte au courant des années 1990 au sud de Téboursouk'; de Vos/Attoui 2015, 91–92, http://rusafricum.org/en/thuggasurvey/DU072/DU072M82/

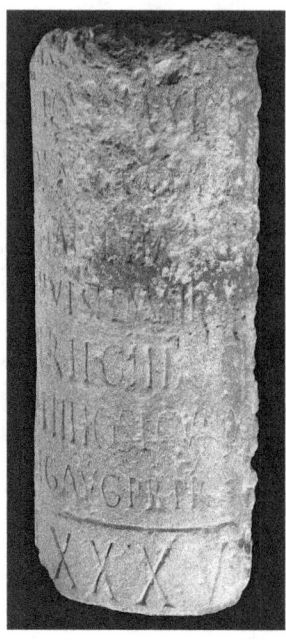

Fig. 11a: Road Carthage-Theveste, 85th Hadrianic milestone. Paris, Louvre Museum, Inv. MND 1589, MA 4123, Dépôt du Cabinet des Médailles, Photo 17-632980 © Musée du Louvre, Dist. RMN-Grand Palais / Daniel Lebée / Carine Déambrosis.

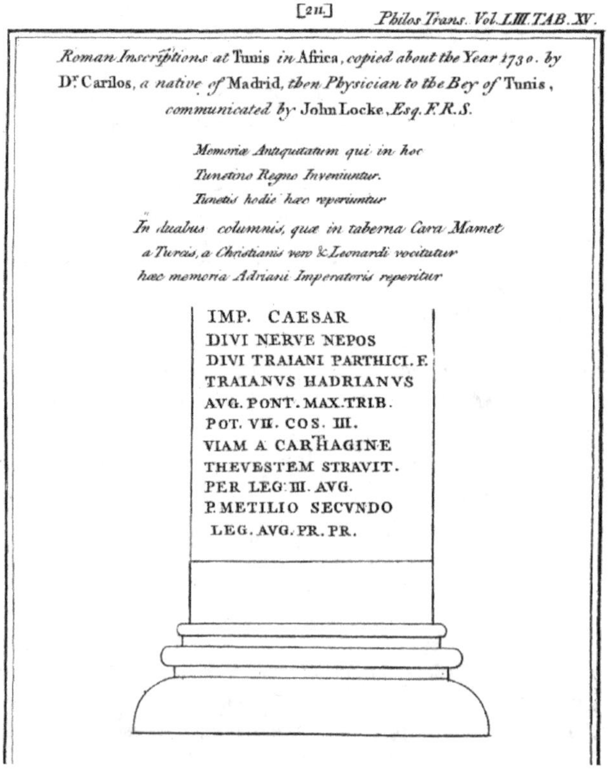

Fig. 11b: Road Carthage-Theveste, 85th Hadrianic milestone, CARILOS 1763, 211, Tab. XV.

Ximénez 1720, Shaw 1757, 156	Falbe apud Letronne 1844, 825	CIL VIII 10081=22071 Letronne, Hirschfeld
PER LEG. III. AVG. P. METILIO. SECVNDO LEG. AVG. PR. PR.	PER. LEG. III. AVG. P. METILIO. SECVNDO LEG. AVG. PR. PR. LXXXV	*vestem strav(it) / per · leg(io-nem) III Aug(ustam) / [P(ublio)] Metilio · Secundo / leg(ato) · Aug(usti) · pr(o) pr(aetore) · / LXXXVI*

Tunis, 'baño de S. Leonardo ó el Caramet'; Paris, Cabinet des Médailles, in the next future to be transferred to the Louvre *réserves* at Liévin.

Dimensions: cylinder H 112 cm, diameter ca. 50 cm.
Ducroux 1975, n. 88: 'entré en 1914, CIL VIII 10048, milliaire, retaillé en épaisseur pour ne garder que la partie inscrite; 12 lignes; les 8 premières peu lisibles; l. 8 cm.'
Letters: similar to the previous item, App. 1. The last letters of lines 2 'IB', 6 G, 7 DO are incised on the moulded frame, as in the 82nd and 90th Hadrianic milestones (App. 1 and 3).
Punctuation: some words separated by points.
Provenance: this milestone was removed from the site Sidi bou Atila and transported by 125 km to Tunis before 1720, where it was copied by Ximénez 'en el baño de S. Leonardo ó el Caramet dos inscriptiones identicas en columnas' without the last line containing the distance-figure. Carilos about 1730 refers to one inscription 'in duabis columnis'(Fig. 11b). The column was probably broken in 2 parts in coincidence with the 4th line. Shaw copied the text of Ximénez' manuscript, without seeing the original, as he explains in his Preface, p. X: 'The Civil War which raged in the Kingdom of Tunis, when I was there, (in the Year 1727) prevented me from seeing the Frigêah, as they call the Western Part of the ancient Zeugitania. I am indebted therefore for the Inscriptions and the Geographical Observations of those Parts to Father Francisco Ximenes, the Spanish Administradôr at Tunis'. He corrected however l. 2 *Nerve* in *Nervae*. Falbe, Danish Consul at Tunis from 1821 added the distance figure, LXXXV, and indicated the damage occurred in lines 2–4 since 1730: his copy was published by Letronne in 1844.[71] Letronne, however, created confusion, saying that a second milestone with distance number LXXXVI discovered recently during an excavation by a French Society at Carthage[72] was transported to Paris, to be offered to the Royal Library. Letronne himself had been director of this Library

---
[71] Ximénez in CIL VIII 10048; Carilos 1763, 211; Shaw 1757, 156; Letronne 1844, 825.
[72] In fact four Roman (CIL VIII 1000, 1029, 1022a, 1066) and one Christian inscription (CIL VIII 1092) had been found on the Byrsa hill during the construction from 1841 to 1845 of a chapel for St. Louis near the Aesculapius temple: de Sainte-Marie 1878, 19, 130, 132.

until 1840. The photograph of the milestone with distance number LXXXV at Paris (Fig. 11a) demonstrates that LETRONNE'S information is wrong and that the distance number LXXXVI of CIL VIII 10081= 22071 has to be corrected in LXXXV; in this way it coincides with CIL VIII 10048. The upper part with the first 3½ lines was not shipped at Tunis. The uninscribed rear half of the central part was chopped off to decrease its weight, as usual in this period, see *infra* App. 6–7 and the uninscribed rear half of a milestone at the 78th mile, abandoned in *Pagus Assallitanus*.[73] The upper right half of the column in Paris shows pick marks and the colour of its surface is altered.

TISSOT saw the fragmentary Hadrianic milestone CIL VIII 10080 = 22062 containing the first 3 lines at the site which coincides with the 86th mile from Carthage, together with CIL VIII 10079 = 22061 (Gordianus, still *in situ*).[74] This is another confutation of LETRONNE'S distance number LXXXVI. At the 89th mile WILMANNS saw another fragmentary Hadrianic milestone (CIL VIII 10036 = 22080).

Why and when the 85th milestone was removed to Tunis remains unknown. Also the question or if it was XIMÉNEZ' initiative or if it was already walled in a door post of the prison of Christian slaves in which the Trinitarian father Francisco XIMÉNES installed a hospital. This prison was just N of Bab Behar, the Eastern entrance of the Medina (now Porte de France), between Rue de l'Ancienne Douane and Kara Ahmed.[75] In the same way three other milestones were reused in Tunis: one of Maximinus, 70th mile (CIL VIII 10047) in the *medres el Andalus*, one of Trebonianus, 20th mile (CIL VIII 10046) in the prison of the H. Trinity and one of Caracalla, 19th mile (BCTH 1897, 436–437) in the El-Houa mosque.

3. 90th milestone, complete except the bottom of the last line, Sidi bou Atila, CIL VIII 22063.

TEMPLE 1835, 353, n. 181	CARTON 1895 n. 51; CIL VIII 22063	DE VOS/ATTOUI 2015, 99–100, here updated with distance numerals and punctuation
	Imp(erator) Caesar / divi Nervae nepos / divi Traiani Parthici f(ilius) / Traianus Hadrianus / Aug(ustus) pont(ifex)	IMP·CAESAR DIVI·NERVAE·'NE'POS DIVI·TRAIANI·PAR'TH'ICI·F TRAIANVS·HADRIANVS

---

[73] DE VOS/ATTOUI 2015, 79–80, Fig. 96, probably pertaining to Philippus Arabs, at the 78th mile.
[74] TISSOT 1888, 349; now disappeared, DE VOS/ATTOUI 2015, 108.
[75] SACERDOTI 1950: map designed by XIMÉNEZ, sent in 1720 to the Sacra Congregazione di Propaganda Fide at Rome, Archive APF, Scritture originali riferite nelle congregazioni generali del 18, 21, 27. 04. 1722, v. 624, folio 166.

Temple 1835, 353, n. 181	Carton 1895 n. 51; CIL VIII 22063	De Vos/Attoui 2015, 99–100, here updated with distance numerals and punctuation
.... AVG. PONT. MAX. TRIB. POT. VII. COS. IIII VIAM A KARTHAGINE HILVESTEM STRAV PER LEG III AVG	max(imus) trib(unicia) / pot(estate) VII co(n)s(ul) III / viam a Karthagine / Thevestem stravit / per leg(ionem) III Aug(ustam) / P(ublio) Metilio Secundo / leg(ato) Aug(usti) pr(o) pr(aetore)	AVG·PONT·MAX·'TR''IB' POT·VII·COS·III VIAM·A·KAR'TH'AG'INE' THEVESTEM·STRAVIT PER·LEG·II·I·AVG P▽METILIO·SECV'ND'O LEG·AVG·PR·PR LXXXX

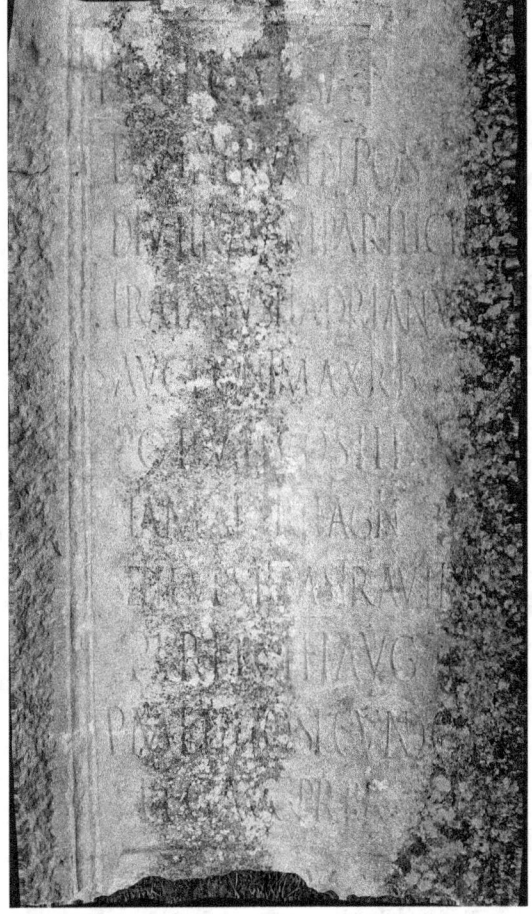
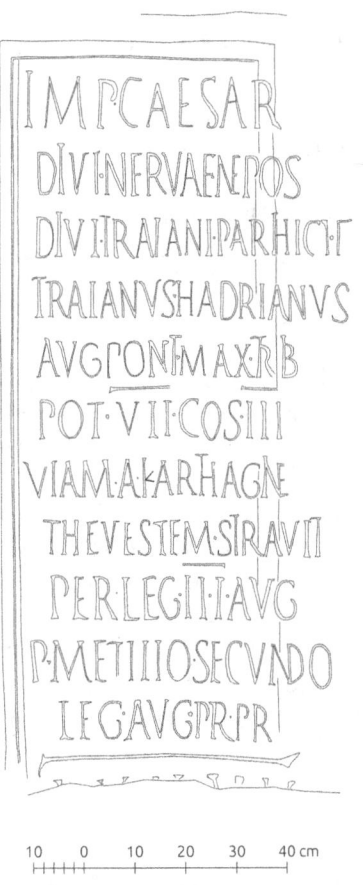

Fig. 12a–b: Road Carthage-Theveste, 90th Hadrianic milestone, removed from Musti in order to sustain Sidi Bou Atila koubba. Photo M. de Vos; 3D modeling and digitalization A. Battisti.

Dimensions: cylinder H 144 cm, diameter 51 cm, epigraphic field: W 49 cm.
Letters: H. l. 1: 10; l. 2: 8.5; l. 3–4: 8; l. 5–6: 7; l. 7: 7–7.5; l. 8 : 6.5–7; l. 9–10: 8; l. 11: 7 cm., *i.e.* 1–2 mm smaller than the letters in the 82ⁿᵈ milestone (App. 1); in the 90ᵗʰ the letter spacing is more compressed. *Nexus*: l. 2: 'NE'; l. 3 'TH'; l. 5: 'TR' and 'IB'; l. 7 'TH' and 'INE', T *longa*; I *longa* in l. 2 and 3.
Layout: The right side of the moulded frame is reduced to lines, and overwritten by the letters of the inscription notwithstanding *nexuses* towards the end of the lines. The width of the epigraphic field (49 cm) is 18cm less than the one of the 82ᵗʰ mile (67 cm). Punctuation: points, erroneously also inside the numerals l. 9 II·I; l. 10: a triangular mark behind P.
Provenance: until at least 1895 the milestone sustained the cupola of the koubba; it is now lying in front of it; its last line preserves only the top serifs of diagonal strokes of the probable numerals: L̲X̲X̲X̲X̲, so it has to come from Musti.

4–5 *Via nova Rusicadensis*, 33ʳᵈ Mile

The two milestones in the garden of the ancient theatre of Rusicade are both discovered in 1870 in the same site – about 1 km to the W of Gastonville (now Salah Bouchaour) – AAA 8.214, or at the 33ʳᵈ mile counting from Cirta.[76] They were published by HÉRON DE VILLEFOSSE, who describes them erroneously as made of marble; in reality they are in white limestone.[77]

4. Skikda, Roman Theatre, garden, *lapidarium*, CIL VIII 10318.

> *Imp(erator) Caesar{e} C(aius) Messius / Quintus Traianus / Decius Invictus Pius F/elix Aug(ustus) pontifex ma/ximus tribuniciae po/testatis cons[ul II pa]/ter patriae [proconsul] / viam imbribus [et vetus]/tate conla<p=B>sa[m cum] / pontibus res[tituit*

Dimensions: cylinder H 79 cm, diam. 39 cm. Letters H 6 cm.
Letters: regular, serifed, cut with large, shallow, round trenches; T *longa* with symmetrical unserifed bar, A with and without crossbar; O oval, P completely closed.

One end of the cylinder is buried, by consequence the last two lines are not visible. L. 4: *F* invisible on the stone.

The name of Decius is in the nominative, and mentions the road repair in the stereotyped phraseology of 3ʳᵈ century milestones (Table 3); the second consulate of Decius dates it to AD 250. The *e* after the nominative *Caesar* is an error of the stone-

---

[76] GSELL/BERTRAND 1898, 27: 'découverte en 1870, à un kilomètre environ à l'ouest de Gastonville, c'est-à-dire au trente-troisième mille'. RATHMANN 2003, 208, 262, notes 474, 745.
[77] HÉRON DE VILLEFOSSE 1875, 412.47 and 48.

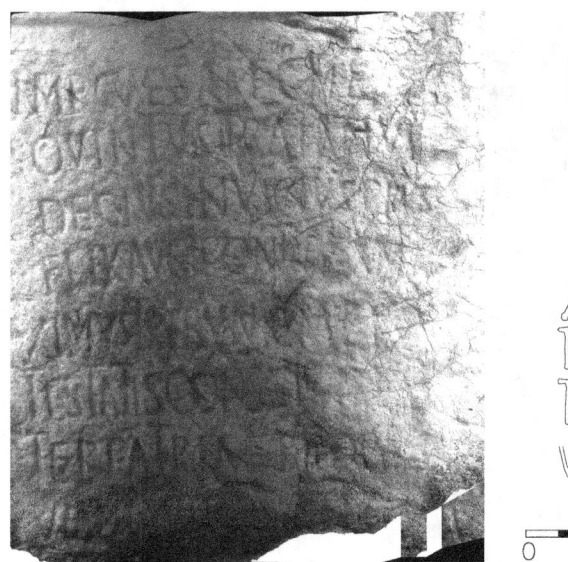 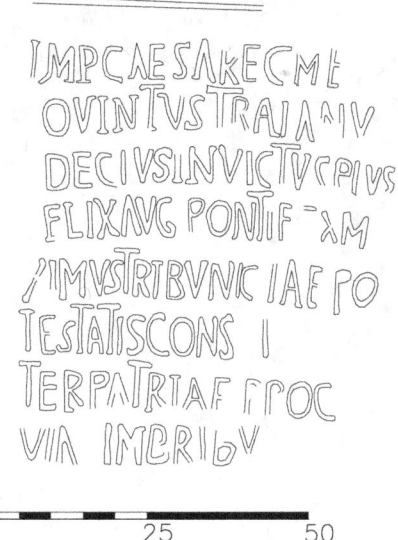

Fig. 13a–b: *Via nova Rusicadensis*, CIL VIII 10318, milestone of Decius (250). Skikda, garden near the Roman Theatre. Photo M. de Vos; 3D modeling and digitalization A. Battisti.

cutter, which was not registered by Héron de Villefosse, nor in the CIL edition. The other two milestones of Decius, CIL VIII 10313 and 10314, are documented by Delamare near the Roman road and the camp of El Arrouch (now el Harrouch). Of course it is impossible to know if Decius repaired all the road, or only its sections near the milestones.

5. Skikda, Roman Theatre, garden, *lapidarium*, CIL VIII 10319.

> D(omino) n(ostro) Fla/vio Const/antio fort/issimo ac / nobilissim/o Caesari / IIIXXX

Dimensions: cylinder H 89 cm, diam. 39 cm. Letters H 6–7 cm; Numeral H 8 cm.
Letters: irregular with large, shallow, round trenches; O perfect circle, 3rd l. from below: i *nana* in *nobilissim/*; A with and without crossbar. The distance from Cirta is in retrograde writing, which is frequent in distance-figures on milestones, and in *instrumentum domesticum* stamps.[78]

The cylinder is buried upside down, by consequence the first three lines are not visible. The first three hidden lines contain the name of Constans Caesar (293–305). Along the road Carthage-Theveste four milestones dedicated to Constans Caesar were

---

[78] Salama 1987, 45, fig. 9 and notes 163–164: list of examples in *Africa proconsularis* and *Numidia*.

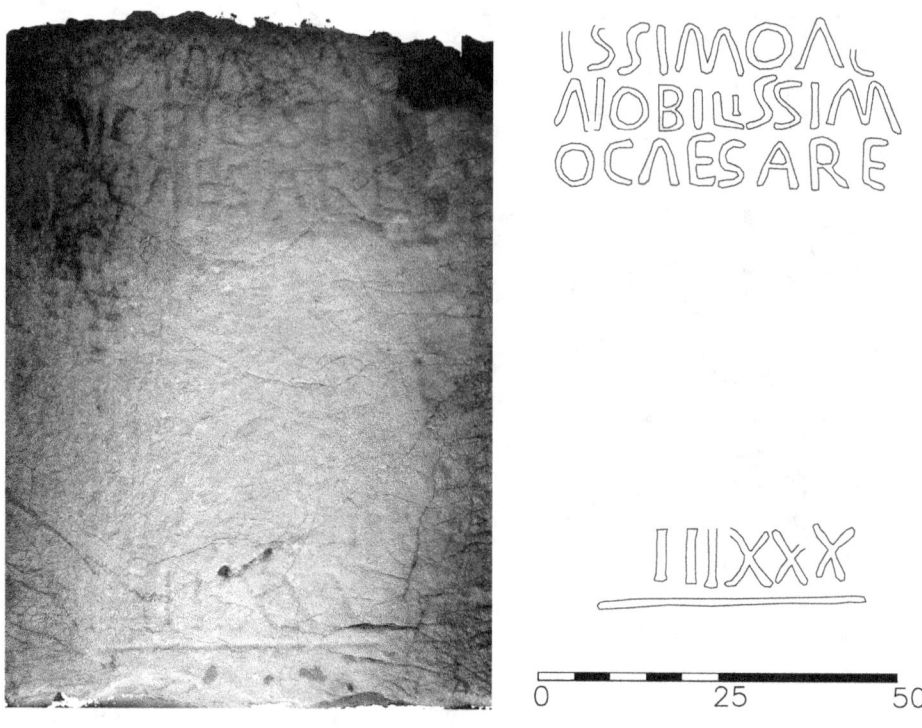

Fig. 14a–b: *Via nova Rusicadensis*, CIL VIII 10319, milestone of Constans Caesar (293–305). Skikda, garden near the Roman Theatre. Photo M. de Vos; 3D modeling and digitalization A. Battisti.

found; further one on the 1st mile of the road from Hippo Regius to Cirta, one on the road Sicca – Thagura and one at Nepheris.[79]

6–7 *via nova Rusicadensis,* El Arrouch

In the Louvre Museum there are two milestones found near El Arrouch (or Harrouch) and transported by DELAMARE in 1845 to Paris in order to save them from destruction. Before being charged on the ship, the not inscribed half of the milestones has been cut in order to decrease their weight, s. *supra* App. 2.[80] The missing half has been integrated after their arrival in the Louvre. The milestones are now packed in order to be transferred to the conservation center under construction at Liévin, alongside the

---

[79] SALAMA 1987, 188, n. 29–32, fig. 9; n. 29 = CIL VIII 22012, is republished by CHAOUALI 2016a, 57–58, fig. 4–5: also this milestone of Constans Caesar presents a retrograde distance-numeral IIXXXX; Salama doubts between 43 and 44.
[80] DUCROUX 1975, Avant-propos, p. IV.

recently opened Louvre-Lens (Pas-de-Calais). For this reason the description is based on photographs and the dimensions are those indicated in the CIL.

6. Paris, Louvre, CIL VIII 10315, DELAMARE 1850, Pl. 47.4; DUCROUX 1975, n. 98.

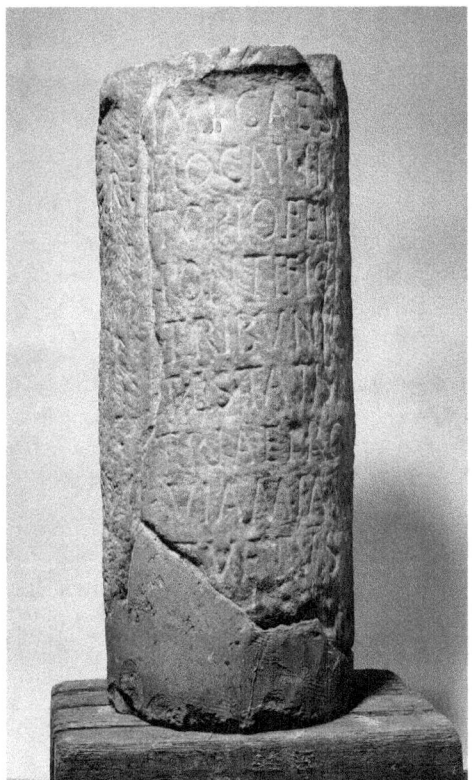 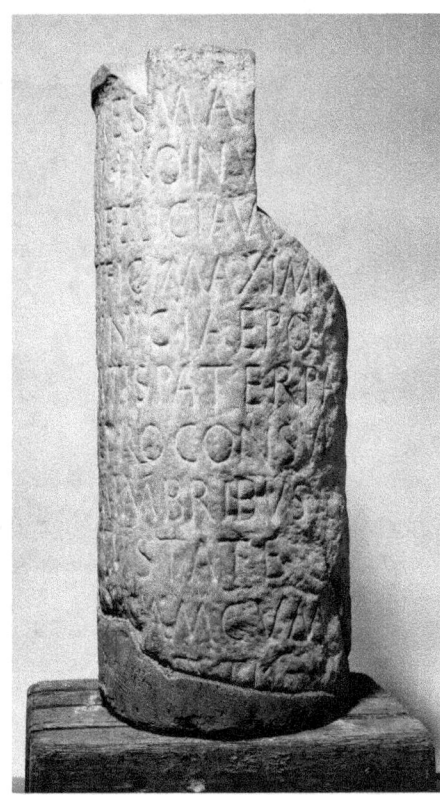

Fig. 15a–b: *Via nova Rusicadensis*, between El Arrouch and Toumiettes, CIL VIII 10315, milestone of Carinus. Louvre-Liévin, Photo 538860 (C) and Photo 632976 (C) Musée du Louvre, Dist. RMN-Grand Palais / Les frères Chuzeville.

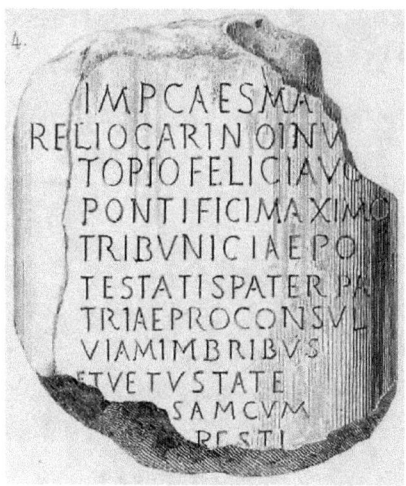

Fig. 15c: *Via nova Rusicadensis*, between El Arrouch and Toumiettes, CIL VIII 10315, milestone of Carinus (282–285). DELAMARE 1850, Pl. 47.4.

Imp(eratori) Caes(ari) M(arco) A[u]/relio Carino Iny[ic]/to Pio Felici Aug(usto) / pontifici maximo / tribuniciae po/testatis pater pa/triae proconsul / viam imbribus / [e]ṭ vetustate / [conlap]sam cum / [pontibus] ṛeṣṭi[tuit

Dimensions: cylinder H 72 cm. Letters H c. 5 cm (copied from CIL VIII 10315).
Letters: monumental, somewhat irregular, maybe because incised on an unsmoothed surface. L. 1 punctuation in CIL VIII 10315 invisible on the photographs. L. 2 *re* seems incised on the 19th c. integrated half. If this is true, Delamare copied the text after the milestone's arrival at Paris and restoration in the Louvre Museum.
Provenance: Milestone of Carinus (282–285), found between the camp of El Arrouch and the Toumiettes, near a square well lined with bricks, which needed only to be cleaned in order to be reused.[81]

---

[81] DELAMARE ms. Sorbonne, IV, p. 248, *verso*, cited by DELAMARE/GSELL 1912, p. 48.4; GUYON 1847, 50.

7. Paris, Louvre, CIL VIII 10320, Ducroux 1975, n. 99.

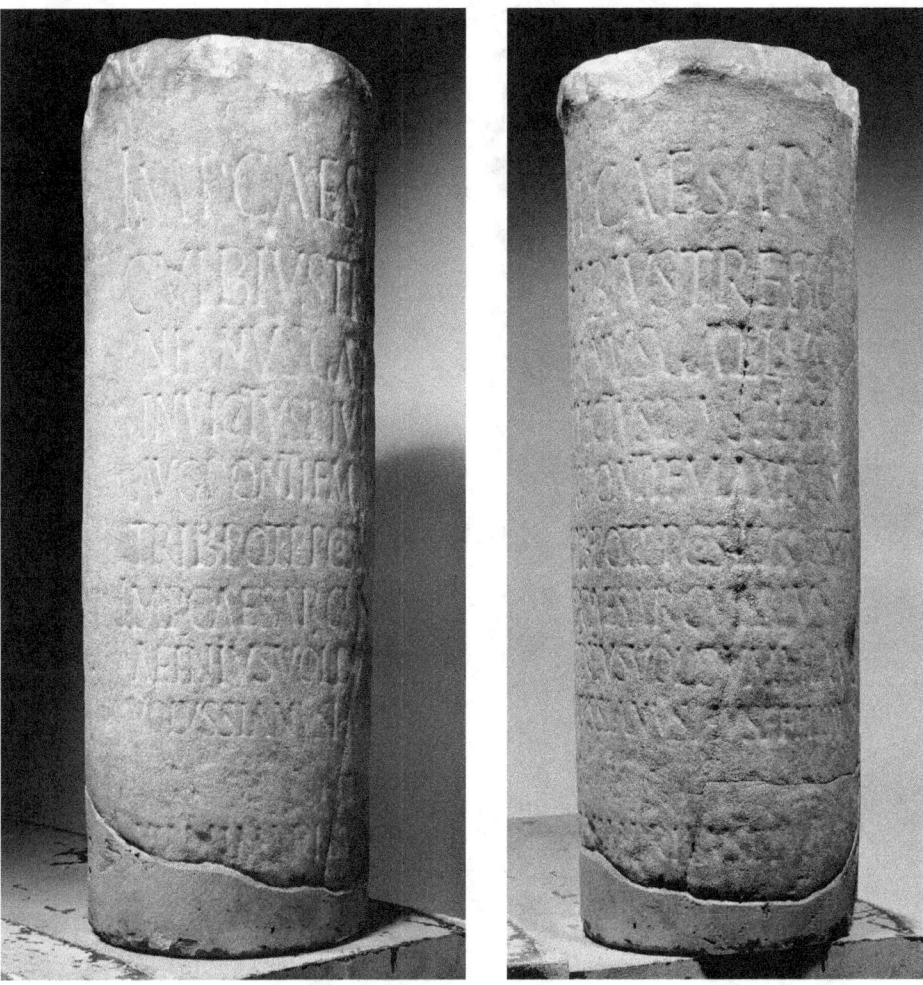

Fig. 16a–b: *Via nova Rusicadensis*, camp of the «condamnés, à l'oued Hammam», CIL VIII 10320, milestone of Trebonianus Gallus and Volusianus. Louvre-Liévin, Photo 538862 (C) and 632977 (C) Musée du Louvre, Dist. RMN-Grand Palais / Les frères Chuzeville.

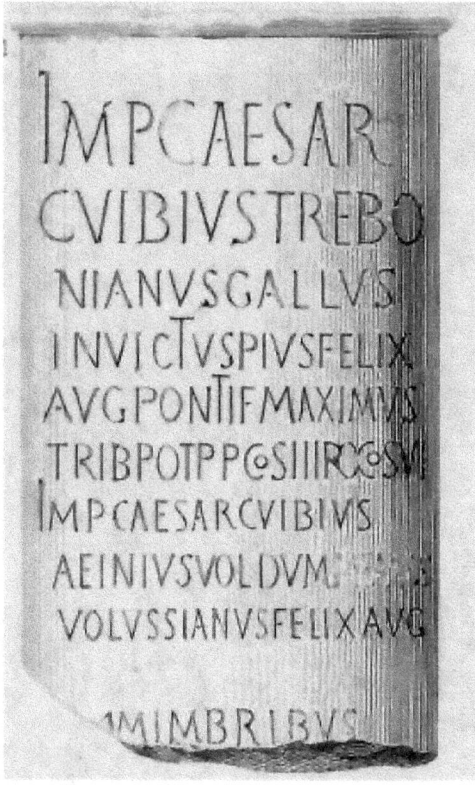

Fig. 16c: *Via nova Rusicadensis*, camp of the «condamnés, à l'oued Hammam», CIL VIII 10320, milestone of Trebonianus Gallus and Volusianus (252–253). DELAMARE 1850, Pl. 47.1.

Imp(erator) Caesar / C(aius) Vibius Trebo/nianus Gallus / invictus pius felix / Aug(ustus) pontif(ex) maximus / trib(unicia) pot(estate) p(ater) p(atriae)co[n]s(ul) II proc(on)sul /Imp(erator) Caesar C(aius) Vibiu(s) / Afinius Voldum{m}ianus / Volus{s}ianus Pius Felix Aug(ustus) / viam imbribus [et ve]/[tustate conlapsam cum] / [pontibus restituerunt

Dimensions: cylinder H 71 cm. Letters H l. 1–3: 6 cm; l. 4–10: 3 cm (copied from CIL VIII 10320).
Letters: cut with trenches triangular in profile; monumental, regular, deeply serifed. L. 1 and 7: I *longa*; l. 4 and 5: T *longa*; l. 6: O of co(n)s *nana*, nexus RO of *proc(on)sul*.
Layout: l. 6 -*sul* outside the frame.
State of preservation: a vertical crack in the right side of the epigraphic field and a horizontal one in the blank space between lines 9 and 10 were created probably during the splitting of the milestone for overseas transport.
Provenance: milestone of Trebonianus Gallus and Volusianus (252–253) found near the camp of the 'condamnés, à l'oued Hammam'.[82]

---

82 AAA 8.226; DELAMARE 1850 Pl. 47.1; DELAMARE/GSELL 1912, 47.1.

Table 2: 38 milestones, 1 *cippus* and 1 slab of the *via nova Rusicadensis*; 1 milestone Stora-Skikda

Toponym colonial and current; n.=number of the milestone in this paper, counting from Cirta, *caput viae*. MP = miles incised on the cylindrical milestone.
AAA = Atlas Archéologique d'Algérie, C = *conlapsam*, motivation formula for restoration.

n.	MP	Toponym	AAA	CIL VIII	DELAMARE 1850 Pl.	DELAMARE/ GSELL 1912	G[OYT1882] S[ALAMA1956, 1987, 2005]	Chronology AD	Emperor/*legatus*	C
01		Le Hamma, Hammet	17.128	10304	125.2	120.2	G p. 160	10.12. 218–9. 12. 219	Elagabalus consul II	X
02	2	Le Hamma, Hammet	17.128	22364	126.4	122.4		237–238	Gordianus, *trib pot* II	
03	2	Le Hamma, Hammet		22367[83]		122.4	S 1987, 21, 98, note 66	28. 10. 312–18. 09. 324	Licinius Aug. alone	X
04	4	Le Hamma, Hammet	17.128[84]	22368			S 1956, 138	218–222 or 222–235[85]	Elagabalus / Severus Alexander	
05	4	Papeterie Brunache, 8 km N of Cirta		22369					fragment	
06	6	fermeOttavi,Bizot	17.129	22370					Hadrianus	
07	6	Hamma		10305	125.4	121.4	G p. 160–61	216	Caracalla	
08	6			10306[86]			G p. 161; S 1956, 132, Pl. 1b	364–378	Valens Aug.	
09	7	Wadi Smendou	17.130	10307	49.3	50.3	G p. 161; S 2005 fig. 19	186	Commodus *trib pot* XI	

---

83 On the backside of CIL VIII 22364, at the 2nd mile *a Co[n]stant(ina)* according to GSELL (*vidi*).
84 'Il n'est pas sûr qu'elle appartient au même (viz. 4ᵐᵉ) mille'. Hamma is a large oasis, the mile distance number varies from 2 to 6.
85 SALAMA 1956, 138 note 3: Elagabalus; SCHEITHAUER 1988, 177: Elagabalus or Severus Alexander.
86 On the backside of CIL VIII 10305.

Table 2 (continued)

n.	MP	Toponym	AAA	CIL VIII	DELAMARE 1850 Pl.	DELAMARE/ GSELL 1912	G[OYT1882] S[ALAMA1956, 1987, 2005]	Chronology AD	Emperor/*legatus*	C
10	[8]	bridge Wadi el Hadjar, near Deux-Ponts[87]	17.131	10296	49.4	50–51.4	G p. 161	124–126	Hadrianus, Sextus Iulius Maior *legatus*	
11	14	Wadi Smendou	8.233	10308			G p. 159–60	220	Elagabalus *consul* III	x
12	14			10309			G p. 159–60	222	SeverusAlexander?	x
13	14			22365			G p. 160	252–253	Trebonianus +Volusianus	x
14	14			22371			G n. 3	239	Gordianus, *trib pot* II	x
15	14			22372			G n. 4	239	Gordianus, *trib pot* II	x
16	14	Wadi Kara Ali		22373			G n. 1	244–249	Philippus f+s a posteriori	x
17				22374			G n. 5; S 1987,131	288	Diocletianus alone *trib pot* V	
18				22375a				310–30. 4. 313	Maximinus	
19	14			22375b					fragment	
20	14			22376			G n. 6	317–326	Crisp(in)us Caesar	
21	14			22377					fragment	
22	15			22378					fragment	
23	18	Condé Smendou, [ZighoudYoucef]	8.230	10310	49.2	50.2	G p. 160	25. 7. 306–28. 11. 312	Constantinus Caesar	
24		between El Arrouch and Toumiëttes	8.219–8.226[88]	10313	47.5	48.5		250	Decius (lower part missing)	[x]
25				10314	47.3	47.3		250	Decius	x

---

[87] CREULLY 1853, 47.
[88] The location of site 8.226 is erroneous, Toumiëttes is 4 km south of El Arrouch, Fme du 3e Bataillon d'Afrique. The error is probably due to the confusion with another military camp indicated as Armée Française on map 8.

Table 2 (continued)

n.	MP	Toponym	AAA	CIL VIII	DELAMARE 1850 Pl.	DELAMARE/ GSELL 1912	G[OYT1882] S[ALAMA1956, 1987, 2005]	Chronology AD	Emperor/*legatus*	C
26				10315	47.4	48.4	Guyon 1847, 50	282–285	Carinus	x
27				10316			Renier 1858,4415		fr. lower part	x
28				10320	47.1		G p. 160	252–253	Trebonianus +Volusianus	x
29				10321	47.6	48.6		?	?	
30	29	W of El Arrouch	8.219	10311			Christol 2013	ante 60	C. Velleius Paterculus *legatus*	
31	29			10312	47.2	47.2			fr. lower part	x
32	29	Crossroad El Arrouch – Gastonville		22379				282–285	Carinus	x
33	33	1 km W of Gastonville, [SalahBouchaour]	8.214	10318				250	Decius *consul* II	x
34	33			10319				293–305	Constans Caesar	
35		El Diss, 15 km S of Skikda	8.205	22380				244–247	Philippus f+s Caes	
36		El Diss, 12 km S of Skikda	8.204	22381			G 155 note 1	247–249	Philippus f+s Aug	
37		11km S of Skikda	8.204	10322					Hadrianus	
38	??			10299			G n. 2	244–249	Philippus f+s a posteriori	
39	??			10300	126.1–2	121.1–2		10.253–260	Valerianus Gallienus	x
40	??	Unpublished					S 1987, 128, n.190	10.352 – end 354	Constantius II + Gallus	
1		Stora-Skikda, villa Lesueur		22382				about 108	Larcius Priscus *legatus*	

Tab. 3: *Conlapsam*, chronology of road/bridge repairs

120	180	210	220	230	240	250	280	320	330	350	360
		1	2	3	3	4	1				1 ?

Table 4: Chronology of all milestones and a slab

ante 60	120	180	210	220	230	240	250	280	290	310	320	350	360
1	3	1	2	3	3	4	6	3	1	2	2	1	1 ?

Table 5: Topographical distribution of the milestones and a slab

MP	2	4	6	7	8	14	15	18	19–28	29	33	El Diss	11 km S of Skikda
n.	3	2	1/3	1	bridge	11	1	1	7	3	2	2	1

Addendum

When the Proceedings were already in press, I discovered Pierre Salama's mportant observations on the *via Rusicadensis* in Annex V at the end of his book *Les bornes milliaires du territoire de Tipasa (Maurétanie Césarienne)*, Roma 2002, 135–137. The Annex distinguishes nine milestones of the *via Rusicadensis* because they are made of marble quarried at Filfila, 20 km east of Rusicade. Eight of these nine coincide with my numbers (Table 2): 13, 17, 28, 26, 32, 34, 36, 40, Salama's 9th milestone concerns an unpublished item of Maximinus Caesar (236–238) at the 45th mile (not in my list); also the slab on the road to Stora is of Filfila marble. The other milestones are made of different types of limestone. Under these are two unpublished: one, between the 17th–18th mile, refers to Philippus and another one at the 17th mile belonging to Severus Alexander, was reused by Constans II Caesar. Salama observes reuse by Constans II Caesar in CIL VIII 22374 (our n. 17) and ascribes CIL VIII 10319 (our n. 34) to Constans I Caesar and indeterminate emperors. Salama's CIL VIII 10258 has to be corrected in VIII 10304 (our n. 1), CIL VIII 22579 in 22379 (our n. 32) and CIL VIII 22384 in 22381 (our n. 36), by consequence Salama's CIL VIII 22381 of an undetermined emperor at the 40th mile has to be another so far unknown item. The opistographic slab of the 48th mile at Philippeville of Filfila marble is not published in BCTH 1917, CCXVI, nor in any other volume of this periodical. Two fragmentary milestones CIL VIII, 10302 and 10303 with undetermined emperor belonged to the *via Rusicadensis* according to Salama, evidently because of the formulation *viam imbribus et vetustate conlapsam cum pontibus restituit*, exclusively used for this mountain road, not far from the sea. The two fragments totalize to 18 the milestones erected in occasion of repairs. Salama's splendid picture (Fig. 22) of the hollow way over the Kentoures ridge gives a vivid idea of the bold construction of this mountain road.

Bibliography

AAA = S. Gsell (ed.), Atlas Archéologique de l'Algérie, édition spéciale des cartes au 200.000ᵉ du Service Géographique de l'Armée, avec un texte explicatif, Alger/Paris 1911.
Albertini 1921= E. Albertini, Fouilles et inscriptions romaines de Lambiridi, *BCTH* 1921, CLXVII – CLXIX.

Barrington Atlas = R.J.A. Talbert (ed.), Barrington Atlas of the Greek and Roman World, Oxford 2000
Benzina ben Abdallah 1995 = Z. Benzina ben Abdallah, À propos d'un pont de la voie de Carthage à Theveste construit, sous Hadrien, à l'entrée d'Ammaedara, BCTH 1995B, 95–100.
Benzina ben Abdallah/Ladjimi Sebaï 2011= Z. Benzina ben Abdallah/L. Ladjimi Sebaï, Catalogue des inscriptions païennes inédites du Musée de Carthage, IV Milliaires, Rome 2011, 117–119.
Bertrand 1905 = L. Bertrand, Un tronçon de voie romaine découvert près de Philippeville, BCTH 1905, 366–367.
Bertrand 1907 = L. Bertrand, Ruines au bord de la voie romaine de Philippeville à Stora, BCTH 1907, 459–460.
Boujarra/Naddari 2010 = A. Boujarra/L. Naddari, Apport de la recherche géoarchéologique à la reconstitution de la voie romaine Carthage-Theveste et des dynamiques de son environnement (le tronçon Jérissa -Haïdra), in: F. Béjaoui (ed.), Actes du 6e colloque international sur l'histoire des Steppes tunisiennes, Sbeïtla, 2008, Tunis, 2010, 106–129.
Briand-Ponsart 2007 = C. Briand-Ponsart, Les «lancers de cadeaux» (*missilia*) en Afrique du Nord romaine, AntAfr, 43, 2007, 79–97.
Briand-Ponsart 2012 = C. Briand-Ponsart, Le pouvoir et la Confédération cirtéenne: priorité au ravitaillement, in: M. Khanoussi/P. Ruggeri/C. Vismara (ed.), L'Africa romana 12, 2012, 623–635.
Briand-Ponsart 2016 = C. Briand-Ponsart, La permanence d'une frontière interne à la Numidie et les Alpes numidiques, in: A. Mbaret (ed.), Le réseau routier dans le Maghreb antique et médiéval, Actes du deuxième colloque international Sousse, 6–8 avril 2015, Sousse 2016, 269–284.
Camodeca 1994 = G. Camodeca, *Puteoli* porto annonario e il commercio del grano, in: Le ravitaillement en blé de Rome. Actes du Colloque international Naples 14–16 Février 1991, Napoli/Roma 1994, 103–128.
Carilos 1763 = Carilos, Roman Inscriptions at Tunis in Africa, Copied about the Year 1730, *Philosophical Transactions of the Royal Society* 53, 1763, 211–228.
Carre 2011 = M.-B. Carre, Les réseaux d'entrepôts dans le monde romain. Étude de cas, in: J. Arce/B. Goffaux (ed.), *Horrea* d'Hispanie et de la Méditerranée romaine, Madrid 2011, 23–39.
Carton 1895 = L. Carton, Découvertes épigraphiques et archéologiques faites en Tunisie (région de Dougga), Paris 1895.
Chaouali 2016a = M. Chaouali, Milliaires redécouverts et inédits du tronçon Thurris – Laribus de la route Karthago – Theueste, in: A. Mrabet (ed.) Le réseau routier dans le Maghreb antique et médiéval, Actes du deuxième colloque international, Université de Sousse, 06 – 08 avril 2015, Sousse 2016, 51–69.
Chaouali 2016b = M. Chaouali, Cinq milliaires d'Afrique proconsulaire, in: N. Boukhchim/J. Ben Nasr (ed.), Peuplement, territoire et culture matérielle dans l'espace méditerranéen, Actes du cinquième colloque international (Kairouan 15–17 avril, 2014), Kairouan 2016, 85–98.
Christol 1994= M. Christol, Le blé africain et Rome, in: Le ravitaillement en blé de Rome. Actes du Colloque international Naples 14–16 Février 1991, Napoli/Roma 1994, 295–304.
Christol 2012 = M. Christol, L'empereur et les cités: la construction de la *Via Nova* de Cirta vers *Rusicade* sous Hadrien, *Epigraphica* 72, 2012, 185–200.
Christol 2013 = M. Christol, Une inscription du Musée de Philippeville (Skikda) relative à l'aménagement de la route entre Rusicade et Cirta (CIL, VIII, 10311 et p. 2138) Caius Velleius Paterculus, légat de l'empereur, AntAfr 49, 2013, 19–26.
Claassen 2009 = J.-M. Claassen, *Cornelius Fronto*: a 'Libyan Nomad' at Rome, *Acta Classica* 52, 2009, 47–71.
Clarac 1847 = F. de Clarac, Musée de Sculpture antique et moderne, II.2. Suppl. Inscriptions trouvées en Afrique et en divers lieux, Paris 1847.
Côte 1979 = M. Côte, Mutations Rurales en Algérie. Le cas des hautes plaines de l'est, Alger 1979.

CREULLY 1853 = CREULLY, Inscriptions de Constantine, *AnnSocConstantine* 1853, 39–80.
CUVIGNY 2018 = H. CUVIGNY, La toponymie du désert Oriental égyptien sous le Haut-Empire d'après les *ostraca* et les inscriptions, VII. Routes, in: J.-P. BRUN/T. FAUCHER/B. REDON/S. SIDEBOTHAM (ed.), Le désert oriental d'Égypte durant la période gréco-romaine. Bilans archéologiques, Paris 2018, http://books.openedition.org/cdf/4673.
DE BOSREDON = DE BOSREDON, Promenade archéologique dans les environs de Tébessa, *Recueil des notices et mémoires de la Société Archéologique du Département de Constantine* 18, 1876/1877 [1878], 382–427.
DELAMARE 1850 = A. DELAMARE, Exploration scientifique de l'Algérie pendant les années 1840, 1841, 1842, 1843, 1844 et 1845, Archéologie, Paris 1850, http://gallica.bnf.fr/ark:/12148/bpt6k664958/f1.image.
DELAMARE 1859 = A. DELAMARE, Étude sur *Stora*, port de Philippeville (l'ancienne *Rusicade*), *Mémoires de la Société impériale des antiquaires de France* 24, 1859, 132–192.
DELAMARE/GSELL 1912 = A. DELAMARE/S. GSELL, Exploration scientifique de l'Algérie pendant les années 1840–1845, Archéologie, Texte explicatif des planches de AD.-H.-AL. DELAMARE, par S. GSELL, Paris 1912.
DELMAIRE 1989 = R. DELMAIRE, Largesses sacrées et *res privata*. L'*aerarium* impérial et son administration du IVe au VIe siècle, Rome 1989.
DE MARCILLY 1853a = M. DE MARCILLY, Notice sur les vestiges de l'occupation romaine dans la cercle de Philippeville, *AnnSocConstantine* 1853, 20–38.
DE MARCILLY 1853b = M. DE MARCILLY, Voie de *Rusicade* à *Cirta*, *AnnSocConstantine* 1853, 32–36.
DEMMA 2007 = F. DEMMA, Monumenti pubblici di *Puteoli*: per un'archeologia dell'architettura, Roma 2007.
DE ROMANIS 2003 = F. DE ROMANIS, Per una storia del tributo granario africano all'annona della Roma imperiale, in: B. MARIN/C. VIRLOUVET (ed.), Nourrir les cités de Mediterranée. Antiquité-Temps Modernes, Paris 2003, 691–738.
DE SAINTE-MARIE 1878 = E. DE SAINTE-MARIE, La Tunisie chrétienne, Lyon 1878
DE VOS 2000 = M. DE VOS, *Rus Africum*. Terra acqua olio nell'Africa settentrionale. Scavo e ricognizione nei dintorni di Dougga (Alto Tell tunisino), Trento 2000.
DE VOS 2013 = M. DE VOS, The Rural Landscape of Thugga: Farms, Presses, Mills and Transport, in: A. WILSON/A. BOWMAN (ed.), The Roman Agricultural Economy, Oxford 2013, 143–218
DE VOS/ATTOUI 2011 = M. DE VOS/R. ATTOUI, Paesaggio produttivo. Percezione antica e moderna. Geografia della religione: un case-study nell'Africa del Nord, in: R. ATTOUI (ed.), When did Antiquity End?, Oxford 2011, 31–89.
DE VOS/ATTOUI 2015 = M. DE VOS/R. ATTOUI, Rus africum 3, le paysage rural antique autour de Dougga: le réseau routier, Bari 2015.
DONDIN-PAYRE 1994 = M. DONDIN-PAYRE, Le capitaine Delamare. La réussite de l'archéologie romaine au sein de la commission d'exploration scientifique d'Algérie, Paris 1994.
DONDIN-PAYRE 1998 = M. DONDIN-PAYRE, La production d'images sur l'espace méditerranéen dans la Commission d'exploration scientifique d'Algérie. Les dessins du capitaine Delamare, in: L'invention scientifique de la Méditerranée, Paris 1998, 223–238.
DOUBLET 1890 = G. DOUBLET, Musée d'Alger, Paris 1890.
DOUBLET/GAUCKLER 1892 = G. DOUBLET/P. GAUCKLER, Musée de Constantine, Paris 1892.
DREW-BEAR/ECK 1976 = T. DREW-BEAR/W. ECK, Kaiser-, Militär- und Steinbruchinschriften aus Phrygien, *Chiron* 6, 1976, 289–318.
DUCROUX 1975 = S. DUCROUX, Catalogue analytique des inscriptions latines sur pierre conservées au Musée du Louvre, CNRS, Musée du Louvre, Dép. des antiquités grecques et romaines, Paris 1975.
DUVAL 1983 = N. DUVAL, L'état actuel de recherches sur les fortifications de Justinien en Afrique, in: Corsi di cultura sull'arte ravennate e bizantina 30, 1983, 149–204.

FOURNEL 1849 = H. FOURNEL, Richesse minérale de l'Algérie, vol. I, Alger 1849.
GALLIAZZO 1994 = V. GALLIAZZO, I ponti romani I–II, Treviso 1994.
GRAMAYE 1622 = I.B. GRAMAYE, Africae illustratae libri decem, in quibus Barbaria, gentesque eius ut olim, et nunc describuntur, Tournay 1622.
GREENHALGH 2014 = M. GREENHALGH, The Military and Colonial Destruction of the Roman Landscape of North Africa, 1830–1900, Leiden/Boston 2014.
GRIRA 2016 = M. GRIRA, Notes préliminaires sur les ponts de la voie Carthage-Theveste, in: A. MRABET (ed.), Le réseau routier dans le Maghreb Antique et Médiéval, Actes du deuxième colloque international, 6- 8 avril 2015 Sousse, Sousse 2016, 103–128.
GSELL/BERTRAND 1898 = S. GSELL/L. BERTRAND, Musée de Philippeville, Paris 1898.
GSELL 1901 = S. GSELL, Les Monuments antiques de l'Algérie II, Paris 1901.
GURT/RODÀ 2005 = J.M. GURT/I. RODÀ, El Pont del Diable. El monumento romano dentro de la política augustea, AEspA 78, 2005, 191–192.
GUYON 1852 = G.L.G. GUYON, Voyage d'Alger aux Ziban, l'ancienne Zebe en 1847, Alger 1852.
HÉRON DE VILLEFOSSE 1875 = A.M.A. HÉRON DE VILLEFOSSE, Une mission archéologique en Algérie, Archives des missions scientifiques et littéraires: choix de rapports et instructions publié sous les auspices du Ministère de l'instruction, des cultes et des beaux-arts le 1er novembre 1873, 1875, 377–491.
VAN DEN HOUT 1988 = M.P.J. VAN DEN HOUT, M. Cornelius Fronto. Epistulae, Leipzig 1988.
VAN DEN HOUT 1999 = M.P.J. VAN DEN HOUT, A Commentary on the Letters of M. Cornelius Fronto, Leiden/Boston, Köln 1999.
KALLALA 2006 = N. KALLALA, Nouvelles bornes milliaires de la voie Carthage-Theveste découvertes dans la région du Kef (Sicca Veneria) en Tunisie, in: P. RUGGERI/A. SIRAJ/C. VISMARA (ed.), L'Africa romana 16, Roma 2006, 1795–1824.
KALLALA 2012 = N. KALLALA, Bornes milliaires inédites de la voie Carthage-Theveste, in: B. CABOURET/A. GROSLAMBERT/C. WOLFF (ed.), Visions de l'Occident romain, Hommage à Y. Le Bohec, vol. 1, Paris, 197–216.
LE BOHEC 1989 = Y. LE BOHEC, La Troisième Légion Auguste, Paris 1989.
LEO AFRICANUS 1550 = G.L. AFRICANO, Della descrittione dell'Africa et delle cose notabili che ivi sono, Venezia 1550.
LETRONNE 1844 = J.-A. LETRONNE, Observations historiques et géographiques sur l'inscription d'une borne milliaire qui existe à Tunis, RA 1844, 820–831.
MASROUHI et al. 2005 = A. MASROUHI/M. GHANMI/M. BEN YOUSSEF/F. ZARGOUNI/J.M. VILA, Halocinèse crétacée et halotectonique tertiaire dans les monts de Medjez el- Bab: nouvelles observations, datations et données gravimétriques; extension des glaciers de sel sousmarins jusqu'à l'est du méridien de Téboursouk, Notes du Service Géologique de la Tunisie 73, 2005, 107–122.
MASROUHI et al. 2014 = A. MASROUHI/O. BELLIER/M. BEN YOUSSEF/H. KOYI (ed.), Submarine allochthonous salt sheets: gravity-driven deformation of North African Cretaceous passive margin in Tunisia – Bled Dogra case study and nearby salt structures, African Earth Sciences 2014. http://dx.doi.org/10.1016/j.jafrearsci.2014.04.032
MAURIN 2000 = L. MAURIN, Hommage à A. Vitellius Felix Honoratus signo Honorius, in: M. KHANOUSSI/L. MAURIN, Dougga, Fragments d'histoire, Bordeaux/Tunis 2000.
NADDARI 2016 = L. NADDARI, La voie Carthage-Theveste dans la pertica de la colonia Flavia Augusta Emerita Ammaedara: le dossier des milliaires, in: A. MRABET (ed.), Le réseau routier dans le Maghreb Antique et Médiéval, Actes du deuxième colloque international, 6- 8 avril 2015 Sousse, Sousse 2016, 71–102.
PAPI/MARTORELLA 2007 = E. PAPI/F. MARTORELLA, I granai della Numidia, AntAfr, 43, 2007, 171–186.
PEKÁRY 1968 = T. PEKÁRY, Untersuchungen zu den Römischen Reichsstraßen, Bonn 1968.

POULLE 1878 = M.A. POULLE, Inscriptions de la Mauritanie Sétifienne et de la Numidie, *Receuil des notices et mémoires de la Société Archéologique du Département de Constantine* 19, 1878 [1879], 313–430.
PRINGLE 1981 = D. PRINGLE, The Defence of Byzantine Africa from Justinian to the Arab conquest, Oxford 1981.
QUILICI 2008 = L. QUILICI, Land Transports, Part I: Roads and Bridges, in: J.P. OLESON (ed.), The Oxford Handbook of Engineering and Technology in the Classical World, Oxford 2008, 551–579.
RATHMANN 2003 = M. RATHMANN, Untersuchungen zu den Reichsstraßen in den westlichen Provinzen des Imperium Romanum, Mainz 2003.
RAVOISIÉ 1846, 1851 = B.A. RAVOISIÉ, Exploration scientifique de l'Algérie pendant les années 1840, 1841, 1842 -Beaux-arts, architectures et sculptures, Paris, vol. I 1846, vol. II 1851.
RENIER 1858 = L. RENIER, Inscriptions Romaines d'Algérie recueillis et publiées en 1855–1858, Paris 1886.
RÖDER 1974 = J. RÖDER, Quadermarken am Aquaedukt von Karthago, *RM* 81, 1974, 91–98.
ROGER 1874 = J. ROGER, Inscriptions de Philippeville, *Receuil des notices et mémoires de la Société Archéologique du Département de Constantine* 16, 1873–1874, 464–466.
ROSTOVTZEFF 1900 = M. ROSTOVTZEFF, Étude sur les plombs antiques, Paris 1900.
SACERDOTI 1950 =A. SACERDOTI, La pianta del bagno di Tunisi detto di S. Leonardo e di Kara Ahmed, *Revue Africaine* 94, 1950, 149–152.
SALAMA 1951 = P. SALAMA, Les voies romaines d'Afrique du Nord, Alger 1951.
SALAMA 1956 = P. SALAMA, Une inscription milliaire à surcharge du Musée de Constantine et les méthodes du remploi épigraphique, *Receuil des notices et mémoires de la Société Archéologique du Département de Constantine* 69, 1955–1956, 131–144.
SALAMA 1987 = P. SALAMA, Bornes milliaires d'Afrique Proconsulaire. Un panorama historique du Bas Empire Romain, Roma 1987.
SALAMA 2003 = P. SALAMA Les métamorphoses d'une inscription sitifienne dans le contexte des remplois épigraphiques, *Cultus splendore*, Studi in onore di Giovanna Sotgiu, Sassari 2003, 835–860 [= Promenades d'Antiquités africaines, Paris 2005, 137–162].
SALAMA 2010 = P. SALAMA, Les voies antiques, in: J. DESANGES/N. DUVAL/C. LEPELLEY/S. SAINT-AMANS (ed.), Carte des routes et des cités de l'est de l'*Africa* à la fin de l'Antiquité, Turnhout 2010, 39–47.
SHAW 1757 = T. SHAW, Travels, or Geographical, Physical and Miscellaneous Observations Relating to the Kingdom of Tunis, London 1757.
STEUERNAGEL 1999 = D. STEUERNAGEL, 'Corporate Identity'. Über Vereins-, Stadt- und Staatskulte im kaiserzeitlichen *Puteoli*, *RM* 106, 1999, 149–187.
TEMPLE 1835 = G.T. TEMPLE, Excursions in the Mediterranean I–II, London 1835.
TISSOT 1888 = C. TISSOT, Exploration scientifique de la Tunisie: géographie comparée de la province romaine d'Afrique, II Chorographie, Réseau routier, ed. par S. REINACH, Paris 1888.
URIBE et al. 2012 = P. URIBE/A. MAGALLÓN/J. FANLO, New evidence on roman water supply in the Ebro valley: the roman dam of Muel (Zaragoza, Spain), in: M. ŻUCHOWSKA, The Archaeology of Water Supply, Oxford 2012, 75–83.
VARS 1896= C. VARS, R*usicade* et S*tora* ou Philippeville dans l'antiquité, Constantine 1896.
WILSON 1998 = A.I. WILSON, Water Supply in Ancient Carthage, in Carthage Papers: The Early Colony's Economy, Water Supply, A Public Bath, and the Mobilization of State Olive Oil, Portsmouth, Rhode Island 1998, 65–102.
XIMÉNEZ 1720 = J. XIMÉNEZ, Diario de Tunez 1718–1720, ms. in the Real Academia de la Historia, Madrid.

Alfredo Buonopane – Chantal Gabrielli
Miliari e viabilità dell'Etruria romana: un aggiornamento e alcune considerazioni

Abstract: Recent researches and new discoveries have shown some critical aspects of the inscriptions engraved on the milestones found in the Italian regio VII (*Etruria*). A new analysis of these milestones is therefore necessary. In this paper we propose that two milestones, placed among the "falsae" by Eugen Bormann (CIL XI 848 * and CIL XI 849 *), are genuine, while we expunge the inscription CIL XI 6665a from the milestones, because it is a *nota lapicidinarum* on a block of marble from Luni quarries. Finally, of the five new milestones, edited after the publication of the CIL XI (1901), we take into consideration three milestones of republican age from Vulci, Orbetello and Lucus Feroniae. The complex problems concerning the road network of northern and coastal Etruria, where some of these milestones are placed, are also examined here. Consequently not only the consular roads (*Via Aurelia nova / vetus, Via Aemilia Scauri, Via Quinctia*), but also the viae minores are considered.

Zusammenfassung: Die neuere Forschung und neue Funde haben einige problematische Aspekte der Inschriften aufgezeigt, die auf den Meilensteinen eingraviert sind, welche in der regio VII Italiens (Etrurien) gefunden wurden. Demzufolge ist eine neue Untersuchung dieser Meilensteine notwendig. In diesem Beitrag schlagen wir vor, dass zwei Meilensteine (CIL XI 848* e 849*), die von EUGEN BORMANN unter die „falsae" eingeordnet wurden, echt sind, wohingegen wir die Inschrift CIL XI 6665a aus dem Kanon der Meilensteine zurückziehen, da es sich um eine *nota lapicidinarum* auf einem Marmorblock aus den Steinbrüchen von Luni handelt. Schliesslich werden von den fünf Meilensteinen, die nach der Publikation des CIL XI (1901) ediert wurden, drei aus der republikanischen Zeit aus Vulci, Orbetello und Lucus Feroniae analysiert. Die komplexen Probleme, die das Straßennetzwerk des nördlichen und des an der Küste gelegenen Etrurien betreffen, wo einige dieser Meilensteine aufgestellt waren, werden hier ebenfalls untersucht. Folglich werden nicht nur konsulare Straßen (*Via Aurelia nova / vetus, Via Aemilia Scauri, Via Quinctia*) untersucht, sondern auch die kleineren Straßen.

Riassunto: Recenti ricerche e nuovi rinvenimenti mostrano che le iscrizioni incise sui miliari delle vie consolari della regio VII (*Etruria*) presentano alcuni aspetti non privi di criticità e suscettibili di ulteriori e più approfondite analisi. In questa sede viene proposta la genuinità di due miliari considerati "falsi" da Eugen Bormann (CIL, XI, 848* e 849*), mentre viene espunto dal numero dei miliari CIL, XI, 6665a, in quanto si tratta di una *nota lapicidinarum* incisa su un blocco di marmo proveniente dalle cave di Luni. Infine, dei cinque miliari editi dopo la pubblicazione di CIL, XI (1901), vengono presi in esame i tre miliari di età repubblicana rinvenuti a Vulci, Orbetello e *Lucus Feroniae*. Vengono poi approfondite le complesse questioni riguardanti la viabilità dell'Etruria settentrionale e costiera, che alcuni di questi miliari pongono. Si prendono, perciò, in esame non solo le strade consolari che attraversano queste aree (*Via Aurelia nova/vetus, Via Aemilia Scauri, Via Quinctia*), ma anche i percorsi secondari.

Nel 1901 veniva pubblicato, a cura di EUGEN BORMANN, il *fasciculus prior* della *pars posterior* del volume XI del CIL, dove sono riunite le iscrizioni relative alle *viae publicae populi Romani regionum Italiae sextae, septimae, octavae*.[1] Per la prima volta, dunque, veniva edita una raccolta, pressoché completa e ordinata in base alle vie consolari, delle iscrizioni incise sui miliari rinvenuti in queste tre regioni augustee, anche se, almeno per quanto riguarda l'area che si prende qui in esame, ovvero la regio VII Etruria, recenti ricerche[2] e nuovi rinvenimenti hanno mostrato alcuni aspetti non privi di criticità e suscettibili, quindi, di ulteriori e più approfondite analisi.

1 Due miliari "falsi", ma probabilmente genuini.

EUGEN BORMANN, seguendo i severi criteri voluti da THEODOR MOMMSEN,[3] ha inserito fra le *inscriptiones falsae vel alienae* due miliari che, grazie all'analisi di nuovi documenti, sono meritevoli di essere nuovamente presi in considerazione e, con ogni probabilità, riscattati.

In CIL XI 848* (fig. 1) EUGEN BORMANN registra un miliario con questa iscrizione:

> imp. caes. d. n. ualenti | pio felici semper aug | ciuitas lun. m. p | imp. caes. d. gratiano | pio fel. semper aug | diui ualentiniani | ciuit. lun., m. p | imp. caes., dño ualentiniano | semp. aug | diui ualentiniani f | ciuit. lun. m. p.

La pietra era stata rinvenuta nella chiesa di San Pietro a Nocchi presso Camaiore (Lucca), ove era reimpiegato come supporto della mensa dell'altare, e poi era stato trasportato nella villa di Nicolao Montecatini Gigli, sempre a Nocchi. Qui, nella prima

---

* Gli autori desiderano ringraziare vivamente PIERGIOVANNA GROSSI che con grande cortesia e amabilità ha messo a loro disposizione disegni e fotografie da lei realizzati, che compariranno in GROSSI 2019, ormai di imminente pubblicazione.
1 CIL XI 996–1014. 6616–6671a; 1401. 8102–8104; si devono poi aggiungere anche i miliari collocati fra le *inscriptiones falsae*, ai quali è dedicato il capitolo LXXX. *Columnae miliariae* (90*- 91*. 843*-849*).
2 Si vedano da ultimi CIAMPI POLLEDRI 1967, 256–272; HERZIG 1970, 50–65; WISEMAN 1971, 27–32; FENTRESS 1984, 72–76; LIVERANI 1985, 279–282; FENTRESS 1985, 123–124; COARELLI 1988, 35–48; BELLI 1988, 43–48; MOSCA 1992, 91–108; MOSCA 1994, 177–184; FABIANI 2000, 397–410; MOSCA 1999, 165–174; CAMBI 2002, 131–135; FABIANI 2002, 393–411; DALLAI/PONTA/SHEPHERD 2006, 179–190; FABIANI 2006; FABIANI/PARIBENI 2007, 404–418; DÍAZ ARIÑO 2015; BUONOPANE/GABRIELLI 2018, 213–224; GROSSI 2019, c.s.
3 MOMMSEN 1900, 532–534.

metà del Settecento, lo vide e lo trascrisse nel suo diario di viaggio il pittore GEORG CRISTOPH MARTINI,[4] il primo *fons* nell'edizione del CIL. Il miliario, oggi disperso, è stato al centro di vivaci dispute sulla sua genuinità ed è stato relegato da BORMANN tra le *falsae vel alienae* con l'espressione *inscriptio videtur in ipso lapide recenti tempore incisa esse miliario*. Le considerazioni con cui BORMANN motiva la sua scelta sono oggettivamente valide: il testo è del tutto simile a quello di un altro miliario, rinvenuto a San Piero a Grado (Pisa),[5] con la sola variante della clausola finale, *civit(as) Pisana* invece di *civit(as) Lun(ensis)*, e, soprattutto, quest'ultima espressione è inserita, diversamente da ogni consuetudine epigrafica, ben tre volte nel testo, subito dopo il nome di ciascun Augusto. In anni recenti FABIO FABIANI ha dedicato a questo miliario alcuni studi particolarmente approfonditi,[6] nei quali non solo analizza criticamente tutta la bibliografia esistente, ma, soprattutto, presenta un documento di notevole importanza, sfuggito a BORMANN.[7]

Si tratta della pagina (fig. 1) di uno "zibaldone" epigrafico redatto da BARTOLOMEO FIORITI, un erudito lucchese, che intorno al 1750 ebbe modo di vedere il miliario e di trascriverlo.[8] Anch'egli afferma che la lapide si trovava "in angulo atrii ejusdem villae" e di aver effettuato l'autopsia: "sic ego legebam". Inoltre sostiene di aver visto sul retro della colonna le lettere *VII / VV MO*. Non credo, dunque, che ci siano dubbi che esistesse realmente un miliario recante un'iscrizione a Valente, a Graziano e a Valentiniano II: alle ragioni addotte da FABIANI[9] aggiungerei che non vedo il motivo per il quale un pittore tedesco e un erudito lucchese, che godeva di buona fama, dovessero creare un falso cartaceo.[10] Penso piuttosto che non si tratti né di un falso su pietra né di un *exemplum recens*, quanto piuttosto di un testo antico, interpolato, incidendovi in età moderna più volte la formula *civit(as) Lun(ensis)*, o per conferire una patente di nobiltà a questo centro o, forse, in seguito a qualche disputa territoriale con centri amministrativi vicini.[11] Espunte dunque le interpolazioni seriori e sulla base del formulario di iscrizioni simili presenti sul già citato miliario di san Pietro a Grado[12] e su due miliari rinvenuti nella vicina regio VIII,[13] oltre che delle letture, purtroppo non sempre sicure, di MARTINI e di FIORITI, gli unici, a quanto pare, che hanno visto la pietra, proporrei:

---

4 Su questo pittore, attivo a Lucca nella prima metà del Settecento, si veda da ultima BETTI 2013; parte dei suoi manoscritti sono stati editi in MARTINI/TRUMPY 1969, dove compare anche la trascrizione di questo miliare (408–409, cfr. 442–443 nt. 100).
5 CIL XI 6665 = InscrIt VII 1, 118.
6 FABIANI 2002, 398–399; FABIANI 2006, 122–129.
7 FABIANI 2006, 125.
8 FIORITI ms. 1613, c. 45r.
9 FABIANI 2006, 126.
10 BUONOPANE 2014, 292–297.
11 FABIANI 2006, 126; si veda anche quanto scrive più oltre CHANTAL GABRIELLI.
12 CIL XI 6665 = InscrIt VII 1, 118.
13 Brisighella (Forlì-Cesena): AE 1932, 60; Campiano (Ravenna): AE 1975, 402 = 1992, 611 = 2006, 441.

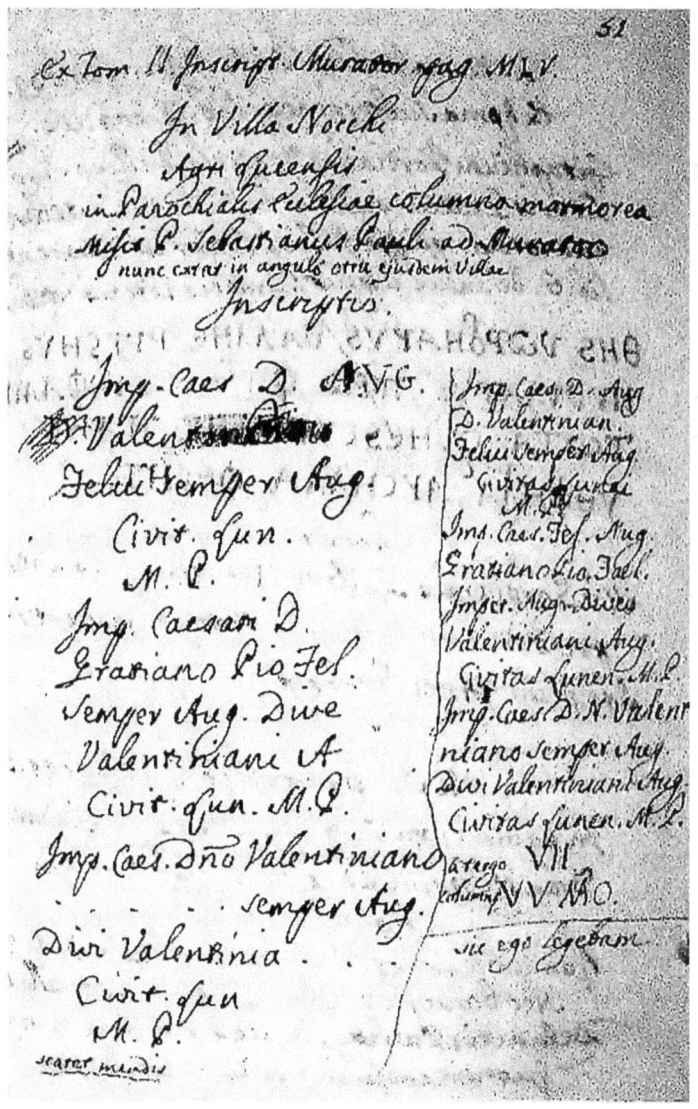

Fig. 1: Il miliario di Nocchi (CIL XI 848*) nel manoscritto di Bartolomeo Fioriti (da Fabiani 2006, 125 fig. 22).

a) in fronte

> *Imp(eratori) Caes(ari) d(omino) n(ostro) / F[l](avio) [Valent]i / Pio / Felici semp(er) A[ug(usto)] / Imp(eratori) Caes(ari) d(omino) [n(ostro)] / [Fl(avio)] Gr[atia]no Pio Fel(ici) / semp(er) Aug(usto) divi / Valentiniani / Aug(usti) filio / [Im]p(eratori) Caes(ari) d(omino) n(ostro) [Fl(avio)] Valentiniano / [Pio] F(e)l(ici) semp(er) Aug(usto) / divi Valentiniani / Aug(usti) filio / m(ilia) p(assuum) [- - -].*

b) ab altero latere

– – – – – – / [– – –]VII[– – –] / [– – –]VV MO[– – –] / – – – – – –.

Un altro caso interessante è rappresentato da CIL XI 849*, che BORMANN pubblica con questa lettura:

Titus Flaminius et Titus Quintius consules Pisae milliario 32 hic posuerunt fines suae ciuitatis

Anche qui la pur lodevole cautela di BORMANN è stata forse eccessiva, dato che, sulla scorta delle affermazioni di GIOVANNI LAMI e di EMANUELE REPETTI, il miliario viene relegato fra le *inscriptiones falsae*,[14] perché ritenuto un "titulum errore vel fraude... factum" sulla base di CIL XI 6671.[15] In realtà già nel XII secolo, in un documento attribuito all'arcivescovo pisano Uberto (1133–1137), il miliario era segnalato nel territorio di Empoli, in una località dal significativo nome di Pietrafitta.[16] Nella carta, oggi perduta, ma della quale esiste un apografo, risalente al 7 marzo 1502 e conservato presso l'Archivio di Stato di Pisa,[17] l'arcivescovo ricorda la presenza di un „lapis marmoreus" che „fuit enim terminus inter nos (Pisanos) et Florentinos qui Petrafitta vocatur" con „istae litterae scripte (sic) Titus Flaminius et Titus Quintus consules Pisae milliario trigesimo secundo". Si tratterebbe, dunque, di una lapide genuina,[18] come confermano sia il fatto che nella trascrizione del testo il nome del console sia stato erroneamente duplicato in una coppia consolare, poiché chi ha eseguito la trascrizione, come talora accadeva, vedeva bene le lettere, ma non comprendeva il testo, sia perché manca il movente per la confezione di un falso.[19] Proporrei dunque:

T(itus) Flaminius T(iti) f(ilius) / Flamininus, / co(n)s(ul), Pisas XXXII.

---

14 LAMI 1758, I, 694; REPETTI 1835, 55–56.
15 Si vedano BUONOPANE/GABRIELLI 2018, 213–224.
16 Sull'importanza toponomastica della denominazione "Petraficta": UGGERI 1991, 21–36.
17 Huberti Archiepiscopi recordationis charta, Archivio di Stato di Pisa, Comune, *Divisione A*, n. 44, cc. 8v-9r; si veda UGHELLI 1718, 355. Fondamentali CECCARELLI LEMUT/SODI 1996, 626–627.
18 Così già CAPECCHI 1987, 35, 37 nt. 4 e MOSCA 1992, 94; cfr. DÍAZ ARIÑO 2015, 99 e BUONOPANE/GABRIELLI 2018, 213–224.
19 Su questa problematica si veda da ultimo BUONOPANE 2014, 291–294.

2 Un miliario da espungere

Singolare è il caso dell'iscrizione così registrata fra i miliari in CIL XI 6665a:

Æ AR
infra
CXIIX

EMANUELE REPETTI, il primo editore,[20] la ritenne un miliario, tratto in inganno sia dal fatto che nelle vicinanze era stato individuato "il selciato di una strada", sia dalla presenza delle lettere *AE*, interpretate come le iniziali di *Aemilia*, da riferirsi al tracciato viario detto *Aemilia Scauri*, sia dalla cifra numerica. Le sue considerazioni furono accolte, nonostante la mancanza di un riscontro autoptico, da BORMANN.

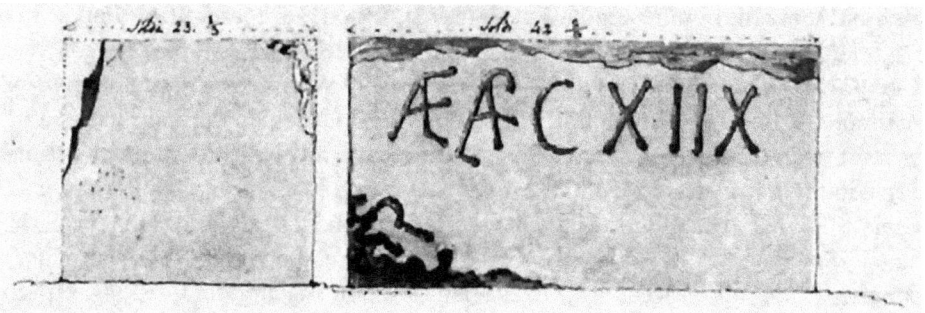

Fig. 2: Il blocco di marmo lunense con *nota lapicidinarum* registrato come miliario in CIL, 6665a (da FABIANI/PARIBENI 2007, 410, fig. 3).

In anni recenti, tuttavia, FABIO FABIANI ed EMANUELA PARIBENI,[21] grazie a accurate ricerche di archivio, hanno ritrovato un disegno di questo reperto (fig. 2), che consente di stabilire in modo inequivocabile che non si tratta di un miliario, bensì di un blocco di cava di marmo lunense, recante una *nota lapicidinarum*, da leggersi "*AE LAP* (?) *CXIIX*".[22]

---

20 REPETTI 1835, 621.
21 FABIANI/PARIBENI 2007, 404, 418.
22 Oltre a FABIANI/PARIBENI 2007, 404, 418, si vedano ora CECCHI 2015, 369, S2; PARIBENI 2015, 375.

3 Nuovi miliari di età repubblicana

Negli oltre cento anni trascorsi dalla pubblicazione del *Corpus* solo cinque nuovi miliari sono stati editi, tre dei quali di particolare importanza,[23] perché posti in opera in età repubblicana. Per rimanere nei limiti di spazio concessi a questo intervento, mi limiterò a una rapida presentazione di queste tre testimonianze, mentre CHANTAL GABRIELLI approfondirà le complesse questioni riguardanti la viabilità, che alcuni di essi pongono.

3.1 Il miliario di *Vulci* (Montalto di Castro, Viterbo)

Rinvenuto a Vulci nel 1958, ancora infisso nel terreno presso l'arco di accesso alla città romana, il miliario (fig. 3 a-c) presenta questa duplice iscrizione :[24]

a) in fronte

    [·] Aur[elius] / [· f(ilius) C]otta, co(n)[s(ul)]. / Ruma LXX.

b) ab altero latere

    ‒ ‒ ‒ ‒ ‒ ‒ ? / *[Ru]ma.*

La datazione del miliario è controversa a causa della non sicura identificazione del console *[·] Aurelius Cotta*: i vari studiosi hanno infatti proposto il 252, il 248, il 200, il 144 e il 119 a.C.,[25] anche se, a mio parere, la presenza di un *chi* calcidico,[26] i segni d'interpunzione circolari e la forma *Ruma*, arcaica e di calco etrusco, per *Roma*[27] mi inducono a propendere per la datazione più alta.[28]

---

23 Gli altri due sono un miliario di Valentiniano, Valente e Graziano (STANCO 1999, 190–191 = AE 1999, 625), rinvenuto a *Lucus Feroniae*, e uno, probabilmente mutilo, recante solo l'indicazione numerica *XXI*, ritrovato presso Montalto Marina (Viterbo), lungo la via Aurelia (CORSI 1993, 173–178).
24 DEGRASSI 1962, 508–510 (= DEGRASSI 1967, 204–206) = AE 1963, 131,2 = ILLRP 1288 = AE 1975, 379 = CIL I² 2931 = KREILER 2011, 109–115 = AE 2011, 60 = DÍAZ ARIÑO 2015, 91–92, nr. 8 = BIANCHI 2016, 152–153.
25 Si veda lo *status quaestionis* in DÍAZ ARIÑO 2015, 91–92.
26 AGOSTINIANI 1995, 53–62.
27 DE SIMONE 2007, 120–128.
28 Ulteriori dati, anche riguardanti la viabilità, in GABRIELLI c.s.

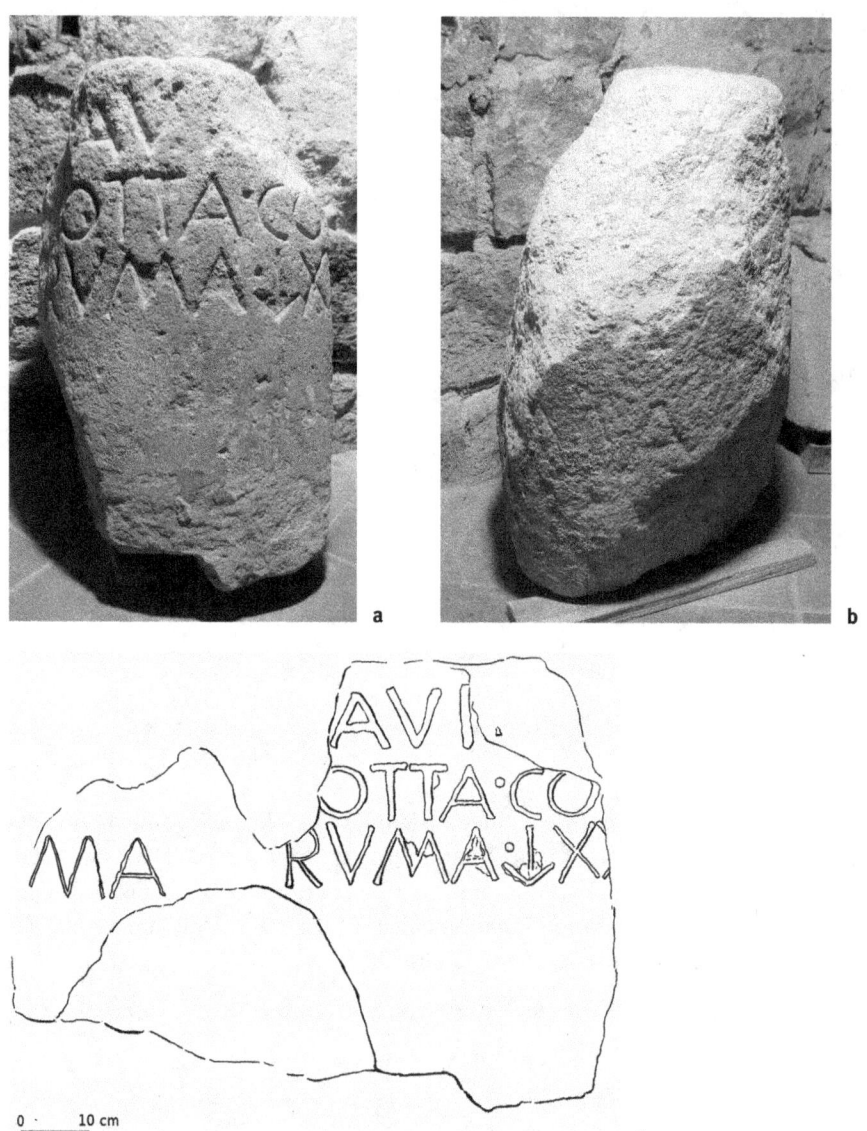

Fig. 3 a–c: Il miliario di Vulci (foto e disegno di Piergiovanna Grossi; su concessione del MIBACT).

3.2 Il miliario di *Orbetello* (Grosseto)

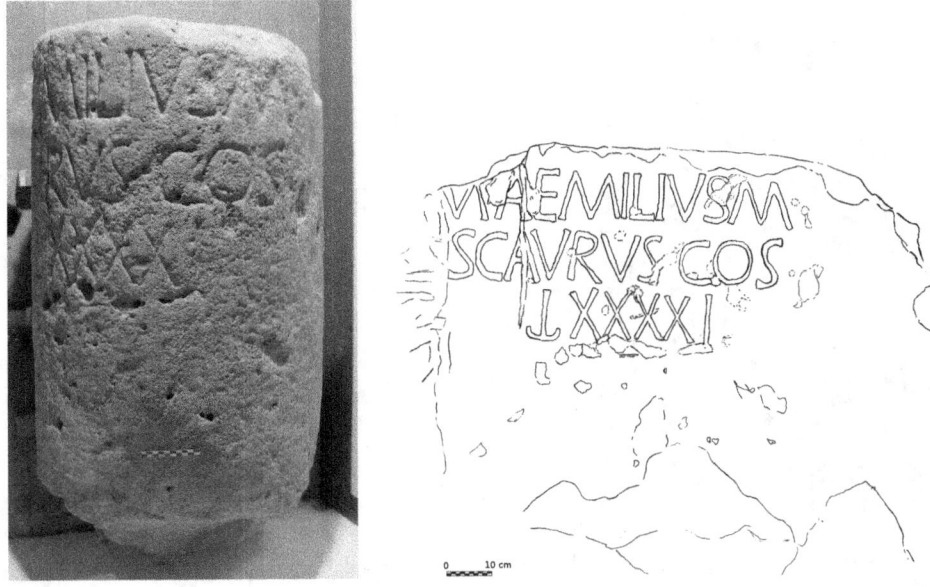

Fig. 4 a–b: Il miliario di Orbetello (foto e disegno di Piergiovanna Grossi; su concessione del MIBACT).

Scoperto nel 1983 durante alcune prospezioni archeologiche nella valle di Albenga, presso San Donato Vecchio di Grosseto (fig. 4 a-b), reca questa iscrizione:[29]

M(arcus) Aemilius M(arci) [f(ilius)] / Scaurus co(n)s(ul) / LXXXXI.

Il console qui ricordato è stato identificato col console del 115 a.C., ma FILIPPO COARELLI, sulla base di un passo di Aurelio Vittore,[30] propone che la strada, cui il miliario appartiene, sia stata costruita non durante il consolato di *M. Aemilius Scaurus*, ma durante la sua censura, ovvero nel 109 a.C.[31]

---

29 FENTRESS 1984, 72–76 = AE 1986, 232 = FENTRESS 1985, 123–124 = CIL I² 2937c = DÍAZ ARIÑO 2015, 92–93, nr. 9.
30 Aur. Vict. vir. ill. 72,8.
31 COARELLI 1988, 38, seguito da PASQUINUCCI 2014, 33; su questo problema DÍAZ ARIÑO 2015, 92.

3.3 Il miliario di *Lucus Feroniae* (Capena, Roma)

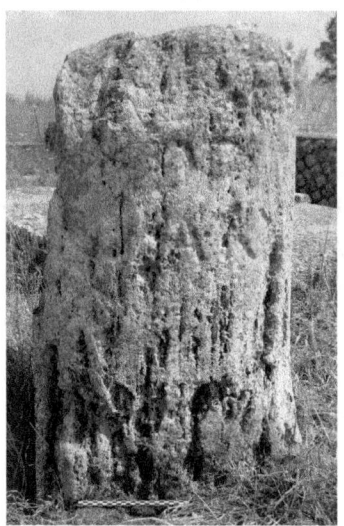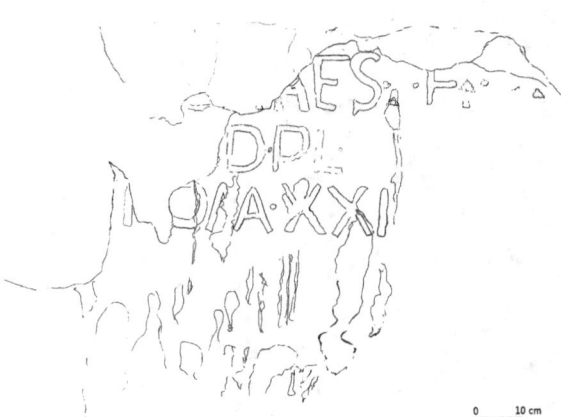

Fig. 5 a–b: Il miliario di *Lucus Feroniae* (foto e disegno di Piergiovanna Grossi; su concessione del MIBACT).

Rinvenuto nel 1956–1958 durante gli scavi archeologici nell'area di *Lucus Feroniae* (fig. 5 a-b) vi si legge :[32]

[P(ublius) Men]ates P(ubli) f(ilius) / [ai]d(ilis) pl(ebis) / Roma XXI.

Un *P. Menates* edile della plebe compare su un altro miliario rinvenuto a Nazzano (Roma),[33] ma non è menzionato in nessun'altra fonte,[34] fatto questo che rende problematico suggerire una collocazione cronologica abbastanza precisa. In base ai dati della paleografia si potrebbe proporre con cautela la seconda metà del II secolo a.C.[35]
ALFREDO BUONOPANE

---

32 STANCO 1999, 191–196 = AE 1999, 626 = DÍAZ ARIÑO 2015, 86–87, nr. 2.
33 CIL XI 6616 = I² 829 (cfr. p. 956) = ILLRP 463 = AE 1999, 194 = DÍAZ ARIÑO 2015, 86–87, nr. 3.
34 BROUGHTON 1951, 467.
35 Cfr. DÍAZ ARIÑO 2015, 87.

Alcune considerazioni sulla viabilità dell'Etruria settentrionale e costiera

Come si è esposto nella prima parte di questo contributo, diversi fattori hanno portato alla revisione di alcuni percorsi viari finora noti che attraversavano in epoca romana la regio VII. In primo luogo la scoperta di alcuni miliari nel secolo scorso ha generato maggiore interesse verso la viabilità dell'Etruria, allo stesso tempo c'è stata anche un'analisi più critica sulla documentazione riguardante mentre questa classe di materiali. Anche se lo sviluppo delle ricerche storico-archeologiche sulla romanizzazione e viabilità dell'Etruria settentrionale romana ha sofferto di una certa marginalità rispetto alla più studiata documentazione dell'Etruria centro-meridionale, negli ultimi decenni si è andata comunque sviluppando un'indagine più accurata di tale territorio, attraverso analisi geomorfologiche, ricerche toponomastiche e di archivio, campagne di scavo e fotografie aeree.[36] La conoscenza dei tracciati viari è ampiamente migliorata grazie anche all'interesse rivolto ai fiumi – ovvero il calcolo della portata dei corsi d'acqua, il fenomeno della sedimentazione, l'innalzamento del livello delle acque del mare, i bacini idrogeologici –[37] tutti aspetti che hanno fortemente determinato l'andamento delle strade con deviazioni o costruzioni di infrastrutture come ponti, non sempre però identificabili *in loco*.[38] La stessa organizzazione romana del territorio, la regolare suddivisione agraria in lotti di pari grandezza, quale conseguenza pratica della centuriazione su aree di nuova acquisizione, ha talvolta determinato l'orientamento di strade, come è chiaramente visibile nella pianura fiorentina.[39] Talvolta era la stessa conformazione del suolo a non favorire la costruzione di percorsi rettilinei e quindi più corti. In Etruria accanto ad una viabilità, per così dire, principale e legata alla costruzione di *viae publicae* ufficiali volute dallo stato romano,[40] dobbiamo considerare anche una viabilità secondaria, di non minore importanza, definita da strade secondarie e vie rurali che intensificarono i traffici e caratterizzarono il tessuto viario sia in aree più interne, come individuato nell'*ager lucensis*,[41] sia lungo le zone costiere. Sono attestati diverticoli della *via Aurelia* nei pressi del *portus Telamonis*[42] e della *via*

---

36 Sulla viabilità dell'Etruria centro settentrionale e costiera in epoca romana a titolo esemplificativo vd. FENTRESS 1984, 1985; TORTORICI 1985; MOSCA 1992, 1994, 1999; CAMBI 2002; FABIANI 2000; FABIANI 2002; FABIANI 2006; sulla colonizzazione vd. CIAMPOLTRINI 1981; COARELLI 1988; TERRENATO 2001; DALLAI/PONTA/SHEPHERD 2006.
37 Richiamo in questo ambito gli ultimi studi di PASQUINUCCI/MENCHELLI 2009; 2012; 2012a; per ulteriore bibliografia vd. PASQUINUCCI 2016.
38 CAMPBELL 2012.
39 La topografia della pianura fiorentina ha permesso di individuare strade il cui andamento segue la centuriazione romana, secondo le documentate ricerche di BACCI 2012.
40 QUILICI 1991, 19.
41 CIAMPOLTRINI/ANDREOTTI 1993, espec. 191; CIAMPOLTRINI 2004.
42 CIAMPOLTRINI 1993.

Aemilia Scauri nei pressi del lago di Porta,[43] a testimonianza di una complessa opera di ridefinizione dell'assetto dei traffici marittimi e la necessità di raccordo con centri dell'entroterra. In questa sede, per i limiti di spazio consentiti, mi concentrerò sull'identificazione della viabilità nell'Etruria settentrionale e costiera, grazie a un'analisi sui relativi miliari. Nello specifico prenderò in considerazione la strada che collegava la costa tirrenica all'entroterra dell'Etruria settentrionale, ovvero la via consolare, denominata convenzionalmente *via Quinctia* dagli studiosi moderni,[44] che partiva da *Pisae*, attraversava la valle dell'Arno e arrivava a *Faesulae*, dove si raccordava con la *via Cassia* proveniente da Roma. Analizzerò poi la viabilità che caratterizzava la stretta fascia costiera ai piedi delle Alpi Apuane[45] e permetteva alla colonia di *Luna* di raggiungere *Luca*, lungo un percorso pedecollinare, e *Pisae* attraverso un tracciato litoraneo (fig. 6).

Su quest'ultima strada infine tenterò di dare alcune risposte agli interrogativi sollevati in merito alla sua individuazione tra *via Aurelia nova* / *via Aurelia vetus* / *via Aemilia Scauri*.[46]

È ben noto come il crescente sviluppo della viabilità sia aspetto strettamente connesso con l'intensificazione coloniaria di aree di recente conquista romana.[47] In Etruria settentrionale e costiera vi fu una densa opera di colonizzazione fra III e II secolo a.C., a seguito di campagne vittoriose su Etruschi che dominavano parte dell'area, attraverso le città di *Pisae* e *Volaterrae*, e sulle popolazioni dei *Ligures*. Polibio e Livio costituiscono le fonti principali per ricostruire le fasi della conquista romana in questa area. Nel 298 a.C. Volterra venne sconfitta,[48] e poco più tardi presso il lago Vadimone (vicino *Horta* – odierna Orte) si tenne nel 283 a.C. una battaglia decisiva contro un'alleanza tra Etruschi e tribù dei Galli Boi. Probabilmente dopo tale data Volterra stipulò un *foedus* con Roma e Pisa diventò *civitas foederata* per poi essere utilizzata nei decenni successivi come base navale per le spedizioni romane in Sardegna e nel sud della Gallia.[49] La penetrazione romana sulla costa tirrenica si affermò con la fondazione della colonia portuale di Cosa nel 273 a.C. e la successiva costruzione

---

43 Si veda quanto scrivo più avanti; cfr. FABIANI 2006.
44 Vd. da ultima MOSCA 1994, 179; MOSCA 1999, 165; la strada è chiamata invece *via Pisana* da LOPES PEGNA 1974, 232–233; LOPES PEGNA 1951, 407–442, in particolare 421 nt. 75; PAGNI 2010, 131. In Sabina è conosciuta un'omonima *via Quinctia*, che congiungeva *Reate* con *Alba Fucens*, raccordandosi con le *viae Salaria* e *Valeria* (Dion. Hal. ant. 1,14) e attribuita al console del 271 a.C. *K. Quinctius, C. f., Cn. n., Claudus* (cfr. BROUGHTON 1951, 158; LIVERANI 1985, 279–282).
45 FABIANI 2006, 45–71; 83–130; 147–155, 156–157 fig. 26.
46 Sulla *via Aemilia Scauri*: LAMBOGLIA 1937; CIAMPI POLLEDRI 1967; FENTRESS 1984; 1985; COARELLI 1988, 38–39; mentre su *via Aurelia nova* e *vetus*: HERZIG 1970; WISEMAN 1971; SORDI 1971; TORTORICI 1985; COARELLI 1988, 42–48.
47 Sulla strutturazione viaria dell'Italia in età repubblicana sono state proposte cronologie distinte: PEKÁRY 1968; HARRIS 1971; COARELLI 1988.
48 Liv. 12,3,8.
49 Pol. 2,27. 3,4,2. 3,56,5; cfr. Liv. 21,39.

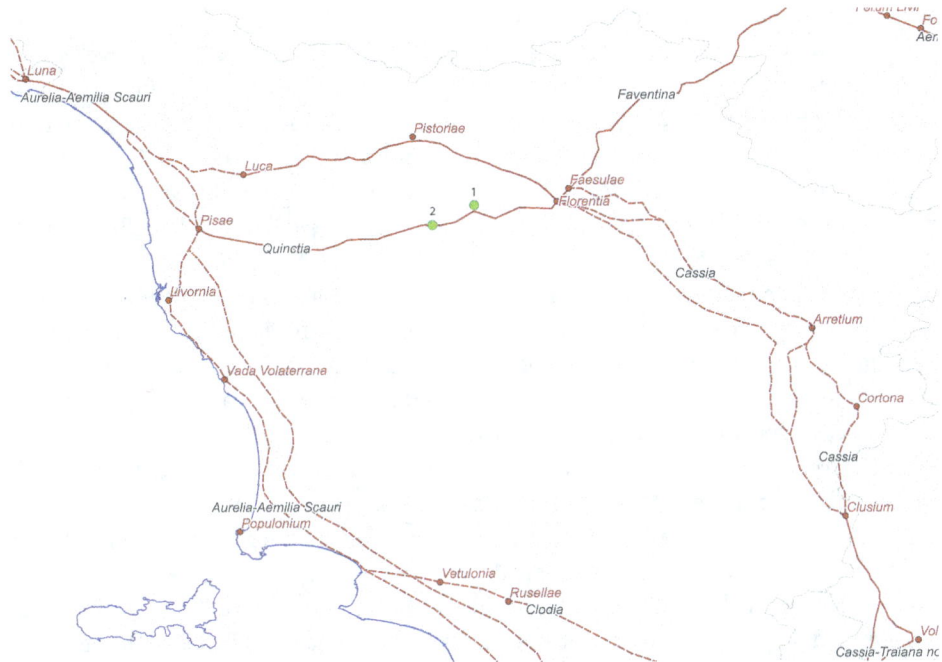

Fig. 6: La viabilità dell'Etruria romana (carta realizzata da Piergiovanna Grossi).

della *via Aurelia* (*Vetus*), attribuita ad un Aurelio Cotta, di assai dibattuta identificazione.⁵⁰ La *via Aurelia* risaliva, con andamento sostanzialmente costiero, verso nord. Costituì in un primo momento l'asse portante della conquista romana dell'Etruria, assieme alle vie minori, sovrapposte alle originarie piste etrusche e successivamente, la linea portante dell'assoggettamento delle tribù galliche e celtiche dell'occidente cisalpino e transalpino. Il primo tratto collegava inizialmente Roma a Cosa, poi la strada raggiunse anche Pisa, diventata base militare per le campagne contro i *Ligures*. Nel II secolo a.C. continuò l'avanzata romana nel territorio dell'Etruria settentrionale e vennero fondate a breve distanza fra loro *Luca* (180 a.C.) e *Luna* (177 a.C.). In questo periodo si ebbe un intenso sviluppo del sistema viario al fine di garantire una migliore connessione sia fra Roma e il nord-ovest dell'Italia che fra l'Etruria settentrionale interna e la zona costiera. La *via Aurelia*, che toccava già i tre porti principali a nord della regio VII, ovvero *Vada Volaterrana*, *Portus Pisanus* e *Luna*, favorendo indub-

---

50 Si veda quanto scrive sopra ALFREDO BUONOPANE; recentemente PASQUINUCCI 2014, 33, accettando tale identificazione propone come date di realizzazione della strada gli anni tra il primo consolato e la censura 252/241 a.C. Considero più plausibile una datazione alta alla luce dell'analisi dei nuovi miliari rinvenuti a Orbetello e Vulci, che sono oggetto di un mio studio in pubblicazione: GABRIELLI c.s.

biamente un incremento nello sviluppo economico dell'area,[51] venne pertanto prolungata attraverso il territorio dei Liguri fino a *Genua* e *Vada Sabatia*, punto estremo di avanzamento verso occidente; il tratto superiore fu condotto da M. Emilio Scauro negli anni 115–109 a.C. (*via Aemilia Scauri*). Sempre nel II secolo a.C. venne creata una seconda strada costiera con un andamento più interno e rettilineo, la *via Aurelia nova*, mentre in epoca graccana si costruì la *via Quinctia* per collegare Pisa all'interna *Faesulae* e successivamente anche alla vicina colonia di *Florentia,* fondata nella seconda metà del I secolo a.C.[52]

Un problema tuttora discusso, relativamente per l'età repubblicana, è rappresentato dall'indicazione della carica del personaggio cui si attribuisce la realizzazione di una strada. Non è chiaro se la citazione della magistratura si riferisca a quella rivestita al momento dell'iniziativa della costruzione della strada o debba intendersi come la più alta carica occupata dal personaggio alla posa dei miliari. Tra gli studiosi vi è chi, come RADKE, tende a negare l'esistenza delle cosiddette vie censorie, riservando il diritto di costruzione delle vie soltanto ai magistrati dotati di *imperium*.[53] Di ben altro avviso appare invece COARELLI, che sostiene invece come per alcuni casi specifici si possa invece supporre che la menzione del consolato vada a indicare la più alta magistratura ricoperta.[54] Emblematico è dunque il caso della *via Aemilia Scauri:* il miliario, rinvenuto nel 1983 *in situ* nei pressi del casale Volta di Rote (San Donato, Orbetello),[55] reca l'indicazione del consolato del suo costruttore (115 a.C.) in contrasto con le fonti letterarie che attribuivano invece la realizzazione della strada alla censura di Scauro (109 a.C.).[56] Il cippo potrebbe allora indicare, secondo COARELLI,[57] che l'inizio dei lavori della strada sia avvenuto a seguito del trionfo riportato da Scauro durante il consolato sulle popolazioni Liguri e si sia concluso con la censura, comprendendo un periodo che va dal 115 al 109 a.C.[58]

L'Etruria sappiamo essere stata oggetto, come del resto anche altre aree dell'Italia, della politica graccana di ridistribuzione dell'agro pubblico. E' ben noto il passo plutarcheo che descrive lo stato di totale abbandono in cui versavano gran parte delle terre di quest'area e il profondo sconforto che provò Tiberio Gracco nell'attraversarle.[59] È plausibile mettere in relazione il potenziamento della viabilità dell'Etruria regi-

---

[51] TERRENATO 2001; PASQUINUCCI 2016, 41–45. Nello specifico sui porti di Pisa e di Volterra vd. PASQUINUCCI 2007.
[52] Sulla dibattuta questione della datazione della fondazione di *Florentia* attribuita a Cesare in età triumvirale o ad Augusto vd. GABRIELLI 2017, 120–121, spec. 120 nt.14.
[53] RADKE 1981, 37.
[54] COARELLI 1988, 38–39.
[55] Vd. più sopra quanto scrive ALFREDO BUONOPANE.
[56] Aur. Vict. vir. ill. 72,7–8: *Consul Liguras Tauriscos domuit atque de his triumphavit. Censor viam Aemiliam stravit.*
[57] COARELLI 1988, 38–39.
[58] Sulla carriera politica di Scauro, figura di spicco tra i Gracchi e Silla: BATES 1986.
[59] Plut. Tib. Gracchus 8–9.

strabile nel corso del II secolo a.C. con l'emanazione di una probabile legge viaria da parte del tribuno della plebe Gaio Sempronio Gracco. Plutarco e Appiano menzionano il potenziamento delle strade come una forte priorità nella attività politica di Gaio Gracco;[60] con molta probabilità la presunta *lex Sempronia viaria* è da intendersi più semplicemente come una disposizione contenuta nella stessa legislazione agraria, resa necessaria dalla divisione dell'*ager publicus* in piccoli appezzamenti.[61] A tale operazione di ampliamento dei tratti viari condotta negli ultimi decenni del II secolo a.C. sembra ricondursi, come vedremo, la costruzione della *via Quinctia* che collegava *Faesulae* a *Pisae*.

L'importanza di una rete viaria come forma di controllo su un determinato territorio continua ad essere una priorità anche in età imperiale. L'amministrazione imperiale enumera la *cura viarum* fra i suoi obiettivi impellenti per le finanze cittadine a garanzia del benessere economico e sociale della collettività.[62] Indubbiamente il sistema viario romano rappresenta un organismo molto complesso. Un recente studio[63] ha messo in luce l'apparato giuridico-amministrativo preposto e istituito appositamente per la cura e la gestione di una particolare tipologia di vie pubbliche, quelle dette anche 'strade municipali', perché non direttamente volute e costruite dallo stato romano ma designate, programmate e gestite da magistrati locali.[64] Talvolta sono gli imperatori stessi a farsi carico della risistemazione dei lastricati viari, usurati dal tempo ma anche dall'incuria, per sollevare da questo onere le debilitate finanze cittadine. Per la regio VII non è chiaro se alla base di tali interventi imperiali ci fosse uno specifico programma di miglioria stradale. Nei decenni successivi a compromettere ulteriormente la viabilità dell'Etruria intervennero anche le continue incursioni barbariche, secondo la testimonianza di Claudio Rutilio Namaziano.[65] Come riporta nel *De reditu suo*, il poeta non esita a risalire le coste dell'allora Tuscia, agli inizi del V secolo d.C., con un'imbarcazione piuttosto che intraprendere un viaggio per terra che potrebbe rivelarsi esiziale e giungere così incolume in prossimità del *Portus Pisanus*.[66]

I miliari, oggetto di analisi e approfondimento, coprono un ampio arco cronologico che va dagli ultimi decenni del II secolo a.C., in piena età graccana, al IV secolo d.C. Ne consegue che motivazioni distinte furono alla base dell'erezione dei cippi, come si evince dalla forma e contenuto delle iscrizioni su di essi incise. In generale

---

60 Plut. C. Gracchus 7,1–2; analogamente Appiano ricorda l'interesse del tribuno verso lo sviluppo della rete viaria italica: App. civ. 1,2.
61 ROTONDI 1912, 311–312; PONTE 2007, 97–99.
62 Sui *curatores viarum*: ERTMAN 1976.
63 CAMPEDELLI 2014.
64 Sulla caratterizzazione giuridica delle *viae publicae* romane: PONTE 2007.
65 Sulla situazione viaria alla fine dell'impero vd. CAVALIERI 2011.
66 Rut. Nam. 1,37–42: *Electum pelagus, quoniam terrena viarum / plana madent fluviis, cautibus alta rigent: / postquam Tuscus ager postquamque Aurelius agger / perpessus Geticas ense vel igne manus / non silvas domibus, non flumina ponte coercet, / incerto satius credere vela mari.* Seguo l'edizione di POZZATO/RODIGHIERO 2011. Secondo LANA 1961, 11–60, il viaggio sarebbe stato compiuto nel 415 d.C.

sulla base della documentazione qui raccolta possiamo affermare che alla necessità, a partire dalla media e tarda repubblica, di tracciare nel territorio il percorso di un nuovo assetto viario e di lasciare memoria sui miliari dei promotori della costruzione e realizzazione di una strada con le indicazioni delle distanze, si affiancano nuovi fenomeni in età imperiale. Infatti a partire dal II secolo d.C. in Etruria vengono registrati interventi imperiali di restauro su tratti dissestati della pavimentazione, casi di reimpiego dei cippi, più spesso accertati in epoca tardoantica, e dediche all'imperatore professate da singole *civitates*. In sostanza con l'assenza del riferimento alle miglia, propria degli ultimi secoli dell'impero, i miliari finirono col perdere l'originaria funzione di indicatori stradali per acquisire un ruolo propagandistico o semplicemente celebrativo.[67] Vediamo ora in dettaglio i singoli cippi miliari e le relative *viae publicae* di pertinenza.

I due miliari della via Faesulae-Pisae

A un'importante arteria di epoca repubblicana, convenzionalmente chiamata *via Quinctia*, che univa Fiesole a Pisa, vanno attribuiti due miliari col nome del console *T. Quinctius Flamininus*.[68] Il primo,[69] rinvenuto a Luciano presso Camaioni, tra Malmantile e Montelupo Fiorentino (Firenze), ritenuto a lungo irreperibile, è stato individuato a Firenze presso la collezione Antinori, collocata nel Palazzo Antinori Aldobrandini di Brindisi, dove è stato possibile effettuarne l'esame autoptico.[70] Questo ha consentito di risolvere alcuni dubbi di lettura riguardanti il numero delle miglia. Infatti in r. 4 lo spazio interessato dalla scalpellatura poteva ospitare al massimo due lettere, mentre, come si può osservare bene anche nel facsimile di RITSCHL, il solco, interpretato come parte di una lettera dagli editori del CIL, sembra essere un segno casuale (figg. 7–8).[71]

L'unica proposta di integrazione della riga sembrerebbe essere quella già avanzata da RADKE, ovvero *Pisas [XL]*, pari a km 59,200 circa, che è con buona approssimazione la distanza tra il probabile luogo di rinvenimento del miliario e il centro di *Pisae*, seguendo la strada lungo la valle dell'Arno denominata "via Antica Pisana".[72] Per

---

67 Sulla casistica della regio VII: FABIANI 2002, 396–397, 403–405, 403 nt. 47.
68 La questione è ampiamente dibattuta con ampia bibliografia nel contributo di BUONOPANE/GABRIELLI 2018.
69 RITSCHL 1862, tav. LVI, b = CIL I 559 = CIL XI 6671 = ILS 5808 = CIL I² 657 (cfr. p. 927) = ILLRP 458 = RADKE 1973, 1432, 1451–1452 (=RADKE 1981, 68) = MOSCA 1992, 93–100 (= AE 1993, 644) = DÍAZ ARIÑO 2015, 97–98 nr. 16, 158 fig. 16. Si vedano inoltre TARGIONI TOZZETTI 1776, 275–278; HIRSCHFELD 1907, 170 (= HIRSCHFELD 1913, 708); LOPES PEGNA 1950–1951, 424; WISEMAN 1970, 136–137, 140 (= WISEMAN 1987, 140–141, 144); MOSCA 1999, 165–166; LOPES PEGNA 1974, 232–233.
70 BUONOPANE/GABRIELLI 2018.
71 BUONOPANE/GABRIELLI 2018.
72 Cfr. LOPES PEGNA 1974, 232–233.

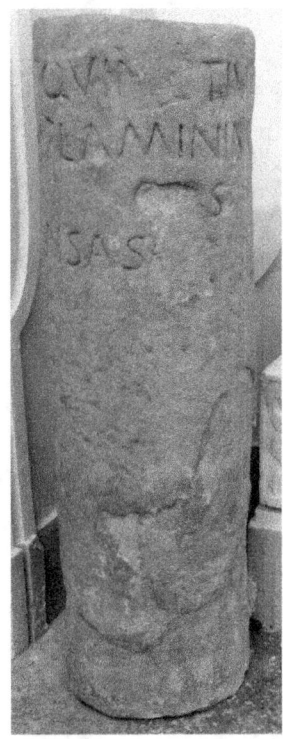

Fig. 7: Firenze, Collezione Antinori, Palazzo Antinori Aldobrandini di Brindisi. Il miliario di
T. Quinctius Flamininus (CIL XI 6671). Foto di Chantal Gabrielli su concessione della SBAP.

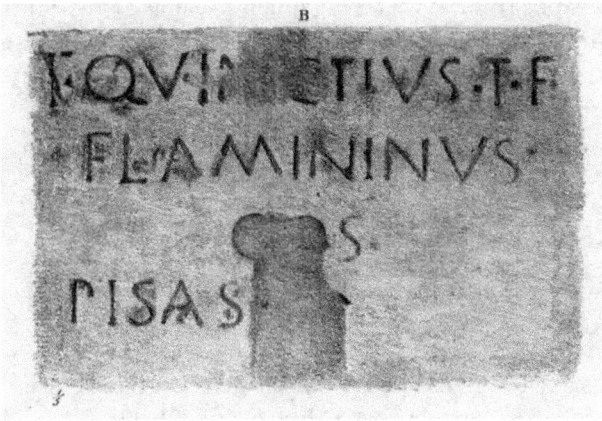

Fig. 8: Il miliario di *T. Quinctius Flamininus* (CIL XI 6671) nel
disegno di Friederich Ritschl (RITSCHL 1862, tav. LVI, b).

quanto riguarda il secondo miliario,[73] che nel Corpus era stato relegato fra le iscrizioni false, un'attenta analisi dei *fontes* ha confermato la sua genuinità :[74] si tratta dunque di un secondo miliario, collocato a XXXII miglia da Pisa, pari a km 47,36 circa, distanza che corrisponde con buona approssimazione a quella che intercorre fra Pietrafitta e Pisa. Possiamo dunque concludere che si tratta di due distinti miliari posizionati uno a 32 miglia e l'altro a 40 miglia da Pisa lungo una strada che venne costruita con molta probabilità dal console *T. Quinctius Flamininus* nel 123 a.C.,[75] sia per le caratteristiche paleografiche del testo sia per il fatto che la realizzazione di opere pubbliche, in particolare le strade, ricevette un notevole sviluppo grazie all'attività politica promossa dal tribuno Gaio Gracco.[76]

La strada Luna-Luca e il miliario 'falso' di Nocchi

Luni era collegata a Lucca con una strada pedecollinare, che con molta probabilità si connetteva alla via litoranea che proveniva da Pisa (*Via Aurelia/Via Aemilia Scauri*) presso il fiume Frigido, nel sito che la tradizione identifica con la *mansio Taberna Frigida*. Lungo questa arteria tra la fine del XVII e gli inizi del XVIII secolo si rinvenne il cippo miliare reimpiegato nell'altare della chiesa di San Pietro a Nocchi di Camaiore (Lucca), ritenuto falso da BORMANN, ma con ogni probabilità genuino.[77] Non conosciamo il luogo di ritrovamento del cippo; per FABIANI sembrava probabile che il miliario potesse avere pertinenza con la strada che collegava Luni a Lucca e, risalendo la Val Freddana, raggiungeva la valle di Camaiore attraverso la località di Nocchi. In realtà potrebbe profilarsi un'altra ipotesi sulla strada di pertinenza del cippo. L'*Itinerarium Antonini*[78] attestava l'esistenza di una antica *via Faventina* che risalendo la valle del Lamone superava la cresta appenninica per scendere nel Mugello e proseguire lungo le valli del Sieve e dell'Arno sino a *Florentia;* da qui poi si dirigeva verso *Luca* via *Pistoriae*. Si tratterebbe di una via di valico e poi di controllo pedemontano del versante appenninico toscano.[79] Durante la guerra gotica Procopio di Cesarea menzionava una sconfitta inferta da Totila all'esercito bizantino avvenuta nel 542 al Mugello,

---

[73] CIL XI 849* = CAPECCHI 1987, 37 nt. 4 = MOSCA 1992, 93–94 = AE 1993, 645 = MOSCA 1999, 165 = MARANGIO 1999, 23 = DÍAZ ARIÑO 2015, 99, con errato rimando a CIL XI 848*.
[74] Si veda quanto scrive sopra ALFREDO BUONOPANE e BUONOPANE/GABRIELLI 2018.
[75] Così già BORMANN (CIL XI 6671), LOMMATZSCH (CIL I² 657), DEGRASSI (ILLRP 458) e MOSCA (MOSCA 1992, 98–99. BROUGHTON 1951, 456, 512. Si esclude dunque la possibilità che si tratti degli omonimi consoli del 198 e del 150; cfr. UGGERI 2015, 138. Sui *Quinctii* si veda BADIAN 1971, 102–111.
[76] HINRICHS 1967, 162–176.
[77] Si veda quanto scrive più sopra ALFREDO BUONOPANE.
[78] Itin. Anton. 30: *A Faventia Lucam mp CXX – In Castello XXV – Anneiano XXV – Florentia XX – Pistoris XXV – Luca XXV.*
[79] MOSCA 1992a.

precisando che la località si trovava ad un giorno di marcia da Firenze; tale indicazione di percorrenza stradale appare in linea con le tappe registrate nell'*Itinerarium Antonini*.[80] Un miliare di questa via si conserva nei pressi di Brisighella (Forlì-Cesena), nella Pieve di San Giovanni Battista in Ottavo, un toponimo che rappresenta una palese indicazione stradale da unire ad altri toponimi che da Faenza sussistono tuttora, dimostrando l'antichità e la vitalità della via.[81] Il miliare, in granito e alto poco più di due metri, era stato reimpiegato come colonna dell'arcata che separava la navata centrale da quella laterale destra. Il testo, in parte nuovamente inciso con qualche parziale modifica, attestava l'attenzione del governo imperiale verso la strada ancora nell'ultimo venticinquennio del IV secolo d.C. La colonna, riportando, infatti, i nomi degli imperatori Valente, Graziano e Valentiniano II, va ascritta agli anni 375–378 d.C.[82] Dal momento che in altri tre miliari, rinvenuti a San Piero a Grado,[83] a Campiano (Ravenna)[84] e a Nocchi (Lucca)[85] ricorrono i nomi degli stessi imperatori (Valente, Graziano e Valentiniano II) con un formulario molto simile, credo si possa prospettare un'altra ipotesi. In primo luogo dato che *Luca*, secondo l'*Itinerarium Antonini*, costituiva l'arrivo della *via Faventina*,[86] non si può escludere la pertinenza del miliario di Nocchi a questa strada o piuttosto a un suo diverticolo. Il vicino cippo di San Piero a Grado potrebbe, in questo senso, testimoniare la creazione di un raccordo con la costiera *via Aemilia Scauri*, promossa sempre negli stessi anni dal governo imperiale. Analogamente il miliario di Campiano mostrerebbe la medesima volontà di prolungare la strada dal *caput viae Faventia* fino a Ravenna. A ciò vada aggiungersi che anche il miliario di Rimazzano, pertinente alla *via Aemilia Scauri* e risalente sempre alla seconda metà del IV secolo d.C., avvalorerebbe l'ipotesi di un'iniziativa congiunta e promossa a livello centrale per rivitalizzare percorsi che facilitassero il collegamento tra Adriatico e Tirreno in ben note fasi convulse dell'Impero.

---

80 Prok. BG 3,5.
81 Lungo il Lamone sussistono ancora a scandire le distanze dal *caput viae*, Faenza, i seguenti toponimi: Quartoletta e Quartolo, Rio di Quarto, Rio di Quinto, Ghiarona e Strada presso Brisighella, San Giovanni in Ottavo, Rio di Pontenono, Santa Maria in Undecimo.
82 KIENAST/ECK/HEIL 2017, 316–317, 319–322, 355.
83 CIL XI 6665.
84 AE 1975, 402 = 1992, 611 = 2006, 441. Sull'iscrizione vd. SUSINI 1974; CENERINI 1992, 49 n. 3; BAZZOCCHI 2006, 320–323, 321 fig. 2.
85 CIL IX 848*, considerato falso, ma probabilmente genuino: si veda più sopra quanto scrive ALFREDO BUONOPANE.
86 Itin. Anton. 30: *A Faventia Lucam mp CXX – In Castello XXV – Anneiano XXV – Florentia XX – Pistoris XXV – Luca XXV.*

Il tratto Luna-Pisae e la probabile identificazione Via Aurelia Nova/ Via Aemilia Scauri

Il percorso fra le *coloniae* di Pisa e Luni costituiva il tratto di un'importante arteria che da Roma conduceva in Gallia *(Vada Sabatia)*. Questo implica una serie di problemi molto dibattuti: l'identificazione delle strade *(Aurelia Vetus, Aurelia Nova* ed *Aemilia Scauri)*, i loro tracciati e relativa cronologia.[87] La strada litoranea partiva da Pisa, lambiva la sponda occidentale del lago di Massacciuccoli, fiancheggiava il lago di Porta, toccava il Frigido per poi dirigersi verso Luni. La *Tabula Peutingeriana* e l'*Itinerarium Antonini*[88] tra Pisa e Luni illustrano le tappe di uno stesso percorso verosimilmente da indentificarsi con il tracciato viario costiero: *Pisae*, mansio di *Fossae Papirianae* (XI miglia – 16,3 Km ca.),[89] mansio di *Taberna Frigida* (XII miglia – 17,8 Km ca.),[90] *Luna* (X miglia – 14,8 Km ca.). La distanza fra le due colonie era pari a XXXIII miglia (48,8 km ca.) e risulta coerente con quella reale fra le due città, qualora si segua un percorso rettilineo e litoraneo. Molto probabilmente la via litoranea nel tratto tra Pisa e Luni doveva identificarsi con la via *Aurelia Nova*, fatta costruire dal console del 200 a.C., C. Aurelio Cotta, come prolungamento dell'*Aurelia Vetus* ;[91] l'arteria collegava Pisa almeno fino al *Portus Lunae*. La doppia denominazione della *via Aurelia* è testimoniata nel II secolo d.C. da un'iscrizione.[92] Gli studiosi si continuano a interrogare se a tale duplice denominazione corrispondessero un diverso tracciato e una diversa cronologia; le fonti antiche non aiutano nell'individuazione del personaggio che legò il suo nome alla costruzione della via, a complicare ulteriormente la questione vi sono anche problemi di specifico interesse topografico per il riconoscimento dei tracciati. Recentemente l'approccio multidisciplinare delle indagini condotte da FABIANI sulla viabilità dell'Etruria settentrionale ha dimostrato che nella pianura apuo-versiliese la via consolare *Aurelia* fosse stata realizzata su un cordone stabile di sabbia fra mare e lagune circostanti. Il tracciato avrebbe avuto un andamento il più possibile rettilineo e diretto, per rispondere alle esigenze militari legate alla costruzione della strada. Venne così superata la *querelle* tra coloro che collocavano l'*Aurelia* nella fascia pede-

---

[87] Per una sintesi sulle ipotesi di datazione e sui percorsi viari: DÍAZ ARIÑO 2015, 91–92 nr. 8; 92–92 nr. 9.

[88] In realtà l'*Itinerarium Antonini* si discosta leggermente dalla *Tabula Peuntingeriana;* riporta, infatti, come cifra complessiva XXIII miglia (34 km ca.) e non enumera la mansio di *Taberna Frigida*. Tale assenza può essere attribuita all'estensore dell'itinerario o a un errore della tradizione

[89] La *mansio* si deve localizzare fra il lago di Massaciuccoli e il mare e prende il nome da un sistema di interventi idraulici secondo un modello che trova la sua più ampia applicazione nell'area della laguna veneta.

[90] La distanza fra *Taberna Frigida* e *Luna* pari a X miglia non appare pienamente convincente, dal momento che il Frigido dista solo VI miglia ca. dalla città.

[91] HERZIG 1970; WISEMAN 1971; sulla rilevanza dei dati archeologici raccolti tramite la fotografia aerea cfr. TORTORICI 1985.

[92] CIL XIV 3610; ILS 1071.

montana e coloro che propendevano addirittura per le prime pendici collinari, dal momento che il nome di una strada, attestata in documenti di età medievale, conservava la memoria di una grande via selciata nella zona invece più vicina al mare, *via Silcia*.[93] Tra i comuni di Montignoso (Massa) e Massa, strada e toponimo (*Silice, in Silice*) sono attestati già nel Trecento; al 1327 è registrata nell'Archivio di Stato di Lucca una causa dibattuta fra le due località per definire i loro confini territoriali in questi termini:

> „...que recta linea contra muragnum eundo usque ad flumen Frigidum recta linea per viam seu stratam antiquam que est per paludes et boscos que via vocatur Silce ..."[94]

Significativa è dunque la presenza nel testo dei lemmi *strata, antiqua* e *silice*, plausibili indicatori della possibile origine romana del percorso. Il riferimento alla *via Silcia* diventa una costante della cartografia storica elaborata fin dal XVI secolo per le perenni controversie di confine tra Massa e Montignoso. Nell'Archivio di Stato di Lucca è conservata una carta che raffigura la situazione relativa al lago di Porta nel 1548, in cui è registrata la *Via del Silice*.[95] Effettivamente tra Forte dei Marmi (Lucca) e Montignoso si rinvennero tracce di un'antica strada: a partire dal XIX secolo nell'alveo del lago di Porta furono avvistati tratti di un selciato stradale, di massi poligonali di pietra locale, generalmente riferito ad età romana,[96] e recenti sondaggi archeologici hanno rilevato una porzione di *via glareata*.[97] Pare verosimile sostenere che il tracciato dell'*Aurelia Nova* sia da identificarsi con la strada litoranea individuata, il cui percorso era collocato a debita distanza dalla zona pedemontana e dalle vallate che solcavano le Alpi Apuane da cui potevano agevolmente essere compiute imboscate dalle popolazioni Liguri. Nel 185 a.C. Livio menziona l'intervento di M. Sempronio Tuditano, che muovendo da Pisa riuscì a sbloccare le comunicazioni

---

93 Fabiani 2006, 87–90.
94 ASLu, Capitoli 21, (anno 1327), 62. Per ulteriori indicazioni documentarie sulle controversie per la definizione dei confini fra Massa e Montignoso vd. Fabiani 2006, 88 nt. 456.
95 Dettaglio della carta del territorio di Montignoso "*secondo lo stato dell'anno 1548*": la "*Via del Silice*" (entro ovale) lungo la sponda occidentale del lago di Porta (ASLu, Offizio Sopra le Differenze di Confine, vol. 568; Gallo 1993, tav. 16).
96 Santini 1858–61, 1, 26; 5, 3, 22. "...lungo tempo fu veduto qua e là sparso il selciato poligono sull'attuale, che oggi dicesi Via del Diavolo, e dove, sopra questo, si formò, nei bassi tempi, il lago di Porta: allorché limpide, e basse ne sono le acque, vedesi ancora la sua direzione ed il suo lastricato a massi poligoni di pietra locale". Così Repetti 1835, s.v. Lago o Stagno di Porta.
97 Per un resoconto del saggio di scavo condotto da Emanuela Paribeni: Fabiani 2000, 404–406; Fabiani 2006, 90–93, figg. 14–15. Già nel 1967 alcuni scavi avevano messo in luce parte del tracciato di una strada romana vicino all'alveo del Lago di Porta nel Padule del Campo di Aviazione: Ciampi Polledri 1967, 271 grafico 3. Anche per Cambi 2002, 131, la primitiva superficie dell'*Aurelia Vetus* era in piccoli ciottoli (*via glareata*).

con il porto di Luni, interrotte dalle locali popolazioni liguri.[98] Non si può escludere, come sostiene PASQUINUCCI,[99] che l'*Aemilia Scauri*, strada anch'essa di raccordo fra Pisa e Luni e realizzata fra 115–109 a.C. da M. Emilio Scauro,[100] seguisse un percorso distinto rispetto alla via *Aurelia Nova*, ovvero pedecollinare la prima, litoraneo la seconda. Sappiamo che la via *Aemilia Scauri* nasce come variante dell'*Aurelia*, destinata al traffico veloce e condotta perciò con un tracciato rettilineo più interno.[101] In realtà la strada pedecollinare tra Luni e Pisa non presenta tali caratteristiche; è probabile allora piuttosto che in questo tratto l'*Aemilia Scauri* abbia seguito il tracciato diretto e litoraneo che forse era già stato dell'*Aurelia;* una tale sovrapposizione viaria sembra, del resto, riscontrabile nel territorio circostante la città di Populonia.[102] Il prolungamento della *via Silcia* a sud del lago di Porta, in direzione di Forte dei Marmi, acquisisce la denominazione *via Emilia* già in carte del XVIII secolo.[103] Questo dato toponomastico confermerebbe che la viabilità romana attraversasse la zona lungo la marina e che la *via Silcia* coincidesse con la via Emilia, mostrando una totale identificazione fra le vie consolari *Aurelia (nova)/ Aemilia Scauri*.

La via Aemilia Scauri e il cosiddetto miliario del lago di Porta

Nei pressi del Lago di Porta, nei primi anni Venti del XIX secolo, venne ritrovato un blocco di marmo, di forma parallelepipeda erroneamente interpretato come cippo miliario, mentre si tratta di blocco di cava.[104] In realtà la scoperta del blocco di marmo avvalora, piuttosto, l'ipotesi che in loco ci fosse un approdo, seppure di minore rilevanza e per imbarcazioni di piccolo cabotaggio, con una funzione di supporto alla strada litoranea e di cerniera con vicini percorsi lacustri e marittimi. Nel 1976 il materiale recuperato dal dragaggio del fiume Cinquale, antico emissario del lago di Porta, ha portato a ipotizzare l'esistenza di un contiguo insediamento, la cui vitalità è accertata almeno fino al V secolo d.C., munito di una fornace per laterizi o di un complesso termale.[105]

---

98 Liv. 39,32,1–2: *Sempronius a Pisis profectus in Apuanos Ligures vastando agros urendoque vicos et castella eorum aperuit saltum usque ad Macram fluvium et Lunae portum.*
99 PASQUINUCCI 2003, 85.
100 Aur. Vict. vir. ill. 72. Cfr. Strab. 5,217.
101 Già l'analisi di SORDI 1971, 305 sul percorso della via Aurelia fra Vada e Pisa rivelava un andamento costiero e una distinzione in tale zona dell'*Aurelia* dalla *via Aemilia Scauri*.
102 PATERA/SHEPHERD/DALLAI/ZANINI 2003, 294–296; DALLAI/PONTA/SHEPHERD 2006, 186–187.
103 FABIANI 2006, 89 nt. 466 e fig. 13.
104 Si vede quanto scrive più sopra ALFREDO BUONOPANE.
105 FABIANI 2006, 93 ntt. 485–486: i numerosi *tubuli* a sezione quadrata, rinvenuti tra il materiale edilizio, rendono plausibile una connessione sia con ambienti termali sia con una fornace (FABIANI 2006, 155).

Un nuovo miliario della via Aemilia Scauri?

In CIL XI 6671a si registra la presenza nel Museo Archeologico Nazionale di Firenze di un miliario della Collezione Medicea, che riporta questa iscrizione:

> Domiiii (!) invi[c]tis(simi) / Constantinus Maximus / [[et Licini]]us semper Aug(usti) / et Crispus et [[Licinianu[s]]] / et Claudius Constantinus, / beatissimus C(a)ess(ar) (!) / iter lapsum ouo/d (!)/ ominino erat d(i)rutum / lungo curia (!) [f]ieri / et restituiq(ue) iusserun[t] / m(ilia) CLXXXII

Il miliario dunque, attualmente ubicato nel Cortile dei Fiorentini[106] (fig. 9), ricorda il restauro di una strada e si può datare tra il 317 e il 324 d.C. per la menzione degli augusti Costantino e Licinio e dei cesari Crispo, Claudio Costantino e Liciniano.[107]

Il luogo di ritrovamento è ignoto, ma nel CIL compaiono due ipotesi. Secondo la prima esso proverrebbe dall'Etruria per il fatto che il miliario indica una distanza in miglia (*CLXXXII*) che si discosta di sole 6 unità dalla cifra presente in un altro cippo pertinente alla via *Aemilia Scauri* e rinvenuto a Collesalvetti (*LI*), in località Crocino (*CLXXXVIIII*).[108] Da questo tratto della via *Aemilia* provengono in realtà altri due miliari: uno falso con analoga distanza del precedente miliario (*CLXXXVIII*);[109] l'altro frammentario e irreperibile, con un numerale che, nonostante la lacuna testuale, pare compatibile con le distanze in miglia segnalate nei miliari limitrofi *([- - -] LXXX[- - -])*.[110] In alternativa il cippo potrebbe essere stato portato in Italia dal medico archeologo Giovanni Pagni, attivo presso i Medici e figura ben nota nell'ambito del collezionismo del *XVII*, che potrebbe aver portato questo miliario, insieme ad altri testi epigrafici, da una località non identificata del Nord-Africa[111] e allora Bormann ipotizza che esso potesse essere collocato presso Theveste, lungo il tracciato della via che portava a Cartagine.[112] Studi recenti condotti da Gunnella e Giua su documenti di archivio inerenti alle acquisizioni epigrafiche del Museo Archeologico e legate ai

---

[106] Al dott. Mario Iozzo, Direttore del Museo Archeologico Nazionale di Firenze, va il mio più sentito ringraziamento per avermi concesso l'analisi autoptica del miliario; ringrazio inoltre i funzionari del Polo Museale, dott.ri Sebastiano Soldi e Miriana Ciacci, per la consulenza sugli Archivi del Museo Archeologico; e la dott.ssa Cinzia Innocenti, funzionario del Centro di restauro della Soprintendenza Archeologia, Belle Arti e Paesaggio, per le ricerche nell'inventario delle schede museali. Senza il loro prezioso appoggio non avrei potuto condurre questa indagine.
[107] Kienast/Eck/Heil 2017, 282–284, 286–291, 293.
[108] CIL XI 6664 = InscrIt VII 1, 117.
[109] Rinvenuto a Collesalvetti, località Rimazzano (Livorno); ora nel Camposanto di Pisa: CIL XI 847*= InscrIt VII 1, 119.
[110] Rinvenuto a Collesalvetti, località Marmigliaio: InscrIt VII 1, 120.
[111] Già Gori 1704, I, 13 n. 11 segnalava la provenienza africana del cippo.
[112] Bormann pare suggestionato da due miliari africani CIL VIII 10047–10048 rinvenuti a Tunisi con i numerali *LXX* e *LXXXV*.

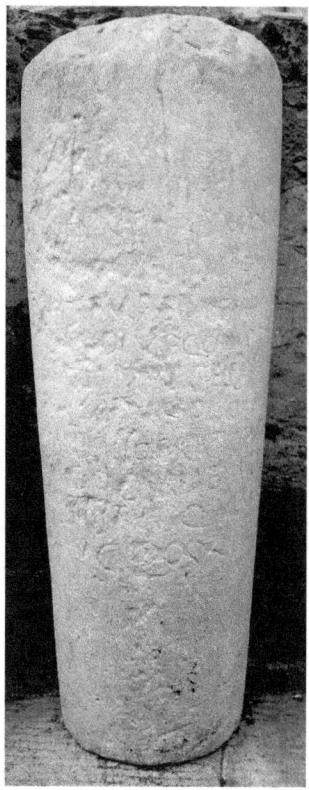

Fig. 9: Museo Archeologico Nazionale di Firenze, Cortile dei Fiorentini. Il miliario della Collezione Medicea (CIL XI 6671a). Foto di Chantal Gabrielli su concessione della SBAP.

traffici di PAGNI mi portano ad escludere tassativamente la provenienza africana del miliario.[113]

Da un controllo sui dati inventariali registrati nell'Archivio del Museo Archeologico Nazionale di Firenze risulta che il miliario (n. inv. 214694) proviene da Roma. Nell'Archivio Fotografico il monumento compare sistemato nelle arcate del giardino, prima della chiusura del corridoio topografico, assieme ad altre lapidi segnalate come "Dono EVELINA MODIGLIANI ROSSI". Con molta probabilità tale indicazione non ha alcuna connessione con il miliario e deve piuttosto riferirsi al resto del materiale presente nella suddetta scheda,[114] mentre la provenienza da Roma appare

---

113 GUNNELLA 2000, 421 e nt. 59, menziona fra le iscrizioni del Nord-Africa portate dal PAGNI unicamente un miliario dell'imperatore M. Iulius Philippus del 244 d.C. (CIL VIII 10049), forse proveniente da Tunisi. Cfr. KÖRNER 2002.
114 Il miliario farebbe già parte della collezione medicea secondo la testimonianza del CIL. Risulta strana la connessione con EVELINA MODIGLIANI ROSSI che sappiamo aver donato, agli inizi del XX se-

confermata anche dai dati conservati nel Centro di Restauro della Sovrintendenza Archeologia, Belle arti e paesaggio di Firenze.[115] Infine il Centro di Documentazione del Polo Museale Fiorentino registra effettivamente, in data 27 settembre 1919, il trasferimento del monumento epigrafico (n. inv. 933) dalla Galleria degli Uffizi al Museo Archeologico di Firenze,[116] eliminando così ogni dubbio sul legame del miliario al dono munifico di EVELINA MODIGLIANI ROSSI. Resta pertanto la possibilità che si tratti di un cippo legato alla viabilità dell'Etruria ed è probabile che si tratti della via *Aemilia Scauri*, che, come messo in evidenza, ha miliari con analoghe distanze.

CHANTAL GABRIELLI

Bibliografia

AGOSTINIANI 1995 = L. AGOSTINIANI, Sui numerali etruschi e sulla loro rappresentazione grafica, *Aion* 17, 1995, 21–66.

BACCI 2012 = M. BACCI, Centuriazione romana: Il caso di Firenze (Florentia), Firenze 2012.

BADIAN 1971 = E. BADIAN, The Family and the Early Career of T. Quinctius Flamininus, *JRS* 61, 1971, 102–111.

BATES 1986 = R.L. BATES, Rex in senatu: A Political Biography of M. Aemilius Scaurus, *PAPhs* 130, 1986, 251–288.

BAZZOCCHI 2006 = A. BAZZOCCHI, I miliari di Ravenna: nuove proposte di lettura, *Mediterraneo Antico* 9.1, 2006, 313–327.

BELLI 1988 = L. BELLI, … Civitas Lunensis Miliarium posuit: Ipotesi intorno a una epigrafe, *Campus Maior* 1988, 43–48.

BETTI 2013 = P. BETTI, Georg Cristoph Martini: Un artista viaggiatore nella Lucca del Settecento, Macerata 2013.

BIANCHI 2016 = E. BIANCHI, Vulci: Storia della città e dei suoi rapporti con Greci e Romani, Roma 2016.

BROUGHTON 1951 = S. BROUGHTON, The Magistrates of the Roman Republic, vol. 1: 509 b.C.-100 b.C., New York 1951.

BUONOPANE 2014 = A. BUONOPANE, Il lato oscuro delle collezioni epigrafiche: falsi, copie, imitazioni. Un caso di studio: la collezione Gazzola, in: A. DONATI (ed.), L'iscrizione e il suo doppio: Atti del Convegno Borghesi 2013, Faenza 2014, 291–313.

BUONOPANE/GABRIELLI 2018= A. BUONOPANE/C. GABRIELLI, I due miliari repubblicani della via Faesulae-Pisae e la viabilità nell'Etruria settentrionale, *SeBarc* 16, 2018, 213–224.

CAMBI 2002 = F. CAMBI, La viabilità, in: A. CARANDINI/F. CAMBI (ed.), Paesaggi d'Etruria. Valle dell'Albegna, Valle d'Oro, Valle del Chiarone, Valle del Tafone, Roma 2002, 131–135.

CAMPBELL 2012 = B. CAMPBELL, Rivers and the Power of Ancient Rome, Chapel Hill 2012.

CAMPEDELLI 2014 = C. CAMPEDELLI, L'amministrazione municipale delle strade romane in Italia, Bonn 2014.

---

colo, al Museo Archeologico di Firenze la storica collezione lapidaria Strozzi conservata fino ad allora nella Villa di Montughi presso Firenze. Le vicende della collezione, con dispersioni e acquisizioni nel tempo, sono delineate da MINTO 1914; MINTO 1920, 40 nt. 5; recentemente GRANINO CECERE 2008, 12.

115 RA 0900270401. Tale scheda, redatta anch'essa nel 1996, conferma pedissequamente i dati contenuti nell'Archivio del Museo Archeologico.

116 Inventario 1825, n. 418.

Capecchi 1987 = G. Capecchi (ed.), Artimino (Firenze). Scavi 1974. L'area della Paggeria medicea; relazione preliminare, Carmignano 1987.

Cavalieri 2011 = M. Cavalieri, La transition de l'Antiquité au Moyen Âge. Le paysage rural en Toscane et dans les régions voisines entre le IIIe et le VIIe siècle, *AntClass* 80, 2011, 199–229.

Ceccarelli Lemut/Sodi 1996 = M.L. Ceccarelli Lemut/S. Sodi, Un "falso documento" falso. Erudizione, riscrittura della storia e aspirazioni socio-politiche in Pisa al tempo della guerra contro Firenze (1494–1509), *Quaderni Storici* 93.3, 1996, 607–630.

Cecchi 2015 = S. Cecchi, Altre notae scoperte tra XIX e XX secolo, in: E. Paribeni/S. Segenni (ed.), Notae Lapicidinarum dalle cave di Carrara, Pisa 2015, 369–370.

Cenerini 1992 = F. Cenerini, Forum Livi, Supplementa Italica, vol. 10, Roma 1992.

Ciampi Polledri 1967 = H. Ciampi Polledri, Via Aemilia Scauri, *SCO* 16, 1967, 256–272.

Ciampoltrini 1981 = G. Ciampoltrini, Note sulla colonizzazione augustea nell'Etruria settentrionale, *SCO* 31, 1981, 41–55.

Ciampoltrini 1993 = G. Ciampoltrini, Il diverticolo dall'Aurelia al Portus Telamonis: un contributo per la tecnica stradale nell'Etruria costiera, *ATTA* 2, 1993, 179–182.

Ciampoltrini 2004 = G. Ciampoltrini, Vie rurali d'età romana nell'ager lucensis: nuove acquisizioni, *ATTA* 13, 2004, 147–156.

Ciampoltrini/Andreotti 1993 = G. Ciampoltrini/A. Andreotti, Vie rurali d'età romana nell'ager lucensis: Contributi dall'alveo del Bientina, *ATTA* 2, 1993, 183–192.

Coarelli 1988 = F. Coarelli, Colonizzazione romana e viabilità, *DArch* 6.2, 1988, 35–48.

Corsi 1999 = C. Corsi, Nuovi dati per la viabilità romana dell'Etruria marittima: un miliario dall'agro tarquiniese, *RTopAnt/JAT* 3, 1993, 173–178.

Dallai/Ponta/Shepherd 2006 = L. Dallai/E. Ponta/E.J. Shepherd, Aurelii e Valerii sulle strade dell'Etruria, in: S. Menchelli/M. Pasquinucci, Territorio e produzioni ceramiche. Paesaggi, economia e società in età romana, Atti del Convegno Internazionale (Pisa 2005), Pisa 2006, 179–190.

Degrassi 1962 = A. Degrassi, Nuovi miliari arcaici, in: M. Renard/A. Grenier (ed.), Hommages à Albert Grenier, Bruxelles 1962, 499–513.

Degrassi 1967 = A. Degrassi, Scritti vari di antichità, vol. 3, Venezia-Trieste 1967, 195–209.

De Simone 2007 = C. De Simone, Il gentilizio latino *Romulus*: Questioni di metodo, *Incidenza dell'Antico* 5, 2007, 117–132.

Díaz Ariño 2015 = B. Díaz Ariño, Miliarios romanos de época republicana, Roma 2015.

Ertman 1976 = P.C. Ertman, Curatores viarum: A Study of the Superintendents of Highways in Ancient Rome, New York 1976.

Fabiani 2000 = F. Fabiani, La viabilità romana tra Pisa e Luni. Nuove riflessioni, in: Da Luna alla Diocesi, Atti della Giornata di Studi (Luni 2001), *Giornale Storico della Lunigiana e del Territorio Lucense* 49–51, 2000, 397–410.

Fabiani 2002 = F. Fabiani, Un miliario falso per una strada vera? Nuove considerazioni sul cippo di Nocchi (Camaiore-LU), *SCO* 48, 2002, 393–411.

Fabiani 2006 = F. Fabiani, «... Stratam antiquam que est per paludes et boscos...»: Viabilità romana tra Pisa e Luni, Pisa 2006.

Fabiani/Paribeni 2007 = F. Fabiani/E. Paribeni, "...qualche schiarimento da alcun pezzo antico che trovisi in avvenire...": Il marmo di Porta, da cippo miliare a blocco di cava, *Epigraphica* 69, 2007, 404–418.

Fentress 1984 = E. Fentress, Via Aurelia, Via Aemilia, *PBSR* 52, 1984, 72–76.

Fentress 1985 = E. Fentress, Il miliario di Marco Emilio Scauro, in: A. Carandini (ed.), La romanizzazione dell'Etruria: il territorio di Vulci, Milano 1985, 123–124.

Fioriti ms. 1613 = B. Fioriti, Zibaldone, ms. 1613, Biblioteca Statale di Lucca.

GABRIELLI 2017 = C. GABRIELLI, I rapporti fra Florentia e Faesulae in età imperiale, in: G.A. CECCONI/A. RAGGI/E. SALOMONE GAGGERO (ed.), Epigrafia e società dell'Etruria romana, Atti del Convegno Firenze 23–24 ottobre 2015, Firenze 2017, 117–134.
GABRIELLI c.s. = C. GABRIELLI, La via Aurelia e il miliario da Vulci di [·] Aurelius Cotta, in stampa.
GALLO 1993 = N. GALLO, Cartografia storica e territorio della Lunigiana centro orientale, Sarzana 1993.
GORI 1704 = A.F. GORI, Inscriptiones antiquae in Etruriae urbibus exstantes I, Firenze 1704.
GRANINO CECERE 2008 = M.G. GRANINO CECERE (ed.), Supplementa Italica Imagines: Roma (CIL, VI) vol. 3: Collezioni Fiorentine, Roma 2008.
GROSSI 2019 = P. GROSSI, Politics, Administration and Propaganda along Ancient Roman Roads in the Center and North Italy, Oxford 2019, c.s.
GUNNELLA/GUIA 2000 = A. GUNNELLA/M.A. GUIA, Agli albori della ricerca antiquaria in Tunisia: Giovanni Pagni (1634–1676), archeologo e medico pisano nel Granducato mediceo, L'Africa Romana XIII. Djerba 1998, Roma 2000, 409–438.
HARRIS 1971 = W.V. HARRIS, Rome in Etruria and Umbria, Oxford 1971.
HERZIG 1970 = H.E. HERZIG, Namen und Daten der Via Aurelia, *Epigraphica* 32, 1970, 50–65.
HINRICHS 1967 = F.T. HINRICHS, Der Römische Strassenbau zur Zeit der Gracchen, *Historia* 16, 1967, 162–176.
HIRSCHFELD 1907 = O. HIRSCHFELD, Die römischen Meilensteine, *Sitzungsberichte der Akademie der Wissenschaften zu Berlin*, 1907, 165–201.
HIRSCHFELD 1913 = O. HIRSCHFELD, Kleine Schriften, Berlin 1913.
KIENAST/ECK/HEIL 2017 = D. KIENAST/W. ECK/M. HEIL, Römische Kaisertabelle. Grundzüge einer römischen Kaiserchronologie, Darmstadt 2017.
KÖRNER 2002 = C. KÖRNER, Philippus Arabs: Ein Soldatenkaiser in der Tradition des antonisch-severischen Prinzipats, Berlin/New York 2002.
KREILER 2011 = B.M. KREILER, Zwei Meilensteine des Konsuls *Aurelius Cotta*, *Epigraphica* 73, 2011, 109–115.
LAMBOGLIA 1937 = N. LAMBOGLIA, La via Aemilia Scauri, *Athenaeum* 15, 1937, 57–68.
LAMI 1758 = G. LAMI, Sanctae Ecclesiae Florentinae monumenta…historiam spectantem continentur, Florentiae 1758.
LANA 1961 = I. LANA, Rutilio Namaziano, Torino 1961.
LIVERANI 1985 = P. LIVERANI, Nota sulla via Quinzia, *ArchCl* 37, 1985, 279–282.
LOPES PEGNA 1974 = M. LOPES PEGNA, Firenze dalle origini al medioevo, Firenze 1974².
LOPES PEGNA 1951 = M. LOPES PEGNA, Itinera Etruriae, *StEtr* 21,1950/1951, 407–442.
MARANGIO 1999 = C. MARANGIO, Il contributo dell'epigrafia alla conoscenza della viabilità nell'Italia romana (1989–1998), *RTopAnt/JAT* 9, 1999, 7–136.
MARTINI/TRUMPY 1969 = G.C. MARTINI/O. TRUMPY, Viaggio in Toscana (1725–1745). Deputazione di Storia Patria per le antiche provincie modenesi, Modena 1969.
MINTO 1914 = A. MINTO, La collezione Strozzi, *Studi Romani* 2, 1914, 57–63.
MINTO 1920 = A. MINTO, Sculture marmoree inedite del R. Museo Archeologico di Firenze, *Bollettino d'Arte del Ministero della Pubblica Istruzione* 14, 1920, 40–48.
MOMMSEN 1900 = T. MOMMSEN, Über Plan und Ausführung eines Corpus Inscriptionum Latinarum, in: A. HARNACK (ed.), Geschichte der königlich preussischen Akademie der Wissenschaften zu Berlin, vol. 2, Berlin 1900, 522–540.
MOSCA 1992 = A. MOSCA, Via Quinctia. La strada romana fra Fiesole e Pisa. I. Da Firenze a Empoli, *RTopAnt/JAT* 2, 1992, 91–108.
MOSCA 1992a = A. MOSCA, La via Faventina. Da Firenze a Faenza attraverso il Mugello e la valle del Lamone, in: La viabilità tra Bologna e Firenze nel tempo: problemi generali e nuove acquisizioni, Bologna 1992, 179–190.

Mosca 1994 = A. Mosca, Problemi della viabilità romana in Etruria, *RTopAnt/JAT* 4, 1994, 177–184.

Mosca 1999 = A. Mosca, Via Quinctia: La strada romana fra Fiesole e Pisa II: Da Empoli a Pisa, *RTopAnt/JAT* 9, 1999, 165–174.

Pagni 2010 = M. Pagni, La romana Florentia, in: M. Pagni (ed.), Atlante Archeologico di Firenze. Indagine storico-archeologica dalla preistoria all'alto medioevo, Firenze 2010, 113–120.

Paribeni 2015 = E. Paribeni, Tabella 1: Notae lapicidinarum su semilavorati di Carrara e su manufatti in marmo lunense trovati fuori Carrara, in: E. Paribeni/S. Segenni (ed.), Notae Lapicidinarum dalle cave di Carrara, Pisa 2015, 375–383.

Pasquinucci 2003 = M. Pasquinucci, Pisa romana, in: M. Tangheroni (ed.), Pisa e il Mediterraneo: Uomini, merci, idee dagli Etruschi ai Medici, Catalogo della Mostra (Pisa 2003), Ginevra/Milano 2003, 81–85.

Pasquinucci 2007 = M. Pasquinucci, I porti di Pisa e di Volterra: Breve nota a Strabone 5.2.5, 222C, *Athenaeum* 95, 2007, 677–684.

Pasquinucci 2014 = M. Pasquinucci, An efficient Communication Network: Roman Land, Sea and River Routes in North-Western Etruria, in: Römisch-Germanisches Zentralmuseum (Hg.), Honesta Missione. Festschrift für Barbara Pferdehirt, Mainz 2014, 33–46.

Pasquinucci 2016 = M. Pasquinucci, Strutture agrarie e allevamento transumante: Emilio Gabba e l'attualita `dei suoi studi storici, in: C. Carsana/L. Troiani (ed.), I percorsi di un historikos: in memoria di Emilio Gabba: atti del convegno di Pavia (18 - 20 settembre 2014), Como 2016, 190–200.

Pasquinucci/Menchelli 2009 = M. Pasquinucci/S. Menchelli, Variazioni climatiche nella Toscana nord-occidentale: indagini multidisciplinari e prime riflessioni, in: E. Hermon (ed.), Société et climat dans l'Empire romain. Pour une perspective historique et sistématique de la gestion des ressources en eau dans l'Empire romain, Napoli 2009, 377–388.

Patera/Shepherd/Dallai/Zanini 2003 = A. Patera/E.J. Shepherd/L. Dallai/E. Zanini, Il Vignale ritrovato, in: C. Macione, A. Patera (ed.), Materiali per Populonia 2, Quaderni del Dipartimento di Archeologia e Storia delle Arti. Sezione Archeologia. Università di Siena, 56, Firenze 2003, 281–313.

Pekáry 1968 = T. Pekáry, Untersuchungen zu den römischen Reichsstrassen, Bonn 1968.

Ponte 2007 = V. Ponte, Régimen jurídico de las vías públicas en Derecho Romano, Madrid 2007.

Pozzato/Rodighiero 2011 = S. Pozzato/A. Rodighiero (ed.), Claudio Rutilio Namaziano: Il ritorno, Torino 2011.

Quilici 1991 = L. Quilici, Le strade romane nell'Italia antica, in: G. Radke (ed.), Viae publicae romanae, Roma 1991, 17–25.

Radke 1973 = G. Radke, s.v. Viae Publicae Romanae, RE, Suppl. 13, 1973, 1417–1686.

Radke 1981 = G. Radke, Viae publicae Romanae, Bologna 1981.

Repetti 1835 = E. Repetti, Dizionario geografico, fisico, storico della Toscana, vol. II, Firenze 1835.

Ritschl 1862 = F. Ritschl, Priscae Latinitatis monumenta epigraphica ad archetyporum fidem exemplis lithographis repraesentata (Corpus inscriptionum Latinarum I: Auctarium), Berolini 1862.

Rotondi 1912 = G. Rotondi, Leges publicae populi romani, Milano 1912 [ristampa Hildesheim 1990].

Santini 1858 = V. Santini, Commentari storici sulla Versilia centrale, vol. 1, Pisa 1858.

Sordi 1971 = M. Sordi, La via Aurelia da Vada a Pisa nell'antichità, *Athenaeum* 49, 1971, 302–312.

Stanco 1999 = E.A. Stanco, Lucus Feroniae (Capena – RM): due nuovi cippi miliari, *Epigraphica* 61, 1999, 190–196.

Susini 1974 = G. Susini, Interpretazioni e deperimento di un'iscrizione antica: l'esempio del milliario di Campiano, *ArchClass* 25-26, 1973/1974, 713–717.

Targioni Tozzetti 1776 = G. Targioni Tozzetti, Relazioni d'alcuni viaggi fatti in diverse parti della Toscana per osservare le produzioni naturali, e gli antichi monumenti di essa, Firenze, vol. 9, 1776.

Terrenato 2001 = N. Terrenato, A Tale of Three Cities: the Romanization of Northern Coastal Etruria, in: S. Keay/N. Terrenato (ed.), Italy and the West: Comparative Issues in Romanization, Oxford 2001, 54–67.

Tortorici 1985 = E. Tortorici, La via Aurelia vetus e la via Aurelia nova, in: A. Carandini (ed.), La romanizzazione dell'Etruria: il territorio di Vulci, Milano 1985, 56.

Uggeri 1991 = G. Uggeri, Questioni di metodo. La toponomastica nella ricerca topografica. Il contributo alla ricostruzione della viabilità, *RTopAnt/JAT* 1, 1991, 21–36.

Uggeri 2015 = G. Uggeri, Il nodo viario di Firenze in età romana, in: V. D'Aquino/G. Guarducci/S. Nencetti/S. Valentini (a cura di), Archeologia a Firenze: città e territorio, Atti del Workshop Firenze, 12–13 aprile 2013, Firenze 2015, 137–140.

Ughelli 1718 = F. Ughelli, Italia sacra sive de Episcopis Italiae et insularum adiacentium, III, Venetiis 1718.

Wiseman 1970 = T.P. Wiseman, Roman Republican Road-Building, *PBSR* 38, 1970, 122–152.

Wiseman 1971 = T.P. Wiseman, Via Aurelia Nova and Via Aemilia Scauri, *Epigraphica* 33, 1971, 27–32.

Wiseman 1987 = T.P. Wiseman, Roman Studies. Literary and Historical, Liverpool 1987.

Patrizia Basso
Excavations in the North of Italy along the *via Claudia Augusta*

Abstract: This paper presents the results of archaeological research carried out during 2014 and 2015 by the University of Verona in Gazzo Veronese, a small town on the Po Plain south of Verona. The excavation focused on the stretch of the *via Claudia Augusta* between *Hostilia* and *Verona*. It has allowed us to understand the technique of construction and the dating of the road. The road was built on an *agger* 10 metres wide, with a drainage ditch about 9 m wide and 1 m deep. Along it, a few tombs were built between the end of the first century B.C.E. and the beginning of the second century C.E. The original gravel surface was removed by agricultural works and dispersed across the surface of the surrounding fields, so that it was possible to follow the road through archaeological survey and to understand its course in relation to the geomorphology of the territory.

Zusammenfassung: Dieser Beitrag präsentiert die Ergebnisse archäologischer Forschungen der Universität Verona zwischen 2014 und 2015 in Gazzo Veronese, einer kleinen Stadt in der Po Ebene südlich von Verona. Die Ausgrabung konzentrierte sich auf den Streckenabschnitt der *via Claudia Augusta* zwischen *Hostilia* und *Verona*. Die Erkenntnisse erlauben uns, die Konstruktionstechnik zu verstehen und die Straße zu datieren. Die Straße wurde auf einem 10 Meter breiten *agger* mit einem Entwässerungsgraben von etwa 9 m Breite und 1 m Tiefe erbaut. Entlang der Straße wurden zwischen dem Ende des ersten Jahrhunderts vor Christus und dem Beginn des zweiten Jahrhunderts nach Christus einige Gräber errichtet. Die ursprüngliche Schotterbefestigung ist durch landwirtschaftliche Arbeiten abgebaut und auf der Oberfläche der umliegenden Felder verteilt worden, sodass es möglich war, dem Straßenverlauf durch archäologische Untersuchungen zu folgen und den Verlauf im Verhältnis zur Geomorphologie des Territoriums zu verstehen.

As my teacher in ancient topography at the University of Padua, prof. LUCIANO BOSIO, used to say, to look for an ancient road, you must use both your mind and your feet. In effect, when studying ancient roads it is crucial, in addition to the analysis of historical sources (literary, epigraphic, itinerary), to carry out research in the field (exca-

---

Article note: I thank Giacomo Sartor and Henry Venner Woodcock for helping in the translation.

https://doi.org/10.1515/9783110638332-020

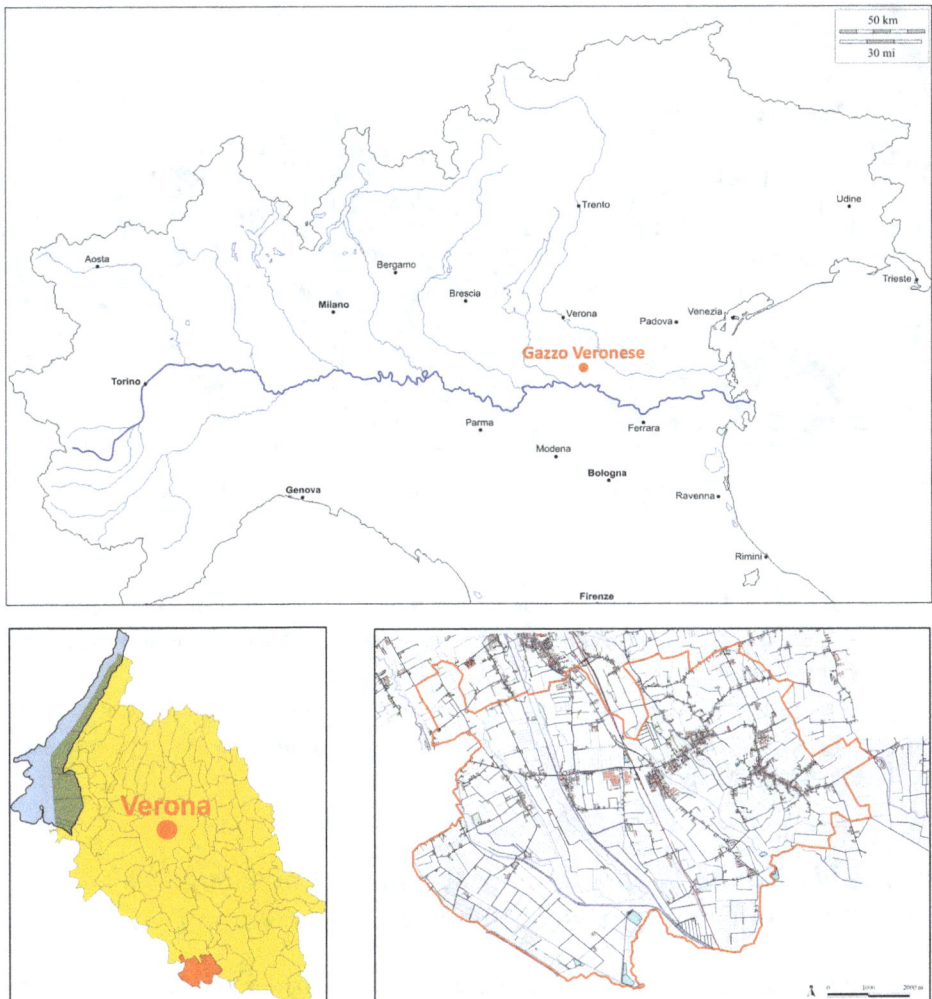

Fig. 1: Gazzo Veronese: position in northern Italy (from d-maps.com) and within the Verona province and municipality's boundaries (revised by Patrizia Basso).

vation and survey), in conjunction with other scientific approaches, such as palaeobotanical and geomorphological analyses.[1]

In particular, I aim to explain the importance of an interdisciplinary approach in road research, presenting the results of a project that I carried out for the University of Verona in Gazzo Veronese, a small town to the south of Verona (fig. 1). This is an

---

[1] On methodology for the study of Roman roads: QUILICI 1992; QUILICI 1994; CHEVALLIER 1998; UGGERI 2000; QUILICI 2004; BASSO 2007; STACCIOLI 2010.

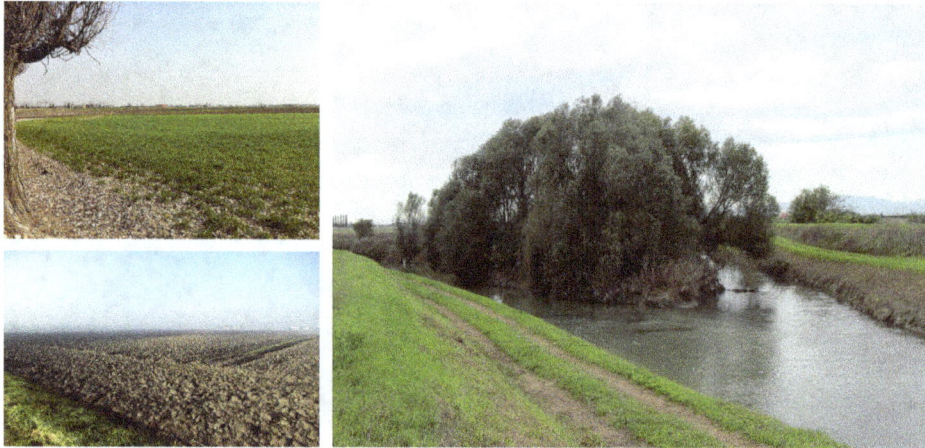

Fig. 2: The territory of Gazzo Veronese: panoramic images (pictures by Patrizia Basso).

agricultural area, free of urban development and therefore ideal for archaeological research (fig. 2). The project seeks, in particular, to study a Roman road that passes through these fields.

Before outlining the results of our research on this road, it is important to introduce the *via Claudia Augusta*,[2] whose problematic identification is the focus of our archaeological investigation.

1 The *via Claudia Augusta*: Current State of Knowledge before the Archaeological Research of the University of Verona

We know the name of the road and the date of its construction from the inscriptions on two milestones: the former came to light in the 16th century in Rablà near Merano (Bolzano) and the latter in 1786 in the church of Cesiomaggiore near Feltre (Belluno) (fig. 3).[3] Both state that the road was opened by Drusus in 16–15 B.C.E. to facilitate the military campaigns against the Transalpine peoples and restored by his son, Emperor Claudius, in 45–46 C.E. to celebrate his father's victories. Nevertheless, the two milestones mention two different starting points for this road: the first quotes

---

2 About the road: Bosio 1991, 82–93; Pesavento Mattioli 2000; Galliazzo 2002 (and in particular Rosada 2002); Czysz 2004; Migliario 2004; Walde/Grabherr 2006 and previous bibliography mentioned therein.
3 About the milestone of Cesiomaggiore CIL V 8002 = IBR 469 = ILS 208 = Basso 1987, n. 36; about that of Rablà: CIL V 8003 = IBR 465 = ILS 208 = Ausserhofer 1976, n. 1 = Basso 1987, n. 41 = CIL XVII/4, 1. The two milestones had already been studied in Guarnieri Ottoni 1789.

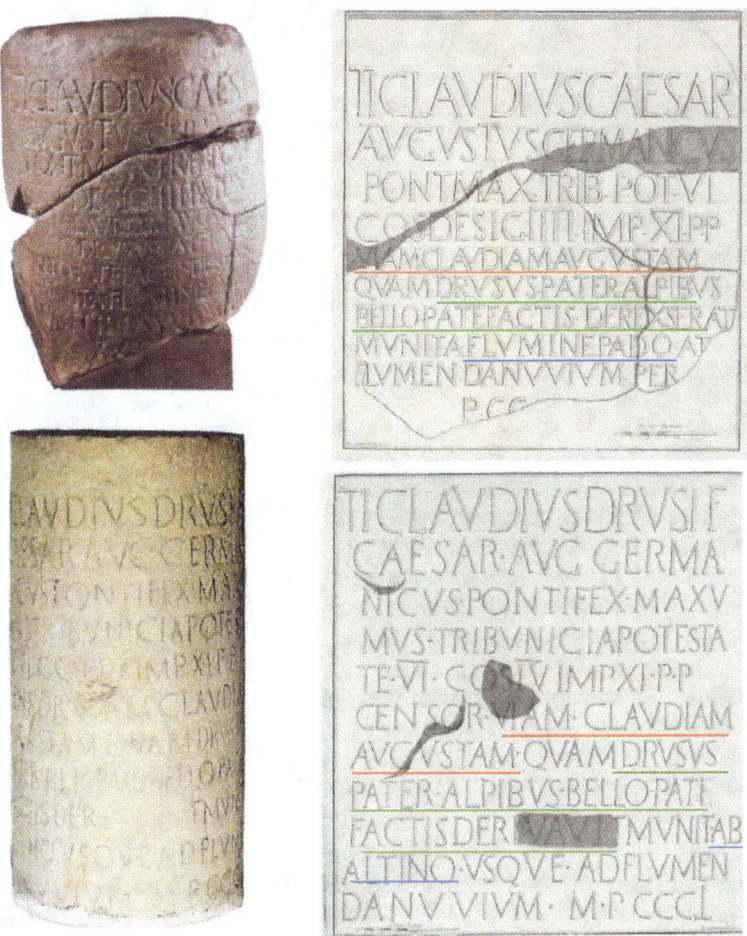

Fig. 3: The milestones of Rablà (Bolzano) and Cesiomaggiore near Feltre (Belluno) (pictures from ROSADA 2002, 39–40; drawings by GUARNIERI OTTONI 1789, revised by Patrizia Basso).

the river Po, while the second names the town of *Altinum*. Because of this discrepancy, three hypotheses on the course of the road have been put forward. According to the first hypothesis (fig. 4, red line), there was only one road from *Altinum* to the Danube through Valsugana and the Resia Pass: in this case, the milestone of Rablà would have mentioned the river Po as a general geographic indicator for the Adriatic coast. According to a second hypothesis (fig. 4, blue line), there were two completely different roads: one would have run from *Altinum* to the Danube through Valbelluna and the Monte Croce Comelico Pass and the other from the river Po through *Verona*, *Tridentum* and the Resia Pass. Finally, according to the third hypothesis, there were

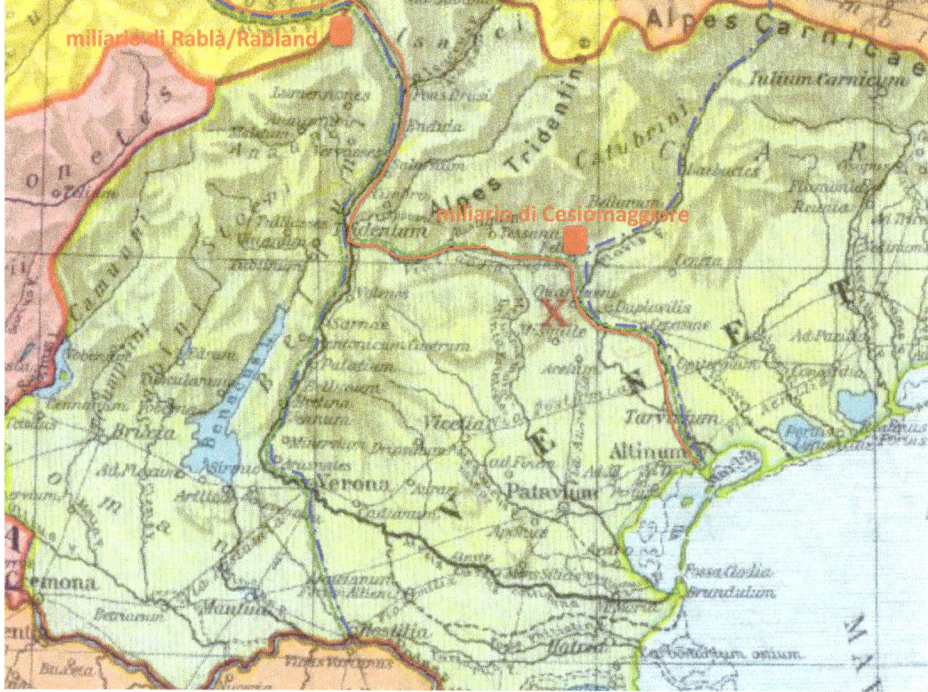

Fig. 4: The different hypotheses regarding the *via Claudia Augusta*'s route and the places of discovery of the milestones in Rablà (Bolzano) and Cesiomaggiore, near Feltre (Belluno) (revised by Patrizia Basso).

two roads starting from two different points (one from the Po through *Verona*, the other from *Altinum* through Valsugana (fig. 4, green line)), which joined at *Tridentum* and then passed through *Pons Drusi* and the Resia Pass.

Additionally, it is worth mentioning a road running from the river Po to *Verona* and *Tridentum* attested by two other milestones, dating back to the 4th century CE, which reappears immediately north of Verona in Valpolicella, specifically in S. Pietro in Cariano and in Arbizzano near Negrar (Verona) (fig. 5).[4] Each of these mentions two different distances, one (*VIII milia passuum*) from *Verona* and a second *(XXXX milia passuum)* from *A P(ado)*, where the two letters "A" and "P" have been interpreted as referring either to the river Po or a road station along the same river, identified as being in ancient *Hostilia*, now known as Ostiglia. *Hostilia*, mentioned by Tacitus as a

---

4 The first milestone is published in CIL V 8048 = BRESCIANI 1942, 87–88 = BASSO 1987, n. 29; the second one has been lost. A picture of it can be seen in BRESCIANI 1942, fig. 1 = BASSO 1987, n. 26. Regarding the two milestones and their possible dating in the 1st century C.E.: CALZOLARI 2005, pp. 410–411.

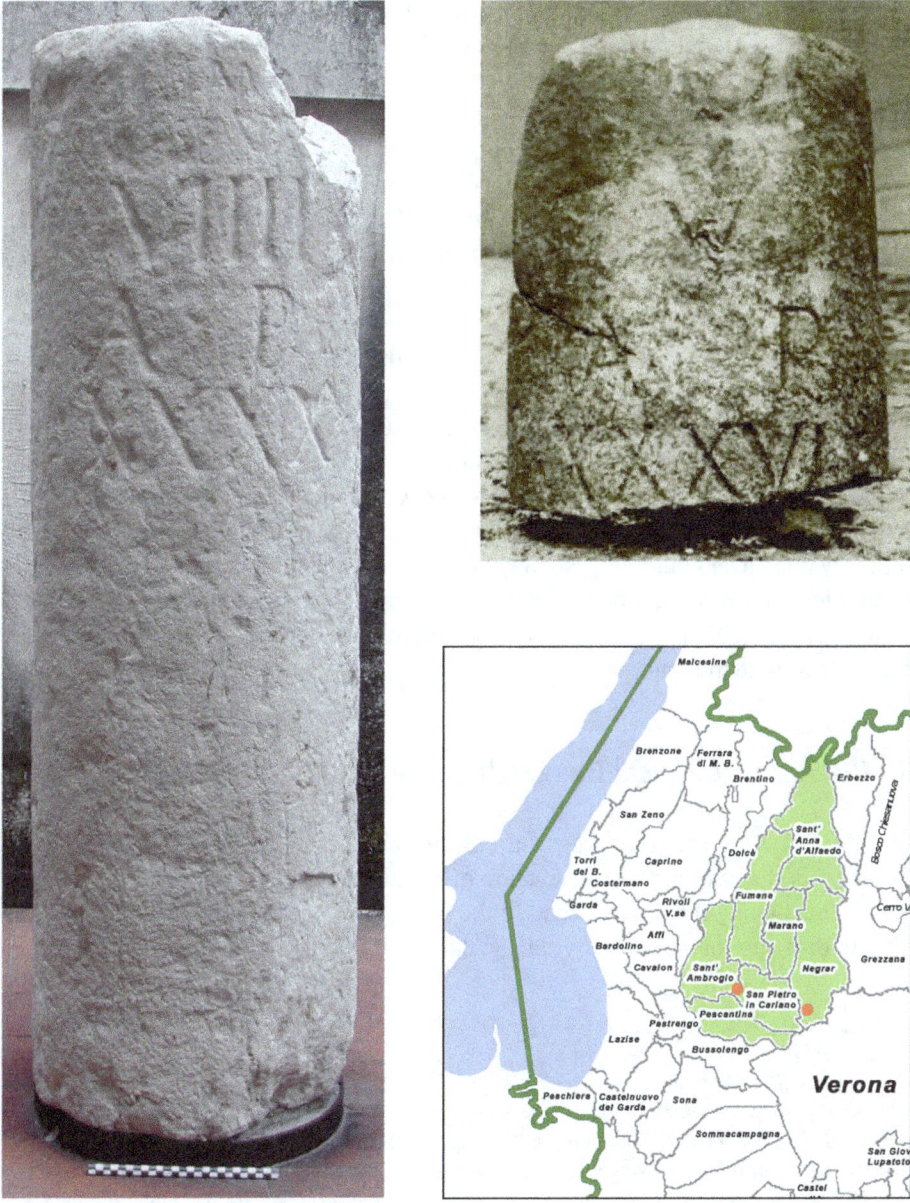

Fig. 5: The Valpolicella (in green) and the place of discovery of the two milestones of S. Pietro in Cariano and Arbizzano (red circle), shown in the pictures (revised by Patrizia Basso; picture of milestone of S. Pietro in Cariano by Patrizia Basso; picture of milestone of Negrar from BRESCIANI 1941–42, fig. 1).

vicus Veronensium,[5] used to be an important crossroads, connected with *Bononia* on one side and with *Mantua* and *Cremona* on the other side. Moreover, important connections with the northern coast of the Adriatic Sea and Ravenna in particular were made both by the river Po and by a road running along the same river (as confirmed by the Tabula Peutingeriana).[6]

The road from the Po to *Verona* is also shown in the Tabula Peutingeriana and further mentioned in the *Itinerarium Antonini*.[7] The distances of *XXXIII* and *XXX* miles mentioned respectively in two *itineraria* match with the 44 km length of the road that now connects Ostiglia and Verona.

Nevertheless, both the route and the date of the road remain uncertain. LUCIANO BOSIO and the majority of scholars believe that the stretch from *Hostilia* to *Verona* was open during the second half of the 2nd century B.C.E., on the basis of historical events that occurred in that period in the *Venetia* and particularly in the territory around *Verona*, when the main road axes of the *regio* were built.[8] Until our project, archaeological confirmation of the correct dating was missing. Moreover, if we exclude a preliminary dig carried out near Ostiglia over 30 years ago, no excavation has ever been conducted on this road.[9] The dig showed that the road was built on an *agger* made of sand, measuring 10 metres in width, however, the work did not reveal any significant evidence to date the road.

2 The Archaeological Research of the University of Verona

In 2014 and 2015, the Department of Cultures and Civilisations of the University of Verona, conducted, under the direction of the author, an archaeological survey and excavations along the ancient road in the territory of Gazzo Veronese, in order to be able to date the road and verify the available data on the construction technique.[10]

---

5 Tac. hist. 3,9.
6 RATHMANN 2016, abb. 14.
7 Regarding the *Itinerarium Antonini*: CUNTZ 1929, 282, 3–4 (within the stretch from *Verona* to *Bononia*); on the *Tabula Peutingeriana*: MILLER 1916, 277–278; MILLER 1962, seg. 4, 4.
8 BOSIO 1991, 61; BIONDANI 2002; CALZOLARI 2005; DA OSTIGLIA A VERONA 2008. On the contrary, BOSIO dates the stretch from Verona to *Tridentum* to the *Caesar-Augustus* age, when the town was becoming a very important beachhead for the conquest of the Transalpine territories.
9 CALZOLARI 1985.
10 The research is part of the GaVe Project ("Progetto GaVe, Gazzo Veronese"), jointly led by the University of Verona, the Central Archaeological Council of the Verona, Vicenza e Rovigo Provinces and the University "La Sapienza" of Rome aimed to reconstruct the rich history of this territory. We thank all the people involved in this project and in particular those engaged in different ways in the work such as the excavation coordinators Ms. VALERIA GRAZIOLI, Ms. MARINA SCALZERI and Ms. ELISA ZENTILINI who also studied the materials. I wish to thank also those who supported the Project: the Mu-

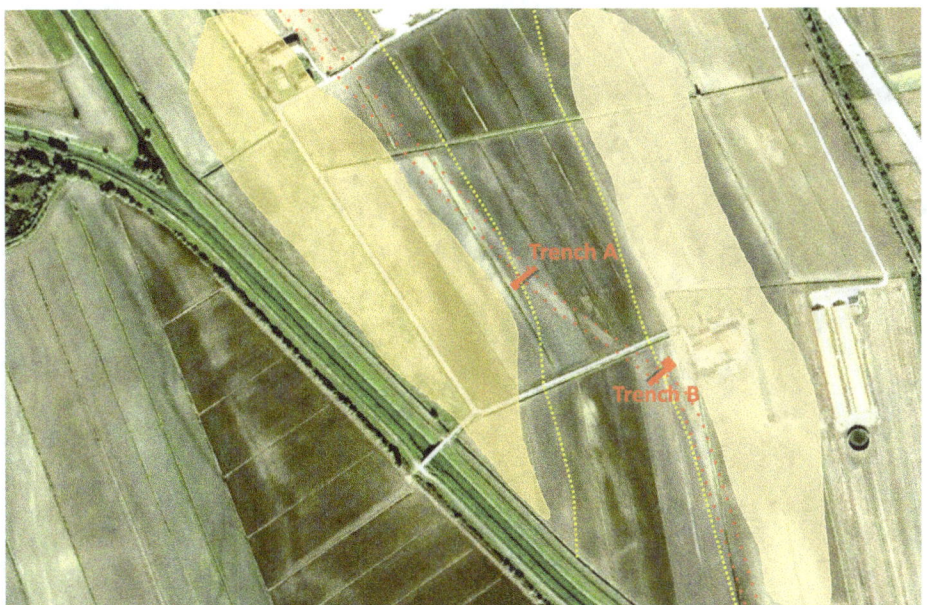

Fig. 6: Aerial photographic trail of the road (dotted red line) and the area of marshland (dotted yellow line) between two sand banks (in yellow) where during our research two trenches were opened: trench A in 2014 and trench B in 2015 (graphic re-elaboration by Valeria Grazioli).

The road was already evident in some aerial photos as a clear linear trace (fig. 6, red dotted line), passing through an area of lower land (fig. 6, yellow dotted line) located between two sandbanks. During the excavations around those features, two long trenches were opened: trench A (55 m x 5 m) was dug in 2014, trench B (60 m x 4 m) in 2015, about 230 m south-east of trench A.

Thanks to the excavations, we were able to understand the techniques used to build the road. The road was laying upon an *agger* (width 10 m) made with local sand brought from a ditch (8 m wide and of a maximum depth of 0.90 m) dug for this purpose. In trench A, this ditch appears on the west side of the *agger*, protecting the road from the water coming down the sandbank (figg. 7a e 7b). On the other, eastern side of the *agger*, there was an area of marshland. The water from the road ran into this marsh, so on this side a ditch was not needed. Also in the second trench (B), we confirmed the same techniques but in this case the ditch is on the east side, while in the west there is an area of marsh (fig. 8).

---

nicipality of Gazzo Veronese, the Reclamation Consortium of Verona, the farm Verallia Saint-Gobain. For the results of our research: BASSO/GRAZIOLI 2015; BASSO/GRAZIOLI/PAVONI/ZENTILINI 2016; BASSO 2017; BASSO c.s.

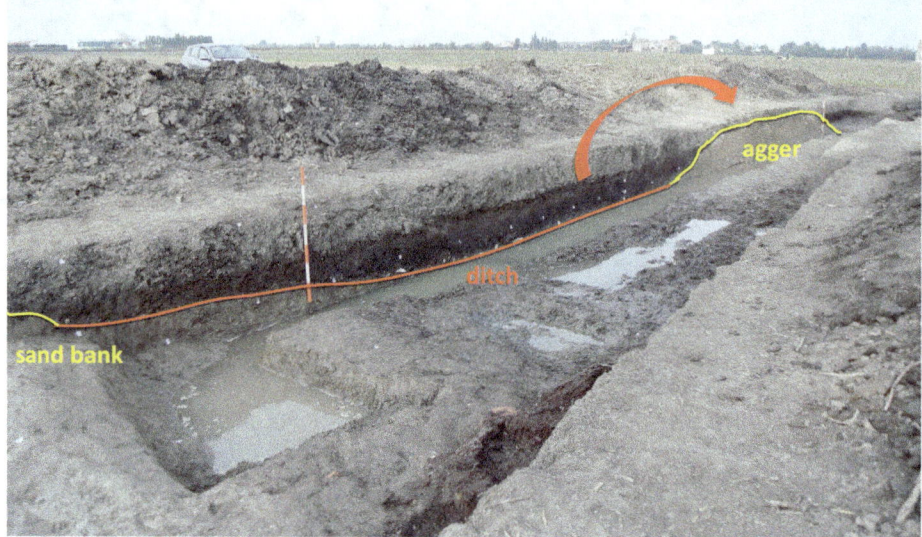
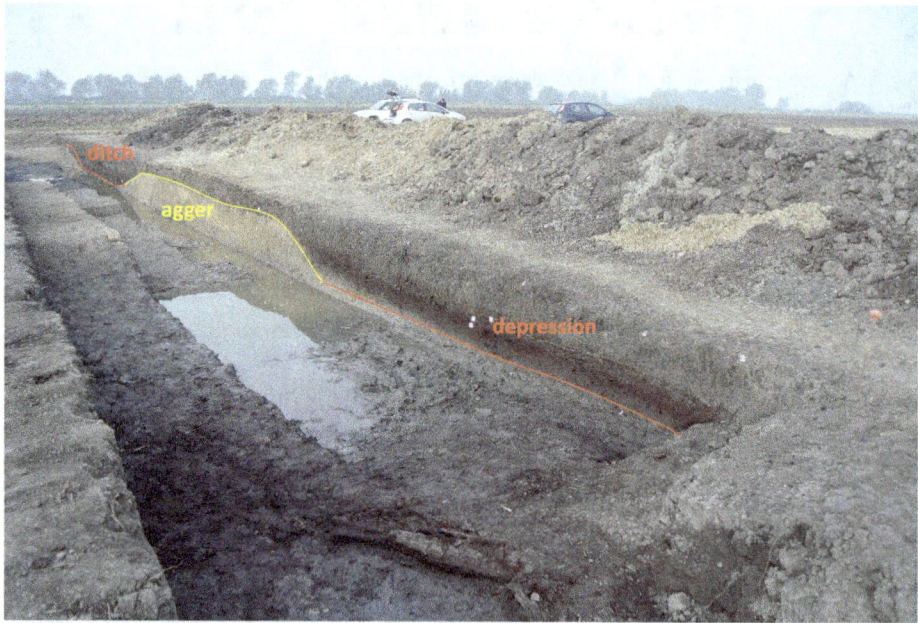

Fig. 7a e 7b: Cross sectional view of the road in trench A from West to East end, from East to West: the *agger*, the ditch, the sand bank and the depression are visible (pictures by Patrizia Basso).

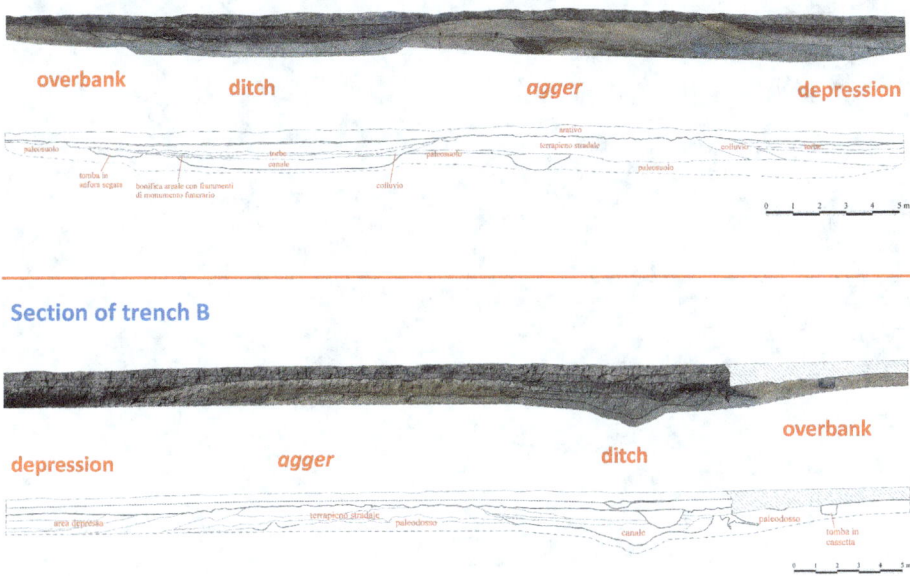

Fig. 8: Cross sectional view of the road in trench A and trench B (graphic re-elaboration by Valeria Grazioli).

On the top of the *agger* lay a layer of pebbles, but this has been destroyed by farmers cultivating the land and dispersed around the area. Only a few traces remain on the sides of the *agger*. By analysing these stones, we learned that they came from the river Adige, which flows about 20 kilometres away.[11] This analysis, together with the fact that the road was wide (10 m), indicates a very complex and expensive construction project, which means that the road was a *via publica*.

Under the layer of the *agger*, the excavations revealed the original geological substratum where a few holes were found, probably from trees uprooted in the preliminary phase of the construction work.

During the excavations, a large number of cremation graves emerged on the sandbank on the other side of the ditch along the road. There are two types of graves: the majority (about 30) in a brick chest, with a few others in cut amphorae (fig. 9). The typical grave goods discovered in the tombs were generally dated between the end of the 1st century B.C.E. and the beginnings of the 2nd century C.E.[12]

Alongside the 2014 and 2015 research campaign, we carried out an extensive survey in large parts of the territory around Gazzo Veronese (45,000 acres). This activ-

---

11 The petrographic investigations have been made by Mr. ROBERTO ZORZIN.
12 BASSO/GRAZIOLI/PAVONI/ZENTILINI 2016, 14–16.

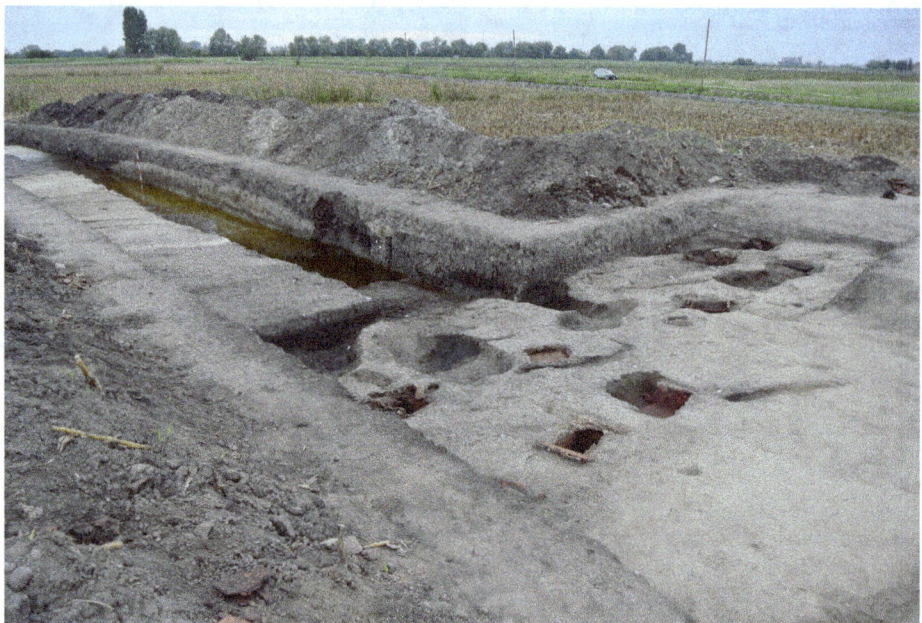

Fig. 9: The graves found in 2015 in trench B (picture by Valeria Grazioli).

ity was conducted in recently ploughed fields with high visibility and at a high level of intensity (with just 5 m between each fieldwalker), with even greater intensity – just 1 m between walkers – where the area appeared of particular interest.[13] The true route of the Roman road was precisely followed thanks to the concentration of pebbles on the fields' surfaces. In some areas the *agger* was still visible, around 20–30 cm higher than the surrounding countryside level.

Thanks to this survey, we discovered the detailed route of the road and we observed the close relationship between the road and the old bed of the river Tartaro, which was straightened in the modern age: so we understood that the road was not straight, as was usual for Roman roads built on a plain, but instead was made up of many segments so as to avoid the ancient fluvial deposits (fig. 10). The road was built in the lower part of these sandbanks, while the higher part, which was safer and more protected, was used for housing and farming.

West of the ancient course of the river Tartaro (fig. 10), corresponding to the linear trail shown in the aerial photography, a dispersion of gravel along the North-North West/South-South East direction has been detected. This band of gravel followed the

---

[13] The survey results integrated the archaeological data already known from previous studies about Gazzo Veronese: Bosio et al. 1994, F. 63, n. 160–189; Calzolari 1986; Calzolari 1989.

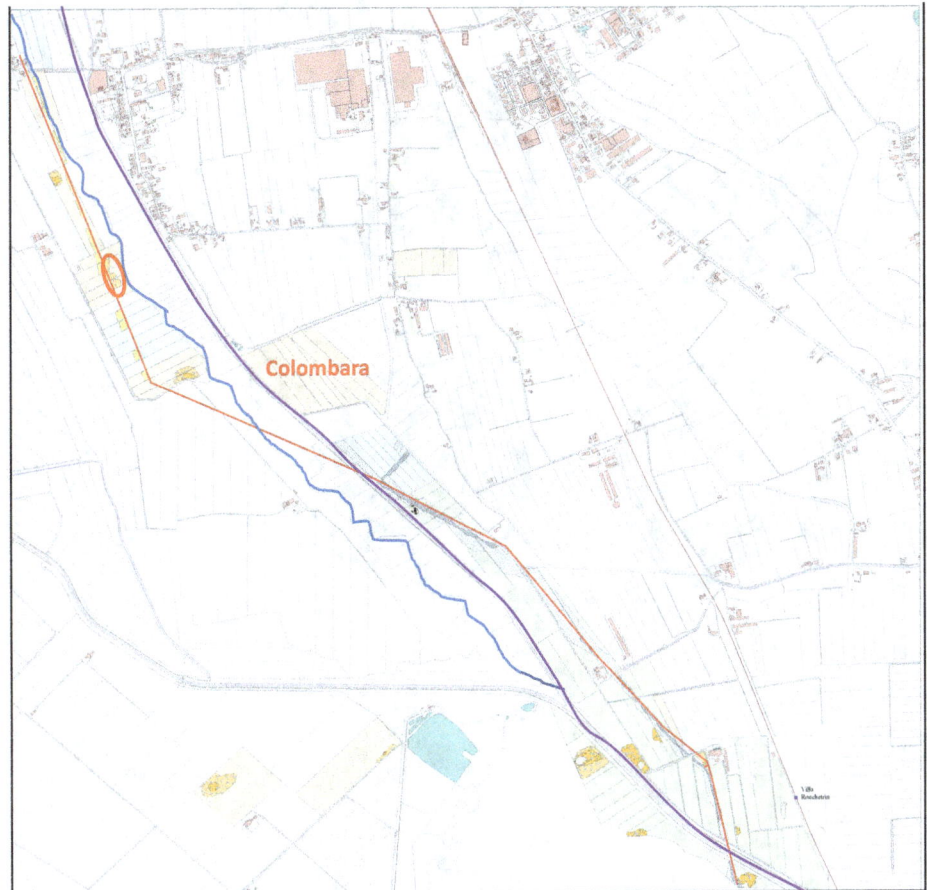

Fig. 10: Road trail emerged on survey (red line) compared to the ancient course of the river Tartaro (blue line), as presently rectified (violet line). Within the red circle a few cremation graves have been found with part of the relevant grave goods (graphic re-elaboration by Valeria Grazioli).

original margin of the sand bank, descending to the old course of the river Tartaro. It shows a clear difference between the lighter band of the old carriageway and the darker and moist band of the lateral ditches, which is clearly evident from the crop marks in the drainage channels between one field and the other (fig. 11). Along this band of gravel we found a few cremation graves, destroyed by ploughing but recognizable by the ash, charcoal and bones from the funeral pyre, which were brought to the surface, together with some elements of the grave goods (fig. 11). This discovery shows

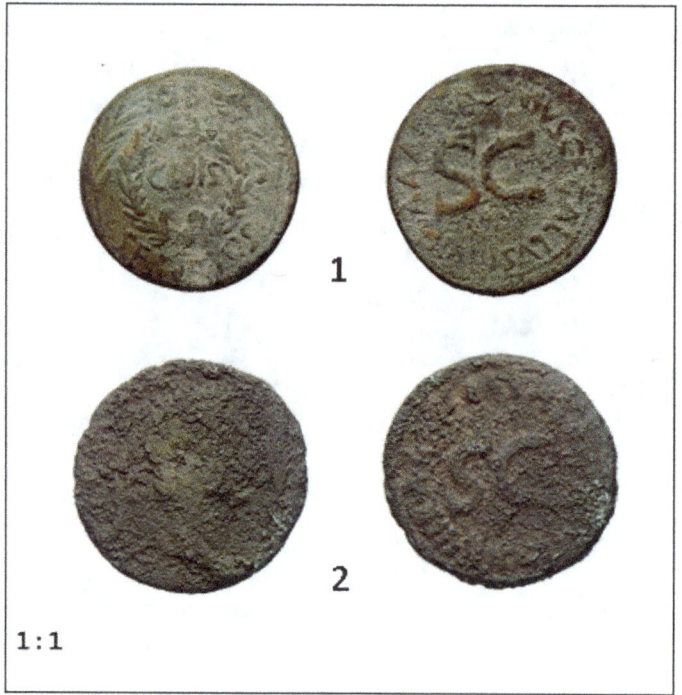

Fig. 11: Two of the four coins from the Augustan age dated 18–5 B.C.E. found in Gazzo Veronese during our research: 1. As of *C. Asinius Gallus*; 2. As of *Augustus* (from BASSO/GRAZIOLI/PAVONI/ZENTILINI 2016, 13, fig. 25).

that this stretch of road was Roman[14] and was part of the same road found during the excavations in the south. These finds allow us to understand that the road crossed the old course of the river Tartaro, turning straight towards the northwest. It is still debated why the road moved from the left bank to the right bank of the river, making it necessary to build a bridge, which we are still looking for by means of geophysical survey. One hypothesis is that the Romans wanted to avoid building the road alongside the left riverbank to respect the Iron-age funeral area in the locality of Colombara (fig. 10), discovered in the recent past.[15]

Thanks to the excavation and the survey, it was possible also to date the road. The most ancient artefacts found in the tombs are four coins from the Augustan age, dated 18–5 BCE.[16] (fig. 11) With appropriate caution, it could be hypothesized that the

---

[14] This hypothesis of the dating of the aerial photographic trace was proposed by CALZOLARI 1989, 102.
[15] BOSIO et al. 1994, 219, n. 177–178.
[16] BASSO/GRAZIOLI/PAVONI/ZENTILINI 2016, 16.

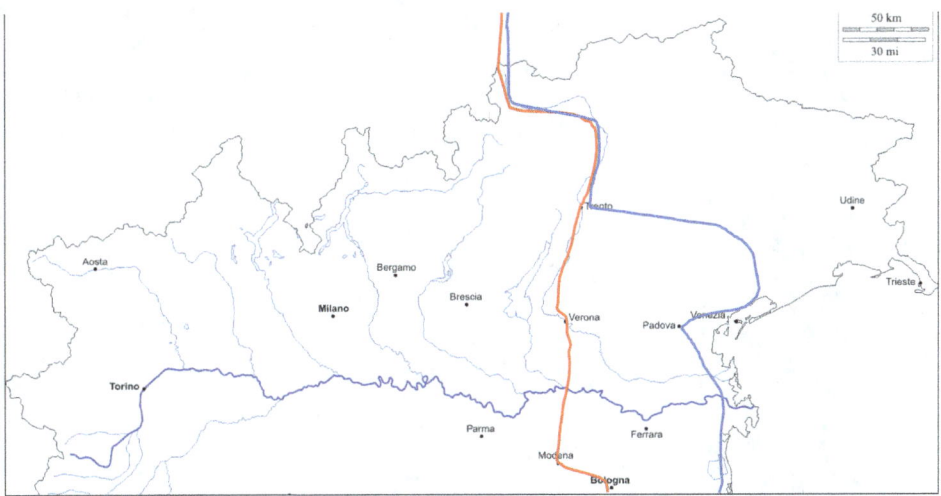

Fig. 12: The two road axes coming from the south and the "Claudia Augusta Padana" (red line) and "Claudia Augusta Altinate" (blue line) (revised by Patrizia Basso).

road was built when Drusus led the military campaigns to conquer the north (16–15 B.C.E.)[17], according to the inscriptions on the two milestones mentioned above.
Dating the road joining *Hostilia* with *Verona* seems helpful in the long and controversial dispute regarding the *Claudia Augusta* road. From the topographical and historical point of view, it is in fact more logical to think that Drusus and his troops travelled along a road directly connecting Rome to the north (fig. 12, red line), rather than through *Altinum* and the Gardena Valley (fig. 12, blue line).

It is worth mentioning that the identification of specific segment of the road from *Altinum* to *Tridentum* at the time of Drusus is only based on the milestone found in Cesiomaggiore, near Feltre. But this milestone has characteristics differing from the other found in Rablà (fig. 3): the shape and the *ductus* are more regular and the stone material is different (limestone / marble), while during the early Imperial period along the same road the milestones were all made from the same stone.[18] So I wonder whether this milestone might be a fake produced in 1700, mimicking the artefact found in Rablà two centuries earlier. Although this hypothesis remains difficult to demonstrate, the emerging dating of the road from *Hostilia* to *Verona* to the Drusian age allows us to think about a new historical point of view for the road itself, suggesting – as mentioned above – that the stretch of road was part of the *via Claudia Augusta*.

---

17 MIGLIARIO 2004.
18 For example, this is the case for Augustus' milestones: GROSSI/ZANCO 2003, 194–195.

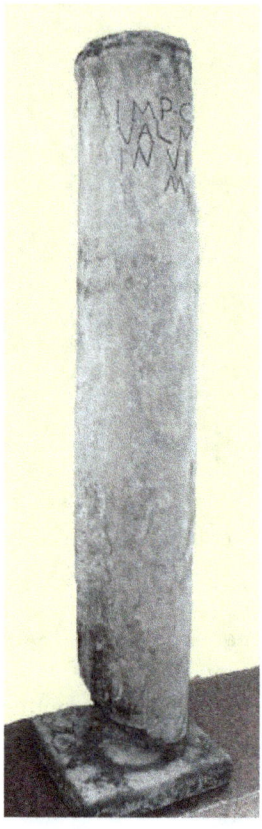

Fig. 13: The milestone of *Maxentius* found in Isola della Scala (picture by Piergiovanna Grossi).

Finally, thanks to the excavations we have also been able to reconstruct the use of the road over time. To this extent too, archaeological sources have to be related to other forms of evidence. In fact, although the tombs we have found are not from the 3rd and 4th century C.E., the above mentioned roadmaps (and in particular the *Itinerarium Antonini* and the Tabula Peutingeriana) and a few milestones show that the road connecting *Hostilia-Verona-Tridentum* was in use during this period. A significant example is a milestone discovered in Isola della Scala, North of Gazzo Veronese, and dedicated to *Maxentius* (fig. 13). This milestone, dated almost certainly to between 311 and spring 312 CE, the time of the fight against *Costantinus*, is related to the other three of the same usurper found along the same route.[19] These indicate the great interest taken by *Maxentius* in the road along the river Adige, in order to counter a possible attack from the Alps jointly launched by

---

19 See the milestones of S. Pietro in Cariano (BASSO 1987, n. 28), Avio (CIL V 8052 = BASSO 1987, n. 32) and Prato all'Isarco/Blumau (CIL V 8054 = IBR 463 = AUSSERHOFER 1976, n. 5 = BASSO 1987, n. 42).

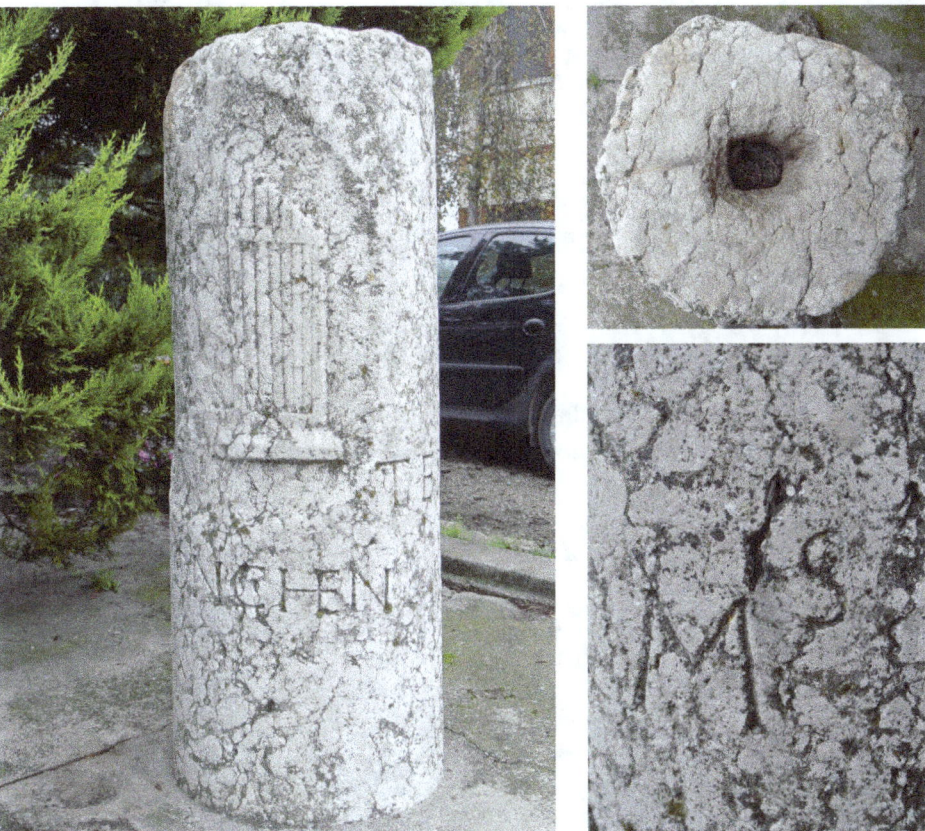

Fig. 14: A presumed milestone discovered in Gazzo Veronese and transformed during the Giusti age. Details of the upper surface and the letter "S" apparently older of the rest (pictures by Patrizia Basso).

his rivals *Costantinus* and *Licinius*, based respectively in *Gallia* and *Illiricum*.[20] As far as milestones are concerned, it is worth mentioning that in Gazzo a cylindrical artefact, made of limestone from *Verona* (112 cm high, with circumference between 129 cm and 139 cm and with a squared recess on the upper surface: 9 x 9 cm) is still visible in the courtyard of a farm (fig. 14). Although it was transformed in the Giusti age (the family was powerful in Gazzo from 1400s–1500s), it is possible to suppose that it was a milestone. Looking at the stone there are also traces of some letters carved on its surface (like the "S "in the picture) which could be part of a longer ancient inscription.

---

20 For a synthesis regarding these milestones, see BASSO 2003, 290. A comprehensive analysis of Maxentius' road policy is in PAVAN 1992.

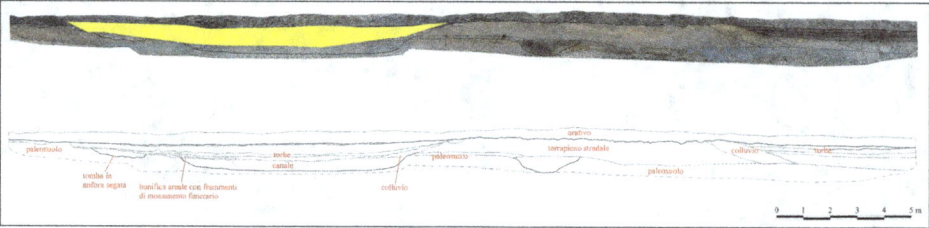

Fig. 15: Cross sectional view of trench A. The layer of peat is indicated in yellow (revised by Patrizia Basso).

The thick peat layers found above the ditch floor (accumulating after the ditch went out of use) during our excavation (fig. 15, yellow) show an early abandonment of the road. These levels have many vegetal remains (branches and trunks), typical of marshy plants (in particular willows, poplars and oaks), analysed by palaeobotanists. Some seeds found by flotation of samples from the deepest layer, are dated to the 8th or 9th century C.E. by radiocarbon analysis. Probably in that time the territory south of *Verona* was covered with marshland and the road was not anymore used, since even earlier, during the final period of the Empire, it was not controlled by a strong central power looking after the complex hydrological maintenance.

Bibliography

AUSSERHOFER 1976 = M. AUSSERHOFER, Die römischen Meilensteine in Südtirol, *Der Schlern* 50, 1976, 3–34.
BASSO 1987 = P. BASSO, I miliari della Venetia romana, Padova 1987.
BASSO 2003 = P. BASSO, La vita tardoantica delle strade romane: gli esempi dell'Annia e della via lungo le valli dell'Adige e dell'Isarco", in: R. FREI STOLBA (Hg.), Siedlung und Verkehr im römischen Reich: Römerstrassen zwischen Herrschaftssicherung und Landschaftsprägung, Kolloquium zu Ehren von Prof. Dr. Heinz E. Herzig (Bern 28–29. 6. 2001), Bern 2003, 283–315.
BASSO 2007 = P. BASSO, Strade romane: storia e archeologia, Roma 2007.
BASSO 2017 = P. BASSO, Recherches récentes sur la voie Claudia Augusta, in: S. ZANNI (Hg.), La route antique et médiévale : nouvelle approches, nouveaux outils, Actes Table ronde internationale (Bordeaux 15. 11. 2016), Bordeaux 2017, 91–108.
BASSO c.s. = P. BASSO, Routes romaines dans la Gallia Cisalpina: nouvelle découverte et perspective de recherche, Actes Voies, réseaux, paysage en Gaule, Colloque en hommage à J.-L. Fiches, (Pont du Gard 14–17 juin 2016), Montpellier c.s.
BASSO/GRAZIOLI 2015 = P. BASSO/V. GRAZIOLI, Indagini archeologiche a Gazzo Veronese lungo la strada romana nota come Claudia Augusta Padana, *Archeologia Veneta* 38, 2015, 63–79.
BASSO/GRAZIOLI/PAVONI/ZENTILINI 2016 = P. BASSO/V. GRAZIOLI/M. PAVONI/E. ZENTILINI, La via Claudia Augusta: recenti indagini archeologiche dell'Università di Verona a Gazzo Veronese (Verona), FOLD&R 370 (www.fastionline.org/docs/FOLDER-it-2016-370).
BIONDANI 2002 = F. BIONDANI, La romanizzazione e la viabilità, in: B. CHIAPPA (Hg.), Isola della Scala: Territorio e società nella media pianura veronese, Isola della Scala 2002, 27–30.

Bosio 1991 = L. Bosio, Le strade romane della *Venetia* e dell'*Histria*, Padova 1991.
Bosio et al. 1994 = L. Bosio et al., Carta Archeologica Veneto, vol. 4, Modena 1994.
Bresciani 1942 = B. Bresciani, Miliari della via Claudia Augusta Padana, *Atti e Memorie dell'Accademia di Agricoltura, Scienze e Lettere di Verona* 20, 1942, 87–90.
Calzolari 1985 = M. Calzolari, Ostiglia. Località Pedemonta. Massicciata stradale di età romana, *Notiziario Soprintendenza Archeologica della Lombardia* 1985, 66–67.
Calzolari 1986 = M. Calzolari, Territorio e insediamenti nella bassa pianura padana del Po in età romana, Verona 1986.
Calzolari 1989= M. Calzolari, Padania romana. Ricerche ambientali e paleoambientali nella pianura tra il Mincio e il Tartaro, Mantova 1989.
Calzolari 2005 = M. Calzolari, "A Pado": la strada romana da Ostiglia a Verona, in: G. Ciurletti/N. Pisu (Hg.), I territori della via Claudia Augusta: incontri di archeologia, Trento 2005, 409–417.
Chevallier 1998 = R. Chevallier, Les voies romaines, Paris 1998.
Cuntz 1929 = O. Cuntz, Itineraria romana. I. Itinerarium Antonini Augusti et Burdigalense, Leipzig 1929.
Czysz 2004 = W. Czysz, 350 Meilen zur Donau: Die römische Staatsstraße *Via Claudia Augusta*, in: "Alle Wege führen nach Rom...", Internationales Römerstraßenkolloquium Bonn, Puhlheim 2004, 101–130.
Da Ostiglia a Verona 2008 = Da Ostiglia a Verona. Archeologia e storia di una strada romana, Catalogo della Mostra, pubblicato a cura dell'Associazione Archeologia Isolana, Isola della Scala 2008.
Galliazzo 2002 = V. Galliazzo (Hg.), Via Claudia Augusta. Un'arteria alle origini dell'Europa: ipotesi, problemi, prospettive, Atti del Convegno (Feltre 24–25. 9. 1999), Feltre 2002.
Grossi/Zanco 2003 = P. Grossi/A. Zanco, Miliari romani nel Nord Italia: materiali, provenienza, lavorazione. L'esempio dell'area veneta e friulana, *Quaderni di Archeologia del Veneto* 19, 2003, 192–202.
Guarnieri Ottoni 1789 = A. Guarnieri Ottoni, Dissertazione intorno al corso dell'antica via Claudia Augusta dalla città di Altino sino al fiume Danubio, Bassano 1789.
Migliario 2004 = E. Migliario, Druso e Claudio fra Resia e Brennero, in: U. Laffi/F. Prontera/ V. Biagio (Hg.), Artissimum memoriae vinculum, Scritti di geografia storica e di antichità in ricordo di G. Conta, Firenze 2004, 279–296.
Miller 1916 = K. Miller, Itineraria romana. Römische Reisewege an der Hand der Tabula Peutingeriana, Stuttgart 1916.
Miller 1962 = K. Miller, Die Peutingersche Tafel, Stuttgart 1962.
Pavan 1992 = M. Pavan, I miliari di Massenzio nella *Venetia* e la sua politica nord-orientale, in: Tipologia di insediamento e distribuzione antropica nell'area veneto-istriana dalla protostoria all'alto Medioevo, Atti del Seminario di Studio (Asolo 3–5. 11. 1989), Mariano del Friuli 1992, 307–311.
Pesavento Mattioli 2000 = S. Pesavento Mattioli, Il sistema stradale nel quadro della viabilità dell'Italia nordorientale", in: E. Buchi (Hg.), Storia del Trentino. II. L'età romana, Trento 2000, 11–46.
Quilici 1992 = L. Quilici, Tecnica stradale romana, Atlante tematico di Topografia Antica, vol. 1, Roma 1992.
Quilici 1994 = L. Quilici, Strade romane percorsi e infrastrutture, Atlante tematico di Topografia Antica, vol. 2, Roma 1994.
Quilici 2004 = L. Quilici, Le strade romane, in: Introduzione alla topografia antica, Bologna 2004, 129–152.

Rathmann 2016 = M. Rathmann, Tabula Peutingeriana: Die einzige Weltkarte aus der Antike, Darmstadt 2016.

Rosada 2002 = G. Rosada, "… viam Claudiam Augustam quam Drusus pater … derexserat…", in: V. Galliazzo (Hg.), Via Claudia Augusta. Un'arteria alle origini dell'Europa: ipotesi, problemi, prospettive, Atti del Convegno (Feltre 24–25. 9. 1999), Feltre 2002, 36–68.

Staccioli 2010 = R.A. Staccioli, Strade romane, Roma 2010.

Uggeri 2000 = G. Uggeri, La viabilità antica, in: G. Bonora/P.L. Dall'Aglio/S. Patitucci/G. Uggeri (ed.), La topografia antica, Bologna 2000, 207–232.

Walde/Grabherr 2006 = E. Walde/G. Grabherr (Hg.), Via Claudia Augusta und Römerstraßenforschung im östlichen Alpenraum, Innsbruck 2006.

Autorenliste

Prof. Dr. Basso, Patrizia, Università di Verona, Dip. Culture e Civiltà, patrizia.basso@univr.it

Prof. Dr. Ben David, Chaim, Kinneret College on the Sea of Galilee, bendavidhm@gmail.com

Prof. Dr. Buonopane, Alfredo, Università di Verona, Dip. Culture e Civiltà, alfredo.buonopane@univr.it

Dr. Comfort, Anthony, independent researcher, associate member of the Centre for the study of Greek and Roman Antiquity, Corpus Christi College, Oxford, comfortam@gmail.com

Dr. Cuvigny, Hélène, CNRS-IRHT, Sorbonne Université – Institut de papyrologie, cuvigny@wanadoo.fr

Ass.-Prof. Dr. Fodorean, Florin-Gheorghe, Babes-Bolyai University Cluj-Napoca, Dept. of Ancient History and Archaeology, fodorean_f@yahoo.com

Dr. Gabrielli, Chantal, Università degli Studi di Firenze, Dip. di Lettere e Filosofia, chantal.gabrielli@unifi.it

Univ. Doz. Dr. Groh, Stefan, Österreichische Akademie der Wissenschaften, Österreichisches Archäologisches Institut, stefan.groh@oeai.at

Ass.-Prof. Dr. Guédon, Stéphanie, Université de Limoges, Faculté des Lettres et des Sciences Humaines, stephanie.guedon@unilim.fr

Prof. Dr. Kolb, Anne, Universität Zürich, Historisches Seminar, kolb@hist.uzh.ch

Prof. Dr. Mirković, Miroslava, Filozofski fakultet Beograd, Seminar za istoriju starog veka, frida@eunet.rs

MER emeritus Mottas, François, Université de Lausanne, mottas@hispeed.ch

Prof. Dr. Parker, Grant, Stanford University, Dept. of Classics, grparker@stanford.edu

Prof. Dr. Petrović, Vladimir P., Académie Serbe des Sciences et des Arts, Institut des Etudes Balkaniques, vladimir.arheolog@gmail.com

Prof. Dr. de Vos Raaijmakers, Mariette, University of Trento, Dipartimento di Lettere e Filosofia, Laboratorio di Archeologia e Scienze Affini, mariette.raaymakers@unitn.it

Prof. Dr. Rathmann, Michael, Universität Eichstätt-Ingolstadt, Lehrstuhl für Alte Geschichte, michael.rathmann@ku.de

Prof. Dr. Şahin, Hamdi, İstanbul Üniversitesi, Edebiyat Fakültesi, hcansahin@gmail.com

Prof. Dr. Sayar, Mustafa H., İstanbul Üniversitesi, Edebiyat Fakültesi, mhsayar@gmail.com, mhsayar@istanbul.edı.tr

Dr. Sedlmayer, Helga, Österreichische Akademie der Wissenschaften, Österreichisches Archäologisches Institut, helga.sedlmayer@oeai.at

Prof. Dr. Speidel, Michael A., University of Warsaw, Institute of Archaeology, mspeidel@sunrise.ch

Prof. Dr. Talbert, Richard J.A., University of North Carolina, Chapel Hill, Dept. of History, talbert@email.unc.edu

Index

Literary Sources

Amm.
21,9,13 — 149 n. 13
Anth. Pal.
9,698 — 157 n. 35
App. civ.
1,2 — 389 n. 60
Aristeid.
26,33 — 10 n. 20
26,51.58 — 9 n. 15
26,101 — 9 n. 14
Arr. an.
1,3,2 — 170 n. 18
2,4,3 — 171 n. 19
2,5,9 — 159
Athen.
3,93e-94b — 40
Aug. epist.
220,3 — 324 n. 10
220,12 — 324 n. 10
Aur. Vict. Caes.
27,3 — 288 n. 45
Aur. Vict. vir. ill.
72 — 396 n. 100
72,7–8 — 388 n. 56
72,8 — 383 n. 30
Balb. grom.
p. 99 — 220 n. 29, 221
Cass. Dio
53,26,1 — 307 n. 24
53,29,8 — 56 n. 16
60,4,5 — 311 n. 39
73,24,1 — 63 n. 51
79,3,3 — 152 n. 20
79,17,2 — 152 n. 18
80,5,1 — 261 n. 40
Cic. Manil.
7,17 — 56 n. 14
Cic. prov.
2,4 — 275 n. 10
Cod. Theod.
15,1,36 — 298 n. 66
15,3,1 — 343
15,3,2 — 343
Curt.
3,4,1 — 171 n. 19
Cypr. sent.
5 — 324 n. 7
Dig.
43,8,2,20–24 — 13
Diod.
19,94,4–5 — 55 n. 7
Dion. Hal. ant.
1,14 — 386 n. 44
3,65,2 — 54 n. 2
3,67,5 — 9 n. 13, 53 n. 1
5,60,1 — 54 n. 3
6,4,3 — 54 n. 3
6,5,3 — 54 n. 3
6,47,1 — 54 n. 3
8,21,2 — 54 n. 3
8,36,3 — 54 n. 3
9,19,1 — 54 n. 3
9,26,5 — 54 n. 3
9,26,8 — 54 n. 3
9,70,2 — 54 n. 3
10,16,4 — 54 n. 3
10,44,2–4 — 54 n. 3
10,46,1 — 54 n. 3
11,33,4–5 — 54 n. 3
15,3,14–15 — 54 n. 3
Est
3,13 — 40 n. 14
8,9–14 — 40 n. 14
Eutr.
8,3,2 — 61 n. 44
Fest.
7 — 171 n.22
14–15 — 61 n. 44
Fronto ep.
2,3,24 — 346 n. 30
Gell.
19,10,1 — 346 n. 30
Geogr. Rav.
4,7 — 261

Hdt.
- 2,72 — 100, 101
- 3,91,4 — 37
- 5,52–53 — 40

Herodian.
- 3,3,7 — 148 n. 5

Herodian., de prosod.
- 3,1 — 101

HA Alex.
- 58,4 — 330 n. 59

HA Aur.
- 14,6 — 195 n. 26
- 22,9 — 195 n. 27

Iord. Get.
- 76 — 216 n. 9

Isid. Char.
- passim — 39–41

Isid. orig.
- 15,1,69 — 307 n. 24

Itin. Anton.
- 30 — 392 n. 78, 393 n. 86
- 134–135,4 — 261
- 184,1–185,3 — 111 n. 14
- 186,1–187,1 — 111 n. 14
- 188,7–189,5 — 111 n. 14
- 190,2–190,5 — 111 n. 14
- 191,1–191,5 — 111 n. 14
- 192 — 111 n. 14
- 192,4–193,1 — 111 n. 14
- 217,5–219,3 — 242
- 261,6–261,8 — 196
- 262,5–262,7 — 196
- 262,8 — 201 n. 43, 210 n. 70
- 416,4–418,5 — 307 n. 20, 308 n. 33
- 418,7–419,6 — 307 n. 20, 308 n. 32
- 419,7–420,7 — 307 n. 20, 308 n. 32
- 420,8–421,7 — 307 n. 20, 308 n. 31
- 425,6–427,3 — 307 n. 20, 308 n. 30
- 431,4–7 — 307 n. 20, 308 n. 30
- 433,1–434,4 — 307 n. 20, 308 n. 34
- 438,2–6 — 307 n. 20, 308 n. 34

Itin. Burdig.
- 565,1–566,8 — 261
- 566,7 — 260 n. 37

Liv.
- 12,3,8 — 386 n. 48
- 21,39 — 386 n. 49
- 37,7,8–15 — 274 n. 7
- 38,15,1–6 — 171 n. 20
- 39,27 — 277 n. 15
- 39,32,1–2 — 396 n. 98

Lucan.
- 6,437 — 277 n. 14

Not. dign. occ.
- 25,21–36 — 324 n. 9
- 25,25 — 328 n. 42

Not. dign. or.
- 36 — 123 n. 39

Ov. trist.
- 3,10,14 — 216 n. 1
- 3,10,25 — 216 n. 1

Paus.
- 1,44,10 — 283 n. 33

peripl. m.m.
- 478 — 161 n. 41

peripl. m.r.
- 19 — 57 n. 20, n. 21
- 20 — 55 n. 10, 57 n. 19
- 47 — 42, 44

Philostr. Ap.
- 3,35 — 55 n. 10

Plin. nat.
- 4,12,80–81 — 218 n. 16
- 4,113–118 — 307 n. 19
- 5,37 — 323 n. 4, 332 n. 87
- 5,98 — 149 n. 13
- 6,141 — 40 n. 12
- 6,26,101 — 55 n. 10
- 6,32,146 — 61 n. 45
- 6,32,160 — 56 n. 16
- 6,219 — 216
- 12,32,63–65 — 55 n. 7, n. 8
- 36,125 — 9 n. 13, 342

Plut. C. Gracchus
- 7,1–2 — 389 n. 60

Plut. Tib. Gracchus
- 8–9 — 388 n. 59

Pol.		4,5,2	219 n. 21
2,27	386 n. 49	4,18–25	55 n. 7
3,4,2	386 n. 49	5,1,4	45 n. 34
3,56,5	386 n. 49	5,3,8	9 n. 13, 11 n. 26
21,35,1–5	171 n. 20	5,217	396 n. 100
Porph. Const., de administrando imperio		7,1,1	216 n. 3
165	102 n. 64	7,2,9	171 n. 19
Prisc.		7,3,13	216
6,13	220 n. 27	7,7,4	273 n. 3, 274 n. 4
Prok. aed.		14,2,8	161 n. 43
4,8	9 n. 17	14,5,4	170 n. 13
Prok. BG		14,5,18	161 n. 43
3,5	393 n. 80	16,4,19	55 n. 7, n. 8
Ps.-Lukian., Macrobioi		16,4,21	56 n. 15, n. 16
15. 18	40 n. 13	16,4,22–24	56 n. 16
Ps.-Lukian. Nero		16,4,23–24	57 n. 20
78	272 n. 1	16,4,24	55 n. 11, 57 n. 21
Ptol.		Suda	
1,1–21	43	π 3037	100 n.58
1,11–12	44	Suet. Claud.	
1,11,4	45	11,3	311 n. 39
1,11,7	45	Suet. Nero	
1,12	45	19	272 n. 1
1,22–24	43	Suet. Otho	
2,1–7,4	43	3,2	306 n. 10, 313
2,1,2	44, 45		n. 43
2,5,1–10	307 n. 22	Tab. Peut.	
4,2,7	323 n. 4, 333 n. 88	1,5–2,2	328 n. 40
5,19,7	61 n. 45	2,2	324 n. 8
7,1,42	44	2,2–3,2	328 n. 39
7,1,44	44	3,2–4,1	328 n. 38
7,1,45	44	6	261
7,4	43	6–7	237
7,5–7	43	Tac. ann.	
Rig Veda		15,12	60 n. 39
1,126,7	36	Tac. hist.	
Rut. Nam.		3,9	410 n. 5
1,37–42	389 n. 66	Theophr. h. plant.	
Sidon. carm.		7,1	101 n. 63
24,5	12 n. 28	Verg. Aen.	
Strab.		6,847–853	9 n. 16
3,3,1–7	307 n. 18		

Inscriptions

AE		1898, 408	172 n. 32
1893, 88	194 n. 16	1904, 72	223 n. 41
1896, 17	258 n. 30	1910, 176	258 n. 30
1896, 18	258 n. 30	1912, 193	276 n. 12

1913, 175	260 n. 37, 263 n. 46	1997, 1363	285 n. 40
		1997, 1365	286 n. 43
1914, 165	315 n. 46	1999, 194	384 n. 33
1927, 151	118 n. 26	1999, 625	381 n. 24
1931, 54	61 n. 42	1999, 626	384 n. 32
1932, 60	377 n. 13	1999, 1397	255 n. 9, 260 n. 35
1936, 51–52	277 n. 16	1999, 1439b	292 n. 54
1942–1943, 105	352 n. 56	1999, 1441	286 n. 42
1944, 70	258 n. 30	2001, 1979	61 n. 45
1946, 38	333 n. 95	2003, 864	306 n. 13
1947, 171	61 n. 42	2003, 1531	258 n. 32
1957, 172	10 n. 19	2004, 1925	59 n. 33
1958, 241	118 n. 27	2005, 1640	61 n. 43
1967, 185	310 n. 35, 316	2006, 441	377 n. 13, 393 n. 84
1967, 198	312 n. 41		
1969/70, 589	279 n. 19	2007, 1639	59 n. 30
1969/70, 607	149 n. 15	2007, 1659	61 n. 43
1972, 487	222 n. 35	2008, 1522	112 n. 16
1973, 475	258 n. 32	2009, 940	6 n. 5
1974, 546	222 n. 36	2009, 1527	149 n. 15
1974, 579	59 n. 34	2011, 60	381 n. 24
1974, 590	298 n. 67	2011, 1146	59 n. 34
1974, 662	59 n. 30	2012, 729	310 n. 35
1975, 379	381 n. 24	2013, 1318	258 n. 32
1975, 402	377 n. 13, 393 n. 84	2013, 1323	260 n. 38
		2013, 1423–24	279 n. 21
1976, 605	260 n. 36	2013, 1425	281 n. 28
1977, 436	315	2014, 579	310 n. 38
1977, 793	168 n. 12	2014, 1031	257 n. 24
1978, 474	258 n. 31	AKYÜREK ŞAHIN/ŞAHIN 2000	
1980, 786	263 n. 48	475	171 n. 28
1980, 792	260 n. 36	BEYAZLAR/CROWTHER 2011	116 n. 18
1982, 778	193 n. 14	CIG	
1984, 792	263 n. 48	I 1558	297 n. 64
1984, 920	118 n. 24	CIL	
1985, 542	315	I 559	390 n. 69
1986, 232	383 n. 29	I 12118	152 n. 16
1987, 612	312 n. 41	I² 657	390 n. 69, 392 n. 75
1987, 837	222 n. 37		
1987, 964	61 n. 45	I² 829	384 n. 33
1991, 1407	277 n. 13	I² 2931	381 n. 24
1992, 611	377 n. 13, 393 n. 84	I² 2937c	383 n. 29
		II 435*	316
1993, 644	390 n. 69	II 401	306 n. 13
1993, 645	392 n. 73	II 759	319
1994, 297	63 n. 51	II 760	319
1995, 1652	343	II 761	319
1996, 1623	61 n. 45	II 2886	6 n. 7
1997, 1344	292 n. 55	II 3167	6 n. 7

Index — 429

II 3221	6 n. 7	III 13626	167 n. 4
II 3271	6 n. 7	III 13813a	258 n. 30
II 4633	314	III 13813b	240 n. 4, 258 n. 30
II 4639	311	III 13813c	258 n. 30
II 4640	12 n. 28, 311 n. 39	III 13813d	258 n. 30
II 4644	317	III 14160,1	60 n. 36
II 4649	314	III 14177,11	152 n. 16
II 4652	312	III 14177,11–12	167 n. 5
II 4655	318 n. 53	III 14207,34	276 n. 12
II 4657	312 n. 41	V 1863	6 n. 7
II 4660	317	V 1864	6 n. 7
II 4667	317, 318 n. 53	V 8002	406 n. 3
II 4677	317 n. 52	V 8003	406 n. 3
II 4679	317 n. 52	V 8048	408 n. 4
II 4680	317 n. 52	V 8052	418 n. 19
II 4682	314	V 8054	418 n. 19
II 4683	312	V 8071	315 n. 46
II 4722	318 n. 54	VI 9557	342
II 4766–4768	317 n. 51	VIII 1000	357 n. 72
II 4805	317 n. 51	VIII 1022a	357 n. 72
II 6206	317 n. 52	VIII 1029	357 n. 72
II²/14, 2332	6 n. 6	VIII 1066	357 n. 72
III 93	60 n. 37	VIII 1092	357 n. 72
III 123	60 n. 36	VIII 2478–2479	329 n. 50
III 204	315 n. 46	VIII 2495	330 n. 63
III 226	157 n. 36	VIII 4204	8 n. 11
III 226–229	167 n. 3	VIII 4484	331 n. 80
III 227	152 n. 16	VIII 4486	323 n. 5
III 228	152 n. 23	VIII 4508	334 n. 98
III 600	6 n. 7	VIII 5358	352
III 857	194 n. 20	VIII 7053	352 n. 56
III 974	157 n. 36	VIII 7959	350 n. 37
III 1627	224 n. 48	VIII 7960	350 n. 39
III 1642	258 n. 32	VIII 8781	333 n. 96
III 1698	240 n. 4, 258 n. 30	VIII 10036	358
III 1699	217, 219 n. 25, 240 n. 6, 258 n. 31	VIII 10046	358
		VIII 10047	358
III 6123	13 n. 30, 276 n. 12	VIII 10047–10048	397 n. 112
III 6358	223 n. 39	VIII 10048	339, 357 n. 71, 358
III 8267	240 n. 6, 258 n. 31	VIII 10049	398 n. 113
III 8268	260 n. 36	VIII 10079	358
III 8270,6	255 n. 10	VIII 10080	358
III 8271	265 n. 55	VIII 10081	339, 340 n. 5, 355, 357, 358
III 8272	265 n. 55		
III 8312	223 n. 40	VIII 10096	368
III 12695	257 n. 24	VIII 10117	343
III 13623–13625	167 n. 5	VIII 10238	330 n. 65
III 13624	157 n. 37	VIII 10296	345 n. 26, 348, 349, 351, 353 n. 63
III 13625	172 n. 32		

VIII 10299	369
VIII 10300	369
VIII 10304	367
VIII 10304–10307	348
VIII 10305	367
VIII 10305–10306	346 n. 32
VIII 10306	367
VIII 10307	367
VIII 10308	368
VIII 10308–10310	348
VIII 10309	368
VIII 10310	368
VIII 10311	369
VIII 10311–10312	347
VIII 10312	369
VIII 10313	361, 368
VIII 10313–10316	348
VIII 10314	361, 368
VIII 10315	363, 369
VIII 10316	369
VIII 10318	360
VIII 10318–10319	347
VIII 10319	361
VIII 10320	365–366, 369
VIII 10320–10321	348
VIII 10321	369
VIII 10322	345 n. 25, 347, 369
VIII 10327–10328	27 n. 10
VIII 12035	344 n. 21
VIII 14386	343
VIII 18017	333 n. 96
VIII 18634	323 n. 6
VIII 18909	352 n. 55
VIII 19852	354 n. 67
VIII 22012	362 n. 79
VIII 22050	355
VIII 22061	358
VIII 22062	358
VIII 22063	339, 355, 358, 359
VIII 22064	367
VIII 22067	367
VIII 22068	367
VIII 22069	367
VIII 22070	367
VIII 22071	339, 340 n. 5, 355, 357, 358
VIII 22080	358
VIII 22173	340
VIII 22212	331 n. 80
VIII 22348	329 n. 51
VIII 22349	329 n. 51
VIII 22364	348
VIII 22365	348, 368
VIII 22368–22370	348
VIII 22370	345 n. 25
VIII 22371	368
VIII 22371–22377	348
VIII 22372	368
VIII 22373	368
VIII 22374	368
VIII 22375	368
VIII 22376	368
VIII 22377	368
VIII 22378	368
VIII 22379	347
VIII 22380	369
VIII 22380–22382	347
VIII 22381	369
VIII 22382	369
VIII 22531	327 n. 32
VIII 22532	327 n. 32
VIII 22533	327 n. 32
VIII 22534	327 n. 32
VIII 22535	326 n. 19, 327 n. 32
VIII 22536	327 n. 32
VIII 26582	353 n. 57
X 5826	195 n. 23
X 7996–8001	8 n. 11
XI 848*	375, 376, 378, 392 n. 73, 393 n. 85
XI 849*	375, 379, 392 n. 73
XI 996–1014	376 n. 1
XI 1401	376 n. 1
XI 6616	384 n. 33
XI 6616–6671a	376 n. 1
XI 6664	397 n. 108
XI 6665	377 n. 5, n. 12, 393 n. 83
XI 6665a	375, 380
XI 6671	379, 390 n. 69, 391, 392 n. 75
XI 6671a	397
XI 8102–8104	376 n. 1
XIII 4549	6 n. 7
XIII 5101	6 n. 5
XIII 5114	6 n. 5
XIII 5144	6 n. 5

XIII 5166	5 n. 1, 6 n. 8	ILAlg	
XIII 6538	223 n. 44	I 3875–3876	349 n. 35
XIV 85	8 n. 11	II/2 4690	352 n. 55
XIV 3610	394 n. 92	ILGR	
XV 7974a	81 n. 42, 82 n. 43	156	279 n. 19
XVII/2, 53	10 n. 22	243	292 n. 54
XVII/2, 157	315 n. 46	244	285 n. 36
XVII/4, 1	406 n. 3	246	273 n. 2
XVII/2, 294	10 n. 19, 274 n. 9	ILJug	
XVII/4, 552–572b	248 n. 20	2, 468	219 n. 24
XVII/4, 571–572	266 n. 56	ILS	
DB		208	406 n. 3
I 12–17	37 n. 5	231	276 n. 12
Eck/Pangerl 2016	59 n. 33	287	319
EKM		1071	394 n. 92
I 482	293 n. 59, 294 n. 60	1409	83
		2281	240 n. 4
Esteban 2013		2541	60 n. 36
Nr. 1124	317	5808	390 n. 69
Nr. 1127	317 n. 52	5834	57 n. 24
French 1988		5863	240 n. 6, 258 n. 31
185	171 n. 28	7159	257 n. 24
186	171 n. 28	9200	217 n. 11
192	171 n. 28	9373	258 n. 30
407–408	172 n. 29	ILTun	
461	172 n. 29	575	352 n. 56
631	172 n. 29	IMC	
852	171 n. 28	285	133 n. 6, 139
855	171 n. 28	437	140
HEp		541–568	133 n. 9
2005, 81	315	569–571	139
Hurtado 1977		572	139
677	310 n. 35	572–574	133 n. 6
IG		573–574	139
II² 5182	284 n. 35	575	139
VII 69	282 n. 31	576–584	133 n. 7
X, II 1009	293 n. 57	585–596	133 n. 8
IGBulg		597	133 n. 5
IV 20141	263 n. 46	645	133 n. 7
IGLS		IMS	
13,1,9071	60 n. 37	I 23–42	255 n. 5
15,2,392	60 n. 36	I 162	258 n. 30
21,94	60 n. 38	II 21–59	255 n. 6
IGR		II 50	246 n. 14
III 880	154 n. 33	II 293	238 n. 3
IK		III/2 37–50	257 n. 21
17/2, 3602	10 n. 19	IV 20–29	248 n. 22
59, 152	6 n. 7	IV 123–128	249 n. 23
		VI 18–20	247 n. 19

VI 195	295 n. 55	I app. 2	153 n. 24
VI 195–206	247 n. 19	I app. 2–3	153 n. 28
VI 196	265 n. 55	I app. 3	153 n. 24
VI 197	265 n. 55	I app. 4	152 n. 23
VI 199	265 n. 55	III 1, 7–10	171 n. 21
VI 200	265 n. 55	III 2, 90c	171 n. 23
Leschi 1949		III 2, 94b	171 n. 23
58–62	332 n. 86	III 2, 95d-e	171 n. 23
59	332 n. 84	III 2, 97a-b	171 n. 23
60–61	332 n. 85	III 3, 159	153 n. 25
MAMA		III 3, 161	153 n. 25
VII 193	277 n. 14	III 3, 162	153 n. 28
Mottas/Decourt 1997		III 3, 163	153 n. 28
348, n° 2	275 n. 11	III 3, 164	153 n. 28
351, n°21	292 n. 55	III 3, 165	149 n. 15, 153 n. 28
Nollé 2001		III 3, 166	149 n. 15, 153 n. 28
177	171 n. 28	III 3, 167	153 n. 28
178	171 n. 28	III 5, 119	11 n. 23
179	171 n. 28	III 7, 11	172 n. 32, n. 34
OGIS		III 7, 15A-15D	162 n. 55
578	154 n. 33	III 7, 15A-18	161 n. 53
707	67	III 7, 15E	163 n. 56, 179 n. 48
Poidebard 1928		III 7, 16A-17	161 n. 54
111	118 n. 25	III 7, 31B	179 n. 47
Puerta 1995		III 7, 37	159 n. 42
Nr. 1	313	III 7, 39	154 n. 32
Nr. 34	312 n. 41	III 7, 41	157 n.34
Nr. 40	312 n. 41	III 7, 42A	157 n. 36
Nr. 155	317	III 7, 42B	157 n. 36
Nr. 173	312 n. 41	Şahin 2009	
Nr. 177	316	131–132	173 n. 40
RIB		Salac 1923	
I 98	15 n. 45	80–83, n. 1	285 n. 36
I 598	15 n. 45	Sayar 2000	
I 707	8 n. 10	19	179 n. 48
I 1463	8 n. 11	SEG	
I 2219–2314	15 n. 45	7, 135	61 n. 42
III 3516–3527	15 n. 45	15, 849	61 n. 42
Rizakis 1998		17, 315	6 n. 7
111, 30a	290 n. 49	24, 1064	59 n. 34
111, 30b	289 n. 46	27, 401	59 n. 34
Roll/Avner 2008		35, 737–38	292 n. 54
271	135 n. 17	35, 753	285 n. 40
RRMAM		35, 754	292 n. 54
I 64	157 n. 34	40, 1523	59 n. 30
I 65 a	157 n. 36	46, 1797	61 n. 42
I 65 b	157 n. 37	51, 1832	13 n. 31
I 66	159 n. 42	61, 588	59 n. 34
I app. 1	152 n. 16		

THOMSEN 1917			VILLENEUVE 2015	
172–173	141		37–38	59 n. 31
176	141		37–40	59 n. 30
177	141		VILLENEUVE 2016	
178	141		20–21	59 n. 31
179–181	141		20–23	59 n. 30
182–184	141			

Papyri / Ostraka

BGU			I 51,17–18. 26–27	77 n. 29
III 709,4	82		I 51,18	76 n. 27
O.Berenike			I 83	77
I 75	100		I 87,14–50	80 n. 36
II 195	92 n. 55		I 91	74
O.Claud.			I 120	73
IV 734–738	93		O.Xer.	
inv. 312	78 n. 30		inv. 574	95
O.Did.			inv. 727	83 n. 48
23	93		inv. 847	101
28	76, 78		inv. 1199	102
28,3–6	77 n. 29		inv. 1212	102
29,9	87		P.Hamb.	
49	83		IV 270,3	93
52	73		P.Iand. Zen.	
61,4	96		53	101 n. 62
400	68 n. 4		55	101 n. 62
O.Dios.			81	101 n. 62
inv. 1460	84 n. 49		P.Kellis I 72,34	95
O.Florida			P.Marmar.	
5	102		r° viii, 37–38	82
O.KaLa.			P.Mich.	
inv. 574	78 n. 31		IX 551,30	87
inv. 619	96		P.Oslo	
O.Krok.			II 33 v° 7	87
I 1	73 n. 20, 75, 95		P.Oxy.	
I 4	73		III 474	80 n. 36
I 10	72 n. 16		VII 1070,39	81
I 13	72 n. 15		XL 2915	97
I 17	93		LI 3642	73 n. 18
I 30,44	72 n. 14		LX 4060,57–58	81
I 41	73, 83		P.Ryl.	
I 41, 74n	84 n. 50		II 78	68 n. 6, 78, 80, 81, 82, 96
I 44	73			
I 47,36	73		PSI	
I 47,52–58	77		VII 862,10–11	101 n. 62
I 47,56	87		P.Worp	
I 50	73		51	73 n. 17, 76 n. 26, 82
I 51	76			

Rom.Mil. Rec.
- 63   246

SB
- XIV 11612   71
- XX 14116,3   100
- XXIV 16187   73

SPP
- XXII 183,76   92